Multidisciplinary Economics

Multidisciplinary Economics

A Methodological Account

Piet Keizer

OXFORD
UNIVERSITY PRESS

Great Clarendon Street, Oxford, OX2 6DP,
United Kingdom

Oxford University Press is a department of the University of Oxford.
It furthers the University's objective of excellence in research, scholarship,
and education by publishing worldwide. Oxford is a registered trade mark of
Oxford University Press in the UK and in certain other countries

First Edition published in 2015

Impression: 1

Published in the United States of America by Oxford University Press
198 Madison Avenue, New York, NY 10016, United States of America

British Library Cataloguing in Publication Data
Data available

Library of Congress Control Number: 2014948662

ISBN 978-0-19-968649-0

Printed and bound by
CPI Group (UK) Ltd, Croydon, CR0 4YY

To Leni, my wife
To Irene, Reitse, and Marian, my children

Welcome to this collection of frameworks of interpretation and learn how to communicate with people who are different

Mission of the Book

After forty years of studying, teaching, and doing research I decided to write this book. During my student period (1965–1972) I felt an increasing sense of dissatisfaction with textbook economics: 'there is something essentially wrong'. Attending many lectures in neighbouring fields led to the experience that in these fields also there was something essentially wrong. In 1982 I submitted my PhD thesis, which contained an institutional explanation of the phenomenon of inflation. With hindsight I can say that this text was the beginning of a long journey towards what I call multidisciplinary economics now. I theoretically integrated two social-psychic variables in a typical economic explanation, namely ideology and militancy of relevant social-economic-political groups. According to the staff, who were responsible for the pass or fail decision, the thesis was good, but not straight economics. This was not a surprise since heterodox economics was not taught, and even forbidden as part of literature lists.

I decided to study sociology, psychology, and philosophy in depth. It led me to conclude that orthodox/neoclassical economics is an analysis of the economic *aspect* of human behaviour rather than an explanation of actors in a real-life economy. So, orthodox analysis cannot unconditionally be applied to real-life economic events. Under the name 'economic naturalism' neoclassical economics, as we know it from textbooks, is doing exactly this: empirical research on the basis of economic aspect-analysis.

When reading neoclassical texts it is remarkable that the essential concepts are not clearly defined. There is much confusion about the meaning of the terms 'economic', 'rational', 'social', and 'logical'. Textbooks do not discuss the philosophical foundation of their approach. For readers, it makes the scope of orthodox economics unclear. In my book I show the partial character of the orthodox paradigm, present careful definitions of the terms just mentioned, and offer a more realistic paradigm and analysis by integrating the three primary human motivations, which are the economic, the psychic, and the social motivation. In the distinction between three irreducible motivations, it is possible to define the concepts in relation to each other. Economic motivation concerns the relationship between man and the natural environment, including other humans, as far as they are considered as just potential valuable natural things. The psychic motivation concerns the relationship between man and his Self. The social motivation concerns relationships between humans and groups of humans, where the fact of being human dominates these relationships. Within groups people are inclined to enjoy solidarity, while in relationships between groups humans are inclined to rival each other. By first developing an aspect-analysis of the psychic and of the social aspect, we can integrate these aspect-analyses in one paradigm, which is about the homo oeconomicus-psychologicus-sociologicus. In this paradigm human nature is less partial and not constant. In every situation the composition of motivations and their relative strength might be different. This variability makes it possible to also develop a macro paradigm, based on the rich material offered by heterodox economics. This paradigm says that macro events are not the result of the aggregation of micro events. Like the micro, the macro level is irreducible and deserves its own paradigm. This paradigm says that reality is an open network of many subsystems, which are highly related to each other. The whole of this open system has properties, which evolve over time, and have a significant effect on the behaviour of persons and organizations on lower levels of analysis. On the lowest level the system has a significant effect on the composition and relative strength of the three primary human motivations.

Heterodox economics, economic psychology, and economic sociology offer much raw material, which is necessary for a shift in the way readers interpret their reality. With respect to the current economic crisis it is obvious that a more pluralistic economics would have led to more realistic policy advice from economists over the last few decades.

When we look at the way leading economists analyse the current economic crisis in Europe, we see that they are educated in a neoclassical way only. Every national economy is approached separately and presented as a firm, which is not competitive enough to operate on the global market. But the European depression came from outside, and many of the national economies are in one and the same depression. They all are pressed by Brussels to cut government expenditures and moderate wages. Because of the interrelationships between the various members of the EU the typical microeconomic analysis of the neoclassical approach create a dangerous downward spiral: less economic growth and less budgetary discipline. Since the EU is a large part of the global economy, this development is a threat for global development. In a climate of depression—not of recession as the neoclassical economists call the situation—price adjustments make a return to a balanced economy improbable. For economists who are not educated in a pluralistic way, which implies comparison between the paradigms of different perspectives—it is difficult to react adequately; their policy advice is always the same, whatever the context of the problems at hand.

The choice in favour of pluralism means that I do not consider myself a modern economist. The modernity project aims at the production of objective knowledge, which is a reliable basis for human action. Neoclassical economics—orthodox economics applied to the real-life world—presents itself as an objective, or at least as a hard and scientific body of knowledge. To me this is beyond humans. Reality is intrinsically an open system, which is permanently bombarded with external shocks. Scientists must not present their analyses as objective and hard. This view contains an element of intolerance: those who say they disagree have not understood it, and have not reached the true scientific level. Pluralism means that knowledge always remains subjective. If many scientists agree with each other, knowledge becomes intersubjective, but never objective. The subject of the scientist will always be involved—it will always be a human construction. Postmodern scientists characterize the failure of the modern project as 'the end of the Grand Narrative'. I disagree; it is only the end of one so-called objective narrative. But every person can always develop his personal grand narrative. Other people might become inspired by particular constructions and begin to participate in the further construction of them. In a democratic world scientists are free to compete with popular schools of thought. It means that competitors should also be offered the natural resources to really compete, and to establish their own essentials and definitions of important concepts. In the medieval and in the modern world essentials were considered to be objective and eternal (essentialism). In a plural and democratic world different subjects tell different stories about the human condition. My book stands in this tradition. One of the consequences is that now and then I start a sentence with 'I' rather than with the usual 'we'.

Target Groups

The primary target groups of the book are the various groups of economists. Most of them are specialized, thereby missing a sophisticated frame for the context of their problems. Of course, the book is also valuable for non-economists, who have a job in which knowledge of human behaviour is important: business administrators, public administrators, lawyers, sociologists, psychologists, and political scientists. Nowadays many PhD economics students don't have a background in economics. This book is an excellent introduction to the fields that deliver the raw material needed for an analysis of the situation of the problems. These students all can profit from the insight the book is offering: that some fields have primarily a subsystem character, while others essentially analyse an aspect-system. The book offers an overview of many relevant currents in the three primary human sciences, namely economics, psychology, and sociology. Knowledge of philosophy is needed to see the broader picture, thereby improving understanding of the phenomena under scrutiny.

ACKNOWLEDGEMENTS

In the first place, I like to thank the referees and editor for their comments. A person who stimulated me to write this book is Brendan Sheehan from the University of Leeds. I learned from workshops, such as the methodology workshops, organized by Sheila Dow from the University of Stirling, the philosophy workshops, organized by the International School of Philosophy of Leusden (the Netherlands), the evolutionary economics workshops, organized by Geoff Hodgson, and a series of lectures on monetary theory by Jan Kregel from the Levy Institute of Bard College, New York. Also, private discussions with Bob Goudzwaard from the Free University of Amsterdam, Mancur Olson from the University of Maryland, and Neil Fligstein from the University of California, Berkeley, were very insightful.

Leni Offringa and Irene, Reitse, and Marian Keizer were always prepared to critically comment on many of my ideas and practical examples. The conversations with Nelleke Verkade about psychology, philosophy, and literature were very valuable. I'm indebted to Leni Offringa for her administrative assistance. And last, I want to mention the students, who followed my lectures, and stimulated me to develop my ideas about human science.

■ CONTENTS

■ LIST OF FIGURES

LIST OF BOXES

Part I
Science, Social Science, Economics

1 Introduction

This book discusses orthodox and neoclassical economics from a methodological perspective and compares them with a series of heterodox economic approaches. We will see that orthodox economics is based on a paradigm that formulates human nature explicitly as economic, rational, and non-social. However, orthodox economics is just a partial analysis of human behaviour. Therefore, it cannot function as a basis for analyses of real-life behaviour. Heterodox economics offers many different analyses and theories, yet is vague about human nature. Orthodox economics is criticized because of its unrealistic paradigm, but heterodox economics does not offer an alternative. By thoroughly discussing psychological and sociological theory, I hope to find the raw material necessary for the construction of a more realistic paradigm. This new paradigm is an integration of the economic, psychic, and social aspect of human behaviour. The orthodox economic model analyses a world in which humans are only motivated economically—this is called *the economic world*. Heterodox economics, psychology, and sociology have not constructed such an isolated abstraction, in which essential factors are ignored. Therefore, I use the material found in these sciences to construct *the psychic world*, and *the social world*, in which only the psychic motivation and only the social motivation respectively plays a role. These worlds are assumed to be closed systems, which means that human behaviour is determined by the world's own mechanism and is not affected by the functioning of other mechanisms.

We define *orthodox economics* as the economics of the economic world. Actors are economic, rational, and non-social. *'Economic'* means that an actor is motivated to maximize economic utilities under the constraint of scarce natural resources. *'Rational'* means that persons have no internal conflict. They have a perfect idea of their true preferences and the willpower to act accordingly. Organizations are perfectly organized and there are no disputes about strategy and tactics. *'Non-social'* means that actors consider each other to be scarce natural resources, with which profitable transactions can be concluded—not as human beings, endowed with a number of human rights and duties. On the basis of this paradigm, economic analyses are developed in terms of market, supply and demand, price, and equilibrium, for instance. *Neoclassical economics* assumes that this economic world analysis can be applied to real-life economies. The reason for this assumption is the following. If households and firms operating in *competitive markets* are irrational or act on the basis of social motivation, they will be out-competed and not survive. So most actors are more or less rational and close to being non-social. When integrating the psychic and the social world we will see that the combination of non-economic motivations in particular might ruin markets, as we know from the economic world.

We also define the term *mainstream economics*. For half a century already mainstream economists are essentially neoclassical economists who have allowed themselves to add psychological and social variables on an *ad hoc basis* to their typical economic explanations. They hope to be able to predict the future without undergoing any sophisticated psychological and sociological analysis. In stable periods they are quite successful, although we don't need sophisticated models at such times. In unstable times, when prediction is needed, they are not successful. Moreover, in many situations they are not able to predict the transition from a stable to an unstable period.

Heterodox economics—defined as non-orthodox economics—rejects this method of isolated abstraction. It prefers to start with a concrete individual (the Austrian School, for instance) or with the actual historical development of an important and stable institution, which can be a large and relatively closed economy. Another important difference is the heterodox idea that reality is dynamic and historical. Every person and every organization is always evolving, which means a permanent change in its properties. Experiences in the past have a significant influence on current and future actions. People learn from their mistakes. They learn to interpret their situation and develop *institutions*, such as habits, routines, and norms. If these appear effective, actors tend to automatize a great part of their behaviour. Institutions, reflecting human experience, are important drivers of human behaviour. Over time they alter under the influence of cultural and technological change. Persons and organizations try to survive by adjusting to institutions, which appear effective in the new order. So, when we compare orthodoxy with heterodoxy we see that heterodoxy is 'based' on developments in culture and technology, while orthodoxy is 'based' on economic motivation, and the consequent drive to improve technology.

A more realistic explanation will be based on a micro- *and* a macro-foundation. It shows the relationship between the different levels of analysis. The lowest level is that of human motivation, while the highest level is that of the economy and the society as a whole. Orthodox economics does not deliver a genuine macro-foundation, and its micro-foundation is partial. Heterodox economics, however, does not offer a genuine micro-foundation, while its macro-foundation is not clearly formulated. This book tries to develop a micro-foundation, in which the economic motivation or aspect is integrated with the psychic and social motivation or aspect. Since neither psychology nor sociology apply isolated abstraction as a research strategy, economists who want to make their micro-foundation more realistic should do this themselves. Moreover, the macro-orientated heterodox economists should develop a historically orientated open macro-system, which is linked to a realistic multi-motivation micro-foundation.

The book presents psychology and sociology as two rich fields, which must be studied by economists. During the last few decades, cooperation between psychologists and economists has led to a growing field, named *behavioural economics*. When we compare it with orthodox economics, it can be characterized as an attempt to relax the assumption of perfect rationality. Behavioural economics, however, is empirically orientated. Essentially, this field misses a careful constitution and analysis of the psyche or mind in a way which is comparable with the orthodox analysis of the economic world. Therefore, it cannot offer a definition of the concept 'imperfect rationality'. When we construct our psychic world, we use pieces of analysis from several psychological perspectives.

Right from the beginning of its establishment as a discipline sociology had a strong focus on the study of real-life economies. Many sociological approaches pretend to produce analyses that are empirically relevant. The reader of the chapters on sociology within this book will discover that the relationship between theory and empirical reality is problematic. A very important problem is the lack of a clear-cut definition of the concept 'social', which is shared by all perspectives. So, we must find out which definition of social fits our analytical goals best. I found this by constructing a social world, which is ruled by the typical social mechanism, and not influenced by the typical economic and the typical psychic mechanism.

As already said, a realistic approach also needs a solid macro-foundation. From psychology we learn that personality theory is about a human person as a whole. Actually, orthodox economics takes the person as a whole, and assumes that he is perfectly integrated. From psycho-analytical psychology we learn that this is just an ideal situation. In reality persons are always wrestling with internal conflicts, which has a significant effect on their behaviour, and also on their behaviour in the economy. From macro-sociology we learn that economies are part of society as a whole. Societies evolve over time, and it is important to discover whether this evolution is characterized by particular cycles or trends. Most macro-sociologists—Weber and Parsons being important exceptions—ignore any link with the micro level. They assume an *autonomous evolution of the whole*, and that persons and organizations should adjust to changes in their circumstances in order to survive. But whole systems do not change without a change in micro-systems, most basically in personal systems. There is always an interrelationship between the different levels. I assume that, with respect to human behaviour, *it is the individual person who is the true agent of change*. Group behaviour always completely depends on the behaviour of group members. Individual behaviour does not always depend on group behaviour. Some agents take the initiative to behave differently—they do not adjust completely to current technology and current culture. They are inventors and innovators, and they are optimistic, while everyone is still pessimistic. Sociologists have paid more attention to the link between the different levels of analysis than economists. They began to work on what is called *network theory*. Now, this approach has also become popular in economics. But there remain essential differences between the sociological and the economic network analysis, given the narrow definition of human nature, being just economic and rational in orthodox economics, and the broad definition of the concept 'social' in sociology.

One of the important heterodox economic approaches is *post-Keynesianism—a typical macro-perspective*. It starts with an essential characteristic of a whole system, in this case an economy with relative small relationships with other economies. The Euro economy, the EU economy, the US economy, and the global economy are good examples in this respect. The Dutch economy is a bad example, as it is strongly interrelated with the

Euro economy. Neoclassical economics analyses national economies like firms, which are operating on a large market. But in Europe a whole series of 'firms' are strongly interconnected and are actually a number of departments of one and the same firm. Now this big firm, who is large relative to the whole of the global market, is in trouble and macro-policy is needed. Genuine macroeconomics takes the Euro economy or the EU economy as a whole. In 2009 this economy was hit by a depression, coming from outside of the EU. Lack of an adequate policy reaction meant that several national economies found themselves in trouble—some economies more so than others, since there is always difference in terms of competitiveness. Macroeconomic disequilibrium led to problems on micro-markets, on some markets more than others. Suppose that construction firms are disproportionally hit by the depression. Workers are fired and their incomes decline. Consumers decide to save more and to pay off part of any debt. Neoclassical economists are inclined to analyse the construction market. On the basis of their analysis they advise reforming this micro-market, expecting that micro-market reform will move the economy into a new upturn. In giving this advice they ignore the macro-character of the depression, and approach the important micro-markets separately. In this book we compare the typical orthodox/neoclassical approach with a whole series of heterodox schools of thought. I also clarify my own position within the methodologically orientated conversations. But the book delivers much material, which makes it possible for readers to discover *their own essential intuitions and views on the economy and society.*

In the methodological literature a distinction is made between reality as a *closed system* and reality as an *open system.* A closed system is—by definition—not affected by external shocks. It has its own mechanism, and the behaviour of the system is determined by that particular mechanism. An open system, however, is permanently shocked by external factors. Not only sudden changes in the atmosphere but also human creativity and free will are examples that illustrate the openness of a system. Systems created by humans are not shock-proof but sources of disturbance. The financial crisis 2008 is a nice example. It shows that an irrational belief in the blessings of a system of free markets turned out to be like a black death. Neoclassical economists assume reality to be a closed system. They apply orthodox, determined models to the open reality and 'solve' this problem by assuming reality to be stochastic. Now they can apply statistical theory, thereby assuming that the constant flow of shocks is not systematic but random. In *the stochastic world* fluctuations around an expected average are a reflection of the *risks*, which are calculable. As soon as we know the risks we insure ourselves against the unbearable ones. Economists who apply the idea of reality as an open system use the concept of *uncertainty* to characterize the essence of the human condition. They argue that the neoclassical risks cannot be calculated. This implies that the conclusion of insurance contracts does not mean that the problem has been solved. Every person or organization should decide about the level of *buffers* they need for their systems to become more shock-proof. In 2008 it became clear to leading economists and politicians that Western banks had based their policies on the neoclassical approach only. Heterodox warnings were not heard or were ignored. Heterodox economists, psychologists, and sociologists advised households, firms, and governments to develop effective institutions so as to minimize the uncertainty. An institutionalized world is more predictable and therefore more stable. However, in dynamic times institutions might also be rigid. Therefore, it is important to understand the micro-macro interactions within a whole system. Every person and every organization, on whatever level of analysis, should develop institutions and build up buffers. There are many types of buffers, such as fat in the human body, mental buffers, economic buffers such as wealth and skills, and social buffers, such as family and friends.

I plea for a multi-motivational analysis of economy and society, and for analysis and modelling of the micro-macro and the agency-structure relationships. However, analyses can become too complex, especially when different aspects are integrated. Therefore, it makes sense to first study the problematic situation on a quite general level. If we analyse the apple market or the market for pears, it might be clear from the outset that a thorough analysis of the irrationality of the buyers and sellers is not that relevant. If we analyse why German, Russian, British, and French politicians and military generals started the First World War, a psychological analysis of the personality of the leaders might be very important. After a type of *pre-research* we can decide on a particular partial analysis, which can be considered as an acceptable attempt to analyse a real-life situation.

The book is organized as follows. It consists of 6 parts and 16 chapters. In the first part the book offers the reader an introduction into the question of what turns knowledge into scientific knowledge. In modern science especially beta-sciences have authority: if statements about nature are labelled with the term 'scientifically proven to be true', hardly nobody doubts it, and it is considered to be part of an objective body of knowledge. In the case of alpha- and gamma-knowledge, however, the character of propositions is quite different. The human world is very complex, and we are all part of it. When we think that we have discovered particular regularities, we begin to use these regularities to our advantage, thereby changing the world. So, even our emotions and thoughts are an intrinsic part of the human world. This phenomenon of *reflexivity* is also characteristic for economics.

Chapter 2 presents a number of methodological issues, as discussed over the centuries. Controversies between schools appear as discussions between two extreme positions most of the time. Many economists do not follow courses in economic methodology, and therefore this book starts with a review of the most important topics. Methodology appears decisive in the understanding of what is science all about, what are serious antagonisms between orthodoxy and heterodoxy, and why psychology and sociology are necessary complements in an economics study. In Chapter 3 the history of economics and sociology is discussed, and we will see that the two disciplines have rivalled more often than cooperated with each other—to the detriment of both. Orthodox and neoclassical economics are inspired by the way physics is built. In laboratories experiments are conducted, in which a number of factors are held constant, to find out what is the effect of variable A on variable B. Economists began to construct thought experiments, based on axioms, which were discovered by means of introspection. This led to the formulation of a series of principles, and an exposition of the market mechanism, which we all know from textbooks. It has given us a logically consistent language of concepts, which describes the operation of the economic motive, the relevance we all recognize from introspection. This research strategy was a reaction to classical political economy, which was an attempt to explain the functioning of 19th-century capitalism. Orthodox economists wanted to formulate *laws of a universal nature rather than empirical regularities in a historically and geographically specified capitalist system.*

Orthodoxy has never been undisputed. Austrians, Institutionalists, Keynes and post-Keynesians, radical and social economists have, each in their own way, sharply criticized it. In Chapters 4 to 9 orthodox and heterodox economics are extensively described and compared with each other. As already mentioned, differences in outcome are highly influenced by differences in methodology and by different contexts in which a particular problem occurs. Some situations can be understood by neoclassical economics better than by post-Keynesian economics, for instance. Imagine that all economies show stable growth, except one economy. All economies have the same institutional framework, except the economy in trouble, which is characterized by a growing monopoly of the unions with respect to wage formation. Then neoclassical economics has more to explain about the situation. But the current crisis in Europe does not result from a lack of competitiveness of some national economies in Europe, but by the global depression 2009, which caused a depression in Europe. Neoclassical economics has no answer to the crisis. Post-Keynesians blame the refusal of leading European economies, such as Germany and the Netherlands, to increase effective demand, the lack of it being the cause of the enduring depression in Europe.

This book shows that economics needs contributions from psychology and sociology. Orthodox economics is strong in analytical form, but weak in content. It is especially weak in its macro-foundation. Heterodox economics, however, is rich in content, but is not clear in its micro-foundation. The book reports an extensive search for explicitly formulated micro- and macro-foundations. Up to now it has been usual to stick to a micro- *or* a macro-foundation. But we need to recognize that there is a dynamic interrelationship between micro-processes and macro-processes: they are each other's foundation. The same holds true for the term 'embeddedness'. Sociologists talk about the social embeddedness of economic processes, while orthodox economists—if thinking about social processes—tend to see social processes as economically embedded. If we consider *economic and social as two aspects of the same phenomenon*—this is what I do in this book—then they are each other's embeddedness.

In Chapter 10 we review seven psychological schools of thought, discuss their methodological characteristics, and see whether economists who want to build a multi-motivational paradigm can use particular parts. An important conclusion of the chapter is that practically all approaches contribute to a better understanding about the way the mind operates. In the review of the biological approach we discuss the body–mind problem. Neurologists tend to reduce the mind to the brain. But *material and mental problems are two aspects of the same phenomenon.* Without a mind there is no brain, and without a brain there is no mind. In the end I construct a psychic world (the mind), which consists of a number of interrelated elements. The functioning of the mind is determined by a mechanism in the same way as the economic world is ruled by a market mechanism. The relation between a person and his/her Self must be maximally satisfying for the person. But limited will power means that this drive is constrained.

In Chapters 11 to 13 sociological contributions that are of value for economists are discussed. Sociologists, more than economists, are pre-occupied with the so-called micro-macro problem. In Chapter 3 we discussed some early sociological contributions. In Chapter 11 we discuss, primarily, contributions of the post-war era. Macro-sociology is about the role of power versus the role of culture. For economists who are searching for a sound macro-foundation, macro-sociology has much to offer. The role of the state and of powerful interest groups are especially important in this respect. During the 1930s, macro-sociology was criticized for lacking a solid micro-foundation. In orthodox economics the micro-foundation contains a statement about the nature of a person. In sociology, however, the micro-foundation is about the permanent interaction within a small group—family, friends, colleagues—that forms, maintains, and changes *common understandings* about the situation within the group and the group's situation.

In Chapter 12 the historical approach is discussed. Most sociologists follow the materialist interpretation of history: that development is the result of technological progress. A minority applies the idealist interpretation. When entrepreneurs apply particular innovative ideas with respect to mental and cultural matters, there will be room for technical and economic development. In the Middle East many countries do not show economic growth, although the population is still very poor. But the minds of the masses are mentally and culturally framed in a way that makes economic competition and cooperation difficult. On the other hand, progressive ideas can only arise if there is some economic growth already. In other words, *materiality and ideality are two sides of the same coin*. Development is a process, in which idealist and materialist progress strengthen each other.

Modernity is based on one particular idea, which says that humans have the potential to develop knowledge, which makes it possible for them to increasingly control their condition. *Pre-modernity or primitivity* means that humans are dependent on gods, and that the ancestors have developed effective ways to deal with them. They have developed a tradition which should be transferred from one generation to the other. Modernity means a farewell to tradition, and a call upon the autonomous and creative individual to develop techniques of organization, production, and lifestyle, which make him happy. Now, some people have entered *the postmodern stage*. They doubt the objectivity and reliability of the systems that are based on modern knowledge. When discussing the structure of knowledge in Chapter 2, we see that *objective knowledge is a modern illusion*. Throughout the book, and definitely also in our discussion about pre-modern, modern, and postmodern, ideas about the structure of knowledge appear decisive in science, and in the way it is applied.

In Chapter 13 multidisciplinary sociology is reviewed and characterized methodologically. When we want to integrate the economic paradigm with the typical psychic and the typical social paradigm this part is of utmost importance. In the economic world there are no psychic and social problems. In the psychic world economic and social problems are absent. If we bring psychic and social problems into our economic paradigm, we need to have a clear idea about the relationship between the social and the psychic aspect. In this chapter it becomes obvious that *the concepts 'social' and 'psychic' also have a negative dimension.* Orthodox economics is often interpreted as the 'dismal science'. But there is nothing negative in this isolated approach. Psychology and sociology might be, when interrelated, the true dismal sciences. If a banker appears to be irrational, we can assume that he cannot survive in a competitive market. But if he meets his colleagues daily, groups of bankers emerge (group in the sociological sense of the word). They develop a common understanding of the situation. For instance: 'governments should not intervene, because free markets are well-functioning allocation-mechanisms', and 'on the free market buyers are responsible for the quality of the good they buy'. The financial crisis shows that bankers' behaviour was not only immoral, but also irrational. They based their decisions upon fixed ideas of their reality, and were narrow-minded when interpreting signs of a coming crisis. It is the combination of irrationality and immorality that led us into a severe depression. The phenomenon of mimesis will also be discussed, which is not necessarily the same as imitation. By discussing psychological and economic sociology we show how concepts as economic, psychic, and social are used by sociologists. The key concept in economic sociology, and especially the new economic sociology, is the *social embeddedness* of economic processes. The term social refers to culture, whereby materialists tend to state that culture is significantly affected by the relative power of relevant groups. The term economic refers to the real-life economy. We will see that, in this context, the combination social-economic is problematic. It suggests that the individual behaviour of market participants and government agencies (economic) is rule-driven (social). If so, the economic aspect of scarcity of natural resources does not play an explicit role. It might turn out that economic sociology is just sociology of the old type. Of course, the sociology of markets is a major complement to the economics of markets, as we know from orthodox economics.

To create the relationship between the economic and the social aspect, a social world is constructed. In this world perfectly rational groups of actors, who are very rich in economic terms, are constantly fighting their status battles. Only relative social power matters. In this way I hope to show what the essence of the concept social means. Group-internal relationships are of a *solidary nature*, while group-external relationships are characterized by *rivalry*. It goes without saying that this is not a description of real-life situations—it is an analysis of the social aspect of human life, and therefore an important piece of the total jigsaw.

In Chapter 14 the typical economic, the typical psychic, and the typical social analysis are brought together in a multidisciplinary economic jigsaw. We first combine the psychic and the economic aspect. Imperfectly rational actors are competing and cooperating with each other. In this world irrational behaviour might sustain, but the economic mechanism operates as a counterforce. Economically motivated cooperation between irrational actors creates even more serious problems than is the case in the economic world, making control mechanisms even less effective. Why should a controller seriously control an agent, who is paying the controller for her monitoring activities? When the crisis began, it appeared that many firms had been over-optimistic in the way they had valued their assets and liabilities. The external accountants had become rich by doing their work in a suboptimal way. Credit-rating agencies played a negative role in the assessment of the credit-worthiness of national economies. Then we combine the social and the economic aspect. A world is created in which rational actors do not only compete and cooperate with each other. They also rival and show solidarity towards each other. In the psychic-social world, economic affluence is combined with irrational and social behaviour of the negative as well as of the positive type. This is a very dynamic world and shows why cruelty and solidarity can be found everywhere. In this world conflicts are not of an economic nature.

Finally a *multidisciplinary economic (MDE) world* will be discussed. It is an integration of the problem of natural scarcity—maximization of economic utilities under the constraint of limited natural resources—the problem of status or social recognition—maximization of status under the constraint of moral rules—and the problem of self-respect—maximization of self-respect under the constraint of limited willpower. It gives an analysis of situations, in which technical and economic problems are integrated with mental and cultural problems. Social processes diminish competitive pressures, and can make irrational practices enduring. Fortunately the opposite can also happen: they can stimulate people to be competitive rather than rivals, trustworthy, and ready to accept particular systems of solidarity. It makes the MDE world extremely interesting. Analyses of a MDE kind are focused on the principal and decisive processes in economy and society. They can explain the rise as well as the fall of families, companies, countries, and regions.

In Chapter 15 a series of applications of the MDE paradigm is discussed. *The meaning of a concept is determined by its context.* It means that the word preference or the word technology has a meaning, which is different in the three worlds as constructed in this book. In the economic world, technological progress is related to the transformation of natural inputs into natural outputs, given the fact that social relationships do not exist and the psychic relationships are perfectly organized already. Orthodox/neoclassical economists discuss technological innovation, and do not mean innovations on the psychic and social terrain—which is a pity. Likewise with concepts, such as rationality, morality, and institutions.

Institutions channel behaviour. They operate as *control mechanisms.* Orthodox/neoclassical economists focus on economic and political control mechanisms. In the MDE world personal and social control mechanisms are added. This makes it possible that the decreasing effectiveness of the personal and social control mechanisms over the last few decades is an important cause of the economic crisis in Europe. Since there is a strong interrelationship between the four control mechanisms, economic and political control might have become less effective because of negative mental and cultural processes.

As already said, every scientific approach needs a micro- *and* a macro- 'foundation'. This book offers ample material to construct a historical analysis of macro-developments, which incorporates the multi-motivational paradigm. In Appendix 10.1 of Chapter 10 we discuss the question of whether or not German monetary experts are traumatized. If we can say this, it would be a major fact, which might be decisive in the process of European economic policy-making at the moment. The MDE model creates many facts which do not exist in the neoclassical world. This makes the extension of the economic analysis with the psychic and the social aspect so important.

A last point about the idea of reality being an open system is the possibility of *temporary closure*. Then, scientists analyse mechanisms, which determine the behaviour of the temporarily closed system. As soon as the mechanisms are explicitly formulated, the system will be reopened and we can analyse how our mechanism changes under the influence of the bombardment of external shocks. In daily practice actors must take the intrinsic openness into account by taking particular measures. *Pre-caution* is key to defend oneself against unpredictable risks. Stocks of capital, in the broadest sense of the word, are the answer. The MDE world appears much richer in *different types of capital stock* than the economic world.

Chapter 16 draws a number of conclusions. Orthodox economics appears a typical aspect-system, in need of extension with psychic and social factors. In this book its micro-foundation—which is the economic world—is extended with the psychic and the social world. Neoclassical economics has no genuine macro-foundation, which makes it difficult to apply its analysis empirically. With the creation of an integration between the economic, the psychic and the social world a realistic analysis of society can be developed that functions as a macro-foundation for an integrated analysis of the economy. Heterodox approaches teach us to make our analyses more dynamic, historical, and open to flows of unpredictable changes from outside our systems.

2 The Character of Science

2.1 Practical Problems and Primitive Solutions

Human behaviour results from a mixture of habits, deliberate actions, emotions, and thoughts about practical and theoretical problems. Part of our behaviour is unconscious and automatized most of the time. Every day we take many decisions, which we experience as unproblematic. Often we even like to have the opportunity to choose between different options—when we buy new shoes or decide about holiday destinations, for example. Besides this, we have to face a number of more or less severe problems. For instance:

- We are poor and unable to find opportunities to earn a better living.
- We live in an area where warfare is not an exception, but the rule.
- Our wife or husband appears to be seriously ill, and the physicians cannot diagnose it adequately.
- We feel depressed although we don't know why.
- We live in an area where earthquakes frequently occur.

We experience these problems, think about them, and talk with other people about effective solutions to these problems. Social life consists, for a large part, of ongoing discussions about daily problems and how to tackle them.

In primitive societies the set of available instruments to solve problems—that is, technology—is rather simple, and the level of prosperity is low relative to what prevails in the Western world today. But primitive people do not necessarily interpret their situation in terms of poverty and backwardness. They might have their *religious interpretations of life* and have developed traditions and habits in dealing with their situation (Girard, 1978). The older generation introduces the younger generation to their religious institutions. This keeps society stable and reduces the number of practical problems significantly.

A typical primitive solution to the problems that seem difficult to solve can be phrased as follows:

We are ruled by gods and we must find out what they want from us. Our ancestors received answers to this question and we must respect them and their traditions. Via socialisation of the next generation we can maintain tradition and keep the gods satisfied. Illness, bad weather and earthquakes must be interpreted as signs of anger of the gods, and in order to please them we must sacrifice things of value—part of the harvest, goats or sheep, and if necessary even some of our children. If our community is attacked by another community, we must be courageous and defend ourselves. Rival gods and devils rule the other communities. So we please our gods most by killing people from rival tribes. Warfare is a battle between good and bad and when we fight against the bad guys our gods are supporting and blessing us. In times of peace our gods give us the resources to have a good living. As long as we maintain our tradition and beseech our gods and ancestors, peace may last.

Priests, medicine men, and headmen run these primitive communities. The first are responsible for a harmonious relationship with the gods, the second for the health of the people, and the third for law and order in the community. Religion-based tradition offers a ready-made solution to a whole series of problems. It leaves a relatively small amount of room for man-made solutions to life's practical problems, such as effective methods to kill wild animals and gather edible plants.

2.2 Western Science as a Product of Modernity

Our knowledge reflects an accumulation of experiences. In the period of the hunters and gatherers (up to about 10,000 years ago) the population was quite stable and the techniques to hunt and to gather did not develop very much. People were nomads and moved from one area to another. They lived at a level of prosperity that was considered as satisficing and there was no incentive to search for improvement. However, increasing scarcity made an increasing number of nomads settle and make a living via horticulture and agriculture. People began to work harder and longer and to search for more effective methods of production (Sanderson, 2000).

A primitive interpretation of the transition from a period of affluence to a period of scarcity refers to increasing anger of the gods. To beseech them, people had to sacrifice more of their harvests and other assets. If we consider Bible stories as historically reliable, about 5000 years BC a man named Abram found he could not believe in gods who could be pleased by sacrificing children. He decided to leave the town where he lived and went to a scarcely populated area, Palestine. In his view there is only one God, who is the Creator of the universe and who loves his creatures. This means that humans are not created to honour their gods by sacrificing valuable assets. On the contrary, they are created to develop the potential of the universe, including their own capacities. Human beings are each other's keepers, not rivals of each other. They must cooperate in their attempts to improve their material and spiritual endowments.

Abram can be considered as a cultural innovator and entrepreneur. His story liberated many people from the fear of gods and devils and taught people to trust their Creator. Human beings are beings of high potential and stewards of the universe. God has given them freedom and responsibility.

This view has become an important pillar of Western civilization (Weber, 1922). The *Judeo-Christian belief system* is based on it. However, new ideas tend to become institutionalized and increasingly lose their original character. In the thousand years from the fall of the Roman Empire until the Reformation, the Roman Catholic Church monopolized the Christian mission in the West, with a negative effect on the development of the intellectual capital of society. The conflict between Galileo and the Church is a famous illustration in this respect. The Church accused Galileo of considering the sun rather than the earth to be the centre of the universe. In other words, the Church did not only claim to have absolute knowledge about the relationship between God and man, but also about the specific way God had constructed the universe. In Box 2.1 we show that the work by Galileo and others was the beginning of what we now call the *Scientific Revolution*.

An increasing number of individuals began to observe their environment, including their Selves, in a more secular way. They made paintings and sculptures that pictured nature and humans as we observe them with our senses rather than as 'sacred' objects. Nowadays we call this development the *Renaissance*. Also, in philosophy people increasingly approached the universe in a more secular way, a phenomenon now called the *Enlightenment*. Thomas Hobbes was one of the famous pioneers, who analysed society in a way that was not inspired by Christian understanding and morality. In Hobbes' time there were many wars, and societies were battlefields rather than well-functioning and harmonious workplaces. Macchiavelli before him, and Locke, Hume, and others after him, developed secular and positive analyses of typical social and political relationships. Physicists became increasingly independent of the Church in their scientific work. Newton is illustrative in this respect; he was a devout Christian, but believed that God had created a universe whose functioning is determined by the operation of a series of laws. God's creation process is now finished, and scientists must search for the laws that explain the mechanisms responsible for the functioning of nature. Bible reading does not give us insights into the functioning of the universe, including human societies. It is as

---

BOX 2.1 THE SCIENTIFIC REVOLUTION

In the medieval period 'science' was highly influenced by Christian theology. The principle source of knowledge was the Bible, and the interpretation of biblical texts about the architecture of the universe was also influenced by Aristotelean cosmology. The dominating paradigm stated that the earth is the centre of the universe, and all other objects circle around the earth. Copernicus (1473–1543) was the first to criticize this axiom. His book *The Revolution of the Heavenly Spheres* (1543) advocates a heliocentric view—the sun as the centre of the universe, and other objects making orbits around it. Afraid of being condemned by the political and clerical authorities, he postponed the publication of his book for about thirty years. Now his book is generally considered as the beginning of the so-called Scientific Revolution.

Later, other astronomers, such as Brahe, Kepler, and Galilei, accepted the Copernican paradigm and started to work in a heliocentric research programme. Galilei (1564–1642) especially, worked on an improvement of the telescope and discovered many novel facts, most of them in contradiction with the official doctrines of the Roman Catholic Church. Galilei was accused of heresy and sent to prison. Finally, he recanted his work, but the story goes that he muttered to himself something like 'nevertheless the earth moves around the sun'.

if God disappeared after having finished His job (*deism*). Now *man is responsible for the management and stewardship of His creation.*

This deist dichotomy made it possible for religious believers and atheists to work on a common project, that is, the modern project that aims at the control of the universe. It is based on *the modern belief that humans are able to discover the laws of nature, including human nature.* It is assumed to lead to a body of knowledge that serves as a reliable instrument to improve the human condition.

2.3 Modern Philosophy of Science

The rejection of revelation as a reliable source of knowledge runs parallel with an increase of our trust in the validity of observation by our senses. The results are called *sense data*, which constitute the so-called *empirical world*. Those who assume that reality only consists of this empirical world are called *empiricists*. For example, in the observation of lightning and thunder, we only see a flash and we only hear a sound. That is all we observe. The religious interpretation that God is speaking to us is not the result of observation and must be rejected as a reliable source of knowledge. We can also observe that the crash of thunder is always somewhat later than a flash of lightning. A secular explanation of this fact must refer to other empirically established facts, not to a god who prefers to show light first.

Other philosophers do not stress the senses as a reliable source of knowledge. According to them the human '*ratio*' ('*pure reason*') structures our thinking about physical and chemical processes that enter the human body via the senses in such a way that we can understand what we see, hear, feel, smell, and touch. Examples of innate structures through which sense impressions come to us are:

(1) the time and space framework;
(2) the cause and effect framework in which every impression is placed;
(3) the categorization of everything in terms of identity and difference;
(4) rules of logic.

Those who consider the human ratio to be the primary source of knowledge are called *rationalists*.

The German philosopher Kant arrived at a synthesis between the empiricist view and the rationalist view. Against the empiricists, he emphasized that empirical reality comes to us as physical/chemical impressions and has no meaning as long as the human mind does not process them into meaningful structured information. Against the rationalists, he emphasized that the human ratio is just a structuring device; so it must structure particular raw materials to transform it into an understandable whole. Hence, knowledge is only knowledge when sense impressions are structured by the mind. In Box 2.2 we show

---

BOX 2.2 REASON

Kant (1724–1804) was impressed by the results of the Scientific Revolution, especially the Copernican Revolution in astronomy (Scruton, 1996). By constantly improving the instruments of observation—the telescope—researchers were able to find more facts, which could be explained by means of analysis and theory derived from the heliocentric paradigm. As a philosopher he became increasingly interested in the way observers observe. What is the human 'telescope' by means of which they observe their empirical reality? By thinking about the way humans think, Kant discovered the 'ratio' or 'pure reason'. This is the capacity of the mind to transform sense impressions into understandable knowledge. So it is a *framing device*—physical and chemical reactions that result from observation are transformed into a categorized world. How the world is framed and categorized is determined by characteristics of the psychic structure and of the economic and social position of a person. Only if we understand our situation are particular emotions triggered, which set us in motion; in other words, we act. Our capacity to understand is, as with all elements of the mind, materially embedded. Somewhere in the brain there is a location that houses this capacity. If this part of the brain is damaged, the person cannot understand his situation anymore, and he does not know what to do.

Kant developed this theory in his book *Critique of Pure Reason*. It was a message to rationalists who considered reason to be the only source of knowledge, and who did not trust sense impressions. In a second book—*Critique of Practical Reason*—Kant develops a moral theory. His moral idea assumes that all humans are essentially equal. Only when we consider (empirical) properties, can we observe many differences, creating inequality. Now, practical reason refers to our awareness of the essential or substantial equality. If people say to each other: 'be reasonable', they appeal to the capacity to judge a situation in a rational and Kantian-moral way.

---

that Kant made a distinction between rationality and morality. In his approach reason refers to the combined capacity of people to be rational and moral.

When developing his synthesis, Kant made a distinction between *a priori knowledge* and a posteriori knowledge. The first category is not based on observation of empirical reality but of the reality of the mind; we call this internal observation. Examples of a priori knowledge are the time and space dimension and axioms of logic like the transitivity rule. Conceptual and analytical structures are based on a priori knowledge. By means of these structures we can observe empirical reality and establish empirical facts. These facts, and the established empirical relationships between these facts, are our a posteriori knowledge. Kant also made a distinction between *analytical and synthetical statements*. The first concerns concepts and systems of logically interrelated concepts. The antonyms (which are the opposites of synonyms) part and whole, specific and general, and the distinction between small and large, are examples in this respect. Syllogisms also represent systems of interrelated concepts. For instance, on the basis of the definition of the concepts 'mortal' and 'human' and the (synthetic) proposition 'humans are mortal', we can deduct the analytical proposition 'humans are not immortal'. Another example of an analytical statement is: orthodox economists assume that people are rational beings. These statements are of an analytical nature, since they are true by definition.

Synthetic propositions state something about reality, be it empirical reality or the reality of the minds of the people. An example of a synthetic statement is: the unemployment rate in the Netherlands in 2004 is 5 per cent and this is caused by the wage inflation rate, which is 2 per cent in the same year.

Kant's synthesis between rationalism and empiricism results from his idea that *synthetic propositions of an a priori character exist*. They especially describe the way the human mind frames reality 'out there'. As we have seen already, the architecture of the mind consists of innate images of time and space, of structures of cause and effect, of categorizations in terms of identity and difference, and of axioms of logic. Results that are in contradiction with these frames cannot be understood. Knowledge of the general characteristics of our mind are a priori, because they are not reality 'out there', and they are synthetic because they are about something real—the mind frame is part of the universe.

Here we must make an important note on the difference Kant is making between *substance and property*. We can only observe properties of things if we have carefully defined a phenomenon. Then we can establish some properties of a particular thing. Suppose we receive some sense impressions of a phenomenon, and we define a category, of which our phenomenon is an element. Then we might conclude that we have observed a swan with the colour black, for instance. If we have defined swans in a way that includes their colour, namely white, then our observed object was not a swan, but something else. If the colour is not part of the definition, a black swan is possible. There are many examples to be given of the problem of how to establish the essence of a thing. For instance, with regard to a group of unemployed people: if an unemployed person is defined as one who receives an unemployment benefit, then many people who are jobless, and are actively searching for a job, are not unemployed. In this case it might be useful to look for a different definition, since many people intuitively feel that all these actively searching people ought to be called unemployed. So, in permanent interaction with each other, people can search for useful definitions, determining the essence of things. Only then we can search for properties of 'unemployed' in a particular place and in a particular period of time. For instance, in the 1990s, many of the Dutch unemployed were older women of foreign ethnicity.

In some currents within social science people resist the problem of ontology. It reminds them of the old times, in which people thought in terms of an objective essence of things. That is, that everything has an objective essence, and we cannot change that over time. This philosophical view is called essentialism. But today many scientists accept that knowledge is not more than a human construction. Thus also with the establishment of the essence or substance of a thing: it is a human construction, and after an intensive discussion we can decide to change some definitions, if we think that this is useful. In this respect it is important to note that Weber worked with the concept 'ideal-type'. To him it expresses a particular idea, and by developing many ideal-typical concepts, such as democracy, capitalism, bureaucracy, we can approach real-life phenomena as complex mixtures of ideal-types.

In conclusion, our mind structures things, but our senses give us the raw material that is to be structured. The raw material is constantly suggesting particular categories to be distinguished and the mind is constantly trying to understand reality by means of the categories that are suggested. So a close cooperation between ratio and senses might lead to a virtuous circle of increasing understanding of our reality. For a deeper understanding of Kant, and for applications of Kant's philosophy of science, see Appendix B at the end of the book. Later in this chapter we come back to the relationship between ratio and sense impression. Then we will see that the ratio is about the form of knowledge—not about the content—while sense impression is about content—not about form. Because form and content are two aspects of the same phenomenon, we can only analytically distinguish, but never empirically separate, the two concepts.

In practice, creative persons 'produce' new ideas by means of which new a priori structures are developed. These structures make it possible to give a new interpretation to our internal and external observations. In Chapter 3 we will see how orthodox economists—in reaction to classical political economists—came up with the idea of an economic, rational, and non-social actor. It led to a different interpretation of reality by means of a logically consistent set of concepts, such as consumption, production, investment, and employment. These concepts were, in contradiction to classical political economy, and, later, with the empirical indicators of the neoclassical economists, not empirically observable.

2.4 **Twentieth-Century Philosophy of Science**

At the beginning of the 20th century, Vienna was an important centre of scientific debate. Scientists of different disciplines discussed their basic philosophies and methodologies in the Wiener Kreis (Vienna Circle). Most of them were so-called *logical positivists.* They were quite radical and anti-metaphysical. Only external observation had to be accepted as a source of information and only logic had to be applied when categorizing sense impressions and relating observed categories to each other. The following example illustrates their view:

(1) Last month an increase in the price of cigarettes was followed by a decrease in the quantity of cigarettes sold.
(2) Last month an increase in the price of butter was followed by a decrease in the quantity of butter sold.
(3) Last month an increase in the price of houses was followed by a decrease in the quantity of houses sold.

Ergo, an increase in the price of a good is followed by a decrease in the quantity of that particular good sold.

A number of specific statements leads to a general statement; this generalization is called *induction*. When we collect more information about price increases and its effect on the quantities sold we can verify whether our general statement is true. As long as *verification* takes place, we hold the general statement to be a true statement. Empirical research makes the list of specific statements longer. Now and then some specific statements will not be verified, but falsified. Is one falsification enough to make one consider the general statement to be false? The reaction of the more sophisticated logical positivists is negative. When we interpret the relationship as a stochastic relationship—that is, we interpret truth not in absolute terms but in terms of probabilities—we only want to know how probable it is that a price increase is followed by a decrease in the quantities sold—the higher the probability, the higher the reliability of the relationship.

A famous opponent of logical positivism is Popper (1968). According to Popper, empirical relationships do not give us any idea *why* the variables are related to each other. So we have no explanation whatsoever. Before we start our observations we first have to formulate a hypothesis to be empirically tested. We need a theory in order to formulate a hypothesis. But we need an analysis in order to formulate a theory and we need a paradigm to define the problematic situation before we can make an analysis of that particular situation. This approach is called *critical rationalism*. The following example illustrates this view.

Suppose a number of people consider themselves to be poor. They accept a job and deliver their labour services in exchange for a particular wage. Then their firm increases its demand for labour. What do we think will happen to the level of the wage rate?

To analyse this situation we must first characterize or define the situation. Assume that the world to be analysed consists of actors—firms and workers in this case—who are motivated to minimize their problem of scarcity; in other words, to maximize their prosperity. The workers are trying to achieve this by offering their labour and the firms by hiring labour and transforming this input—together with other sorts of input—into production that can be sold on the market for a profitable price. An analysis of our situation in terms of demand for and supply of labour shows an excess demand in the market. On the basis of our economic definition of the situation and our analysis of this situation in terms of demand and supply, we can *logically deduct* a theory that states that wage levels will rise in case of an excess of demand for labour over supply. Now we can specify a hypothesis that can be tested empirically: the increase of the wage rate is a positive function of the size of the difference between the quantity of labour demanded and the quantity of labour supplied.

What if there is excess demand for labour but wages do not rise and the hypothesis is falsified? Then we must conclude that the combination of definition of the problematic situation, analysis, theory, and the particular specification of the hypothesis has been false. Scientists must change assumptions—one by one—in order to see whether the explanation of the situation improves.

Lakatos (1970) elaborated on the Popperian criticism by showing that analysis and theory are always part of a group of analyses and theories, which is based on a common *paradigm*. For example, evolutionary economics is a research programme that is based on an evolutionary view of life. The evolutionary paradigm states that every system is an organism, which evolves over time. Through the operation of the mechanism of natural selection a system can only survive if it adapts to changing circumstances sufficiently. On the basis of this paradigm an analysis is made which is applied to the economy. So, a specific evolutionary theory could be: those firms that spend a significant part of their budget on the research and development of new products have a chance of surviving the process of satiation of the demand for the prevailing good. Empirical testing of this statement can show whether the correlation between the R&D budget share and survival within a particular period of time is statistically significant. If not, then researchers who are working in the evolutionary economic research programme will not give up their typical evolutionary approach, but continue with their search for evolutionary theories that can withstand the empirical test.

Kuhn (1970) described and analysed the history of scientific research and discovered that changes in the research paradigm or switches of researchers from one school of thought or research programme to a different one, is not a rational process. In other words, it will never be rational to shift. The researchers who stay within the programme because they believe that the programme will finally prove to be fruitful are not less rational than those who leave the programme and start working on the basis of a different paradigm.

Within social science, the *Methodenstreit* (battle of methodologies) was not only about induction versus deduction, and about prediction versus causal explanation. According to Weber (1904), the world is too complex to be successful in terms of prediction or causal explanation. Human action can only be understood if we are aware of the *world-view of the actors*. For example, the behaviour of Muslims can only be understood if we know the typical Muslim view of the world. The world-view operates as a framework of interpretation or paradigm. It offers people a tool for understanding their environment rather than explaining or predicting it. Only then they can be rational in the sense of calculating costs and benefits of their different actions and choosing the best one.[1]

Logical positivists heavily criticized the application of the Weberian idea of *understanding* (in German: 'verstehen'), especially in its specification in terms of *participative observation*.[2] Subjective judgements of the researcher would make the achievement of objective knowledge impossible. The interesting thing here is the fact that the Weberian idea of 'verstehen' is quite similar to the Lakatosian and Kuhnian idea of the 'verstehen' of researchers when working within their research programmes. So the social scientific method defended by Weber in the 1920s is a forerunner of the 'discovery' by Lakatos

[1] In the 1980s the idea of a world-view entered the economics scene when Tversky and Kahneman (1986) analysed the so-called framing of decisions.

[2] Most people are not really aware of their world-view. Therefore, it is difficult to ask people about it through questionnaires. An alternative option to gain information about the world-views of people is participative observation. This means that researchers live among the people who are the objects of research for a while. By participating in their daily lives they hope to discover the world-views that determine that particular culture.

and Kuhn of the role of a paradigm in scientific research. It also means that there is a clear parallel between the non-rational behaviour of scientists when choosing a particular research programme, on the one hand, and the non-rational behaviour of humans with respect to their 'choice' of world-view on the other. When comparing this result with the reaction of empiricists, in particular towards religious dogmas, the difference between religious and scientific beliefs is less pronounced than they would like us to believe.

2.5 Three Philosophical Questions

When thinking about reality and ways to acquire knowledge about it, three principal questions can be distinguished.

1. How can we define the nature or essence of reality?—The field of study that deals with this question is called *ontology*.
2. How can we collect information about it? In other words, what are reliable sources of information?—This field of study is called *epistemology*.
3. How can we structure the acquired information into meaningful and practically applicable pieces of knowledge?—This field is called *methodology*.

The three questions are interrelated and cannot be answered completely separately from each other.

2.5.1 ONTOLOGY

Before we start collecting and structuring information, we must define the nature of the situation. One particular situation can be imagined and presented in many ways. Nuclear physicists regularly work on the basis of a picture of the universe as consisting of independent atoms. They may proceed to analyse the inside of an atom, making further distinctions between different parts of the atom. Evolutionary biologists work on the basis of a picture of the universe being an organism that consists of a functionally interrelated set of organs. They may proceed to analyse an organ, making further distinctions between different parts of the organ. Orthodox economists work with an image of the universe interpreted as a series of rational and non-social individuals who are trying to maximize their utilities under the constraint of scarce natural resources. In our chapters about heterodox economics, psychology, and sociology we will see that ontology is decisive in understanding the differences between the various schools of thought.

The choice of ontology implies a particular interpretation of the problem. It is constitutive as well as limitative. In the case of orthodox economics it constitutes a framework that is fitted for the job of analysing the omnipresent problem of scarcity. It is limitative in the sense that it makes it impossible to analyse, for instance, the omnipresent social problem of human rivalry.

2.5.2 EPISTEMOLOGY

Information about our reality can be obtained in different ways.

(1) Introspection; humans have the capacity to observe the content of the mind in order to make analyses of flows of emotions and thoughts. When thinking systematically about these flows and trying different interpretations of it, people learn about themselves and the motivations that set them in motion.

(2) Intuition; it can be defined as a voice inside us that gives us an answer to problems that are too complicated to be understood by deliberate analysis. The content of the intuitive reaction is based on the personality, his social context, and past experiences that are related to similar problems. Apparently, humans have the capacity to store experiences in a very concise way. They do not remember the situations in which they developed feelings in terms of 'yes' or 'no', or in terms of 'be careful now', 'do it fast', or 'do it only together with other people'.

(3) Logical thinking; the ratio is the capacity of humans to frame every impression in a logical framework, thereby applying automatically rules of classical logic.

(4) The capacity to (empirically) observe the outer world by means of the senses.
Logical positivists tend to ignore information acquired from introspection and intuition. Although there is no difference in principle between internal and external observation, it must be admitted that thoughts and emotions are more difficult to observe than external objects, such as chairs, tables, and motor cars. Moreover, if asked for the results of introspection people might not be honest because of strategic reasons.

2.5.3 METHODOLOGY

The information we acquire must be structured and processed in such a way that we can attach meaning to it, and make it applicable to the solution of practical problems. Important distinctions that are made to structure information include the following.

(1) *Particular versus specific versus general.* If Messi scores a goal for Barcelona, this can be considered as a particular event. If in Europe black football players score more goals than white players, this can be considered as a specific fact. If, on a world level, black football players score less goals than white football players, this fact is more general, compared with the former fact, which is more specific.

(2) *Induction versus deduction.* Induction takes place if we draw conclusions from a series of particular events and formulate statements on a more general level. For instance,

we have observed 100 swans and they all appeared to be white. Inductive 'logic' leads us to the conclusion that all swans are white. Deduction takes place if we logically deduct a particular statement from a general statement. If, for instance, I believe that all Chinese people like table tennis, and my friend is Chinese, deductive logic leads me to conclude that my friend likes table tennis.

(3) The universe can be imagined as a *hierarchical structure of levels.* It is difficult to establish the highest and the lowest level. The architecture of our mind makes it impossible to imagine what is finite and what is infinite. Therefore, we can never establish absolute boundaries in terms of the highest and the lowest level of analysis. Some physicists are constantly splitting natural elements into smaller pieces and others are searching for the boundaries of the universe—without finding absolute boundaries, of course.

While physicists are trying to split elements, chemists are trying to cluster atoms and molecules. Biochemists study the behaviour of very complex chemical systems that appear to be the material aspect-system of living systems. Biologists study the behaviour of all kinds of organs and organisms. Last but not least, sociologists study the behaviour of groups, organizations, institutions, and societies at large. By imagining such a hierarchy we have a major instrument for ordering and systematizing the universe. Distinguishing a particular level makes sense only if the phenomena on that level have some stability. For example, chemists are inclined to consider the level of the molecule to be the most stable one when explaining chemical processes. Biologists tend to consider the gene as the most stable level when analysing biological processes.

(4) *Reductionism, holism, and institutionalism.* Reductionism states that an explanation of phenomena on whatever level of analysis must always be found on the lowest level possible. It means that physics is the most fundamental science, in its search for explanations of everything on the subatomic level. In orthodox economics, reductionism means that all economic phenomena must be explained by referring to the economic behaviour of individual human beings. In sociology it means that all social phenomena must be explained by referring to the interaction between two or a few human beings. This approach is called *methodological individualism.*

Holism, in contrast, means that explanations of phenomena on whatever level must be formulated on the highest level possible. For economics, the highest level possible is the global economy. For sociology, the highest level possible is the global society. This approach is called *methodological collectivism.*

There is a third position somewhere in between the two positions just mentioned, that is, *methodological institutionalism.* It argues that levels of explanation are not necessarily the highest or lowest levels of analysis. The best level of explanation is that closest to the level of analysis which can be considered as the most stable one. The following example will clarify this view. Suppose we want to explain the development of the wage rate of the Dutch economy over the period 1950–2000. Neoclassical economists adhere to the individualist methodology and analyse the situation in terms of individual human beings who are economically rational and non-social agents. The wage rate of an economy is an aggregate of the wages earned by the members of the Dutch working population. Neoclassical economic theory of individual behaviour explains why employers are offering higher wages when they have difficulty in filling their vacancies, while employees supply more labour services in case of rising wages. When we aggregate these individual reactions for the economy as a whole, we can conclude that wage developments are determined by the size of the excess demand or excess supply on the Dutch labour market.

A holistic approach means that the Dutch economy is presented as an important part of the global economy. It implies that Dutch developments are highly affected by global developments. In our case, we can speculate as follows: the excess demand can be perceived as part of a general excess demand on all markets of the global economy. Dutch firms may not be prepared to increase their wage level so as to compete effectively in the global market.

An institutional approach, however, does not automatically turn to the level of the individual or to the behaviour of the group as a whole. It looks for the level closest to the level of the Dutch economy that is the most stable. Assume that the institutions that shape labour relations on the central level of the Dutch economy are the most stable. This means that the central organizations of unions and employers' organizations—in permanent consultation with the government—decide which wage levels are socially acceptable. Their policies have a strong effect on the development of the actual wage rate. The typical neoclassical explanatory factor, excess demand or excess supply on the macro-labour market, may play a role in the formulation of union policies, but the power of the Dutch union movement plays an independent role as well.

(5) Induction and deduction can be interpreted as two stages within one process of knowledge development. The following example illustrates its *circular character*. Time series of unemployment and inflation show the Dutch economy following a particular pattern over the period 1960–2000. These series are calculated by aggregating the observations of particular unemployed persons and by aggregating the observations of price increases of goods produced. The next step concerns the correlation between the two time series. Statistical analysis leads to conclusions with respect to the correlation coefficient and its degree of significance. Assume that the coefficient that expresses the ratio between changes in unemployment and inflation is statistically significant and has a negative value. Then we can conclude that inflation has a negative effect on unemployment, or that unemployment has a negative effect on inflation, or that there is a third factor which affects both variables, although in a different direction. When we correlate the two variables for many countries and many time periods, we can formulate a general empirical law, expressing a negative relationship between them. This generalization is the inductive phase in the process of theory development. When measuring the two variables we implicitly answer the question of the definition of the two phenomena. When explaining their interrelationship we must use these definitions in our analysis of the situation. This analysis must function as a basis for a theory explaining the relationship

between unemployment and inflation. In economics the dominant research programme is the neoclassical one. On the basis of introspection, neoclassical economists accept the motivation to diminish scarcity as much as possible as the principal human drive. They develop an analysis that leads to a coherent set of theories of economic behaviour. Unemployment is interpreted as the quantity of labour supplied that is not hired by an employer, although the wage that is minimally claimed by the supplier is lower than the market wage. This interpretation leads to a specific definition of an unemployed person. Time series used when testing a neoclassical theory should be the result of calculating the number of unemployed persons on the basis of this definition. Having derived the correct definitions of the concepts involved in our analysis, we can deduct which persons do belong to the set of unemployed persons and which price increases do belong to the set of price increases defined as inflation. This is the deductive phase in the production of reliable knowledge: logically deducting the particulars that belong to the defined set of phenomena on the basis of their definitions.

In practice, many researchers just accept the framework of interpretation of a particular school. They adjust to 'the literature', and participate in a discussion within a particular context, including all its imperfections. Moreover, most of the time they accept the statistics, as published by 'official' institutes, without scrutiny.

Within a particular framework many specifications can be derived and empirically tested. But there may come a moment when the possibilities of a particular analysis become exhausted. Then scientific progress needs conceptual innovation. The creative process that leads to scientific novelties is called *abduction*. It leads to a redefinition of the problem by using, for instance, a different metaphor. An important example of a novelty in economics is the introduction by Veblen of a biological metaphor. He imagined the economy to be a complex whole of organs, which is subject to the mechanism of natural selection. Only a few economists followed Veblen in his evolutionary approach, but today a growing number of economists are working within the evolutionary economics programme in a way that was suggested by Veblen about a century ago.

(6) An important distinction is that between *closed and open systems.* If we opt for a mechanistic and atomistic ontology and search for universal and eternal laws that determine the course of nature, we consider the universe as a closed system. God created it as a 'perpetuum mobile', and then moved on. Now the universe functions in a constant manner forever. Scientists must discover the laws that determine natural behaviour. People can take the mechanisms as described by natural laws into account when developing their strategies, but they can never change them. We can, however, also opt for an organic ontology and interpret the universe as an ongoing process of evolution. Some characteristics will slowly disappear, while other characteristics emerge. In that sense the universe is an open system: new elements or new characteristics of existing elements can be created, and existing elements and characteristics of existing elements can disappear, making the universe different from what it was in the past and will be in the future. For instance, according to the evolutionary paradigm in biology life did not exist from the very beginning of the universe. Particular chemical compositions—especially carbon

compounds—appeared necessary and sufficient for the emergence of living organisms. Now humans are considered to be the most complex organism. But there is not any reason to assume that the human is the end of history. New and more sophisticated forms might emerge.

Difference in ontology—mechanistic or organic, for instance—affects the epistemology that is accepted and the methodologies that are applied. In a mechanistic approach, logical thinking and mathematical modelling is a frequently used methodology, based on a rationalist epistemology. In an organic approach, a broader view of epistemology and methodology is required. Intuition and judgement are principal sources of valuable knowledge, while, besides quantitative methods, qualitative methods are used to improve our knowledge. Abduction as a method leads to the trying out of new metaphors by scientists.

2.6 **Modernity and Postmodernity**

Modernity assumes the possibility of developing reliable knowledge about our reality. Logical positivism or empiricism works with sense data, thereby accepting the axioms of classical logic. Other approaches are based on a framework of interpretation, consisting of a series of axioms, which are considered as evidently and obviously true. The two main views differ in what they consider to be the foundation of knowledge: sense data or empirical evidence versus the realism of the a priori axioms, established by careful introspection.

Postmodernity criticizes the modern idea of objective knowledge and of the duality of nature. Duality means that many concepts are defined in such a way that a phenomenon can be characterized by one *or* by the other, such as induction or deduction, individualistic or collectivistic, and external or internal observation.

According to postmodernists, knowledge is a human construction, and therefore fallible. Even mathematics consists of human constructions of ideal forms, which do not exist in reality.[3] For example, a circle has particular characteristics that are essential. In practice, circles do not exist; the form of a concrete football is never a perfect circle. Risks can only be calculated in a statistical, stochastic world; never in the real world. It means that the ideas of creative individuals are the foundation of knowledge. They are giving us stories about human experiences; their imagination is the true source of knowledge. As social psychology and sociology are telling us, individuals always live in interaction with other people. In ongoing interaction people also develop common knowledge, which is shared by a group of people.

---

[3] It is important to understand that we act upon pictures of the real world. Nevertheless, these pictures are part of the real world, at least in their consequences.

Subjectivity does not only play a role in the formulation of a new foundation or paradigm. It is also decisive when judging the results of the empirical testing of a hypothesis. In other words, the philosophical foundation determines the (human) nature as well as the statistical criteria, which decides whether a particular empirical result is plausible or not.

Bashkar (1975) offers a new approach, in which he tries to find a position between two extreme positions: the objectivity claim from the logical positivists and empiricists on the one hand, and the relativism of the postmodern scientists. His views, now called *critical realism*, can be summarized in a number of propositions.

(1) *There is reality 'out there'*; there is a reality independent of what we experience. By means of accumulating experience, we can try to approach reality, which will never be known completely.

(2) *There is reflexivity*, making reality transitive; human perceptions are part of reality as a whole, and affect reality significantly by means of human expectations and interventions. A good example is the Marxist prediction that capitalism will turn into socialism in a revolutionary way. Many workers believed Marx, and were motivated to make the revolution come true. This made many conservatives and liberals anxious, and prepared to give in to the claims of union movements. If nobody had championed the analyses of Marx, would there have been welfare states in Europe?

(3) *Causal structures do exist,* and are therefore real; reality is more than the empirical surface. Behind the empirical scene there are forces at work, which are responsible for particular behaviours. The gravitational force as well as the sexual force can be experienced, and are important parts of what we experience as reality.

(4) *Reality is stratified*, which means that different levels can be distinguished. First, the real level, which consists of powers, tendencies, and mechanisms. Second, the actual level of experimental events, which take place in laboratory experiments, and in complex conjunctures outside the laboratory, such as econometric models. Third, the empirical level, which consists of events that are observed by the senses. In Chapter 4 we will discuss economics, and the meaning of the so-called economic force or motivation (real level), the substitution and wealth or income effects (actual level), and statistics about measured prices (empirical level).

(5) *Reality is differentiated,* which means that different causal mechanisms are operating simultaneously. In Chapters 4 to 13 we will see that neither the typical economic nor the typical psychic and social mechanisms work alone. No mechanism can explain empirical reality. They all have their own actual world.

(6) *Reality is an open system,* which means that not all variables can be identified. In particular, human intentionality and creativity make any system indeterminate.
Bhaskar's sophisticated analysis of reality makes it possible to discuss the differences and similarities in ontology between the various philosophies of science. Therefore, his work must be considered as a step forward: don't exclude different sorts of 'reality' on a priori grounds.

2.7 **Causality and Reason**

A last problem to be discussed is the difference between the concepts cause and reason. In Chapter 4 we will see that orthodox economics assumes the ontology, which says that humans are economic and rational actors. If the price of a good rises, an economic and rational actor is motivated to lower the quantity of the good that he is demanding. Now we say that the change in behaviour—lower quantity demanded—is caused by the change in price (*immediate cause*), but also by the fact that the actor is economic-rational (*ultimate cause*).

Do humans have a reason to change their behaviour in case of a price rise? Not necessarily. Imagine a landowner falls in love with the wife of one of his tenants. She does not react in a way that is acceptable to the landowner. Now his social prestige is at stake. To show his power he decides to fire her husband. The causes of his behaviour cannot be called reasonable. In the first place, we can wonder whether the satisfaction of his sexual drives is rational or not. Nobody but the landowner can answer this question. But the firing of the husband is definitely immoral in the Kantian sense. Therefore, we can say that his action is unreasonable.

Reason supposes the presence of a person with a ratio and enough willpower to act according to what the ratio tells him is good for him.[4] Moreover, reason supposes the presence of a moral consciousness, which tells the person that, on the level of essence, all men are equal. A reasonable act is based on a rational and a moral consideration. Now reason can be defined as the capacity to be reasonable. In contrast to that, causes refer to motivation, to forces, which drive people in one or another direction. It implies that a rational person has his drives under control, and a reasonable person is a rational person who has adopted the Kantian rule of morality (see also Box 2.2).

2.8 **The Structure of Knowledge**

As has been said already, knowledge is structured information. This section is about the ways we logically structure our information. The philosophical discourse shows the emergence of a consensus on a few basic elements.

2.8.1 PARADIGM

When we experience a practical problem, we first have to define the essence of the problem and establish the context in which it will be analysed. A paradigm is an answer to

---

[4] In Chapter 10 we will present a more sophisticated analysis of the mind.

the ontological question of what is to be considered as real and existent. In orthodox economics all practical problems are defined as problems of scarcity and placed in a situation in which many rational and socially independent individuals face problems of scarcity and are inclined to do everything that helps them to diminish it. The way situations are defined is a matter of ontology and results in the formulation of a paradigm. The typical sociological paradigm, for instance, is the statement that all human behaviour is socially learned behaviour. A typical sociological definition of the situation is the imagination of our world as consisting of groups of people, in which group-internal relations are characterized by solidarity, while group-external relationships are characterized by rivalry.

2.8.2 ANALYSIS

When we have defined our problem and placed it in a proper context, we can make a systematic analysis of the situation. When we have characterized the problematic situation by scarcity and have defined scarcity as the relationship between needs and resources that can satisfy these needs, we start an analysis on the basis of these two basic concepts. The concept of analysis means 'a distinction between'. Economists make a distinction between a need and a resource. Next, they make a distinction between a combination of needs and resources that leads to a supply of scarce goods and a combination of needs and resources that leads to a demand for scarce goods. In this way economists develop a language of 'a priori' concepts such as demand, supply, price, exchange, market, and value. Sociologists make a distinction between different groups, which operate in an arena, where they have their status battles. Every group suggests to other groups that they are superior, and that the others are inferior. Within firms there is an ongoing status battle between different departments. In markets there is an ongoing fight between different firms or groups of firms. In contrast to economics, which analyses relationships between firms in terms of competition and cooperation, sociological theory analyses these situations in terms of arena, solidarity and rivalry, and status. The government is always one of the important players. Social processes may lead to relevant civil servants becoming part of the established group. In this way, firms who have the capacity or potential to produce nuclear energy can be successful in convincing civil servants responsible for energy policy of the advantages of producing nuclear energy. Other firms, who produce wind energy, try to convince the same civil servants of the danger of nuclear energy, and of the great advantages of wind energy. If the wind lobby is successful, they gain in prestige (status) at the cost of the nuclear energy lobby. All activity, also so-called economic activity, is, in the end, social activity: it must lead to as high a status as possible.

Careful analysis of problematic situations gives us a logically consistent set of concepts that helps us interpret the problematic situation systematically.

2.8.3 THEORY

Now we have defined and analysed our situation, we can deduct from it a series of coherent theories. When we take our typical economic analysis as an example, we have interpreted the world as consisting of a very large amount of competitive markets. If this set of markets is in equilibrium, allocation of scarce resources is optimal. Then, a further improvement can only be reached via more sophisticated production technologies. This means that economic problems can be interpreted in terms of market disequilibria. Moreover, we know that price adjustments affect the quantities demanded and supplied and can enlarge or diminish the size of a market disequilibrium.[5] On the basis of this analysis we can formulate a whole series of theories—general statements about the relationship between two or more variables. Thus, unemployment can be interpreted as a labour market disequilibrium and be related to the price of labour, which is the wage rate.

2.8.4 HYPOTHESIS

Suppose our practical problem concerns a person who has been searching for a job for a long time without success. The typical economic theory states that her unemployment is caused by her supply wage being too high. This general statement can be tested for our problematic situation. So we can formulate a hypothesis stating that the Dutch economy over the period 1982–2004 is characterized by a stable relationship between the rate of unemployment and the level of the supply wage rate. If the coefficient representing the ratio between the supply wage level (or its growth rate), on the one hand, and the unemployment rate, on the other, is significant, the value of the coefficient reveals something about the size of the wage decline that is necessary to diminish the unemployment rate significantly. So our job searcher is advised to offer her labour for a lower wage. Then her chances of getting a job will increase.

From the former analysis we can conclude that the structure of knowledge has four basic elements: Paradigm, Analysis, Theory, and Hypothesis. We can summarize this result with the acronym *PATH*. In Figure 2.1 we have sketched a research process, including feedbacks. In case of a falsification of the empirical hypothesis the failure can be

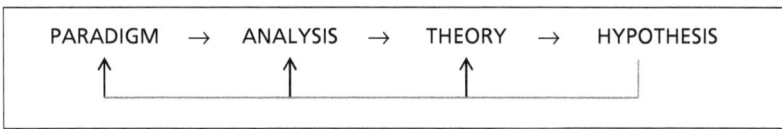

Figure 2.1. The Logical Structure of Knowledge

---

[5] In Chapters 6 to 9 we will see that economic approaches, based on a different paradigm, will offer us different analyses, theories, hypotheses, and empirical facts.

found in every element of PATH. In Chapter 10 we discuss the concept irrationality. Then, it becomes clear why researchers almost never criticize their own paradigm, and are not open for conversations with scientists who work in another programme.

In the next two sections we will deal with the organization of the process of knowledge production.

2.9 **Strategies of Specialization**

When studying the universe, we can stress its unity and think about its nature. When we want to profit from our knowledge in terms of higher levels of well-being, however, this is not enough. Therefore, we must make an analysis of the universe—make a distinction between various parts of it. A first and major distinction is that between the natural and the non-natural world. Another distinction is that between the material and the non-material world or between the non-living and the living world. All these antonyms are not necessarily identical. Imagine our world to consist of solid, liquid, and gaseous material. These elements manifest themselves in the form of stone and metal, water and other types of liquid, and in different sorts of gas. All these elements are subjects which are related to each other in particular ways. *Materiality* is, however, only one aspect of our reality. The other aspect is *ideality*. In every subject there is a built-in power that determines the direction in which the elements are moving. This power is an expression of the idea that is embedded in the material side of reality. Particular atoms are inclined to cluster into molecules. Particular molecules are inclined to cluster into more complex ones. Particular combinations of molecules, especially organic materials, are capable of functioning as the body of a living being: bacteria, bacilli, plants, animals, and human beings. So every 'being' has a material and an ideal aspect.

In practice, the division of labour within the scientific community is not efficiently organized and no single criterion is able to explain which discipline is doing which task so as to achieve an optimal functional structure. This chaos results from the tendency of scientists to group together around a particular discipline, to become independent of other disciplines, and to rival them, rather than to cooperate with other groups in a serious attempt to achieve an integrated whole of knowledge.

2.9.1 SUBSYSTEMS VERSUS ASPECT-SYSTEMS

To better understand processes of specialization in terms of *aspects* of nature rather than of real-life phenomena we will explain the difference according to the systems approach. Here, the universe is a whole system, which operates on the highest level of integration and generalization. Now we can formulate specializations by making distinctions between different subsystems. For instance, society can be divided into a number of institutions:

family, economy, government, education, and religion. These institutions are subsystems of society as a whole. In chemistry we can subdivide processes into organic and inorganic processes, and in biology we can focus on plants or on animals.

In general, we can define a system as a set of interrelated elements. Then a *subsystem* of a whole system can be defined as a system of which the elements are a subset of the whole system, but the character of the interrelationships is the same for both systems. However, we can also make a distinction between different aspect-systems. For instance, we can analyse the economic aspect of human life. The same human behaviour can be approached from different perspectives, for instance from the social point of view. In general, we can define an *aspect-system* as a system of which the elements are the same as in the whole system, but of which the interrelationships represent only one aspect of the whole.

When we take two subsystems together we move from a more *specific* to a more *general* system or analysis. When we take two aspect-systems together we move from a more *partial* to a more *integrated* system or analysis.

In Figure 2.2 we have presented a picture, which shows the principal difference between a subsystem and an aspect-system.

In Figure 2.3 we have pictured a figure, which shows four types of systems, a categorization which is based on the set of elements and the set of aspects, reflected in the character of a particular relationship. The types are specific-partial (A), specific-integral (B), general-partial (C), and general-integral (D).

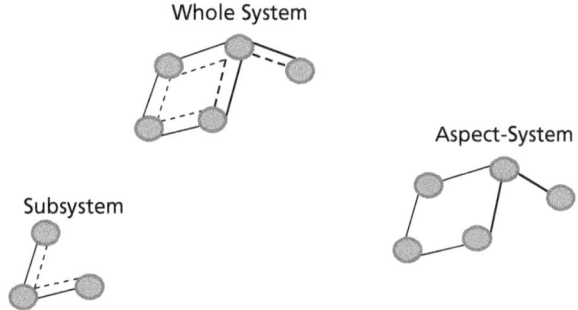

Figure 2.2. Subsystem versus Aspect-System

No. of aspects / No. of elements	Partial	Integral
Specific	A	B
General	C	D

Figure 2.3. Different Types of Systems

In Chapter 4 we will see that neoclassical economists are permanently mixing up the different types. This is due to their basic error in approaching real-life economies (sub-system) with the orthodox economic analysis, which reflects an aspect-system.

2.10 **The Organization of Human Science**

We can discuss the organizational pattern of science from two points of view, namely from a *historical perspective* and from a *logical point of view*. When we give a historical account we can understand why the current division of labour is quite chaotic. However, a logical account of the current situation makes us more aware of the gaps that must be bridged when improving the quality of interdisciplinary research.

So, if we define human science as the discipline that aims at the explanation of human behaviour, and we imagine a situation in which humans live in their environment, then three types of relationships can be distinguished. A human being has a relationship with his natural environment (1), with his fellow humans (2), and with his Self (3). Economics studies the first, sociology studies the second, and psychology the third relationship. In real life every step is determined by all three relationships simultaneously. When a person is looking for a job, he may do it primarily to make a living (economic aspect), but, unavoidably, his choices are co-determined by his social and his psychic drive. When a person subscribes to a workshop on 'personal growth', the psychic aspect may represent the principal motive, but, unavoidably, the economic and the social aspect play a role as well. If the workshop is very expensive the person might hesitate to subscribe to it, and if his social environment is sharply disapproving these types of activities he may decide not to go. As long as we analyse a particular aspect in isolation from other relevant aspects, we cannot apply the theory to the empirical world. As soon as we have integrated the three primary aspects, we have a much more realistic theoretical tool, which might produce empirically relevant results.

Two other disciplines can also be interpreted as aspect-disciplines within human science, namely *history* and *geography*. History is focused on the role of time in human life, whereas geography is about the role of space. Although the historical aspect plays a role within economics, psychology, and sociology, only in history is it at the centre of the discipline. So with geography: the aspect of space plays a role in economics as well as in psychology and sociology, but only in geography is the spatial aspect at the centre of the discipline.

All other areas or fields within human science can be interpreted as subsystems of the aspect-systems just mentioned or as aspect-systems of aspect-systems. Ethics, for instance, is about the moral aspect of life, which is an aspect-system of the social aspect-system of human life. Political science can also be considered to be an aspect-system; then it is about the political or control aspect of human life. When derived from psychology as well as from sociology and economics it is an aspect-system of an aspect-system. The first is about self-control; the second about control of society or parts of it; and the third is about economic policy of individuals, households, firms, and governments. Many other studies within social science can be interpreted as studies of subsystems of society. Anthropology, European studies, industrial sociology, social policy studies, and business administration are examples in this respect.

2.11 **Methodological Pluralism**

What we accept as reliable knowledge is, to a large extent, a social product. We all face our reality as something big and strange and we tend to feel very uncertain about what we know about its functioning. Therefore, we tend to accept as reliable knowledge only those parts that are accepted by many people, or at least by groups of authorized experts. The fact that knowledge is a human product makes it impossible to reach the level of objectivity. It always remains subjective. If many 'subjects' agree upon the acceptability of some statements and regularities, it becomes intersubjective, but it always remains fallible. In this text we have seen that we can only observe and collect information by means of frameworks of interpretations. People develop habits and conventions with respect to the way they frame and interpret their situation. This means that the choice of frame will always remain subject to debate (see Box 2.3). In real life some frames dominate

---

BOX 2.3 CHOICE OF FRAME

In social science the idea of framing plays a very important role. From Kant we learned that our mind—whether we are conscious of this process or not—frames our situation when observing empirical reality. But the way in which we frame our practical situations is influenced by our psychic, social, and economic status. A person's psychic status can be characterized by a strong sensitivity towards uncertainty, implying a strong desire for protection by a father figure, for instance. For a person who lives in a social context that is characterized by collectivism—Latin America, for instance—this need for protection is satisfied more easily compared with social contexts that are characterized by individualism—the United States, for instance. If a person is very rich he can invest his wealth in many different assets, creating a strong feeling of safety. Then his need for certainty and protection is satisfied, and the person lives a happy life. But if—by revolution, for instance—the person is robbed of all his property, the lack of certainty and protection becomes a severe problem, since he might not have built up psychic and social buffers against uncertainty.

Whether basic needs are satisfied or not is decisive in the formation of frames. Strong personalities who are rich tend to frame the world in more liberal ways. They analyse their actual situation in reference with this liberal anchor or benchmark. They easily detect differences between the actual and the 'normal' situation, and call these differences 'disequilibria'. Weak personalities, who are not very wealthy, tend to frame the world in more conservative or collective ways. They are inclined to interpret their actual situation in reference to a more conservative anchor. Under the influence of experiences, frameworks of interpretation evolve. On the personal level these changes are relatively minor, since the first years of our childhood are very important and more or less fix someone's frame. On the societal level, however, economic and social developments can affect the frameworks more significantly.

other frames. Historically, we see that some frames do not survive, others adapt and survive, and new frames emerge. In a liberal and democratic society, individuals are free to choose. For a scientific community this principle means the freedom to choose one's own framework of interpretation. Fair competition and effective cooperation can be expected only if we are able to organize power-free communication between all people interested in scientific enquiry.

When we compare the three boxes in this chapter—about Scientific Revolution (2.1), about Reason (2.2), and about Choice of Frame (2.3), we see three important elements of scientific knowledge, in which interrelationship is still subject to hot debates within philosophy of science. The first element stresses the relevance of 'bare' facts. The second is about the role of human thinking, and the third is about the role of personalities in their economic and social context. Science should respect all three elements in their interrelationship.

3 Genesis and Development of Economics and Sociology

3.1 Introduction

Within modern Western thought three different types of science can be distinguished: natural science, life science, and social science. Natural science studies physical and chemical processes. Life science studies chemical processes within living bodies and the behaviour of plants and animals. Social science analyses human behaviour, while taking the results of the other groups of sciences as a description and explanation of the human environment. When humans are insufficiently aware of their context, environmental problems, including health problems, are the result. Our book focuses primarily on social science, leaving this environmental context out of consideration.

As we saw in Chapter 2, modern science is a reaction to the dominance of religious doctrines. In the first millennium after the birth of Christ, in Western Europe the Roman Catholic Church not only dominated the way people interpreted the world of the supernatural; it also dictated the way people had to interpret human society and the way they had to behave in the here and now. In Europe in the second millennium, social philosophers started to analyse society from a more secular point of view. Because human morality was considered to be the main difference between animals and humans, they were called moral philosophers. They created images of society that could function as paradigms for social scientific research programmes. In this sense, moral philosophy appeared to be fertile ground for the development of a flourishing social science.[1]

In this chapter we will show which paradigms were developed in this respect. Developments in society in the 18th and 19th century stimulated the development of analysis of sectors of society, especially the economy. Classical political economy, for instance, can be seen as a reflection of the increasing significance of the upcoming bourgeoisie. Thereafter, we will show how neoclassical economics and classical sociology grew out of political economy, both intending to improve the scientific value of the analyses constructed thus far.

[1] Ekelund and Hebert (1990) gives a lengthy overview of the various schools of thought that dominated economic dogmen history.

3.2 **Modern Moral Philosophy as the Foundation of Social Science**

Thomas Hobbes was the first moral philosopher to analyse society in a secular way. He worried about the loss of orthodox Christian faith. According to him, the Church was the institution par excellence to keep people's behaviour under control. Religion was the primary disciplining institution and secularization meant that people would become jealous, see others as rivals, and be inclined to struggle against each other constantly. The only answer to secularization was the acceptance of a *strict social hierarchy* and a *person with absolute power*. Hobbes lived in the 17th century, a period of monarchs who wielded absolute power. Therefore, his book, *Leviathan*, is considered to be an apology for the status quo (Hobbes, 1651) (see also Achterhuis, 1988).

John Locke was another famous philosopher. In Locke (1689) he was more optimistic about the future than Hobbes and did not foresee huge social and political clashes. First, he considered the moral ideas that were advocated by the Church as innate to human beings. Although losing faith in the existence of a personal god and in the reality of hell and heaven, people do not lose automatically their *conscience*. Moreover, a possible way to avoid outright violence between people is the *exit option*, which means that some people leave the arenas of conflict and migrate to other areas (Locke, 1689).

Jean-Jacques Rousseau was another famous philosopher. He lived in the 18th century and was not very optimistic about the future. In contrast to Hobbes, however, he did not advocate absolutism as a way out of the chaos that constantly threatens our society. Rousseau considered the *inequality between the different classes* as the main source of conflict. By being tied up in a straitjacket of roles that are determined by the prevailing class structure, people lose their original characteristics. Rousseau (1755) reveals his principal idea: the true and harmonious human nature returns if we are able to establish societal structures that reflect the idea of human equality.

Of course, there were more famous philosophers. But, with hindsight, we can say that each of the three philosophers just mentioned can be characterized as typical of a particular current of thought.[2]

Hobbes, then, is the *conservative* who views man as a being that can only flourish within a strict hierarchical order, which is the natural order as in the world of animals. The capacities of people appear to be unevenly divided, which makes some people suited for being leaders and others for being followers. In the 17th and 18th century the philosophical debate was especially focused on the question of whether a democracy would be preferable to a monarchy. Conservatives were of the opinion that families who had shown excellent skills in defending and controlling a country must have the right genes and traditions to do this job. The elite have the responsibility to educate the masses, and

---

[2] A historical person's ideas and writings never perfectly reflect a particular ideal-type of thinking. As a matter of illustration, however, we can use the philosophers, as mentioned in the text, for our goal.

teach them the right values and norms of life. If necessary they are morally allowed to maintain law and order by coercion.

Locke is the *liberal* who views man as a being that always maintains a balance between care for his own Self and empathy for the poor. On the basis of the first characteristic, he is inclined to avoid or even prevent severe social conflicts. An individual is supposed to search for the best opportunities of having a prosperous and peaceful life. So man must be left free to develop his capacities. On the basis of the second characteristic, free people are expected to voluntarily transfer resources to the poor, preventing the emergence of sharp class divisions. When guaranteeing that every exchange is voluntary, a country becomes prosperous.

Rousseau is the *socialist* who considers hierarchical structures to be a bottleneck, restricting people from developing their true capacities. These hierarchical structures are not only found in the political field, but also within large firms and in markets when the large firms have out-competed the smaller ones.

These descriptions not only contain the prototypes of three currents of social and political thought. They also represent mechanisms that steer an orderly, a free or an equal society.

In the ideal-typical conservative world, the mechanisms are *moral suasion* and, if necessary, *political coercion*. They must create order, make social life predictable, and trigger private initiative within legal restrictions and fair treatment of everyone, according to his merits.

In the ideal-typical liberal world, the mechanism is *free exchange* between people, who can freely enter and exit every place, where they can meet other people to communicate and to transact. In such a society everyone will agree that private property must be protected; otherwise exchange would not make any sense. Freedom for the individual to develop his capacities and to build up his own wealth is fair as long as it is not the privilege for a happy few, but for everyone. That makes *voluntary transfers* from the rich to the poor another mechanism. It is based on sympathy and it narrows the gap between the different classes within society.

In the ideal-typical socialist world, the mechanism is *democratic decision-making* concerning all issues that have an important effect on the lives of the people. Politically, democracy is the expression of the true equality between people. Economically, true equality is expressed by an equal distribution of the necessities of life. This equal treatment makes social conflict superfluous, thus creating the necessary order.

All these currents of thought admit that the three principal issues in social analysis are order, freedom, and equality; and that these three issues are strongly related to each other. The difference between the social and political currents, however, can be summarized as follows. Suppose society shows a negative spiral of growing disorder, inequality, and lack of individual freedom. In such a situation a conservative prefers a strategy that, first, leads to regaining strict order, under the condition of a re-establishment of a natural hierarchy. If order is restored, freedom and some equality will return automatically within the hierarchical constraints of the natural order. A liberal, however, would prefer a strict order in the sense of a protection of private property rights. If they are efficiently protected, and make private initiative in economic affairs profitable, order and some equality will automatically return within the constraints of individual freedom. A socialist prefers a government that establishes a societal structure that offers equality to the masses of the people with respect to the basic necessities of life. Social and political stability returns and will create the necessary conditions for individual freedom and order.

In Sections 3.3, 3.4, 3.5, and 3.6 we will show how social science emerged from moral philosophy.

3.3 **The Emergence of Classical Political Economy**

Scientists began to analyse the functioning of society as it evolved in Western Europe and North America in the second half of the 18th and the first half of the 19th century upon the basis of the moral philosophies, as discussed in Section 3.2. In the *feudal society* of the medieval period, the main groups were the landlords, the peasants, the government, and the Church. To an increasing extent, they were challenged by the upcoming traders and manufacturers. The government apparatus was headed by monarchs and the landlords possessed the land, which was the most important economic resource. The peasants worked on the land and they were allowed to keep part of the produce. The landlords took the rest and sold it on the markets. Besides offering peasants the opportunity to earn a small living, the landlords were responsible for their safety. The maintenance of the Christian civilization was the responsibility of the clergy—they had to morally persuade the nobility to materialize their responsibilities towards the peasants. Feudal society was hierarchically ordered and well regulated— by legislation as well as by customs.[3] When the process of industrialization had its principal take-off, two new classes emerged: the bourgeoisie or capitalist class and the proletariat or working class. The traders and manufacturers increasingly resisted strict governmental regulation of their activities. The levying of import duties especially was a thorn in their flesh. These political conflicts triggered an ongoing debate between two groups or positions. On the one hand, there were those who considered protected trade not only a typical landlord interest, but also as beneficial for society as a whole—*mercantilism*. On the other hand, there were those who considered free trade not only a typical capitalist interest, but also as beneficial for society as a whole— *economic liberalism*.

Adam Smith is the most famous defender of free trade. He was a moral philosopher who applied Lockean principles to the analysis of an economy. Free individuals tend to serve their own interests, but are also able to develop *moral sentiments* (Smith, 1759).[4]

---

[3] It is important to note that the control of the elite, over themselves as well as over the masses, was far from perfect.

[4] This book—*The Theory of Moral Sentiments*—analyses the mechanism of voluntary transfers on the basis of sympathy. In another book, *The Wealth of Nations* (1776), Smith analyses the mechanism of free

The first motivation dominates when buying and selling goods, capital, and labour on the market. When the local community asks for charity, moral sentiment motivates people to contribute. While the first drive leads to a smooth functioning of markets, the second drive diminishes inequality and class conflict. After Smith, economists such as Ricardo, Malthus, and Marx made analyses of the functioning of the capitalist system as it operated during the 18th and 19th century in the Western world. We now call these economists *classical political economists*. The term classical suggests a link with the Greek and Roman secular and natural philosophy. The term political suggests that the analyses were primarily made to serve a political end: how to develop a system of production that creates prosperity for some or all classes. Some economists were pessimistic about the potential for a capitalist system to create lasting prosperity for all classes—Marx, for instance. Others were not optimistic about the future of capitalism as a vehicle towards any prosperity—Ricardo and Malthus, for instance. Smith, however, was optimistic about the results of a capitalist economy. He paid much attention to the necessary institutions that must make prosperity in a free market society possible.

The analyses of the classical political economists had a common definition of the situation: an economy is a game where capitalists, workers, landlords, peasants, and the government are the main players. In a capitalist economy the capitalists are the owners of the most important means of production. They take the decisions to invest in production capacity and they hire workers if needed and fire workers, if they are no longer needed. The landlords own the land and they rent the land to peasants as long as it is profitable. The government is responsible for law and order and therefore allowed to monopolize the right to use violence and to levy taxes.

These analyses aimed at an explanation of the level of production and the distribution of income over the different classes. The outcomes of the analyses of the various economists differ significantly, however.

Adam Smith developed the idea of a free market that functions *as if* there is an invisible hand that makes quantities demanded and quantities supplied equal to each other. If there is an excess of demand, a price increase will lead to a lower level of the quantity demanded and a higher level of the quantity supplied. In case of an excess of supply the opposite will happen. In other words, if prices are flexible, markets show a tendency towards equilibrium. As long as governments do not interfere with this adjustment mechanism, all markets tend towards their equilibrium. It means that a system of self-interested actors tends towards an optimum situation for the economy as a whole. Smith's optimism about the possibilities—not only in reaching an optimum for the economy as a whole, but also in achieving economic growth—was especially based on the expected positive effects on labour productivity of a process of ongoing division of labour (Smith, 1776).

exchange, which is the market mechanism. See Appendix D at the end of the book for a more detailed discussion of the writings of Adam Smith.

BOX 3.1 WTO

In order to avoid tariff wars as occurred in the 1920s and 1930s the General Agreement on Tariffs and Trade (GATT) was created. From 1947 on, it organized a series of negotiation rounds that resulted in tariff reductions. In 1994 the World Trade Organization (WTO) was created. Membership of this organization put greater obligation on countries to observe the established rules.

   Every country has an interest in tariff reduction by other countries, but prefers to protect its own interests, by means of trade barriers. Protection is often justified by the 'infant-industry' argument. If a firm has just been created recently, it is unable to compete with the establishment in that particular sector. For developing countries this argument may be a relevant one. Temporary protection can make it possible to become a mature firm that can survive in a competitive environment. The WTO is the global platform where members can negotiate about the fairness and efficiency of the existing tariff walls.

David Ricardo (1815) improved Smith's theory of international trade by showing the relevance of comparative advantage rather than absolute advantage.[5] So, even countries that are the least productive in the production of whichever good can profit from international trade. Applied to the current process of globalization it means that rich as well as poor countries profit from a regime of free trade—the basic 'axiom' of today's WTO (UN World Trade Organization) (see Box 3.1 about the WTO). Nevertheless, Ricardo was not optimistic about the possibilities of ever growing economies. Because of population growth, to an increasing extent, less productive land must be used for the production of food. This leads to structural increases in food prices, negatively affecting the purchasing power of the (minimum) wages. Besides this effect, Ricardo acknowledged that the idea of what must be regarded as a minimum subsistence level is not only a biological, but also a cultural affair.[6]

Robert Malthus (1798) stressed also the negative effects of population growth on the possibilities of increasing prosperity per capita. Increasing production leads temporarily to increasing wages. But a higher level of prosperity would lead to an improvement of the health care for children and subsequent decline in their death rates. This means that the amount of resources per capita does not rise in the long run. Therefore, most people would always remain on a minimum level. This theory describes, more or less, the current poverty trap in many African and Asian countries.

Karl Marx (1872) made a distinction between different stages of development of the capitalist system. In the early phases of industrialization competition prevails, but in

---

[5] Smith had stated that a country must specialize in the production and trade of goods that could be produced at the highest level, compared with other countries. Ricardo, however, stated that countries must specialize in goods which are most advantageous relative to other goods; in other words, where opportunity costs are the lowest.

[6] When prosperity increases, the lowest incomes must increase as well to prevent people with low incomes from becoming marginalized. For example, if a growing number of children in a village or in a particular neighbourhood of a big city entertain themselves in a more luxurious way, the children of low-income parents will not be able to participate in social activities anymore if minimum incomes are not raised proportionally.

later phases the scale of production becomes increasingly decisive with respect to the question of which companies survive and which go out of business. Capital accumulation leads to concentration in the industrial markets. Increasing shares of production are spent on investment goods, implying a decreasing share for the production of consumption goods. Wages are set at their minimum level because of the overall unemployment (permanent excess of supply of labour). The application of new technologies of production makes an ever-growing level of production possible. The character of technological progress leads not only to an increasing capital coefficient (amount of capital divided by the amount of production), but also to a lower level of employment. Because wages are permanently at the minimum level, the excess supply of labour cannot be diminished via a decrease in the wage level. Actually unemployment—a reserve army in the terminology of Marx—will increase, fuelling the class-consciousness of the workers. Marx is pessimistic with respect to the chances of survival of the capitalist system, but he does not regret its predicted downfall. On the basis of his socialist political philosophy, he considers private ownership of means of production as an anomaly in a modern society. A 'retour à la nature' for Marx means the abolition of the class conflict. When the property rights of the means of production are transferred to the people as a nation, the human drive to compete with each other will die and cooperation and solidarity will make it possible to maintain high levels of prosperity.

Classical political economists have the following characteristics in common:

(1) They analyse *the economy as a real-life system*—the economy as we know it from our daily lives and as it is discussed in the media. The economy is approached as a subsystem of our real-life society—not as an aspect-system that analyses society from the typical economic perspective.

(2) They do *not intend to produce universally valid economic theories*, but stick to the analysis of the capitalist system of their own times, the 18th and 19th century.

(3) They all have a strong focus on the explanation of *production and distribution*, trying to answer the question whether a capitalist system can bring prosperity to nations.

(4) Their epistemology is more or less *rationalist*. On the basis of a notion of self-interest of persons and of groups, an analysis is developed of an a priori character rather than an empirical account of what happens.

The answers given to the principal questions differ widely. The reason for this diversity must be found in their methodological differences. The following differences are important in this respect:

(1) Smith focuses on an analysis of the production process and the increase in efficiency that can be achieved when implementing a greater division of labour. Competition in free markets leads to the survival of the fittest companies—those that implement labour division in the most efficient way. His analysis has a *micro-character* and is based on an idea of the drive of individual entrepreneurs, workers, and consumers. Smith did not analyse technological innovation, but his focus on labour division made him an optimist.

(2) Ricardo's pessimism results from the idea of a *constant fertility of land*. Some pieces are fertile, while others are less. If we introduce the possibility of agricultural technological progress, the result turns out to be different. His analysis has a more *macro-character*, especially analysing factor income distribution.

(3) Malthus' pessimism results from the idea of *increasing health care for children* in case of increasing wage incomes. This affects the size of the population, making it necessary to feed more people. However, if we assume that an increase in income leads to a lower birth rate, prosperity in terms of income per capita rises. His theory has a clear macro-character.

(4) Marx is quite explicit about the philosophical foundations of his economic analyses. His methodology is *collectivist* in nature. Classes conflict with each other—not persons. Personal behaviour is determined by the class to which the person belongs and class behaviour is determined by the structural characteristics of the situation of the economy as a whole. These characteristics are determined by the system to which the economy belongs and its stage of development. Marx's pessimism with respect to the survival of capitalism is directly related to his methodological collectivism: society consists of two rival classes and only when this conflict is solved will there be lasting peace and prosperity.

Technological progress as a main factor determining the wealth of a nation is, surprisingly, absent from classical political economy. When we observe economic developments in the 20th century—long- term economic growth especially triggered by technological innovation—we can conclude that this absence is a serious omission. Many classical political economists were not very explicit in their methodology. Smith was a liberal who was inspired by Locke and Hume. Marx was a socialist and was inspired by Rousseau. But Ricardo, Malthus, and many other economists were not explicit in their philosophy and the way in which they derived their analyses from it.

Later economists, such as John Stuart Mill, Stanley Jevons, and Carl Menger, considered the lack of universality in classical political economy to be a major flaw. In Section 3.4 we will deal with these critics and the main characteristics of the alternatives that they developed.

3.4 From Classical Political Economy to Neoclassical Economics

John Stuart Mill (1874) was one of the first to give an indication in which direction improvements could be achieved. Later, John Neville Keynes and others elaborated on his work and tried to formulate an alternative approach. Now, it is generally agreed that the formulation of Lionel Robbins presents most clearly what is now called the orthodox research programme (Robbins, 1932). Here, economics is not about the real-life economy anymore. It focuses on the natural scarcity aspect of human life and it aims at the formulation of laws of a universal and eternal character, like the laws of nature as formulated in Newtonian physics. The law of gravity, for instance, holds in Europe as well as in China; it held thousands of years ago, and will hold in the future. According to orthodox economists, social science must aim at the discovery of laws of nature, in particular human nature. So economists must abstract economic theory from place and time and focus on the ways in which people deal with their problem of scarcity of natural resources.

For a growing number of economists natural science functioned as an example to be followed. When physicists and chemists set up their laboratory experiments, they attempt to isolate one factor from other determinants of a particular phenomenon. By varying the isolated factor and keeping other factors constant, they can observe its effect. This is *the method of isolated abstraction*. By imitating natural science, economists wanted to isolate the economic aspect from other aspects of human behaviour. Economists should study the omnipresent phenomenon of scarcity, which is defined as the relationship between human needs and resources capable of satisfying these needs. When abstracting from other aspects it is illuminating to formulate explicitly which are the other aspects. We can distinguish three primary aspects, namely the economic, the social, and the psychic aspect. Economics focuses on the relationship between humans and their natural environment. Sociology is about the relationship between humans, who recognize each other as such, while psychology is about the relationship between a person and his Self. The term 'economic' refers to the problem of scarcity of natural resources. The term 'social' refers to the problem of 'the status in the eyes of the other', while the term 'psychic' refers to the problem of 'the respect of a person for his own Self' or 'self-respect'.

Generally speaking, any human action is always motivated economically, socially, and psychically. Imagine a white person, living in Texas, who wants to sell a piece of land. A black person shows interest and is willing to pay the demand price. The white vendor, however, refuses. The economic motivation implies that there is a price that is acceptable to the seller—his reservation price or demand price. An economic and rational actor would be happy with the buyer. The social motivation, however, implies that the buyer must fit into the culture of the group of landowners in the region. The psychic motivation implies that the transaction must contribute to the vendor's self-respect. If a person has developed a clear picture of his 'true Self' being a reasonable person, an act of discrimination diminishes his self-respect. Only in primitive cultures does discrimination, as required by the gods, increase self-respect. When looking at the content of the US Constitution, the USA is not a primitive country. But people imperfectly adjust to ruling institutions, and form subcultures, which can be very primitive. In our example, discrimination is triggered by the social motive, while it is constrained by the economic and possibly by the psychic motive.

Orthodox economics abstracts from the social aspect by assuming social relationships to be non-existent. Relationships between people are economic in nature. They regard each other as owners of scarce resources and engage in trade with each other if the exchange is beneficial for both. Social relationships emerge if people recognize each other as humans. Then they form groups and behave as social beings. Such recognition can have positive as well as negative effects. If individuals recognize each other as members of the same group, they express their solidarity with each other. If, however, they recognize each other as members of a different group they rival each other in terms of status. In orthodox economic analysis, people are not members of groups; they operate as individual persons.

Orthodox economics also abstracts from the psychic aspect by assuming that every individual has perfect control over the Self. In other words, every person is a perfectly integrated personality, who has enough willpower to control his emotions and act according to what he truly prefers. Thus, the person is perfectly rational and emotions only play a role when establishing the deliberately considered preferences.

What is left is the economic problem—the tension between needs and natural resources that can satisfy these needs. This problem can never be solved completely—scarcity can only be reduced. An extensive analysis of the scarcity problem must lead to the formulation of economic laws. These laws are observable only in the isolated world as constructed by economists, just as physical laws only hold in the isolated world of laboratory experiments. Economic laws are valid irrespective of time and place and reflect that scarcity is and will always remain part of human life. We can summarize economics as an aspect-system as follows:

Economics is about everything
But not everything is economics.

As already said, Lionel Robbins formulated the characteristics of the neoclassical research programme in a way that is generally accepted. We can present his view on the philosophical characteristics of economics in the following way.

3.4.1 ONTOLOGY

The world consists of non-social and psychically perfectly integrated individuals who face the omnipresent phenomenon of natural scarcity.

3.4.2 EPISTEMOLOGY

Individual human beings are rational actors who take their decisions on the basis of deliberately collected information. Among them are scientists, who formulate axioms by means of introspection and by the application of rules of logic.

3.4.3 METHODOLOGY

Behaviour, as observed on all levels of analysis—markets, market economies, global economy—must be explained by aggregating the behaviour of individuals. This is called methodological individualism or reductionism.

To further present the orthodox economic research programme in terms of its methodology, we use the idea that the structure of knowledge consists of four elements. The first part consists of an ontological statement about the reality we are explaining, which is called a 'paradigm'. The second part consists of an analysis that is derived from the paradigm. A third part consists of theoretical statements that are derived from the analysis of the situation. A fourth part consists of hypotheses, which are specified statements about the empirical reality of our problem. We can expose the orthodox economic research programme in these terms now.

3.4.4 PARADIGM

Every human being maximizes the level of satisfaction of their needs (the utilities he is deriving from the consumption of goods), under the restriction of the available scarce resources.

3.4.5 ANALYSIS

Scarcity is defined as the relationship between needs and resources able to satisfy those needs. In some cases individuals combine needs and resources, resulting in a demand for goods—when buying products in a grocery shop, for instance. In other cases individuals combine needs and resources resulting in a supply of goods—when supplying products in a grocery shop, for instance. The place where supply and demand meet each other is called the market. In this way a neoclassical economist builds a consistent set of concepts—a language—that makes it possible to analyse a problematic situation.

3.4.6 THEORY

From the statement that utility maximization is conducted under the constraints of scarce resources it is possible to logically deduce a negative relationship between the price of a good and the quantity demanded (deduction!). In the same way we can deduct a positive relationship between price and quantity supplied. It also means that price fluctuations have an effect on the difference between the quantity demanded and the quantity supplied. So, in case of market disequilibria flexible prices can bring a market back into equilibrium.

3.4.7 HYPOTHESIS

If we had been able to construct such a market in a laboratory, we could have measured the strength of the different reactions of the quantities demanded and supplied in case of price fluctuations. In modern experimental economics attempts in this direction are being made.[7] However, it is practically impossible to find people who play the role of an economic, rational, and non-social actor. Moreover, participants are always aware of the artificiality of the situation—a disadvantage compared with physical/chemical experiments.

In Section 3.5 we will deal with economists who disagree with the neoclassical strategy of isolated abstraction.

3.5 The Institutionalist Critique of Neoclassical Economics

Especially in the United States, the Institutionalists disagreed with the neoclassical philosophy. According to them, it makes no sense to search for laws that only hold in isolated worlds, but will never have any practical value. In physics, only laws that operate in the empirical world play an important role. What oxygen atoms are doing in a world that only consists of oxygen atoms and what hydrogen atoms are doing in a strictly hydrogen world does not tell us anything about the functioning of water. Only studying the effects of water in different circumstances can tell us something about the characteristics of water. So with human behaviour: only studying real-life situations makes sense.

By rejecting the method of isolated abstraction, these economists studied the functioning of real economies and 'discovered' that *there are no universal and eternal laws* describing economies in general. So the views of the neoclassical economists were

---

[7] Experiments with the 'ultimatum game' show that sociology students and economics students score differently. Economics students act more in line with their economic rational paradigm, where sociology students live, to a certain extent at least, in a social world. By way of clarification: the ultimatum game is played by two players. One player must divide a particular amount of money between the two, and the other can refuse the amount of money that is offered to him. But in case of refusal neither party receives money. Economic theory predicts a transfer of one euro, while in sociological theory the idea of fairness plays a role, leading to a division of the amount of money closer to a 50–50 distribution.

challenged and some attempted to formulate an alternative philosophy. The critique can be summarized in the following points:

(1) Because universal and eternal laws concerning human behaviour do not exist, social scientists must search for adequate descriptions of historical processes in real-life societies.

(2) The motivations of human beings cannot be derived from a constant human nature, but are triggered by the structure of their environment.

(3) Agents are rational only to a certain degree; different types of instinct and habit are significant drives in this respect.

Thorstein Veblen was one of the first and most important of the group of *Institutionalists*. Veblen (1899) stresses the relevance of an organic ontology rather than a mechanic one. Therefore, he advocated the use of biological metaphors more than physical ones. In particular, the process of natural selection, as described by Darwin in his attempt to explain the evolution of species, was applied to social economic processes. When people are driven by instincts and habits, especially *habits of thought*, a change in the environment means the selection of those who appear to be the fittest—they will survive. Applied to the economy it means that firms whose habits of thought, which is their *corporate culture*, appear to be the fittest in the evolving economic, social, political, and natural circumstances will survive at the cost of the firms with less advantageous habits.

Institutionalists such as Mitchell and Kuznets focused on the necessity of developing reliable empirical facts. When the description and explanation of a real-life economy is the principal aim of economics, we need to know the basic empirical facts of our subject matter in the first place. They worked especially on the construction of macroeconomic statistics. This gave Kuznets the opportunity to formulate his ideas about the existence of long-term business cycles.

Commons has become well-known for his work on the legal foundations of a market and a market economy (Commons, 1924). He started his analyses with the concept 'transaction', and stated that every transaction must be backed not only by a private but also by a *social contract*. The private contract must arrange the conditions of the transaction and the social contract must organize the protection of the property rights and the guarantee that the terms of the contract will be complied with. While market behaviour is an aggregate of *private action*, the construction and compliance of the social contract is the result of *collective action*.

Clark criticized the neoclassical habit of interpreting capital costs as fixed costs, as opposed to labour costs being variable costs (Clark, 1936). From the point of view of a firm this might be an adequate interpretation. From a societal point of view, however, capital costs are the variable costs—by saving and investing we can build up capital in varying degrees. When we do not reinvest, the value of capital will decrease. Labour costs, however, must be interpreted as fixed—firms can fire people, but society cannot.

Because the Institutionalists remained a rather small group, they were not able to develop a mature alternative to neoclassical philosophy. Therefore, they never became a prestigious group of economists in the academic world.

3.6 **From Classical Political Economy to Classical Sociology**

In Section 3.3 we discussed the characteristics of classical political economy, whose aim was to explain a real-life economy, being a subsystem (not aspect-system) of a real-life society. Its ontology is rather mechanistic, and its epistemology is rather rationalist. Its dominant methodology was to develop a static analysis of particular historical stages of economic development, especially the capitalist stage of the Western countries in the 18th and 19th century. In Section 3.4 we described the reaction of many economists who wanted to be more scientific, and to formulate universal and eternal laws about the economic aspect of life, which is the omnipresent phenomenon of scarcity. Other social scientists, however, reacted quite differently to the results of classical political economy. While focusing on the economy, they did not take its societal context into account. Moreover, they produced mostly rationalist analyses of a metaphysical nature— the invisible hand and phenomena of that sort. Positivist criticism by Comte stimulated others to start with the establishment of so-called *social facts* and a positivist explanation of them. Comte is seen now as the founding father of the independent discipline of sociology.[8] His work was the start of what we now call classical sociology.

What has become familiar under the heading of classical sociology is a group of sociologists whose thought shares a number of characteristics, but also differs greatly in a number of other respects. Their shared characteristics are the following:

(1) The economy can be understood only if it is placed in its social and political *context*.
(2) There is such a thing as *society*; its functioning can be studied by analysing the interrelationships between the different institutions of which it is constituted.
(3) Human life must be interpreted as a *historical process*; empirical relationships differ significantly when different stages of development are compared. We can imagine, for instance, that in one period wages strongly react to changes in the unemployment rate, while in other stages hardly any reaction can be detected.
(4) Human behaviour is *social behaviour*: individuals behave according to the group norms set by society at large. Culture creates a difference in behaviour of young

---

[8] Although Comte is generally regarded as the founding father of sociology, the empiricist or positivist methodology that characterizes him was not followed by most sociologists of the second half of the 19th and the first half of the 20th century.

versus old, of men versus women, of French versus Americans; individuals learn to behave in a socially desired way.

So, ontologically, there is a marked difference between neoclassical economics and classical sociology. While the first imagines a world of individuals, the second imagines a world that consists of groups. Classical sociology opts for a *collectivist or institutionalist methodology*. An individual is not interpreted as an independent person, but always as a member of a group. Individuals adjust to the roles the social environment imposes on particular group memberships. The stable elements in society are not individuals—they come and go—but groups. A few examples will illustrate this *social fact*.

(1) The group of blacks in the USA, especially in its relationship with whites, may be generally perceived as having very particular characteristics. For instance, they may be perceived in a white-dominated society as unintelligent, lazy, emotional, sensitive to rhythm, and be subject to many other prejudices and judgements. If a person is born as black in the USA, it is very difficult for him to ignore the way his social environment judges him as a group member more than as an independent person.

(2) The role of women in Muslim countries such as Saudi Arabia, especially in its relationship with the men in that world, is carefully defined. Women are expected to cover their heads when outside their home and are generally subordinated to men. They must obey men and do their duty. For an individual woman it is almost impossible to deviate from the norms that are dominant in these societies. Openly kissing a male stranger is even dangerous.

(3) The Dutch football team has typical characteristics relative to other national football teams. Dutch football players are expected to play technically well and always be on the attack. If not, they are simply not selected and will never be offered a position in the team. These characteristics are quite stable and not adjusted to the particular characteristics of individual players. So, when talking about top football at the Dutch national level, the style or culture is more stable than individual characteristics.

As well as a number of shared characteristics, classical sociologists also have clear differences, especially with regard to the different ways in which they present the process whereby history evolves. We will deal with two sociologists who differ in the analysis of the mechanisms responsible for possible progress, namely Marx and Durkheim.

Marx's paradigm is derived from his *historical materialist view* on the course of history. To understand this view, we first have to briefly set out the dialectical mechanism sketched by Hegel. In Hegel's view, every period of history can be characterized by a particular idea that dominates the way society is controlled: the thesis. Those who have a different idea about the way society must be controlled are the opponents, who try to persuade the powerful of their idea: the anti-thesis. Historical events are thus the result of the conflict between the thesis and the anti-thesis. The thesis represents the status quo and is of a conservative character. The anti-thesis represents the will to change and is of a progressive character. According to Hegel, those progressive powers that fit into the necessary historical progress towards more organic unity on the global level will

---

BOX 3.2 GLOBALIZATION

The national economies have become increasingly interrelated to each other. Not only the financial markets and the goods markets, but also labour markets show increasing flows of migration. From a social point of view we see the emergence of a global arena. People are increasingly confronted with each other, and start ranking the different groups and nations. Western culture is considered as dominant, but there are challengers, such as Muslim or East Asian cultures. From a political point of view we see a multipolar system arising.

  After the Cold War, the USA was the only dominant power. Nowadays China challenges American power, and the Arab world especially is quite active on the global platform. Economic and social processes are intertwined, of course. Current problems that result from globalization are the global financial crisis, the migration flows to Europe and their consequent ethnic conflicts, and the conflicts created by Russia in its attempt to return as a global leader. These problems make the constitution of a global government necessary, but also impossible. No party is sufficiently neutral to build trust and legitimation. Nevertheless, the role of the UN has grown over the years, and it is generally expected to grow in the near future.

---

win the battle and establish a new status quo. In the subsequent period, this position is challenged by the next anti-thesis. This process continues until the end of history is achieved: *global organic unity* (see Box 3.2).[9] Fichte criticized Hegel's idealism, stating that it is not ideas but material positions that conflict: the production and distribution of wealth at each stage of development being dominated by particular groups. This conflict and its resolution determine the course of history—not ideas about how to run a particular society.

  Marx adopted Fichte's interpretation of history and analysed the different stages of economic development. His analysis of capitalist economic development has become especially famous. A capitalist system arises out of a feudal society. *Technical progress*, especially with respect to transport, and later with respect to the production of manufactured goods, gives traders and manufacturers a progressive advantage over the dominant class, the landlords. The upcoming class, the bourgeoisie, becomes richer and increasingly invests its capital in the production and trade of goods. They press the government to deregulate the economy and give the owners of the means of production the freedom to produce and trade what they consider profitable. In the early phase of capitalist development markets are characterized by many relatively small firms. Competition is severe and prices more or less reflect the scarcity of the goods produced and consumed. In a later phase, however, the scale of production has a strong effect on the production costs, making firms with a larger volume of sales able to sell more cheaply and therefore be more competitive. Smaller firms go bankrupt and their market shares are taken over by the remaining big ones. *Accumulation of capital* thus leads to *concentration of capital.*

---

[9] The process of globalization is illustrative in this case. While globalization of the economy is a quite progressive process, social and political globalization is a stagnating process in many respects. This asymmetry creates severe conflicts that must be solved in a progressive way in order to approach the global organic unity à la Hegel.

According to Marx, technical progress is characterized by increasing capital intensity and an increasing capital coefficient. If these characteristics are in accordance with a statistical description of a particular economy, it is easy to show that the average profit rate is declining. The consequence is an ongoing process of concentration until all production is in the hands of only a few capitalists. An important condition in this respect is a constant wage rate rather than an adjustable one. Since there is a large number of unemployed people, wages are at the lowest level—that is, the minimum subsistence level, necessary for the reproduction of labour energy.[10] A constant wage rate means that a declining profit rate cannot be countered by a decrease in the wage level. Typical neoclassical adjustment processes do not work, and the capitalist economy finally collapses.

In Marx's analysis the class conflict between capitalists and workers is the principal conflict determining the course of history. The means of production are owned by capitalists, not by workers. Since the capitalists are forced to use their profits to finance investments, is it impossible for them to let the workers share in the increasing value of these assets. Only a *collectivization of the ownership of means of production* would make it possible to reach equilibrium between the production of investment goods and of consumption goods. Marx considered capitalism to be a progressive system compared with the feudal system: it is necessary, and leads to an enormous increase in technical production know-how. It means that, upon a revolutionary change in property relations—from private to collective ownership—it will be possible for a socialist society to reach the stage of affluence quite soon after the revolution, because, in the stage of affluence, the reason for human rivalry disappears. This, according to Marx, is the end of history.

Durkheim developed his analyses and theories on the basis of a quite different ontology (Durkheim, 1893). He saw history as a *process of ongoing differentiation*. This is also the case with human societies: earlier primitive societies were transformed into modern societies through the application of technical innovations in the production process. To prevent a Hobbesian war, society should develop processes of integration that counter processes of disintegration. Primitive societies such as hunter-gatherer and horticultural societies were characterized by their use of primitive production techniques. Societal integration was achieved through a primitive religion. As outlined in Chapter 2, gods in a primitive religion are assumed to be arbitrary despots, who demand to be assuaged. If they are not praised enough, they might punish people, for instance, by creating internal-group conflict. Gods also have to fight against other gods or devils, who reign over other groups of people or societies. In this way, primitive beliefs create and maintain a structure of groups and societies characterized by internal solidarity and external rivalry. Because a primitive society is small and homogeneous, its solidarity is mechanical in nature—the priest is responsible for a good relationship with the gods,

---

[10] Workers offer labour services, which consist of physical and mental activity. After some time their bodies and minds get increasingly exhausted and depreciated. Therefore, they are in need of regular maintenance, and must eat, drink, and have some rest. Marx called this the necessary reproduction of labour.

and the ruler is responsible for law and order. Parents are responsible for the socialization and education of children in the tradition of their culture. The ordinary people have to obey the rules set by the ruling elite—mainly priests and rulers. At the stage of horticultural societies, there were reasons for people to evaluate their production techniques and try to intensify their use of land and improve their economic productivity. In later stages, the transformation of agrarian societies into industrial ones triggered a process of differentiation and specialization.[11] As well as the advantages in terms of growing production and consumption, there was a great threat of disintegration. Modern societies are, however, rather complex phenomena and it is far from clear how a sufficient degree of cohesion can be maintained. According to Durkheim, a modern society cannot be organized mechanically as can a primitive society. A modern society must be compared with a human body, which is a very complex system of physiological processes. The body is an organism that consists of a series of organs that are functionally interrelated to each other. When we use this biological metaphor for organizing a human society we must make structures that represent 'organs'—that are important functional specializations. Then, society must *create platforms of consultation*, where these organs can communicate with each other about the functioning of the organism as a whole. The government must be held responsible for the organization of the functions and their interaction. Because the functioning of organs is highly dependent on the good functioning of the organism as a whole, consensus must and can be reached.

The way in which labour relations in north-western Europe are organized reflects this Durkheimian functionalism. Labour conditions are highly influenced by tripartite consultations and negotiations between unions and employers' organizations that are officially recognized by the government. Only after having reached consensus can society function well—as long as there are conflicts between the different functions society is 'ill'. *Exchange of information* and *moral persuasion* are the tools that must be used to bring the relevant organizations in line with each other.

When we compare Durkheim with Marx various differences are important. While Marx stresses the class conflict in a capitalist society, Durkheim sees the functional specializations of any modern society, whether capitalist or not, as its main characteristic. This implies that Durkheimian disintegration can only be overcome through consensus among the relevant functional representations about the functioning of society as a whole. Marxian disintegration can be overcome only by a victory of the proletariat over the capitalists. The difference is thus essentially of an ontological character: material interests versus ideas ruling the world. According to Marx, conflicts must lead to a winner and a loser, while, according to Durkheim, conflicts must be solved by communication

---

[11] Evolutionary philosophers and scientists also see the shift from simple to more complex societal organization as the most important characteristic of our history. Technological progress is based on an increasingly complex system of knowledge. It leads to ongoing differentiation in our occupational and professional structures. In primitive times the medicine man took care of all health-care activities. If we compare this with the organization of a modern hospital we can easily see the difference.

and reaching consensus. Marx's moral philosophical roots can be traced to Rousseau, while Durkheim's analyses are rooted in the moral philosophy of Hobbes.

Two other sociologists dominated the debates in the first half of the 20th century: Weber and Parsons. In the following we will briefly discuss their main contributions.

Weber developed a macro view of the functioning of societies in general and of economies more specifically, characterizing human history as a *process of rationalization* (Weber, 1922; Ritzer, 2008) Primitive societies can be characterized by traditional behaviour. People accept the rules set by the elite, so as to discipline their emotional selves. When they faced economic problems, people increasingly thought about more sophisticated techniques of production. This process of economic rationalization became a growing source of deliberation about other aspects of society.

While orthodox and neoclassical economists typified man as an economic being, in Weber's ontology he is assumed to be, primarily, a social being. Society is not an aggregate of individuals, but a set of interrelated groups. Each group has its own specific culture, which is integrated, to various extents, with other groups through an overarching common culture. This integration is always far from perfect; society's unity is constantly threatened by internal conflicts. Christians may have values that differ from those of Muslims, and religious groups may have values that are different from those of atheist groups. Within the economy, capitalists may have different views compared with those of groups of workers.

When trying to explain the functioning of society, Weber acknowledged social life to be very complex. Because he considered it impossible to predict human behaviour, it was also impossible to predict the behaviour of workers, firms, and consumers. The search for causal explanations was too difficult to succeed. He therefore developed a different epistemology: if we try to *understand the way people understand the world*, we can understand their behaviour. So, in contrast to searching for causes, he advocated a search for reasons. For example, when we know of a person that she is a woman and a Muslim, we understand the reason why she is wearing a headscarf. Or, when a person who is member of a socialist union operating in a capitalist society participates in a strike and claims a higher wage, we know that his claim is just a means to finally reach the ultimate goal: the overthrow of the capitalist regime. As soon as we understand the socialist world-view, and the socialist view of capitalism, we understand the behaviour of a socialist worker during a strike.

If we discover a group of people with a strange culture, we need to understand this culture first. An effective method to increase our understanding of a different culture is so-called *participative observation*. The researcher becomes a member of the group and lives his or her daily life among them, thus increasingly learning the rules (norms) of the group and the view they have of their world. A good example is a modern hospital. There are many groups of staff, including physicians and different sorts of managers. They all have their own culture—that is, their own interpretation of the situation (in Chapters 9, 11, and 13 we will deal more extensively with the concept of culture). Physicians consider managers to be servants—they must support the work done by physicians. Managers, on the other hand, have developed the idea of being the coordinators and controllers of the work done by physicians. If the members of the two groups never imagine themselves as members of the other group, they will never learn to understand each other. If they were to observe each other in a participative way, growing understanding of each other's distinctive role may result.

Weber applied his approach to the problem of economic growth. In the first half of the second millennium, he reasoned, most parts of the world did not show any economic progress. From the 16th century onwards, Western European economies started to grow. Why did it happen in that part of the world and why did it happen in that period? Weber's answer was that a growing group of people adopted the typical *Protestant world-view*. To understand this relationship we have to find out what this view means. Weber discovered that Protestants considered humans to be the stewards of the earth. Their thinking went: 'God has given us the freedom and responsibility to develop our talents and to use the potential of the universe to our own advantage and to the advantage of our fellow humans. We must save a large part of our income to finance high levels of investment and production. We can trust God that he will bless us when we work hard.' Their activities had a strong positive effect on the opportunities of other people. In the Netherlands it resulted in the Golden Age, which made this country a world leader.[12]

Parsons can be considered as the sociologist who prepared his discipline for a transition towards a more micro-orientated approach. When we explain history from a macro point of view, we implicitly make assumptions about the basic drives that set people in motion. Without any idea about the motives of people we cannot explain *why* they react to changes in their circumstances. An orthodox economist explains why people consume more in case of an increase in income by referring to the human drive to maximize utilities by consuming goods. But, in a less partial and more general approach, we must specify more carefully the different drives that force humans in different directions.

Parsons (1937) used the systems approach to clarify a particular situation. A system is a set of interrelated elements. When explaining societal developments we can distinguish between three different systems:

(1) the personality system;
(2) the social system;
(3) the cultural system.

The first system relates the different elements that can be distinguished within a personality: its body, its goals, its relationships with other people, for instance. The social system ranks the different roles within society. A role reflects the general expectations with respect to the tasks and functions of particular positions. Examples of rankings are the interrelationships between management and staff and the rank and file in a firm, or

---

[12] Hall and Jones (1999) discuss modern empirical economic growth literature, which shows a correlation between areas in the Third World that are highly influenced by Western European culture and current growth figures.

the relative position of the parents and the children in a family, and that of the politicians and the citizens in a nation state. The cultural system relates the different persons,
groups, and institutions, and integrates them in one, overarching system by means of a
set of common views or maps, values, and norms. Thus, modern Dutch culture is characterized by small power distances between different hierarchical levels and the Dutch are
quite individualistic and feminine in their social relationships. Latin American culture,
however, is much more masculine and shows large power distances in its hierarchies
(Hofstede, 1980) (in Chapter 13 we will discuss the typical Hofstede dimensions of culture more precisely). In the Parsonsian approach, the personality system, the social system, and the cultural system are highly interrelated. Imagine that an increasing number
of Dutch firms were managed by American CEOs. These people import views and values
from their American cultural system. This would affect Dutch cultural systems. These
changes would trigger changes in the Dutch social and personality systems. The role of
shareholders may change under American influence, which leads to adjustment in the
personality of Dutch managers, for instance.

Later Parsons (1951) sought to establish the necessary conditions for a system to survive and stay integrated.[13] Therefore, he made a distinction between aspect-systems and
subsystems. Every subsystem can be interpreted as a set of interrelated aspect-systems.
For a subsystem to function well, all aspect-systems must function well. Now persons,
organizations, and institutions can be considered as subsystems of society at large. They
are constituted by a series of necessary aspect-systems. Parsons distinguishes four:

(1) Every subsystem must have an aspect-system that takes care of the input–output
relation with his natural environment; Parsons call this system 'adaptation'; we
calls this *the economic aspect-system.*

(2) Every subsystem must have an aspect-system that produces a goal; Parsons calls
this system 'goal-attainment'; we call *this the psychic aspect-system.*

(3) Every subsystem must have an aspect-system that establishes a generally
accepted stratification; Parsons calls this system 'integration'; we call it *the social
aspect-system.*

(4) Every subsystem must have an aspect-system that maintains control over the whole
of the system; Parsons calls this system 'latency'; we call this *the political aspect-
system* or the system of governance.

Parsons (1978) places human society within the system of the universe. Now the
physical-chemical system offers us the necessary 'adaptation'. The so-called organic
system (which is the embodied mind) offers us the goals, and human society delivers
the necessary integration between the different social systems. Finally a 'telic' system
offers us meaning and a set of values and beliefs that results from our thinking about the

---

[13] Parsons uses a language which is not used anymore. Therefore, I have translated his concepts into a
language that fits the text of this book.

meaning of the universe. This analysis leads to a whole raft of interrelated systems, which produces goals, means, social integration, and meaning.

In summary, we can conclude that Parsons has offered us a systematic treatment of the typical actions of individual persons (1937), of typical interaction patterns at the level of societies (1951) and of the universe as a whole (1978). No other social scientist has ever produced such an impressive analysis of the human condition; reason enough for the prestigious American Sociological Association to call Parsons the greatest sociologist of the 20th century.

3.7 Economics in the Interbellum: The Macro Revolution of Keynes

While macro-orientated sociology was searching for micro-foundations, economics was in need of a macro-foundation for its micro-orientated theories. As we saw in former sections of this chapter, classical political economy has a bias towards laissez-faire policy. If governments do not interfere in market processes many invisible hands steer the economy as a whole towards equilibrium. Neoclassical economists increasingly ignored the aspect-character of their research programme and assumed that neoclassical analysis and theory are accurate descriptions and explanations of the behaviour of real-life markets and market economies. In other words, on the basis of the neoclassical paradigm, a macroeconomics had developed *assuming* that a free market economy is always close to equilibrium. If one micro-market should face disequilibrium, the excess of demand or excess of supply is too small to push the economy as a whole into disequilibrium. Other markets are buffers dampening the diffusion of excesses. This macroeconomics is called *classical theory* and it explains why governments must abstain from intervention in the macro economy. One important political implication was the claim for budget equilibrium: government expenditures must always be equal to government receipts. There is, however, one market which is not small relative to the economy as a whole: the money market. Every transaction is an exchange between a particular good and money. Thus, if the money market is in disequilibrium, all markets are affected by it. Therefore, government intervention in the money market is necessary.

At the beginning of the 20th century most Western economies applied the gold standard as their monetary system. The substantial characteristic of a gold standard—not a property—is the fixed relation between the value of the amount of gold in the hands of the central bank and the value of the amount of money in circulation. Fluctuations in the amount of gold in the vaults of the central bank guaranteed that money creation stayed in line with the real needs of the economy. When, in 1929, the Western world faced a crash on the New York Stock Exchange, with disastrous effects on the functioning of their economies, it meant an enormous challenge to classical theorists. The whole

Western world went into a deep depression. Investments decreased while interest rates were almost zero. Production and employment decreased although prices of goods and wages appeared flexible, and were adjusted in a downward direction. In many countries politicians increasingly ignored classical policy advice—they abandoned the gold standard, accepted budgetary deficits, and tried to protect national production via import restrictions.

Some economists, however, had expressed their doubts about the classical theory before the Wall Street Crash and the Great Depression. Besides Marx, it was Hobson especially who stressed the possibility of *under-consumption*. In times of recession and depression, wage decreases may affect the macro level of consumption negatively. Workers tend to consume a higher share of their income compared with capitalists. So, a shift in the income distribution from workers to capitalists, which often takes place when the economy moves from an upturn into a downturn, leads to a lower level of consumption.

But the greatest attack came from John Maynard Keynes. He criticized most fundamentally neoclassical philosophy, and came to very different macroeconomic policy conclusions (Keynes, 1936). He was interested in an explanation of the functioning of the real-life economies of his time—not in the development of aspect-systems and the formulation of universal and eternal economic laws like the neoclassical economists. His ontology, epistemology, and methodology are quite different. While the neoclassical foundations of the macroeconomic classical theory are derived from a mechanistic and atomistic ontology, Keynes assumes an organic world, which is evolving and never reaches complete equilibrium. His epistemology is less rationalist and offers room for knowledge acquired from instinct, intuition, and judgement. Methodologically Keynes tends to a collectivist rather than an individualist position. In order to make his attack as effective as possible he attempted to show the *in*stability of a free market system by changing only a minimum of neoclassical assumptions. Therefore, it looks as if Keynes' theory does not differ very much from neoclassical economics. In his collected writings, however, we discover a Keynes who is philosophically quite different from the neoclassical paradigm.

As already said, Keynes approaches human societies more organically and historically. His agents are not perfectly rational and socially independent and do not have perfect knowledge about their capacities and needs and about the characteristics of their environment. Keynes only abstracts from variables that are less important for the explanation of the phenomena under study—he does not isolate typical economic factors from non-economic factors. Because of the open character of his 'reality', humans have to make their decisions under *uncertainty*. It means that they lack important information to make reliable predictions of future events. Therefore, they must fall back on other 'sources of information'. When entrepreneurs must decide whether or not to invest they like to have estimations of future costs and revenues. In unstable periods especially, these estimations are unreliable, however. Then entrepreneurs fall back on their *'animal spirits'*, which tell them to invest or not to invest. Entrepreneurial optimism and pessimism is significantly affected by the general mood of the entrepreneurs, considered as a collective. So with the group of financial investors: when buying and selling financial assets on the stock exchange, individual actors are very sensitive to the general climate of optimism or pessimism of the investors as a collective.

Keynes analysed the functioning of a later stage of the capitalist system. He called this stage *'managed capitalism'*. Important sectors of industry are no longer characterized by severe competition. Prices of goods are set via mark-up methods. Wages are the result of collective bargaining rather than being determined by supply and demand on the markets. Because of increasing prosperity the propensity of the masses of workers to consume declines. This makes under-consumption a permanent threat and the system prone to depression. The nominal interest rate tends to be close to its minimum level. We can conclude that, in the stage of managed capitalism, macro prices are less sensitive to excess of demand or excess of supply on the markets.[14] The invisible hand has become less effective, making intervention from outside the system necessary, once the system is in a depression. According to Keynes, it is the government that must intervene by stimulating government expenditures financed by money creation. Budgetary deficits must be accepted in the short term and will wither away when economic growth is restored by the collective stimulus.

To present the methodology of Keynes more schematically, we use our methodological concepts as explained in Chapter 2.

3.7.1 ONTOLOGY

Reality is an open system; we have imperfect knowledge about its functioning, and humans are irrational to different degrees, which means that they are inclined to always make the same mistakes. Since humans are not only economic, but also social, beings, mistakes are made group-wise: herd behaviour. In the course of history societies evolve organically, not mechanically.

3.7.2 EPISTEMOLOGY

Keynes was not an empiricist. He saw that ideas rule the world. In other words, the frames of interpretation and analysis of brilliant intellectuals are the source of knowledge. So, we can say that Keynes was an idealist in the philosophical sense of the word. But he never considered knowledge as something objective, as earlier idealists tended to do.

---

[14] Keynes assumed that macro prices, such as the goods price, the wage rate, and the interest rate are fixed in the stage of managed capitalism. But he also showed that during a depression prices might decline without having a positive effect on production, income, and employment.

3.7.3 METHODOLOGY

Keynes was a methodological collectivist. He considered the historical evolution as a process that can only be influenced by the ideas of intellectuals, but not by individual behaviour. If there are 100 persons unemployed and there are just 50 jobs, because of a depression coming from the outside, then there will be 50 persons unemployed. By working hard some can move from the group of unemployed to the group of employed, but then some other persons must move in the opposite direction.

If economies are doing badly, it is the task of the government to intervene. Governments should be led by small groups of wise people, who judge the situation on the basis of their knowledge of different perspectives.

3.8 **Post-War Economic Growth in Western Europe**

When the Second World War was over there was a strong awareness in Western Europe that radical solutions to societal problems had to be prevented. From conservatism we can learn that order is an important condition for a prosperous and fair society. But too much conservatism creates resentment among the working class. From socialism we can learn that equality is an important condition for a prosperous and orderly society. But too much socialism creates resentment among the middle class. From liberalism we can learn that individual freedom is an important condition for a prosperous, fair, and orderly society. But too much freedom creates resentment among both the working and the middle class. The key to peace and prosperity is to be found in a balance between order, equality, and freedom.

From the functionalist and conflict approaches in classical sociology, politicians have learned to build a *corporatist structure* that organizes the ongoing societal debate between the important occupational and professional organizations. In north-western Europe the outcome of the consultations and negotiations was a strong commitment towards the construction of a steady *welfare state*. This state had to guarantee all citizens social participation and economic welfare at a decent level. Private property can only be protected effectively in a society without large groups of outsiders and have-nots. These guarantees can only be maintained if the population is healthy and well-educated. To meet these conditions the government has to organize an effective system of health care and education that is accessible for all citizens. For those who appear to be unable to care for themselves, an extensive system of social protection must prevent people from 'falling through the net' (De Swaan, 1988).

From neoclassical economics, politicians have learned to adopt legislation necessary for a well-functioning free market sector. The freedom to start a business is a strong incentive to work hard, and save and invest capital. It appears an efficient way to reach higher levels of prosperity. From Keynes, politicians have learned to implement anti-cyclical budgetary and monetary policies, besides another series of legal measures.[15] If not, free market economies can get into a depression, while having no mechanisms to recover. That would mean a serious threat to the survival of individual freedom as a main institution. From neoclassical economics politicians have learned to implement competition policies. From Marxian economists they can learn that anti-trust policies will turn out to be a failure. There is, especially in the manufacturing sector, a strong tendency towards concentration and monopoly power, which will be abused.

Western European countries, especially those countries that had become members of the European Union, have implemented policies as mentioned above. Because of the success of the EU, membership has become extremely popular among the European countries that are not yet members. The main characteristics responsible for this unprecedented success can be summarized as follows:

(1) A structure of consultation that is responsible for order and equality.
(2) A welfare system that is the result of the ongoing consultations and negotiations.
(3) This welfare system produces health care, education, and social protection for all citizens.
(4) The government is responsible for the protection of private property.
(5) The government is responsible for the implementation of anti-cyclical budgetary and monetary policies.
(6) The government is responsible for the implementation of anti-trust policies, so as to prevent unacceptable market power of private organizations.
(7) The government is responsible for the adoption of legislation that makes a flourishing capitalist sector possible; a sector that offers employment for all workers.

If societies meet these conditions, the capitalist sector has the potential to produce the goods that are warranted by the mass of the people. Competition between firms will force them permanently to improve their production methods and products. This results in technical progress which is the basis for ongoing increases in labour productivity. It leads to wage and profit increases. If profits are used to finance new investments, the business sector will remain solvent and competitive; in other words, growth will be sustainable.

Because of its success, the EU area became attractive for an increasing number of people outside it. The number of member-countries increased rapidly, and the number of people from other areas in the world, who migrated to the EU area also increased significantly. Their goals were clear: prosperity; their means were also clear: accepting relatively low-paid jobs. But social integration became increasingly a hot issue, as expected when using the analysis by Parsons. The economic competition in the labour market between foreign people and the low-skilled insiders has become an issue of great importance. It might lead to a falling apart of the EU as we know it now (December, 2013).

---

[15] These anti-cyclical policies should prevent the economy from falling into a depression. Once in a depression these anti-cyclical elements are not, however, strong enough to get the economy out of the depression. Then, an increase in effective demand is necessary. (For an extensive treatment of the theories of Keynes see Chapter 8.)

Part II
Economics

II.1 **Introduction**

Most economics textbooks are of an orthodox nature. Neoclassical theory dominates academic teaching; even macroeconomics is transformed into aggregated microeconomics. Alternative approaches are hardly mentioned, and a methodological comparison between orthodoxy and heterodoxy is never made. Even the methodology of the orthodox approach itself is not spelled out. The use of the basic terminology is quite sloppy and the ontological difference between economic, social, rational, and logical is not discussed. This is problematic, since a careful treatment of the axioms of a particular school of thought gives necessary insight into its scope: when it can be applied, and when it can definitely not be applied.

In this introductory section (II.1) we will first describe two ideal-typical methodologies, which are used in economics, and which should be discussed at length in teaching programmes: the orthodox versus the heterodox methodology. The first is based on a metaphor derived from Newtonian physics. The second is based on a metaphor derived from biology, and applied to evolutionary, Austrian, post-Keynesian, and, to a certain extent, Marxian, economics and social economics.

In Section II.2 we present orthodoxy and heterodoxy at the highest level of abstraction and we discuss the axioms that define orthodoxy. Heterodoxy is defined as the opposite: everything that is not orthodox.

In Section II.3 we discuss the relevance of so-called ecological awareness. Important orthodox economic principles are essentially deducted from physical and psychological principles. Economists must be aware of the environment of their analysis.

In Chapter 4 we discuss orthodox microeconomics. The setup is in line with most textbooks, but the emphasis is on the methodological properties: in this case an axiomatic system, including a large number of logical implications. It leads to a series of principles of a partial nature. The idea of a free and competitive market is explained in terms of a series of necessary conditions, altogether, defining the concept of the perfectly competitive market. Then we discuss a number of imperfectly competitive markets: oligopoly, monopoly, monopsony, and bilateral monopoly. The orthodox analysis of government behaviour is explained, and the effects of it in case of market failure. Economic analysis of government behaviour triggered an orthodox analysis of institutions, which became known as new institutional economics (NIE). In contrast to original institutional economics (OIE) (or American institutionalism) NIE does not recognize that economic processes are taking place in a social-cultural context. NIE assumes that every phenomenon has an economic foundation, not the other way around. So, cultural rules are established if they are considered to be economically efficient. We will see that two headmen of NIE, North and Williamson, have added step-by-step OIE elements in their analyses. In Section 4.5 public choice is discussed quite thoroughly—from a methodological point of view, of course.

In Chapter 5 we show that orthodox macroeconomics is essentially aggregated microeconomics. When discussing the heterodox Post-Keynesian approach in Chapter 8, we will see that the consequent denial of the existence of any collective entity has far-reaching consequences, also with respect to economic policies.

In Chapter 6 we discuss two approaches, which focus on entrepreneurship and evolution, thereby applying heterodox methodology.

In the first place, we present evolutionary economics. The Darwinian model of natural selection, as we know from biology, plays a crucial role in the evolutionary approach to economic problems. But there are other, more sophisticated, evolutionary models, which include typical human elements.

In the second place, attention will be paid to Austrian economics. Menger is considered to be one of the founding fathers of this school. Besides his typical Austrian work he developed important analytical tools, which became part of the orthodox economic framework. Menger considered this framework as an isolated, partial abstraction, and was also interested in real and historical work, thereby applying heterodox methodology. Although this approach contains several evolutionary elements, it is very much against any collective entity. Its methodological individualism implies that, ontologically speaking, collective entities do not exist except in the mind of human individuals, who all bear responsibility of whatever collective action. Politically and economically Austrian philosophy led to the foundation of libertarianism, a strong current in the USA. Where orthodox economics has developed public choice as a typical economic approach to public action, the Austrians have developed their own 'public choice'.

In Chapter 7 we explain why radical economics, although barely taught in the Western world, is still a successful scientific project. The radical view on the developments in the global economy are worth noting.

In Chapter 8 we will present the post-Keynesian approach, which is the opposite of the Austrian School. While Hayek is one of the founding fathers of the Austrian School, Keynes is the founding father of post-Keynesian economics. He was a typical heterodox economist, and developed an alternative to orthodox macroeconomics on the basis of methodological collectivism. In other words, human nature is not a constant entity, but a variable, which is significantly affected by 'the situation'. Even if a macro-situation looks fine on the empirical level, irrational behaviour makes the system unstable, thereby making regulation by the government necessary.

In Chapter 9 we will discuss a number of economic analyses, which assume that economic processes are socially embedded: social economics. In some cases the analyses are typical economic, but include some social elements: socio-economics. In other cases economics is defined as behaviour in the economy, which is ruled by (social) institutions.

II.2 The Ontological Difference between Orthodox and Heterodox Economics

The ontology of the orthodoxy can be explained as follows. Once God created an orderly nature, and then He disappeared. If humans want to improve their condition, they must try to discover the laws which rule nature, including human nature. So, although at face value there is much diversity and change, from a metaphysical perspective there is a world of constant forces, which drive entities to do what they do. Physics is the primary science, to which all other sciences can be reduced. Leading economists in the 1870s were inspired by Newtonian physics and began to use the Newtonian picture of the universe—eternal movements of planets and moons around the sun—as a metaphor to develop an economic science, which searches for universal and eternal laws of human nature. According to this view, the universe is a closed system, completely determined by its own laws—nothing can disturb its course from the outside. Scientists should discover these laws, and increasing control over natural forces will improve the quality of human life considerably.

In the ongoing search for laws, classical logic, mathematics, and statistics are major tools to quantify important relationships. Application of these tools can only take place under the assumption of homogeneity of the basic categories, which are distinguished. So, if we distinguish two goods, namely apples and pears, then we assume that all apples are of the same quality and weight; the same holds for the pears, of course. Even in this example we all know that every apple is unique and cannot be considered as identical to other apples. The same holds for workers. No worker is identical to another worker. The problem remains, even if we carefully distinguish between different qualities, that homogeneity is an ideal-typical construction, which cannot be found in the empirical world. The assumption of homogeneity makes it possible to imagine a stochastic world. In the closed world relationships endure. But since we do not know all the forces that drive entities at a particular moment, there is always a chance that behaviour deviates from the behaviour that is expected, given the theoretical relationship. If we have modelled the most important factors, derived from the primary forces, these deviations are unsystematic. If our predictions are quite accurate all the time, we know that we have found the most important forces in operation. Then we are able to calculate the risk that the actual value is different from the predicted one.

Orthodox economics is a closed model of a special nature. It is not only closed because economists think that reality is a closed order. It is also the isolation of the economic motivation from motivations that play or should play a central role in psychology and sociology that makes the orthodox analysis a closed system. This method of *isolated abstraction* means an *intrinsic closure* of the economic world from the psychic and the social world.

The opposite of orthodoxy is, by definition, *heterodoxy*.

In the first place, reality is not closed, but *open*. It means that we will never be able to describe and explain everything. In other words, it will always be possible to be surprised. It is not even certain that reality can be exposed as a system—that relationships really exist. They are just *human constructions*. So, our lives are ruled by *fundamental uncertainty*. Over time, we are able to accumulate experiences, and discover new temporary and local relationships.

In the second place, we saw that orthodoxy stresses the fact that nature is ruled by principles of a universal and eternal nature. Heterodoxy assumes that reality is essentially *dynamic and historical*. Everything changes—every thing changes—all the time. Applied to human experience, we see that our knowledge about reality changes reality 'itself' (*reflexivity of knowledge*). Moreover, we notice that we can only externally observe things if we have first developed a framework of interpretation of the relevant situation (*subjectivity of knowledge*). In the third place, we must acknowledge that knowledge is a *social phenomenon*. We can only communicate our experiences in terms of a language that can be understood by other people. In other words, scientific results must always be formulated in a language that is known and accepted by the community in which scientists operate. Therefore, we must consider language as a very important institution. It makes communication possible, but it also constrains it. Individuals might have experiences for which there are no words in English or in orthodox economics.

But even if communities have a commonly understood language, it does not mean that the meaning of concepts used are fixed over time. In other words, concepts and language are *fluid*. Imagine that a free market economy is in a depression. For unemployed people their situation is very difficult. If they have been able to save some money, they can support themselves for a while. But after some time, when the savings are spent, these people are in trouble. Let us compare their situation with unemployed people in a welfare state in depression. In the first place, the latter receive an unemployment benefit. In the second place, a welfare state, co-responsible for full employment, will intervene in the economy in such a way that unemployed people can apply for vacancies again. So, if a free market economy transforms into a welfare state, the meaning of unemployment transforms too.

In the orthodox/neoclassical world mathematics and statistics are major tools to develop applicable knowledge. In the heterodox world the application of quantitative methods is a serious problem. If the meaning of a particular concept—let say unemployment—changes over time, and is different in various locations, time series and cross-section analysis makes less sense. The meaning of a concept, more than a precise statistical definition, is decisive for people to react to. Change in meaning changes the result of the estimation of equations. It makes statistical results inconclusive.

So, reality is constantly changing. Is the quality of it increasing over time? Progressive people assume that this is true; conservative people, however, assume that there is a swing from better to worse, and back to better times. In this discussion we will see that the schools of economic thought, known as heterodox, differ greatly in their answer to these sorts of questions. Some are just assuming history as a sequence of stages. Others assume that there is ongoing evolution without any clear direction. The historical approach is the opposite of the logical approach, as we know from the orthodox methodology. In the end we will also conclude that logic and history do not exclude each other. They even need each other in a common attempt to develop a practically valuable theory.

II.3 **Ecology**

We can make a distinction between two parts of the universe, namely 'humans' and 'non-humans'. The last category consists of physical objects, such as rock, earth, metal, and liquids, and living organisms, such as plants and animals. Together they are the environment of human beings and constitute the *human habitat*. Actually, the person who makes economic decisions also lives in a body and has a mind, which are structured in particular ways. The decision-maker has to deal with these structures. Now we face a typical ecological problem: physical, chemical, biological, social, and psychic structures surround us; they affect us and our decisions affect our surroundings. It is very important to be aware of the interrelationships between different sorts of structures that constitute our environment. For example, if we eat a lot of potatoes and meat, we apparently like the food because of its excellent taste and smell. But it has consequences for the physiological and psychic processes in our body and our mind. If the long-term consequences are quite negative, it is undesirable to continue eating that much of just a few foods, while ignoring others. The study of the interrelationships between the human systems and their environment is called ecology.

Now we have introduced *ecological awareness*, we must deal with a few ecological principles first. Thereafter, we will see that these principles must also be applied to our consumption and production behaviour.

Every scientific theory needs an analysis of the relevant situation. An analysis can only be made after we have interpreted the situation; otherwise, we won't know how to start. The search for fruitful interpretations is a creative process, in which the scientist can use interpretations of earlier scientists in his own field or scientists in other fields. Our text is based on the idea of the universe being one world. Now we add to this the idea of a world that is '*inspired materiality*'. Human beings are embodied minds (the mind lives in the body) and the same holds for animals and plants.

Another idea is to picture the universe as a system, which consists of many subsystems and many aspect-systems. A system is defined as a set of interrelated elements, where every element is a manifestation of 'inspired materiality': a human being, a human body, a cell, an atom, an electron, and so on. The universe is the largest system; in fact, it is the whole system. When we assume elements to be inspired entities, the system as a whole is an *organic system*, a living system, which expands or contracts, or, more generally, which *evolves*. In an organic system, the elements are heterogeneous. When we take the human body as an example, the lung is different from the heart, and the kidneys differ from the legs, and they all have different functions. So with human society—it can be interpreted as an organism, which consists of different organs; family, economy, government, and education, for instance.

When studying the ecology of the universe, in which the human being must function well, we can trace a few important principles. Two of them will briefly be discussed now. The first is the principle of *homeostasis*. It refers to a 'mechanism' in organic systems, which describes a continuing process of adjustment of systems to changes in their environment.

We can imagine a situation of equilibrium of the system as a whole, where all subsystems and aspect-systems are in equilibrium. As already said, elements in an organic system are heterogeneous. Equilibrium means: an optimal composition of a number of different elements that constitute a particular substance. If a system is not in equilibrium, it does not function optimally. If some elements that are part of a malfunctioning system feel below par—in the language of economics, these elements experience a relatively low level of utility—they are motivated to change their position until the system has returned to equilibrium. As a matter of illustration we can take a badly functioning football team. Some players appear dysfunctional, and others express their irritation about their play. Finally, some players leave the team and search for more comfortable positions.

The second is the principle of *entropy*. This holds that natural processes are characterized by an inherent tendency towards dissipation of useful energy. This principle is often interpreted as a force within systems that transforms order into disorder. In other words, every system needs some maintenance; otherwise it disintegrates. So, if we apply this principle to the human body and the human mind, we must feed them, otherwise they disintegrate. With respect to the body, this idea reflects our daily practice of eating and drinking, and the use of clothing. With respect to the mind, we can refer to problems of psychic disintegration in case of people who are imprisoned and put into complete isolation, for instance. With respect to firms, it is not only workers who need to restore themselves after having delivered some effort; machines also need regular repair and maintenance. When dealing with a number of economic principles we come back to this ecological principle.

When taking the two ecological principles together, we can derive a few important conclusions:

(1) Every system needs a particular *composition* of different sorts of elements.
(2) There is an optimal *distribution* in the number of elements that are part of the system.
(3) *Maintenance* is necessary to keep the system integrated.

We will illustrate this by means of a few examples.

(a) Imagine that a particular organ in the human body has the following optimal composition: 6 units of protein, 4 units of vitamin, 3 units of carbohydrate, 2 units of fat cells, 19 units of water, and 17 units of oxygen. If the actual composition deviates from its optimum, the organ functions less efficiently. A malfunctioning organ has negative effects on the functioning of the system as a whole. A person with a malfunctioning organ feels bad and is motivated to change his behaviour: the person decides to eat and to drink more healthily, or to dress himself more warmly, and, if necessary, to take some medicine.

(b) A particular group of people has the task of building a house on the basis of a design made by an architect, and has the following optimal composition: 2 carpenters, 1 plumber, 3 electricians, 2 plasterers, and 3 unskilled workers. If the actual composition differs from the optimal one, the group will function less efficiently. Of course, it is possible to build the house if there are only 2 electricians or only 1 carpenter, but a more optimal composition of the team will increase the efficiency.

(c) A Board of Directors of a large multinational company is composed of 4 business economists, 2 psychologists, 3 lawyers, and 2 sociologists. We can wonder whether this composition is the optimal one. In some cultures it is very important to have good lawyers with different specializations on the Executive Board. In some fields the production technique is quite specific and is it important to have some engineers on the Board. We can also look for a balance in personalities within the Board: 10 people with a high degree of masculinity in a Board of 15 people may be too much. More femininity on the Board might improve the efficiency of the process of decision-making.

When looking at this problem from a historical point of view, we observe that our knowledge has become more sophisticated over time; at least our knowledge with respect to physical and chemical processes. It means that we are able to construct newly composed and therefore more efficient systems. Our machines are very different from the machines of hundreds of years ago. The human body of the younger generation differs from the bodies of the older generation when they were young. When looking at sports results we see a marked difference, reflecting increased health. People from the northern part of the world are taller, and if people from the North adopt children from the South, they become much taller than their brothers and sisters who stay in the South. So, we can conclude that technological progress affects the optimal composition of systems. This means that maintenance and renewal of systems must imply an ever-increasing sophistication: a constant change in the composition as a result of growing knowledge.

In Chapter 4 we will show how we can derive a series of important economic laws from our ecological interpretation of the universe. Then, we will only discuss human behaviour, while leaving the analysis of animals, plants, and natural elements to other texts.

4 Orthodox Microeconomics

4.1 Introduction

In Chapter 3 we saw that neoclassical economics is a reaction to classical political economy (CPE). The first neoclassical economists considered CPE as too political and not scientific enough. They saw Newtonian physics as an example of true science, and wanted to develop a series of principles that ruled the economy. From the very beginning there was lack of unanimity about purpose and scope of the neoclassical programme. The founding fathers, such as Mill (1874) and Menger (1883), saw it as an isolated abstraction, which needed to be complemented by non-economic analyses of human behaviour. Otherwise, the analysis could not function as a theoretical foundation for empirical research. Later economists, such as Jeverson and Marshall, were more 'pragmatic'. Jeverson considered competition as an incentive for market participants to be as rational as possible and to ignore social aspects, to avoid being out-competed. Marshall considered labour markets as an arena where non-economic factors were too important to be left out of the analysis. We see that, from the beginning, economists did not work consistently on the basis of one pure ideal-type of approach. They added non-economic variables to their analysis on an ad hoc basis, or used the orthodox analysis, notwithstanding its methodological problems, as a basis for their empirical research.

In Section 4.2 we will explain in more detail what we mean by orthodox economics.

4.2 The Economic World

In the economic world actions are economic in nature. There is only one problem in this world, which is the omnipresent problem of scarcity. *Scarcity* is defined as the ratio between the needs of actors and the resources that are available to satisfy these needs. All actors are motivated to minimize this ratio as much as possible.

To isolate this drive from the operation of the social force, we assume that there are no social relationships. All relationships between people are of an economic kind. So, if someone enters a shop, the shopkeeper is just a scarce resource for him, not a human being with a set of inalienable rights and duties. If there had not been any shopkeeper, but just a vending machine, it would not have made any difference to him. This implies, for instance, that he does not care whether the shopkeeper is male or female, black or white.

There is no social distinction; neither rivalry nor solidarity between different religious or ethnic groups, between employed and unemployed, young and old, healthy and sick or handicapped people. Every actor is an independent individual without any social identity and without any social right or duty.

To isolate the economic force from the operation of the psychic force, we assume that actors are rational. This means that every actor is a perfectly integrated personality. The person has a stable preference structure, in which all preferences are ranked according to their priority. The rational person's behaviour is based on deliberately collected information about the costs and benefits of every possible strategy. Emotions play a role when establishing what is desired and preferred. For example, if your beloved grandmother gave you a watch, it has much value for you. The emotion—the memory of your grandmother—makes the watch to a very valuable object for you. A rational approach to this problem would be as follows: first establish the value you attach to this watch. Assume that this value is 10,000 euros. If another person offers you 10,001 euros, it is rational for you to sell the watch. If the price that is offered is lower than 10,000 euros, it is not rational to sell. An example of an emotional action is the following: you are shopping and suddenly you see a pair of very nice shoes; the size appears exactly right. You decide to buy them immediately, without even asking the price; you simply use your credit card. This is not a rational but an emotional action. There is simply the emotion of immediate desire, without any deliberate weighing of costs and benefits.

Besides the economic, non-social, and rational characteristics, a fourth condition has been formulated, namely that classical logic can be applied to economic analysis. Classical logic is based on a couple of axioms, of which the law of identity is an important one. This law says that a = a. This sounds logical, but when we apply it, we must be aware of the following problem. Suppose that trade unions declare a strike. They do this in almost all economies in the world, and on a regular basis. Now we are going to count the number of strikes in the different countries and compare the results with each other. In our calculations we give a strike the symbol 'a'. According to applied classical logic, a strike is a strike. So, if we observe five strikes, the total is five. But in practice, one particular strike is never the same as another strike. In other words, it is not true that a = a, when applied to real phenomena. The content or meaning of the concept 'strike' is different for different countries and it changes over time. By applying classical logic straightforwardly, without careful research as to the homogeneity of the phenomena that are categorized, we can make serious mistakes.[1]

In conclusion, we can say that the economic world is based on four axioms:

(1) Persons are *economic* actors: they are driven by the economic force, leading to a maximization of utilities, derived from the consumption of goods, under the restriction of the available resources.

---

[1] See Appendix A at the end of this book for more information about the logical world.

(2) Persons are *non-social* actors: they do not recognize each other as bearers of human rights and duties.

(3) Persons are *rational* actors: their behaviour is based on a deliberate account of their preference-ordering and the costs and benefits of all options available.

(4) *Classical logic* can be applied when analysing the relationships that exist in this world.

4.3 **Orthodox Microeconomic Analysis**

4.3.1 DEMAND AND SUPPLY

As explained in Section 4.2 economics is about the relationship between humans and non-humans. Taken from the human perspective, there is a tension between the two substances, which is characterized by scarcity. Scarcity implies a suboptimal composition of the physiological structure of the body and of the psychic structure of the mind. To reduce this tension there are two possible reactions.

In the first place, part of the available resources can be consumed. This means that utility is derived from goods, thereby satisfying needs. The more goods are consumed, the closer the person comes to his physiological and psychic optimum. If this optimum is reached, and the person continues with the consumption of a particular good, the utility derived from the last unit of the good consumed (which is called marginal utility) will decrease. In economic analysis it is assumed that an increase in the total level of consumption leads to a decrease of the marginal utility of a particular good, given the level of consumption of other goods. In other words, if the composition of the physiological and the psychic structure is optimal, an increase in consumption of one good can only lead to decreasing increases in the level of utility. If the person would continue increasing his consumption of that good, given the amount of consumption of other goods, the marginal utility will become zero or even negative.

The relationship between the level of consumption and the level of the marginal utility is called *the first law of Gossen* or the *law of diminishing marginal utility*. This relationship is shown graphically in Figure 4.1, where U is the amount of utilities and Q the amount of goods consumed.

If a person increases his consumption of all goods which are desired, while leaving the composition intact, the level of utility may increase. Of course, the amount of resources available is an effective restriction. So, a maximum amount of utilities is reached as soon as all resources are used up, while leaving the optimal composition of the physiological and psychic structure intact. This is *the second law of Gossen*, saying that every euro spent in whatever direction should create the same amount of utility. In many textbooks this is called the rational spending rule. In Figure 4.2 we show the optimum as described by

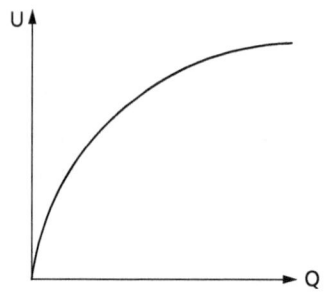

Figure 4.1. The Law of Diminishing Marginal Utility

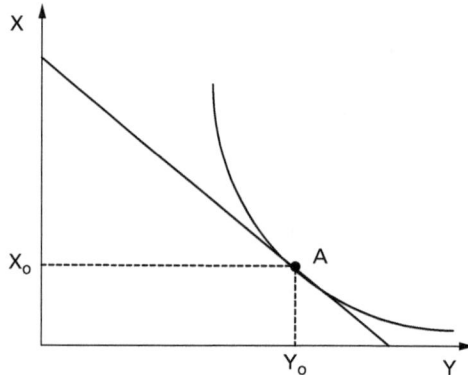

Figure 4.2. The Second Law of Gossen

this second law. Imagine an individual actor, who can choose between good X and good Y. The prices of the two goods are given. Also, the amount of scarce resources available to our actor is given. The straight line, regularly called the budget line, represents the relationship between the prices and quantities of the goods, and the budget available. The preferences of the individual actor are expressed by the curve, which shows the combinations of good X and good Y, to which the individual is indifferent. The second law of Gossen says that the individual's allocation of resources is in its optimum in the tangent point of the line with the curve.

In the second place, we can increase the amount of resources by sacrificing utilities. By combining a series of inputs in an optimal way, we maximize the net increase of utilities and add these to our productive resources. For instance, we can produce apples by combining an apple orchard with a store, an office, and a number of people: some fruit pickers, some transporters, and some retailers. This production process leads to a particular quantity supplied of apples, which can be bought by other people. Given the state of production technology, there is an optimal composition of inputs, which leads to a maximum of output. If we now increase the volume of one sort of input, while the volumes of the other inputs are given, the increase of the output will decrease. This relationship is called the *law of diminishing marginal returns*. This relationship is shown

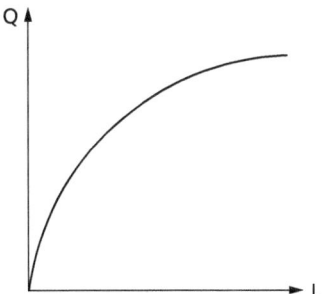

Figure 4.3. The Law of Diminishing Marginal Returns

graphically in Figure 4.3, where Q is the volume of production and L is the amount of the variable input factor that is used.

The three laws discussed so far reflect the same phenomenon. There is an optimal composition of resources, which produces the maximum level of utilities—in the consumption as well as in the production process. Suboptimal composition implies a lower level of utilities. There is some *substitutability* between the different inputs, however. Imagine, for instance, a motor car, of which some parts are made of plastic. If plastic is not available or has become more expensive, rubber may do just as well. In some cases substitution is hardly possible, while in other cases goods have almost perfect substitutes.

Complementarity is the opposite of substitutability. On holiday, a tent is a substitute for a hotel; so with apples and oranges when eating fruit. When apple pickers use a particular tool, there is an optimal composition of pickers and tools. But if we attract more workers while not extending the number of tools, the volume of production will not increase in correspondence with the number of workers. Again, there is substitutability, but it is imperfect. In other words, there is some complementarity. In the example of a pen with ink in it, the two elements are perfect complements. Both are completely useless without the other.

Imagine there is technological progress, which means that we can add more value to a given amount of scarce resources. Now we can apply the second law of Gossen to the production process. When the profitability of the last unit of input in whatever direction is the same, we have maximized the value that is produced and the level of utilities that can be derived by consuming this good.

4.3.1.1 Demand theory

Consumers are motivated to maximize the utility they derive from consuming goods, but consumption implies the sacrifice of scarce resources. If the value of the resources that must be sacrificed increases because of an increase of the price of a particular good, utility maximization requires substitution of this good by another good, whose price has not increased. So a price increase implies a decrease in the quantity demanded of a particular good. The negative relationship between the price of a good and its quantity

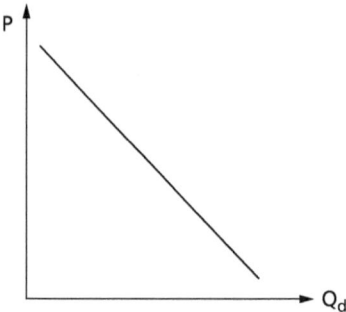

Figure 4.4. The Law of Demand

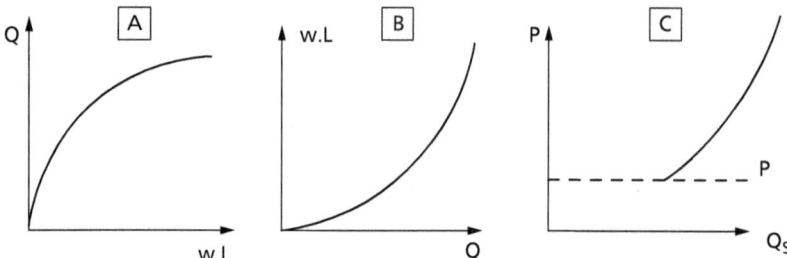

Figure 4.5. Derivation of the Law of Supply

demanded is called demand, and is described by *the law of demand*.[2] Figure 4.4 presents this law graphically, where P is the price of the good and Q(d) is the quantity demanded. The curve shows the maximum price a purchaser is willing to pay when buying a particular amount of the good. If the price a buyer has to pay is relatively high, the utilities sacrificed by not consuming other goods are relatively high as well. This is called the *opportunity cost* of buying this good. At every point on the demand curve the price is a *reservation price*, which is defined as the highest price a buyer is willing to pay. If the price of the good is higher than the reservation price—in other words, above the demand curve—the opportunity costs are too high to buy the good, since the purchase would not maximize utility.

4.3.1.2 Supply Theory

The derivation of the supply curve from the curve that shows the law of diminishing marginal returns is presented in Figure 4.5. In Figure 4.5A we have presented the law

---

[2] As soon as a change in the price implies a significant change in the real value of the total amount of resources, there is a so-called income effect (change in the quantity demanded for a good as a result of a change in the real value of the available resources). This can (partly) compensate the substitution effect as described in the law of demand.

of diminishing marginal returns, multiplied by the (constant) wage rate. In Figure 4.5B we have drawn the inverse of the function presented in 4.5A. In Figure 4.5C we have drawn the marginal cost curve, which represents the slope of the curve in Figure 4.5B. It represents the supply curve as far as the marginal costs are higher than the average total costs.[3] As long as the price of the good to be produced (P) is higher than the marginal costs of producing another unit of output, the production of the latest good is beneficial to the firm that produces it. As soon as the price is lower, however, no economically rational firm will produce the good. If the firm cannot influence the price of the good, the marginal cost curve reflects the quantities produced and supplied by the firm. In other words, the marginal cost curve is the supply curve. Now we can formulate the so-called *law of supply*: if the price of a good (P) increases, the quantity supplied of that good (Q(s)) will increase as well.

4.3.1.3 The Market as the Meeting Point of Supply and Demand

Both supply and demand are relationships. Supply relates the price of a particular good to the quantity supplied. Demand relates the price to the quantity demanded. Economic and rational buyers are somewhere on the demand curve; economic and rational sellers are somewhere on the supply curve. There is one combination of price and quantity in which all market participants are in their optimal position. This is the point at which the two curves intersect. Here the market is in equilibrium. This market equilibrium is shown in Figure 4.6.

Imagine that the actual quantity supplied is lower than optimal, given the market equilibrium price. Then suppliers have an incentive to increase the price and the volume

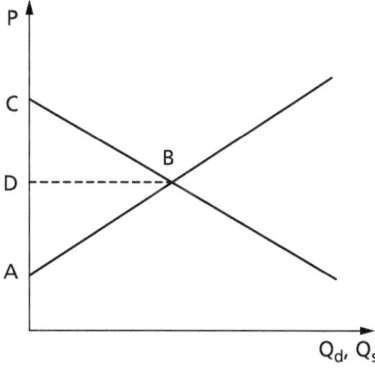

Figure 4.6. Market Equilibrium

---

[3] If marginal costs are lower than the total average costs, these costs will decrease in case of production increase. In other words, profits still increase in case of production increase. Profits are maximized as soon as the marginal costs have become equal to the average costs.

of production, until the actual quantity is equal to the optimal one. The same holds for the buyers: if the actual quantity demanded is higher than the optimal amount, they act suboptimally. They can increase their marginal utility by substituting the product for another consumption good.

Buyers like to stay below the demand curve, and sellers like to stay above the supply curve. The area indicated by ABC in Figure 4.6 is a sort of bargaining area. In our analysis we assume that markets are competitive, meaning that competition drives sellers to a price that is just sufficient to pay the equilibrium price for all the inputs that are necessary for the production of the good, including the reward for their own capital (normal profit). This price is equal to the market equilibrium price. In such a situation, the price sellers receive for the goods they sell is equal to the marginal costs. So their marginal returns (which is the price they receive) are higher than or equal to their marginal costs. The total difference, which is equal to the area ABD, is called *producer surplus*. This surplus can be used to finance the fixed costs of production. The price the consumer of the marginal unit has to pay is equal to the maximum price the consumer is willing to pay (his reservation price). But for all other goods that are bought, the consumer pays a price that is lower than his reservation price. The difference between the amount of money that is paid by buyers, and the amount the buyers are willing to pay for the quantity of the good that is sold, is called *consumer surplus*. In Figure 4.6 the area DBC represents this surplus.

In a market economy, there are many markets. We have shown that competition between market participants leads to a price and quantity sold that is equal to the equilibrium level. Here, all participants are in their optimal position, which means that their utilities are maximized, given the total amount of resources available. So, an economy as a whole has allocated its scarce resources optimally if all markets are competitive and in equilibrium. This situation is called *general equilibrium*.[4] In Section 4.3.2 we discuss the phenomenon of competition in more detail, and especially explain the concept of perfect competition.

4.3.2 PERFECT COMPETITION

As we saw in Section 4.3.1 competition drives market participants to equilibrium. In general, we can say that competition between persons exists if both want to be the owner of one and the same good. Then there must be a mechanism that leads to a decision about who becomes the owner. If there is a dictator, he can decide to give it to the person he prefers. In case of free markets, there is no dictator or planner. When analysing market processes we assume that every resource or good has an owner, and that property rights are perfectly guaranteed by a government. An owner can decide to sell a good, and other

---

[4] When we go from a market to a market economy, it is a shift from a specific to a general system. It is not a shift from a partial to an integral system. In the economic world all systems have a partial nature.

people can try to persuade him to sell it to them. They can offer him a high price, for instance. If there are many other people who are interested in that particular good, they may bid against each other to see whose willingness to pay is highest. But the owner must recognize that he is not necessarily the only one who owns this particular type of good. So, we are in a situation where a number of demanders as well as a number of suppliers compete with each other for having a particular amount of the good. Of course, the good must be scarce. Otherwise, everyone can take as much as he desires, without paying any price. So, in an economic world without dictators or central planners, a process of competition drives buyers and sellers to a combination of prices and quantities of the different goods, which is optimal for all parties. In such a situation we call the allocation *Pareto-efficient.*

Now we are going to discuss the conditions that must be met to achieve a Pareto-optimal allocation. We call this situation *perfect competition.* It is the ideal-type of a free market economy as described by orthodox economics. The strategy of constructing an economic world, which is presented as a free market society, where all markets are perfectly competitive, is chosen for two reasons. In the first place, it shows under which conditions prices of goods will perfectly reflect their natural scarcity. In the second place, the series of conditions that must be met to reach optimal allocation of scarce resources shows why real economies fail to reach it; or why it may not even be desirable to ever reach this point.

The following conditions are substantial elements—not properties—of the concept of perfect competition.

(1) There are *many demanders* for the good, which is supplied. 'Many' means so many that no one can influence the price. If a new buyer enters the market and is willing to buy goods, this has no effect on the price. In other words, the volume of production that is demanded by one participant is very small compared with the volume of production that is offered for sale in the market as a whole.

(2) There are *many suppliers* of the good, which is demanded. 'Many' means so many that no one can influence the price. If a new seller enters the market and is willing to sell goods, this has no effect on the price. In other words, the volume of production that is supplied by one participant is very small compared with the volume of production that is offered for sale in the market as a whole.

(3) Market participants have *perfect information* about their true preferences and about the satisfaction-generating capacities of the goods that are supplied. It means that they never run any risk and act on the basis of complete certainty. By means of this assumption we avoid the influence of the risk we always face when taking decisions on the basis of imperfect information. In practice, of course, purchases can always turn out to be better or worse than expected.

(4) In every market, where many demanders and many suppliers meet each other, the goods to be traded are *homogeneous* in the eyes of the buyers. So, there is no competition over the quality of the good. If companies are supplying a series of goods with different qualities—let us say a series of cameras of different quality—for every

quality there is a different market, each characterized by many demanders and many suppliers.

(5) There is *free entry and free exit*. In other words, it is costless to move from one market to another; or, for newcomers, it is costless to enter a market for the first time. In practice, there are many problems when entering a market: you may need a licence; start-up investments can be extremely large; you are unknown to the potential buyers; insiders have vested interests and may try to create insurmountable barriers. The same with exiting a particular market: if an employer wants to fire a number of people, this might turn out to be a costly affair, because of customs or legislation that forbid quick firing. Free exit and entry means that there is perfect mobility of production factors.

(6) All actors are *one-man businesses*. This means that all relationships are market relationships, and firms are just bundles of contracts that are concluded by the owner of the firm. Each (freelance) worker has a contract with a firm, arranging exactly the labour service that is delivered, and a precise specification of the labour conditions—not only the work conditions but also the wage and other forms of reward. In practice, however, a very important function of firms is the formation of a group in the social sense of the word. These groups develop a culture, which makes it possible to trust each other's way of operating. This makes it less necessary to specify everything in explicit contracts. If the workers of a firm are really a team, it is not necessary to formulate explicitly all the tasks before signing a contract. If the firm is not only an economic but also a social entity that has reached a stage of perfect harmony, the individual members of this group can perfectly trust each other. Then everyone can handle many unforeseen problems in a way that fits the expectations of the group as a whole. In a world including (intra-firm) social relationships, firms can also compete with each other by investing in an image of trustworthiness—for workers as well as for customers. Now we have introduced an element of heterogeneity in our model that does not fit the idea of perfect competition. Therefore, in our core model we abstract the idea of firms being teams. In organization economics, as well as organization sociology and organization psychology, we see how we can create a more realistic picture of firms.

(7) The analysis *abstracts time*. It is a static analysis, which means that all actions take place at one and the same moment. This suggests that we are perfectly adjusted to our circumstances at every moment in time. In other words, we are always in equilibrium. In practice, circumstances change all the time: there is an ongoing process of technological progress, our preferences regularly change and new discoveries of valuable natural resources take place. To be in our optimum position, we must therefore constantly adjust to the new possibilities and new desires. In our analysis of perfect competition we assume that all these processes of adjustment do not take any time. If we want to make a dynamic analysis, we introduce lags in our relationships. If we discover, for instance, that the price of a particular good has changed, we buy less of that good after some time, but not immediately. If we discover that

the quality of a particular good is lower than expected, we hesitate about what to do. It is only after some time that we may take the decision to buy a close substitute. So, if we really take time seriously in our analysis, and we recognize that our knowledge is less than perfect, we will introduce the phenomenon of *learning* into our analysis. We can learn from past experiences and from the mistakes we make. To formulate this more accurately, we take history seriously, the story of our failures and successes. This recognition means that it is possible to think that we have reached an optimal allocation of our resources although we may discover at a later moment that this was not true.

(8) The analysis *abstracts space*. We assume that all activities happen at one and the same place. This assumption is meant to keep intact the idea that a particular good has just one price. Therefore, we have to disregard the problem of the scarcity of space. It is always a costly affair to go from one location to another. Since every activity takes up space somewhere, firms cannot perfectly compete only with the price of a particular good—there is always the distance that must be bridged between the place of the demander and the place of the supplier. Therefore, one supplier is always geographically closer compared with another supplier. So, for a demander in the real world there are no 'many suppliers' at the same distance. The same holds for a supplier: there are no 'many demanders' at the same distance. When introducing the element of space, we actually introduce geography as an important element into our economic analysis. In the core model, however, we leave it out, so as to maintain the statement that prices perfectly reflect natural scarcity, and that for every good there is just one price.

(9) There is a government that guarantees *private property rights*. Imagine someone goes to a shop and takes some products and walks away without having paid for them. Some people really do this, but if we all did it, the economy could not function anymore. Production means adding value to particular scarce resources and selling the finished product. But if products are not sold, but simply taken away by others, the production would mean only losses, not profits. So, we are not coming closer to our optimum. The guarantee of private property rights is an extremely important institution, which must be 'produced' by the community. In political philosophy this issue is heavily debated and different ways of producing such an institution are discussed. In the Western world most people hold the government responsible for the maintenance of this institution.

In summary, the economic world is a construction that consists of four axioms. Perfect competition as an ideal-type of market structure is a construction that consists of nine assumptions. If a particular situation meets the conditions that are formulated in these axioms and conditions, the conclusions of our typical analysis hold. The most important conclusion of this orthodox economic analysis is: *the allocation of scarce resources is optimal, and prices perfectly reflect natural scarcity*. So, if the rent for rooms is 500 euros, nobody can blame the supplier for exploiting tenants. If the price of bread is 4 euros, making it impossible for many poor people to buy it, nobody can blame the bread seller. It is natural scarcity rather than powerful people, who determine the price.

When reviewing the list of axioms and assumptions we must recognize that they are not realistic. This implies that prices never perfectly reflect natural scarcity, but in some cases several axioms and assumptions are quite realistic. Moreover, we have a clear-cut idea of how to improve the practical situation so as to make the allocation of resources more efficient. Finally, we can look for situations in which it is even undesirable to structure society as a free market society. Then our analysis gives us insights into the way society must be restructured. As a matter of illustration we imagine the following situations:

(1) Assume that the natural wage rate, which is the equilibrium price on the labour market, of a number of particular low-skilled jobs is below subsistence level. Now some people cannot supply their labour service anymore. If they are unable to do a different job, they are structurally unemployed. For these people there is no place in our economic world. They cannot feed and shelter themselves and after a while they die. If we introduce a social world into our economic world, the outcasts might group together, and develop revolutionary and criminal activities. From a moral point of view this is unacceptable. To study this problem we need to analyse social relationships and give them a place in our analysis.[5]

(2) Imagine a particular good has negative effects on the health of the consumer. There are many goods that are strongly desired and consumed, but are bad in their effects. People who lack self-control still buy these goods. After a while they become addicted to these goods and they need an increasing amount of the good to keep the degree of satisfaction at the same level. A free market society offers people ample opportunity to become addicted and stay addicted for the rest of their life. In order to understand problems that result from imperfectly rational people, who lack control over their Selves, we need to analyse psychic relationships and give them a place in our analysis.[6]

Before we deal with the way in which we can make our economic analysis more realistic, we first discuss two phenomena that play an important role in every economy. In the first place, there are the problems of the various types of goods, such as club goods, common goods, merit goods, and public goods, and, in the second place, we have to deal with the problem of externalities.

---

[5] Social economics and socio-economics are concerned with this kind of problem.
[6] Behavioural economics analyses this kind of problem.

4.3.3 NON-INDIVIDUAL GOODS AND EXTERNALITIES

So far we discussed only the production and sale of individual goods. An individual good is defined as a good that can only be used by the owner. Other people, who did not pay for it, can be excluded from consumption. A second element in the definition of an individual good is the 'rivalry' of consumption. If someone uses the good, other people cannot use it anymore. So, excludability and rivalry are the elements that make a good into an individual good.

Goods characterized by excludability and non-rivalry are called *club goods*. Here we can think of tennis clubs, where only members of the club are allowed to use the courts. As long as there is no congestion, the use by one member is not at the cost of the use by other members later.

Goods characterized by non-excludability and rivalry are called *common goods*. Here we can think of oceans, and also fish. If everyone were free to catch as many fish as they wanted, this would lead to over-exploitation, and in the end there would be no fish stocks left. A more optimal allocation can be reached by establishing an organization composed of all countries with a fishing industry, which declares itself responsible for this area. In other words, the oceans need to be owned by a person or by an organization or a group of countries, who/which will act responsibly. Ostrom (2005) discusses situations where a community can solve problems without government intervention, and without explicitly formulated private or public property rights. In the world of economic, rational, and non-social actors there are no solutions without government intervention. Here, actors would be forced to act in accordance with community interests. If we assume, as we do in Chapters 11, 12, and 13, that actors are also social beings, the analysis is very different. Social relations can be negative as well as positive. Imagine a neighbourhood in which people from different religions and ethnicities are living. Their common good is an area without noise nuisance and dirt in the streets. If the different groups feel resentment towards each other, it is difficult for them to cooperate in order to solve the common problem. Suppose there is no discrimination and prejudice, the families could decide to set up a neighbourhood association. By organizing consultation platforms people come to know each other, and become increasingly prepared to work on improving the quality of the neighbourhood.

Production factors have become increasingly mobile. During the last few decades, capital has become very mobile all over the world. But labour flows—especially from poor to rich areas—have also become a global phenomenon. This development is a threat to stable communities. Bauman (2005) analyses the growing divide between the globals and the locals within each community, making the production of common goods more problematic. But the orthodox solution of government intervention also becomes more problematic because of the growing social conflicts. The European Union, for instance, has set fishing quota in an attempt to prevent over-exploitation. Now European fishermen feel forced to do their work outside the EU zone, and so go to African waters and out-compete the local African fishermen. In Chapters 11, 12, and 13 we will discuss this sort of problem more thoroughly.

Goods that are characterized by non-excludability and non-rivalry are called *public goods*. Here, we can think of a system of dikes protecting a country against floods or a police force that protects people against the activities of criminals. If there is a system of dikes, it is not only those who contributed to the cost of construction, but also people who did not pay who are protected (non-excludability). The fact that someone feels safe because of the dikes does not mean that others cannot feel safe anymore. So the consumption of the good by one is not at the cost of the consumption by another person (non-rivalry). It appears difficult to arrive at an optimal allocation of resources when producing public goods. It is especially difficult to discover consumers' willingness to pay (their reservation price). A private organization cannot produce public goods and offer them for sale on the free market. It does not have the legal right to force citizens to pay for the use of the good. So, the government must at least organize the sale of the good and determine the price paid by the users. If the government, therefore, asked individual citizens about their willingness to pay, everybody would deny their need for protection. In practice, governments estimate the need for dikes in various ways, on the basis of which they decide upon the budget to be spent on their construction. Thereafter, taxpayers have to pay the bill.

As we know, there are no social relationships in the economic world. All relationships, even between humans, are of an economic kind. That is the reason why it is ontologically impossible to expect the formation of culture. In the real world we find social and cultural phenomena all the time. Culture is a public good itself. Moreover, it can also solve the problem of the coordination and production of public goods. To illustrate the importance of having a careful analysis of the social and the psychic world, we will discuss the example of full employment. In the economic world this good is neither a public, nor a common, good. It is not a good at all, but just one of the outcomes of an economy in equilibrium. If we assume that the people of a nation form a community with a common understanding of its situation, full employment might be an important goal. When we analyse a situation in which full employment can only be reached if the macro-wage level decreases, a (prisoner's) dilemma exists in a world of economic, rational, and social beings. A free market cannot solve this problem, since wage-cutting by unemployed workers is not accepted by employed people (the so-called insider–outsider problem, which is a typical social dilemma). Every worker would prefer all other workers to accept a drop in their wages rather than accept a decline in his own wage. Thus, the free rider reaches his goal maximally: full employment without a wage drop. In Figure 4.7 we

OTHERS ME/WE	YES		NO	
YES	100	I 100	−100	II 0
NO	150	III 50	0	IV 0

Figure 4.7. Full Employment as a Public Good

OTHERS	YES		NO	
ME/WE				
YES	150	I 150	100	II 50
NO	50	III 100	0	IV 0

Figure 4.8. Full Employment as a Common Good

have presented the dilemma by means of a pay-off matrix, showing the effects of the two options with respect to the required wage moderation: yes or no.

In a world where the social aspect plays a role, an economic world analysis will always be ineffective. A common understanding of the situation, among workers and between workers and firms, can be the basis for a social and economic solution. The Dutch economy in the period 1945–2000 is a good example. Economic institutions had solved the social conflict between labour and capital, which is so typical for a capitalist free market system. A consultation economy was institutionalized and a welfare state system was organized, on the basis of consensus between worker's organizations, employer organizations, and government. By permanently influencing each other's views and preferences, no organization of workers was inclined to play the role of free rider. Because of this cultural change, the pay-offs in the wage moderation were different. In Figure 4.8 we have presented the solution to the problem, where full employment must be interpreted as a common good.[7]

4.3.3.1 Merit Goods

In the literature on public economics the phenomenon of *merit goods* is often discussed. In the economic world, merit goods do not exist. There is no reason for an economic and rational actor to subsidize other economic and rational actors, who know their own interests very well and are perfectly capable of serving them. In the real world, however, there are many examples of goods that are subsidized by institutions in order to stimulate their consumption. Economic and rational actors don't have a motive to order their government to subsidize merit goods or to penalize demerit goods. To understand the universal character of merit goods, we have to wait for a detailed discussion of psychological and sociological theory. In Chapter 14 we will bring the three worlds of economics, sociology, and psychology together, and then we will better understand phenomena such as merit goods.

---

[7] Strictly speaking, the Dutch system of consultation is also based on government legislation. But the system as a whole, including government incidence, is based on a common understanding that emerged over the period 1945–1959 (Visser, 1989).

4.3.3.2 Externalities

There is a second problem in our economic world, namely the phenomenon of externalities. There are economic activities, which have effects, not only for the two parties involved in a trade, but also for third parties. For instance, a factory produces goods and sells these goods on the market. Production implies the sacrifice of scarce resources, but the goods are sold against prices that must at least cover the costs. When selling the good, the buyer pays for all the costs. He only buys it as long as his willingness to pay (the benefits he is expecting from the consumption of the good) is at least equal to the price. So far the allocation of resources is optimal. However, many production processes produce smoke, or waste water that must be drained off. This leads to polluted air, rivers, and soil in the neighbourhood of the factory. This is a cost for people other than the buyer of the good and therefore they are called *negative external effects*. There are also positive external effects. For instance, in some cities there are areas with beautiful houses. If people take a walk and enjoy this beauty, this is a benefit for people other than the owner of the house. A system of markets cannot handle this problem of externalities. A government must intervene and develop legislation that decides who is responsible for the negative effects. For instance, if a family lives in a house and produces a lot of noise, the law must decide whether this family has the legal right to produce noise or if the neighbours have the legal right to peace and quiet. In the first case, the neighbours must take measures to solve their problem. In the second case, the noise-making family must take measures to solve the problem of their neighbours.

However, in the simple versions of the economic world the government is a deus ex machina. It is not a normal economic and rational actor. It functions as a kind of benevolent dictator, and has perfect control over the execution of the rules that are adopted and implemented. A more realistic view on government will be discussed in Section 4.5. For the moment we will illustrate that an introduction of the psychic and the social aspect will change the analysis of economic externalities significantly. If air and soil are polluted and local people are poor and from an ethnic minority, it might make latent conflicts manifest. Another example concerns the way women are clothed in the public space. Some Muslim women wear a niqab, which irritates other women, since they experience a niqab as a symbol of oppression. Some ultra-Western women wear, especially in the summer, hardly any clothes, which is a source of irritation for other people. How can we solve these conflicts? When we assume that actors are also social beings there are possibilities of creating a common culture that prescribes, more or less, the cultural restrictions. Then the government can formulate a number of basic rules, which are generally accepted, making monitoring and maintenance practically possible.

A last example is historical. Belgian firms are polluting the river Maas close to the Dutch border. So, only Dutch have to face negative external effects from Belgian behaviour. A typical orthodox economic reaction is the idea that the Dutch pay the Belgians so much money that they are prepared to reduce their pollution to a level that is acceptable for the Dutch. In other words, the Belgians are free to pollute the river, and the Dutch must seduce the Belgians into stopping. If we approach the situation from a social and ecological point of view, we might see two countries as from one and the same (European) culture. Rivers are flows of water where plants and fishes live. Citizens are only allowed to throw polluted liquids in the river if the European community decides that the pollution is not too bad, and if the cause of the pollution is very important for the European economy. This example illustrates, again, the relevance of a realistic ontology.

* * *

So far, our economic world is a reflection of the idea that the economic force is the only force in operation. Moreover, it is assumed that there are no barriers to reaching a situation that is not only optimal for each actor, given his situation, but also optimal for the economy as a whole. In other words, we have created a world where the famous 'invisible hand' operates freely.

Now we are going to describe a strategy that makes our picture more realistic. We will sketch a more sophisticated world without changing the basic axioms of the economic world.

4.3.4 TOWARDS A MORE REALISTIC ANALYSIS OF THE ECONOMIC WORLD

Now we will relax a number of conditions, and show that this makes the orthodox picture more realistic. In the first place, we allow just a few demanders and/or suppliers to operate on a market. We saw that the assumption of many buyers and many sellers implies that market participants cannot influence the level of the price, which is determined by supply and demand. Subsequently, the price determines the quantity demanded, the quantity supplied, and the quantity sold. But in practice there are many markets with just a few demanders and/or suppliers. Oil markets, for instance, are oligopolistic markets: a few companies, including state monopolies, supply so much oil that they can influence the price. There are even markets characterized by one demander and one supplier, both having a significant influence on the price. European labour markets are an example in this respect, where unions and employers' organizations bargain about wages and conclude collective labour contracts, which are valid for all workers in a particular industry or profession. In all these cases the price is not necessarily equal to the market equilibrium price. In that case the allocation of resources is not optimal. A perfectly competitive market would have driven participants to more efficient deals. But, in case of imperfect competition, participants have *market power*.

An instrument that can create market power is advertising. Suppliers can suggest that, even if their product is technically perfectly homogeneous, their particular brand is different and more interesting. By linking the product to particular famous persons or groups of people especially, advertising can trigger social forces—but this takes us outside the economic world. Aesthetics plays a role too. When offering cosmetics in beautifully coloured and interestingly shaped bottles, the product as a whole has become different, even if the content of the bottles remains the same. If the consumer recognizes these differences, suppliers have created a niche in the market, which is not characterized by perfect competition.

In the second place, we relax the assumption of perfect information, and adopt the condition of *imperfect information*. When we inform ourselves about the different options of spending, we do not collect information until we know everything. So, after a while we stop searching and take a decision, which is based on the information available. It means that we never know for sure whether we have taken the right decision. What if we had searched a bit longer? Then we might have discovered a very nice opportunity to spend our resources in an extremely efficient way. If we plan a holiday, we might first decide to go to a Mediterranean country, for instance. We surf on the internet for luxurious but cheap apartments, close to nice beaches, where many sports facilities are offered. After a while, we have collected a number of options and decide to stop gathering information. After an in-depth debate about the costs and benefits of the different options, we take a decision. The procedure is a rational one, except for the decision to stop collecting options. So, we always run the risk of missing a more efficient option.

In the third place, we do not abstract time any longer, which means that the adjustment of actors to circumstances are not complete and costless anymore, but incomplete and time- and cost-consuming. When making a dynamic analysis, we take into account the fact that processes of adjustment take time. So, if our income has decreased, we must adjust our consumption. If we abstract time, we actually assume that everything takes place within one moment of time and that the change in income leads to a change in consumption at the same moment. A *dynamic analysis*, however, describes adjustment processes over time. So, when our income has decreased at moment t, consumption decreases at moment t+1. As long as we keep assuming that our information is perfect, the dynamic approach describes our history and the way we perfectly adjust to changes in our circumstances. The more we can anticipate changes in our circumstances, the faster we can adjust when these changes occur. When we link our introduction of time with the introduction of imperfect rather than perfect information, adjustment processes become more complicated. Then, we regularly discover that we have made mistakes. Hopefully, we learn from our mistakes so as to avoid history constantly repeating itself.

In the fourth place, we do not abstract space any longer. When we accept that space is real and that every activity must take place somewhere, it is clear that *transportation costs* are going to play a role. Then, one potential trader is always closer compared with another trader, and has an advantage to others in the cost/benefit calculation of a particular market participant. Space matters, since it is costly to bridge spatial distance.[8]

---

[8] Space also matters because it is a scarce good. Every 'thing' which is anywhere must be somewhere and takes space.

Every economy consists of a very large number of exchanges. In every exchange space is involved. To reduce scarcity, we must also reduce transportation costs. This can be achieved by locating one's consumption or production activities near to other important activities. Hence, the *geographical clustering* of activities results from our attempts to minimize the costs of transporting goods. Moreover, we observe an increasingly sophisticated transportation technology, reducing transportation costs significantly and changing the factors that are decisive in the choice of location. If natural resources, such as gas and iron ore, are important, firms look for a location near the place where these resources are exploited. If a firm wants to attract many highly educated workers, it locates itself close to beautiful areas where people like to live and to spend their leisure time in a comfortable way. Economics that focuses on the role of space is called geographical or spatial economics.

In the typical economic analysis, a government is (implicitly) assumed, which is held responsible for the protection of private property. But economic actors who do not acknowledge social relationships will not recognize the authority of a government. Why should an economic, rational, and non-social actor suddenly become moral and accept rules formulated by another person? If economic actors install a government to protect private property, they all hope for protection of their own property, while always trying to get valuable assets, 'owned' by others, for free. In this case an effective system requires an extensive and expensive monitoring system. But this system consists of non-social actors, which means that they don't understand the meaning of bribery. Some people offer monitoring agents money in exchange for services, which is just profitable business. Other people organize their own protection. In practice it means that:

1. Many people have a gun (as is the case in the USA).
2. Many people have a contract with a private security agency (as is the case in many Latin American countries).
3. A large number of criminal organizations all over the world intimidate people by offering them so-called protection.
4. Many government agencies are unreliable, since they also employ economic, rational, and non-social actors.

Real actors are not only economic, but also social actors. They have the capacity to develop feelings of sympathy for each other and accept rules, which are set by a government, that appear to be rather fair and efficient. In sociology, the increasing acceptance of rules set by a government is called legitimization of legal authority. Countries with badly developed positive social relationships have no social foundation for the development of a legal system. Consequently, economies cannot grow because of a lack of trust with respect to the protection of private property. Countries with a low-trust society include Somalia, Sudan, Afghanistan, and Iraq, for instance.

In Section 4.3.5 we will discuss a number of market structures, which are characterized by imperfect competition as a result of few demanders and/or suppliers.

4.3.5 IMPERFECTLY COMPETITIVE MARKET STRUCTURES

In the economic world there are only market structures, no market cultures. Actually, there is one implicit culture that embeds all market structures, which is the common understanding that all market participants are economic and rational actors. It also means that everyone 'knows' that he and all the other actors are permanently exhibiting optimum behaviours while competing with other actors. This implicit culture is perfect, which means that every participant accepts the rules of the game completely. In introductory textbooks the government is assumed to be an exception. It is pictured as a benevolent dictator, who offers perfect protection of property rights.

Now we discuss a number of market structures, namely oligopoly, monopoly, monopsony, and bilateral monopoly. In all cases we present the simplest analysis, which means that history and geography do not play a role.

4.3.5.1 Oligopoly

An oligopoly is a market structure, characterized by perfect competition, except that there are just a few suppliers. In our presentation we assume two suppliers, supplying a homogeneous good. Technological progress has made it possible to produce a very sophisticated good, and our suppliers are the first to consider producing it. We assume that both suppliers are equally efficient, and know the optimal production level. Both did market research and came to the conclusion that there is just enough market for one supplier. In this situation there are four possibilities. Supplier A decides to take the risk and start the production programme, while supplier B decides not to take the risk. The result is that A is generating big profits, while B has to chase other investment opportunities. The second possibility is that A decides not to take the risk, while B does. The third possibility means that both take the risk, and the fourth possibility implies that both do not take the risk to produce the sophisticated good. In Figure 4.9 we have presented a pay-off matrix of the four options of the two suppliers.

A \ B	YES	NO
YES	−100 −100	200 0
NO	0 200	0 0

Figure 4.9. Homogeneous Duopoly

We see that the possibility of both producing the good is the worst. The best options are the two in which there is just one supplier who takes the initiative to produce the good. But this free market structure does not offer a solution to the problem of coordination. In a more realistic analysis we may assume that one supplier is more efficient than the other, and that both suppliers know this. Another possibility is that A is a risk lover, while B is a risk averter. In that case A produces the good, while B goes in search of other opportunities. We can also assume that the suppliers start a close cooperation, in which both do part of the job of producing and selling the good. Then the structure has transformed into a monopoly.

4.3.5.2 Monopoly

Monopoly is a market structure which differs from perfect competition in two respects, namely there is just one supplier, and barriers of entry are prohibitively high. So, there is no competition that drives the cost curves downwards. Moreover, there is no reason for the monopolist to set a price on the level of the marginal revenues which should be equal to marginal costs. He can afford a higher price. The only effective restriction is the demand curve: he cannot force buyers to accept a combination of price and quantity that lies above the demand curve. Of course, he can try to shift the demand curve to the right by means of impressive advertisement campaigns. In Figure 4.10 we have presented a graph of the price and quantity formation in a monopoly structure. The equilibrium price is P(e) and the equilibrium quantity sold is Q(e). It goes without saying that, in case of a monopolist who is not only economic and rational, but also a social being, the curves might be different.

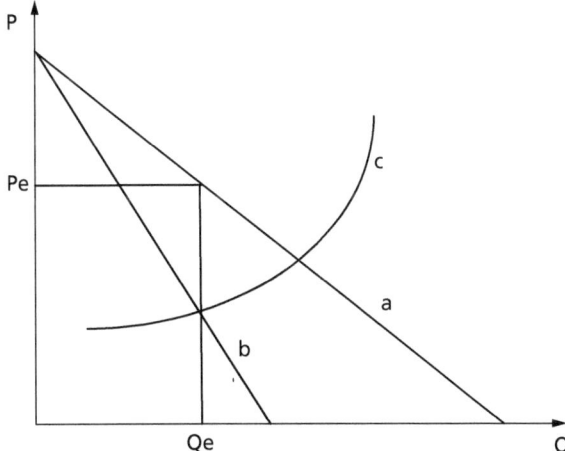

Figure 4.10. Monopoly

a: demand curve; b: marginal revenue curve; c: marginal cost curve

4.3.5.3 **Monopsony**

Monopsony differs from perfect competition in the fact that there is just one demander, while there are many suppliers, and that the barriers to entry are prohibitively high. The demander goes on demanding more goods until his marginal revenues are equal to his marginal costs. In Figure 4.11 we have presented the monopsony case. The S-curve represents the supply curve, and the S^1 represents the marginal costs for the demander. The D-curve represents the demand curve and D^1 reflects the marginal revenues for the demander. Point Q(e) shows the quantity demanded and the quantity supplied in case of equilibrium. Point A is the point on the supply curve, which fits the condition of the demander: marginal costs are equal to the marginal revenues. So, P(e) is the price 'set' by the demander. While in the monopoly situation the price is higher than it would have been in a perfect competition case, in Figure 4.11 we see that the price as set by the demander is lower than the perfect competition price. In both free market structures Pareto-optimum is not reached. Also, it holds here that a monopsonist, who is not only an economic and rational actor, but also a social being, might react differently.

4.3.5.4 **Bilateral Monopoly**

This market structure is characterized by one demander and one supplier. In Figure 4.12 the market situation is presented graphically. The S-and the D-curve are the supply and demand curve respectively. The S^1 and the D^1 curve are expressions of the marginal costs and the marginal revenues curves for the demander, and the marginal revenues and marginal costs for the supplier respectively. Q(a) is the equilibrium quantity supplied and demanded. P(S) is the price claimed by the supplier and P(D) is the price claimed by

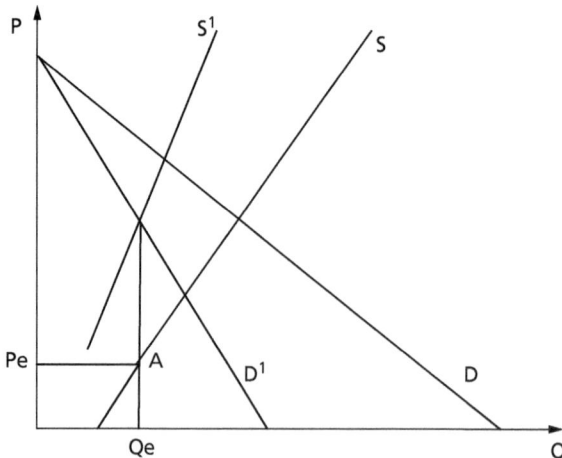

Figure 4.11. Monopsony

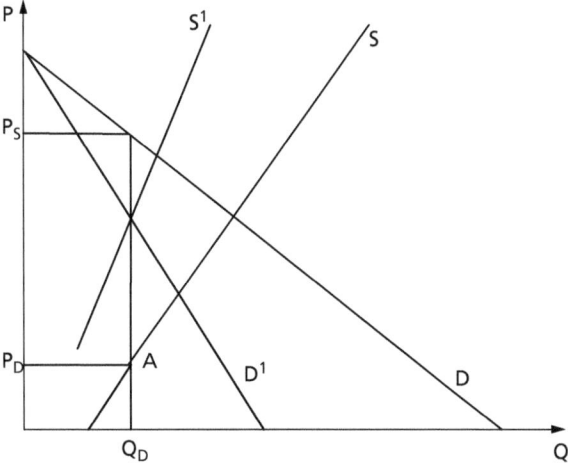

Figure 4.12. Bilateral Monopoly

the demander. In the simplest version of the economic world there is no solution to the coordination problem.[9]

Imagine that the labour market in a particular large area is structured this way. For instance, the labour market for coal miners in Great Britain was characterized in this way. In the first period of coal mining the firm was the only demander in a large area, and since there were very few other jobs available, the structure was pretty much characterized by monopsony. Wages were very low, and the opportunity costs for the workers almost nil. Over time, workers founded unions who represented almost all coal miners. Then the structure of the labour market transformed into something like bilateral monopoly, at least with respect to wage formation.

A more realistic version of the economic world would be a world in which time and space play a role, and where there is not one demander, but a few spread over the whole world. If the distance is far, and transportation technology unsophisticated, we can interpret the situation as a series of monopsonies. But if capital and people are increasingly able to move from one location to another, the situation changes structurally. In general, capital is more mobile than labour, which makes capital more powerful in its relationship with labour. Now we are in the midst of a process of globalization, capital has become extremely mobile, and some parts of the global labour force have also become more mobile. These movements have led to structural shifts in the power relations in the world, triggering social and political conflicts. Unfortunately, the typical economic analysis is unable to analyse the psychic and social effects of these movements. This is far from ideal because of the strong interrelationships between the economic, the psychic, and the social. Now economics is just a partial analysis, unfit to develop knowledge

---

[9] See Chapter 9 on social economics for a solution to the problem of bilateral monopoly in a world of economic, rational, and social actors (Keizer, 1982).

about the complex relationships in the (global) economy. In Chapter 12, on the historical approach in sociology, we come back to this issue.

4.4 **New Institutional Economics**

4.4.1 INTRODUCTION

In the simple analysis of the orthodox economic world it is assumed that all actors are perfectly informed, even about future developments. Future markets perfectly register the perfect expectations of actors. In this section we relax this assumption and introduce the assumption of *imperfect information*, meanwhile leaving the assumption of perfect rationality intact. So, all economic actors are permanently making mistakes. As soon as they discover them, they adjust and store the new information in their memory. In general, we can say that some people overestimate particular developments, such as their income, while others underestimate these developments. In some periods many people may be optimistic about the development of particular variables, while in other periods many people appear to be more pessimistic. On average, however, the typical orthodox economic relationships hold. Imperfect information in the economic world means that this world is also *a probabilistic world*. The laws hold with a high degree of probability. Individuals become more economy wise during their life, but the aggregate of individuals does not learn fast.

Knight (1921) made a distinction between risk and uncertainty. *Risk* is related to the size of the deviations of actual values from the expected values. By means of probability theory the relative size of the deviations can be expressed in numbers. Economic and rational actors are able to know the risks they take by buying particular goods, or accepting particular jobs, or by investing in a particular firm. Some actors are risk-averse and go for a low-risk/low-profitability profile, while others are risk loving and opt for a high-risk/high-profitability profile. *Uncertainty* in the sense of Knight, however, means that actors are unable to make a reliable analysis of the (near) future. In a depression, for instance, it is impossible for consumers or investors to make particular estimations of their employment and income. This leads to lower consumption and investment, and if governments try to stimulate the economy by means of tax cuts, the actors might save the increase in their disposable income. Only if the depressed spenders are offered a clear future perspective will they spend more.

Langlois (1984) calls the Knightean uncertainty *parametric uncertainty*; actors are uncertain about the value of the parameters of the equations in the model that describes the actual situation. Others use concepts, such as *fundamental* and *radical uncertainty*, to stress the difference with the probabilistic notion of risk. Uncertain actors do not have any reliable analysis and model of the (near) future.

Now we have introduced the assumption of imperfect information, it is important to find out how actors search for reliable information. *Daily life experiences* are an important source in this respect. So people build up their own rudimental 'model' of their environment. It consists of series of *correlations,* such as 'when I'm friendly to potential customers, they buy more than if I'm distant towards them'; 'when I see that goods prices go up, the nominal wage rates always follow with a time lag of a year'; 'in periods of tough monitoring of my workers, I see that the number of shirkers increases'. People are inclined to develop series of *habits* on the basis of experienced correlations: always friendly to customers, reluctant with respect to price increases, or less visible methods of monitoring. When actors talk with each other, they can exchange experiences and might agree that particular rules are in their common interest. In this way they develop *routines* and *conventions* with respect to customer orientation, attitudes towards unions, or monitoring practices, for instance. The adoption of rules will save information costs and avoid every actor reacting to every bit of new information and trying to reinvent the wheel.

In the following subsections we discuss the phenomenon of property rights (4.4.2), the market as an institution (4.4.3), and markets and firms as governance structures (4.4.4). Then we will show that new institutional economics (NIE) is a reaction to original institutional economics (OIE), as we explained in Chapter 3. It appears that there is an important difference between the two strands. We also discuss the critique of NIE, including the shifts which two big men of NIE, Williamson and North, have made in the direction of OIE.

4.4.2 PROPERTY RIGHTS

Imagine an economic world without a reliable system of property rights. Every individual is inclined to appropriate particular things, but other people do not recognize property claims. If some persons are producing valuable goods, others come and take them. Especially if the takers are more powerful, this greatly discourages the producers, and they call organizations of robbers the mafia. The producers are also inclined to erect their own organizations, to protect the goods they see as their property.

No good is perfectly excludable and the world is full of rivalry. In Chapter 3 we have seen that Hobbes (1651) describes the chaos in society as a war of everyone against everyone else. If the producers are able to cooperate and develop a strong army and a strong police force, the power of the mafia can be reduced. When discussing the Austrian approach in Chapter 6 we will see that some of them—the libertarians—assume that there will be a flourishing market for protection services. Economists, who characterize themselves as NIE economists, assume the existence of a government, which has developed a legal system, and a judicial system, which is responsible for the monitoring and enforcement of such a system of property rights. Because of imperfect information this system does not function perfectly well. Also, here we can discuss the costs and the benefits of a protection system. Policing services are scarce and the benefits must outweigh the costs. So, if there is much theft in a rich neighbourhood, the government might decide that rich people must take care of the protection of their own property. Only if the mafia is really threatening people physically, might this typical economic approach advise sending police to observe the situation.

Alchian and Demsetz (1972) have argued that *private property rights* are to be preferred to common or public property rights. In the case of common property the owners do not have a strong incentive to undertake the necessary maintenance, and to prevent devaluation. Economic history shows many examples, of which the tragedy of the commons is the most familiar one. Large pieces of land in the neighbourhood of villages and towns had no owner. Every person was allowed to graze cows on the land. Increasing population and wealth led to overuse of this common property, degrading these areas. In 15th-century England landowners decided to enclose these areas, and make it part of their property. Alchian and Demsetz (1972) see this as a profitable action. Currently, we can give the example of the seas and the oceans. There is no owner and nobody, except a few action groups, such as Greenpeace, feels responsible for this area. Overfishing is the result.

Suppose a group of countries decide to cooperate and erect a body, which declares itself responsible for the oceans in the world. They develop a series of codes of behaviour and decide to keep these rules. Other countries, however, are not bound to these rules and profit from the lower level of competition in the whale fishing, for instance. Actually, the only way the problem of overfishing or pollution of the oceans can be solved by a *public body* would be if it was a global public body. The problems of establishing such a body will be discussed in more detail in Section 4.5.

In Section 4.3.3 we discussed the distinction between individual goods, club goods, common goods, and public goods. This distinction runs parallel with a distinction we can make between private, shared, common, and public property. The argument in favour of private property rights is typical of the economic world. Only in the case of pure public goods might public property be an efficient option. However, actors are not perfectly rational beings, and are social beings, in the positive as well as in the negative sense of the word. This makes the Alchian–Demsetz solution of an almost complete privatization an unrealistic one. In the real world we see many hybrids or even triads: combinations of property systems. Ostrom (1990) has analysed many forms, in which private persons execute activities, whether a particular good is owned by a club, a local community, or by the central government. She shows that the question of who is the owner is not always decisive when it comes to judging the efficiency of the organization of allocation processes. When persons are irrational and many social conflicts exist in the organizations of society, no property structure satisfies. If people are motivated to bear responsibility for a particular situation, the question of the property right loses its top priority.

In Section 4.4.3 we will discuss the market as an institution.

4.4.3 THE MARKET AS AN INSTITUTION

In the real world regular encounters between actors appear to create a sense of commonality. But in the economic world this commonality only means that all participants know that the others are economic, rational, and non-social too. As long as buyers and sellers are free to choose a contract partner there is competition between the various buyers and between the various sellers. But as soon as a buyer and a seller perceive each other as attractive business partners, they might have a mutual interest, especially if the buyer is interested in a contract concerning the delivery of goods over a long period.

Suppose a motor car firm owns an assembly line, and purchases many motor parts. So, the firm operates on the market of components as a buyer. In the *principal-agent theory* the firm is called the principal. He orders a component, which cannot be produced by the firm, but is necessary for the assembly of a motor car. The producer of the component is called the agent. He has the expertise to produce and deliver the part. This cooperation is also characterized by a *conflict of interest*. The principal wants to have high quality for a low price, while the agent wants to deliver a good of reasonable quality against a relatively high price. Moreover, the situation is characterized by *asymmetry of information*. The principal orders for a good, but does not have the knowledge to monitor its quality. The agent, however, is supposed to have the knowledge necessary for the production of high-quality goods. Only in case of long-term contracts is it worth setting up a costly quality assessment system, and confronting the deliverer with the results.

With respect to the attributes of the actors, the principal-agent theory is a typical orthodox economic theory. It assumes *opportunistic behaviour*, which means that relationships between market participants are of a strict economic nature; social relationships do not exist. If the agent discovers that particular problems with the good cannot be monitored by the principal, the agent will cheat the principal. A boss of a department of a firm, for instance, cannot monitor his subordinates every day all day; there is always discretionary room for the subordinates to use their working time to serve their own interests. This is called *shirking behaviour*. It also assumes that rationality, although perfect, is bounded because of the limited capacity of the mind to store information. People can only be rational within the limits of the information available.

With respect to opportunism we can distinguish between an ex ante and an ex post variant. Ex ante opportunism means that the principal is cheated before the contract has been signed. If a vacancy must be filled, and some of the applicants have undergone training in application skills, these people are able to hide their weaknesses: lack of knowledge or bad personality characteristics, for instance. They seduce the principal into making a wrong choice, which is called *adverse selection*. Ex post opportunism means that agents, after having signed a contract, are cheating the principal. Top managers can easily take money from their principals (shareholders, for instance) by arranging high bonuses and by organizing meetings at exotic places. This phenomenon is called *moral hazard*.[10]

In the economic world characterized by imperfect information rules are developed, which form *an institutional framework*. This framework channels the actions of the individuals, thereby reducing the information costs and making the world more predictable. The rules emerge out of regular contact between traders, and are transmitted over the

---

[10] Moral hazard is a strange word in this context, because there is no morality in the economic world.

economy as a whole. As long as the rules are perceived as efficiency-enhancing they will endure. The rules are about holiday periods, about the speed of working, the conditions of payment (once a day or once a week or month), for instance.

It is impossible to formulate complete contracts in which every contingency is foreseen. This means that both parties, but especially the principal, must carefully monitor the transactions, so as to minimize costs of cheating. In the economic world it is impossible to solve this problem: monitoring systems can never be perfect, and must be executed by opportunistic people. If monitoring systems are developed to monitor the monitoring system, the problem will not be solved. The costs of monitoring will strongly rise, while the benefits might be negligible. In Figure 4.13 we have drawn two curves, expressing the marginal costs (MC) and the marginal benefits (MB) of monitoring activities (q(m)). The situation of the profitability of monitoring is the same as with the costs of research and of the collection of relevant information in general: we know the costs, but we don't know the benefits of a next unit of monitoring.

History shows many examples of cheating. In some economies this phenomenon makes economic growth impossible; in other countries we see that prosperity and cheating goes hand in hand. It is difficult for NIE to explain these relevant differences. OIE, however, had less difficulty in understanding why, in some countries, cheating is more widespread than in other countries, and why the phenomenon is, in some countries, a more serious barrier than in other countries. In Section 4.4.5, on NIE, we will pay attention to the revival of OIE, and show that their stronger focus on the cultural and legal context offers a different and more realistic explanation of market institutions. Now we continue with a discussion of the NIE view on governance structures.

4.4.4 GOVERNANCE STRUCTURES

In Section 4.5 on public choice we will discuss public governance structures such as political democracy and government bureaucracy. Now we deal with private

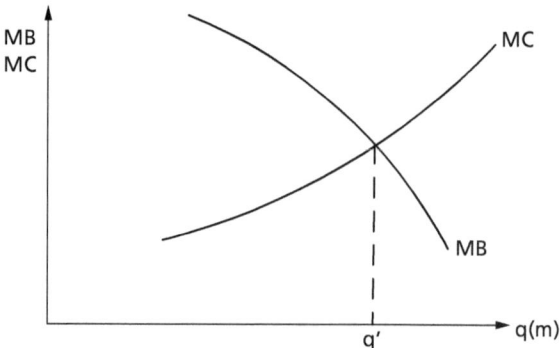

Figure 4.13. Optimal Volume of Monitoring Activities

structures, and focus on the difference between market and firm as two ideal-types of governance systems. The perfect market has been described in Section 4.3.2 on perfect competition. In this market society every person is a one-man business and every transaction is a market transaction. We have seen that externalities are a problem in such a society. Fortunately, as long as everything has a private owner the costs of externalities will be minimized. According to Coase (1960), the market is able to solve the externality problem in all cases where transaction costs are negligible: *the Coase Theorem*. Imagine two persons are neighbours with different lifestyles and tastes. One person is a scientist and studies every day all day. The other is a drummer in a band, and practises his skills quite often. It is important to establish that silence is not a problem for the drummer, while sound is definitely a problem for the scientist. It makes the scientist the party who must take the initiative. He goes to the drummer, and asks him which compensation is required to get the drummer reduce the noise. If he has alternative venues in which to practise his skills, his not-playing-at-home is a nice benefit. On the other hand, the scientist might decide to study somewhere else if there is no viable alternative. In this way, both parties weigh costs and benefits and accept a deal where marginal costs are equal to marginal benefits. A more complicated example is the following situation. The river Rhine flows from Switzerland through Germany to the Netherlands. In Germany large chemical firms are polluting the river. The German chemical industry pays some costs and gets large benefits, while the Dutch are only confronted with costs of pollution. The Coasean solution to this situation suggests that the Dutch must pay at least part of the costs of limiting the pollution.

So, the role of the government is limited to the protection of property rights. According to Alchian and Demsetz (1972) even a firm is a market. Thus, whatever the legal structure of a production organization, we can consider firm-internal relations between economic actors as market relations. The owner of the firm possesses a bundle of contracts: a number of contracts about the delivery of components and other inputs, a number of contracts about the transportation of goods, and a series of contracts about labour services. All contracts are bilateral and on a voluntary basis. In this world slavery is just a contract signed by two parties, who agree with each other on a series of transactions, including a transfer of autonomy.

This view does not differ from the traditional neoclassical view of a firm being interpreted as a production function. The firm is a legal construction, which brings capital and labour together in an optimal way, as long as the context is a competitive market. In such a situation the state of the production technology determines capital intensity and the productivity of capital and labour.

Williamson (1975) has refined the transaction cost approach, and formulated conditions, which make firm-internal transactions more efficient than market transactions. He accepted the general axioms of opportunism and bounded rationality, and found that three conditions were decisive when it comes to the decision to make or to buy a good. If the firm takes the decision to buy a good, it means that the contract on which the transaction is based is a market contract. The decision to make a product means that the 'contract' on the basis of which the transaction takes place is a firm-internal contract.

The first condition is *asset specificity*, which means that goods that are very typical for the firm must be produced by the firm itself rather than be bought in. So, it would be strange if Shell were buying the process of oil refinery, since this is its own core business. On the other hand, it might be very efficient to source out the cleaning of the headquarters, the maintenance of the copy machines, and the running of the in-firm restaurants.

The second condition is *frequency*. The more frequently a transaction takes place, the more efficient is a firm contract. If a hospital is located in an area where there are hardly people who suffer from malfunctioning kidneys, it is not efficient to hire kidney specialists. In this case it is more efficient for the hospital to conclude a contract with a hospital in the nearest city, which allows our hospital to send their kidney patients for proper treatment.

The third condition is *uncertainty*. The more uncertain the quality of the transaction, the better it is that the good is produced by the firm itself. We can illustrate this condition by means of the following example. The Dutch company Gasunie produces gas, and distributes it over a large area. Gasunie also buys gas from Gazprom, a Russian state enterprise. Because Russian state enterprises are regularly used by the Russian government as an instrument for her geopolitical goals, the gas delivery is uncertain. For the Gasunie this fact is a reason not to be too dependent on Russian delivery.

If the transaction cost approach suggests that the buy option is the most efficient one, it assumes that the market-economic context functions well, and that outsourcing is a real possibility. If the approach suggests that the make option is the most efficient one, it assumes that the firm is able to handle the new tasks efficiently.

Williamson (1967) warned that a firm can become too large, and cannot be efficiently controlled anymore. To understand his arguments we must realize that a firm is supposed to be more efficient in the exchange of information than a market. Not every contingency can be foreseen in market contracts. Within firms, consultation of different departments is easier to organize. Frequent personal contact leads to growing understanding. If a firm increases in size there might come a moment when the information flows are too complex to manage. In that case, the firm's size has become suboptimal and dysfunctional because of ongoing misunderstandings between different parts of the firm. Eventual suboptimality means that the make option is less optimal than the buy option.

The NIE approach is a typical orthodox economic product. It is analytically strong but far from realistic. By excluding irrationality and positive and negative sociality, NIE analysis might ignore the most important function of a firm, which is the creation of *trust*. In Chapter 10 we will see what irrationality really means. In Chapters 11, 12, and 13 we will point out what we mean by positive and negative social relationships. Only after having developed the proper psychological and sociological analysis will we be able to show that ongoing communication between different groups within a firm can transform irrational subcultures into a common rational firm culture.

In Section 4.4.5 we will discuss the revival of OIE, and its critique of NIE. We will see that OIE has significantly influenced some big men of NIE.

4.4.5 THE REVIVAL OF OIE

As we have explained in Chapter 3, the Institutionalists criticized the orthodox idea of isolated abstraction and the search for universal and eternal laws of nature. According to them there are no such laws, and we must interpret human behaviour from a historical perspective. Culture and technology were considered as the two drivers of the evolutionary process, which change structure and the performance of economy and society permanently. Markets, as well as other institutions, emerge in particular historical situations, and only by studying their technical, social, and economic context can we understand why and how institutional frameworks function. According to Veblen, the most important institutions are the *habits of thought* of people. Commons (1924) came up with the idea of the transaction being the basic unit of analysis—thirteen years earlier than Coase (1937), who is considered as the father of the transaction cost approach. But Commons placed the analysis of a transaction in a legal context. Without a well-functioning system of legislation no transaction can be executed in the way agreed by the parties. Coase and other NIE economists implicitly assume a perfect system of property rights, which does not exist, either in practice or in an NIE world. The analysis of Commons can be called a multidisciplinary analysis. He distinguished three aspects with respect to contracts, which arrange a transaction. In the first place, the contract must fulfil conditions of *mutuality*, which means that all parties involved must profit from it. In the second place, it must fit into a *social context*, contributing to what generally is seen as just. In the third place, it must contribute to the creation or maintenance of *order*. There are strong parallels between Commons' analysis of the three aspects of a transaction, the political philosophical analysis of the three political-philosophical principles, which are liberalism, socialism, and conservatism, and the multidisciplinary analysis of the three worlds as we are developing in this book. In Chapter 15 we come back to this parallel.

While NIE participates in the discourse within neoclassical circles, a number of economists, among them Hodgson, were trying to improve and elaborate on the ideas of OIE, and compare the results with the analyses of NIE. According to Hodgson (1988), the NIE view on a firm fails to indicate what the main reason is for the establishment of the firm. He thus argues that the failure can be brought back to a positivist idea of information. In the NIE approach, information consists primarily of facts and correlations between facts. However, not all the expertise of experienced people consists of facts and correlations between facts. Hodgson stresses the fact that information is more than factual knowledge. As we saw in Chapter 2 on the philosophy of science, knowledge starts, logically speaking, with an idea, formulated in a paradigm. Then an analysis is derived from that paradigm, and theories are derived from the analysis. Scientists who work in different research programmes cannot easily communicate with each other. This also holds for experts in firms, who have different views on how to tackle a particular problem. If groups of experts are hired and offered a place in the office, their daily communication might create a *common understanding* of the way in which particular problems should be fixed. The market cannot easily coordinate this process. A firm is a superior institution in this respect.

For Hodgson, the firm is a *protective enclave*, where workers can develop feelings of loyalty and trust. Both characteristics imply a reduction in information costs, including monitoring costs. If a firm operates in a trust society, this context makes it easier to develop and maintain trust within the firm. So, the cultural context plays an important role with respect to the functioning of individual firms; it influences its cost-benefit analysis of the different transactions significantly.[11]

For Ullmann-Margalit (1978) the question of market versus firm is not about efficiency as Alchian, Demsetz, and Coase suggest. It is a matter of power and control. The leadership of a firm is not trying to maximize its profits, but the size of the firm. The larger the size, the more power and prestige the leadership of the firm has with regard to other players in the field. It means that not technology, but control, is the most important instrument. A permanently growing organization faces increasing problems of control. We saw that Williamson (1967) paid attention to the *limited span of control*. Many company leaders are strongly status-driven and irrational in their attempts to maximize the rate of growth of their company (Kets de Vries, 2006). As long as their rivals in the market are also irrational, such a tactic might not lead to immediate bankruptcy. But for the whole of a sector this could be disastrous. In Chapter 10 we will discuss the problem of irrationality in more detail. In Chapters 11, 12, and 13 we will give the problem of status a thorough treatment.

When orthodox economists study the phenomenon of institutions, they get into trouble. Institutions are rules of behaviour. We all know from experience that most rules have a moral connotation. If one concludes a contract, we know by intuition that breaching the contract is a bad thing. There might be good reasons for doing so, but the breaching act in itself is morally bad. So, the typical economic construction that social relations do not exist is definitely not a realistic assumption. When rules are the topic of research the social aspect of human life cannot be ignored anymore. Two important economists, Williamson and North, show a slow but steady move from NIE to OIE. Williamson started with an analysis of costs without any context: the parties were assumed to minimize the transaction costs when deciding upon the governance structure. Later, Williamson recognized that the outcome of contracts between private parties is influenced by the legal structure. Legislation is essentially about the formal rules of the game. So this limits the possibilities of private parties to arrange whatever they want.

---

[11] North is one of the gurus of NIE, while Hodgson is a typical OIE guru. In the discourse between these two economists, North increasingly admitted the role of culture and institutions. Compare North (1981) with North (2005) and see the differences.

Legislation not only limits people; it also creates a protected area, where the government guarantees rights that result from contracts. But legislation is not the result of private contracts. Governmental laws are based on collective decision-making. In Section 4.5 we will see that a nation, which consists of individuals without any common understanding, creates severe Arrow paradoxes. Intuitively we know that we always and everywhere operate in a social and cultural context. And it is this context that influences legislation and governance structure significantly. In Williamson (1998), a scheme is offered, presenting four levels of social analysis:

(1) Informal institutions, such as habits, customs, norms, and religion.
(2) Formal institutions, as formulated in legislation.
(3) Governance structures, channelling the allocation of goods.
(4) Resource allocation on the basis of cost-benefit analysis.

NIE is about the way level 3 influences activities on level 4. Alchian and Demsetz (1972) start with an analysis of the allocation of goods (level 4), which leads to the conclusion that the free market is the superior governance structure (level 3). The legislation of level 2 is a formalization of rules, which make a free market possible; it is mostly meant to guarantee private property rights. Level 1 is the cultural level, which is completely endogenous. It results spontaneously from ongoing market interactions, and serves to make the economic market processes more efficient. The typical OIE starts with level 1. Historical processes are driven by a permanent interaction between technological and cultural processes on the macro level. Legislation is a formal reflection of the culture at a particular moment (level 2). Within the context of the informal and formal institutions on the macro level, private actors develop their governance structures, so as to enlarge their power and control (level 3). Within these structures, private actors make their cost-benefit calculations to see which strategy is the most beneficial—that is, leads to a maximum of power and control (level 4).

The schedule in Figure 4.14 offers a nice instrument, not only showing the differences between OIE and NIE, but also showing how syntheses can be created between the two poles. OIE focused on analyses of level 1, 2, and 3, and presented these as alternatives to typical neoclassical analyses of allocation of scarce goods. NIE started as an outright orthodox analysis of institutions. But both strands influenced each other, and the four-level analysis has the potential to bring the groups closer to each other. Rather than going just top-down *or* bottom-up, several feedback loops are imaginable. When we treat the evolutionary approach as one of the heterodox views, we will discuss the problem of efficiency versus persistence. Evolutionary economics refuses to accept that the course of history, described by the evolutionary mechanism, can be called efficient. Persons and organizations which survive are not necessarily the most efficient.

Even if consensus between OIE and NIE could be reached, the problem of human nature remains a severe bottleneck between orthodoxy and heterodoxy. To deal with this problem we need an extensive treatment of psychology and sociology, in order to answer the question of what is the motor which drives persons, organizations, and societies.

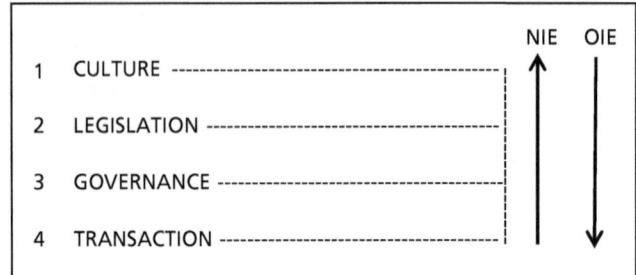

Figure 4.14. The Four Levels of Williamson

We illustrate Williamson's schedule by means of a case about the Dutch health-care system, as presented in Box 4.1.

An economic analysis of a system ignores the problem of rivalry between the different groups that play a role in the system. If there is room in the system to develop many different governance systems, the orthodox economic analysis suggests that they compete with each other, and the most efficient governance systems survive. But if we look at the system from a psychological and sociological point of view, we see many governance systems rival each other to get control over important parts of the system. We give an example, which is linked to the case in Box 4.1 and illustrates the controversy between an economic analysis focused on efficiency and a psychological-sociological analysis, which is focused on power and control.

Some commercially orientated medical specialist companies are constantly growing in size, and become regionally organized, such as a particular firm, which organizes a team of cardiologists somewhere in the northern part of Netherlands. They work in several hospitals and coordinate their work. Some hospitals offer the more regular and highly standardized treatments, while, in one large hospital, more advanced interventions take place. The hospitals, however, complain. They see it as their task to define their own strategy and compete or cooperate with other hospitals. How can they find out whether the cardiologists are doing their work efficiently and to a high level of quality? In this way the discussion gets bogged down in endless chit-chat about performance indicators, making it problematic to establish whether the cardiologists or the boards of the hospitals are the true power and control freaks.

Economists tend to calculate the optimal allocation of resources, and, when confronted with a principle such as solidarity, they calculate the difference in efficiency between systems without solidarity and the efficiency of systems based on the principle of solidarity. The difference is interpreted as the price of solidarity. In our chapters on sociology we will see that this kind of reasoning is flawed. By not taking the social force into account, we ignore the negative social and economic effects of not applying the rule of solidarity. Of course, too many solidarity rules create moral resentment among the middle class, leading to negative social and economic effects.

BOX 4.1 DUTCH HEALTH-CARE SYSTEM

Current Situation—December 2013

Level 1

Strong solidarity between young and old, rich and poor, and between healthy and unhealthy.

Level 2

Every health insurer ought to accept every client who applies for a policy; no premium differentiation, except on the basis on income: high incomes pay a higher premium. The insurer is obliged to offer a broad package of care.

Level 3

A very complex system of commercial and non-commercial one-man businesses, companies of medical specialists of a particular kind, hospitals, and other types of institutions; some organizations are small, while others are very large; health insurers and hospitals profit from economies of scale; there are just a few very large health insurers, which buy health-care services for their policy holders; no state-owned organizations.

Level 4

Daily transactions are on the basis of contracts between clients and health insurers and between health insurers and health-care deliverers. Clients are free to choose their favourite insurer, and the care they need as far as offered by their insurer.

Current Policy Issues—A Few Examples

Level 4

A more transparent system of premium payment, so the client is more aware of what he is paying for.

Level 3

To increase the number of medical specialists with a labour contract with the hospitals, at the cost of specialist who are one-man businesses, or have a labour contract with a specialist company, which has a goods contract with a hospital; reason: they are cheaper. Counter-argument: they are less productive.

Level 2

To increase the dependence of premiums on the income level of the client, so as to increase the solidarity of the rich with the poor.

Level 1

Less solidarity with the elderly people; example: people older than 85 are not entitled to get a new hip; this policy issue is taboo in politics; specialists on the work floor have to take these sorts of decisions.

4.5 **Public Choice**

4.5.1 INTRODUCTION

So far, orthodox microeconomics has been about private choice, where individuals choose, free markets coordinate their decisions, and the price mechanism determines prices and quantities sold. Now we will discuss public choice, which is the way in which aggregates of individuals decide about the allocation of (public) goods (Mueller 1989).

We will see that there are different approaches within public choice. This chapter focuses on the typical orthodox economic approach. After having presented this body of knowledge, we will criticize it by discussing a few other views.

The basic axioms of the orthodox economic public choice are usually formulated as follows:

(a) Individuals have preferences, which they rank and compare.
(b) These orderings are transitive, which means that they are logically consistent.
(c) Resources are scarce.
(d) Individuals are economic and rational, which means that they are maximizing the net benefits of every action; it implies that there are no social relationships; all relationships between people are of an economic kind.

With respect to the demand side in the public 'market', it is assumed that voters have prior knowledge about the quality and the price of the goods that are supplied (1), and their preferences are fixed exogenously, which means that they are not influenced during the process of decision-making (2).

With respect to the supply side, it is assumed that aggregates of individuals, or so-called collective entities, can be treated as unitary actors (1), and that politicians are maximizing their utility function, which just contains the number of votes during an official election (2).

The question of whether public choice has an ideological bias or not regularly comes up. The answer is that all theory is derived from a particular analysis, which is based on a particular idea. So, ideology is unavoidable. When economists use the orthodox framework as a theoretical basis for empirical research, then this research has a classical liberal bias: economic and rational individuals without social ties. When we criticize this approach we will see that the alternative views have different ideological biases.

The section on public choice is set up as follows. In Section 4.5.2, we discuss the institution of *direct democracy*. Arrow (1951) has shown that, under intuitively acceptable conditions, which appear to be typical orthodox economic conditions, there is no stable solution. A major topic of discussion is the question whether we should prefer the *unanimity rule* or *the simple majority rule*. In Section 4.5.3, we discuss the institution of *representative democracy*. Downs (1957) was one of the first who analysed the allocation of votes over different programmes. In case of the simple majority rule we see that the concept of the *median voter*—like the concept of the representative consumer and producer—plays an important role. In Section 4.5.4, we will present the analysis of Niskanen (1971, 1973) with respect to the behaviour of bureaucratic leadership. We will also discuss critique coming from sociological corners. In Section 4.5.5, the interest group analysis of Olson (1965) is presented as a typical orthodox economic one. Individuals are willing to become members of an interest group if the net economic benefits are positive. It means that group leaders should design policies that give members private benefits. Also, in this case we will shortly discuss sociological critique. In Section 4.5.6, we introduce the assumption of *imperfect information*, which creates room for the influence of ideology, as defined by Downs (1957). Also very important in this respect is the idea of Frey (1983) that we should improve the competition between economists, so as to improve the quality of the advice from individual scientists as well as from collectives of economists, such as research institutes. In Section 4.5.7 we discuss the new political macro economy.

4.5.2 DIRECT DEMOCRACY

The typical economic approach implicitly assumes that all citizens accept the initial distribution of wealth and the institution of direct democracy. Democracy is defined as a coordination system, in which every citizen has one vote. Arrow (1951) analysed the problems of coordination and we will see that his assumptions are inspired by the idea of the economic world, as explained in Section 4.2. Arrow's axioms are:

(1) Actors have an unrestricted domain, which means that all logical preference-orderings are allowed.
(2) The Pareto criterion for efficiency is valid; if each actor prefers c to b, then society at large would prefer c to b.
(3) The choice between two options is independent of irrelevant alternatives; in other words, the context of a binary comparison does not play a role in the choice of the citizens.
(4) No individual should determine the collective decision (non-dictatorship); we can add to this axiom that citizens are not allowed to sell their right to vote (no-market condition).

On the basis of these four axioms Arrow formulated his *Impossibility Theorem*: no democratic institution is able to generate a stable solution for its coordination problems. So, it is impossible to derive a collective welfare function from a series of private welfare functions.

Wicksell (1896) was one of the first economists who analysed not only the unanimity rule, but also the simple majority rule. Wicksell felt attracted to philosophies that put the independent individual at the centre of considerations and analyses (see, for instance, the Austrians, as discussed in Chapter 6). To him it was a bad idea to give a majority of a particular constituency the possibility to overrule a minority. Actually, the only rule that guarantees that no one will be overruled, is the unanimity rule. Others, however, saw a comparable problem with the unanimity rule: if everyone has a veto, one person can block all others in the production of the good that is essential for their existence (Dunleavy, 1991; Frey 1978, 1983). Buchanan and Tullock (1962) have become famous for their constitutional economics, in which they distinguish between public goods, which represent principal rights that must be guaranteed in the Constitution on the one hand,

and public goods of less importance, which could be decided upon by means of the simple majority rule, on the other hand.

Usher (1982) gives a telling image of the problem of democratic decision-making. He analyses a constituency, which consists of three persons, each with a portfolio of assets. They regularly trade with each other, but some problems are collective in nature and cannot be solved by their markets. Two persons propose the simple majority rule. The other person refuses, since it is easy for him to anticipate many problems, especially the threat of a large transfer of resources from him to the other two. In such a situation every coalition is unstable, since another minority can always offer another coalition party a larger transfer. It goes without saying that the richest party is the minority, which will be stripped. Rawls (1979) has shown that, under particular conditions, the two poorer parties are not interested in a transfer of all the assets of the rich party; they would lose their cash cow. In his theory Rawls does not recognize the existence of negative sociality, which could imply a more than 'optimal' redistribution.

Since its ontology ignores the existence of social relations, the typical economic approach to democracy does not recognize fundamental human rights. As we have seen in Section 4.4.2, private property rights—consumption goods as well as capital goods—are always implicitly assumed. This gives applied orthodox economics its classical liberal bias. Hayek (1978) highlighted a difference between Anglo-Saxon and Continental liberalism. The first expresses more or less the British situation a few centuries ago. Parliament, with its House of Lords and House of Commons, was seen as the protector of the people against the arbitrary operations of the king. In modern parlance, parliament should protect the people from government intervention. The second expresses the situation on the European Continent a few centuries ago. Society was characterized by ongoing social conflicts: the nobility, the Church, the tradesmen, the factory owners, the workers, the landowners, and the peasants. Governments were supposed to install order in such a way that all, or at least a large majority, of the people could accept the situation.

In the second view, the government should not solve the social conflict, which divides the country, by functioning as an instrument in the hands of one or a few social groups, which suppress the other groups. As the history of industrial relations in north-western Europe shows, it is possible that different pressure groups have learned to *communicate with their 'enemies'*, and try to find a solution to the conflict that is beneficial for all parties. We come back to this in Section 4.5.5 on pressure groups. Chapter 11 will deliberately discuss the conflict sociology and the consensus sociology as the two macro-sociologies.

4.5.3 REPRESENTATIVE DEMOCRACY

To avoid a never-ending Arrowian bedlam it makes sense to create some order in the whole of the preference-orderings of the citizens. They can form political parties, which design programmes based on a particular ideology (Downs, 1957). In regular elections parties compete with each other to get as many votes as possible. If a party gets the majority of the votes, it can form a cabinet to lead the government and to rule the country until the next election. If no one gets the majority some parties can form a coalition by making compromises.

Now we will discuss a number of characteristics of a representative democracy. One of the first who analysed the process of party competition is Hotelling (1929). He imagined a beach with two crossings. Close to each crossing the beach is quite crowded, but the area in between the two crossings is thinly populated. Now there are two ice-cream vendors. One takes the crossing at the left side, and the other takes the right crossing. The problem for the vendors is to find the location on the beach which offers them a maximum of sales, while it is assumed that ice creams are a homogeneous good. Suppose the right vendor discovers that the left vendor has located his stand just in front of his crossing. He gets the idea that, for him, a location a little to the left would attract more buyers from the thinly populated middle. Later he discovers that the other vendor has done the same—for him a move to the right. At the end of the day both vendors have placed their stands beside each other, in the middle of the beach, where just a few people are sunbathing and playing.

In this example there are two crossings and two vendors. We can imagine situations with many crossings and many vendors.[12] Downs (1957), De Swaan (1973), and Frey (1978) have contributed to the theory of a multi-party representative democracy. The distribution of the voters over a continuum of policy options is a very important determinant of the political outcome. In Figure 4.15 we have presented a number of different distributions of votes over a series of policy options, showing the effect of the distribution on the policy chosen. In Figure 4.15A we see a normal distribution. If there are two parties, both are inclined to shift to the position of the median voter, which is the marginal voter of the right or of the left block (M). In the other distributions it is probable that there are more than two parties, and coalition formation is probable.

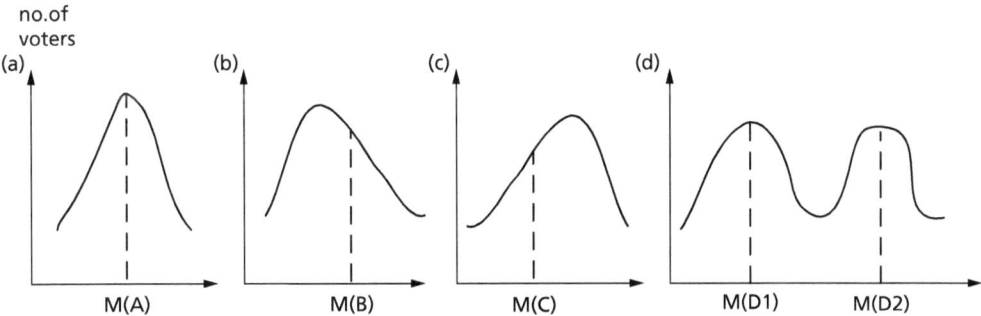

Figure 4.15. Various Distributions of Votes over a Policy Option

---

[12] Nowadays we see many vendors walking along the beach with a bag, so as to seduce people to buy an ice cream. This solution can be compared with the practice of canvassing in politics.

In Chapters 6 to 13 we introduce new paradigms and analyses, which relax the strict assumptions of perfect rationality and non-sociality. Then we will see that analyses, also of situations in the political sector, differ. For now we continue with analyses on the basis of the typical economic world axioms and discuss a few problems in the aggregation of individual preference-orderings.

If all preference-orderings were the same, the collective-ordering would be the same as all these private-orderings. If every individual-ordering is unique, we know from Arrow that there are no stable solutions. An important reason for this impossibility is the assumption that there are no social relationships. It means that there is no common understanding among the citizens of their situation. Chapters 11 to 13 explain that this is very unrealistic. In many cases there are just a few independent policy areas, such as 'economy' and 'ethical issues', which play a role in a particular election. Quite often one cluster of problems dominates the electoral battle. Then there might be a difference of opinion, but not on which topic. In a case of so-called multidimensionality of political goals, decision-making is a problem that can hardly be solved. But as soon as a nation is characterized by a strong culture, differences of opinions can be pictured along one or two continua. Most of the time economic matters play a decisive role. Some people strive for a sober welfare state, while others prefer just a minimum of social security. When discussing the question whether the tax rates should be increased or not, it is easy to reach a compromise. More technically expressed, a society without a strong culture, which narrows the gap between the different groups, shows plural-peak patterns in the distribution of voters along a policy continuum (Figure 4.15D). But if, as in Scandinavia, most people prefer a welfare state, the distribution shows a single peak. In Figure 4.16 we have presented both situations. The first picture (I) shows a plural-peak pattern, where, for instance, many people don't want a welfare state at all, and many people have a strong preference in favour of a well-developed welfare state. In this situation it is difficult to formulate a compromise. The second picture (II) shows the easier situation: parties move to a median position.

Another problem with respect to the aggregation of individual preference-orderings is the *difference in intensity* of the preferences. Some people prefer a tax cut and a less liberal abortion policy. But, for them, abortion policy is much more important than tax policy. For other individuals the ranking is the other way around. One way of solving the problem is the introduction of a point system. Every voter gets ten points and is allowed to distribute these points over different topics. In Figure 4.17 we have presented two tables, one showing the usual one-point system (I), and the other a ten-point system (II). As we can see, the outcomes differ. In system I option A is the winner, while in system II C is the winner.

A last point is the possibility of organizing vote trading, which can reduce the lack of an integrated culture and differences in intensity. Van den Doel (1978) gives an example from Dutch political history, which illustrates the phenomenon of vote trading. In 1917 the Dutch parliament consisted of three main groups: socialists, confessionals, and Anglo-Saxon liberals. Two issues dominated the debates, namely the introduction of universal suffrage and the recognition of private (mostly confessional) education. The preferences of the parties are presented in Figure 4.18.

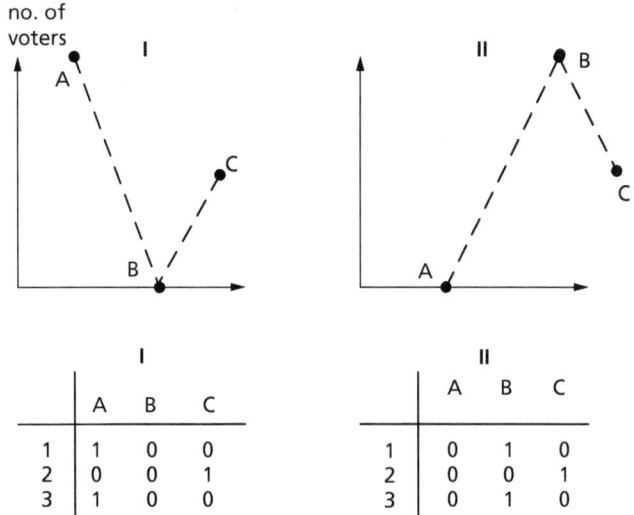

no. of voters

I		A	B	C
1		1	0	0
2		0	0	1
3		1	0	0

II		A	B	C
1		0	1	0
2		0	0	1
3		0	1	0

Figure 4.16. From Plural to Single Peakedness

I

Option / Voter	A	B	C
1	1	0	0
2	0	0	1
3	1	0	0

II

Issue / Voter	A	B	C
1	5	2	3
2	2	1	7
3	4	3	3

Figure 4.17. A One-Point versus a Ten-Point System

Issue / Voter	Universal suffrage	Private education
Socialists	++	–
Confessionals	–	++
Liberals	–	–

Figure 4.18. Vote Trading

We see that the socialists had a strong preference in favour of universal suffrage, while the confessionals had an intense preference in favour of the recognition of private education. The liberals were against both proposals. Without vote trading there would not have been a solution. The socialists and the confessionals, however, decided to do a deal: the socialists promised to vote in favour of private education, while the confessionals promised to vote in favour of universal suffrage. And so it happened.

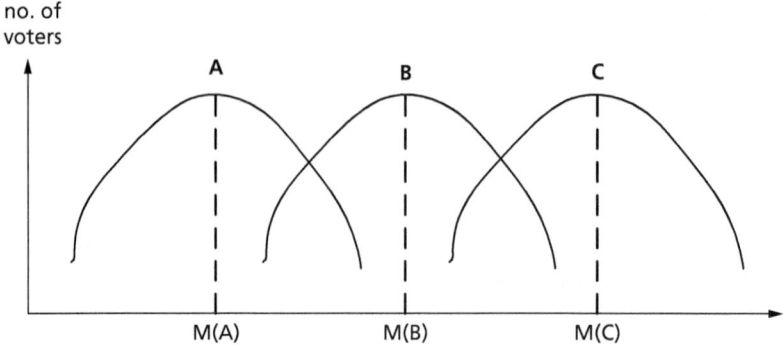

Figure 4.19. Vote Distribution in a Culturally Fragmented Society

We have seen that the construction of a median voter is very important. It is the voter of a set of 101 voters, where there are 50 voters on each side, who can decide which side will tip the scale. In Figure 4.19 we have pictured a distribution of voters, where the median voter is smaller than the modal voter (A), is equal to the modal voter (B), or is larger than the modal one (C). If society consists of three competing groups, we can picture the distribution of the voters over a policy continuum as is done in Figure 4.19. Then, political parties are inclined to choose one of the groups as their 'own' constituency, and take the local median voter as their target point.

In Section 4.5.4 we will discuss the functioning of a bureaucracy.

4.5.4. BUREAUCRACY

Not only democracy, but also bureaucracy, is a new field for economists of the orthodox and neoclassical type. In sociology and political science the topic has been discussed widely, but not on the basis of an economic and rational voter. When non-economists talk about the new economic contributions, they see it as the rational actor model most of the time. When going through their comments, we can see that most non-economists don't make a clear difference between 'economic' and 'rational'.

Niskanen (1971) was one of the first who applied the orthodox economic axioms to the phenomenon of a bureaucracy. He defined a bureaucracy as a non-profit organization, which is financed, at least in part, from a periodic appropriation or grant. He assumes that all bureaucrats are rational and selfish maximizers of their utilities. A bureaucratic organization consists of a hierarchical structure of bureaus. A leader of a bureau is assumed to maximize the size of his budget. The larger his budget, the larger will be his own income and the possibilities of growth. All bureaus are in a sort of ecological competition with each other, all strictly run in a top-down way. In this way, a bureaucracy is exactly the opposite of a free market.

Niskanen wanted to show that a government organization is a monopolist, which always produces more than is efficient. Therefore, he used the orthodox economic apparatus. Each bureau has a single sponsor, which provides a budget in return for a whole package of outputs. The personnel of the bureau have a monopoly with respect to the knowledge of the costs and benefits of the outputs. The sponsor compares the actual output with the output that was promised in the contract. Bureaus can never expand their output to a level that would imply a decrease in total welfare: a sponsor would never finance this output. The expansion stops when the total costs of a particular programme are equal to the total benefits of that programme. This rule differs from the rule that prescribes that its marginal costs are equal to its marginal benefits, which is an efficiency rule in the case of individual goods supplied in a market.

In Figure 4.20 we have presented Niskanen's idea of budget maximization under constraints. In case of competition, the size of the programme would have been OC (optimal size of the programme). But in the public sector there is monopoly, which implies a programme size of OD (monopoly size of the programme).

Niskanen has given an example of a programme which could, to a certain extent at least, be split in smaller pieces, making the programme as a whole more efficient. The sponsor of the London Metropolitan Police asked the London police force not to pay so much attention to drunken people in public. In the next period the costs of the organization declined significantly. In this case, the public good 'public safety' is cut into several pieces, among them the good 'no public drunkenness'.

Downs (1967) and Dunleavy (1991) offer an analysis with a broader focus. Now both approaches will be discussed and contrasted with the typical economic approach. Downs defines a bureaucracy as a large organization, in which the productivity of the bureaucrats cannot be directly evaluated. He assumes motivational diversity, and distinguishes between a series of self-interested and altruistic motivations. On the basis of these drives, Downs distinguishes five personality types: the climber, the conserver, the zealot, the advocate, and the statesman. Bureaucracies show, as all organizations do,

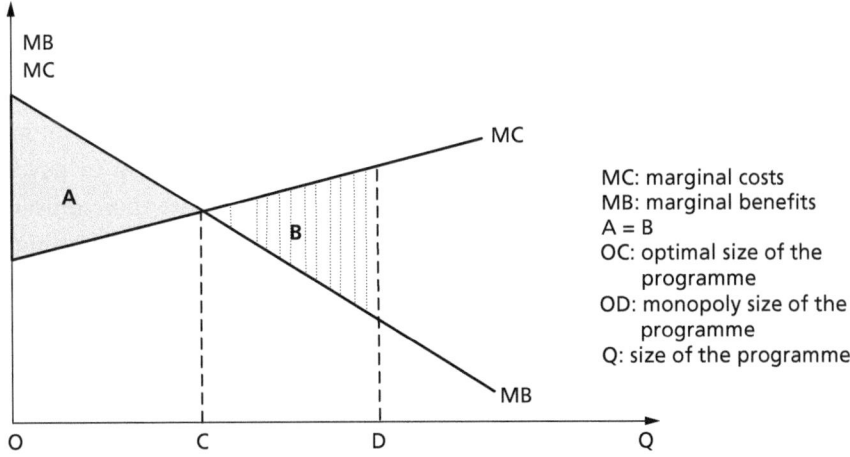

MC: marginal costs
MB: marginal benefits
A = B
OC: optimal size of the
    programme
OD: monopoly size of the
    programme
Q: size of the programme

Figure 4.20. Niskanen's Theory of Oversupply

lifecycles. Every stage in this cycle is characterized by one or a few personality types, which dominate the organization. The function of particular personalities is to bridge the gap between principals and agents of a particular bureau. People with a strong sense of order, especially zealots, people with a mission, and conservers, can organize unity within a particular bureau.

In Niskanen's construction, the assumption of perfect unity and control is not a realistic one. A bureaucracy that consists of economic and rational bureaucrats suffers from principal-agent problems. Agents are professionals, who know how to fix a problem, while the principal who has hired them—because he himself lacks the necessary skills—is supposed to evaluate them.

Dunleavy (1991) criticizes Niskanen and states that the continuing establishment of new bureaus (bureau-shaping behaviour) explains the growth of a bureaucracy. Bureaucrats with a staff function are especially motivated to have their own bureau with its own budget and staff. These bureaus create a nice working environment for the staff, with regular consultation meetings rather than a quite impersonal machine-like executive office. These bureaus discover problems in administrative processes and in the programming of the executive stage, and try to get these problems on the agenda of the bureaucracy rather than operating in the front office.

Both Downs and Dunleavy are critical of the typical economic public choice and try to develop a multidisciplinary approach. Downs is looking for a solution to the coordination of decisions, other than the command structure, in which the commanders have perfect control over the rank and file. The personality of the leader plays an important role in his approach (see also Kets de Vries (2006), discussed in more detail in Chapter 10). Dunleavy's bureau-shaping theory explains bureaucratic growth in a way which differs from Niskanen's explanation. Actually, Dunleavy is explaining the growth of the organization and its budget indirectly, namely through an ever-more complex organization. Moreover, Dunleavy does not focus on money income, but on all sorts of labour rewards, including nice working conditions. While Niskanen talks about budgets, Dunleavy analyses organizational structure.

The main difference between Niskanen on the one hand, and Downs and Dunleavy on the other, is that the latter two do not accept the picture of an individual as an economic and rational utility maximizer. Both bring in psychology to make the analysis more realistic. But both are not clear in their ontology. In other words, we need a more sophisticated analysis of the psyche to be brought into the analysis. Downs is using personality theory, which is based on psychoanalysis (see Chapter 10), and Dunleavy seems to implicitly use self-development analysis (see Chapter 10), which might explain bureau-shaping behaviour in terms of the drive for a place, far distant from the front office, where people can safely develop their assumed Self.

In Section 4.5.5 we will deal with the phenomenon of interest groups.

4.5.5 INTEREST GROUPS

The public choice literature on interest groups shows a series of approaches, among them the typical economic one. Olson (1965) is a good example of this approach. Therefore, we will discuss his 'logic of collective action' in more detail. Then we will give a short presentation of the pluralist, the corporatist, and the new right view, so as to compare and contrast them with Olson's orthodox/neoclassical economic view.

To develop an *economic logic of collective action* Olson assumes that actors are economic, rational, and non-social. In the case of public goods, collective action is needed. Private actors who are interested in the production of particular public goods might consider the formation of a pressure group. But there is a prisoner's dilemma now. Those who sacrifice resources by establishing such a group, or become members and pay their contribution, press the government for the production of a good, while non-members cannot be excluded from the use of it.

However, in the real world we see many interest groups and their lobbyists in cities, such as Brussels and Washington. To Olson this can be explained as follows. In the first place, it holds that the smaller the groups, the easier it is to overcome the prisoner's dilemma. In relatively small groups, people execute some control on each other, and persuade each other to become members.[13] In the second place, leaders can create private benefits for members, so as to discriminate between insiders and outsiders. In the third place, some members gain a great deal, making them prepared to contribute significantly to the lobby. In the fourth place, Olson sees not only negative, but also positive selection incentives. A negative incentive is the social pressure from insiders, as we saw in the first point he made, for instance. Examples of positive incentives are friendships and a sense of belonging that an interest group gives to the members. In the fifth place, leaders can promote strong group discipline.

According to Olson, these restrictions lead to unequal levels of group influence over policy-making, which persist for long periods of time.

The *pluralists* have a different view on the net effect of lobby groups on government policy. They do not assume that individuals are rational and non-social. Competition on the lobby market means that the best survive, whether they are rational and non-social or not. They see many relatively small groups competing with each other. If a particular interest is strongly organized, the incentive to develop countervailing power is also strong. The smoking industry is a good example in this respect. It has a well-organized lobby, but there is countervailing power from health organizations, influencing government policies. Another example is the employer's lobby, which triggered the establishment of unions. According to pluralists, the net effect of all these pressures is a well-informed government, rather than it leading to a reallocation of resources.

---

[13] Olson is assuming non-social actors, except in this case; this is not very consistent.

The *corporatists*, however, stress the fact that power relationships in the economy are very unequal, and key economic interests also unequally represented in the political centres. In the capitalist class struggle, groups are based on a common class membership, including its ideology, thus creating solidarity among the members. In order to solve the class conflict these interest groups should develop a common structure of consultation. If they succeed in creating consensus about their common long-term interest, the government can profit from this social basis.

The *new right people* criticize Olson by saying that interest groups are not involved in the production of public goods. According to them, there are hardly any public goods, and people can always be excluded from the use of particular goods. Only national defence and the judicial system might be examples of public goods. Most of the time lobbying is about private interests, and about leftist attempts to redistribute money from the rich to the poor. But redistribution is definitely not a public good; it is legal robbery, which creates inefficiency in the allocation of scarce goods.

Taken together, we see that the application of the orthodox economic world to the world of politics does not lead to an explanation of the phenomenon of interest groups. Olson implicitly uses some sociological elements, making it possible for an interest organization to survive. But as soon as interest groups enter the market that limits their services to the production of private benefits for their members, they will win the competition with typical Olson interest groups. The pluralists, like Olson, are using micro-sociology to explain the existence of interest groups (see Chapter 11) rather than establish their analyses on the basis of an economic and rational actor. They also implicitly assume that the societal context, in which many small groups operate, is a stable one. The corporatists, however, establish their analyses on a macro-sociological basis, namely the consensus sociology (see Chapter 11). In other words, the main interest groups can organize a social basis, on which government and economy can function well. The new right approach is actually the only one which really sticks to the axioms of the economic world. Essentially, the concept 'public' does not exist. Individuals cooperate or do not cooperate with each other, and that's the whole story. In Chapter 6 we will give a presentation of the Austrian School. There we will see that extreme right-wingers advocate that even the protection of property rights can be coordinated by a free market.

If scientists introduce a government that forces people to vote, to pay taxes, and to stick to rules, this is not the economic world anymore, and we actually enter the social world. An analysis can only be made if we first define the social world ontologically—as we do in Chapter 13. Otherwise, we stay on the level of ad hoc science.

In Figure 4.21 we have presented a sketch of the relationships in the political sector as far as is relevant in the process of collective decision-making.

Up to now we have not only assumed that actors are perfectly rational, but also that they are perfectly informed about their economic world. The alternative approaches in the public choice literature do not use the concept of rationality versus irrationality at all. In Chapter 10, where we discuss in detail what psychology can mean for an economist,

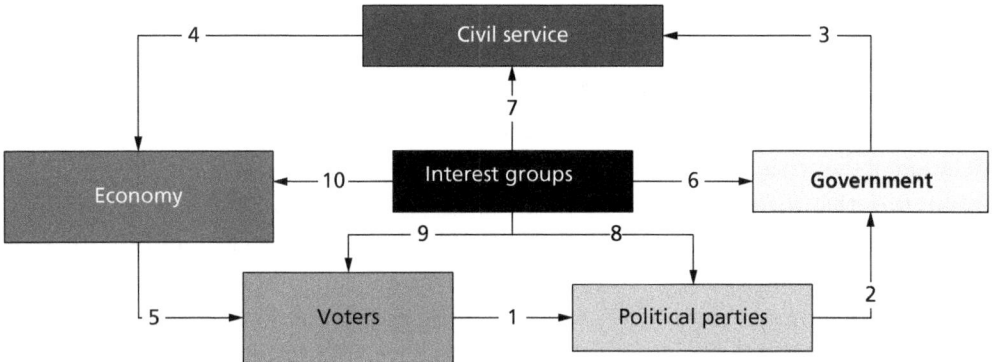

Figure 4.21. A Politico-Economic Model

we will discuss the idea of rationality and show that social theory should include the idea of humans being imperfectly rational.

4.5.6 IMPERFECTLY INFORMED ACTORS IN THE PUBLIC WORLD

The assumption of perfect information is made in order to start with a simple analysis. Now we relax this very strict assumption.

Our modern world is characterized by enormous stocks and flows of information. But the main problem is how to select and structure those pieces of information that are really relevant for the solution to the problem at hand.

In Chapter 2 we have seen that knowledge consists of four parts, namely paradigm, analysis, theory, and hypothesis (PATH). It means that, from a logical point of view, an understanding of the problem starts with the formulation of a paradigm. This means that an explicit ontology must be formulated. In our public world this is an important task of the media. Many media, such as newspapers and TV programmes, do not clearly formulate their ideology. They suggest that they offer the news in an ideology-free manner, and that the 'colour' of the medium can be extracted from the editorial comments. In earlier times the media in Europe were highly pillarized. Every pillar had its own explicitly formulated ideology, which delivered the ontology necessary for the definition and selection of the news. Now most Dutch media are significantly influenced by neoliberal ideology. In this seeming ideology-free world of politics, the modern voter is constantly zapping between the different media and has become a floating voter. It means that people do not accept the prefabricated structures of the pillars anymore. However, most of them are not able to solve the problem of selection of what they see as important information. In this situation many voters are unable to protect themselves against the influence of *hidden ideologies* in the world of information. The European economic crisis can serve as an interesting example in this respect. It started with a crisis in the deregulated global financial market. In Europe, growth figures were and still are lower and unemployment rates higher than ever after the Second World War. There is no inflation anymore. However, the neoliberal ideology has become the dominating view in the financial world, and in the world of universities and media. Without being explicit about it, important neoclassical and monetarist axioms are used in their interpretation of the crisis. Two hidden assumptions will be discussed shortly. The first is the assumption that the government is a consumer household, which should not borrow money on the capital market. It means that the government budget should structurally be in equilibrium, where equilibrium means that total expenditures are equal to current revenues. A more Continental-liberal view on government budget policy is different, but almost nobody explains and applies this view. The result is that most citizens think that budget discipline is identical with budget equilibrium as calculated in the neoliberal way. The second hidden assumption is the neoclassical/monetarist idea that a market economy is always close to its equilibrium. There is a business cycle, which shows changes in the growth rate; in some periods the rate is a little higher (expansion), and in other periods the rate is a little lower than the trend (recession). Over time the monetarists have developed a set of monetary instruments, by means of which the central bank can control the macro economy. Now the European economy shows a severe decline, the dominant view has no language to analyse it, and no policies to tackle the problem. In Chapter 8 we will discuss the fact that the current situation (2013) should not be characterized by the term 'recession', but by the term 'depression'. The political consequences are far-reaching.

These examples show that ideology plays a very significant role in the public world. It is important to know that one of the factors, making people adhere to one ideology rather than to another, is the way they look at their personal interests. Thus also with interest groups: they formulate particular interests, and people who support the ideology behind it, become members. People who have invested large amounts of money, for instance, are justifying their interests by supporting a neoliberal political party.

If we assume imperfect information in the economic world, the adoption of an ideology is an effective way of structuring flows of sense impressions. In the economic world the ideology says that everyone is economic and rational and everyone knows this. This leads to a clear idea of what the interests of the actors are. In Chapter 7 on radical economics we will see that changes in the axiomatic structure lead to a completely different picture: no equilibrium, ideology matters, and a dynamic that leads to the end of a free market economy. There are capitalists who are influenced by radical economic ideas—in the West as well as in the East. They regularly stress the necessity of particular government interventions. Most capitalists, however, advocate a reduction in government regulation as far as possible. In Chapter 10 we treat a series of psychological approaches, and we will see that individuals are not all the same, as is suggested by the economic orthodoxy: economic and rational. They can also be portrayed as irrational searchers of their true Self. In Chapters 11 to 13 we discuss a series of sociological approaches, and we will see that social structure and culture affects individual behaviour significantly.

Now we will finish our section on public choice with a model of the political sector, which shows that the implicit assumption of the economic world—there is a government who operates as a benevolent dictator—needs to be relaxed.

4.5.7 NEW POLITICAL MACRO ECONOMY

Public choice contains a micro-level and a macro-level analysis. Micro public choice is about the behaviour of the individual voter, politician, bureaucrat, or member of an interest group. On the basis of the orthodox economic axioms, an analysis is made of them and their economic interaction. Macro public choice is about the whole of the public world, and focuses on the economic interactions between the main constituent parts. It is important to note that orthodox macroeconomics is based on a micro-foundation, which is the familiar set of axioms about the individual person. In Chapters 7 and 8 on heterodox radical and heterodox post-Keynesian economics we will see that genuine macroeconomics has a macro-foundation.

The macro level concerns decisions on the level of groups, including the government, which take decisions on the basis of their own interest. In the economic world an omniscient and benevolent dictator takes the decisions. In public choice democracy is assumed, which means that every person has one vote, while a vote market is forbidden. It is important to note that the democratic decision rule is derived from the idea that every individual has a series of inalienable rights, thereby reflecting the essential equality of man. In sociology more attention is paid to this idea. In orthodox economic public choice it is just the 'one man, one vote' rule that makes a political system a democratic one.

The economic approach says that voters look at the economic performance of the economy as a whole, and hold the ruling parties responsible for it. In fact, the voter assumes complete control of the government over economic development, which is indicated in the literature as the *short-sightedness of voters*. Politicians compete and try to maximize the number of votes in the next election, which is called *myopiness of democratic politicians*.

Suppose a political system consists of two political parties, competing for the votes of voters, who look at two economic issues, namely the rate of unemployment and the rate of inflation. One party rules, and the other is the opponent, and is constantly challenging the ruling party. Now we can present the situation in a way that looks very much like the situation of a consumer who chooses between two options. The consumer has his utility function and his budget constraint. Here the ruling party wants to be as popular as possible, but the economic performance functions as a restriction. In Figure 4.22 we have presented the situation. The indifferences curves, which are concave to the origin, show combinations of unemployment and inflation, for which a particular percentage of the electorate is indifferent. A shift of such a curve to the left and below makes the share of the electorate that votes for the ruling party larger. The curves that are convex to the origin show the relationship between the rate of unemployment and the rate of inflation

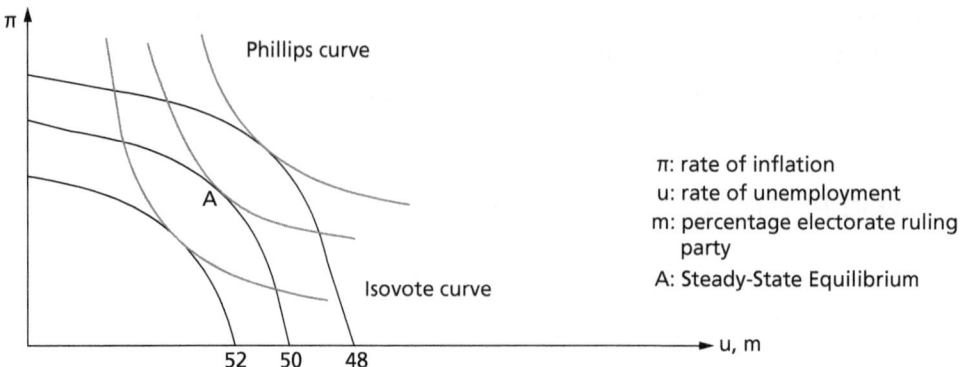

Figure 4.22. Steady-State Equilibrium in the Political Sector

at a particular moment. The points where the two curves have the same slope are equilibrium points. But only equilibrium combinations between inflation and unemployment that give the ruling party a majority of the votes are acceptable to the government. If these combinations do not lead to a majority of the votes for the ruling party, government policies will be changed to get the inflation-unemployment curve down to a lower equilibrium point.

The situation in the USA in October 2012 can be clarified by Figure 4.22. At that time, Obama, the candidate of the ruling party (the Democratic Party), had the lead by just a few percentage points. Political experts expect Obama to win the elections if he is able to get the unemployment rate down without an increase in inflation in the weeks just before the election.

In the form of equations we have the following two-equation model:

$$POP(t) = a.u(t) + b.\pi(t) + POP(aut) \quad a \leq 0; b \leq 0 \tag{1}$$

$$\pi(t) = c.1/u(t) + \pi(aut) \quad c \geq 0 \tag{2}$$

POP = popularity, expressed in the number of votes.
u = rate of unemployment.
π = rate of inflation.
aut = the autonomous part.

In the economic world individuals are economic and rational and they know that all other individuals have the same nature. In Chapter 5 on orthodox macroeconomics we will see that, in such case, there is just one interpretation of the relationship between inflation and unemployment. In the short run the relationship is an inverse one, and in the long run there is just one equilibrium level of the rate of unemployment, the so-called natural rate of unemployment. As soon as we leave the economic world, as we do in the heterodox part, both equations are different. The structure of the market for 'economic knowledge' is definitely not a competitive one. There is one school of thought that dominates the educational programmes at universities. It means that civil servants of ministries, and members of staff at research bureaus, and in large firms, and banks, are programmed in a particular way, and have barely learned to look at economic problems in different ways. Strong psychological and sociological barriers prevent academics operating as *interest-free intellectuals* who aim for truth rather than the interests of the powerful groups. Before we look at a whole series of different heterodox approaches, we will sketch what we mean by orthodox macroeconomics.

5 Orthodox Macroeconomics

5.1 Introduction

The concept 'macro' can be understood in two ways. In the first place, it refers to the *level of analysis*, which can be the level of a country, a region, such as the Eurozone, the EU economy, or the global economy. To an increasing extent, national economies have become so dependent of each other that they are not macro economies anymore. In the second place, it refers to the *level of explanation*. Then we interpret every phenomenon as part of a bigger whole. So, if we want to analyse the latest developments in the Dutch economy, we place them in the context of the Euro Area, or even in the context of the EU economy. If we want to understand developments in this context, we place the Euro Area or the EU economy in the context of the global economy. More specifically, when we search for causes of the Euro crisis, it makes sense to mention the reason why the global economy was hit by a financial crisis, which started in the USA.

Orthodox macroeconomics, however, approaches every phenomenon from the smallest unit, which is the individual. So, individuals are going to markets, meet other individuals, and, if it is profitable for both sides, individuals trade with each other. A national economy consists of many markets. But the same holds for the Euro Area, and the global economy: they all are aggregates of individual activities. Applied to the Euro crisis the orthodox analysis does not focus on the Euro Area as a whole, and as part of the global economy. It focuses on the competitiveness of individuals and firms, and therewith on the competitiveness of a national economy. The Germans and the Dutch are clearly using the micro-economic methodology of orthodox macroeconomics when analysing the Euro crisis. When applying the macroeconomic methodology, it is not difficult to understand why countries such as the USA and the BRIC countries (Brazil, Russia, India, and China) are irritated, and blame the EU for a lack of cooperation in solving the global prisoner's dilemma.

In this chapter we discuss orthodox macroeconomics. First, we discuss the basic principles, and a set of equations, which form the core model of it. Second, we show the consequences for phenomena, such as business cycles and inflation, production growth, and income distribution.

As explained already, orthodox economics starts with the economic, rational, and non-social actor, who tries to reduce scarcity as much as possible. We have seen that this paradigm leads us to supply and demand analysis, and to the price mechanism, which makes markets tend towards equilibrium. The allocation of scarce resources is optimal if all markets are characterized by perfect competition. The axioms that make this microeconomic approach an appropriate basis for an analysis of a macro economy are the assumptions that *all persons and firms are small relative to the market as a whole, and that all markets are small relative to the whole of the economy.* It means that bankruptcies of persons and firms do not create market disturbances, and that a disequilibrium in one market cannot create significant disturbances in other markets. It also means that the market economy as a whole can only show temporary disequilibria as a result of a change in an exogenous variable. When discussing the orthodox business cycle theory, we go into more detail with respect to cyclical adjustment processes.

There is, however, one market that is not small relative to the economy as a whole, and that is the money market. Money is involved in all market transactions. Whatever the good, including labour and capital services, it must be paid with money. Therefore, the money market is a typical macro-market. If the money market is in disequilibrium, it has significant effects on the economy as a whole. In Figure 5.1 we have presented this micro view on a macro economy graphically. The picture shows many micro-markets. The interrupted lines suggest many more micro-markets. Below this set of very small markets we have placed one macro-market, which is the money market.

In the orthodox economic approach prices are flexible, because actors are assumed to have a strong economic force or motivation. This makes markets alert with respect to changes in their environment. They are also assumed to be rational, which means that

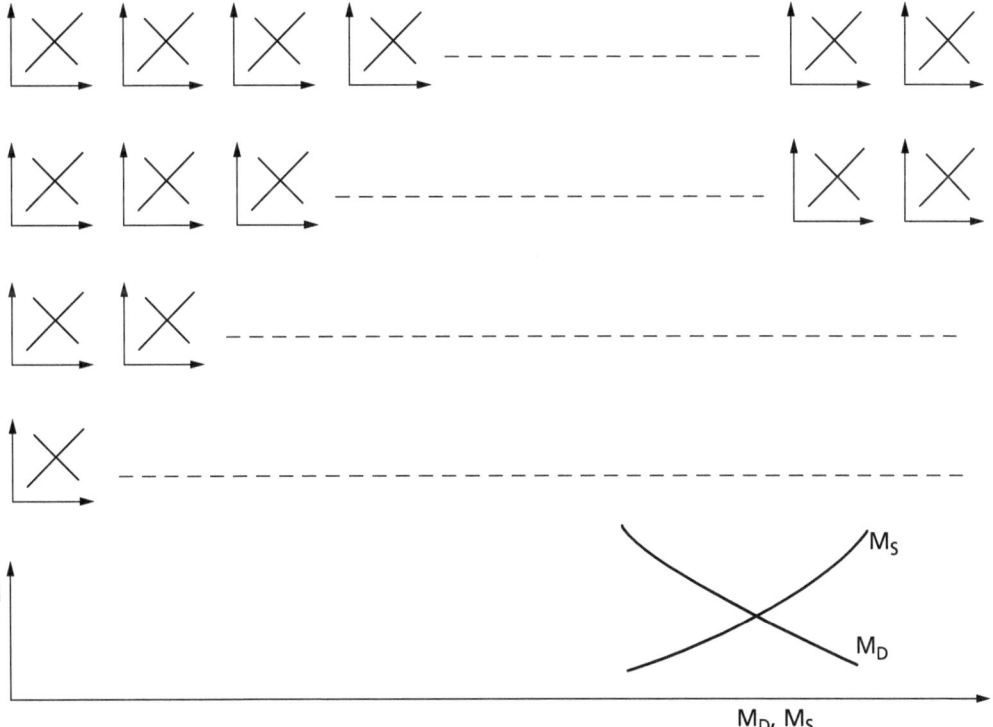

Figure 5.1. The Macroeconomic World

they are able to select the goods that maximize their utility over a relatively long period of time. So, if the price of the good that turns out to be satisfying true needs decreases, our actor is strongly motivated to find out whether it makes sense to consume more of the good. Economic and rational actors react flexibly. Actors who are not driven by a strong economic force, or are not rational, might react more slowly, making the price mechanism less effective with respect to the allocation of scarce resources.

The money market is a special market. In the economic world private banks are the money creators. They do not only store savings, and lend it to firms. Since they have discovered that many people do not substitute their savings and bank deposits for coins and notes, banks lend more than the amount of savings and cash from the clients. This difference means an increase of the money in circulation. Economic and rational actors will change their amount of savings, if the reward for it, which is the interest rate, changes. An increase in the amount of savings implies a decrease in the quantity of money demanded, because the opportunity costs of keeping assets in the most liquid form are equal to the interest rate. The higher this rate, the stronger the economic motivation of banks to lend money to their customers, and the weaker the economic motivation of spenders to borrow money from the market.

Most neoclassical economists are of the opinion that the private banks should be controlled by a central bank, which is responsible for an optimal amount of money in circulation. In Chapter 6 we will see that the Austrians defend a monetary system that is 'ruled' by free markets.

As we have seen, the economic world is not meant to be a reliable picture of real-life economies. It is just a construct, which shows the operation of the economic motivation or force. So, the installation of a central bank does not fit the axioms of the economic world.[1]

What has been said about money markets also holds for the foreign currency markets, a special type of money market. We can imagine that the economic world develops institutions, which make the transaction costs lower. In Chapter 4 we discussed this phenomenon under the label new institutional economics. For now we can just state that everywhere in the world particular goods became money, and if traders wanted to trade with people in a different currency area, they had to sell their own currency and buy the foreign one. Of course, these markets should be free markets, where the relative price of the currencies is flexible. This system is called the *system of floating currencies*. All currencies compete with each other; some are stronger than others. A process of concentration might lead to one currency used in all areas in the world, which is apparently the most efficient solution.

An extreme variant of orthodoxy is the new classical economics (NCE). This school assumes that adjustment processes take place very fast and smoothly. Economic and rational actors are motivated to process the latest information of their activities immediately. If the media announce voluminous lay-offs in a particular firm, shareholders

---

[1] The Federal Reserve System in the USA is responsible for the execution of monetary policy. The system is owned by a series of very large US banks. In other words, it is private. The government has the authority to appoint the chairperson, however.

immediately react by selling their shares. They can only find actors who are willing to buy their shares if they accept a not-too-small drop in the price of the shares. In this way the market always reflects efficient prices and quantities. If workers discover that they might be fired, they immediately begin to search for another job, or search for possibilities of retraining themselves, or consider the erection of a one-man business. If they get fired and they do not react at all, we can conclude that these people are voluntarily unemployed, or not unemployed at all.

The analyses of the NCE are based on the assumption that actors have *rational expectations*, and react quickly to changes in the economy. With respect to the monetary policies in the USA there are many interpreters who interpret the words spoken and the texts written by the chairman of the FED. Also, his face expressions are carefully studied. This gives information to the FED watchers, which is immediately reflected in many financial prices and quantities. It is important to note that the NCE assumes that every actor frames information flows according to the principles of the economic world.

In this NCE world there is always (almost) equilibrium on all markets. The macroeconomic department of the Chicago School has become famous for its NCE approach. They apply this analysis to the free world, discover that real-life economies show many markets in disequilibrium, and come to the conclusion that real-life economic processes are apparently channelled by institutions designed by people who did not understand economics.

The functioning of the economy as a whole can be presented in a series of equations. Quantities demanded and supplied are a function of the price of the good, and all markets are in equilibrium, which implies that the economy as a whole is in equilibrium.

The relationship between the labour and capital market on the one hand, and the goods market on the other, is called the production function. The mathematical form, which expresses the economic principle of easy substitution best, is the Cobb–Douglas function:

$$X(t) = A(t) \cdot K^{\alpha}(t) \cdot N^{(1-\alpha)}(t)$$

Investments always have two sides. On the one hand, they lead to an increase in the demand for goods. On the other hand, they lead to an increase in the capital stock, which represents the production capacity. Therefore, we need the definition equation:

$$I_{(t)} = dK / dt$$

to relate the production function to the demand for goods function. In orthodox analysis the spending effect is considered to have already taken place in the short run. The capacity effect, however, takes place in the long run. It is important to notice that the long run is defined as the period necessary for a free market economy to turn back to equilibrium after a particular shock. In the methodology literature, the concept of time, which is linked to effects that are constructed in the world of economic logic, is called *logical time*. When discussing heterodox macroeconomics we will see that post-Keynesians, for instance, are using *real time*. In other words, a short run means one or a few years. A medium run means about five to ten years, and a long run is about ten years and longer.

In the *short-run analysis* the size of the capital is a constant; and so with the level of technology. It means that the production function can be presented as:

$$X = N^{\alpha}$$

The behavioural equations, together with the equilibrium conditions are:
Goods market:

$$
\begin{aligned}
Y &= C + I \\
X &= N^{\alpha} \\
Y &= X \\
X &\leq Xcap
\end{aligned}
$$

Y = quantity demanded (goods)
X = quantity supplied $\left(\text{goods}\right)$
N = employment
C = volume of consumption
I = volume of investments
$Xcap$ = short run production capacity
aut = autonomous component

Labour market:

$$
\begin{aligned}
N_{(D)} &= b \cdot w + N(D)(aut) \\
N_{(S)} &= d \cdot w + N(S)(aut) \\
N_{(D)} &= N_{(S)}
\end{aligned}
$$

$N_{(D)}$ = quantity demanded $\left(\text{labour}\right)$
$N_{(S)}$ = quantity supplied $\left(\text{labour}\right)$
w = wage rate
$b \leq 0; d \geq 0.$

Capital market:

$$
\begin{aligned}
I &= e \cdot i + I(aut) \\
S &= f \cdot i + S(aut) \\
I &= S
\end{aligned}
$$

I = investments $\left(\text{physical}\right)$
S = savings $\left(\text{flow}\right)$
i = interest rate
$e \leq 0; f \geq 0$

Money market:

$$
\begin{aligned}
M_{(D)} &= g \cdot i + M(D)(aut) \\
M_{(S)} &= h \cdot i + M(S)(aut) \\
M_{(D)} &= M(S)
\end{aligned}
$$

$M_{(D)}$ = quantity demanded $\left(\text{money}\right)$
$M_{(S)}$ = quantity supplied $\left(\text{money}\right)$
$g \leq 0; h \geq 0$

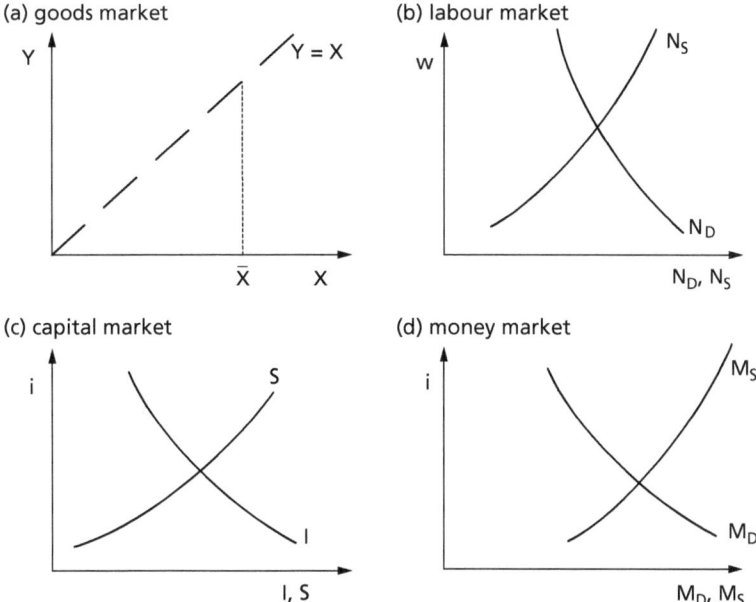

Figure 5.2. Short-Run Orthodox Macro Model

An important assumption behind this model is that competition on the currency market means that only currency systems that are able to maintain price stability will survive. It means that there is no difference between the nominal and real values of the entities. If we relax this assumption by introducing imperfect information, or even imperfect competition, we would construct a different model of the money market. In Figure 5.2 we have presented the four markets graphically.

The economic world shows business cycles. We will discuss a theory, which is developed on the basis of the assumption that small disequilibria are possible, and a typical NCE business cycle theory, based on the idea that market economies are permanently in equilibrium.

5.2 **Business Cycles and Inflation**

When taking the monetary sphere explicitly into account, the classical theory comes to the conclusion that, in equilibrium, there is a complete dichotomy between the monetary sphere and the real sphere of production and employment. We saw that the money market is a macro-market, in contrast to all other markets. This implies that small disequilibria on the money market may have significant effects on all other markets. Wicksell (1898) was one of the first to describe the transmission mechanism responsible for the effect of a monetary disequilibrium on the economy as a whole, and show

how the economy is able to return to its equilibrium. His analysis starts with a situation in which all markets are in equilibrium. Then a couple of banks set their interest rate at a level that is lower than the equilibrium or natural rate of the capital market. This makes it attractive for investors to borrow money and to invest it in financial and physical assets. Investments increase, stimulating production and consumption. Since the labour market was in equilibrium already, this leads to an increase in the price level of goods rather than an increase in the volume of goods. Later, Pigou in the 1920s and Patinkin in the 1950s developed a more general theory about the transmission between the money sector and the real sector. The result remains the same, however. An increase in the money supply implies a higher real balance (M/P) in the hands of the public, which leads to a series of wealth and substitution effects, which ends up as an increase in the general price level. So, in equilibrium the real value of the money in the hands of the public (M/P) is constant.

Fisher (1911) was the first to formulate the so-called quantity theory of money, often presented by the following equation:[2]

$$M \cdot V = P \cdot T \qquad M = \text{quantity supplied of money}$$
$$V = \text{velocity of circulation of money}$$
$$P = \text{general price level}$$
$$T = h \cdot X \qquad h = \text{average number of households}$$
$$X = \text{level of production / income}$$

Later Robertson, Marshall, and others formulated this equation a little differently:

$$L = k \cdot P \cdot T \qquad L = \text{quantity demanded for money}$$
$$k = L / P \cdot T$$

The second equation is an answer to the question why people do *not* immediately use the money, while everyone knows that holding wealth in terms of cash does not give any reward. According to the orthodox theory, people need cash, because it takes too much effort to plan all the inflows and outflows of money perfectly well. So, a buffer of cash is needed to pay bills in time.

Keynes appeared to be the main critic of this classical theory. He considered V as unstable in unstable periods, such as during the Great Depression. Monetary policy could not be effective in helping us out of a depression. Even if the interest rate fell to almost zero, consumers and investors would not be triggered to spend their money.

---

[2] T is the real value of the transactions in a particular period. The more consumption and production households, the more often money is needed for financing transactions.

Their pessimistic expectations with respect to jobs, incomes, and sales prevent them becoming active.

Many economists were impressed by Keynes' analysis of the depression, and, in practice, many Western governments adopted part of Keynes' policy advice after the Second World War. Meanwhile, other economists were still working on an improvement of the classical monetary theory. Friedman (1956) came up with a restatement of the quantity theory of money. His argumentation in favour of V being quite stable runs as follows. If the economy is close to equilibrium, V can increase only as long as L is positive, and T can only increase as long as the production capacity is not completely utilized. But as soon as L is at its bare minimum and all the factors of production are used, price increases can only be caused by an increase in the money supply. Friedman estimated a demand for money function with many elements as explanatory variables. The most important were the aggregate of the permanent incomes of the households and the interest rate. According to Friedman, the function appeared stable for a long period in the United States. It brought Friedman and Schwartz (1963) to the conclusion that the Great Depression was the result of errors made by a few men who controlled the American monetary system. They accepted a decrease in M with one-third in the first half of the 1930s. Consequently, it is not a surprise that the free market system could not function properly. Active monetary policy would have prevented the American economy from falling into a depression.

Although Fisher (1911) did not work on the dynamics of the transmission mechanism, he had already assumed a statistical relationship between wage inflation and unemployment. Later, Phillips (1958) published an article about this relationship, which he estimated for the period 1861–1957. He found an inverse relationship between the two variables. Although this relationship is generally interpreted as an empirical relationship, close reading of the article leads to a different conclusion. Many years which Phillips did not consider to be 'normal' years, where their combinations of wage inflation and unemployment did not fit the plotted curve, were deliberately excluded from the time series used in the published results. In some years there had been rumours of a war, or an actual war, and in other years the government had intervened in the process of wage formation or strikes had led to lower production and higher wages. This means that this empirical study is based on Phillips' idea of a normal period, which is a period in which individuals are economic and rational, and the markets are free and close to equilibrium. These typical orthodox axioms should lead to a linear relationship between the two variables.[3] In Figure 5.3 we have presented two lines, each with a different slope; both slopes are possible.

Orthodox theory cannot explain the relationship of Phillips, which is a curve convex to the origin. The downward stickiness of the growth rate of wages is especially remarkable. In our discussion of post-Keynesianism in Chapter 8 we come back to this issue.

---

[3] There are no a priori reasons why the relationship should be a curve that is convex or concave to the origin.

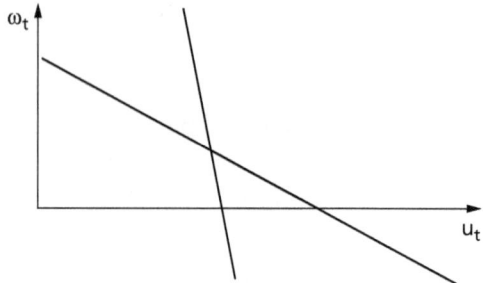

Figure 5.3. Orthodox Phillips-Like Relationships

Friedman (1968) criticized the way in which the Phillips relationship was interpreted politically. Many economists suggested that there was a trade-off between inflation and unemployment, and that politicians could freely choose a point on the curve which they favour. So, the price of lower unemployment is a higher rate of inflation, and vice versa. According to Friedman this was only the case in the short run. But as soon as individual workers and capitalists discover that government-demand policies create inflation, they adjust their expectations, and claim an income increase so as to be compensated for the loss in purchasing power. So, the curve shifts upward, which means that both wage inflation and unemployment have become higher than expected so far. If the government continues its attempts to reach an unemployment level that is structurally lower than the natural rate, expectations adjust and income recipients claim an even higher increase, so as to be compensated for the loss of purchasing power. Friedman draws the conclusion that, in the long run, the curve is transformed into a vertical line. Long-run equilibrium is reached—by definition—as soon as the unemployment rate is on the natural level, while inflation depends on the stubbornness of the government. It is essential to recognize that, in this orthodox approach, time is not historical, but logical. Long run means the period necessary for the market economy to adjust to shocks coming from outside the system. It might take many years, and still, by definition, it's not the long run, because the system of free markets is not yet in equilibrium. When discussing heterodox economics we will see that economists such as Keynes and others are using historical time. Friedman's relations are called the *expectations-augmented Phillips relations*. As long as these analyses are not applied to the real world, there is no problem. But looking at the relationship between wage inflation and unemployment during the 1970s and 1980s, we do not see a negative relationship nor a vertical line, but a positive relationship. Neoclassical and monetarist economists began to search for an explanation in terms of not-economically-motivated institutions, which were responsible for the growing stagflation. Other explanations were and are still blocked by typical orthodox axioms, which were assumed to be beyond doubt. When discussing other theories we see that it is not wise for economists who want to become empirically relevant to stick to unrealistic axioms.

According to the monetarist view, only monetary policies can prevent sharp fluctuations in production and unemployment. The monetarists consider the government to be a consumption household, which should aim for a balanced budget. Only a central bank, which operates independently from the government, has the expertise and the right incentives to implement monetary policies with price stability as the only target. Friedman is impressed by the difficult-to-control time lags between the occurrence of problems and the moment they are fixed. Therefore, he rejects discretionary policies by monetary experts. Monetary matters are too complicated, and it is better that the experts develop *policy rules,* meant to stabilize the cycles of production. Rational individuals take these rules into account when taking their decisions. Friedman proposed a rule of a month-by-month check of money growth, which should be between 3 and 5 per cent on a yearly basis. Of course, such a rule is context-dependent and must be adjusted regularly.

When we discuss heterodox approaches we will see that the monetarist position is heavily criticized. But even other orthodox economists criticize the monetarist explanations. In the first place, economists who adhere to the supply-side economics view criticize the monetarists for their focus on the demand side of the money and the goods market. Supply-siders assume that, in a free market economy, it is essential that economic actors have strong incentives to work, to save, and to invest. In that case, the macro demand for goods will always adjust to the supply of goods. If workers and capitalists decide to cooperate in the production of particular goods they are inclined to spend the incomes they earn. If some people decide to save, the market mechanism will induce other people to invest. In this way all production will always be sold.[4]

It is obvious that supply-siders also assume that all markets are always close to equilibrium. It also means that the cyclical fluctuations, resulting from changes in exogenous variables, are too small to pay attention to. This view is more or less the same as the new classical economics approach. This assumes that expectations are perfectly rational, and that adjustments hardly take any time. So, fluctuations in the rate of production growth and in the rate of unemployment are not signs of disequilibria, and therefore there is no reason for a government to intervene. If the government makes the mistake of intervention, economic and rational actors anticipate the negative effects, thereby making government policies ineffective. The only effect a government can have is the crowding out of private activities. In other words, a substitution takes place of public activities for private activities; a substitution which will definitely be at the cost of the wealth of a nation.

In Section 5.3 we will discuss the orthodox growth theory.

---

[4] Actually the supply-siders fall back on a very old law from classical theory, which is Say's law: supply always creates its own demand.

5.3 **Orthodox Growth Theory**

We saw that, according to classical, neoclassical, and new classical economics, the wealth of a nation is determined by the productivity of the factors of production, and that a free market economy offers the economic and rational actors the strongest incentives to work, to save, and to invest. Orthodox economics assumes that economic rationality means that actors are very sensitive to changes in their economic context. So, if the price of a particular good increases, actors are inclined to switch to a substitute, whose price did not change. We call this switch *substitution*. So with factors of production: if the wage rate increases while the interest rate is constant, entrepreneurs are inclined to implement more capital as a substitute for labour. In the orthodox world all markets are assumed to be perfectly competitive, which means that all firms choose a production level that meets the condition of *constant returns to scale*. This requirement implies a linear and continuous function, which is twice differentiable.[5] A mathematical function, which relates the volume of capital and labour with the volume of production, thereby assuming perfect substitutability and constant returns to scale, is the Cobb–Douglas production function:

$$X(t) = A \cdot (\sqrt{K(t)} \cdot \sqrt{N(t)})$$

X = volume of production

K = volume of capital

N = volume of labour

A = state of production technique.

Figure 5.4 presents the situation in which entrepreneurs choose their optimal production technique: the relationship between K and N, producing a particular amount of X. The curves are indifference curves and the slope of the straight lines expresses the relative factor price: w/i, whereby w is the wage rate and i the profit rate. The lines are called iso-cost lines. Applying the second law of Gossen, which we discussed in Chapter 4 when explaining consumer behaviour, we see that the slope of the indifference curve is expressed as:

$$dX/dN/dX/dK$$

In other words, the slope reflects the ratio between the two marginal factor productivities. Where the tangent of the line and of the curve are equal to each other, we have a point of equilibrium, and a change in the relative price leads to a change in the ratio between the volumes of capital and labour (see the shift of the straight line in Figure 5.4, leading to the equilibrium points 1, 2, and 3). In this analysis we have implicitly assumed

---

[5] A linear homogeneous function means that the volume of production doubles if the volumes of capital and labour are doubled.

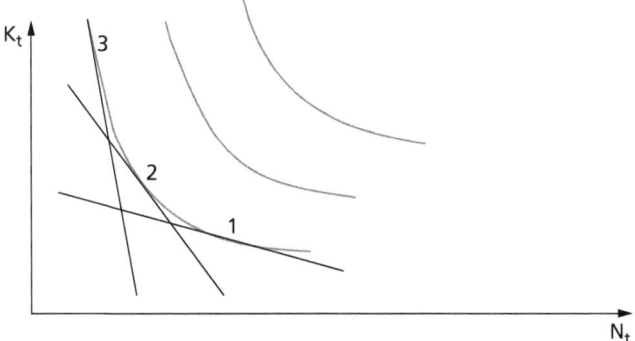

Figure 5.4. Economic Growth as a Result of Factor Substitution

that there is no technical progress. In such a situation economic growth can only be the result of factor substitution.

Now we develop a simple orthodox model of economic growth, which does not only show the role of factor substitution, but also the fact that the savings rate does not play a role in the determination of the rate of economic growth; a surprising result indeed.

Imagine a closed economy without an explicit account of government action. The expenditures of actors consist of consumption and investment (1). The income of the actors can be used for consumption, and that part of income that is not consumed is called saving (2). The production function is of a Cobb–Douglas type (3). Investment is defined as an increase in the stock of capital goods (4). The capital output ratio (K/X) is indicated with an (a) (5). The savings are a fixed share of the income (s) (6). The growth rate of the labour force is indicated with the letter (n) (7). All markets are in equilibrium (8). When we take these assumptions together, it gives us the following model:

$$(1) \quad Y = C + I \qquad \text{definition equation}$$
$$(2) \quad X = C + S \qquad \text{definition equation}$$
$$(3) \quad X = \sqrt{K} \cdot \sqrt{N} \qquad \text{technical} - \text{economic equation}$$
$$(4) \quad I = dK / dt \qquad \text{definition equation}$$
$$(5) \quad a = K / X \qquad \text{definition equation}$$
$$(6) \quad S = s \cdot X \qquad \text{behavioural equation}$$
$$(7) \quad N_{(S)} = N_{(S)} \qquad \text{behavioural equation}$$
$$(8) \quad I = S \qquad \text{equilibrium condition}$$

We can conclude from the model that the growth rates of Y, X, S, I, and K are all the same. It is easy to show that the value of this rate of growth is s/a. Equilibrium on the labour market means that the employment grows at the same rate.

So, in equilibrium holds that

$$s/a = n$$

What will happen if the saving rates increase? It is impossible to have a higher rate of growth, since the growth rate of the labour force is the effective constraint. But we can expect a lower interest rate, which is an incentive for investors to substitute capital for labour, leading to a higher capital output ratio. So, an increase in s leads to an increase in a, until the ratio s/a is back to the level of n. An increase of n as a result of an increase in immigration, for instance, will lead to an excess supply on the labour market, which lowers the wage rate. This is an incentive for the investors to substitute labour for capital, leading to a lower a. This process of adjustment goes on until s/a is equal to n again.

Now we introduce the state of technology as an exogenous variable. In Figure 5.5a we present the relationship between the production level and the level of the capital stock, being an expression of the law of diminishing marginal returns. If we divide both variables by N, we get a relationship as presented in Figure 5.5b: labour productivity (X/N) is related to capital intensity (K/N).

The law just mentioned holds for the short run, which means that the employment level is constant. As long as we assume constant returns to scale, the same relationships also hold for the long run, in which both factors of production are assumed to be variable.

Now we assume technical progress, which means that the curve shifts upward: a higher level of labour productivity is reached, ceteris paribus the capital-output relationship. Mathematically it can be proven that the slope of the curve is equal to the marginal productivity of capital (Kuipers and Wilpstra, 1983). It means that a free market economy, which is characterized by perfect competition, is in equilibrium when the tangent of the curve is equal to the profit rate. In Figure 5.5 we have shown a straight line with a slope equal to the interest rate; in other words, the marginal productivity of capital is equal to the interest rate. So equilibrium is reached in A.

Hicks (1963) made an analysis of economic growth in which he wanted to separate the influence of factor substitution on the one hand, and technological progress on the other.

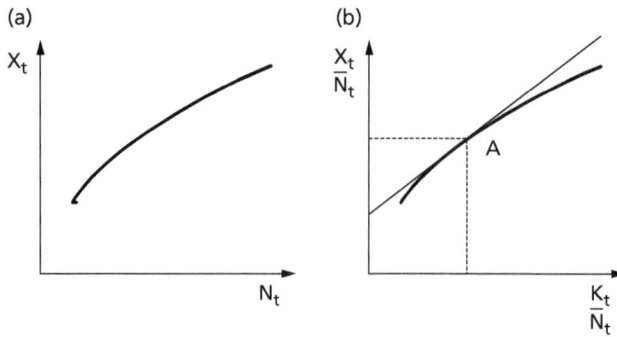

Figure 5.5. A: Law of Diminishing Marginal Returns; B: Constant Returns to Scale

As we saw, factor substitution is a typical orthodox element, and the only factor in an orthodox analysis without technological progress that causes growth. In Figure 5.6 we have drawn two other curves, illustrating the effect of technological progress. If we keep capital intensity constant (no factor substitution), we can read along the vertical axis the effect of technological progress on labour productivity X/N. In Chapters 7 and 8 we will see that other economists, such as Marx and Harrod have developed other analyses and other concepts and definitions, leading to different conclusions. There we will see that neutral technological progress is defined as the situation in which capital productivity and profit rate are constant: a definition which reflects a different view on what the important issues are in a capitalist system.

A last question to be discussed is if the saving rate still does not play a role in the determination of the rate of economic growth in an analysis with technological progress. We take the equilibrium condition with respect to the various growth rates as our starting point. The equation says that s/a = n. Now we introduce technological progress into our model. So-called exogenous growth models treat technological progress as an exogenous variable. Its growth rate is determined by forces outside our model. Suppose that technological progress means a growth rate of labour productivity of b. Then the equilibrium equation is s/a = n + b. However, is it realistic to assume that b has nothing to do with the behaviour of economic actors in the model? *Endogenous growth theory* is developed to show that the answer must be negative.

Romer (1990) takes the orthodox idea of economics as the science of optimal allocation of resources as his starting point. New information and knowledge are scarce goods, and if the profitability of investments in R&D is attractive, newcomers enter the market and invest more in the 'production' of knowledge. In the economic world it makes no sense to exclude these investments and production from the rest and call it exogenous. A world economy which consists of competitive markets will show an optimal amount of resources spent on invention, innovation, and education. The market also takes care

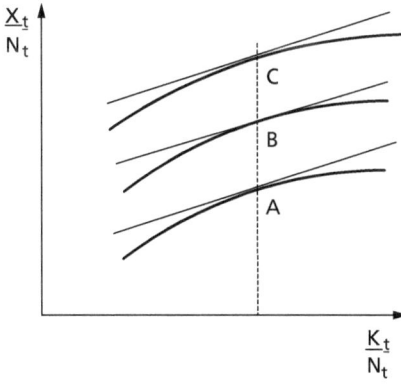

Figure 5.6. Neutral Technological Progress in the Sense of Hicks

of the diffusion of novelties. The government is responsible for the protection of property rights. So the inventor must have the possibility of keeping his findings to himself.

The Romer analysis fits the orthodox world. He developed a series of analyses on the basis of the assumption that the level of technology is the same all over the world. Romer (1990) searches for an explanation of the empirical fact that there is no convergence between the growth rates of poor and rich countries. He highlights a difference between the technology level of an economy, which is the same in all countries on the one hand, and the capital intensity (K/N) in all the firms in a particular country on the other.[6] It might be possible that the two do not form an optimal combination. Imagine that an American firm, which is characterized by the American level of technology, including its optimal combination of smart physical capital and smart labour (human capital), invests in Chad. Most of the workers they attract are indigenous Chad people. Even if these people have the proper qualifications, it might be true that their lack of general knowledge makes them less suited to operate the capital stock. If all the people in the world with the proper qualifications were equally productive, the speed of knowledge diffusion would determine the speed with which poor countries could catch up with the rich. According to Romer, this cannot explain the actual difference in rates of growth of labour productivity between rich and poor countries.

The typical economic world approach to the problem of economic growth fails to explain the differences in income per capita. The endogenous growth theory tries to find out where the main barriers to prosperity can be found. Is it in the market for R&D, or in the market for education? The problem lies somewhere in the building up of human capital. According to Romer and others, knowledge is neither a pure individual nor a pure public good. It is non-rivalling, and temporarily excludable. The government must take care of the protection of property rights, including inventions and innovations. Because this protection will never be perfect, the government should consider subsidizing R&D activities. For every person or firm these activities are very risky— researchers cannot plan discoveries, and it might take many years and millions of euros to conclude that the whole project is a failure. If we all agree that R&D and education are very important for society to function well, government involvement is an option. A careful analysis of the market for R&D, of education, and of the market for information (the media, for instance) is needed to find out how to improve the record of poor areas. A simple picture of marginal costs and marginal benefits of information, which should indicate what is the optimum amount of information, is not a proper reaction to this important problem.

In Chapter 4 we discussed how orthodox economics has treated the phenomenon of institutions. This might lead to a better answer to the question of the ultimate sources of economic growth, rather than just calculating private labour and private capital productivity. The institutionalization of society at large will appear an extremely important

---

[6] In terms of Figure 5.6 all countries are characterized by one and the same curve, but firms take different positions on the curve.

production factor. Historically, we can say already that Europe, and later the West in general, has been so successful just because of its institutions. We also saw that a strict economic approach to institutions is insufficient to understand particular severe barriers to growth. Irrational subcultures can lead to civilizations that have the power to hinder economic growth for centuries. But that can be discussed only after we have looked at psychological and sociological approaches and developed an analysis of irrationality and positive and negative sociality.

In Section 5.4 we will discuss neoclassical empirical practice.

5.4 **Neoclassical Empirical Research**

5.4.1 ECONOMICS AS AN EMPIRICAL SCIENCE

The founding fathers of orthodox economics—such as Mill, Pareto, Walras, and Menger—saw themselves as constructors of an aspect-system. But from the very beginning there were authors, such as Marshall and Jevons, who considered the orthodox analysis as applicable to at least the market sector of an economy. According to Jevons, the competitive nature of a free market makes it impossible for firms to be driven by motives other than the economic one. Marshall did not agree with Jevons as far concerns the labour market. Labour services are inseparable from the worker, and therefore it cannot be treated as a good, like apples and wood.

Most economists could not resist the temptation to test economic theories empirically. Although Robbins (1932) formulated orthodox economic philosophy in a way that found general agreement, most economists discussed daily practice just from an economic point of view. If Robbins' famous quote 'economics is neutral between ends' were straightforwardly be applied to the real world, it would give numerous outcomes, which can hardly be understood. It would mean that all drug addicts enjoy their drugs, and use them voluntarily, and that the wealth of the world would increase greatly if the Americans, the Chinese, and the Russians all decide to increase their military expenditures significantly.

The main problem of the empirical application of an aspect-theory is the fact that the meaning of the term 'economic' changes drastically. Orthodox economics is about human needs and their satisfaction. Neither needs nor their satisfaction can be observed by the classic senses. In other words, orthodox economics is *not* an empirical science. Applied to the concepts consumption and investment, we see that there is a significant difference between the theoretical and empirical interpretation of the two concepts. Theoretically, consumption means the derivation of utility from a good and investment means the sacrifice of goods by means of which more consumption goods can be produced. When we look at the empirical definitions of consumption and investment—goods bought by family households and goods bought by production households respectively—the difference between families and firms is based on a non-economic argumentation: we all know that, economically speaking, firms also consume and families also invest. In general, we can say that all goods have a consumption and an investment aspect.

The mixing up of economic theoretical concepts and empirical (statistical) concepts leads to strange outcomes: a single mother with three children receives an allowance benefit, and uses it to bring her children up decently: a good example of an investment in the theoretical sense, but a typical example of consumption in the empirical sense. If politicians decide to cut the allowance benefits to a biological minimum, it is because they interpret it as pure consumption, not as a necessary investment for a sustainable family and society.[7]

These problems of interpretation were exactly the reason why the fathers of orthodoxy constructed their isolated abstractions. They disagreed with the American Institutionalists, who offered empirical analyses as an alternative to the classical theory that dominated the 19th century. Robbins' book was accepted as the bible of orthodoxy and can be considered as an important warning against materialist definitions of the term 'economic'.

This move from the subjectivist idea of satisfaction of needs to the objectivist idea of empirically observable stocks and flows of goods became increasingly supported by economic theoretical and methodological views. Three examples illustrate this move.

In the first place, Samuelson (1950) introduced the concept of *revealed preferences*, by which he meant to say: we must consider every purchase and sale as a revelation of the true preferences of the actors. Money costs and money benefits are a good measure of the disutility and utility as experienced by the actors. If a medical specialist decides to take an hour's walk, the personal value of this walk can be expressed by his hourly wage, he were receiving if he would have worked one more hour.[8] In this way money is an ideal yardstick. Actually, Samuelson abstracts from the problem of irrationality and ignores the problem of socially motivated destructive activities, such as robbery, espionage, gossip, and social and military warfare. When discussing the problems concerning the measurement of economic growth we come back to this problem of mainstream economics.

In the second place, Friedman (1953) tried to solve the empirical problems by falling back on the empiricist tradition of the logical positivists, as discussed in Chapter 2. He advocates the idea that the theoretical construction that has led to the empirically testable hypotheses is unimportant. Theory functions like a rocket, which must bring a satellite into orbit around the earth. In this example science is not interested in the rocket as long as it fulfils its function well. Scientifically relevant is simply the question of whether the empirical theses are predicting the future well. In Section 5.4.2 our discussion about the successes and failures of econometric modelling comes back to this issue.

[7] In orthodox economics social considerations do not exist. If we discuss sociological theories about the economy, solidarity and fairness might enter the floor as appropriate arguments.

[8] This walk is not assumed to be a complementary good, delivering necessary relaxation.

The switch from aspect-theory to empirical variables also led to a series of practical problems. In the first place, *the problem of identification* can hardly be solved. Economic theory is about entities such as demand and supply, and quantity demanded and quantity supplied. An empirical researcher can only observe the quantity sold, however. So, if the quantity sold of a particular good changes, it is impossible to find out the reason for this shift. It can be a shift along the demand or along the supply curve, or a shift of one or both of these curves. Frequently, neoclassically orientated empirical researchers assume that the market is in equilibrium, which means that changes in the quantity sold are always the result of changes of the curves. In monetarist research this assumption is quite usual. By assuming that the money market is in equilibrium the monetarist must observe the quantity supplied, and then he knows by assumption the quantity demanded. In the heterodox part we will deal with the post-Keynesian theory, where we will see that the measurement of the quantity demanded is quite decisive in the whole discussion about the effectiveness of monetary policies vis-à-vis the effectiveness of fiscal policies—not unimportant in these days of a severe macroeconomic crisis. Moreover, the researcher knows from his theory that many demand curves shift under the influence of a change in the wealth of the demander. So, he should take the partial character of the demand and supply functions into account. This solution creates two problems. The first is the way wealth should be measured. The second problem is the question of which variables besides wealth are affecting the location of the demand and supply curves. By taking an isolated abstraction as theoretical foundation this question can never be answered satisfactorily.

In the third place, empirical measurement requires an appropriate definition of the concepts, which must be measured. Definitions cannot be observed, and must be derived from a satisfying theoretical instrument. Since orthodox economics does not offer such an instrument, the problem is to find adequate definitions. A few examples are given to illustrate this problem.

(1) The measurement of the unemployment rate is highly problematic. The definition of the concept depends on the analysis, which is made of the phenomenon. Different research programmes have their own definitions. Given a particular definition the observation might also be problematic. Quite often statistical bureaus publish estimates rather than the results of measurement. Then the problem shifts to the way the statisticians estimate their variables. The problem is linked to the difficulties with the observation of quantities demanded and quantities supplied. A liberal approach to the measurement of the quantity supplied implies that people who do not actively search for a job, whatever the job characteristics, and do not show strong motivation in job interviews, are not truly unemployed. In alternative approaches women who search for a part-time job taking up 50 per cent of the working week, but meanwhile work on a 25 per cent basis, are unemployed for 25 per cent, although they might not be eligible to receive an unemployment benefit. Also, workers who applied for a job many times, but always experienced

outright discrimination, and therefore stopped applying for a job, must be calculated as unemployed. In the 1990s the OECD came up with an estimation of Dutch unemployment between 5 and 25 per cent. Recently, an economic statistical bureau estimated the unemployment among Dutch young people with non-Western background at 20 per cent, while in the same period a social statistical bureau came up with an estimation of 40 per cent. With respect to the measurement of the quantity demanded, the number of registered vacancies is taken as an indicator of the difference between the level of the quantity demanded and the level of employment. We all know from practice that many important vacancies are not registered, and that a firm may create a vacancy as soon as it meets a promising worker. Statisticians defend themselves by saying that they are especially interested in changes in the variables, more than in absolute sizes. Alas, because the quantity demanded can hardly be measured, it is difficult to imagine that the changes in an indicator would give us a reliable picture of changes in the quantity demanded.[9]

(2) Inflation figures play a very important role in macroeconomic policy matters. Originally inflation meant an increase in the price of a fixed basket of goods, together with a proportional increase in the amount of money in circulation, produced in a closed economy. Competition between banks and rivalry between different income groups are two principal causes. In the economic world an increase in the amount of money in circulation is a necessary condition for having inflation. In Chapter 8 we will see that this is not the case in a post-Keynesian world. So, in order to calculate this price increase we must have a list of all the goods that are produced and consumed. In practice, however, only the prices of private consumption count. But the prices of the goods and services, delivered by education and health care, for instance, are not calculated. A large part of the budgets in these sectors are financed by the government. Through direct and indirect taxation the citizens pay for the total package of these services. These packages are not fixed. In practice, there is a permanent change in quantity and quality of these baskets, making it impossible to calculate price changes. The way in which these baskets are financed makes privately received net incomes decline and privately financed consumption goods become more expensive. The last element is called inflation, but this empirical 'fact' is very different from the theoretical notion of inflation. As soon as the consumption price index increases, many workers and investors want to be compensated for the decrease in purchasing power of their net nominal wage income. But the registered increase is definitely not a correct reflection of inflation, but also the result of a way of financing ever-growing packages of educational and health-care goods and services.

---

[9] Statistical reports always talk about demand for and supply of labour, while they mean the quantities demanded and supplied. For a neoclassical macro-econometrician this difference is not important: the demand and supply curves do not shift in their model endogenously. In heterodox macroeconomics, however, the difference is very important.

Another problem with the measurement of inflation is the way in which increases in the price of import goods are interpreted. Macroeconomically speaking, it means national impoverishment, and should be paid by some people. When it affects the price level of private consumption goods, it is called inflation, which must be compensated, of course.

The measurement problem originates from the fact that price calculation is difficult in many cases. Moreover, nobody is buying the same basket time and again. Goods are never perfectly homogeneous. Every copy is different from another copy, and over the years the quality of the goods is changing. In many cases the quality is increasing, but quite often the quality is decreasing. If we compare the capital goods in the British factories of the 18th century with the current capital stock, the quality has increased significantly. If we compare dentist or psychiatric services of two centuries ago with current practices, the change in quality is amazing. In the Netherlands the quality of the paint that is used in the construction sector has decreased the last few decades. It appeared that the high-quality paint was very unhealthy for the customers. So, quality reduction happened, as a result of environmental quality improvement. How to calculate inflation in such a case? In the 1990s an American commission under the chairmanship of Boskin wrote a report on this problem, and estimated that inflation should be measured as an increase in the general level of the goods prices minus 2 per cent. This percentage is caused by the so-called *substitution bias* and the *quality change*. The substitution bias means that price increases are an incentive to substitute a cheaper good for the more expensive variant. With respect to inflation there is another serious problem. Which basket do we take? Some say: take the basket of a modal worker, but others plea for a broader basket. One of the causes of the financial crisis 2008 was the fact that the American economic officials worked with a basket of consumption goods, ignoring strong price increases of financial and real estate assets. A different interpretation of the significant rises of the prices in the asset markets points to an increase in scarcity of bonds, shares, and homes. In other words, price rises as a result of increased scarcity cannot be interpreted as inflation.

(3) How can we observe a bubble in a times series of a particular price index? To answer this question we must first define a bubble. The most common definition says that a bubble is a price increase, which is the result of unrealistic expectations with respect to a particular price. It means that a strong increase will undoubtedly be followed by a strong decline. In other words, there is an important difference between the actual price and the price, which is of a more structural nature, expressing the true scarcity of the good(s). The problem is that we don't know what the natural price is, and therefore we don't know whether a strong price increase is the beginning of a bubble. If, after a while, a significant price increase is followed by a strong price decline, we all tend to say: it was a bubble. But what if the price decline is the result of discretionary policy of an authority? This was the case with the decline in home prices in the USA in 2008, which was the beginning of the financial crisis and subsequent global depression. In this case it was an increase

in the interest rate by the monetary authorities that was an incentive for many home owners to offer their houses for sale. The reason for the FED to increase its nominal interest rate was its idea that bank credit was too cheap. Neoclassical/ monetarist economists blamed the institution for setting the actual interest rate lower than the natural rate, creating an inflationary environment. But how did these economists measure the level of the natural rate of interest? They must have *estimated* equations derived from their theoretical apparatus. But heterodox economists tried to *measure* the global savings and the global investments, and came to the conclusion that the low rate of interest was the result of a persistent excess supply on the capital market. So, the FED decision to increase its interest rate was not a wise decision. The lesson we can learn from this case is that different views of a problem lead to different definitions, measurements, and estimations. The consequent policies lead to a different reality, making it difficult to find out, in an empirical way, which view is the more realistic one.

(4) As we saw in the foregoing sections, orthodox economics assumes that fluctuations in prices and quantities take place in the neighbourhood of market and market economy equilibrium. In a market economy especially, price flexibility is essential for staying close to equilibrium on all markets. Changing prices mean shifts *along t*he demand and supply curves of the various macro-markets. In some periods all these markets show an excess demand: the economy is in an expansionary stage. In other periods all macro-markets show an excess supply: the economy is in a *recession.* Not long ago economists were used to make a distinction between recession and *depression.* A recession was defined as a regular decline in the growth rate, while depression was a more than regular decline, caused by pessimism among spenders with respect to the medium-run future. In the discussion about the continuing crisis the term depression has disappeared. Mainstream economics has no depression theory, and therefore the phenomenon does not exist. There are even authors who started to talk about the Great Recession of the 1930s rather than the usual Great Depression. Even sharp fallbacks in growth rates and strong increases in unemployment are called recession. When China faced a decline in its growth rate of production from 12–14 per cent to a level of 6–8 per cent, neoclassical-empirical terminology just observed a very flourishing economy. This is not a minor issue; not 'just semantics'. According to the theory of Keynes, which will be discussed in Chapter 8, the turn from expansion and boom towards recession and depression is not just a matter of actual growth rates of production. It is linked to the emotional state of the consumers, investors, and workers. In a recession the overoptimistic expectations of the boom turn into more realistic views on the near future. In a depression, however, the more down-to-earth expectations are turned into pessimism about the medium run. In Chapter 8 we will see that government policies in a recession differ from the policies necessary in a true depression. So, the disappearance of the term depression has dramatic effects on the policies proposed and discussed. The dominance of the

neoclassical approach has changed the language in which the crisis debate takes place, thereby ignoring a number of serious policy options.

(5) On the level of the firm many concepts are problematic. Accounting as a discipline has the task of attributing numbers to values and values foregone. There are many ways of calculating costs and revenues, of profits and of capital. The government has a strong interest in the way these concepts are measured, and has developed systems of calculation so as to tax and to control firms. Different countries and regions have different cultures in this respect. Multinational companies struggle with the problem that divisions, which are located in different areas, must apply different accounting rules. When interpreting consolidated balance sheets of a multinational company we must realize that different rules give different pictures of the whole of the company.

The problems of transforming theoretical notions into empirically measurable notions are huge. Does it mean that empirical research is useless? *No*, but it is dangerous to create an empirical world that is separated from the theoretical context in which it plays a role, and from which it has taken its definition. Moreover, theory determines the meaning of concepts, but a theory without any empirical part cannot have meaning for our daily life. When the theory is just about an aspect-system especially, economists must work on the development of a realistic theory of the subsystem 'economy'. Only then does work on an improvement of the empirical world make sense.

We have illustrated the measurement problems by the examples of unemployment and inflation. But actually all concepts are problematic, such as poverty and inequality.

5.4.2 ECONOMETRICS

It is interesting to see that one of the founding fathers of econometrics was a Dutch physicist, who wanted to show that capitalism was an unstable system (Tinbergen, 1935). Tinbergen was a socialist, and estimated an investment function, with business profits as a main explanatory variable. He showed that investments could not satisfactorily be explained, and that the investment function was not a stable function. Now we can give two explanations for this result. In the first place, private investments appear the most volatile variable in a macroeconomic model. In the second place, the main result of macro-econometrics is the finding that many functions appear rather stable in stable periods, while many functions appear unstable in unstable periods. Tinbergen estimated his investment functions in the 1930s, which was a very unstable period as we know. Nowadays we are facing the same problem: the Euro Area is in a depression, and many functions, especially the consumption and the private investment function, are unstable. Keynes agreed with Tinbergen that a full-fledged capitalist system is too volatile, but rejected the idea of econometric modelling as an important instrument for economic policy. His theoretical work was meant to support economic policies in a different way.

After the Second World War Western economies stabilized, and econometrics became increasingly popular, influencing policy decisions significantly. We will give a few examples to illustrate its importance: one example from the money market, one from the labour market, and one from the goods market.

(1) Friedman and Schwartz (1963) did research on the stability of the demand for money function, and came to the conclusion that, over a long period of American monetary history, the velocity of circulation (V) was a stable function of a series of variables. The political relevance of this outcome was clear: it meant that the relationship between the money supply on the one hand, and the level of production and the goods price on the other hand, was a stable relation. So, monetary policy makes sense—not only in times of expansion and boom, but also in times of a downturn. This implication stood in sharp contrast to the theory of Keynes and the empirical numbers of the Great Depression. Friedman blamed the American authorities for having accepted a decline in the money supply during the downturn. Expansionary monetary policies in the early years of the crisis would have prevented such a strong decline in the level of production. Friedman's analysis was meant to be an attack on the position of Keynes during the 1930s. According to him, the decline of the money supply was not the result of bad monetary policies. The interest rate was at its lowest, which means close to zero. It was the pessimistic expectations of the consumers and investors that made them reluctant to demand bank credit. Nowadays Keynes is not taught in the university textbooks anymore (see Section 5.6 on economic education), and his interpretation is not studied in the crisis discourse.[10] Friedman versus Keynes: an important debate, which cannot be solved by empirical research only.

(2) Keizer (1993) gives an overview of union economics, which is a part of labour economics. This field of study was developed to offer an alternative to the multidisciplinary field Industrial Relations. The author criticizes the typical neoclassical methodology that is used. In general, the union economics approach can be summarized by the following assumptions: the economy as a whole can be described by the general equilibrium model as developed by Walras (1); governments do not interfere in the process of wage and price formation (2); there are no employer's organizations; every employer bargains about wages for himself (3); the unions are operating as one union on the level of the economy as a whole; the union has the monopoly right to bargain about the wage level (4). Empirical research with respect to the influence of the unions on the level of wages and unemployment is based on an analysis of the economy, based on the assumptions just mentioned. Without unions there is no unemployment. In reality we see fluctuating rates of unemployment. The logical implication of this research set up is that unions are

---

[10] Economists regularly come up with so-called Keynesian views: 'we must not forget to stimulate growth'; 'we must lower the tax tariffs and increase wages so as to stimulate growth'. But this is not Keynes.

responsible for eventual unemployment. The conclusion is clear and can easily be shown by a simple micro-picture of labour demand and labour supply. The unions have the power to set the wage level above the market-clearing level. Unfortunately, they almost never use their power in a responsible way, but blame employers and government for the creation of unemployment.

When reading union economic texts closely, authors are regularly aware of the implicit ideology of this research strategy. Nickell and Andrews (1983) write in the end that their result is 'hardly a surprise'. They warn the reader, saying that it is 'a mistake to conclude that a sensible response to this fact would be to attempt to weaken the power of the unions' (Nickell and Andrews 1983: 206). They continue by claiming that institutional changes are necessary to distribute responsibility for wages and employment among employers, workers, and government. In the language of union economics, they advocate breaking up the employer's monopoly right to manage, which means the monopoly right to decide upon the level of employment. But their advice is not based on any theoretical analysis; on the contrary. A better research strategy is to replace the Walrasian model for a more realistic picture of a macro economy, and to give the three parties a place in the model. Only then it can be demonstrated which party should be responsible for what.

In Solow (1985) we see the same phenomenon—an author who is not convinced of the effectiveness of the neoclassical methodology, but nevertheless stay within its paradigmatic boundaries. When discussing the issue of wage undercutting by unemployed people, Solow says: 'I, personally do not find it hard to imagine that the unemployed do so little undercutting of the wage because they think it is an improper or undignified thing to do, and because they would not like others to do it unto them if roles were reversed, and they might be next time. But I realize full well that this is not the way economics is supposed to model the world, and I mention it only as a Galilean remark, (i.e.) something muttered to oneself)' (Solow, 1985: 413). In Chapter 9 we will come back to the issue of efficient labour relations.

(3) Neoclassical growth theory uses the orthodox growth theory as the foundation for empirical research into the causes of the (lack of) growth of nations. In Section 5.3 we explained that, on the basis of the orthodox economic axioms and the assumption of perfect competition, the growth of production is determined by the rate of technological progress and the rate of growth of the labour force. The orthodox analysis assumes a high rate of substitution in case of changes in the price structure. The familiar Cobb–Douglas function can be applied if the substitution elasticity is equal to one. Empirical research has increasingly been focused on the technology variable. When looking at the neoclassical production function—$X = A.K^{\alpha}.N^{1-\alpha}$, where A represents technology—we see that technology means the cluster of factors effecting economic growth besides the stock of capital and the volume of employment. Technology means the knowledge of how to combine capital and labour in the most efficient way. The knowledge and skills that are used to achieve the optimal combination are the result of continuing research. In current empirical

research, technology is almost identical to beta-knowledge. In the Anglo-Saxon world the term science means physics, chemistry, and mathematics. Social science is not a science, and cannot contribute to the efficiency of organizations. If a social scientist has invented a particular idea or analysis or procedure, he cannot go to the patent office and ask for registration. So, when economists use the number of patents as an indicator of technological progress, it's only the hardware that counts—not the programming of the mind, which might have become more efficiently organized. Orthodox economics is isolated from psychic and social processes. It means that psychic and social technology does not play a part in the analysis of an economist, and economic growth is not related to improvements in the psychic and social technology.[11] So, in Greece, which has been in severe trouble for a couple of years now (2013), neoclassical economists do not advise politicians and leaders in civil society to improve institutions, other than the liberalization of markets. Europe has worked on social technology for a long time. The mutual understanding of employers and employees has significantly increased over time. But these important matters remain out of sight because of the paradigmatic boundaries. Africa needs modern hardware: computers, internet access. But they also need a reduction in the ongoing struggles between classes, ethnicities, and religious groups for a spread of prosperity across the continent. But the option that better beta-technology might particularly improve the efficiency with which the rivalling parties are able to kill each other, is not part of neoclassical research. The focus on education and research, stimulated by the development of endogenous growth theory, is undoubtedly important. However, in the areas of social science especially, strong positivist trends lead to the production of waste rather than of improving the efficiency of thought structures in the minds of people.

Time and again empirical results show that some relationships are quite stable in stable periods, such as in the 1950s and 1960s. But in unstable periods hardly any relationship shows stable and reliable results; even private consumption cannot be predicted these days.

Besides the problem of prediction, there is the question of whether economic growth, as it is measured by the gross domestic product (GDP), is an acceptable yardstick for human well-being. This problem will be discussed in Section 5.5.

5.5 Economic Growth, Happiness, and the Good Life

Although the GDP per capita is generally criticized as an appropriate yardstick for human well-being, it still plays an important role in politics. The reason is that it is considered as

---

[11] Chapter 15 discusses these types of technology more thoroughly.

a good indicator for the economic and (potential) military power of a nation. Moreover, there is a clear link with the amount of paid work, which is of great interest for the mass of the people.

Meanwhile, many researchers, not only economists, have tried to make calculations that give a better indication of human well-being. A famous index is the *Human Development Index (HDI)*, developed by a group of scientists under the auspices of the United Nations (1990). Besides a variable such as the GDP per capita, which is considered to be an indicator of the access to resources, the index takes into account factors such as education and longevity. From the 1970s onwards there has been growing awareness of the importance of environmental quality. Even if we do not attach value to entities such as animals and plants as such, they are important inputs for humans, and need some care. To express the quality of the environment, researchers have developed an indicator called *ecological footprint* (Amielsky and Rowe, 1989). It is an attempt to indicate the biologically productive area needed to produce the resources used and absorb the waste generated by a population. This area can be considered as the demand for 'nature'. This demand can be compared to the supply of nature, which is the biological capacity to reproduce resources and to absorb waste. As long as there is an excess demand, we call this the *ecological deficit*.

A last measure of growth is the *Index of Sustainable Economic Welfare (ISEW)*, constructed by Daly and Cobb (1989). It not only contains economic and ecological aspects, but also takes the social aspect into account. The distribution of work and income are the most important indicators in this respect.

All these measures of growth are empirical. They can be interpreted as an attempt to bridge the gap between the subjectivism of orthodoxy and the objectivism of the neoclassical theory. The simple GDP approach is generally rejected as a reliable measure of human well-being. It is interesting to note that many researchers stick to objectivist measures, meanwhile taking other-than-economic aspects into account. Actually, we so need one more step: not only to include non-economic elements, but also to include the subjectivist nature of well-being, also called happiness.

Veenhoven (1984) developed a questionnaire to find out people's level of happiness. He tried to distinguish between *short-term excitement* and *long-term satisfaction*. People living a life full of exciting experiences are not necessarily happy people. Drugs addicts have their excitements too. People who work hard and love their work might reach high levels of long-term satisfaction. The happiness literature shows that the happiest people live in the northern part of Europe. Experts link this result with the presence of social democratic and confessional welfare states. This result from empirical research requires careful interpretation. Do particular types of welfare states lead to long-term satisfaction? Or is it the other way around? Or can we find a third variable that explains the correlation between happiness and type of welfare state? Again, neoclassical economics cannot give a satisfactory answer to that question. It lacks a realistic picture of the basic human drives, and therefore it doesn't know what satisfies people most. The only answer the neoclassical economist can give is: the more resources, the higher the chance to satisfy basic needs. For an economic and rational actor this holds true. But in following chapters we will see that this picture needs to be revised. This book makes a distinction between three primary drives, which are the economic, the social, and the psychic drive. In the end we integrate three partial analyses, which are built upon the three types of motivation.

In Layard (2005), the same distinction is taken to search for happiness factors. Without any analytical-theoretical instrument empirical research delivers many intuitively interesting results. Together with the results of other happiness researchers we can conclude that, in general, psychic and social factors determine whether the amount of resources available has weak or a strong positive effect on human well-being. In Section 15.4.1 we come back to this issue.

Now we will discuss the way typical economics textbooks are dealing with the problem of using an aspect-analysis as a theoretical instrument to explain events in the real world.

5.6 Academic Education of Economics

A giant in economics textbooks is one written by Samuelson. The first edition was published in 1948, and the book is still relevant. In the 15th edition (1995) the author looks back and reflects upon the philosophy behind his textbook. He explains why he does not pay attention to different schools of thought, and just focuses on mainstream economics. He writes: 'people differ about economic policies—each convinced that its view of the simple truth is the one-and-only correct version'. 'In the long run the facts win out. The fanatical simplicities perish in the Darwinian struggle for survival of useful principles' (Samuelson and Nordhaus, 1995: xxxix). In Chapter 6 we also discuss the evolutionary economic approach. There we will show that Samuelson interprets Darwin incorrectly and confuses the efficiency from the orthodox economic world with the persistence in the Darwinian world.

He also states that economics is about the economy (subsystem, not aspect-system!), and explains why he treats microeconomics rather than macroeconomics first: in this way we show the micro-foundations of macroeconomics. Samuelson pretends to give 'a fair and impartial review of the thinking of the intellectual giants of our profession' (Samuelson and Nordhaus, 1995: xxxvi–xxxvii). When we look at the attention paid to giants such as Marx, Schumpeter, and Keynes, it is difficult to maintain that maximally half a page per giant is fair and impartial. The giant of evolutionary economics—Veblen—is not even mentioned. The most problematic issue is the fact that the axioms of the neoclassical approach are not discussed, making it impossible to criticize Samuelson's economics fundamentally. That macroeconomics has a micro-foundation is not the issue. But that Samuelson does not even mention that microeconomics has a macro-foundation is not fair and impartial. In Chapter 6 we will come back to this point.

Another famous textbook is that written by Bernanke and Frank (2010). McDowell and Thom are co-responsible for the European editions. The difference between the original American editions and the European editions is not analytical-theoretical; it has to do with descriptive statistics and organizations, which play an important role in economic policy-making. Also this book is straightforwardly neoclassical. There are no macro-foundations of the microeconomics, and the microeconomic problems are not complicated by the introduction of irrationality and positive and negative sociality. So, principles of international trade are illustrated by trade between Paul, Maria, and Thom, and not by trade between the USA and Cuba, or by trade between Indian and Pakistan. Irrational subcultures, which can dominate particular local markets—no black home-owners in this area, for instance—are ignored. With respect to macroeconomics something remarkable happened in 2010. In the middle of the global crisis the authors decided to remove the one-page text about Keynes. The book deals with a so-called Keynesian analysis of a short-run adjustment process on the goods market—but offers a typical neoclassical interpretation of Keynes' contribution.

Another remarkable change in the 2010 edition, compared with the 2006 edition, is the absence of the Taylor rule. This 'rule' describes the behaviour of the central bank, and says that its real interest rate is a negative function of the current output gap (the difference between potential and actual output) relative to the potential output gap, and a positive function of the difference between the actual inflation rate and the target inflation rate. To put it simpler, the higher the production and the actual inflation, the higher the real interest rate, which the central bank is counting on for its customers.[12] This is remarkable, because one of the authors, Bernanke, is the chairman of the FED. Apparently he did not appreciate a separate equation describing (or prescribing?) central bank behaviour.

Nowadays, also textbooks on the introductory level are more specialized. In many educational programmes there is no general introduction anymore, and students start their economics study with micro- or macroeconomics. This is a pity, because it makes clarification of the interrelationship between the two levels of analysis less probable.

When we look at the microeconomics texts at the introductory level, we see that no attention is given to the axioms that describe the typical orthodox economic approach. When we take Perloff (2012), for instance, there is nothing that makes it clear what particular school of thought the author has chosen, and what the limitations of his approach are. There are no definitions of the term 'rationality', and its difference from the terms 'economic' and 'logic'. There is no mention of the abstraction of the social context. Nevertheless, the author states that 'an economic model is a simplification of reality that contains only its most important features' (Perloff, 2012: 26). This view suggests that the

[12] Taylor calculated the coefficients and the autonomous component of the real interest rate for the USA to be 0.5, 0.5, and 0.02 respectively (Taylor, 1993). In the years just before the 2008 financial crisis, Taylor warned the FED to raise its interest rate. The FED kept its rate relatively low for another few years. When it actually raised her rate, it was followed by a series of events, which led to the global depression.

neoclassical analysis is an appropriate theoretical instrument for understanding real-life economic processes. But the book does not say this explicitly, and, consequently, this view is not explained and defended.

The language which is used makes it difficult, if not impossible, to criticize the approach. Important concepts of rivalling approaches are used, but in a different sense. The meaning of the term 'social' is reduced to 'the aggregate of individuals', abstracting the essence of the term as it is used by sociology.[13] Also, the term 'uncertainty' is used, but not in the sense that is usual; namely as the opposite of risk. In the neoclassical language there is no place anymore for the phenomenon of fundamental or non-parametric uncertainty (see also Chapter 6 on the Austrian and Chapter 8 on the post-Keynesian school of thought). A last serious problem in this typical orthodox microeconomics book is the use of the terms 'cause' and 'effect'. An economic and rational actor is assumed to have allocated his resources optimally. If his income increases, he is assumed to allocate the additional resources over the different goods in an optimal way. So, if he buys a new car, an orthodox economist says that, in this case, the income rise is the cause and the purchase of a car is the effect. Although this is right, it is not the end of the story. The rise in income must be considered as the immediate cause. Then the fact that our actor is economic and rational is the ultimate cause of the action. In the economic world this cause is always the one and only cause. So why always repeat the obvious? The reason is that explicit notice suggests that other ultimate causes are possible; causes which are not considered by orthodox economics.

In another famous microeconomics textbook (Frank, 1994) most of the errors made in Perloff (2012) are also made by Frank. At one point there is a marked difference. Frank pays more attention to the latest findings of behavioural economics under the heading of cognitive limitations of human behaviour. He discusses very important concepts, such as perception, framing, judgemental heuristics, and biases. These are important insights and will be discussed in Chapter 10. Actually, there just one problem with these phenomena. In the book by Frank they are discussed in a separate chapter, which is called supplementary. It suggests a study of these is just a nice side path rather than a principal critique or extension of the orthodox paradigm. In Chapter 10 we will link the so-called cognitive limitations with the concept of rationality, and develop an idea of what we mean by 'degrees of (ir)rationality'.

From the popular introductory textbooks on macroeconomics we take the book by Blanchard (1997). It is one of the more sophisticated and eclectic ones, in contrast to most other books, which are more standardly neoclassical, as is their interpretation of the so-called Keynesian short-run analysis.

Blanchard makes a distinction between short run, medium run, and long run. As we know, neoclassical analysis uses the notion of logical time rather than real time. Blanchard uses both interpretations of time simultaneously. On the one hand, he defines

---

[13] In Chapters 11, 12, and 13 we will see that the sociologists use the term 'economic' not in the orthodox sense, but always in the heterodox sense.

the short run as a period of about one year. On the other hand, he defines it as the period within which the goods market adjusts itself to changes in the money market. This mechanism can be clarified by means of the famous IS-LM diagram. Blanchard takes the typical neoclassical model as presented in Sections 5.2 and 5.3, and builds a Keynesian element into the neoclassical goods market model: private consumption does not react to the interest rate, but to the level of national income. The model of the money market remains a typical neoclassical model: the adjustment process on the money market takes no time. So, an economy is always located somewhere on the LM-curve. In Figure 5.7 we have pictured this model. The IS-curve shows the combination of interest rate and national income, for which it holds that I = S. The LM-curve shows the combination of interest rate and national income, for which it holds that L = M. In this analysis the price level of the goods is assumed to be constant. It means that there is no difference between the nominal and the real values of the variables. Suppose that the quantity supplied of money increases. Since we have assumed that this variable is not dependent on another variable of our model, we can simply say that the money supply has increased; in other words, a shift of the LM-curve to the right. It implies a change in the equilibrium combination of income and interest rate from S via S′ to S″. The move from S to S′ shows the immediate effect of a change in the money supply on the quantity demanded for money. The move from S′ to S″ shows the short-run adjustment on the goods market.

Actually, this is quite an orthodox construction. Two adjustment mechanisms are distinguished and placed in a logical time sequence, while in reality both mechanisms are taking place simultaneously. Blanchard assumes that the money market adjusts immediately, but in periods of depression this is not true. The beginning of the analysis—the central bank increases the money supply—is quite artificial. In the real world the central bank can only increase the amount of money in circulation if firms and consumers are demanding bank loans, which they might do if the interest rate is set at a lower level. So, a real-time sequence runs as follows. Suppose that both the goods and the money market are close to equilibrium. If the labour market is in equilibrium firms are not inclined to increase their investments. If the labour market is not in equilibrium, they invest if they are in an optimistic mood. They demand more investment goods and more cash. If the

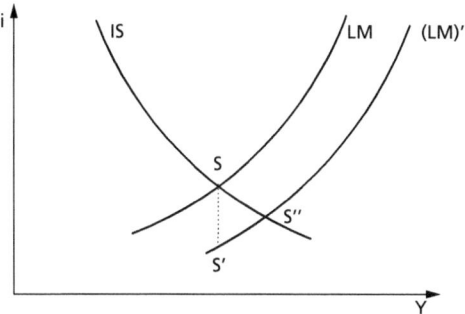

Figure 5.7. Effect of ΔM on i and Y

banks are also optimistic they are prepared to finance the investments. So, the quantity demanded and quantity supplied of goods increases. So with the quantity demanded and the quantity supplied of money. The adjustment processes continue until full employment is reached. We see that this real-time approach offers us a different picture.

Blanchard also distinguishes a third adjustment mechanism, which describes the way the prices on the goods market adjust to the wages on the labour market and vice versa. These medium-run adjustment processes take time; according to Blanchard it might take about a decade before the wage–price spiral ends up in an equilibrium situation on both markets. Again, the construction of logical time—the time necessary for a particular mechanism to create market equilibrium—is mixed up with the construction of real time. When Blanchard takes the logical time method, the analysis is focused on the way the adjustment process takes place. When he focuses on a real-time analysis, he should create room for a series of complexities. By artificially staying within the equilibrium analysis—supply and demand curves do not shift—he avoids these complexities.[14]

The wage-setting behaviour depends on the price-setting behaviour and vice versa. In a strict orthodox-neoclassical model, markets are setting prices, not firms. Every firm and every worker must accept the market conditions, which express the natural scarcity of goods and labour. In Blanchard's analysis, however, alien elements play an important role. Unions are assumed to be powerful and able to set wages. Firms are powerful as well, and are able to set prices, thereby using the so-called mark-up method. With respect to wages Blanchard refers to ideas of dual markets, efficiency wage, and collective bargaining to give an indication of why the labour market does not function as an ideal-typical competitive market, and why adjustment to new equilibria takes so much time.[15] With respect to prices Blanchard refers to ideas, such as mark-up pricing, which means that market power offers firms the opportunity to fix the mark-up (difference between selling price and cost price). It means that the profits they earn are not affected by the competitive pressure. In Figure 5.8 we have presented a figure that reflects the different processes of adjustment. The analysis is about the relationship between the real-wage rate and the rate of unemployment. Given the goods price level, unions set their nominal wages, and employers hire workers, according to their demand for labour, given the level of the goods price and nominal wage level. Unions are inclined to set their

[14] The method of logical time analysis is a good orthodox economic instrument. It clarifies the operation of mechanisms one by one. But daily reality is so different—mechanisms do not get the time necessary to bridge the gap between the actual and equilibrium level of prices and quantities. This complexity forces the researcher to select those adjustment mechanisms that run quite fast, and leave out ideal-typical mechanisms that run slowly or not at all. In Chapters 7 and 8 we will discuss the radical economic and the post-Keynesian approach, and see that it is not just the typical price mechanisms that can dominate macroeconomic developments.

[15] In heterodox approaches we see that new equilibria will never be reached, since adjustment processes affect the position of the new equilibria. In other words, policy is like shooting a moving target, as the moves of the target are difficult to predict. Blanchard uses heterodox elements, but keeps within the borders of equilibrium analysis. He implies that disequilibrium is always caused by price and wage stickiness. In Chapter 8 we will see that price and wage stickiness is not the cause of disequilibria according to Keynes' theory.

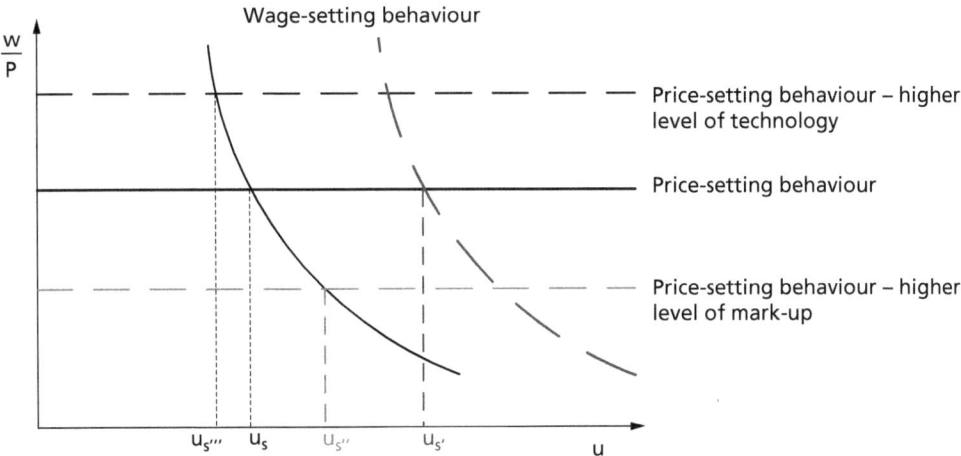

Figure 5.8. Mechanism on the Labour Market

wages lower in case of higher unemployment. If unions are setting the wage rates on a level that is higher than the market-clearing wage, there will be structural unemployment. If union power increases, the wage-setting curve shifts to the right, leading to a higher level of structural unemployment (shift from u(s) to u(s')). If firms increase their mark-up, structural unemployment increases from u(s') to u(s''). This increase forces unions to accept the decline in the real-wage level. The interaction between firm and union leads to a medium-run 'equilibrium'. In this case, the meaning of the term equilibrium is different from its meaning in a strict orthodox economic analysis. Here it refers to a persistent situation with a particular level of structural unemployment.

Blanchard also distinguishes a long run. In terms of logical time he defines it as the period necessary for an economy to adjust to its long-run trend. Growth theory is meant to explain why some countries grow on average 1 or 2 per cent, while others grow 8 or even 10 per cent for a long time. In the typical orthodox theory all markets are—by definition—in equilibrium in the long run. If there are inefficient institutions on the labour market, which do not disappear for a long period of real time, the equilibrium on the labour market shows a high rate of equilibrium unemployment. In this typical mainstream interpretation equilibrium does not mean the same as in orthodox economics—that quantity supplied and quantity demanded are equal to each other; it just means that the situation does not change over a long period of real time. In heterodox economics the term equilibrium would definitely not be used for such circumstances. Then unemployment is called persistent.

Technological progress is the principal determinant of economic growth. Figure 5.8 shows that, in the case of technological progress, the line that represents price-setting behaviour by firms shifts upwards. If unions do not claim higher nominal wages, just because of a higher labour productivity that results from technological progress, the level of employment increases, leading to a lower level of structural unemployment (a shift from u(s) to u(s‴). The implicit assumption is that growth of labour productivity leads to a lower price level, thereby increasing the purchasing power of the given nominal wages.

The book is impressive; many generations of economists have been introduced to macroeconomics this way. But there are a number of flaws that must be mentioned.

In the first place, we have seen that the mix of logical time and real time is confusing. Neoclassical economics is based on the idea of logical time, and of partial abstractions. The meaning of the various terms, such as 'equilibrium', is based on this notion. If this type of analysis is mixed up with real-time analysis, conceptual confusion is probable.

In the second place, the orthodox idea of Walrasian equilibrium is the point of reference. When applying this to the real world, we can't introduce just a few 'alien' elements, such as union power, or workers with an idea of fairness, while ignoring employer power and government incidence with respect to the protection of private property rights, for instance. The real world is characterized by an institutional framework, which is supposed to channel behaviour, which is multi-motivated. There is no possibility of modelling irrationality from the side of the employer, and culture is very local and limited to employed workers. It is one ad hoc element after the other, with arbitrary results. Deviations from equilibrium values are assumed to be so small that the positions of the supply and demand curves do not change. In Chapters 7 and 8 we will see that this is an unrealistic assumption.

In the third place, Blanchard's analysis represents a closed and restrictive system, and appears stable. Even if the equilibrium unemployment is high and rising it will not lead to chaos, war, and dictatorship. If we introduce the psychic and the social world, and integrate it with the economic world, negative social forces might become too strong for social peace to be maintained in case of high unemployment.

Blanchard (2011) is a European edition, written together with Amighini and Giavazzi. It contains a chapter about the crisis during the period 2007–2010. The explanation is in compliance with the analyses presented. In other words, the crisis has had no influence on their way of looking at macroeconomic developments. In a series of so-called pathologies, Blanchard indicates he views the crisis as a recession, and discusses the high public debt as a serious problem. In his analytical terminology it is very clear that only private actors can invest, and that balanced budget is the most desirable outcome of fiscal policies. The unemployment records are not discussed as a serious problem, and the issues of distribution of income and wealth are not even mentioned. Inflation is a problem, while the threat of deflation is not discussed. When the government borrows money, only the costs in terms of future taxes are discussed. Apparently there are no benefits. When discussing fiscal policies, there is no difference between a decrease in tax tariffs and an increase in the autonomous expenditures. The possibility of financing government investments by means of money creation—not a bad idea in times of debt pay-offs—is not mentioned at all. Financial regulation, an important issue in current policy debates, is not part of the preferred package of measures.

The most remarkable fact is the complete absence of labour market problems. In the USA, it has been a long time since wages have increased, notwithstanding a continuing growth in labour productivity. There is no room for the role of labour relations and for the absence of social peace in many countries, which might make it problematic to reduce the depression. The conclusion must be that the book does not discuss alternative approaches at all; it basically reflects the policy options that are considered by the economic experts in power.

The last point of discussion is about one of the icons of mainstream macroeconomics, which is the Phillips curve. In its original form it is an empirical relationship between the rate of change in the wage rate and the inverse of the unemployment rate (Phillips, 1958). The data set is about the UK economy during the period 1861–1957. In Figure 5.9 we have presented the curve.

The most remarkable difference between the orthodox economic relationship of the two variables and the result in Figure 5.9 is the downward wage rigidity in case unemployment increases significantly. Phillips does not derive this relationship from orthodox economics. He just considers the relationship as an expression of 'normality'. He discusses the years in which the situation is not normal. More than a third of the years must be considered as abnormal. As we saw already, in some years the increase in import prices appear relatively high. In other years there are strikes or other signs of union incidence. Also, the years characterized by government influence on the wage rates are called abnormal years.

Lipsey (1960) pretends to offer an orthodox foundation of the Phillips relation: wages increase in case of excess demand, and do not increase in case of excess supply. The wage rigidity is not explained, which is not a surprise, since it does not fit the idea of humans being economic and rational actors. During the 1960s the normal relationship disappears. Hines (1964) offers an ad hoc explanation by adding a variable to the wage equation, expressing the assumed increase in union power. Hines tries out a series of indicators with respect to the incidence of strikes: the number of strikes, the length of the strikes, and combinations of the two. The results appear statistically significant. Keizer (1984) offers a review of this literature, and discusses the problems in more detail. For the moment we conclude that the lack of a social-cultural context in the analysis leads to

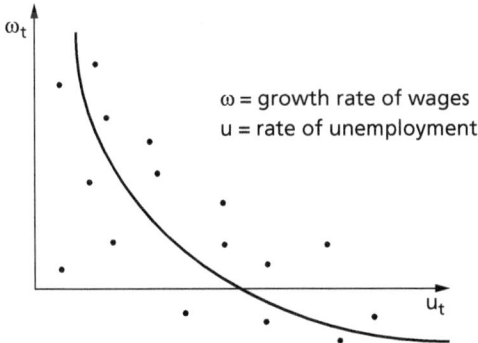

Figure 5.9. The Phillips Curve

unacceptable ad hocery. Strikes are not necessarily an expression of power. There is even literature outside the mainstream economics that argues just the opposite.

Without a clearly formulated paradigm, analysis and theory prejudice rules rather than scientific method. During the 1970s we see a positive relationship between the rate of change in the money wage and the rate of unemployment. The oil crisis led to a sharp increase in the import prices of non-oil producing countries. In many European countries the welfare state expanded rapidly, not only in terms of growing rights, but also in terms of the use of all these rights. According to orthodox theory, an increase in taxes and social premiums lead to a shift of a part of the burden by workers to employers. Figure 5.10 shows the typical orthodox picture of a competitive labour market, where the macro-market shows the aggregated micro supply and demand curves. An increase in the tariffs of taxes and social premiums leads to an upward shift of the supply curve. Along the vertical axis we have plotted the gross real wage, while workers are supposed to think in terms of net real wage. We see that the real wage increases, while the level of employment decreases.

There will not be any unemployment; marginal workers leave the market because of the decrease in the net wage rate. But if we take the European institutional context of wage and employment determination into account, both variables are significantly influenced by this context. When discussing heterodox approaches we will see that an increase in taxes and premiums does not necessarily increase the power of unions, and that it can also increase the resistance of employers' organizations.

We see that the Phillips relation is not an empirical relation anymore. The interpretation has moved from a long-term empirical relationship to being a short-run theoretical relationship, occurring in normal times. Abnormal times lead to a shift of this curve, for instance as a result of an additional money impulse, an increase in import prices, or a spontaneous increase in union power. In the long run all markets are—by definition—in equilibrium. So the relationship becomes a vertical line on the level of natural or structural unemployment. This equilibrium is characterized by an inflation rate that is equal

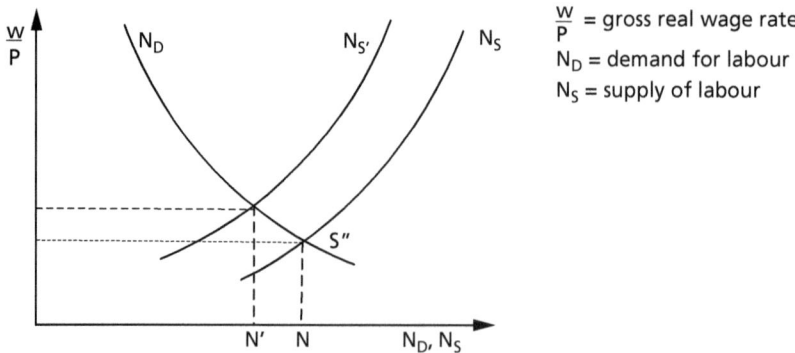

Figure 5.10. Effect of an Increase in Tax/Social Premium Tariffs on the Levels of Gross Real-Wage Rate and Employment

to the expected rate of inflation, and by an unemployment rate that is accepted by the government. As long as these two conditions are not met, the Phillips relation keeps on shifting to the right and upwards.

5.7 Epilogue: The Crisis as a Turning Point?

In this chapter we have seen that the orthodox economic analytical instrument—which explains the operation of the economic force—functions as the micro-foundation for orthodox macroeconomics. The psychic and social context is not mentioned, because the constructors of this economic world intended to develop an isolated abstraction rather than an abstraction from less important factors. After the Second World War this analytical framework became the basis for most of the empirical research. Time and again this application led to inconclusive results, even in so-called normal periods. The Phillips curve is the icon of empirical macroeconomics. However, it shows downward wage rigidity in a free market economy. As a consequence, econometricians—less bound to economic theory—began to try out non-economic variables. Without a clearly formulated paradigm and analysis, this ad hoc additions of non-economic variables to a strict economic theory does not give enduring results and will not improve our knowledge of the fundamental mechanisms that rule the empirical world. In stable periods mainstream economics is not able to predict the emergence of instable periods. Moreover, since it is not able to explain why the regime has changed, it is not able to develop an effective therapy, that would help us.

According to the neoclassical macroeconomists, the current crisis is—as expected—the result of bad policy behaviour by the American central bank system. The FED waited too long to implement the necessary increase in its interest rate. An earlier increase, as 'prescribed' by the famous Taylor rule, could have prevented the bubble on the home market. When the crisis started governments intervened and took over many risks from the large banks. It did not wait until many banks went bankrupt, thereby preventing survivors taking over viable parts of the losers. When the global economy turned into a (great) recession, central banks all over the world had to stimulate productive activity by lowering their interest rates. Meanwhile, governments had to abstain from any intervention. Unfortunately, several governments stepped in, gave their big banks large money infusions (recapitalization), and stimulated the autonomous demand for goods. No wonder that the crisis aggravated: financial markets began to distrust governments, whose debts had sharply increased.

Our economies are still in crisis and mainstream economists, who dominate the scientific economic world, are not able to present a systematic policy approach. Now public opinion and young economists are pressing for change, including change in the education of economists. In the following chapters we will see whether oppressed heterodox economics offers a viable alternative.

6 Evolution and Entrepreneurship, an Evolutionary and an Austrian View

6.1 Introduction

In Section 3.2 we have seen that heterodox methodology means that there are no constants in nature, including human nature, to which an analysis can be reduced. Local and temporary constants can function as theoretical foundation of explanations of historical events and periods. In orthodox methodology the individual person is the level of explanation, whatever the problem. In heterodox methodology, however, reality is layered, which means that there are many levels of explanation.

If we look at the problem of poverty in Africa, for instance, orthodox economics approaches the problem on the basis of a theory with respect to the economic behaviour of an individual person. So, Africa is poor because many Africans are poor, which can be explained by the fact that many Africans do not save and invest. Heterodox methodology, however, does not stick to the individual level, but searches for a complex of factors, to be found on a whole series of levels. For instance, in some African countries it might be the role of primitive religion, while in other countries it might be corrupt clans of politicians that block progress. It might also be that the image of Africa in the eyes of non-Africans is quite negative. And, as a last example, African poverty might be the result of historical development, which has given Africa the function of suppliers of cheap raw material and cheap labour in the whole of the world economy, making it difficult for the population to gain skills.

An important implication of the absence of constant relationships is that reality has a historical character. Nobody knows who is responsible for the fact that reality exists, and how it all started. May be it was God who shouted 'bang', and suddenly there was reality. What we know is that we live our lives in a world, including all its possibilities and impossibilities, that has been cultivated by our ancestors. We know that we live in a context that is influenced by the choices taken in the past. We are *locked-in*, so to speak, in our history. The literature analyses such a situation in terms of *path dependence* and *hysteresis*. Imagine a person grows up in an orthodox Protestant environment. Her unconscious is institutionalized in a particular way, which is an important source of automated reaction patterns. Later she meets many people with different habits of thought, and step by step she becomes conscious of her implicit knowledge, and that of her fellow humans. They all appear heavily influenced by their past (path dependence), and they all have difficulty deleting this structure, and starting anew (hysteresis).

The various heterodox economic programmes differ from each other in the way they deal with the two characteristics just mentioned: everything evolves (1), and the evolution takes place in a place and time framework (2). In other words, heterodox economics is about evolution and context. In Section 6.2 we will discuss evolutionary economics.

6.2 **Evolutionary Economics**

6.2.1 INTRODUCTION

The Greek philosopher Herakleitos considered reality as something, which is always moving—'panta rei'. Applied to humans he said that *rivalry* is the drive that keeps humans going. It means that people are motivated to improve their situation, especially in comparison to the situation of their 'fellow' humans.

Some philosophers, such as Hegel, Marx, and Fukuyama, assume that the living world develops towards a final end. This teleology is criticized by other philosophers, who say that evolution is a blind process; in some periods we see progress, followed by periods that are characterized by regress.

In evolutionary economics both positions are defended. Some economists approach the world as an open system, which has—by definition—no final end. Others are more deterministic. A move that is determined by a limited number of interrelated forces has a final goal, and it is the task of scientists to discover the basic trends towards the 'eternal equilibrium position'. Some scientists divide history in periods and approach each period as if it is a closed system. Dynamic analysis can be used to describe essential mechanisms that determine the course of history during that particular period.

Veblen must be considered to be the founding father of evolutionary economics. He was inspired by Darwin's analysis of the evolution in the living world, and he used Darwin's *model of natural selection* as a metaphor for his ideas about the evolution of the economies in the developed world, especially the American economy. Veblen did not copy Darwin's model, but extended it by means of *feedback and feed-forward mechanisms*, which makes Darwin's analysis more suited for a description of the evolution of economy and society.

We will first set out the Darwinian model of natural selection. Then we discuss the feedback and feed-forward mechanisms. A more specific analysis of the American socio-economic evolution in the end of the 19th century and the beginning of the 20th century by Veblen illustrates what he meant by an evolutionary approach in economics (see Section 6.2.5).

After the Second World War, and especially from the 1970s onwards, economists paid increasing attention to the phenomenon of technological progress. New institutional economics (NIE) could not explain inventions and innovations in a satisfactory way. It triggered a return of original institutional economics (OIE) (see Chapter 4 for an exposition of new institutional economics; see Chapter 3 for a short introduction of OIE). The main concepts used when explaining technical development are discussed. At the end of Section 6.2 we briefly discuss the role of evolutionary economics in an attempt to create a synthesis between heterodox and orthodox currents.

6.2.2 THE DARWINIAN NATURAL SELECTION MODEL

Darwin wondered how some species of animals could survive, while others couldn't. The general answer is *adaptation to changing circumstances*. But which mechanism is responsible for this process of adaptation? Darwin's explanation runs as follows:

1. There is variety in the population of a particular species.
2. Circumstances change regularly.
3. Those members of the population with characteristics that fit the latest circumstances best will survive; in other words, they are selected by nature. These characteristics are replicated, and are called replicators.

This model of natural selection can be applied to social and economic phenomena. Imagine a long war breaks out. Before this event people with high education tended to survive. But in wartime other characteristics, such as physical and mental strength, fit the changed circumstances best and will be replicated.

6.2.3 SELECTION IN THE WORLD AFTER THE EMERGENCE OF HUMANS

In the world prior to human intervention the Darwinian model might describe the evolution of species accurately. The emergence of the human species had enormous effects on our world. In the first place, humans have developed methods to improve their characteristics. So the increasing quality of the replicators affects the situation significantly. In the second place, humans have intervened in the environment, making their world increasingly a better place. In Figure 6.1 we have presented a procedure of selection in which changes in the variety as well as in the circumstances play a role in the selection.

In the first period there are two types of people in environment E1, namely, * and ~. Then the environment changes, because of a severe economic crisis, for instance, which

E1	E2	E3	E4
*		>	
*		>	
*	*	>	>
*	*	>	>
*	*		>
~	~		>
~	~		
~	~	x	
	~	x	x
	~	x	x
			x
			x
			x

Figure 6.1. General Evolutionary Model of Selection

leads to environment E2. Members of the population with characteristic * have a hard time, and not all of them survive. For members with characteristic ~ the crisis offers good opportunities. So, they have no problems replicating. Now the members with the characteristic * especially begin to use their time by improving their characteristics. Pregnant women become more careful of their lifestyle, and, after having given birth, they show more commitment to raising and educating their children well. The new characteristics are indicated with a >. So, in the third period, we see that people with characteristics > appear the better survivors. Meanwhile, the environment changes again. Because of a massive immigration of unskilled workers the environment E2 transforms into E3. We see that most of those who changed their lifestyle survive. Now the members with characteristic ~ appear to have a hard time. A few are able to change their characteristics into × and survive. Unfortunately, the other members do not survive. In the last period in this example—E4—we see that some members of both groups have decided to change their environment by means of migration. This increases their survival chances.

We see that actors do not only adjust to changing circumstances, but that they also influence their characteristics as well as their circumstances, an element that is not part of the typical Darwinian approach.

Nelson and Winter (1982) criticized the orthodox economic analysis about firms and the way they operate on markets. The orthodox assumption of economic actors being rational implies that firms react to changes in the market situation adequately, for instance through price adjustment. In practice, many firms are not that flexible. Over time they have developed systems of rules, and have automatized various sorts of *routines*. These routines are very stable, or sticky. When circumstances change, the firms with routines that fit the new situation quite well will survive. Other firms might not survive.

We see that firm-specific routines play a gene-like role. They are the organizational memory, and are the most stable unit in the whole process. In the general literature about institutions the most stable institutional or cultural unit is called *meme*, and its methodology is not individualist or collectivist but institutional (see Chapter 2 for an explanation of methodological institutionalism). According to Nelson and Winter, there is, besides the price mechanism, another mechanism of adjustment. In practice many firms have set an aspiration level of profit, and if the actual level is below the aspired level, the R&D budget will increase (a nice example of a routine). By increasing the quality of the production process and of the products, they are trying to lower the costs and to increase the quality of the goods they are supplying. If some firms are successful, their strategy is *imitated* by others.

6.2.4 ECONOMICS OF TECHNOLOGICAL CHANGE

According to the dominating neoclassical economists OIE lacked theoretical and mathematical rigour. Therefore, there were hardly any resources for OIE economists to make their analyses more sophisticated. Orthodoxy even developed a macroeconomic growth theory, based on its well-known axioms of economic, rational, and non-social actors. The logical implication of a neoclassical analysis of competitive markets is that markets are always and everywhere close to equilibrium. So long as the government does not intervene and disturb the market mechanism, economic growth is at its maximum. Because technology is a given in a simple orthodox economic analysis (see Chapter 5), it is impossible to study the economic conditions necessary for improving the state of technology.

Increasing growth problems in the 1970s was the reason for a growing number of economists to spend their energy in the endogenization of technological change. Or, in other words, how can we promote the production of technical inventions and apply these novelties to the economic process of production and consumption, which is called *innovation*?

These economists discovered that neoclassical analysis does not offer the theoretical tools which make it possible to understand the process of technological change. In an earlier discussion about the problem of imperfect information, behavioural economists criticized the neoclassical concept of 'optimal amount of information'. In a typical orthodox economic analysis, every quantity sold is determined by its marginal costs and its marginal benefits. So, a searcher continues to search for information until the increasing marginal costs are equal to the decreasing marginal benefits (see Chapter 4). But in reality nobody knows what he will find in the next period. In other words, marginal benefits cannot be established. This is not only true for a consumer who is searching for the best camera, which can be bought for an acceptable price. This is also true when establishing 'optimal' R&D budgets. Marginal benefits might increase. If someone is searching for a needle in a haystack and he is sure that there *is* a needle, the longer he searches, the greater the chance that he will find the needle in the next period. But R&D departments search for the yet unknown, which makes it impossible to calculate the profitability of their work.

Most evolutionary economists are quite optimistic about the effects of large R&D budgets. Much empirical research is done to prove the statement that innovation is key for sustainable growth. The big problem with empirical research in this context is the (almost) impossibility of measuring technical quality. The number of patents is considered to be an indicator for the amount of innovations. But one innovation plus another innovation is not equal to two innovations. Innovations are too heterogeneous for such a simple addition. To understand this problem it makes sense to refer to the structure of knowledge, as explained in Chapter 2 (the PATH structure). It is probable that innovations on the H-level are less influential than innovations on the P-level. Inventions in the beta-sciences are mostly about stronger, faster, and bigger. Inventions in social science are focused on completely different things. In Chapter 2 we have given an example of a social-cultural invention: the switch from a primitive to a Jewish-Christian-Humanist paradigm.

In order to improve our knowledge about the character of invention and innovation, we will discuss in more detail a number of important concepts in the evolutionary economics of technological change.

(1) At a particular moment one particular scientific programme dominates the research of a particular intellectual and scientific community. The hard core of the programme consists of its paradigm, which is that part of the analytical and theoretical instrument which is not questioned. The analysis consists of a series of logical implications. Step by step, this construction can be improved and extended, making the theoretical statements more consistent with the knowledge structure as a whole. At last we can improve the empirical specification of the theoretical relationships. It might lead to better empirical results with regard to the explanation of the past, or even to the prediction of the future. At all levels researchers can discover *novelties*. In physics, Higgs found that there must be a particular particle which should be the foundation of all materiality. In 2012, researchers who worked on the project said they had found this particle.

In sociology, the 'experience of one God, who loves its creatures' was a novelty with enormous effects on social relations (see Chapters 2 and 12.) In economics, Ricardo's discovery of 'comparative advantage' as the key concept in the orthodox economic explanation of international trade flows was a novelty. And last, psychology became an independent science when James introduced the idea of perception rather than just empirical observation (see Chapter 10).

(2) If a novelty takes place on the level of analysis (A) or theory (T) or means a better formulation of the empirical indicators of the phenomenon under research (H), persons who feel committed to that kind of research read the results with approval and store them in their minds. This is a *learning process* of a relatively easy kind. What if the opponents of the dominant research programme have improved their paradigm? Suppose the change means that their basic axioms have become more convincing, even in the eyes of some researchers of the dominant club? This might

mean a serious challenge to the 'rulers' of the scientific world. Suppose that the paradigmatic change leads to changes in analysis, theory, and hypothesis in such a way that the empirical results have become significantly better? Again, some researchers might change group. But others might feel motivated to apply more sophisticated (quantitative) methods to prove the superiority of their own paradigm. It means that paradigmatic change is a not just a rational affair. Whether a particular researcher sticks to his old paradigm, or really changes his paradigm, is not a strict logical and rational matter, but depends on his personality and his social-cultural context (see Chapters 10 and 13).

(3) Most of the time groups of specialists fight battles in which *status* plays a more important role than the technical quality of their knowledge and skills. In the innovation literature there is a continuing discussion about the organization of scientific research. If, for instance, every new specialization develops its own organization, and is located in its own building, and never meets members of another specialization, status battles might continue for decades. But if different programmes in one and the same specialization, or different but neighbouring specializations, are located in the same building, cross-fertilization and increasing common understanding of the problems under research might take place. So far, the dominant idea is that the *disciplinary distance* must be neither too small, nor too large. Otherwise, people are too homogeneous and all apply the same protocols, or ignore each other, even if they share rooms (Nooteboom, 2004). So, we can imagine an optimal disciplinary distance, given the context in which researchers operate. This context evolves over time, of course. In Box 6.1 we have described a case in which it becomes clear how difficult it is to organize necessary cooperation between economists, who are attracted by different research programmes.

The learning processes in science are illustrative of the way people learn in their daily lives. Using the distinction between the P, A, T, and H-level again, we see that changes on the P-level are the most difficult ones to accept. As a matter of illustration a few examples are presented.

(a) The official medical world is furiously against any recognition of what is called alternative medicine, or paramedical practices.

(b) The inhabitants of a monocultural neighbourhood are inclined to exorcise newcomers who belong to a different culture; even if they just eat different food or wear different clothes.

(c) Different ministries, dealing with one and the same problem in a different way, are not inclined to regularly sit together to see whether they can rationally communicate about the matter. For instance, if the level of the social security premiums is the problem, the Ministry of Social Affairs undertakes an analysis which is centred around the concept of fairness, while the Ministry of Finance gives its analysis with the government budget as the central variable, and the Ministry of Economic Affairs analyses the problem from the perspective of competitiveness.

BOX 6.1 PROBLEM-BASED LEARNING (PBL) AS THE LEARNING ENVIRONMENT

In April 1983 I moved to Maastricht University as the first member of staff to help erect an Economics Faculty. One of the ministerial conditions was an educational programme with a so-called PBL format. According to the PBL philosophy, the learning process should start with a series of practical problems, presented in a number of tasks, to be executed by the students. Groups of about ten students, under the chairmanship of another student, should work on these tasks. During the group meetings a tutor should be present to guide the learning process. Every task should be dealt with in a prescribed way: the so-called 7-step. Step 1: read the task and formulate one or a few problems; step 2: brainstorm about the possible factors that might be responsible for the problem; step 3: try to make a coherent analysis of the factors that have been found; step 4: transform a number of questions into learning goals; step 5: go home and read literature that might answer your questions; make notes of it, so as to be able to report to the group during the next meeting; step 6: students report their findings during the next meeting, and discuss whether they have solved the problem adequately; step 7: if students and/or tutor are not satisfied with the results so far, they must start anew. If the group fails again, they must ask for help from an expert, who can show them how to solve the problem.

It goes without saying that reality is multidisciplinary. Suppose that a task is about a company which faces disappointing sales. This problem is interesting from a macro, a micro, a marketing, and a strategic point of view, at least. So, different types of specialists should cooperate in the construction of the task, including the formulation of an answer model and literature that is relevant for the students to study. From the moment that full professors were hired and made responsible for a particular sub- or aspect-discipline, cooperation became a problem. They began to blame each other for not understanding each other's discipline. Moreover, many full professors could hardly hide their disdain for the other's methodology. It made the organization into an arena where status battles were fought.

In such a situation three strategies can be followed. (1) The staff must not only be trained in PBL philosophy and skills, but also in multidisciplinary economics. Moreover, their research should be assessed in terms of multidisciplinary research. (2) The organization cancels the idea or paradigm of PBL. (3) Every specialization has its own course, while leaving the integration to the students. Maastricht did not choose an explicitly formulated strategy, but its practice comes close to the third one. Main restriction: staff's interest in a career—which is determined by mono-disciplinary research performance rather than educational performance—comparable with other economists in the world.

In the Netherlands even the central bank regularly advises about the social security system. These institutions do not only have their own analyses, but even their own data. How do these groups make progress in their common understanding? A common view might emerge if the different ministries decide to regularly meet with each other to see whether they are able to develop an integrative model in which several key concepts play a role. So, regular communication between institutions must lead to an analysis in which the interactions between different variables play a decisive role. Looking back it is difficult to establish one moment of transformation from groupthink to common think. It is a process, and the new properties *emerge* rather than are 'installed' at a particular moment.

A learning process is not only a cognitive affair—just storing information in the memory. At every moment we are bombarded with sense data. And we can only live with this fact if we are able to immediately select those data that are relevant for that moment.

Over time we learn how to select (which knowledge structure must be used in which situation). This process becomes increasingly automatized. Sense data which fall outside the automatic framework of interpretation and analysis are not stored, and often not even observed (see Chapter 10). The framework operates as a *comfort zone*. Strong emotions block an eventual change in the framework. Some students feel comfortable with the idea that they are not good at mathematics. They think that they are a good judge of their own lack of talent and have learnt to circumvent inconveniences. The idea that mathematics is doable, for them, creates uncertainty and anxiety, since it would imply going beyond their comfort zone. Consequently, just following lectures in mathematics leads to confirmation of the comfortable idea that 'math is not for me'. Innovation in the organization of the learning environment could mean an enormous increase in the productivity of (mathematics) education, if it takes not only cognitive, but also psychic-social factors into account (see also Box 6.1 about the system of problem-based learning).

It is not only in education, but also in other institutions of the economy that these problems play an important role Imagine a tribe lives on a steppe in Kenya. They make their livelihood from herds of cows. Changes in the climate cause unacceptably low levels of food. Some individuals begin to set up small experiments in planting particular crops. The leadership of the tribe warns against change: cancelling traditions might trigger the anger of the gods, who may fear loss of prestige. On the other hand, the frustration about the low food productivity is growing. The situation can be understood by using the typical evolutionary method of *cumulative causation*. Over time the frustrations grow, and the fear of angry gods drops. So, at a particular moment frustration becomes stronger than fear, leading to a turn: a transformation of the economy from cattle breeding to agriculture.

A last point to be discussed is the way in which transformations take place. Two possibilities can be distinguished: the *evolutionary* and the *revolutionary* way. Another distinction, which is not very different, is the distinction between *spontaneous* and *designed* change.

Imagine a society where people work in a hierarchy, and transactions between departments within the hierarchy are institutionalized. North Korea comes close to this situation. Then a few workers begin—secretly—to grow some crops, and organize a voluntary exchange of crops between themselves. Other workers hear about this, and start their own businesses too, and organize markets. This process shows the emergence of properties of a different economic order, namely that of a free market. This is an evolutionary and spontaneous process. Nobody intended to change the economic order. They are just doing business, driven as they are by self-interest. Suppose the hierarchy discovers these illegal actions, and intervenes by means of the police. In reaction, the workers, who had become, increasingly, businessmen, organize themselves and revolt. If they are supported by many other workers, their revolution might be successful. They take over the political institutions and make private property, and ownership of productive resources, legal. Then the intended switch from hierarchy to free market has taken place in a revolutionary way.

What if the economic order is a mix of *market* and *hierarchy*. What do we call this mix? To answer this question we must realize that the concepts 'hierarchy' and 'market' reflect particular ideas; ideas which determine the substance of the ideal-types of hierarchy and market. So, if the economy shows a mix and the people agree consciously with this practice, it must be based on a particular idea. For instance, north-western people feel attracted to the ideal-type of a *welfare state*. The idea behind this type of society is that two principles—individual freedom and social justice—are not enemies of each other; on the contrary, they strengthen each other. It leads to a synthesis, and to a society, which functions better than a hierarchy or a free market society. Now a new concept has born with a firm substance—a novelty.

6.2.5 THE RETURN OF ORIGINAL INSTITUTIONAL ECONOMICS (OIE)

Hodgson must be held responsible for the increasing attention paid to the role of institutions, and the contribution to it of the American Institutionalists. In Chapter 3 we paid attention to this group. Now we will discuss Veblen's evolutionary view of the dynamics of institutions in more detail.

Because Veblen did not accept the neoclassical axioms, he was an outcast in the world of economists (Veblen, 1899). He considered the world to be an *open* and *dynamic* system. Not only the natural but also the social world shows a permanent interaction between natural and social actors respectively. Social interaction results in social institutions, which are rules that make life more understandable and controllable. According to Veblen, *habits of thought* are the most important institutions. They determine social structure, and therewith they determine which groups compete with each other. Within a group social interaction takes place in a positive way, and leads to a common framework of thought. Between groups interaction takes place in a negative way—an ongoing status battle.

The dynamics of social interaction is characterized by what Veblen called *cumulative causation*. He applies it to American society at the end of the 19th century and the beginning of the 20th century. At that time there was a process of accumulation and concentration going on in the industrial sector. Products and production processes were of an increasing level of quality and quantity. In the firms technicians formed an important group, and they had developed a culture of what Veblen called *workmanship*. They were proud of the quality of their products, and were in constant rivalry with groups in the firm who were responsible for the organization of the production process and the selling of the products. Marketers were responsible for the selling of the products and tried to influence the unconscious of potential customers with the idea of society as a *consumption society*. Life does not mean working and job satisfaction. Life is leisure and consumption. How can we, marketers, stimulate the consumption? By suggesting, via advertisements, that the status of a person or of a group depends on his consumption style. This suggestion—Veblen calls it *emulation*—means that no one has ever enough;

there is always reason to consume more—more than your rich neighbour. Now Veblen is back to Herakleitos' 'panta rei': the eternal desire to be superior as the driver behind the habit of thought as it emerged in the minds of the American people.

Nowadays we see that the organizers and sellers are increasingly winning their battles against the technicians. Sometimes it looks as if it is only in countries such as Germany and Japan that the role of technicians is still important. In the Dutch education system it is clear that the social group 'technicians' are increasingly losing their battle against the organizers and sellers. The worst effect of this conflict is the decline in number of high-quality technicians, including teachers, who are willing to fight against a decline in quality. At universities, popularity and prestige have become the guides when doing research, at least in social science.

6.2.6 THE FUTURE OF EVOLUTIONARY ECONOMICS

The return of OIE, and growing attention on Veblen's work, has enriched economics as a science. Two matters that were stressed by this approach are very important. In the first place, the idea of *reality as an open system* must be taken seriously. The role of novelties in the explanation of technological progress is a result of it. Later we will see that the Post-Keynesians are on the same page with respect to this issue. In the second place, is the idea that *reality is historical*. Current behaviour is always and everywhere influenced by events and choices in the past, and by expectations and anticipations about the future.

Notwithstanding these two notes, it is important to make partial analyses on the assumption of a closed world. Of course, these pieces of knowledge are not descriptions of the empirical world. But they might function as necessary parts of a more integrative model. Actually, it is difficult if not impossible to make models of an open system. The unknown cannot be modelled; only be represented—per scenario—by a given entity, which operates as a source of unpredictable impulses.

Many evolutionary economists are wary of metaphysics and don't accept introspection as an important source of knowledge. But this method of internal observation is a necessary part of knowledge. Without metaphysics and introspection we wouldn't have any idea of the forces that drive us. Without them, we cannot accept the existence of an economic or a social force; and so with the sexual force and the force of gravitation. It means that we cannot accept logic and mathematics, and we cannot make a distinction between substance and property, as we learnt from Kant; there is no substance. One of the consequences of this fear is the reluctance to accept the (evolutionary) idea that all living things are driven by a force that aims at the *maximization of the chance to survive*. When we accept the assumption of the existence of such a drive, we should ask the question: what should survive? Of course, in very poor countries people try to survive physically, although many fail and die relatively young. But in more developed countries other goals might also play an important role, such as self-esteem and social prestige. We need a broader model, which includes psychic and social analysis, to show the consequences of this result of internal observation.

A second problem with evolutionary economics, as it manifests itself today, is the lack of analytical rigour. Temporary and local closures are necessary, and clear-cut definitions of concepts are of utmost importance. Just a rejection of neoclassical definitions of concepts such as 'economic', and 'optimal' is not acceptable. Important concepts such as 'social' and 'rational' are used in a sloppy way, or not used at all. Founding father Veblen made 'the habits of thought' a key element of his work. If we would understand why people are motivated to stick to this habit, it is necessary to analyse the social and the psychic problem first (see Chapters 10 to 13). We will see that the analysis of the psychic world offers a nice answer to the problem of the stickiness of thought habits.

In Section 6.3 we will discuss the Austrian approach.

6.3 **Austrian Economics**

6.3.1 INTRODUCTION

In Chapter 3 and Chapter 4 we have seen that John Neville Keynes and John Stuart Mill criticized the classical political economists for their analyses of 18th- and 19th-century economies: place- and time-dependent analyses rather than a serious attempt to formulate universal laws of an economic nature. Carl Menger (Vienna) took their criticisms seriously, and began to construct an analysis of an individual consumer, thereby assuming that human actors have a constant nature, namely an economic one. Economics should focus on the relationship between a human subject and a non-human object, which is based on the idea of scarcity of valuable objects. For a correct interpretation we must take into account also the fact that humans can be approached as non-human objects—when they are offering their labour service, for instance.

Objects have value because subjects, who possess resources, attach value to them. This *subjective approach* to the problem of value is opposed to the old idea of the classical political economy, which assumed that labour input expressed in time units is the objective basis of value for an object. Later Von Wieser and Von Böhm-Bawerk developed analyses of costs, benefits, and markets on the basis on Menger's individualism and subjectivism.

Not only in Austria, but also in England, and later in the United States, 'Austrians' took this individualist and subjectivist approach as the starting point of their analysis. In England Von Mises and Von Hayek worked on an analysis of real-life market processes, and their philosophical and ontological underpinning. In the USA, people such as Kirzner

(1973) continued the Austrian tradition. We will see that Joseph Schumpeter does belong to the Austrian School, although his work shows properties which are less individualist than most Austrians appreciate. Nevertheless, Schumpeter is too important to be ignored.

6.3.2 PRAXEOLOGY AND HISTORICAL DEVELOPMENT

Menger applied the idea of isolated abstraction to social science. If every social science takes its part in the division of labour, social science as a whole will flourish in a way comparable to physics and chemistry. So, for economists a subject is just an economic subject, and economists study the relationship between subject and objects, which are approached as non-human. As long as there is scarcity of resources that can satisfy human needs and desires, economic action makes sense. In the chapter on orthodox economics we have seen that Menger's consumer theory logically implied the *law of demand*: if the price of a particular good decreases (increases), the quantity demanded will increase (decrease). In Figure 6.2 we see two pictures, one of price formation in the marginal analyses by Menger, and the other of price formation in classical political economy. In the first picture the variables are of a subjective nature. A shift of the demand curve affects the price level proportionally. In the second picture, prices and values are objective entities. A shift of the demand curve as a result of a change in the subjective valuation of the consumer does not affect the price of the good.

Menger's idea of individualism and subjectivism, and the way he developed an economic analysis of it, is called *praxeology*: the general science of human action, applied to economics. Robbins (1932) formulated the principles of praxeology, and criticized the objective and materialist definitions of the opponents. Economics should focus on scarcity rather than on production, as measured by statisticians. In other words, economics is an aspect-science rather than an explanation of a subsystem.

So far Menger is an orthodox economist—not a neoclassical one. Besides his orthodox work, he worked also on an approach to real-life historical processes. In this work he did

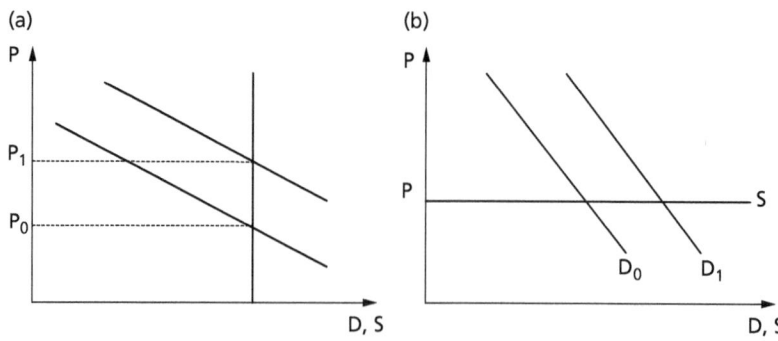

Figure 6.2. A: Menger; B: Classical Political Economy

not make a distinction between different aspects of human behaviour, and took every real person as responsible for his Self, independent of his context. So, he avoided discussions on rationality and sociality. An individual person who is operating in a free society can be held responsible for all his actions, except a child, who falls under the jurisdiction of his parents.

When comparing this Austrian approach with the basic version of the orthodox economic world, we see the following differences.

(1) The Austrians assume that individuals have *knowledge* of their own tastes and of the opportunities to satisfy their needs; orthodox analysis assumes that subjects have perfect information about their preferences and their situation, including the future.

(2) The Austrians assume that individual persons have their own *interpretations* of current events and the actions of others; orthodox analysis assumes perfect information, which implies that everyone has the orthodox economic world as his frame.

(3) The Austrians assume that human persons have their *expectations* about future events, and the reaction of others upon it; orthodoxy assumes perfect information about the future, which implies a perfect functioning of future markets.

(4) The Austrians assume the existence of *entrepreneurs,* who are alert to new and profitable opportunities previously unrecognized. In the basic orthodox world there is no room for entrepreneurs and novelties. In this world there are only one-man businesses, which are perfectly informed.

If imperfect information is assumed, all subjects are supposed to search for information about future developments in an optimal way. Imperfect information implies that humans live in a stochastic world. Fortunately, the risks of human actions can be calculated. Austrians assume very imperfect information, creating emotions of uncertainty (Knight, 1921). In Chapter 8 we will return to this subject.

So, the Austrian world is an open world, full with heterogeneous people and goods. Competition is a discovery procedure—it drives the process of coordinating individual plans. In the economic world preferences and technology are givens, but in the Austrian world nothing is a given, and everything is a process. Entrepreneurs strive for profits, as a reward for noticing some lack of coordination in the market. Profits must be interpreted as an incentive for the discovery of new knowledge. In orthodox economics allocation is perfect as soon as equilibrium is reached. In the Austrian approach perfect coordination does not exist. Economic life implies an ever-continuing search for novelty.

6.3.3 SUBJECTIVISM

Menger's praxeology stresses the subjective character of costs and benefits. It's all about utility and disutility, experienced by individuals in the end. Von Wieser took Menger's analysis as his starting point. Individuals always choose between different options. Assume that there are two options: option A and option B. Both have costs and benefits, and the options can be compared by their net benefits. An economic actor will choose A if its net benefits are higher than those of B. Von Wieser called the net benefits of the option that is not chosen the *opportunity costs* of the option that is chosen.

Von Böhm-Bawerk extended Menger's praxeological analyses of consumer behaviour to the capital market. He asked himself the question of why people postpone their consumption and save part of their income. He assumed that individuals have a time preference for consumption. They prefer consumption now to consumption later. So, if the economic system requires savings the savers must be rewarded for that. If the interest rate goes up, people intend to save more, and vice versa. In this way Von Böhm-Bawerk worked out a marginal analysis of capital supply. A marginal analysis of the demand for capital runs in terms of the marginal productivity of capital, which must be equal to its marginal costs. In the case of a perfectly competitive market these marginal costs are equal to the interest rate.

Now we will give a few examples of subjective valuation of prices, which means that they are expressions of the judgements of consumers of a particular good.

(1) The salaries of a number of very good football players in Europe. Whatever the organization of the markets that play a role in the football sector, it is the appreciation of a very large number of football consumers that makes the salaries extremely high. The principle of the winner who takes all, is based on the subjective preferences of many consumers, who prefer a game between Barcelona and Real Madrid for the third time in a short period rather than a match between Austria Wien and FC Zurich for the first time. The preference is based on the consumer's own observations, and few watchers feel badly about the extremely high wages of the players.

(2) The salaries of many bankers, who are involved in the arrangement of mergers and acquisitions in the world of big business. There are league tables of top firms and top investment banks. A top firm only wants to deal with a top bank, and both businessmen and bankers are used to being paid well. The games these people play belong to the social rather than to the economic world. Nevertheless, an Austrian economist would only ask whether there are enough consumers who are willing to pay for the goods and the bank services offered by these top organizations. If so, the production process is well developed, since competition on the market always motivates top organizations to avoid too much waste. Psychological and sociological analyses are not made; Austrians just see persons who are free and responsible for their selves and their subjective appreciations.

(3) When an Austrian makes a cost-benefit analysis, he applies the principle of opportunity costs. Most cost-benefit analyses made by research bureaus do not do it that way. They just take statistics of 'relevant' variables, all expressed in money, place the costs opposite the benefits, and so calculate the 'price' of important phenomena, such as immigration, membership of the EU, adoption of the euro,

and equality. These 'objective' analyses ignore the costs and benefits in case of the absence of immigration, the absence of the euro, and so on. So, a fair judgement upon the basis of a comparison between different options is not given in this type of quantitative study.

Shackle (1955) considers human behaviour to be unpredictable. The human mind is seen as capricious. Such a position raises the question of what an economist should do. In the first place, economists should try to improve the quality of quantitative measures. We all know that the GDP is a bad measure of the wealth of a nation. Fortunately, there are economists working on an improvement, such as the valuation of housework and the raising of children. Nevertheless, most of these measures are expressions of objective rather than subjective criteria. In the second place, economists can operate as consultants for consumer households, firms, and government agencies, and advise them not only in quantitative, but also in qualitative terms. In an open world with heterogeneous subjects the role of econometrics can only be a small one. An Austrian economist wonders why this discipline is necessary and unavoidable now.

6.3.4 THE MARKET AS A COMPETITIVE PROCESS

If a seller meets a buyer and they decide to a particular transaction, the trade takes place—by definition—in a market context, which means that there might be other sellers and buyers transacting a comparable good. If participants discover that there are other sellers or buyers with whom they can exchange goods in a more profitable way, a free society allows these people to do just that. Every transaction needs a contract. It contains information about the quality and the price of the goods. It should also answer the question of who is responsible for an acceptable delivery, including the after-sales service, for instance. In this way the transfer of property rights is arranged properly.

In Chapter 4 we have seen under which conditions a market can be called perfectly competitive. Austrians, however, are not interested in perfect competition. Where neo-classical economists are inclined to support anti-trust legislation in case of imperfect competition, Austrian economists stress that concentration on markets is the consequence of a competitive market. The most efficient firms survive, and have the incentive to stay keen on efficiency because of the ever-existing possibility of newcomers. They call this contestable competition. Only if the barriers of entry are prohibitively high might an Austrian consider government action. We come back to this issue later in this chapter.

According to the Austrians the future is uncertain and actors can only develop particular expectations of it. In more sophisticated orthodox models imperfect information is assumed, including about the future. But in this approach future markets are trading risks, thereby making it possible for risk averters to make accurate calculations. For Austrians these markets mean that some parties 'buy uncertainty'. The current crisis shows how dangerous it is if there are many big uncertainty lovers.

A last characteristic of the Austrian world is the central position of the entrepreneur. In its basic formulations the orthodox economic world does not recognize the specific function of entrepreneur; all subjects are assumed to economize on the relationships between input and output, given the state of technology and the preferences of the consumers. In orthodox macroeconomic growth theory technological progress is assumed, thereby implicitly assuming that producers are constantly applying the latest inventions.

Schumpeter was one of the first economists to give the entrepreneur a central role in his market process theory. In situations of disequilibrium especially they go against the wind and try to make profits by applying *new combinations* in their construction of the goods and in their production methods. So, especially in recessions, when sales and profits drop, some firms do not only compete with cost reductions. A different strategy to increase profits at the cost of the competitors is the introduction of *innovations*. When others discover the entrepreneurial activities of their competitor, they try to imitate him. This process of imitation is responsible for a quick dispersion of the latest technology.

In the section on evolutionary economics we saw that entrepreneurs are the creators of novelties. Also, in the Austrian approach entrepreneurship plays a pivotal role; it stresses that it refers to a function, not to a person, being the owner or the top manager. It means a constant search for innovative ideas about products and production methods. In the literature it is stressed that this search function is linked to the willingness of the searchers to risk failure.

Orthodox economics does not describe historical processes, but is focused on an optimal allocation of scarce resources. Austrian economists—as is the case in evolutionary economics—are focused on an explanation of processes. In their worlds it is impossible to calculate optimal budgets for R&D and other categories of expenditures. In both worlds some entrepreneurs survive, while others go bankrupt. Alertness and luck are important elements in the destiny of businesses.

Orthodox economics defines perfect competition in the context of a market with many perfectly informed suppliers and demanders who are trading a homogeneous good. As already said, Austrians do not work with the concept 'perfect competition'. They assume that entrepreneurs always try to improve their competitiveness by producing goods that (slightly) differ from those of the competitors. Even if there are just a few suppliers and demanders, competition can be fierce. In case of a monopoly the monopolist might feel the threat of newcomers. It means that if a monopolist actually exploits his monopoly position by gaining high profits it might be an incentive for others to enter the market and supply the same goods for a lower price.

So, under particular conditions even a monopoly can be an efficient solution. This is the case when the barriers of entry and exit are quite low. But if we imagine a producer of nuclear plants being a monopolist on the global market, and the demand for nuclear plants to be high and rising, the situation is quite different. The price the monopolist is setting determines the quantity demanded and the quantity sold. The profits are high, but potential newcomers face extremely high costs of entry. It takes a new firm a long and costly period before it has the expertise and the materials needed. Meanwhile, the monopolist can decide to lower its price a bit to discourage the investments by newcomers. In this way an established monopolist does not have a strong incentive to work hard on a permanent improvement of the quality of product and production process, including the quality of the processing of the dangerous waste.

6.3.5 INSTITUTIONALIZATION OF FREE MARKETS

Market transactions are based on a contract. There are two important problems, however. In the first place, it is impossible to foresee all transaction problems and arrange them effectively in the contract. In the second place, there is the question of what to do if the other party is breaching the contract. In a historical approach there are no universal solutions to the two problems just indicated. Problems always occur in a place- and time-dependent context. Most of the time transactions take place in a region administered by some sort of government. In a free society the government is the authority which should protect private property rights. Most Austrians advocate this solution. The first problem—the impossibility of specifying all contingencies—is solved by the (spontaneous) emergence of rules which makes clear to contract partners what they should do in particular circumstances.

For instance, in winter ponds might be frozen, and many people take their chance to skate and have fun. Some skaters are newcomers and skate in any direction. Most skaters have been doing it for years, and are familiar with the implicit rules which channel typical Dutch skating. There is no government with legislation, and there are no statutes, or similar, which inform newcomers about the rules of traffic on ice. Nevertheless, the spontaneously emerged rules work well most of the time.

The following story can be found in a novel by Follett (1989) about English society in the 12th century, and illustrates the idea of spontaneous rule-formation. A young orphan, responsible for her little brother, is able to borrow some money, and buys a few sheep. Every season she clips her sheep, and colours the wool in fashionable red. Italian wool buyers travel through England now and then and buy her wool. Then she faces a very bad year, without much wool. She asks the Italian wool buyers to pay her for the wool she promises to deliver them next season. Some people from her village react negatively: we never do this sort of stupid thing. Others, on the contrary, react with more enthusiasm: this is a great idea; we will do the same. For them this is the very beginning of a future market.

Stimulated by this entrepreneurial attitude some local people start a discussion about the possibility of organizing a market every year, where many traders with many goods can come and meet each other. Again, some people feel this to be a threat: foreign people visit our village on a regular basis? Others, however, love the idea of growing business.

One of the most internationalized markets is the money market. Over the course of time some goods appeared to have a comparative advantage over other goods to fulfil the function of money. The value of money must be stable and the money should easily be transported and stored safely. Silver and gold appeared to be superior to other materials. 'Banks' began to make coins, and later banknotes. Coins have the advantage of their intrinsic value. Notes have just nominal value, and can only be issued by organizations which are trusted by large groups of people. In some periods silver and gold functioned as money. Sometimes the price of gold, expressed in silver, was a flexible one, and dependent on the relative scarcity of the two precious metals. It meant that many businessmen were constantly speculating with respect to the composition of their portfolios. In other periods governments decided to fix the gold price, expressed in silver. In this monetary system people were inclined to melt gold or silver, dependent on which metal was undervalued, and sell it on the market for gold or silver. Famous in this respect is the *law of Gresham*, which says that in case of fixed exchange rates 'bad money always drives out good money'. As soon as gold became scarcer, it was melted and the system became a silver standard. The law shows that that only spontaneous rules work effectively; they emerge because the market participants see them as facilitating business transactions.

Austrians like to tell the history of money and money creation. They see the story as proof of their ideas about free markets. In the 19th century governments adopted a gold standard. Banks bought gold by means of currency, and put the gold in their vaults. So far, so good. Then banks discovered that most clients trusted them and never substituted gold and gold coins for their notes. It meant that much gold stayed in the vaults of the bank, seemingly a waste of scarce resources. They decided to lend money to businessmen. It meant that they received an account, which could be used for payments, but also as a substitute for coins and notes. Again, most banks appeared successful in remaining trustworthy to their clients. From that time just a fraction of the money in circulation was covered by gold in the vaults of the banks. If all clients went into a collective panic, and wanted to substitute gold for their nominal money, the monetary system would collapse. Monetary history shows bank runs on a regular basis, which illustrates the Austrian idea that government intervention in the money market is not a good idea, and fractional reserve banking plus governmental guarantees is a very bad combination. A free market would mean that every bank is competing with other banks to get and maintain the trust of its clients, who are interested in reliable information about the balances of their banks. In times of instability and uncertainty clients are inclined to transfer their nominal money to banks with a more conservative lending policy. But as soon as governments intervene and take over risks from private banks, the latter feel free to lend money as much as possible.

Today (December 2013) the European economy is still in a depression, while many large banks are less solvent and liquid than is necessary now. All the governments of the EU countries, and other important countries in the world reacted to the financial disaster of 2006–2008 with strong interventionist measures. Many banks appeared to be *system banks*—banks which most experts think are too large to go bankrupt without a complete collapse of the system as a whole. The reaction from the American Tea Party, a libertarian movement, shows that the Austrians are still influential: government, don't support Wall Street. The Tea Party expects to be able to build a new and better financial system upon the ruins of the current one.

6.3.6 INSTITUTIONS OF A FREE SOCIETY

Austrian political philosophy portrays society as a large number of free and independent individuals. As long as persons have not reached their adulthood, parents are responsible for their behaviour. But as soon as they have become adults, they are free and responsible for themselves. Every individual is unique and a source of creativity, spontaneity, and free will—he is a *motor of change*. This idea of a human person is quite different from the ideas about an individual in other approaches, such as the neoclassical, and Marxist philosophy. In these schools of thought individuals are just chains in a large system. The neoclassical individual is determined by his given and constant economic nature, just responding to economic incentives. The class to which a Marxist individual belongs determines his reactions, just responding to social incentives.

In Section 6.3.7 we will briefly discuss the so-called Calculation Debate between the Austrian Von Mises and the Socialist Lange in the 1920s.

6.3.7 THE CALCULATION DEBATE

The Interbellum (1918–1939) was a period of revolution and rumours of a war. Only the Russian Bolshevik Revolution of 1917 appeared a 'success'. It stimulated Austrians to discuss in detail the advantages and disadvantages of a free market economy versus a centrally planned economy. Given the Austrian ontology, it is not a surprise that they advocated the free market economy, most fervently by Von Mises. His opponents were Lange and Taylor (1938), who defended systems of state planning. Two aspects dominated the debate most prominently, namely the way the systems generate reliable information about prices and qualities of goods on the one hand, and the incentives for individuals to search for profitable activities in the system on the other. Von Mises argued that consumer interests should be the focus of the system of production and allocation of investment and consumption goods. He also argued that consumers themselves have the best knowledge about their own needs, and certainly better than a government agency. Only a system that is decentralized to the level of the individual is fed by reliable information, and gives the participants the strongest incentive to perform well. Lange's argumentation runs via the waste that results from competition. There is much advertising with information that presses people to buy rather than one-time useful information. Moreover, there are many bankruptcies because of a lack of coordination on a central level. In case of macroeconomic disturbances, countervailing measures taken by a central government can prevent much unemployment and poverty.

The Austrians recognize the existence of so-called *social facts*. Chapter 11 contains an exposition and explanation of this concept. For now, Austrians think of the *interpretations* individuals make of their environment, or of the awareness of statistical artefacts about their society. Both the interpretations as well as the statistical artefacts can be wrong; nevertheless, they affect individual behaviour significantly.

On the basis of this picture of an individual person Austrians analyse the functioning of a free society, and the negative effects of government intervention, which is based on misperceptions of what an individual really is and is doing, if he lives in freedom. Why should a government intervene in the first place? An Austrian only accepts the existence of pubic goods and externalities as a possible argumentation. However, there are hardly genuine public goods to be found. In the Netherlands the system of dikes is a good example. Here, the Austrians advise the government to keep the administrative system as decentralized as possible. Looking at the Dutch system of democratically chosen district water boards, they have listened to the Austrian advice. Other approaches, such as the economic sociological approach (see Chapter13), interpret income and wealth distribution as a public good. They mean to say that it is an important characteristic of the society in which people are living. Therefore, it influences the well-being of people, whatever their place in the social ranking. Austrians do not recognize society as an entity which could claim resources from an individual. Some Austrians see physical security as a public good, which should be produced by the government. But other Austrians, such as Rothbard, consider the production of these goods to be private matters. As we know from situations in Latin America, many ordinary people protect themselves by means of heavy metal fences around their house and garden, and the richer ones make use of private armies. Also, the USA uses private firms for dangerous actions in the war in Iraq and Afghanistan.

As already said, Austrians do not accept ideas about freedom other than their individual freedom from government intervention (except the protection of property rights). So they are not prepared to accept redistribution of scarce resources as a public good and refuse to recognize the existence of *merit goods*. When discussing other heterodox approaches we will see that a different ontology leads to a different analysis and different policy advice, be it for individuals or firms, or for the government.

Is a free society in the Austrian sense a stable and orderly one? Rothbard considers such a society as natural—in compliance with human nature. It is in the nature of a human individual to feel challenged by individual freedom, and to do everything possible to serve his own interest. As soon as a particular order leaves some freedom to individuals, they learn what it is to be free, and don't stop claiming more freedom until they are liberated from all unnecessary government intervention.

Hayek is less optimistic and considers it necessary that all persons agree with what he calls the *'rule of law'*. This law says that every individual has a set of inalienable rights, especially property rights, and we should not interfere with the rights of others. Only if we agree with this law and act accordingly, is a free society guaranteed which offers all people the opportunity to become wealthy.

In dictatorial countries dictators are inclined to serve their own interests, and people in general are assumed to serve the dictator's interests. In democratic countries every voter is assumed to serve his own interest, including by voting for particular government transfers. Groups of voters are driven to form coalitions with groups of voters with comparable interests, and try to gain at the cost of minorities (*the tyranny of the majority*). According to Hayek, the right to vote should be limited to those who can be regarded as responsible enough not to play these sorts of robbery games. He himself had a limit in mind in terms of age—older than 40 years, for instance.

The Austrian approach can be characterized as *individualistic* and *atomistic*. The first property should be taken literally: a person is a unity and should not be divided analytically in two or more parts, as some psychological currents are doing. The second property says that human nature does not change when a person regularly interacts with other persons. In Chapter 11 we will discuss, among others, the symbolic interactionist approach. There we will see that social relationships differ from strict economic relations, and that human nature appears as a variable, which also depends on the social context. We can compare social relations with chemical relations. When a chemist combines a series of atoms, he discovers that, under particular conditions, a number of atoms become a molecule with its own properties, different from each of the atoms.

But Austrians regard relationships between people not as social in the sociological sense of the word. All relationships are strictly voluntary, and based on a subjective cost-benefit analysis. Human nature is and remains strictly economic. Social duties do not exist, but if people feel sympathy with the poor in their own family or in their own neighbourhood, they can do *charity* work, of course.[1] As long as it is beneficial for a person to be member of a group, he will stay. As soon as his cost-benefit analysis shows that it is not beneficial for him anymore, he will quit. In Chapter 11 we will see that, in a sociological analysis group, membership might change a person's view of the world, and therewith what he experiences as cost and what as benefit.

6.3.8 SCHUMPETER AS A SPECIAL CASE

In his famous book *Capitalism, Socialism and Democracy* Schumpeter presents a view on historical economic development which differs remarkably from 'mainstream Austrianism' (Schumpeter, 1943). In his exposition he shows—like Marx—that, during the course of time, the capitalist market economy transforms from a competitive to a more oligopolistic and monopolistic market economy. Large companies imply that the number of managers necessary to plan production and sales increases significantly. It might lead to growing effectiveness, but these hierarchies lead definitely also to growing inequality. The intellectual elite especially will increasingly

---

[1] See Keizer (1990) for an exposition of the Austrian view on a welfare state.

oppose this tendency. In particular, sociologists have learned to think in terms of planning and control, and cannot accept outcomes of spontaneous processes, which are not humane. They see it as their task to improve the structure of society, such that all persons can participate in all aspects (see Chapter 11 on sociology as an emancipatory science).

They will develop several strategies, such as the establishment of unions, democratic political parties, and international cooperation between emancipatory movements, to change societal structure and culture.

Schumpeter was not negative about these strategies and hoped for a balanced mix of capitalist markets and state planning. A free society is only sustainable if the entrepreneurial function in the free market sector is combined with a government which is able to reduce the anti-capitalist sentiments that result from severe inequality.

6.3.9 AUSTRIAN MACROECONOMICS

Austrians are optimistic about the economic results of a free market economy. Disequilibria are not a bad thing and mean an incentive for entrepreneurs to intensify their search for novelties. If many entrepreneurs are prepared to take incalculable risks and innovate their products and production methods permanently, the economy can recover from recessions and flourish. Only government interventions are able to frustrate these market processes. Hayek, for instance, constructed a business cycle theory in which he considers the central bank to be the source of imbalance, leading to sharp fluctuations in the level of production and employment. If the central bank sets the bank interest rate on a level lower than the natural rate, firms borrow more money and increase their investments. Since economies are always close to equilibrium, this spending impulse will soon lead to inflation. Workers react to it by claiming higher nominal wages. If their unions are successful, wages might increase significantly. An increase of consumption as a result of wage increases is a reason for firms to further increase their prices. This wage–price spiral stops as soon as the central bank moves to a more restrictive monetary policy, and increases the bank interest rate. Lower investments mean a lower level of production and employment. The rise in unemployment breaks the wage–price spiral, and the economy turns back to her original position, close to equilibrium. If unions get a state-guaranteed monopoly-right-to-bargain about the wage level, the cyclical fluctuations will become larger.

Hayek's conclusion is that business cycles with their booms and busts result from changes in the structure of (factor) prices. Therefore, a bust should not be reduced artificially by a governmental spending impulse (message to Keynes). Spontaneous market processes will solve the problem in the end, whereby unemployment functions as an incentive for workers and unions to lower their wage claims.

It is typical for Austrians to ignore the attempts of others to empirically test Austrian business cycle theory. For them, numbers on spending, production, income, and unemployment are meaningless statistical aggregates. For one person unemployment has meaning, which differs from the meaning of it for others. A rich person who is unemployed for half a year does not experience his position in the same way as a poor person who has already been unemployed for several years. In such a case one plus one is not two. Austrians develop business cycle theory to show to others that, even in a downturn, government intervention is undesirable, and that busts do not occur if money markets are free and competitive.[2]

6.3.10 CONCLUSION

Menger is generally considered to be the creator of the marginalist revolution and the founding father of the Austrian School. Economics can design thought experiments, comparable with the laboratory experiments of physicists and chemists. Imagine that human persons have just one motivation, which is the economic force. In this economic world humans react only if the volume of the scarce resources available or the prices of the goods change (see Chapters 4 and 5). Besides his praxeology Menger worked on a better understanding of the historical developments of markets as institutions. The way in which he worked out his real-life analyses is different from the typical neoclassical way of straightforwardly applying orthodox economics to the real world. When reading typical Austrian descriptions and explanations of historical processes, it is remarkable to see that the psychological and sociological aspects are mostly ignored. Economic action, interpreted as the economic aspect of human action, has become identical to actions in the sector 'economy'. Austrians never use the concept rationality, and their use of the concept economic is different, because of the different ontology. Although realistic psychological and sociological assumptions are not taken into account, economic analysis is applied to the real world. These real-world descriptions lead to the conclusion that free markets are superior to any form of government action, except the protection of property rights. While the neoclassical school at least tries to empirically test their theories by means of objectivist data, the Austrians reject any attempt to empirically test their theory. They consider themselves right because of the *obvious validity of the axioms* chosen in their praxeology. If they were taking the psychological and sociological axioms seriously they would have discovered that there are more principles ruling human behaviour than the individual drive to be free and independent from government interference. In Chapter 10 to 13 we will see which other axioms might play a significant role in the lives of humans.

---

[2] The American central Bank (FED) is set up by large private banks and is independent from the government. Hayek agreed with Friedman that the FED was not active enough in the period 1929–1932. He blamed himself for his silence when the FED was not active in the period just mentioned. Actually Hayek is not—as nobody is—a typical Austrian. Every economist is unique in his combination of analyses, which is quite in compliance with the Austrian paradigm. They just have a series of axioms in common.

A last point worth noting is the fact Austrian texts are mixtures of positive and normative analysis. Their praxeological axioms are considered as real, but at the same time the Austrian message to the world says that we *should* act according to their axioms. Even countries which have not listened to the Austrians for a very long time now, have flourished for many decades. Austrians have just one answer: it is all about the subject with his needs and satisfaction, and such can only be experienced by people, not empirically proven by large data sets about objects.

7 **Radical Economics**

7.1 **Introduction**

In Chapter 3 we have given a short exposition of three ideal-typical political philosophies, which can be distinguished. The radical approach in economics is based on socialist philosophy, which sees Rousseau as one of his founding fathers. According to him, a human being becomes increasingly alienated from his Self when living his life in a modern society, which is characterized by ongoing social conflict. Different philosophers have taken this idea about modernity and alienation and placed it in a historical perspective. Some picture history as a story of humankind, who develops increasingly complex and realistic ideas about its condition. According to Hegel, this process of ideological progress is moved by an ongoing conflict about the ruling idea. It leads to the development of new ideas about the nature and functioning of societies. According to philosophers such as Fichte and Feuerbach, this dialectical process should be applied to material rather than ideological progress. This switch is not difficult to understand: they lived in a period of revolutionary turmoil when growing masses of workers became impoverished, although the Industrial Revolution led to growing production.

The headman of the radical approach is Karl Marx. He started his research with a sketch of the hunting and gathering epoch, where small groups of nomads lived from animals and plants, while wandering from one region to another in search of a decent living. For them the earth was common ground, and they lived in affluence: on average they needed just a few hours per day to hunt animals and to gather plants. The rest of the time was spent playing and organizing religious rituals. The main coordination mechanism was clear: every person delivers input according to his capacities, and takes output according to his needs. Inequality was expressed in terms of status and organizational function only. In the following stages of development an increasing number of people faced scarcity of natural resources. Many people became settled and developed the idea of property rights. The first settlers did not pay for these rights—there were no owners; only the idea of a common good. They protected their resources on an individual basis. But they increasingly discovered that a 'public' body with the monopoly right to protect all private property is more efficient. The different stages of historical evolution are distinguished on the basis of their mode of production. Marx focused his main analysis on the capitalist stage.

The main characteristics of the capitalist mode of production are the following. Some people own capital, while the mass of the people just own their labour power. In

186 MULTIDISCIPLINARY ECONOMICS

other words, the population consists of two groups: the haves and the have-nots. The capital owners, or capitalists, have the opportunity to start a business and hire workers. The workers are forced to search for a job, offered by a capitalist. This inequality is the source of all conflicts in a system that produces ever-growing amounts of goods by combining capital and labour and letting them cooperate. By means of an extensive capitalist-economic analysis Marx pretended to show that the scarcity experienced by the mass of the people is the result of capitalist institutions rather than a natural phenomenon for people with limited capacities. In Section 7.2 we will present the economic analysis of Marx in more detail. We will see that Marx predicts an impressive growth in production, but that the capitalist system will come to an end because of a permanently rising inequality in income and wealth. He used a series of concepts, which are not accepted by adherents of today's radical economics, a branch of economics that takes Marx's analysis as its starting point, but reaches different results. In Section 7.3 we will discuss a few authors who aim at making Marx's analysis up to date. To illustrate that radical economics has practical value, we will deal with a few radical explanations of the financial crisis that started in the period 2006–2008. When comparing the results we see a significant difference as compared with the neoclassical explanation, including different policy advice. In Section 7.5 we conclude our story about the radicals by summarizing the methodological differences between neoclassical and radical economics.

7.2 **The Economics of Marx**

For a proper understanding of Marx's analysis,[1] it is useful to realize from the beginning that many workers are assumed to be unemployed. Marx had in mind the situation in England in the middle of the process of industrialization. A large outflow of people from the agricultural sector led to a permanent reserve army, which made it possible for the capitalist to stick the wage rate at the level necessary for a worker to keep his health on an 'acceptable' level. So, whatever the situation the wage rate just fluctuates around subsistence level.

It is necessary to explain two other assumptions. The first is the assumption that only labour is really productive—the so-called *labour value theory*. Land is only productive if workers cultivate it. Capital goods are only productive in the form that is produced by labour. It does not mean that Marx is against any payment for capital, but it is just a passive factor, which is increasingly affluent rather than scarce. The second assumption is that the analysis is not about everything that is produced and used; it is only about

---

[1] For an introduction to the economics of Marx see: Mandel (1974), Nentjes (1983), Hegelund and Hebert (1990), and Backhouse (2002). For the original text see Marx (1872).

commodities, which are goods produced for sale on the market. In the early period of manhood every economic activity was focused on the production of goods for one's own use. With the emergence of markets, merchants and traders became the mediators who made markets function well. With the introduction of factories, workers were forced to work long hours for the capitalist, which made it impossible for them to have a business of their own.

Now the analysis of the production process in a capitalist economy runs as follows. Capitalists take the initiative and buy investment goods, such as machines and buildings, and hire labour power. These two sorts of production factors are called *productive capital*. In the production process the inputs are transformed into outputs in the form of commodities. When these commodities are sold on the market, capitalists receive money. After having paid the workers, the capitalist hope for profits as high as possible. In Figure 7.1 we have pictured this production process.

We see that the labour power, which is hired, produces the commodities. Marx expresses the value of a commodity in terms of the average labour time needed for the production of one commodity. We also see that the capitalist is paying the workers for their labour: the wage rate (w) is the amount of money per unit of labour time. Because there is almost always an excess of supply on the labour market, capitalists can pay the lowest wage possible, which is the subsistence wage. This amount of money is necessary for the worker to revitalize himself and be able to work the next day. There is a marked difference between the value produced by the worker and the wage, which is called *surplus value*. The ratio of surplus value and the productive capital is called the *rate of exploitation*.

For Marx, technological progress is the main factor that makes economic growth possible. Capitalists compete with each other by investing ever larger amounts of capital in physical capital (accumulation). The larger the scale of production the lower the average total costs, which makes it possible for larger firms to out-compete smaller ones (concentration). The capital intensity (K/N) as well as the capital-output ratio (K/X) are structurally rising. Although labour exploitation is the source of profits, Marx assumes that capitalists are constantly trying to substitute K for N. Nentjes (1983) shows that if capital intensity grows faster than labour productivity, the profit rate will show a structural

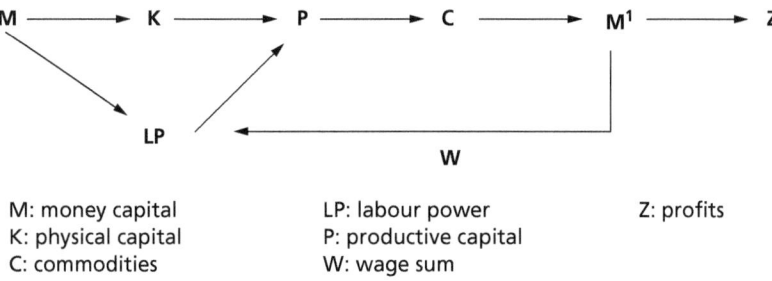

M: money capital   LP: labour power   Z: profits
K: physical capital   P: productive capital
C: commodities   W: wage sum

Figure 7.1. Capitalist Production Process

decline. The following definition equation shows this result. The wage rate is assumed to be constant on the level of subsistence.

$$z = (X - W)/K = (X/N - w)/K/N$$

z = profit rate (volume of profit divided by physical capital stock); X = volume of production and income; W = wage sum; K = volume of physical capital stock; N = volume of employment; w = wage rate.

In Figure 7.1 we have sketched one turnover: from money (M) to productive capital (P) to commodities (C) to money again (M^1). During every turnover the capitalist is receiving money without spending it: $M^1 - W$. This money is idle and can be hoarded or used for the purchase of financial assets or held in the form of a savings account. The money leaks out of circulation, and is a source of disturbance. The workers are assumed to consume all their wage income, but capitalists are searching for a profitable investment for the surplus value, produced by the workers but not received and consumed by them.

In periods of recovery and boom capitalists are inclined to invest most of their financial capital. Profits will rise and so will investments, mostly paid by internal funds. Unfortunately, many capitalists act this way, which creates *over-accumulation*. So long as the increase in production capacity grows with the same rate as the demand for commodities, there is no problem. But in the analysis by Marx the wage rate hardly fluctuates, and the employment shows fluctuations around a declining trend. This means that every boom ends as a result of *under-consumption*, and over time the crises become more severe.

The capitalist economy suffers from a constant threat of under-consumption, which triggers capitalists to permanently search for new markets. On the one hand, they search for markets where they can buy cheap raw materials, and, on the other, they search for new commodity markets, to sell their production. Successors of Marx have based their *imperialism theory* on this search (see Chapter 11.1.2 on Marxian sociology). In order to compare the Marxian view on the labour market with the typical neoclassical view, we can look at Figure 7.2. The supply and demand curves are quite short, reflecting the idea that the fluctuations in the wage rate are relatively small. Supply and demand show a structural shift to the left; demand under the influence of technology and supply as a result of high rates of starvation among the labour population.

Capital markets are characterized by a constant tendency towards excess supply, leading to low interest rates. Even if these markets are close to equilibrium, we must realize that the labour market is far from equilibrium. In Figure 7.3 we have presented the situation on the Marxian capital market in such a way that makes a comparison with neoclassical theory easy: quantity supplied and quantity demanded are functions of the price of capital. The supply and demand function is not elastic with respect to the interest rate, and the equilibrium is not restored by a change in the interest rate, but by shifts of the supply and demand curve, under the pressure of a change in production and income.

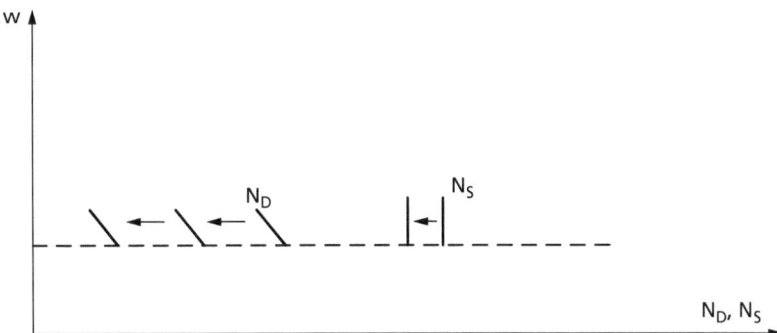

Figure 7.2. Marxian Labour Market

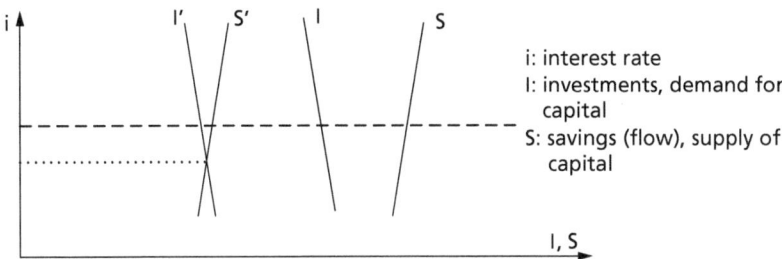

Figure 7.3. Marxian Capital Market

We will summarize a couple of theoretical statements which are logically implied by Marx's analysis.

(1) The law of accumulation and the falling rate of profit.
(2) The law of increasing concentration of capital.
(3) The law of a growing industrial reserve army.
(4) The law of the increasing misery of the proletariat.
(5) The law of increasingly severe crises and depressions.

The fourth law has not been discussed so far; it is only mentioned as the reason for the shift of the labour supply curve to the left. It is directly linked to the third law. We can easily imagine what it means for the neighbourhoods where the proletariat lives if an increasing number are unemployed and without any means of living. Diseases, theft, and alcohol addiction would become the rule rather than the exception; an environment which would make it increasingly difficult for the employed to do their job and raise their children properly.

We have seen that there are significant similarities and differences between the neoclassical analysis of a capitalist economy and the analysis made by Marx. Both are axiomatic and assume that individuals are rational and economically motivated. But Marx assumes that individuals are also socially embedded in the group of people with the same position in the production process. In the early stages of capitalism individuals are grouped along ethnic and religious lines. They are taught to obey superiors and threatened with imprisonment. Later workers become increasingly class conscious and organize themselves to fight for a different mode of production. In the neoclassical theory individuals have no social nature and stay individuals, whatever the circumstances. No culture can change this. The constant human nature in the neoclassical approach implies that history just shows ever-returning cycles around a particular 'equilibrium'. In Marx, history has a beginning and an end. There are no universal and eternal laws of nature except *the law of motion*, which determines the course of history. In our section on evolutionary theory we saw that this approach also interprets reality in a historical way. But evolutionary theory does not assume that the course of history is predetermined. Evolution is a process without a clear goal—philosophically speaking it is not teleological. Marx's analysis, however has. For Marx, history is the story about the social and economic conflict. After the split between the haves and the have-nots has closed at the end of the mature stage of capitalism, we will all live in peace and in affluence forever.

Marx's analysis is of a collectivist nature: the whole of society develops in a particular direction. Individual capitalists and workers have to adjust or will not survive. A worker can only offer his labour power and consume his wage. A capitalist only use his capital in the most profitable way, otherwise he would not survive as a capitalist. In some periods it means that capitalists hold a large part of their capital in the form of money capital. In periods of recession and depression especially they prefer to wait to invest until times have become more promising. *Workers cannot wait*, however. They need their daily meals, and cannot postpone necessary consumption for a couple of years.

Different paradigms and different analysis means different theories. When we compare the five laws of motion with the orthodox and neoclassical laws, we see essential differences. Neoclassical laws are of a universal and eternal nature and are focused on the behaviour of an individual worker, consumer, or investor and intend to describe the economic aspect of human behaviour. Marx's laws of motion describe the development of an economy as a whole through the different stages of development of the capitalist mode of production, being part of the historical development of the whole.

In our chapter about orthodox economics we have seen that neoclassical economists assume that the orthodox laws about the economic aspect can be applied to the real-life economies. After the Second World War they began to empirically test their theories, and in the chapter about orthodox economics we have given a number of examples, showing that the results were not impressive. It triggered these researchers to increasingly add non-economic variables to their equations. Marxist economists pretend to develop empirically testable hypotheses. But, therefore, they should develop their own empirical counterpart. They need statistics about the size of surplus values, average labour time, and average intensity of the efforts made by workers. However, the transformation of Marxist empirics into neoclassical empirics appeared to be a terrible problem. In Section 7.3 we will see that many radical economists today just accept neoclassical statistics and skip typical Marxist constructions, such as the labour value theory.

BOX 7.1 INTERMEZZO: A VERY CONCISE ECONOMIC HISTORY OF CONTINENTAL EUROPE: 1850–1950

Marx wrote his work in the second half of the 19th century. It is not necessary for a theory to be internally and externally consistent in order to be politically important. The dominant neoclassical theory proves this; and so with Marx's theory. Although it was heavily criticized straight from the beginning, it was very influential. For many workers Marx was a hero and a saviour. He described what they experienced as their daily life: scarcity as something created by institutions, the inequality between haves and have-nots, and the lack of choice for workers, who were completely caught by the capitalist mode of production. Marx offered workers a perspective—a frame; there is hope, you must unite and fight, and in the end these oppressive institutions will be transformed into institutions which reflect the substantial equality of all men.

Marx was also active in the development of an international network of socialists and communists. This movement organized a couple of Socialist International meetings. One was about the role of the unions versus the role of the political party.[2] The unions should fight for improvement of labour conditions, including social security. The political party should fight for a system of general suffrage, and for the design of a system of social assistance and systems of education and health care accessible for all. A second meeting discussed the issue of revolution versus evolution. The orthodox socialists stuck to the analysis of Marx and strived for a socialist revolution, together with the unions, of course. The so-called revisionists saw possibilities in a step-by-step improvement of the situation. Later they were called social democrats. A third strategic issue was the question of whether a country could strive for transformation in an environment of capitalist countries, or if revolution (or evolution) should take place on an international level.

Most Continental European countries chose a national and reformist strategy, where the political party was seen as the primary organizer of the reform. Political democracy and the step-by-step building up of a welfare state should be the main results of this process. Such a welfare state is built upon the commitment of the government to strive for full employment, full access to health care and education for all, and a social system, which offers people who become old, sick, handicapped, or unemployed the care they need.

When, in 1989, the Berlin Wall broke down and Western socialists discovered that socialist dictatorship had not led to a communist state, the option of a socialist centrally planned economy was off the agenda.

Before we go on with radical economics as it manifests itself today, we will present Box 7.1, showing the practical effects of Marx's economic analysis.

7.3 **Current Radical Economics**

Today radical economists take the hard core of Marx's analysis of exploitation and conflict in a capitalist society and try to develop more realistic analyses of the different types of capitalism and welfare states. Problems related to the labour value theory are barely studied anymore, and the definitions of the concepts that are the basis of the official statistics are accepted.

The radical element consists of the idea that as long as there is a voluminous capitalist sector, government services are constantly threatened. After the Second World

---

[2] The idea that the unions should take the lead in the organization of the revolutionary process is called syndicalism.

War many Western countries introduced elements of a welfare state. This made it difficult to find out whether the stability of the welfare state results from the countervailing power of the government, or whether the capitalist sector is a stable system that must defend itself against too much government intervention. In the 1960s there was a debate between economists from Cambridge, England (in particular Robinson and Pasinetti) and economists from Cambridge, USA (in particular Samuelson and Solow). In the literature the debate is called the *Cambridge Capital Controversy*. As always in a conflict between a dominant and a subordinate party the establishment is hardly aware of the attacks of minorities. But in this case two highly prestigious members of the neoclassical school defended their analyses against attacks by the radical minority. A very short summary of the neoclassical position runs as follows: human nature is economic and rational. As soon as the situation of an individual changes he adjusts by changing quantities and prices of scarce goods in such a way that a new equilibrium has been reached. So every individual is always close to his equilibrium. If we study economic processes on a macro level, we can simply aggregate all the individual actions. So, a macro economy is always close to its equilibrium and prices reflect natural scarcities. This also holds true for scarce production factors such as capital and labour. An economy can be presented as a multi-market model, in which all prices are simultaneously determined.

The radical critique runs as follows. There is not one constant human nature. As long as the mass of the people lives in poverty they are economic, rational, and belong to a group in the same position in the process of production. In the capitalist mode of production, the mass of the people are forced to offer their labour power to capitalists, who hire workers to make their capital profitable. So the 'constant' nature of workers drives them to maximize their wages and the level of employment. But in other modes of production—a welfare state in a period of affluence, for instance—human nature might be different. Then workers might be inspired by good workmanship, for instance. So, the variable 'nature' of humans depends on the historical stage of development of the economy.

Historically, capitalist economies started with a severe inequality in the distribution of productive resources. The labour market is characterized by a fluctuating excess supply, which makes the worker powerless relative to the capitalist. Workers are just commodities, and if the capitalist expects a recovery he invests in his physical capital stock and hires workers. He takes the surplus value as his profit. But after a while the capitalist discovers that many other capitalists have done the same on 'his' market. Over-accumulation means that the profit rates decrease, making the capitalists more cautious. In this way physical capital and profit rates fluctuate strongly, and so with the unemployment rate. But there is no equilibrium at all—just a historical development with sharp fluctuations and structurally decreasing profit rates and increasing amounts of jobless people. Prices are not reflections of natural scarcity; they just show the stop–go actions of capitalists in search for profits. In this historical process the profit rate at time t affects the value of K at time t + 1, which has an effect on the profit rate at time t + 2. If we assume that all markets are—at every moment—close to equilibrium, and we calculate equilibrium values, we need the profit rate to calculate the capital stock, and we need the capital stock to calculate the profit rate. The neoclassical economists solve this problem in a static equilibrium model, in which both endogenous variables are calculated simultaneously. The radical economists blame the neoclassical economists for their ahistorical approach, thereby denying that even the initial distribution of wealth and income is not a reflection of natural scarce capabilities.[3]

There is another problem with the neoclassical theory. If wages are almost constant, while profit rates are constantly fluctuating—one cycle might take many years—the question arises as to whether profit-maximizing capitalists should constantly switch production technique, a phenomenon that cannot be observed empirically, since K cannot be measured independently.

As always in a debate between parties who are unequal in terms of status, although the minority was right—even according to the neoclassical economists in the end—the majority did not change their paradigm, although they recognized the claims of the radical minority.

A very recent contribution to radical economics is Piketty (2014). By presenting an incredibly large number of statistics about income and wealth inequality in many countries and over a very long period of time, he shows that a combination of low growth and increasing inequality is the rule, and the combination of high growth and relatively low inequality—as in the period 1945–1980—is the exception. Piketty focuses especially on the increasing wealth of the top 1 per cent in the Anglo-Saxon world. But Europe is going in the same direction. Over the last few decades we see the emergence of a group of managers who earn super salaries. The savings rate of these salaries is quite high, and these savings are used to finance a rapidly growing capital stock. The inheritance flows are rising now, and mark the beginning of a rentier society.

In his calculations Piketty focuses on economic capital that is tradable. Since human capital is not tradable—except in societies where slavery still exists—it is not part of his concept of 'capital'. Also, public capital, whether it is tradable or not, is excluded from the figures.

His interpretation of the low growth–high inequality combination is based on a couple of 'laws':

(1) His first fundamental law of capitalism states that the capital share in income is equal to the rate of return on capital multiplied by the capital income ratio. However, it is easy to see that this is not a law at all; it is just an equation, which is true by definition (later in the book he recognizes this mistake, but does not correct it).

---

[3] Piketty (2014) considers the Cambridge Controversy to be a minor point. He states that the neoclassical economists increasingly admitted that there are short-term disequilibria, thus differing from the heterodox view, which stresses the long-run development to be a difference in degree rather than in principle. In this chapter we have explained that there is a methodological difference between the two strands, which is very important. Cambridge (USA) uses logical time when analysing the difference between short-term and long-term analysis in the context of an equilibrium analysis. Cambridge (UK), however, uses historical time in a historical context. So the USA economists assume that short-run disequilibria do not have an important effect on long-term equilibrium values. In the historical time analysis long term is just a time sequence of short-term actions. Piketty ignores this major difference.

(2) His second fundamental law of capitalism states that the capital income ratio is equal to the savings rate divided by the growth rate of output and income. In Chapter 5 we saw that neoclassical growth theory, in which the neoclassical savings function is replaced by a simple Keynesian savings function, gives the same equation, which holds in case of goods market equilibrium. Although Piketty interprets this equation as a long-term law of capitalism—more precisely an asymptotic law—it does not sound very historical. In the neoclassical theory, goods market equilibrium has already been reached in the short term. But Piketty states that an adjustment of the capital income ratio to changes in the savings rate and in the growth rate of output and income takes several decades. Apparently, production technology is hardly flexible. It is important to see that the model used to deduct this 'fundamental law' of capitalism is of a ceteris paribus type. Important social, political, and institutional developments are not taken into account.

(3) The law of cumulative growth states that even a low annual growth rate over a very long period of time gives rise to considerable progress. This law is of an arithmetic type. In mainstream textbooks we find comparisons between two families, the Spends and the Thrifts. They have the same income, but the first family has a low savings rate, while the other has a relatively high savings rate. Within a few decades the difference in wealth is impressive.

All these laws culminate in one essential formula: capitalism is characterized by r > g, whereby r is the rate of return on capital and g is the rate of growth of output and income. Since r reflects the rate of growth of K, r > g logically implies that K/X is growing. In other words, capital productivity is decreasing. According to Marx and Piketty it means the beginning of the end of the capitalist system. Economic growth is a necessity. We have to intervene in the system so as to make it not only just, but sustainable. Piketty proposes a global wealth tax, or a European wealth tax, as a start of a necessary transformation of the global economic system. His contributions trigger the following comments.

In the first place, it remains to be seen whether large market disequilibria can only be tackled by a (global) tax. The financial crisis 2008 has taken so much time to be solved as a result of bad European budget policies. In the future we could try to convince the G-20 to coordinate global effective demand policies so as to reduce the depth of the depression. In the second place, we can doubt whether a structural increase of the capital income ratio makes a free market economic system unstable if it is stabilized by financial regulation and effective demand policies. Suppose that many rich countries strive for zero economic growth on ecological grounds. Growing amounts of saving lead to very low interest rates. It means that the rate of return on capital can be very low as well—it should just reflect a kind of risk premium. It is even thinkable that the value of capital may shrink, because the opportunity costs might even be lower. The macro wage rate can remain constant or decrease a little—this is not a problem, when taken from a macroeconomic perspective. Technological progress leads to a structural increase in labour productivity, which creates the room for a structural increase in the capital share. If rich countries become increasingly characterized by a growing number of part-timers, there is even more room for increases in capital productivity.

In the third place, besides accumulation the statistics show also a process of concentration of wealth. As long as there is a low-income class, severe inequality is a social problem. Unfortunately, the analysis does not include mental and social relationships, and cannot, therefore, say anything about the effectiveness of measures taken by private, collective, and public agents. At one point Piketty discusses a psychological/sociological phenomenon, which is the time preference of agents. But he considers—without argumentation—this as too simple a solution for the problem of inequality. If agents in the world of mergers and acquisitions and in the world of finance were operating on a longer-term perspective, it would reduce the magnitude of fluctuations in many variables, such as share prices and bonuses for top managers.

In the fourth place, Piketty concludes from the data that a small group of top managers earn top salaries, including huge bonuses. Quite often they are alumni from prestigious universities in the USA and UK, and form well-functioning networks with each other. They are highly linked-in, so to speak. In this case we can understand the functioning of the top manager markets only from a sociological perspective. In Chapter 13 we will give an overview of sociological market theory (Section 13.3.4).

In the fifth place, Piketty links growing inequality with the capitalist system. So, (partial) expropriation of privately owned (productive) resources might counter this development. From sociology we know, however, that in every societal system there is a tendency towards growing inequality—including in terms of rights and duties. The iron law of Michels as well as the elite theory of Pareto argue in these terms (see Section 13.2.2). According to Pareto—the same person who became well-known in orthodox economics for his contributions to welfare economics—persons are driven to become members of an elite who dominate organizations and societies at large. They thereby use so-called justifying ideologies so as to convince the rank and file that inequality is to their advantage. So, also in command economies there will be a drive from democracy to oligarchy, ending up with severe inequalities in the spheres of income and wealth. It means that we have to develop analyses of economic systems in which the economic aspect is integrated with analyses of the psychic and social aspects. Otherwise, we simply don't know why inequality is bad (or not), nor how it affects the performance of societies.

In the sixth place, Piketty rejects the isolation of economics from other social sciences. It can advance only in conjunction with them. The social sciences know too little to waste time on foolish disciplinary squabbles. As I have argued in Chapters 2 and 4, integration of disciplines can only take place when a scientist carefully defines his concepts; in this case concepts such as economic, social, psychic, rational, and political. If not, he lacks a scope through which he looks at the empirical part of reality. If we want to interpret the enormous amount of important statistics, as presented by Piketty, we should develop such a multidisciplinary framework of interpretation and analysis first.

* * *

For radical economists, a main task for the government is to function as a countervailing power in such a way that the whole of the economy is a stable system (Saros, 2008). An important assumption is that, without the stabilizing influence of the government, the capitalist free market sector stagnates, and recessions and depressions will often occur. But individual capitalists are driven to maximize their free space to do business. Their minds are framed by the neoclassical idea that a free market economy is a stable system. It is relevant to ask what the views of the employers' organizations are. In the Netherlands there is one organization that represents a very large portion of the companies (VNO/NCW). The ideology of this institution is very moderate. The leadership accepts the idea of a moderate welfare state, and just fights for enough freedom for the companies to serve their interests and flourish. In other words, they search, together with the union movement, for a balance between market and government. Scandinavia is a paradise when it comes to social peace and an egalitarian distribution of income, without destroying the capitalist part of the economy. But in many other countries with a large free market sector employers' organizations and unions are still involved in a social conflict, although Labour has had some success in the design of some elements of the welfare state (Mediterranean Europe, for instance). The focus of the radicals is about the unequal distribution of wealth and income and on the lack of autonomy for the individual worker, who cannot voluntarily choose whether or not to accept the labour conditions.

Bowles and Gintis (2011) disagree with the neoclassical economists in their emphasis on the selfish character of human beings. According to this paradigm every contact between people is of a competitive nature. Even marriages are considered as a contractual relationship, in which both partners are constantly calculating the costs and benefits of their relationship. Bowles and Gintis's research (2011) is focused on the cooperative nature of a human being. If we are able to develop institutions that trigger our sense of cooperation, we will be able to improve the efficiency as well the justice of our system. Many people who belong to the lowest class are negatively triggered. The incentives to cooperate are so weak that they remain in a vicious circle. Unskilled, drug-addicted young persons, not living in a family context anymore, are seduced into finding their living in the black sector. What positive incentives can the community offer these people, who are socially embedded in a criminal scene, to shift from a destructive to a more constructive attitude towards their Selves and towards society at large? So with people from the upper class: many are socially and culturally embedded in such a way that they are highly involved in the capitalist case. In this way a capitalist firm remains a platform of social conflict. The shareholders, quite often investor funds, the members of the Board and the members of the Council of Supervision regularly consult each other, thereby developing identical frames, and see the rank and file as something which must be controlled rather than as a source of information and motivation for the benefit of the company as a whole. The Anglo-Saxon liberal idea of shareholders being the only stakeholders makes the company into a cash cow for the shareholders. If we stress the cooperative nature of humans, companies that are considered to be a meeting point for several stakeholders will be more efficient in the end. The modern credo in this respect is: people, profit, and planet. It stresses the idea that free market firms are areas of cooperation between different interests in society. Of course, these firms need profits so as to be able to continue their business. But in many markets competition is not so fierce and people and planet can really play a role, especially if consumers become increasingly conscious of the conditions under which their consumption goods are produced.

Cohen (1995) stresses the moral aspect of capitalism, and especially its undemocratic character. Marx was morally aroused by the daily practice of capitalist industrialization, and called the rate of surplus value the exploitation rate. So, capitalism exploits people and is exploiting the planet, which is not the same as exploring it. Where neoclassical theory assumes that every resource has an owner, mostly private owners, the radical view takes a different position. Its historical character means that the analysis starts with a planet which is the habitat of plants and animals. They have not developed a system of private property rights. When humans enter the scene, they are nomads, wandering from one region to another. Later most of the people *settle*, and consider land as a common good, 'owned' by the community that has settled there. History has become a history of economic and social conflict, as in the animal world. Groups put their flag somewhere, enclose the area, and say: from now on this is our property—as if the world is up for grabs. Human history is the story of the permanent flow of conquests. The land, which is the 'property' of the USA, is conquered and taken from the indigenous (Indian) people. The enduring conflict between Israel and Palestine started in this way: some Jewish settlers wanted to buy a piece of land, but the land was common ground and was not for sale. Then Jewish settlers just started their business there. Later the state of Israel was proclaimed, and considered to be the legitimate owner of a particular area—even by the United Nations. Also the North and the South Pole are attractive areas to be occupied by states. As a last example we mention a group of unpopulated islands between Japan and China. Both countries claim authority over these islands. The Japanese conjecture the presence of unexploited raw materials close to the islands, and try to give their stagnating economy a new impulse by becoming active in this contested region (2012–13): a typical aggressive act necessary to save a capitalist economy. Another and possibly more effective method might be to discuss the history of the countries, which were occupied by the Japanese during the Second World War. If Japan is able to make true peace, which is more than an armistice, maybe in the future more East Asians might buy Japanese cars and other manufacturing products. The radical mission is how to develop economic institutions that are not aggressive. Full-fledged capitalist structures always create unequal trade relations. Multinational companies, having the knowledge and the skills to explore and exploit the soil, the water, and the air, always have the advantage in their negotiations with poor and unskilled people who 'own' parts of the earth, which might be full of scarce raw materials. And if these people are not willing to sell or hire land to the companies, the contested area becomes a source of social, political, and military conflict.

A last point in this respect is the place for new generations. If a child is born into a family who belong to the have-nots, he will be caught in that position. Who will invest in his upbringing and education? If capitalism rules the world, and all space is already occupied by some groups, there is no place in our global society for poor newcomers anymore. If people attach value to democracy, capitalism should not rule the world.

Cohen also stresses the importance of what he calls worker autonomy. Marx saw a difference between economic relations and human relations. He saw that capitalism stresses the economic aspect, thereby ignoring the human aspect. Labour is seen as a commodity, and whether labour service means that a group of workers must make a series of ice creams or that women are prostitutes, or children also work ten hours per day, does not make any difference—it is just a market transaction, which leads to profits. A second problem is the fact that workers are increasingly just chains in a system, which produces as much as possible. Far-reaching specialization leads to boring activities, which are quite routinized, until machines take over these activities. Then workers must practise new skills and learn to routinize different but still boring activities. For a worker it is good not to think about the activity—just do the routine. According to Marx, this leads to the *alienation* of the workers. Their true nature cannot be developed in such an environment. Essentially, each worker wants to develop his talents, and enjoy the fruits of it. But the capitalist system requires a completely different attitude.

Hodgson (2001) blames Marx for his neglect of a well-formulated theory of transition from one mode of production to a better one. There is a structural development of rising unemployment and declining profit rates, making an increasing number of workers conscious of the position of their class. Communist unions and political parties should closely cooperate in their attempt to overthrow the government. The young Marx was an activist who wanted to help accelerate the transition. But when Marx wrote his *Das Kapital*, he based his analyses and theories on a deterministic description of the coming of a wind of change. Marx's theory is unclear with regard to the relationship between conscious action and the predetermined character of history.

Today, radical economists have drawn the conclusion that Marx's analysis of capitalism has changed our social and economic reality. To avoid the apocalypse many individuals and organizations have developed institutions to make the capitalist system more stable. Up to 1989 many people in the West were still communist, and strove for a system of central planning. But when the Berlin Wall came down and the daily reality of people living under socialist dictatorship became clear, central planning was not an option anymore. A different question is whether governments can stimulate or limit private spending and investments in particular.

Two big issues remain, and deserve the attention of radical thinkers. In the first place, the capitalist mode of production produces ever-growing *inequality* in income and wealth. In the second place, capitalism considers humans as commodities, which means that *human dignity is at stake*. With respect to the first problem two groups of economists worked on this issue. Under the flag of *analytical Marxism* a group of people wanted to approach capitalism in concepts borrowed from neoclassical economics (Elster, 1998; Van Parijs, 1996). Actors in the economy—individuals as well as groups—are economic and rational. Without typical Marxist concepts such as dialectical materialism and forces of production, they come to the conclusion that a capitalist economy does not offer a decent living for everyone. Democracy requires substantial equality of all people, and therefore the community, represented by the government, ought to develop countervailing systems. One of the ideas is the introduction of a basic income. It means that every citizen receives a minimum income from the state, enough to live at a subsistence level. Every person who wants to have additional income can search for a job. People who don't have the qualifications for that—too old or too handicapped—must accept that this is an impossibility for them. This policy leads to a more egalitarian society, where hardly anybody will end up as homeless.

Another group operates under the flag of *market socialism*. They are searching for solutions in which the advantages of a market are combined with elementary socialist axioms, such as substantial equality. They see the core problem of capitalism as the shareholders being the owners and most important controllers of the firm. A capitalist firm is meant to maximize profits and workers are just instruments in the hands of the capitalists, who do not care about the workers' human dignity. This governance system should be changed fundamentally, without losing the informational role of the market. In Continental Europe different sorts of stakeholder models have been developed so as to protect the firms from Anglo-Saxon short-term shareholder value influences.

A third group is working on the issue of human dignity, and is primarily about *worker autonomy on the firm level*. In large organizations especially, bureaucratic structures bridge the gap between the top and the rank and file. This makes it difficult for workers to bear any responsibility, and to think about innovations in the products and in production processes. Large organizations promote cheating behaviour. Budgets are large, and the top employees earn high salaries and give each other interesting options and bonuses. Why not use some resources for goals other than firm goals? Endeburg (1998) and Romme (1999) have done research with respect to the idea of *self-management* of teams and organizations. Typical psychological concepts, such as actual Self, true Self, and willpower, can also be applied to teams and organizations. *Sociocratic methods* are developed to manage processes of consultation and decision-making. They applied these methods to learning processes in university as well as higher vocational education. (See the Box 6.1 in Chapter 6.) But in capitalist enterprises this idea was also successfully implemented.

In Figure 7.4 we have pictured the cyclical and structural development of a capitalist economy, be it the economy of a country, a region such as the European Union, or the global economy. The picture shows the destruction of a capitalist system. Potential employment refers to the employment that a modern socialist economy should have offered people, making it possible for them to live a decent life. So the difference with the

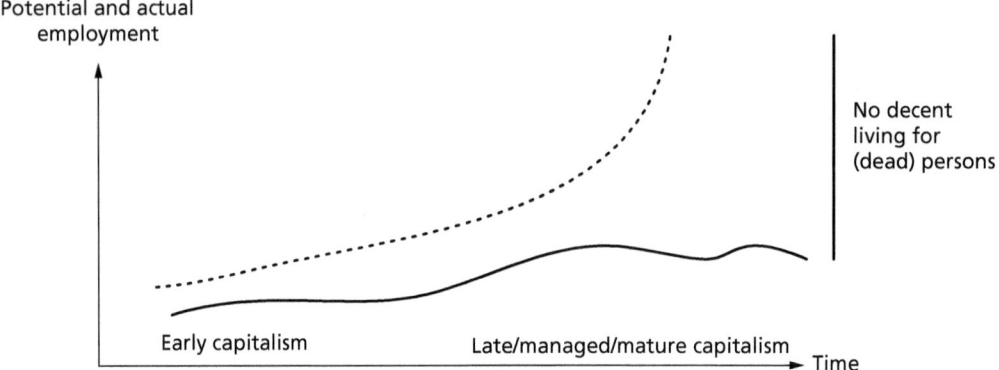

Figure 7.4. Increasing Difference between Actual Employment and Potential Employment

actual employment shows the number of jobs and people who are unemployed plus the people who died because of a lack of opportunities. In the early stage of capitalism competitive markets are the rule. There is unemployment, and it fluctuates around an average. In later stages the fluctuations become stronger and unemployment is structurally higher. Workers are subject to increasing pressure from capitalists to work as machines.[4] There are no social services for the unemployed. This is the situation described and explained by Marx. Now we all know that a centrally planned economy does not lead to true democracy. Therefore, the big issue for radical economists is how to tame the driving forces of capital. In Figure 7.5 we have pictured the relationship between capital on the one hand, and different realms of society on the other.

According to Marx, the economy is the sector which determines the way other sectors of society are functioning. So, capitalists are powerful enough to determine governmental action. They dominate the programmes of research and education at universities, and the main task of the government is to protect private property; a task which is paid by the population as a whole.

The course of history after 1850, however, shows a development which might not be in line with Marx's prophecies. Marxist economists, however, explain all these developments in the realm of social security and assistance, education, and health care as matters which continue the existence of capitalism with its profit maximization at the cost of decent worker compensation. The institution of marketing appears a very successful attempt to frame the minds of people and let them believe that shopping and constantly buying new products is more than just fun. Products shape a person's identity and signal his status (Sheehan, 2010). The economic developments in the last few decades show that

---

[4] As a matter of illustration, I give the following example. At a Dutch university, also a large and bureaucratic organization, workers are not allowed to fix a very small problem of electric-power failure. They must wait for a day or so, until the central facility service has fixed the problem. Meanwhile, nobody can do his work. So, even if the government takes over tasks from capitalist firms the problem of alienation cannot be solved without changing the culture and structure of the organization.

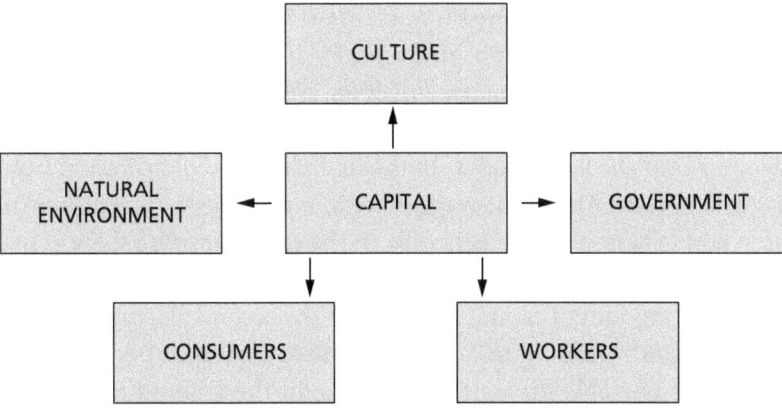

Figure 7.5. A Capitalist Economy Means a Capitalist Society

the whole idea of a welfare state is just a temporary interval, resulting from a temporarily successful full employment policy in a couple of north European countries. In Section 7.4 we will discuss a few economists who have given a radical explanation of the crisis of 2006–2008 and its far-reaching consequences.

7.4 **A Radical View of the Financial Crisis 2008**

Neoclassical economists assume that a free market economy is a stable system, and all problems in the actual economy result from market-alien elements, such as governments and unions, which are backed by legislation. Radical economists take the opposite position and assume that a capitalist economy is an unstable system, and all problems result from a lack of countervailing powers, such as governments and unions.

Globalization has taken place on a scale that is unique in history. From the 1970s onwards the mobility of goods, capital, and labour has increased significantly. The financial markets especially are almost completely globalized now. It means that private financial institutions, such as banks, pension funds, investor funds, and new institutions, such as hedge funds and private equity, are operating on the global level in a professional and sophisticated way. These developments imply that many firms all over the world are subject to the scrutiny of financial experts. Huge amounts of money are constantly moving around in search for higher profits. On the labour markets increasing flows of workers are searching for a job: in many countries many ethnicities are at work. Even the goods markets are globalized to an extent which is unique. Globalization means that both factor markets are characterized by excess supplies, which put a downward pressure on the wage and the profit rate. Meanwhile the capital stock is growing strongly.

According to the radical theory, the situation in the first decade of the 21st century was ripe for the next crash and depression. Huffschmid (2007) analyses the main forces that are responsible for the crisis which started in 2008, and which should therefore be regulated. According to him there are two reasons why the global stock of financial assets has grown so strongly over the last decades. In the first place, a redistribution from poor to rich has taken place. A decline in the wage share in many Western countries implied an increase in the profit share (or more generally in the capital income share).[5] Because the savings rate of capitalists is significantly higher than that of workers, this redistribution has led to a growing amount of capital supplied. In the second place, pension premiums have grown significantly, leading to large amounts of capital in pension funds. These developments are responsible for a strong increase in the amount of global capital in search of a profitable investment.

The 1980s and 1990s were characterized by strong deregulation of financial markets, and new types of funds with aggressive strategies were developed. In the first place, so-called *private equity funds*, which buy non-quoted firms, restructure them, and sell them within a period of two to seven years. In the second place, so-called *hedge funds*, which buy high-profit–high-risk assets in quoted stocks. Both strategies are aggressive: very rich funds are threatening firms by warning them not to withstand their offers. Every firm knows that, in such a case, much publicity, generated by the rich fund, might create a self-fulfilling prophecy: shareholders will be willing to sell their shares for attractive prices. After a fund has bought the firm they split it up in several pieces, cut large amounts of debt into some pieces, and declare them bankrupt. What is left gets a new leadership—people whose minds are framed by Anglo-Saxon views on governance.

More generally, we can say that the financial world has become an unstable system. Funds promise capital suppliers high profitability, and try to realize this by activities that must be profitable in the short run. Speculation on the asset markets, including real estate, has become a popular activity. Funds themselves are borrowing much credit from banks, thereby accepting very low solvability ratios; in other words, using *high leverage*. Many funds have their headquarters located offshore, which makes supervision by official controllers, such as central banks and other authorities, difficult. Taken together, Huffschmid comes to the conclusion (2007) that a global power shift has taken place— from labour to capital—making the global economy very unstable.

After the crash Crotty (2009) came up with more or less the same explanation. He stresses the role of the deregulation of financial markets, which had led to a *fragile system* characterized by:

(1) *Lack of transparency*—political control could not be developed along with the integration of the global market; actually all countries should cooperate so as to close all escape routes.

---

[5] Profit share is defined as Z/X, while the profit rate is defined as Z/K, where Z is the amount of profit, X the volume of production or income, and K the volume of the physical capital stock. So, increasing profit shares are not contradictory to declining profit rates.

(2) *Perverse incentives*—as soon as parties involved in a transaction conclude a contract in which a firm is taken over, for instance, they give themselves fees and bonuses. They do not wait until it has become clear whether the contract improves the quality of the business over a longer period.

(3) *Excessive risk*—taken from the perspective of an individual bank or fund, the acceptance of excessive risk for the intermediate and long run is economic and rational. Every other market participant is forced to also take excessive risk because of fierce competition. This is exactly how free markets operate.

(4) *Liquidity is a waste*—every actor operating on a competitive market is motivated to reduce liquidity as much as possible. Every form other than cash gives a reward. So, it is always beneficial to hold wealth in the form of short- or medium-term financial paper rather than cash.

(5) *Contagion*—the idea behind mergers and acquisitions is that bigger is better; the reason is simple: the economic interests of capitalists and groups of lawyers, accountants, and bankers involved in big deals are highly dependent on size. Moreover, very big banks do not only compete with each other; they also cooperate with each other every day, because their customers do business with each other. In this way the system as a whole is dependent on big institutions. It creates a situation of banks, insurance companies, and funds which are too big to fail and too big to save.[6] A system with hardly any buffer is very fragile. One small incident can create a fatal series of incidents.

The fact that these developments have been described by radical economists quite accurately is remarkable. Looking back we can see that, in the period 1973–2013, the wage share significantly decreased in OECD (Organisation for Economic Co-operation and Development) areas, and especially in the USA, and that a redistribution has taken place from poor to rich. Peterson (1994) has already shown that a silent depression has taken hold, affecting four out of five American families. A remarkable fall in the investment in infrastructure and the tax policies of the Reagan Administration were the beginning of this development in the wrong direction.

The image of Americans is that of big spenders—workers who consume more than they can afford, leading to ever-increasing consumer credit loans. When the radical analysis says that the US economy suffers from under-consumption, mainstream economists react by laughing rather than by serious comment. But, according to the radical analysis, higher wages would have given workers the opportunity to buy the necessary goods without so much consumer credit. It would stimulate physical investments rather than speculative bubble-creating trades in financial assets. The capitalist system forces people to act as they do. A systemic change would create more stability, which would solve problems of government budget and balance of payments. In the financial world the change in system must lead to a control of the banks and other financial institutions.

---

[6] The terms 'too big to fail' and 'too big to save' are mine, not Crotty's.

The central banks should give up their independence from the government, since this independence makes them a defender of the interests of capitalist institutions.

In Section 7.5 we draw a number of conclusions.

7.5 Conclusion

Radical economics is based on socialist philosophy, which has as its principle the substantial equality of men. Persons might have very different properties—one is highly talented, while another is severely handicapped—but on the level of substance (see Chapter 2) we are all equal. It means that we must formulate a couple of inalienable human rights and duties which hold for every person. As long as there is affluence of resources while productive resources are common property, there are no conflicts in society. In early and primitive times this situation was realized. But when scarcity of resources grew, and people began to settle and to 'privatize' productive resources, history began to be, and is still, characterized by a conflict between the haves and the have-nots. On the basis of this paradigm Marx analysed the historical dynamics of capitalism. In line with the orthodox economic paradigm he assumed individuals to be economic and rational. But, in contrast to this view, he also considered individuals to be social, in the sense of being members of a group of people with a similar position in the production process. He considered historical dynamics to be a description of a process of conflicts between two parties. The party that builds its power on the latest skills with respect to production techniques always turns out to be the winner. This means that technological progress is the primary source of economic growth. In the capitalist system the conflict is between capitalists (the haves) and workers (the have-nots). Marx's analysis shows that, under particular conditions, the capitalist system destroys itself. At the beginning of the system there is excess supply on the labour as well as the capital market. Over time both excesses grow in size. So, compared with the orthodox analysis, which assumes that we are always close to equilibrium on all markets, radical economics offers a typical *disequilibrium analysis*. While orthodoxy formulates laws of a universal and eternal nature, reflecting the economic aspect of life, Marx formulates a series of laws of a historical nature: they describe the historical dynamics of the capitalist production process. The system ends in misery, and will be transformed into a new mode of production. Since the problem of scarcity has been solved, there will be no clashes between haves and have-nots anymore.

At several points Marx's analysis appeared to be problematic. His labour value theory especially made empirical testing of his theories difficult, if not impossible. Another problem concerns the possibility of a structurally falling rate of profit. It is not difficult to formulate the conditions under which capitalism will not survive. But because of the difficulty of measuring the value of the capital stock, establishing whether or not capitalism can survive remains problematic.

Marx's analysis appeared very attractive to many people, and challenged the establishment of the haves. It motivated the have-nots to organize themselves, and to help history to get to its end. It created fear in capitalist circles and it reminded Christian confessionals of their own ideas about social justice. All these incentives created a continuing process of reform of the capitalist system into something different. It meant that reality changed; a typical example of the transitivity of reality and an interesting illustration of historical dynamics.

Radical economics, as it functions today, is highly influenced by the idea that the labour value theory is not a practical doctrine, and that a centrally planned economy functions badly because of insurmountable problems of information and motivation. It focuses on the question of how a capitalist free market economy can be stabilized by the development of countervailing powers. The main threat to its stability comes from the categorical income distribution, which tends to structurally squeeze the wage share. Both the capital and the labour market tend to increase excess supplies. In Marx's analysis the non-economic sectors are strongly influenced by the typical capitalist culture of profit maximization in the economy. Marx did not see any development in the non-economic sectors, which could lead to a more balanced relationship between sectors. In Chapter 11 we will see that sociological neo-Marxists work on this issue, leading to very different results. Economists stick to the necessity of changing the income distribution, and to regulating markets. In a last section we discussed the contributions of radical economists to the debate about the current crisis. We saw that their analyses all lead to policy recommendations in terms of structural change by means of legislation.

When we look critically at the contributions of Marx and his successors, their typical methodological collectivistic approach lacks an explicitly formulated micro-foundation. Human 'nature' might be dependent on the context in which humans operate. Nevertheless, it is still important to formulate this connection between circumstances and human motivation explicitly. Marx makes a distinction between economic and human relations. But his analysis is only about the economic relations. The increase in class consciousness, and the consequences of it for the ultimate revolution, are unclear. In this respect it is important to note that the economic history in Western Europe shows a different course. So with the role of the human psyche in the story of capitalism—by assuming rationality of individuals and economic groups, psychology is ignored. The implication of this omission is that only structural or systemic change can lead to improvement. The bare micro fact that persons and small groups can learn from a new view or paradigm and begin to look at their daily reality in a different way is ignored as well. However, this reframing of important parties might be the essence of historical dynamics. In Chapter 10, we will see that humans are strongly motivated to withstand reframing if it means a strong loss of face. The current crisis is one big demonstration of the irrationality of people: neoclassically framed minds have great difficulty in recognizing that their frame was a main cause of the systematic misinterpretation of economic processes.

Marx distinguished human relations, but he forgot to analyse the negative side of sociality: whatever the context, humans are motivated to rival 'the other'. For Marx, status battles might take place, but they are completely endogenous, which means that they are always triggered by economic conflicts, and not the other way around. Therefore, they have no independent effect on historical economic development.

A last point of critique is the following. Marx analyses capitalists, who are constantly maximizing their profits. Marx also stresses the importance of technological progress. But the role of the entrepreneur is not highlighted. In Chapter 6, we saw that Schumpeter makes the entrepreneur the hero of the capitalist system. He is the inventor and innovator of products and production processes. The role of an individual, who is different to other individuals, is pivotal. The entrepreneur is the true agent of change. But this idea can also be applied to non-economic sectors: the political, the cultural, the environmental, and the spiritual entrepreneur, offering society examples that could be followed. In other words, historical change needs individuals who make a difference.

In Chapter 8 we will discuss post-Keynesian economics.

8 Post-Keynesian Economics

8.1 Introduction

This school of thought is the result of work by economists who take Keynes as their starting point, and aim at improving his theory and applying it to the current stage of development of modern capitalist economies.[1] Keynes' work is a reaction to the classical theory, which we now call neoclassical macroeconomics. Neoclassical theory could not explain the Great Depression of the 1930s. Keynes did not agree with the axiomatic approach of the classical economists, and developed an analysis with a different foundation. His main thesis is that a free market economy, once in a depression, has no mechanism to bring the system back to equilibrium. In Section 8.2 we will discuss the philosophical principles applied by Keynes. In contrast to the orthodox and neoclassical approach, which is based on the principles of methodological individualism, Keynes' analysis is based on the principles of methodological collectivism. Behaviour of individuals is explained by their economic situation, which results from developments in the whole of the economy. In Section 8.3 we will show the basic elements of the analysis, deducted from his collectivist paradigm. This analysis will be compared with the neoclassical analysis. In this way we will show that wage rigidity is *not* the reason for eventual persistent unemployment. In Section 8.4 we will present the reaction of the neoclassical school to Keynes' contributions. Some economists tried to bring Keynes within the Walrasian general equilibrium framework, and showed that his 'General Theory' is about a special case. Others did the same and showed that the General Theory is just about the short run. The New Classical Economic School presented Keynes' work as an unsuccessful attack on the sound principles of homo oeconomicus. Their analyses show that, in the economic world also, actors may be confronted with high levels of voluntary search unemployment, and with bubbles in the world of asset markets. In Section 8.5 we discuss the ideas of Leijonhufvud, who constructed a theory of corridors. If the economy is in a stage that is characterized by a high level of employment and actors are not negative about the future, the system appears stable. However, if the level of employment is quite low, and actors are pessimistic about the future, the system does not have an equilibrium-restoring mechanism. This situation might turn out to be socially unacceptable, and therefore not stable. In Section 8.6 we deal with what is called new Keynesian economics. In this corner economists accept that a free market

---

[1] Skidelsky (2009) gives a good introduction to Keynes' thinking.

economy is not a stable system and can show enduring unemployment. But, in contrast to Keynes, they search for a micro-foundation able to explain this disequilibrium on the labour market. They try to explain rigidity of wages and of interest rates, suggesting that such rigidity is enough to explain equilibrium unemployment. In Section 8.7 we discuss the analyses made by post-Keynesians, a name which was coined by Eichner and Kregel (1975). They laid a foundation for a macro- and micro-analysis on the basis of Keynes' methodology. Its starting point is a situation in which actors are *uncertain about the future*, while knowing what happened in the past. In principle every market is in disequilibrium, which means that there is unemployment and less than full use of production capacity. But in their analysis the term (dis)equilibrium is unpopular, since it suggests that people know at every moment the so-called equilibrium values, which are assumed to be constant. In real life, however, nobody has a clear supply and demand picture of their situation in mind. Important contributions about financial markets and about labour and goods markets, offered by economists, such as Kregel, Minsky, Akerlof, Shiller, and Dow are discussed. In Section 8.8 we draw a number of conclusions with respect to the question of whether post-Keynesian economics offers a satisfying alternative to the neoclassical mainstream approach.

8.2 The Methodology of Keynes

Keynes criticized the methodology of the neoclassical approach in many respects. As a reminder we present a shortlist of its main characteristics (see also Jespersen, 2009). The neoclassical ontology says that the world is a closed system, which is completely determined by a few mechanisms. More specifically, the economic world is determined by the market mechanism that always and everywhere coordinates the decisions of economic and rational actors. In simple models actors have perfect information, including about the future. In more sophisticated models information about the future is imperfect. So, actors always run the risk of expectations that may not be completely realized. Fortunately, there are markets where people can 'sell' their risk, and buy security. Actually, they live in a stochastic world. Since this world is quite stable and predictable, risks can be calculated. Economic and rational risk lovers like to gamble, while risk averters like to minimize the risk they run as much as possible. In this way, every actor is always close to his optimum.

Keynes' methodology is very different. He considers the world to be an open system, which has an organic rather than a mechanic character. Actors are badly informed, especially about the future. This makes it difficult for them to be rational. Emotions (*animal spirits*) take control over a person. In some periods actors are quite optimistic with respect to profitable opportunities. In other periods, however, they are quite pessimistic, making them more passive.

While the neoclassical methodology takes the human nature of an actor as a constant—always economic and rational—Keynes founds his approach on the characteristics of an economy as a whole. He assumes that human nature adjusts to its environment, which is the state of the economy. While neoclassical theory pretends to produce universal and eternal laws, such as the law of supply and demand, Keynes focuses his analytical work on an explanation of a particular situation in the real world. His 'General Theory' is meant to explain why capitalism, as it manifested itself in the Western world in the first half of the 20th century, was an unstable system.[2]

Now we will go into more detail with respect to the concepts 'open system' and 'organic system'. As we said already, an open system means that reality is not a completely determined whole. Our knowledge is far from complete, and many elements and relationships are simply unknown. We don't even know what we do not know. At any time we can be surprised. A tsunami might unite a particular group of people and solve their social conflicts, and a violent dictator might become a benevolent dictator overnight. This means that people should always be prepared to face completely different and difficult situations. If all actors frame the world according to neoclassical principles, the world system becomes very fragile, and does not take negative surprises into account.

An organic system is the opposite of a mechanic system. While this system is characterized by constant elements and relationships, an organic system consists of permanently evolving elements and relationships. No person or organization stays the same over time, nor does their relation to other elements. The *organic approach* comes from biology; the human body can be considered as an organism, consisting of a number of organs, which all have their specific function. Let us take the liver as an example. Over time it evolves, which means that some characteristics disappear and others appear and dominate the way the liver functions in the body. If a person is an alcoholic, a medical expert can see how the alcohol has affected the organ. In this way we can describe the history of every element in the world. They emerge, grow, flourish, decline, and die. If we make historical and geographical comparisons, we see that practice and meaning of phenomena are subject to permanent change. If we compare dentist practices across regions and over time, we see an impressive progress has been made in some areas; so with psychiatric services, and computer technology.

Continuing changes in the quality of our reality make it difficult to conduct quantitative research. Reality is fundamentally heterogeneous, and if we want to apply mathematics to describe relationships between constructed entities, we must be aware that these entities are not homogeneous at all. So with the relationships: we might describe them by means of continuous functions, but we simply don't know whether our reality allows us to be described as such.

---

[2] The term 'general' means that the theory is not only about a special case, such as a situation of depression. It holds for all phases of the business cycle, as it manifested itself in the Western world in the first half of the 20th century. When we read about the general equilibrium of Walras, the meaning of the term 'general' is different. There, it means always and everywhere in the economic world, not in the real world.

A real-life example can illustrate this problem. In the Netherlands the government has a group of civil servants who must deliver forecasts with respect to the Dutch economy a few times per year. In election time all political parties can hand in their programme, and the group, called Centraal Planbureau (CPB), calculates the effects of the proposed policies on a series of important variables, such as unemployment, economic growth, and budget deficit over a period of 30 years. In 2010 there were elections, and because of the crisis the issue of large cuts in government expenditures, as required by the European Commission, was the most important issue. It appeared that the Liberal Party, which proposed large cuts and lower social premiums, performed best in terms of employment in 2040. This remarkable result can be explained by the following properties of the econometric model of the CPB model. First, the European Commission required large expenditures from *all* European countries, especially the countries that had introduced the euro as their currency. But the budget cuts of the other European countries were not taken into account. On the contrary, exports were expected to grow relatively fast. Second, the model assumed a relatively large wage elasticity with respect to employment. Although an elasticity is only valid in the case of small changes of the variable in the denominator, the calculations were based on large changes in the labour costs over a very long period. Decreases in private consumption were assumed to be compensated by relatively strong export growth, and eventual union reactions or changes in the political scene in the Netherlands or in other European countries—as a result of enduring wage cuts—were not part of the model. The political effect was that the classical liberal party (VVD) was constantly telling the people that they were the employment creators. This party became the largest for the first time in their existence. A post-Keynesian CPB would never have made such a mess of quantitative methods.

It is difficult to represent an evolving world in numbers. During the 1930s Keynes discussed the role of quantitative methods with Tinbergen, one of the first econometricians. Tinbergen was a socialist and wanted to show that private investments could not be predicted because of their volatile character in a capitalist system. Keynes agreed with the result, but questioned the econometric instrument. According to him, many other relationships might turn out to be unstable too. So, although Keynes was a mathematician by education, he rejected this tool as an important instrument for predicting human behaviour.

Besides the ontological characteristics of reality being open and organic, Keynes criticized the idea of the homo oeconomicus. He did not consider human nature to be a constant, and therefore did not believe it could function as a fixed point of reference or anchor in the explanation of any economic phenomenon. As we have seen in Chapter 2 it is typical for methodological collectivism to take the macro level as the level of explanation, whatever the level of the phenomenon to be analysed. Keynes had a debate on this problem of individualism versus collectivism with Hayek. For Hayek, macroeconomic phenomena are just an aggregation of microeconomic phenomena. Does it make a difference for an unemployed person whether he is one of few or one many people who are unemployed? Every individual has his own unique capacities, and can decide to search for a job, or to start his own business. In many countries people earn their living by just selling oranges from their own garden, or by buying the necessary equipment to become a shoe polisher. Social security systems must not discourage people from taking action. But Keynes disagreed with Hayek's strict individualistic approach, which denies the existence of such a thing as society, whose condition affects the chances of individuals significantly. Hayek recognized a few exceptions of his rule that governments should not intervene. First, he acknowledged the necessity of having a system of property rights which should be guaranteed by the government. Second, he advocated a monetary policy, implemented by a central bank whose independence from the government should be arranged by legislation. Third, Hayek advocated census suffrage: only people older than 40 years of age should have the right to vote, so as to guarantee that the government not intervene in the economic process.

Hayek was Austrian and was asked by the London School of Economics to come to England to organize the resistance against the strong influence of Keynes on the outcomes of policy debates. During the Great Depression Hayek did not offer a satisfactory explanation of the severe decline. Not only goods prices, but also wages, appeared flexible. So government and unions could not be blamed. It took a while before economists, such as Patinkin and Friedman, came up with a neoclassical and monetarist explanation of the Great Depression. Friedman in particular blamed the central banks for not having implemented expansionary monetary policies.

In Section 8.3 we will discuss the economic analysis, as developed by Keynes. Then we will come back to Keynes' position in the debate about the effectiveness of monetary policies in periods of depression.

8.3 The Economic Analysis of Keynes

In Chapter 4 we explained that orthodox economic analysis is about the economic aspect of human life, and not about the real-life economy. Neoclassical economics is an application of orthodox analysis to the real world, which appears to be a problematic strategy. Keynes set himself to analyse the real-world economy; not in an attempt to develop universal and eternal laws, but to find explanations for important economic phenomena in a particular region and during a particular period of time. For Keynes these were the economies in the Western world during the first half of the 20th century. He wanted to explain why economies showed strong fluctuations in variables such as production, employment, inflation or deflation, and government debts.

In contrast to the neoclassical view, Keynes had the idea that a free market economy is an unstable system—an idea he derived from his open and organic system axioms. The natural instability of a free market system makes it necessary for the government to intervene in case of a depression. Because of the dominance of neoclassical thinking, not only among economists, but also among laymen, we will constantly compare his ideas with the familiar neoclassical ones.

The neoclassical approach starts with a statement about a constant human nature—the economic and rational actor—and develops a theory of demand and of supply on this micro-foundation. Every micro-market has its own price mechanism, which guarantees that the market will always be near equilibrium. The picture of the demand and the supply function, with a point of equilibrium where the two curves cross each other, is the most telling expression of the neoclassical approach. It makes it clear that price flexibility is a necessary and sufficient condition for a market to stay close to equilibrium. The conclusion that this also holds for an economy as a whole seems plausible. As soon as we make a dynamic description of a market process, however, we discover that, even in a neoclassical approach, the market mechanism does not only mean a shift along the curves, but also of the curves themselves. If firms and families notice a decrease in their incomes, demand curves shift to the left. If the price mechanism works and prices drop, this has a negative effect on incomes, leading to a further downward shift of the demand curves. Famous neoclassical economists, such as Friedman, bring in positive expectations about the near future. They assume that consumers and investors assume that the decline in their incomes is just temporary, and they do not adjust their spending behaviour. It implies that curves do not shift and the price mechanism functions well. But what if a general decline in incomes is interpreted as the beginning of a period of recession and, possibly, of a depression? Then the shifts of the curves on the goods, the capital, and the labour market do prevent an 'automatic' return to equilibrium. Then consumers and firms prepare themselves for a crisis of at least a couple of years. They save and pay off part of their loans. This is not a mechanic, but an organic, reaction to changes in the general climate of the economy.

Keynes is, besides his organic and open system ideas, also a methodological collectivist. This means that even small changes in the aggregates can affect the general economic climate. If many people were optimistic or even over-optimistic, a small change can affect the mood of many people. They all read the newspapers and use internet to stay up to date. In this way, 'society' can create a downturn, making many people pessimistic, and reduce their spending, for instance. In this way, a small shift triggers a large shift. According to Keynes, a free market economy does not have a mechanism that can turn pessimism into optimism. As long as there are no positive shocks from outside the economic system—the news that Israel and Palestine has reached a peace agreement, for instance—depression maintains its hold.

According to the orthodox analysis, shifts along or of the curve are relatively small and can be ignored. These assumptions are meant to isolate markets from each other, so as to promote the idea that every market can solve its own coordination problem. On the macro level there is just one true macro-market, which is the money market. Money is involved in every transaction, and it means that the government should be responsible for an optimal amount of money in circulation. In the chapter on orthodox economics we discussed the distinction between short run and long term. Together with their idea of logical time rather than real time, we see that orthodox economists come to the logical implication that a market economy might show small disequilibria in the short run, but in the long run all markets are cleared. It is important to stress that this conclusion is true by definition. As long as a market economy is not in equilibrium, it has not reached the long run.

Keynes rejects this orthodox and neoclassical strategy. His analysis is about the real world, and Keynes uses real time rather than logical time. He rejects the distinction between short term and long term. In reality subjects take decisions on the basis of their expectations about future economic developments. Some people have a horizon of one or two years. Others, especially firms, when deciding to buy investment goods have a longer horizon. But the analysis is just about the decisions people take, period after period.

According to Keynes, markets in the Western economies during the first half of the 20th century are not quite isolated from each other. Goods markets are characterized by imperfect competition, and many firms in the manufacturing sector are quite large, and strongly connected to other large and small firms in various other sectors. Some are even too big to fail: if they go bankrupt, many other firms, buyers as well as suppliers of the firm in trouble, are going to go bankrupt as well. Also, labour markets are strongly connected with each other. Especially through the unions, which organize workers along occupational and sector lines, changes in the wage rate somewhere trigger changes in the wage rate everywhere. For the financial markets hold that the mobility of capital and the many substitution opportunities create a highly interrelated network of markets. Even in the financial world many markets are characterized by imperfect competition. The financial crisis of 2008 shows that many firms in the financial world were considered too big to fail.

As already mentioned, Keynes starts his analysis of an economy at the level of the economy as a whole. He considers subjects as economic actors, living in an environment which is imperfectly known. In some periods people are optimistic about their future incomes from labour and capital. In other periods they are pessimistic about their economic performance. We know that neoclassical economists assume price flexibility, which they consider necessary for a market and a market economy to function well. According to Keynes, price flexibility on the macro level is *not* important. When discussing new Keynesian economics we will discuss this matter in more detail. For the moment we just state that prices in the Western world in the first half of the 20th century were quite sticky, except during the Great Depression. But Keynes showed that price flexibility will not lead to a recovery of a depressed economy: wage cuts will affect the level of demand for goods and labour negatively, and cuts in wages as well as goods prices will leave the real wage rate more or less unchanged.

The most important propositions of Keynes about the determinants of production, income, and employment are the following:

1. The level of production is determined by the level of effective demand, which is the total of discretionary expenditures.

2. The level of employment is determined by the level of the production, given the state of technology.

When we compare these statements with the neoclassical theory, we see remarkable differences. In this approach employment is determined by the size of the labour force, while production is determined by the level of employment, given the state of technology.

To understand what is meant by effective demand, we need to make a distinction between regular so-called *non-discretionary expenditures* on the one hand, and *discretionary expenditures* on the other. Keynes assumes that the level of production and income shows a secular trend, around which the actual level follows a cyclical pattern. In Figure 8.1 we have presented the secular and the actual levels. In neoclassical pictures there is also a trend in the potential production, which is the level of production necessary for full employment. In Keynes' approach this trend is affected by fluctuations in the actual production. In the neoclassical approach, changes in the number of unemployed do not affect the quantity of labour supplied. In Keynes' approach, unemployed people might become discouraged or ill, thereby affecting the level of potential production.

Figure 8.1 clarifies what we mean by secular (also called regular) non-discretionary expenditures. Households and firms consume and invest on a regular basis, and these expenditures are determined by their regular income, and not by their potential income as the neoclassical theory suggests. In addition to this regular part, subjects are inclined to add a *discretionary element*: in times of expansion and optimism they consume and invest more, and in times of recession and pessimism they spend less. This addition is called *effective demand*.

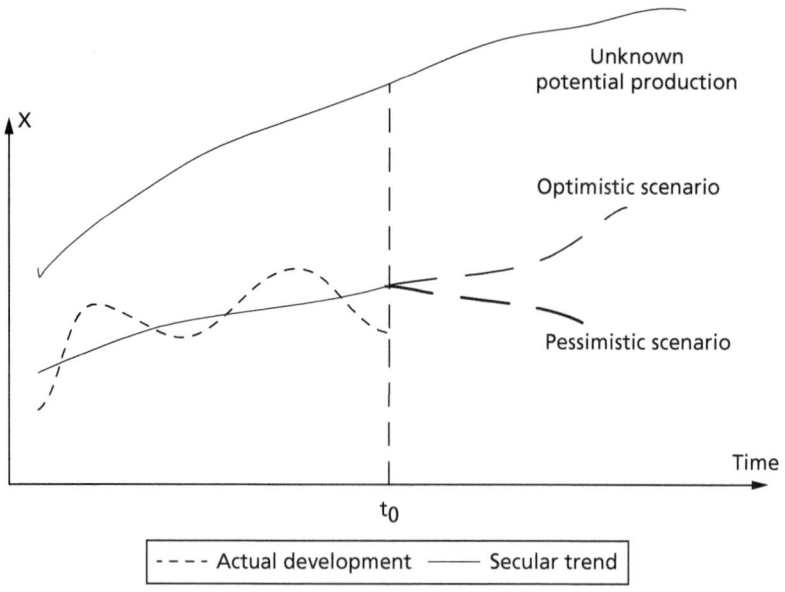

Figure 8.1. Secular Trends and Actual Levels of Production according to Keynes

Now we formulate a small and simple model expressing the idea of Keynes that effective demand determines the level of output. If the level of output is not enough to offer all workers a job, then the economy needs a stimulus—coming from outside the model—to create more employment. The consumption is determined by the regular income (X) and an exogenous part. So with the investments. We assume that the goods market is in equilibrium. This leads to the following set of equations:

$$C = c \cdot X + C(au) \qquad \text{behavioural equation}$$
$$I = a \cdot X + I(au) \qquad \text{behavioural equation}$$
$$Y = C + I \qquad \text{definition equation}$$
$$X = C + S \qquad \text{definition equation}$$
$$Y = X \qquad \text{equilibrium condition}$$

Solution of this model leads to the following characteristic of the equilibrium situation:

$$X = 1/(1-(c+a)) \cdot [C(au) + I(au)]$$

The second proposition relates the level of production to the level of employment. To keep the analysis simple we apply a linear and positive connection. In Figure 8.2 we portray this situation. In the first quadrant we see the so-called *Keynesian cross*. In the second quadrant

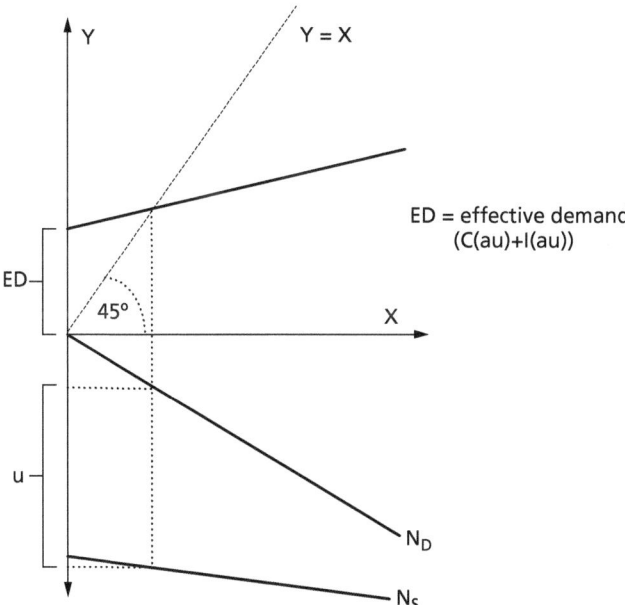

Figure 8.2. Derivation of the Relationship between Effective Demand and Unemployment

we have pictured a simple labour demand and labour supply curve, which are also positively related to the regular level of production.[3]

Now we will deal with the analysis of the capital and the money market. The demand for capital depends on the level of investments. When we apply the neoclassical marginal analysis, a firm will increase the amount of investments until the benefits of the last euro spent has become equal to its costs. The flow of net benefits is primarily determined by the *expected revenues* of the firm, discounted over a number of years, and the costs are primarily opportunity costs, which are determined by the interest rate on the capital market. Neoclassical analysis stresses the effect of changes in the interest rate. Keynes, however, considers the interest rate as only one of the cost elements. The expected revenues, however, is the primary variable, determining the level of investment. So, an expectation about the growth of profits is the decisive variable. In times of optimism I(au) is relatively high, while in times of pessimism the entity is relatively low.

With respect to saving (= that part of income that is not spent) neoclassical theory develops a marginal analysis of the decision of households and firms to save. The conclusion is that the flow of saving increases where there is a higher rate of interest. Keynes, however, considers saving to be a residual. In optimistic periods people like to spend and to borrow, while in pessimistic times households and firms prefer to save a larger part of their income. In Figure 8.3 we have presented both views in a typical neoclassical way, showing the functioning of the price mechanism. Figure 8.3A shows the neoclassical view that the mechanism works well, while Figure 8.3B shows that the mechanism does not work. The interest rate is not determined by the demand for and the supply of capital; part of the saving will not be used. It implies that the demand for goods is lower than the production. So, in the next period we will expect a decline in the production and income. This means a lower level of saving—leading to a shift of the supply curve to the left, until

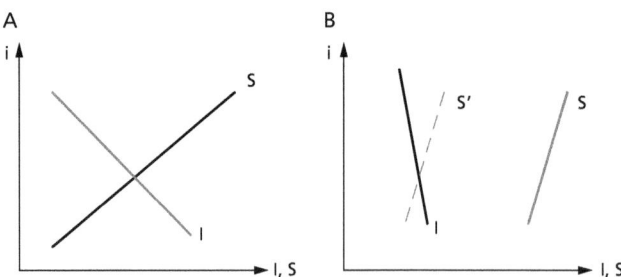

Figure 8.3. A: Neoclassical Capital Market; B: Capital Market according to Keynes

---

[3] In a neoclassical analysis the demand for goods refers to the relation between the quantity demanded of a particular good and its price. When the (post)-Keynesians use the concept demand, they do not necessarily mean that relationship. It might be the relationship between quantity demanded and a different variable, such as production or employment. The same comment holds for the concept of supply.

the saving has become equal to the level of investment. Then the equilibrium of the goods market implies a lower level of employment.

The same procedure will be followed by analysing the money market. In our chapter about orthodox macroeconomics we have seen that the nominal money demand is primarily a function of the nominal income. This claim is explained by the idea of the *transaction motive*. The higher the income, the more money is needed to finance the transactions. A second motive people are supposed to have is the *precautionary motive*: we never know what will happen in the near future, and therefore it makes sense to have a buffer in case of bad events. The neoclassical theory says that the size of the quantity demanded, based on the precautionary motive, is dependent on the interest rate. As long as a subject holds part of his wealth in cash, he is not receiving interest payments. The higher the interest rate, the higher the opportunity costs of having cash.

According to Keynes there is a third motive to hold cash, which is the *speculative motive*. It does not play an important role in neoclassical analysis. The reason is that an economy is assumed to stay close to its equilibrium. So, in case of a recession most speculators expect an expansion, and in a stage of expansion most speculators expect a recession. In such a situation it is difficult to make profits out of price fluctuations in financial assets. Speculation plays a significant role only in a case of uncertainty. Then, there is more difference in the risk assessments as well in the risk preferences. Suppose that the interest rate is quite low. There are no clear signals of a recovery. Many financial investors substitute cash for non-liquid financial assets, since they expect a further decline in asset prices. As we have seen in our model of the goods and labour market, there is no automatic mechanism that leads the economy back to equilibrium. So, financial investors keep waiting, meanwhile holding relatively large amounts of money. If the central bank is trying to increase the amount of money in circulation, it must take into account that people just store additional amounts of money in so far as they think they need it. Especially in times of depression, it appears to be difficult to enlarge the amount of money in circulation. Few consumers and firms are prepared to increase their debts by borrowing money, which makes it difficult for the central bank to create money. According to Keynes, the only way of stimulating the economic activity is a combination of fiscal and monetary policy. The government increases the effective demand (C(au) + I(au)) and finances the additional expenditures by means of money creation by the central bank. Then an increase in economic activity, accompanied by additional transaction money, will turn expectations from pessimistic to optimistic, creating private effective demand. In Figure 8.4a we have presented Keynes' money theory. To make it easy to compare his approach with the neoclassical one, we have presented the neoclassical theory in a Keynesian as well as in a neoclassical way (Figures 8.4b and 8.4c respectively).

In Figure 8.4a we have presented the idea that an economy fluctuates across a relatively low level of production and income. Changes in the interest rate have a strong effect on the quantity demanded for money. The money supply function (M = M(au)), expresses the idea that the central bank supplies a particular amount of money, which

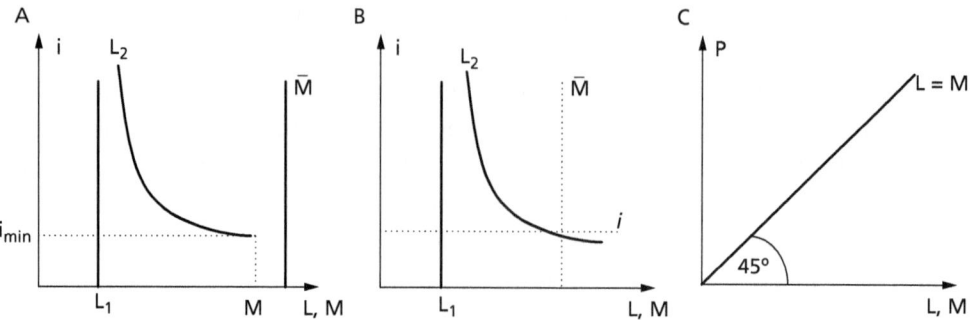

Figure 8.4. Keynesian (A) and Neoclassical Money Markets (B, C)

is not dependent on other variables in the model. Part of the amount of money in circulation is meant to be used for the payment of the transactions (L1), and the other part of the cash is motivated by considerations of precaution and speculation (L2). There is disequilibrium on the money market. Not all the money supplied is demanded. So the actual amount of money in circulation is smaller than the amount of money supplied by the central bank. The level of the interest rate is 'determined' by money market forces, including the interest policy of the central bank. The actual amount of money in circulation is determined by the quantity demanded for money (L).

The current situation (December 2013) in the USA, the EU, and Japan exemplifies this case. The nominal interest rates are close to zero, and so with the inflation rates.[4] So, the real rate of interest is almost negative. Nevertheless, consumers and investors are not taking out additional loans because of a lack of confidence in the future. It means that the amount of money in circulation does not increase, notwithstanding the extremely low interest rate. The conclusion is that monetary policies are ineffective in an economy in depression.

In Figure 8.4b we have pictured the neoclassical money market. In contrast with Keynes' analysis there is equilibrium. Because the capital market functions well the economy will not fall in a liquidity trap.[5] In Figure 8.4c we have presented a different picture of the neoclassical money market. It shows the typical neoclassical proposition that there is a proportional relationship between the general level of goods prices and the amount of money in circulation. Since the neoclassical money market is—by assumption—always in equilibrium, the line does not only relate M to P, but also L to P.

---

[4] Here we use the habit of central banks to define price stability as an increase in the general price index of 2%. See the discussion about the Boskin Report in Chapter 5.

[5] The liquidity trap refers to the situation in which subjects are inclined to hold onto cash and wait until the economy begins to grow again. It means that everyone is waiting for everyone else, while nobody takes the initiative. This is the reason why the government should take the initiative to increase its effective demand.

If we compare Keynes' analysis of the relationship between the different markets with the typical neoclassical analysis we can draw a few politically relevant conclusions.

According to Keynes, none of the macro-markets has a price mechanism that is able to restore equilibrium if the economy is in a not-too-small disequilibrium. All these markets show adjustments also in terms of shifts *of* the curves rather than only as shifts *along* the curve as a result of a price adjustment. So if there is a lot of unemployment, and the expectations of consumers and investors are quite negative, the government is the only institution that is large enough to affect the effective demand sufficiently to turn pessimism into optimism. Shift of the demand for goods leads to full employment in the end.

According to neoclassical economists, all markets have their own price mechanism. So, if there is unemployment wages should go down. If there is inflation the growth of the money supply should be restricted. If institutions are making it difficult to adjust quantities and prices in case of disequilibrium, deregulation should create more room for markets to function properly. In Section 8.4 we will discuss the reactions of a number of neoclassical economists to Keynes' analysis.

8.4 **Neoclassical Reactions to Keynes' Analysis**

Hicks (1937) wrote an article in which he placed Keynes' analysis in a neoclassical framework. According to him, his own approach was more general, and Keynes, as well as his classical opponents, were just explaining special cases.

To understand Hicks' construction we must be aware that his so-called IS-LM analysis is based on the neoclassical ontology. The world is a closed and orderly system. There are a few mechanisms which are responsible for the coordination of activities. In the world of economies this is the price mechanism, which coordinates market activities. There are regular shocks, which disturb market processes. Prices are flexible and able to trigger the necessary adjustments, but it takes time. The government is able to accelerate these adjustment processes in a market-conform way. The interest rate is the most important price; it should fluctuate in such a way that the economy as a whole returns to equilibrium. Monetary policy can influence the interest rate in such a way that the necessary adjustment processes take less time. During the adjustment process the volume of production and income is lower than their equilibrium values. To speed up the adjustment process, fiscal policy can change the level of production and income directly.

In this view the level of production and income (X) is the target, and the level of the interest rate (i) is an important instrument. The popular IS-LM analysis relates these two variables to each other, under the condition that the goods market as well as the money market are in equilibrium (I = S and L = M, respectively). Now we get the following model:

$I = a \cdot i + I(au)$	$a < 0$	behavioural equation
$S = b \cdot X + S(au)$	$b > 0;$	behavioural equation
$L = d \cdot X + e \cdot i + L(au)$	$d > 0; e < 0;$	behavioural equation
$M = M(au)$		behavioural equation
$Y = C + I$		definition equation
$X = C + S$		definition equation
$Y = X$		equilibrium condition
$L = M$		equilibrium condition

In Figure 8.5 we have presented the IS-LM model graphically. The goods as well as the money market are in equilibrium at $(X(e), i(e))$. Since $X(e)$ is lower than potential production $X(pot)$, there is unemployment. If the government increases the effective demand the IS-curve shifts to the right, leading to a higher level of production and income and to a higher interest rate. If the central bank increases the amount of money in circulation, the LM-curve shifts to the right, also leading to an increase in the level of production and income, but in this case the interest rate decreases. The horizontal part of the LM-curve shows the situation in which the theory of Keynes is topical. The vertical part of the LM-curve shows the situation in which classical theory is topical.

After the Second World War most Western countries introduced a particular specification of the idea of the welfare state. The main principle of the welfare state says that the government is co-responsible for the well-being of all citizens. On a more specific level it meant that governments try to reach and maintain full employment and develop a social

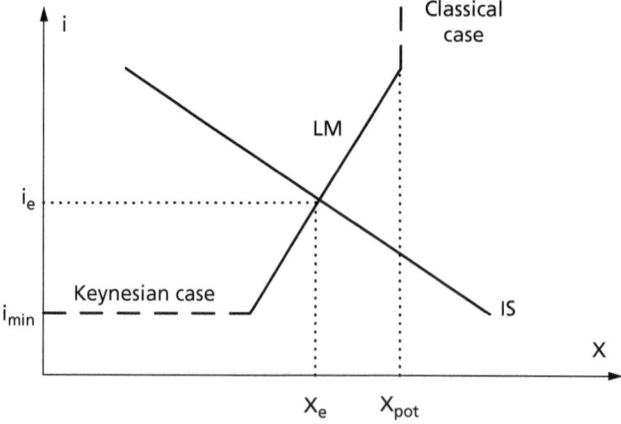

Figure 8.5. IS-LM Analysis

security system. The implementation of these policies appeared to affect the effectiveness of fiscal policy, an important full-employment instrument. In case of an expansion turning into a recession, the increase of unemployed persons leads automatically to an increase of government expenditures and a decrease in government revenues. In other words, the welfare system functions in an anti-cyclical way. If the recession turns into the next stage of an expansion, the decrease of unemployment leads to lower unemployment benefits and higher tax revenues: again an anti-cyclical effect. In the period 1950–1973 most Western economies were rather stable; small increases in economic growth in the stages of recovery and expansion alternated with stages of recession. During this period the idea that the business cycle had become obsolete gained ground: there will never be severe depressions anymore. Economists have constructed a tool, which makes it possible to manage economies. Econometrics calculates the quantitative relationships, making fine-tuning possible.[6]

Hicks (1937) interpreted Keynes' analysis using the general equilibrium framework. But Keynes used the concept 'general' differently. His famous book *The General Theory of Employment, Interest and Money* pretends to offer an employment theory. He called his theory 'general' because it holds for all the stages of the business cycle: the upswing as well as the downswing. In contrast to this theory, the (neo)classical theory is about an economy close to equilibrium. All subjects have more or less the same expectations of and reactions to predictable developments in the interest rate. There is no effective demand, which depend on pessimism or optimism among the potential spenders. The IS-LM model is made by engineers, who live in a mechanic and stochastic world, while Keynes is an economist, who is aware of a series of important features of the open and organic world in which we live. The long enduring stability of the economic system over the period 1950–1973 suggested that we really lived in a closed, mechanic, and predictable world. It explains why this IS-LM mechanism has become and is still one of the most important totems in modern macroeconomics (Dow, 2002). In Section 8.5 we will discuss the ideas of Leijonhufvud on the existence of corridors. Then we see that, from the Keynesian corner also, there were attempts to bridge the gap between Keynes and the neoclassical economics (Leijonhufvud, 1968; Howitt, 2002).

After 1973 economic events showed that, in a long period of more or less full employment, labour power had grown too much. Labour relations, as they were institutionalized, appeared ineffective in keeping the economy close to full employment. Later we will show that, in the period 1980–2006, we faced a long period of relative stability, which ended because of a ineffectively controlled capital power. In the sociological chapter about modernity and postmodernity we will discuss the whole *idea of control*, which has already dominated Western thinking for a very long time, more thoroughly.

---

[6] Before the Second World War, business cycle theory distinguished stages of recovery, expansion, recession, and depression. Under the influence of many years of almost full employment, neoclassical economists have abolished the term 'depression'. Even now the EU economy is in a true depression, they keep saying that Europe is—now and then—in a recession. So, whatever the situation, depressions will apparently not return.

Phillips (1958) pretends to have found a stable empirical relationship between the growth rate of nominal wages and the rate of unemployment. In Chapter 5 we have already discussed and criticized this article. From a political point of view the Phillips relation has played an important role, especially the suggestion that there is a trade-off between inflation and unemployment. Lipsey (1960) shows that the empirical relationship, stable or not, can be derived from a neoclassical analysis about the labour market. In case of excess demand there is a tendency to increase the wage rate above the eventual increase in price inflation and labour productivity. In case of excess supply there is a tendency to decrease the wage rate. Friedman (1968) blamed the Keynesians for using an expectations theory, which does not fit the orthodox economic paradigm. Rational workers do not accept wage levels which are not compensated for inflation. The so-called adaptive expectations theory, used by Keynesians, suggests that workers conclude labour contracts that set the nominal wage for a period of one or two years. After this period they conclude a new contract. Then they claim a nominal wage that is adjusted for past price inflation. It means that they lose purchasing power in a period of increasing inflation. Neoclassical economists call this *money illusion*: during every period of the contract, workers are not aware that there is—again—inflation. This irrational behaviour does not fit the rationality concept as used in the neoclassical approach. To Keynes and Keynesians it is not at all clear why workers are irrational if they accept a lower real wage in exchange for a higher level of employment. If this cut in real wages occurs through inflation they at least know that the cut applies to all workers (Negishi, 1979).

In the 1970s economists from Chicago used the neoclassical idea of rational expectations in their apology of the free market system being a stable system. According to this new classical economics (NCE) approach markets are always in equilibrium. As soon as there is new information about economically important events or expectations about future events, many subjects react by selling some goods and buying other goods. In this way prices almost immediately adjust to the new situation. In sophisticated versions, it is not necessary that all actors react immediately. Some people spend more time collecting and analysing new information than others. This means that markets are always in equilibrium, given the information available. When the information spreads throughout the economy, relative prices keep changing.

It is clear that NCE brings us back to the simple economic world of orthodox economics. Every subject is economic and rational. Every subject is completely free to choose whatever he prefers. If a so-called unemployed person stays at home and applies for jobs, but so far has not found one that fits his preferences, he is definitely voluntarily unemployed. There are always vacancies in the lower segments of the labour market, including vacancies which can workers create themselves. This way of typical classical reasoning implies that the labour market is always in equilibrium; the axioms of the economic world lead unavoidably to this conclusion. It is not the result of empirical research.

To summarize and conclude this section, we have seen that neoclassical economists do not understand why Keynes' work is a scientific revolution. They don't understand the methodological differences. His analysis is about the real world, and this world has characteristics which are very different from the characteristics as described by the neoclassical ontology. Keynes' world is open and organic, and uncertainty plays an important role in the decisions actors take. Detailed quantitative analyses of future developments are impossible, and the most important decisions, which are the investment decisions, are based on animal spirits.

Neoclassical economists did not change their paradigm under the influence of Keynes. They still stick to their closed and mechanical world, and a market economy which is always close to equilibrium. Small price adjustments are enough to let the markets turn back to their equilibrium. In this picture they make some room for what they see as typical Keynes: in the short run markets might face disequilibrium. To them Keynes is wrong when suggesting that markets might not return to equilibrium. The labour market returns to full employment as long as institutions do not prevent (rational) workers competing by offering their labour service for a wage that is lower than the current market wage. We will come back to this problem at a later stage in this chapter.

8.5 Leijonhufvud's Idea of the Corridors

Leijonhufvud was dissatisfied with the way Keynes' work was interpreted by neoclassical economists, such as Alchian and Phelps (1970) and Phelps (1972), who were looking for a micro-foundation of the IS-LM analysis. Keynes' revolution was exactly focused on the problem of a fixed human nature. He was looking for a sound macro-foundation, as well as for microeconomic analysis. According to Leijonhufvud, the IS-LM analysis is part of a Walrasian equilibrium framework, except for the figure of an auctioneer and the assumption of flexible wages. For him, the Walrasian framework is only meant as an ideal state and a search for conditions necessary for the ideal state to become real. Leijonhufvud developed the idea of a *cybernetic approach*, which means the development of a system of causes and consequences, including feedbacks and feed-forwards, and of anti-cyclical as well as pro-cyclical effects. The system as a whole is myopic and without any long-term goal. There might just be forces or attractions to certain points of references, such as full employment. But there might be strong pro-cyclical tendencies, such as the quantity adjustments as described by Keynes. Even in the case of flexible prices the adjustment processes take time, and meanwhile there are adjustments in the points of 'equilibrium' as well. The more difficult it is for market participants to interpret particular price changes, the more time market adjustment processes take, and the higher the chance that quantity adjustments complement price adjustments.

In an orthodox-economic analysis of a market, changes in the price of a good as a result of an excess supply or excess demand are relatively small, including in terms of income effects. There is no relationship between a particular price change and an eventual shift *of* the curve. So, the supply and demand curve are fixed, and the price changes as long as there is disequilibrium on the market. In the case of perfect competition this equilibrium will be reached given the circumstances of the market. Besides criticism of the assumption that non-economic circumstances are given, there is the problem that macro-markets function differently compared with micro-markets. If wage rates are falling because of excess supply on the labour market, this decline affects the level of demand for goods significantly. Technically speaking, the demand for labour shifts downwards, making it more difficult to achieve equilibrium. According to neoclassical economics the disequilibria are relatively small, and small changes in the wage rate do not seriously affect the position of the demand for labour curve. The firms which invest in, produce, and hire labour expect the next recovery pretty soon, and do not change these vital decisions on every whim. Leijonhufvud states, however, that economists don't have the slightest idea whether a particular price change should be called small or large, which means whether a particular price change affects the expectations of households and firms significantly or not. According to the new classical economics all economic and rational actors have the same frame of interpretation—they all interpret their world as the typical orthodox economic world, and interpret particular changes in prices and quantities of goods in the same way. Sometimes there is expansion, and after two or three years we all know that this phase will be followed by a recession. When the recession is happening, many experts will inform the public: 'yes, now we face a recession, but don't worry, because the recession will not take very long'. According to Leijonhufvud, however, the situation is multi-interpretable. In Figure 8.6 we have presented the development of the growth rate of the production of a particular economy. In Figure 8.6a we see that the variable shows a series of cycles which are easy to predict. Most people expect a

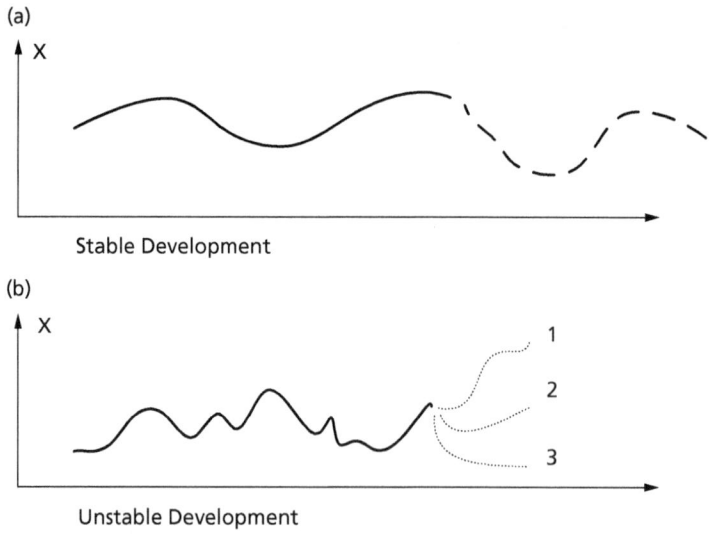

Figure 8.6. Different Interpretations of Future Development

simple extrapolation, which is indicated by the interrupted line. In Figure 8.6b, however, the cycles are less regular, and the picture suggests that a sudden increase or a sharp decline is not excluded. The figure presents three options. In the first interpretation the latest fall is an incident, followed by a recovery, which is interpreted quite positively. In the second interpretation the latest fall is interpreted as a negative change in climate for a longer period than just the next stage of a cycle. The cycles will remain on a lower level of production. In the third interpretation the latest fall is interpreted as the beginning of a very serious decline, which might not stop soon. It goes without saying that the three interpretations imply different strategies.

According to Leijonhufvud, the second interpretation implies that the economy stays in its corridor. The fluctuations do not affect basic attitudes and beliefs with respect to the future. The context of the economy does not show remarkable changes, which worry the speaking heads. So, everyone expects a continuation of the development so far. The third interpretation shows a move from one corridor to a lower one. Apparently there were events in the institutional context of the economy, or developments in the technological sphere, which give the experts the idea that the economy will not grow as fast as it did in the past. In the first interpretation experts are uncertain about the future, and are not able to assess the change in context adequately. But on one point they agree: the future will be good.

The work of Leijonhufvud is very important, and the determinants of a corridor should be an important area for future research. It is clear that social-moral as well as psychological factors do play an important if not a decisive role in the determination of the strength of the lower and upper bound of a particular corridor.

8.6 New Keynesian Economics

The IS-LM analysis shows that combinations of fiscal and monetary policy can be found, which bring a free market economy back to full employment. The level of wages and goods prices are exogenous and are thus taken as a given. Relatively small changes in the interest rate are enough to stimulate private investments. To speed up the process of adjustment the government could increase the effective demand. But, according to the neoclassical establishment, automatic stabilizers in the government budget are enough to stimulate the economy.

Over time the IS-LM analysis has been increasingly criticized. In many Western countries the government has declared itself responsible for maintaining full employment. This commitment contributed to a long period in which the economies stayed close to equilibrium on all markets. Wages and prices appeared flexible, at least in upward direction. When these economies faced external shocks during the 1970s the real wage rate appeared sticky in a downward direction, notwithstanding growing unemployment. This is the reason why an increasing number of economists began to formulate a 'Keynesian' micro-foundation for Keynes' statement that a free market economy, once in a depression, does not have the mechanisms to lead the economy back to full employment. The discussion is *not* about the question of whether or not an economy with a politically strong union movement and a growing welfare system is stable. It is about a free market economy, and the question is whether we can explain price stickiness. We will give three examples of analyses which pretend to have given an explanation of price stickiness in a free market environment.

In the first place, the explanation of interest-rate stickiness by Stiglitz and Weiss (1981). They analyse the relationship between a bank and a client who wants to finance his investment by means of a bank loan, thereby using the principal-agent structure. Every investment project has a certain risk. If the project fails the borrower cannot pay back the capital sum to the bank. So, the bank must form expectations with respect to the risk of default of a particular project. The higher the expected risk, the higher the interest rate the bank claims. But the higher the interest rate, the higher the risks of the projects that are presented to the bank for financing. Now the situation is framed as follows: there is asymmetric information. The borrower is supposed to know the risk of the project, while the bank is supposed to have incomplete information about it. In this principal-agent structure there is the danger of adverse selection: a relatively high interest rate selects the gamblers among the investors, while the more prudent investors postpone or cancel their investment plans. There is also the danger of moral hazard: borrowers who have already a relationship with the bank switch to more risky projects. Taking these considerations together banks might decide to be more reluctant to increase their interest rate, even when there is excess demand for loans. This bank behaviour is called *credit rationing*. It shows upward price stickiness, explained by gambling investors. We can doubt whether this behaviour can still be called rational. Another disadvantage of the credit-rationing hypothesis is the lack of social action, which might reduce the information asymmetry between principal and agent.[7]

A second example is about wage stickiness, explained by Shapiro and Stiglitz (1984). They also use a principal-agent structure, characterized by asymmetric information. The principal has set up a monitoring system, to see whether agents are shirking or not. But the monitoring costs are high, and the control is imperfect. However, if a worker is caught in an act of shirking, he is fired. If the unemployment rate is relatively low, the cost of being caught and fired is not that high. The worker will find a next job relatively easily. To increase the costs of being caught the employer might give his worker a wage that is higher than the current market wage. This is an incentive for workers not to shirk so much. In other words, they become more productive, which might justify a higher wage on strict economic grounds.

A problem with this explanation is the following. Shapiro and Stiglitz leave the social element out of their analysis. They show that wage stickiness also occurs in a typical

---

[7] In Germany banks have a representative on the Board of large firms that borrow large sums of money from them.

economic world. But the real world is more than that, and it would be realistic to bring in the social aspect. Then we would see that this can also explain wage stickiness, but in a more realistic way. In a social-economic approach we might picture a firm as a hierarchically ordered series of groups. Now the principal-agent structure can also be applied to situations close to the top: groups of top managers, who have their individual and group goals (shirking), and force their own agents (workers on a lower level) to serve the manager's interests rather than the long-term firm interest. Top managers can easily shirk, since they can hardly be monitored (controllers and controlled are members of the same group). If, nevertheless, some top managers are caught and fired, they don't suffer a loss of reputation, but are offered a good job by members of their social network who work in other firms.

A third example is given by Akerlof and Yellen (1986). They explain wage stickiness as follows. Employers are supposed to be economic and rational actors. Workers, however, are also supposed to be social actors. They are a group in the sociological sense of the word. They are inclined to have solidarity with their colleagues, while not having solidarity with the unknown unemployed people outside the firm. The employer is offering a wage that is considered by the workers to be fair. Workers are inclined not to shirk when wage levels are considered fair. But if there are newcomers in the economy who offer themselves for a lower wage, the insiders threaten the employer with shirking in case of wage cuts. Wage competition is not part of the worker culture. Since the employer is rational and economic, he knows that shirking workers are not efficient. So, he will continue paying relatively high wages, which he considers efficient, and the workers fair.

The problem with this efficiency wage theory is the following. Akerlof and Yellen introduce the social aspect but in a very partial and specified way. Only workers are social, and they only show solidarity amongst their own group. The employers do not experience this; for them, workers are like machines, whose productivity can be measured accurately. If individual workers are not contributing to the profits of the firm, they are fired. Firms are analysed isolated from any social context. In Chapters 11, 12, and 13 we will see that there are more fundamental approaches to these sort of problems. It will appear that a strict neoclassical approach, which interprets firms not as teams but as a set of socially isolated persons, will not suffice to explain the real-world behaviour of people.

8.7 Post-Keynesian Economics

8.7.1 INTRODUCTION

During the 1970s a number of Keynes experts decided to formulate a new paradigm and a new series of analyses. According to them, many economies were out of balance because of the oil crisis of 1973, and neoclassical theory was not suited to deal with the macroeconomic problems of the time. They coined their approach post-Keynesian economics—thereby stressing that much could be learned from Keynes, especially his idea that every period needs its own analysis. When discussing Keynes we saw that he tried to analyse the real world of the Western capitalist economies of the first half of the 20th century. Meanwhile, institutions were changed as well as the state of technology and the level of wealth of many people. His ideas were caught and placed in a neoclassical framework of interpretation in the first decades of the post-war period. The post-Keynesians saw it as their mission to liberate Keynes from this framework and to develop analyses and theories upon the paradigm of the open, organic, historical, and real world, rather than an economic world that models the economic aspect of life.[8] We will see that analyses of human behaviour can only be made if the open world is closed for the moment of the analysis (temporary closure), and that the organism called economy can only be understood by searching for mechanisms that control it (temporary determination). The interpretation of analysis and mechanism is different from those in the neoclassical world: in the post-Keynesian world it is definitely a human construction. Closed and determined worlds are just semi-finished products, which might be of help in the construction of a realist and context-dependent theory.

8.7.2 THE MACRO-GOODS MARKET

In our open world the future is uncertain. There are hardly any reliable empirical relationships, and actors who take initiative must form (subjective) expectations, based on their animal spirits. When actors discover that their expectations have come true, they tend to continue with their actions until actual outcomes differ from the expected ones. The most important decisions are the investment decisions taken by entrepreneurs. When they are optimistic about the future and decide to increase their investments, to hire more workers and to increase their production, the economic process gets a boost. If they decide to postpone their investment plans, and stick to the regular levels of production, the economy stays on a level, which might not be enough to offer all job seekers employment. If entrepreneurs, however, are pessimistic about the future and decide to decrease production and to fire workers, these actions give the economy a negative shock. Regularly, orthodox analysis of the macro-goods market is presented by means of the AD-AS analysis, where AD is the aggregate demand and AS the aggregate supply of goods. Given the amount of money

---

[8] During the 1980s there was confusion about the terminology with respect to the various approaches which used the name of Keynes. See Kuipers (1985) for a sophisticated analysis of macroeconomic processes, in which he defines post-Keynesianism as 'price stickiness'. Now we all agree that this is not the right use of the term 'post-Keynesianism'.

in circulation, aggregate demand and aggregate supply of goods determine the level of the goods price. So, inflation can only occur if the central bank accommodates it by increasing the amount of money in circulation. Post-Keynesians have developed an alternative for this analysis: the so-called D-Z analysis. Many actors take many decisions quite automatically. Consumers who receive a wage, which tends to grow about 2 per cent every year, for instance, tend to consume 2 per cent more every year. So with subjects who decide to produce and invest. But actual changes always deviate from this regular development. It makes actors consume or produce a little less or a little more.

If actual values are higher than warranted values, and there is a climate of optimism growing, private investments especially grow faster. The reason is that the investors expect a higher price for the goods they are producing and selling. Investment decisions are always followed by the decision to hire more workers and to produce more goods. This means that there is a positive relationship between the expected goods price, the demand for and the supply of goods, the level of production, and the level of employment.[9] If consumers have more confidence in the future because of an increase in their income, they may also decide to increase their discretionary consumption expenditure. This leads to higher production and employment. Since post-Keynesians want to explain the level of employment more than the level of production, they have developed a function that explains the relationship between the demand for goods (D) and the level of employment (N).

The supply function shows the relationship between the supply of goods Z and the employment level. While D is based on expectations, the supply function is based on the actual cost structure, which is supposed to be well known to the producers/investors. Over a whole range of production and employment levels the actual price of the goods is quite constant. The reason is that, in the context of an economy that is not in equilibrium, firms face a rate of utilization which is not very high. So, increase of production does not need additional investment. In the case of increasing employment and production the average costs might even decline, until the utilization rate approaches 100 per cent. Then the actual price as set by the producers will increase, together with the amount of employment and production. In Figure 8.7 we have presented the two functions graphically. In times of optimism the D-function shifts upward, while in times of pessimism the function shifts downward.

Post-Keynesian economics starts with an analysis of the economy as a whole. Cycles of pessimism and optimism affect its development strongly. On the basis of macro-analysis it is possible to develop *post-Keynesian microeconomics*. Firms are supposed to operate on imperfectly competitive markets, and are unable to predict the future of the markets in which they are operating. In practice, we see that large firms are applying the *mark-up*

---

[9] As already said, the concepts demand and supply are not necessarily the same as the neoclassical demand and supply, which are derived from the orthodox laws of demand and of supply.

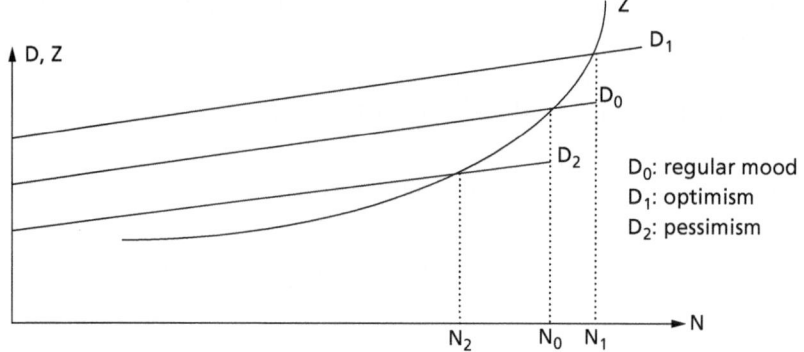

Figure 8.7. D-Z Analysis

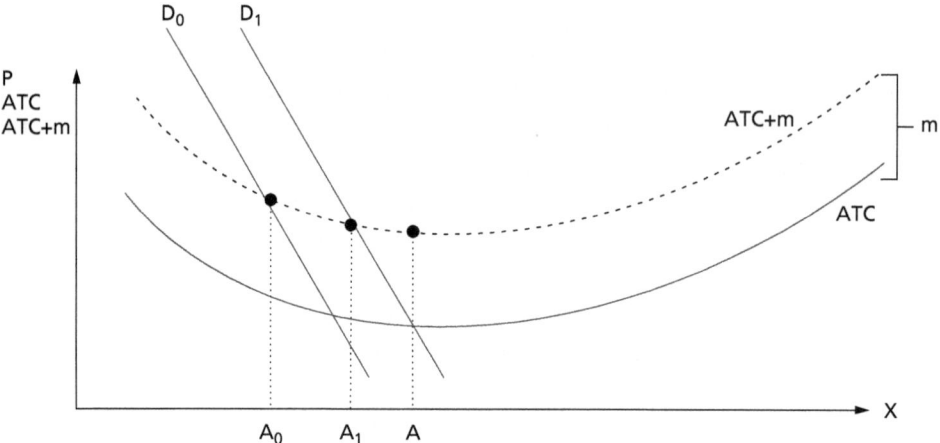

Figure 8.8. A Firm Operating on a Market during a Depression

pricing method. It means that, in their situation with so many uncertainties, firms fix a number of important variables. The price they are going to set is calculated by fixing the profit per product, which functions as a mark-up above the average total costs.

In Figure 8.8 we have presented the familiar average total cost curve for a firm. A stands for the production level, which is characterized by constant returns to scale. Neoclassical microeconomics analyses situations right of this point most of the time. Post-Keynesians analyse situations left of point A. This has the peculiar characteristic that the average costs decline if production increases. The more production the lower the price can be. It makes clear that firms profit significantly from a shift of their (neoclassical) demand curve; not only from a shift along their curve by setting the price on a profit-maximizing level. No firm can shift its demand curve if we take the quality of the goods, as perceived by the customers, as a given. Cycles of optimism and pessimism can. And the government is the only actor which is large enough to affect the position of the demand curves, thereby influencing the mood of the spenders. In Figure 8.8 we have presented an ATC-curve, an ATC plus mark-up (m) curve, and an expected demand curve.

∗ ∗ ∗

Harrod (1939, 1948) developed a growth theory upon the basis of Keynes' analysis. He can be considered as a post-Keynesian 'avant la lettre'. In his model of the goods and capital market, saving is a fixed part of income (S = s. X), and the capital coefficient is constant (K = a. X). It is easy to show that, in case of equilibrium, the growth rates of the capital stock, the investments, the saving, and the production and income are all **s/a**. Harrod calls this the warranted growth rate. The goods market is in equilibrium, while there is no mechanism that assures full employment. So, the warranted growth rate is smaller than or equal to the potential growth rate, which is the rate of growth of production and income in case of full employment. The actual rate of growth reflects the growth rate as it actually is: fluctuating around the warranted rate of growth (see Figure 8.9). Harrod uses Keynes' distinction between discretionary and non-discretionary expenditures to clarify the difference between warranted and actual growth. If the discretionary expenditures are zero, the actual rate is equal to the warranted rate. But if spenders are optimistic, they increase their expenditures, independent of the development of their regular income. In this case the gap between the warranted rate and the potential rate becomes smaller, and might be bridged after a few years. Then, in the language of Harrod, the economy has reached the *Neoclassical Golden Age*. As long as the warranted rate is smaller than the potential rate, Harrod calls such a period *the Limping Golden Age*. If the warranted rate is equal to the potential rate, but the workers or their unions do not accept the real wage level as it exists at that moment, Harrod calls this situation the *Bastard Golden Age*.

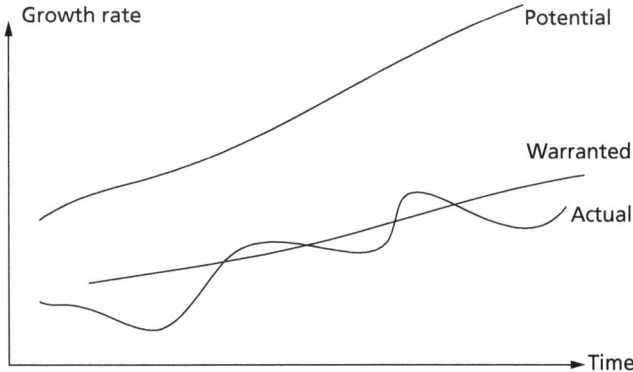

Figure 8.9. Actual, Warranted, and Potential Rate of Growth

According to neoclassical theory there is only one level of the real wage rate that fits full employment—the so-called natural rate of real wages. Post-Keynesian analysis considers the outcome as historically determined rather than something natural. If people had developed other habits, and experienced different events, the real wage rate could have been significantly higher or lower. Suppose that the unions had decided to increase their financial power, and required higher contributions from their members. In such a situation the saving rate of the wage recipients had increased, as well as the supply of capital. It means that the profitability of capital had decreased, and capitalists—among them the unions—must have accepted lower profits.[10]

When discussing the orthodox economic growth literature (Chapter 5) we saw that—by definition—an economy is in equilibrium in the long run. Then the actual growth rate is equal to the potential growth rate, which is determined by the growth rate of the labour force (n) plus the rate of technological progress (t). This leads to the following equation:

$$s/a = n + t$$

The actual rate fluctuates around the potential rate, creating some unemployment in the downswing and some inflation in the upswing. Given the automatic stabilizers in welfare budgets and the tax revenues, only monetary authorities should implement discretionary stabilizing policies. The central bank is constantly fine-tuning the interest rate so as to keep the actual growth rate of production close to its potential rate.

On the basis of the post-Keynesian growth literature policy advice is different. If the warranted rate differs from the potential rate, the government can try to create a more optimistic investment climate. It can increase its discretionary investments, which might lead to a higher level of production. Such policies must be communicated effectively to the spenders. Their expectations must be changed from regular to optimistic. If the government is successful private spenders take over and increase their discretionary consumption and investment expenditures.

Harrod also considers stable and unstable situations of warranted growth. In Figure 8.10 we have presented a stable (Figure 8.10a) and an unstable situation (Figure 8.10b). In the stable situation we see that, in the case of increasing growth, the growth rate of investments is lower than the growth rate of savings. In the unstable case the opposite holds. In the stable case we might say that the optimism among physical investors is

---

[10] Post-Keynesian economics is basically about a closed economy. It means that capital cannot flow to more profitable economies. Currently we see that global savings have significantly increased, which is one of the reasons why the rewards for capital are relatively low in the world. Bubbles in the asset markets show temporary exceptions.

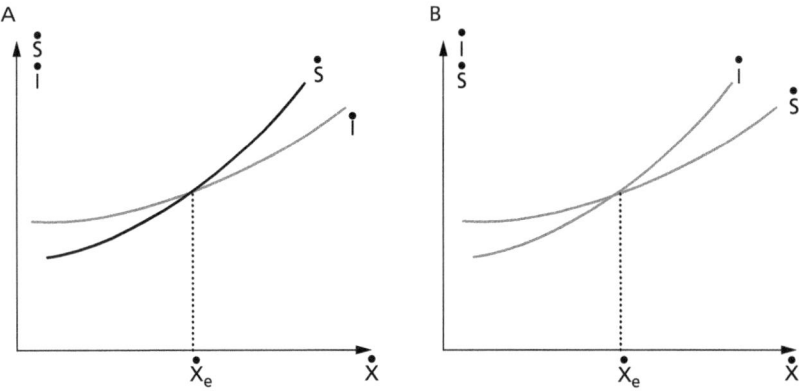

Figure 8.10. A: Stable Economy; B: Unstable Economy

weaker than the pessimism among the consumers, who save and financially invest much of their increase in income.[11] In the unstable case a government spending impulse has successfully created a climate of optimism among private firms and households. The consequence is that the demand for capital grows faster than the supply of capital via saving and financial investments. Without shocks from the environment of the model this process continues until the actual rate has reached the level of the potential growth rate. If the growth rate continues to rise it is not the volume but just the nominal value of production and income which grows; in other words, there will be inflation.

∗ ∗ ∗

Keynes' General Theory is about capitalist economies without a government that has declared itself responsible for full employment. Keynes foresaw that capitalist economies, managed by governments who operate according to his ideas, will function differently compared with the way he had analysed these economies. Keynes (1943) warns there may be a wage–price spiral if the economy approaches full employment. The best solution to this problem is the implementation of economy-wide wage policies. In boom times the government should regulate the wage level so as to prevent wage increases being too high. In the post-war period many European countries followed his advice.

In Section 8.7.3 we discuss the way post-Keynesians analyse the labour market.

---

[11] The EU economy is quite closed, and shows a warranted growth rate, over the last five years, which is significantly lower than the potential rate of growth. Other regions in the world show higher growth rates, which leads to a stimulus for the EU economy via the exports. Nevertheless, the actual rate of growth does not increase because of pessimism among European spenders. The Dutch economy is a perfect example (December 2013).

8.7.3 THE MACRO-LABOUR MARKET

The neoclassical approach assumes that employers are economic and rational profit maximizers, operating on a competitive labour market. They all have a labour demand function, expressing the negative relationship between the wage rate and the quantity demanded. The wage rate is determined by supply and demand on the labour market, and is a given for each employer. Given the demand and the wage rate, the quantity demanded is determined by and equal to the marginal productivity of labour. In Figure 8.11 we have presented this neoclassical idea. In Figure 8.11A we have pictured the market situation, and in Figure 8.11B we see the situation of one employer operating on the labour market (w(au), N(opt)).

Post-Keynesians, however, disagree. To them there is no macro-labour market mechanism. What they mean to say is that the price mechanism does not function well as a coordinator of market transactions. Prices are not determined by the supply and demand of a particular good. In times of pessimism individual employers are forced to stay below the neoclassical labour demand curve, due to a demand constraint. This situation is pictured in Figure 8.11B: the actual combination of wage and quantity demanded is (w(au), N(pes)), where 'pes' refers to pessimism. The neoclassical employment level can only be reached in case of optimism ('opt').

For the economy as a whole, however, the macro-labour demand in particular does *not* reflect the orthodox economic principle of the law of demand, which, as we saw in our exposition of orthodox economic analysis, expresses the substitution effect. So far as there is substitution, it is between capital and labour. Post-Keynesians stress, however, the complementarity between the two factors of production. Besides the substitution effect, there is a significant income effect: in case of a wage cut in a closed economy the demand for goods, and therefore the level of production and employment, will decline.

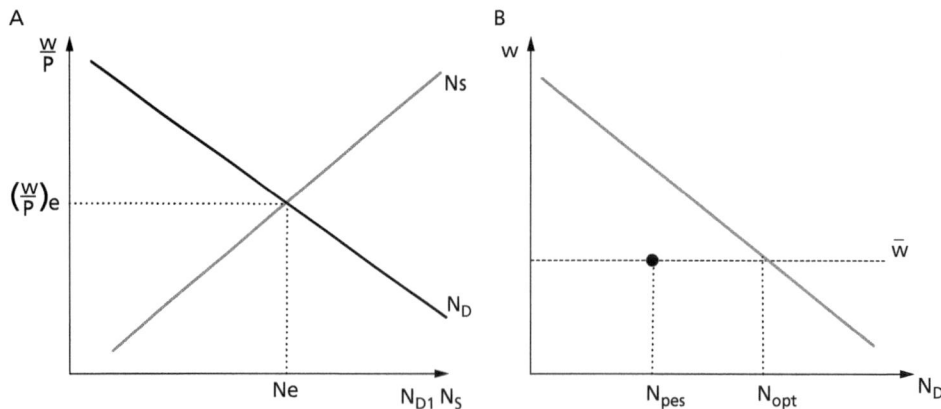

Figure 8.11. A: Neoclassical Labour Market; B: Post-Keynesian Labour Market in a Neoclassical Framework

Two elements are important now. In the first place, Keynes assumed that prices of goods and labour are sticky, and in a depression interest rates are sticky as well. In the second place, whether wages and prices are sticky in a depression or not is not an important issue. A capitalist economy cannot help itself returning to equilibrium on all markets, whether the goods prices and wages are sticky or flexible. Now we will discuss the first element.

In our D-Z analysis we have presented the idea that in an open,[12] organic, and historical world, sticky prices imply that the quantity demanded for labour is not determined by supply factors, but by the effective demand (C(au) + I(au)). We saw that effective demand is based on expectations with respect to the future. If the economic sentiments move from regular towards optimistic, spenders will consume and invest more. This leads to a shift *of* the D-function (and to a shift of the spending line in Figure 8.2). Given the Z-function it implies a higher level of the quantity demanded for labour. Now we can portray the relation of effective demand to quantity demanded for labour—see Figure 8.12. To show what happens with the unemployment level in case of changing effective demand, we make a curve representing the supply of labour. The neoclassical curve shows a positive relationship between wage rate and quantity supplied, expressing the effect of substitution of work for leisure—the opportunity costs of leisure have been increased in case of an increase in the wage rate. Post-Keynesian theory is different, but there is not one clear alternative. Neoclassical price effects are replaced by quantity effects most of the time, and animal spirits, such as optimism and pessimism, also play an important role. So, in case of an increase in the wage rate, it might be interpreted as an increase in the scarcity of workers, and trigger the animal spirits of the unemployed, encouraging them to start looking for a job again. Since it is difficult to statistically establish the number of active seekers who are still looking for a job, the position, as well as the slope of the line representing labour supply, cannot easily be determined.

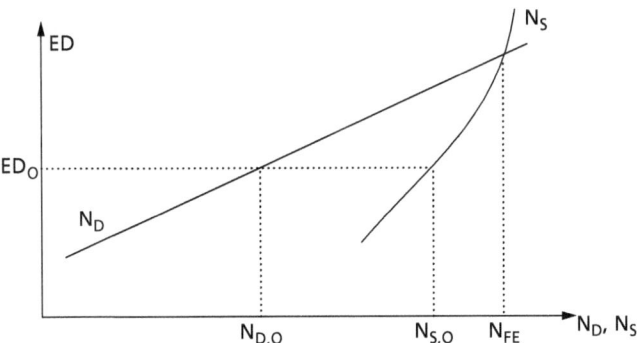

Figure 8.12. Post-Keynesian Labour Market in a Post-Keynesian Framework

[12] Be aware that the assumption of a closed versus an open economy is not identical to the philosophical assumption of a system being closed or open.

Figure 8.12 shows that both the quantity demanded and the quantity supplied react to a change in the effective demand. It goes without saying that if the effective demand keeps increasing, the increase in the quantity supplied will become increasingly smaller. We have presented the typical post-Keynesian demand and supply curve, and show that the coordination task on the labour market is executed by the effective demand. In times of depression we know that private spenders decrease their discretionary expenditures, and the government has to step in and take over the function of creating equilibrium on the labour market.

The second element to be discussed is the question why an eventual wage decline in case of a depression will not lead to full employment again. This topic is discussed by Keynes in the famous chapter 19 of his *General Theory* (see also Welsh 1987). In Figure 8.13a we have presented a neoclassical picture of the labour market, which suggests that, in case of unemployment, a real wage decline will lead to an increase in the quantity demanded. The decline must go on until the quantity demanded has become equal to the quantity supplied.

However, in the post-Keynesian world a real wage decline will be interpreted by the workers/consumers as a sign that the economy faces bad times, and that they have to change their behaviour. It means that a lower income will not be interpreted as an incident, and they will decide to decrease their level of consumption. The firms discover that their expectations with respect to the price and the sales of goods are too optimistic and adapt their investment behaviour. So, the change in the level of effective demand implies a change in labour demand. This is the reason why a decline in the wage rate brings the economy off the neoclassical demand curve. In Figure 8.13b we have portrayed a situation in which the absolute value of the positive effect of a shift along the demand curve (substitution effect) is equal to the absolute value of the negative effect of the decline in effective demand. In Figure 8.13c we have presented a graph that shows the effect of the effective demand in case of a depression, where pessimism rules the expectations of the spenders. The income effect will be stronger than the substitution effect.

Neoclassical economics attaches much value to substitution effects. If an economy is not very closed, and international trade has a significant effect, increases in the goods price might lead to lower exports and higher imports. For relatively closed economies,

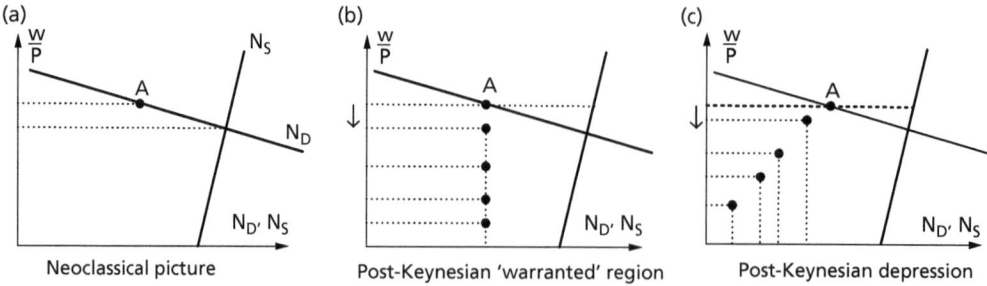

Figure 8.13. Neoclassical and Post-Keynesian View of the Labour Market Adjustment Process

such as the USA and the EU, this effect is not strong. But if the real wage rate increases, and labour costs increase, it might also affect the properties of the production technology applied. Real wage increases are an incentive for producers to switch to more labour-saving techniques. Post-Keynesian analysis assumes that these substitution effects are not very important, and can—in a simple analysis—be ignored.

The two approaches differ significantly about the desirability of prices being flexible. Neoclassical analysis is completely built on this assumption. Rigidity with respect to the wage rate is seen as the main cause of unemployment, and can only be the result of the incidence of government-backed unions (Hayek, 1931, 1984). For Keynes and post-Keynesians the macro wage rate should be a stable entity, only reacting to structural changes in the labour productivity. The Great Depression shows that wages as well as goods prices declined without a significant effect on the course of production and unemployment. A stable wage rate does not mean that the wage structure must be stable. On the micro level wages should reflect relative scarcities, as they are manifest within a particular institutional context. In case of a structural and increasing excess demand for computer experts, for instance, their wages should be increased; and so with structural and increasing excess supplies, which should lead to a decline in the relevant wages. But, macroeconomically, nominal wages should not react to general increases in the excess demand for labour. If the general goods price increases, and the nominal wage rate does not change, a decline in the real wage (given the level of the productivity of labour) functions as an automatic stabilizer.

In Section 8.7.4 we will discuss the post-Keynesian financial world.

8.7.4 THE MACRO-FINANCIAL MARKET

In Chapters 4 and 5 we have explained the typical neoclassical analysis of the capital and the money market. Wicksell offered an analysis, in which he brought the two markets together. Figure 8.14 shows the way in which the nominal interest rate is responsible for stability on the financial market. The addition sum of the nominal value of the saving (a flow) and the increase in the amount of money in circulation in a particular period is the total amount of money available in a particular period that can be borrowed. The additional sum of the nominal value of the investments and the increase in the amount of money in circulation that is demanded by the subjects (a flow) is the total amount of money that has been borrowed. Wicksell's analysis is called the loanable fund theory.

As we know, the neoclassical analysis assumes that prices are flexible enough to bring all markets close to equilibrium, which means that the level of production offers all job seekers employment. If the monetary authorities increase the amount of money in circulation, it will not lead to an increase of the level of production, since this level is already at its potential level. It will only lead to an increase in the level of the prices of goods

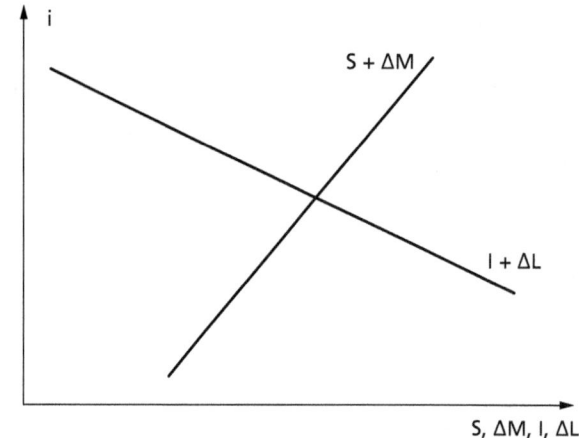

Figure 8.14. Wicksell's Loanable Fund

(inflation). We also saw that the so-called quantity theory of money formulates the typical neoclassical monetary theory—later called monetarism:

$$MV = PT$$

where M is the amount of money in circulation, V is the velocity of circulation of money, P is the level of the goods price, and T is the real value of the transactions. V is supposed to be a constant, and so with the level of production that is the potential production which has a strong effect on T. So, every increase in M leads to an increase of P, which implies the *neutrality of money*. Money just facilitates trade, and does not affect the allocation and distribution of scarce resources.

Schumpeter and Keynes developed a different idea about the role of money. They interpreted the modern economy—for them the Western economy during the first half of the 20th century—as a *credit economy*. It means that money creation takes place when a bank decides to give—on request, of course—a firm a loan. In other words, money in circulation is the result of an action of the private actor, thereby always creating a liability. Without debts there is no money in circulation; this money is called *inside money*. The neoclassical view on money creation is different. Money comes from outside the economy, namely from the central bank. The monetarist literature often uses the metaphor of a helicopter which is constantly showering the economy with notes and coins. Every year the amount of money in circulation must grow in order to finance the growth of production that is for sale. The monetarist money is called *outside money*, and is interpreted as an exogenous variable, while post-Keynesian theory considers money to be an endogenous variable: if there is no demand for loans from private actors, there will not be any growth in money in circulation.

In the monetarist analysis banks are just intermediate institutions, which bring savings and money creation to the actors who demand capital and money. But in the post-Keynesian view banks have increasingly become independent players on the financial markets, who are trying to maximize their profits. If it is not in their interest to lend to private actors, they don't do it. If it is in their interest to lend more, they will seduce potential borrowers with all means available. So, the financial system has become a very complex world, in which several anti-cyclical *and* several pro-cyclical reactions take place. There are neither auctioneers nor helicopters to manage these complexities.

Minsky (1982, 1993) offers an explanation of the intrinsic instability of the modern financial system. He underscores the typical post-Keynesian view that profit expectations of investors are the core variable in the capitalist system. Positive expectations lead to larger purchases of investment goods and financial assets, both financed by bank loans. This implies an increase in commitments to pay these back in the future. Profit realizations of investors offer the borrowers the means to really pay back the loans. Western economies show a structural inflationary bias because of the commitment of governments to strive for full employment. So in the pattern of waves from optimism to pessimism and back to optimism that determined capitalist development before the Second World War, there is a bias in the direction of optimism. According to Minsky, shifts in the *mental modes of actors* lead to shifts in the mode of finance of investors. He distinguishes between the *hedge*, the *speculative*, and the *Ponzi mode* of finance. The hedge mode implies that the flow of interest and redemption should be financed by the regular cash flows of the borrower. The speculative mode implies that the interest payments can be paid out of the regular cash flows, but that the borrower assumes that at the time of the final redemption the lender is prepared to roll-over the loan. The Ponzi mode of finance implies that even the interest is paid out of new loans. This scheme can only endure as long as the price of the assets, which are bought by means of the loan, increases over time. Ponzi schemes work as long as an increasing number of people are willing to participate in the scheme. Only then is the owner of the scheme able to pay an attractive rate of interest—all paid out of the deposit of new participants.

The *financial instability hypothesis* of Minsky says that, in a long period of enduring optimism, there will be a gradual shift from the hedge mode via the speculative mode to the Ponzi mode of finance. Borrowers increasingly believe that this period will never end—we have reached a new era. Banks also accept low or even extremely low solvability and liquidity ratios. In the period before the 1980s it was quite normal for the central banks to set minimum liquidity reserve percentages. But the central banks increasingly lost their function of controller and became just one player in a huge financial game. Neoclassical analysis is based on the philosophical idea of reality being a closed system. The economic system is determined by economic forces, and decisions to buy and to sell are well coordinated in a free market system. The differences between actual and predicted values can be understood by the assumption of the world being a stochastic world. Risks can be calculated, and buffers in terms of own capital and liquidity are actually a waste of resources—cash on the table so to speak.

Minsky foresaw and explained why such a development in modes of finance could not continue forever. The increasingly fragile system needed just a relatively small shock in order to collapse. Intuitively, people knew that such a fragile system was an extreme risk. Whatever the shock, within due time the system will collapse—the so-called *Minsky moment*. The idea that, even in case of many Ponzi-like systems, there is actually no problem can be called a *typical irrational idea*. The fall of Lehman Brothers in 2006 can be called the Minsky moment: suddenly all optimism was gone, and many investors started to sell assets and to pay off loans. In 2008 the problem had become so big that the real sector of production and employment faced a growing lack of loanable funds for their regular business. This was the beginning of a global depression.

Shiller (2002, 2007) interprets bubbles in the course of asset prices as an expression of irrationality of investors. To him, it is our uncontroversial experience that 'what goes up must go down'. Experts know this from their professional training. Nevertheless, many people behave according to the rule that increasing prices will continue to increase. This irrationality makes it necessary to introduce legal rules so as to restrain the hubris of investment managers. Shiller discusses four human shortcomings. The first is called representativeness heuristics, which means that it is difficult for humans to imagine that times will change, while most experts don't understand why this is the case. The second is the problem that some features of the situation are constantly highlighted and become salient for our actor. The media play an important role in the diffusion of salient features. But experts almost always operate in groups, and discuss the latest developments with each other on a daily basis. In such situations there is a strong pressure to conform to the prevailing views about the causes and effects of particular developments. Other very important facts, such as income distribution and a lack of effective demand, are systematically ignored. Currently, most politicians and mainstream economists discuss the budget deficit and government debts every day.

A third shortcoming is the fact that people who have built up skills and experience extract self-confidence from past success. Why change a winning team? The successful strategy will be continued, until things go really wrong. A last human shortcoming is wishful thinking. Humans are inclined to think that what they so eagerly want is feasible. Most of the time this is a mistake, which has negative consequences.

This summing up of human shortcomings seems somewhat arbitrary. It is not clear what the common denominator is, and what exactly is irrationality. The post-Keynesian world is chaotic, and few stable empirical relationships exist. Consequently, it is not obvious that experts have learnt that what goes up, must go down is always true. From the idea of chaos we can only derive that empirical variables go up and down in an unpredictable way. So, if people are rich and like gambling with part of their wealth, an unregulated financial market is one great casino. It is unclear why we should call the gamblers irrational. The degree of irrationality is a characteristic of the mind, and can only be observed by introspection; that is, by the person himself. When carefully defining the concept of rationality, a person can increasingly discover by self-reflection whether or not his behaviour is essentially irrational.[13]

Neoclassical and new classical economists disagree with Shiller and state that even the most volatile movements can be explained by means of theories based on the economic and rational actor. Before we explain economic action, and disagree with the typical neoclassical stories, we should develop an alternative for the neoclassical homo oeconomicus. In Chapter 1 we stated that neoclassical economics can only be improved by changing the axioms on rationality, sociality, and logic. After we have dealt with psychology and sociology, we will show how we can imagine an integrated world where the economic, the psychic, and the social aspect are interrelated.

If we compare Shiller's approach with that of Minsky, there is a remarkable difference. In Shiller's world actors are irrational because they keep buying assets as if their prices will rise forever; they take the risk of facing a sudden downfall in the prices. In Minsky's world actors are irrational because they keep buying assets and reduce their buffers in terms of solvability and liquidity. So, in case of a sudden downfall they don't have the means to finance setbacks and they go bankrupt. In the neoclassical literature this is still considered to be rational, because actors know that most governments will bail them out in case of bankruptcy.[14] The dispute about rational and irrational behaviour can only gain in quality if psychological research of the Kets de Vries type will be executed on the basis of a careful analysis of the mind and a clear definition of the phenomena of rationality and irrationality.

Akerlof and Shiller (2009) discuss the term animal spirits extensively. Keynes used it in his General Theory to indicate that, in times of uncertainty, actors do not have reliable information about the future. Then they use their animal spirits, which tell them to be optimistic or to be pessimistic. Akerlof and Shiller use the concept of animal spirits as the dual of the rational calculator. They discuss several examples of an animal spirit. In the first place, they interpret confidence as a positive animal spirit. It is an emotion upon the basis of which actors take decisions, although they were not able to calculate whether the net benefits of the decision are positive. In a climate of optimism many investors are confident that the actions they take will turn out to be beneficial. In the neoclassical analysis actors just react to prices, but we have demonstrated at length that in the post-Keynesian approach optimistic or pessimistic spirits are decisive for future economic development. Akerlof and Shiller even analyse a *confidence multiplier:*

---

[13] In Chapter 10 we discuss the analyses and therapies as developed by Kets de Vries (2006). His work is especially focused on the irrationality of CEOs. See also this chapter for the architecture of the internal world or mind. And see Chapter 2 for the distinction between introspection and external observation. The role of empirical testing is less decisive than is the case in the neoclassical approach.

[14] Many neoclassical economists don't like discussions about their rationality axiom. For them the postulate is not a serious attempt to be realistic, but only part of a theoretical apparatus, which is as simple as possible. This apparatus is necessary to generate empirically testable hypotheses. If the tests are negative, neoclassical economists search for an improvement of the empirical fit by changing elements of the so-called protective belt—never by changing elements of the hard core. For them empirical results are decisive, not the realism of the axioms. According to heterodoxy the world is an open and organic system, and stable empirical relationships only exist in a stable institutional context.

if confidence is growing and leads to a wave of investments, the results will be positive, which promotes further increase in confidence.

In the second place, they interpret fairness as an animal spirit. Experimental economics shows time and again the existence of moral sentiments. Akerlof uses fairness among insider workers as an explanation for the phenomenon of rigid wages, as we saw in a former section. In this case fairness is restricted to the solidarity between workers, while they are assumed not feel any solidarity with job seekers—an assumption which might play a role in American labour relations practice. In Continental European practice these animal spirits play an important role in wage bargaining on professional sector and national level; in these cases the spirits are not that restricted.

In the third place, Akerlof and Shiller mention corruption and bad faith as animal spirits. The moral constraints that are based on moral sentiments become less strict, partly because of a series of scandals, such as with Enron, which shows that the elite at the top of very large companies are bad guys, who like to fool the masses. These scandals can function as a trigger for many people to lose confidence and become corrupt as well.

The problem with the interpretation of animal spirits as the opposite of rational calculation is the following. It implies that, in stable periods, animal spirits are not necessary to guide actors in their decision-making. We can calculate costs and benefits in the way suggested by neoclassical theory. We are economic and rational, and we find stable empirical relationships, and behave accordingly. The stable period will never end. According to Minsky, it is precisely because of the stability that people draw wrong conclusions: 'this is a new era, and we don't need buffers anymore'. Akerlof and Shiller do not develop an analysis of the mind and do not carefully define the concepts of animal spirits and irrationality. They also forget to develop a typical social analysis. This implies that fairness comes out of the blue. But it is unclear what it has to do with animal spirits.

It might be a better idea to define the concept human spirits on the basis of an analysis of the mind (see Chapter 10). There we see that everything is emotional, which means that it is based on emotions. On the one hand, we have the spirit to reduce scarcity as much as possible. On the other, we are driven to maximize our status in the eyes of relevant others. In Chapter 10 we argue in detail that we are also inspired to respect our Self, and to protect the Self against attacks. One of the most important human spirits is the drive to use our ratio to control the other spirits. This is the rational element in our mind. This emotion is based on instinct and intuition. Every living entity is equipped with a strong drive to survive and to manifest itself. This can be called instinct. Over time animals and humans experience and learn from it. In this way they develop intuition, which tells them what to do in different kinds of situations. This can be interpreted as an instinct-based frame or paradigm, which defines the situation. In the post-Keynesian world situations are extremely complex and the result of particular strategies is very uncertain. Our intuition is able to store rules of behaviour which appear to be successful. Humans are not always conscious of the rules they have stored; most institutionalized behaviour is automatized. The most general frameworks are determined by our embodied personalities. Processes of socialization determine which engrained rules are developed into more specific and particular rules, such as: 'never cross the street without first looking left, followed by looking right'. In Chapter 10 we discuss a few basic themes, as formulated by Jung, which dominate our life. Personality and socialization determine the basic frameworks of interpretation. The institutionalization of life implies that life is less chaotic than it would have been without the institutionalized frames of interpretation.

Now we turn back to the dispute between neoclassical and post-Keynesian economists. Neoclassical economists assume that their economic and rational actors have enough information to make responsible decisions. If actors make mistakes, they have sufficient information to correct their behaviour. Their rationality lets a system of free markets coordinate buy-and-sell decisions satisfactorily. Individuals can have their personal rules: they don't need anything from society except the protection of property rights. Post-Keynesians, however, consider reality to be an open and organic system. Failures of actors can be large, threatening the functioning of the economy as a whole. This makes economy-wide institutions, in particular government regulation, necessary. In Chapter 14, where we bring the different worlds together, we will see that there are more control mechanisms than just the neoclassical personal rules and the post-Keynesian legal rules which can play an important role in controlling society at large.

In Section 8.7.5 we will briefly discuss two typical post-Keynesian positions in the debate about the current crisis.

8.7.5 THE POST-KEYNESIAN POSITION IN THE CRISIS DEBATE

The media report on the course of the crisis every day. They appear to have a very important function in the crisis debate. They constantly *frame* the situation in which problems arise, and even co-define the 'real' problems. Almost everybody agrees with the proposition that the crisis started in the financial sector, and that the financial problems are not solved yet. The credit crunch of 2008 pushed the global economy into a depression. Some countries began to stimulate their demand for goods, but others, such as the EU, began to cut their government expenditures. In the north-western European media the neoclassical view dominates. Every day the media tell people that government expenditures should be cut.[15]

The paradigm or human spirit behind the neoclassical view is the idea that there is a lack of competition on the financial markets. More competition would lead to more transparency with respect to the properties of the different financial products. That

---

[15] In the Netherlands there is a small shift visible in the opinions of the popular media-economists at the moment (December 2013). The negative effects of the cuts in government expenditures are increasingly clear to them. Now they advise the government to lower taxes tariffs and social premiums and to increase wages in an attempt to stimulate private spending. These proposals fit the Hicks (1937) interpretation of Keynes' analysis, as expressed by means of the IS-LM analysis. We have explained that this

would make it easier for economic and rational actors to choose a risk profile that fits their preferences. In case of trouble every actor must accept the consequences of their participation on the financial markets. Competitive financial markets imply that regulation is inefficient. Moreover, large government budgets, budget deficits, and debts are inefficient too; they crowd out and limit the room for profitable private activities. Individual economic and rational actors know better than the government what is in their interest. The cause of the crisis is the monetary policy by the American central bank, the FED. For a long time it kept the interest rate too low. When the central bank discovered its mistake and increased its rate, banks interpreted this as a sign that the new era was over. They stopped relending all the funds, and began to improve their own reserve position. The famous credit crunch had started. When the governments of the USA and the EU had to bail out a number of big banks, it brought the financial position of the governments into disarray. The crisis will be over as soon as the national governments cut their expenditures so much that financial markets become confident and lend their money for not-too-high rates of interest.

The post-Keynesian position is quite different. Unfortunately, the paradigm or frame is rarely presented in the Western media. Minsky is hardly taught at universities in the compulsory bachelor's programmes, and the idea of animal spirits, frames, and irrationality is almost completely ignored. The generations of economists educated after the 1980s have never heard of it, and are unaware of the different methodology of Keynes. When the economy is in a depression, post-Keynesians consider interest rate policies to be a minor issue. In terms of Leijonhufvud we can say that the Western economies are out of their stable corridor, which kept the economies close to full employment. The immediate cause of the crisis might be a change in the interest rate, leading to a process of deleveraging (Leijonhufvud, 2009). The ultimate cause of the crisis, however, is the long period of over-optimism, which made the financial world careless. It lobbied successfully for deregulation, making it possible to lower liquidity reserves and the size of its own capital. The irrationality in this process is the lack of buffers, which are needed in any system that operates in an open and organic world. Until the crisis, most production and employment systems were more or less healthy. The breakdown of the financial system created a strong decline in the levels of production. This was disastrous for the confidence of private spenders. Governments had to intervene and take over dubious financial assets. But the real problem is the reluctance of consumers and investors to take risky action again. The solution is not an expansionary monetary policy—not a so-called 'zirp', which means *zero interest rate policy*. The government should reregulate the financial world more or less

analysis fits the neoclassical methodology. Keynes and the post-Keynesians, however, stress the pessimism among households and firms. That means that a wage increase will not stimulate consumption, but savings and the paying off of loans. So with lower taxes and social premium payments: firms might lower their prices, but not increase their investments. The European economy, and definitely also the Eurozone, is in a depression, and only governments are big enough to give the economy such a boost that optimism might return.

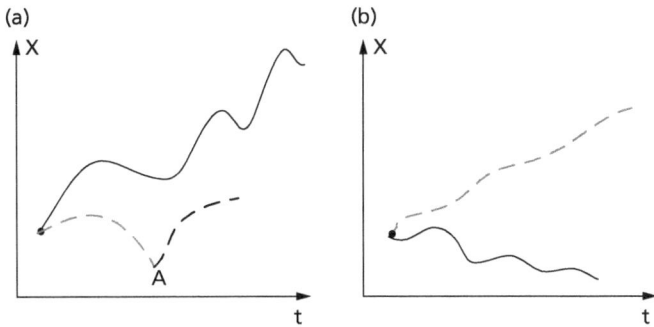

Figure 8.15. A: Production Growth in a Free Market Economy according to Neoclassical econo-mists and post-Keynesians; B: Production Growth in a Regulated Market Economy according to Neoclassical economists and post-Keynesians

in the way as happened in the 1930s, and stimulate effective demand (C(au) + I(au)). According to Keynes, the 1930s required an increase in public investments. Kregel (2009) discusses why Japan could not solve their liquidity trap problem during the period 1989–2013, and also advocates a reregulation, together with a stimulus in the effective demand.

If we financed the increase in public investments in a monetary way, the amount of (outside) money in circulation will increase without an increase in liabilities. The gov-ernment should therefore issue bonds or other financial papers with a never-ending period and an interest rate of zero; the central bank must be obliged to buy these assets. In Figure 8.15 we have presented two pictures, one reflecting the spirits of neoclassical economists, and the other of post-Keynesian economists. In Figure 8.15a point A means that the government intervenes with an increase in effective demand so as to prevent a socially unacceptable further decline.

8.8 **Conclusion**

Post-Keynesianism finds its starting point in Keynes' work. He analysed the function-ing of the capitalist system, especially the system as it functioned in the first half of the 20th century. His methodology is very different from that of the orthodox neoclassical approach. The world is considered as an open and organic, and not a closed and mechanic, system. For Keynes, the world to be analysed is the real world; not a world which only reflects the operation of the economic force. In other words, it is a subsystem rather than an aspect-system. His methodology is a collectivist rather than an individualist one. Where the neoclassical approach assumes the constant economic and rational nature of humans as the (microeconomic) foundation of its analysis, Keynes considers human nature as a variable, depending on the (collective) climate for investors and consumers.

In his analysis, the spending climate (optimism versus pessimism) determines whether consumers and investors spend more or less than the non-discretionary expenditures, which are dependent on their regular incomes. Total discretionary expenditures are called effective demand. The level of the wage rate does not play an important role in the explanation of the strong fluctuations in production and employment. It is determined by variables outside the model, which are highly influenced by its historical development. If policy was directed on downward wage flexibility, it would not lead to full employment, but to lower levels of production and employment. It would lead to increasing pessimism and a further decline of the effective demand. Keynes foresaw that, in a time where governments are committed to maintaining full employment, wage inflation would need to be prevented by an incomes policy.

After the Second World War neoclassical economists tried to encapsulate Keynes' ideas and give them a place within the typical neoclassical framework. The IS-LM analysis is a good example in this respect. So, Keynes' work was increasingly interpreted as an analysis for special situations, or as a short-run theory.

Leijonhufvud constructed two corridors. Both consist of an upper and a lower boundary, within which the volumes of production and employment evolve. A first corridor implies a cyclical development close to full employment. A second one channels the development of production and employment on a much lower level of employment. The first corridor exists because a capitalist private sector, combined with a welfare system, contains so-called automatic stabilizers. In the case of a small decline in the level of employment an increasing number of workers receive an unemployment benefit, thereby stabilizing consumption. In the case of a small increase the opposite occurs: a decreasing number of unemployed people receive a benefit. If there is, however, a strong and negative shock, which brings the economy out of its corridor, the automatic stabilizers are not strong enough to counter the pro-cyclical effect of a decrease in confidence in the future of the economy. Consumers and investors spend less, and if their incomes (wages, benefits, profits) increase they use it to increase their savings and to pay off part of their debt. In a capitalist economy without a welfare system the decline could go on until a revolution takes place. A sober welfare system makes it possible for an economy to be more or less stable at a lower level of production and employment, which is not enough for maintaining full employment.

The new Keynesians look for a solid micro-foundation in their explanation of enduring disequilibrium in a free market system. They ignore the macro- or collectivistic nature of Keynes' methodology and focus on the question of why prices are rigid. They seem to implicitly assume that less rigidity would lead to a higher level of production and employment—a statement which would not have been supported by Keynes.

Post-Keynesians do not question the methodological principles of Keynes. They just work them out in a way that fits modern times. The period 1950–1973 was a long period of economic growth with a level of employment close to full employment. In this new stage of development of capitalism the role of wages changed significantly.

The full employment commitment of the government gave the economy an inflationary bias. It means that the European institutions of collective bargaining, developed to prevent wage decreases in case of a depression, prevent inflation-creating wage increases; at least as long as the economy is channelled by Leijonhufvud's first corridor. Nowadays (December 2013) the European economy is clearly in the second corridor, and responsible unions must prevent too much wage moderation, and should press the government to stimulate effective demand by an increase in its own (investment) expenditures.

When reading Minsky we discover that without an external negative shock the economy can shift from a corridor. A long period of success makes people less alert and less responsible. They increasingly invest in more risky ways. Not only consumers and buyers of investment goods, but also financial investors and banks, increasingly create more liabilities relative to their assets. So, an economy in the first corridor becomes increasingly fragile. Then, a small external shock is enough to cause a financial and economic disaster.

We also discussed the contributions by Shiller and by Akerlof and Shiller. Shiller bases his analysis on his proposition that it is an uncontroversial fact that 'what goes up, must go down', at least in the case of asset prices. The behaviour of asset buyers appears to be irrational: they assume that a price rise will be followed by further increases. This way of arguing is disputable. The following example illustrates why this argumentation is flawed. Dutch home prices have been rising for decades. Nobody knows exactly when this rise will come to a halt. Several factors play a role in the formation of the price of a house, while the future is unknown. It implies that the purchase of a house for a price that is higher than it was in the previous period is not irrational. People are only irrational if they finance their purchase in an increasingly risky way and do not have a large enough buffer to handle the situation in case of a change in income and/or costs; if this occurs, they are, nevertheless, angry with everyone except themselves. Otherwise, people are just risk lovers.

Akerlof and Shiller discuss the concept of animal spirits extensively. We looked at a few examples, namely confidence, fairness, corruption, and bad behaviour. They also discuss money illusion and storytelling. The common denominator, which makes these issues expressions of animal spirits, is difficult to find. Akerlof and Shiller suggest at least a relationship characterized by a lack of information. In a world with perfect information these phenomena would not happen. We have suggested a relationship characterized by instinct, intuition, and the ontology of paradigm and frame. These elements function as a necessary context within which information is understandable—*embedded information* so to speak.

We draw the conclusion that the difference in methodology is decisive in an explanation of why post-Keynesian analyses, theories, and policy advice are so different. It is uncertainty that rules the open and organic world. This permanent uncertainty cannot—by definition—be approached by extensive analysis and calculations that will find out what to do. Animal spirits rule the behaviour of people. At this point post-Keynesians should cooperate more with institutional and evolutionary econo-mists. The latter also start with uncertainty, but see this as a basis on which to develop rules of conduct. People always develop cultures which imply a common understanding of the situation. This gives people a tradition, based on their personal and group experi-ences, and functions as a rich source of rules, which help them to deal with unknown situations. Our chapters about sociology deal extensively with this way of handling problems of uncertainty.

With respect to the current crisis we see the following typical difference between the two opposing approaches. Neoclassical economists see the interest rate policy of the FED as the main cause of the crisis. Post-Keynesian economists consider the deregulation of the financial world over a period of about two decades as the main cause of the increas-ing fragility of the financial world. The credit crunch should be countered by a recapi-talization of the banks by the governments. But this is not enough. Now the (European) economies are in a depression, Kregel emphasizes the necessity of an increase of the effective demand by the government. In Figure 8.16 we have summarized the difference in analysis between the neoclassical and the post-Keynesian approach with respect to the question of whether a free market economy is a stable or an unstable system. The presen-tation is a typical neoclassical one: demand and supply interpreted as expression of the

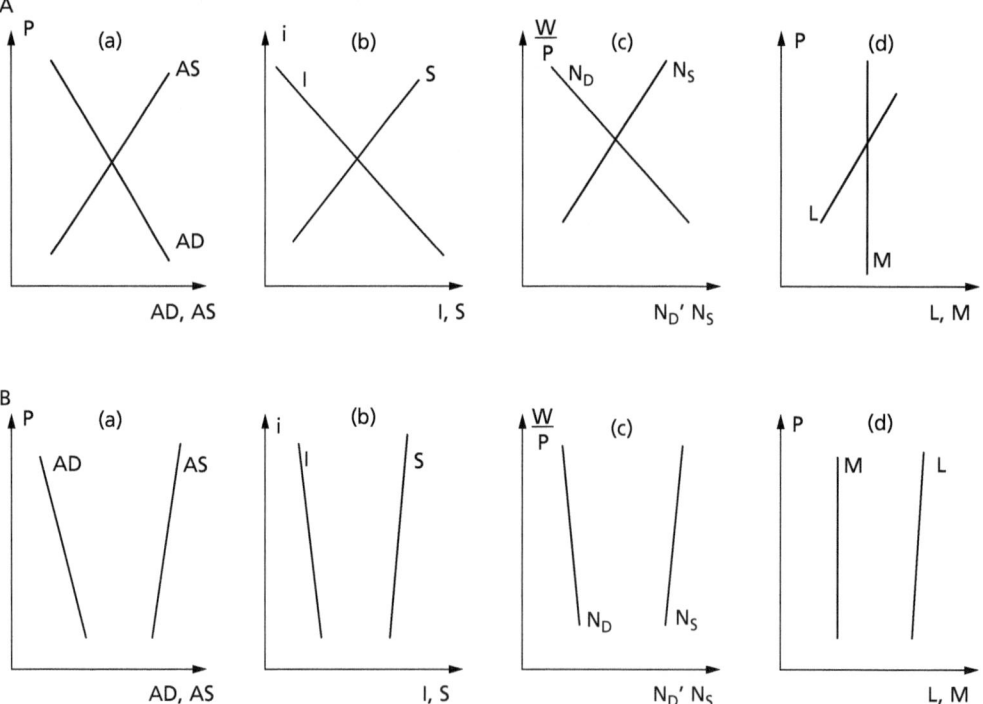

Figure 8.16. First row: Neoclassical Analysis of a Free Market Economy; Second row: Post-Keynesian Analysis of a Free Market Economy Outside the First Corridor, Presented in a Neoclassical Framework of Demand and Supply Functions; (a) goods market; (b) capital market; (c) labour mar-ket; (d) money market

orthodox laws of demand and of supply. In an economy in disequilibrium, where uncertainty rules, the results appear very different. These pictures can definitely not function as a totem for the neoclassical tribe.

The most important problem of the post-Keynesian approach is, however, the lack of a clear formulation of variable human nature. It is clear that the economic climate, which is expressed in terms of optimism and pessimism, can change, with far-reaching consequences for the situation of individual persons. But there is no analysis of the relationship between the state of the economy and the state of the minds of the people. Which forces potentially move people? Which forces develop in which type of situation? A depression might trigger irrationality—suicide rates increase in economically bad times, for instance. People might become more corrupt and fraudulent and more prejudiced against foreign groups in a depressed economy. In our chapters on psychology and sociology we will discuss these questions in more detail. It will appear that sociology especially contains more analysis of the relationship between macro-level and micro-level phenomena: the so-called agent-structure problem.

In Chapter 9 we will discuss social economics.

9 Social Economics

9.1 Introduction

Social economics has a long history already. O'Boyle (1996) gives an overview of the discipline, and shows that many perspectives and strategies are brought together under this umbrella. The common denominator is the idea that economic life is socially or even religiously embedded. It is a mix of normative and positive analyses. The difference between the two is less apparent than it seems at first sight. Positive analyses can be judged on the basis of methodological norms, and normative analyses of actual events and processes might be derived from generally accepted norms and values. If humanist and Roman Catholic economics offer a blueprint for a better world, many Western citizens might support these ideas. Then humanist and Catholic economists have the task of making analyses and models so as to make clear which instruments can be used to reach particular goals. John Stuart Mill is seen as one of the founding fathers of modern social economics (Mill 1848, 1874). He criticized a simple use of the utility concepts. He made a categorical distinction between economic utilities (pleasure), social utilities (moral norm maintenance), and aesthetic utilities (judgements, based on forms that touch our emotions positively). According to Mill, there are no common denominators that make it possible to calculate total utilities; the three different categories cannot be reduced to each other. O'Boyle (1996) considers Marx, Schumpeter, and Keynes to be leading figures in this field. These economists have been discussed already, and Marx will be discussed in our sociology chapter also, as an important sociologist. Methodologically, however, this group of figures is far from homogeneous. There must be something different, which makes social economics a separate strand of economics.

The latest overview on social economics is the handbook edited by Davis and Dolfsma (2008). In their introduction they make it clear how they see the position of the field, especially in relationship with several other social or socio-economic approaches. They highlight a difference between the early social economy, the current social economics, socio-economics, and new social economics.[1] *Social economy* stands for the field of research that is focused on not-for-profit activities, serving particular economic goals. This field still exists, and nowadays we can think of foundations, cooperatives, and

---

[1] The concept social economics is used in two different ways. Social economics as used in the title of this chapter means the total of the different strands just mentioned. We call this social economics in the broad sense. Social economics in the narrow sense of the word refers to that part that uses the social character of human behaviour, including economic behaviour, as its axiom.

associations, active in the field of sustainability, civil society, and common goods. *Social economics* (in the narrow sense of the word) is defined as the field which not only deals with social economy as it has just been defined, but also with typical problems of so-called mixed economies and societies: besides a large collective sector, there is also a large free market sector. Davis and Dolfsma approach their subject from a typical sociological paradigm: economic life is socially embedded. The term economic refers to the economy, being an important sector of society. So developments in consumption, production, and employment, for instance, are explained by reference to the social and moral context of the economy. People tend to buy consumption goods that create status within the group to which they belong. People search for jobs that create social approval, and if a person is unemployed while living in a group where unemployed people are blamed for being unemployed, this is terrible for him. So, the starting point of every analysis is the social structure or network in which the various actors play their social roles. Then this analysis is applied to networks in the economy, while the inequality between different actors or organizations is emphasized.

Another approach within broad social economics is *socio-economics*. Here the starting point is orthodox and neoclassical economics. An increasing number of economists recognize that social life is not completely endogenous and determined by economic factors, even in the economy. They look for variables of a social character, and add these to their economic analysis. The last mentioned approach is called *new social economics*. According to Davis and Dolfsma (2008), this field is essentially the opposite of what they define as social economics. It approaches social life in the economy as an institution, which is economically embedded—an institution that enhances the efficiency of economic life. In Chapter 4 we discussed new institutional economics (NIE): the orthodox economic theory of institutions. In Chapter 6 we discussed original institutional economics (OIE): institutions are socially embedded and affect economic performance significantly. In the field of social economics we see the same difference, which makes it possible to distinguish between *original social economics (OSE)*, on the one hand, and *new social economics (NSE)* on the other. The subject matter of institutional and social economics is practically the same. Methodologically speaking there is a difference: OIE is strongly influenced by the evolutionary philosophy, while OSE is methodologically more pluralistic.

To illustrate the differences between the various approaches defined so far we take the example of globalization. We show that different paradigms and analyses lead unavoidably to different policy advice.

Marx foresaw increasing globalization. For him, this process was unavoidable, because large firms—under the pressure of competition—would never end their search for new markets: markets of raw materials and other inputs as well as sales markets. Multinational corporations would go to undeveloped and underdeveloped regions in the world, in order to profit from cheap inputs, and to create markets for their products. If not, they would lose the competitive struggle—as others will definitely go. The NIE approach, although on the basis of a different methodology, comes to the same conclusion: globalization is unavoidable. Economic actors will never stop improving their economic position. So, globalization offers the expansion of human horizon, and technological progress will make it possible for the masses to constantly travel around, and to profit from the comparative advantage of so many economies. Since cultures, including the cultures of economic life, are embedded economically, it is obvious that the culture and institutions of the most competitive persons, organizations, and countries also win the cultural and institutional battle. According to the radical economic approach, accumulation and concentration of economic power in the hands of a few multinational corporations will create countervailing powers in the hands of a few globally operating unions. Only a global welfare state can prevent a global class struggle. The orthodox economic approach, including the NIE view on the origin of institutions, prefers a different strategy. Inefficient institutions, which make the economy less competitive, should be deregulated. The interference of the government through rules and taxation should, especially, be systematically reduced. Only then our economies can compete on the global market.

Social economics in the narrow sense of the word (OSE) offers a different view on the process of globalization. It does not lead to one global economy with one global economic culture. Cultures and institutions are social phenomena, and express the social preferences of a particular group of people. If they prefer more government influence, this does not make the economy necessarily less efficient. On the contrary, governments and market sectors are quite complementary (Fligstein, 1998; DiMartino, 2008). Public goods such as dikes, and semi-public goods such as roads, railways, and digital infrastructure, are extremely profitable capital goods. Large parts of a system of social protection can be interpreted as a profitable long-term investment—investment in human capital. If a single mother with a few children receives a social assistance benefit from the state, this benefit has a strong investment character. Imagine what happens with the children in case of 'no assistance', and compare your image with the productive adults who grow up on a material basis delivered by the community. As long as a community is prepared to pay for costly investments through so-called social services, and consciously enjoy the benefits of a well-institutionalized economy and decent society, there is no problem in terms of competitiveness. So local cultures have costs *and* benefits, and it is up to the people how they keep things in balance. In Chapters 11 to 13 we will go into more detail when discussing matters such as the McDonaldization of the world economy.

The set-up of this chapter on social economics in the broad sense will be as follows. In Section 9.2 we will discuss the methodologies which are used in the different variants of social economics. We will see that the field is characterized by the relationship between 'economic' and 'social', where the meaning of the two concepts differs significantly between the different variants. In Section 9.3 we will discuss the concept of institution and the various analyses that can be derived from it. In Section 9.4 we will present a series of contributions, theoretical as well empirical, which are characteristic of what we call socio-economics. In Section 9.5 we discuss the philosophical roots of the social-economic approach by presenting the views of Adam Smith and Amartya Sen. In this we shall see that social economics already is very old, but still has great relevance. In this section we also present the views of

Sen on the current crisis and see why social economics is a fruitful way of approaching economic processes. Section 9.6 concludes. Section 9.7 contains a methodological intermezzo, which clarifies why the book continues with an exposition of psychology and sociology.

9.2 The Methodology of Social Economics

The axiom of social economics in the narrow sense of the word is the statement that *economic behaviour is socially embedded*. Several variants of social economics are all variations—small modifications or extensions—of this ontological truth. In Chapter 13 we will see that this is also the core axiom of economic sociology. The only difference between the two approaches is that social economics is constructed and developed by economists, and economic sociology is the result of research by sociologists. When discussing sociology we will present several views on the meaning of the concept 'social'. For the moment we translate the term into 'relations between persons and groups of persons'. In this section on methodology we will discuss a few contributions, which try to analyse the idea of social embeddedness, and we will see that agents are not completely moulded by social structure. Persons are assumed to be independent to a certain extent, and bring their personal identity to the ongoing social interaction.

In the first place, we will discuss the contribution by Davis (2008). He makes a distinction between a liberal society view and a social justice view. The first mentioned view defines individuals as atomistic, autonomous actors, who like to have as much individual freedom as possible to serve their own interests. In analyses of society the free individual is the starting point. In other words, liberals prefer methodological individualism as their scientific methodology. The social justice view is the anti-pole of the liberal view. The behaviour of persons is socially determined, whereby they willingly accept behavioural 'restrictions' with regard to fairness and equality. Persons prefer a society that offers them not only freedom from too much government interference, but also freedom from want. To understand the character of a particular society they prefer methodological collectivism as their scientific perspective.

Davis tries to combine the two views. He is inspired by Giddens (1986) and Granovetter (1985), two sociologists who worked on the interrelationship between the agent and the structure in which he operates. In Chapter 11 we will deal with these two authors in more detail. For the moment we stick to an explanation of Davis's view, which is expressed in Figure 9.1.

The arrow indicated by number 1 tells us that socially embedded persons influence their social structure by consistently behaving in particular ways. In constant interaction, members of the group or network increasingly affect each other's way of organizing and managing their own preference-orderings. So, in one and the same process social identity and personal identity are shaped. The arrow indicated by number 2 tells us that

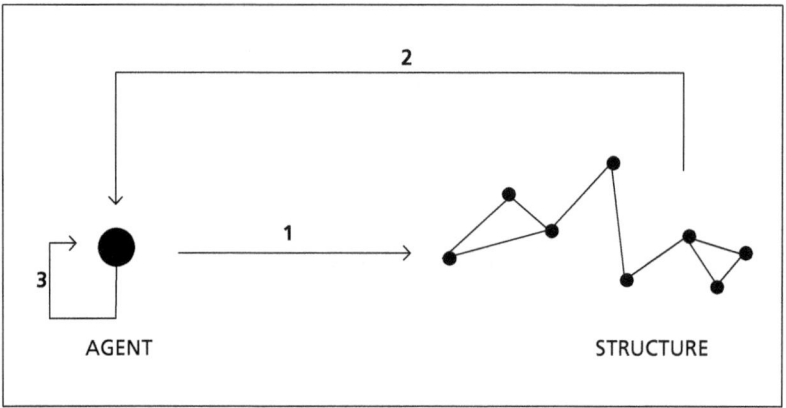

Figure 9.1. Simultaneous Shaping of Personal and Social Identity

every person is highly influenced by the social identity of the group to which they belong. In this way, a reconciliation has taken place between the autonomy of a person and the way his identity has been determined by his social environment. The ongoing interaction between individuals and groups triggers persons to constantly reflect on themselves. Without reflexivity, the figure shows a mechanism in the strict sense of the word. When we assume reflexive persons we approach social interaction in an organic way: vivid and more difficult to predict. This reflexive element is indicated with arrow number 3.

When presenting evolutionary economics, we explained why Veblen is the founding father of this discipline. He introduced the idea of downward and upward causation—taken together this is the idea of circular causation. The term downward refers to arrow 2 and upward refers to arrow 1 in Figure 9.1. He interpreted the recursive practice from 2 to 1 and back to 2 as a learning practice of an evolutionary and historical character. We saw in the text on evolutionary economics that persons and groups can never turn back, only go forward. History will be part of our memory (conscious or unconscious) forever. According to Lawson (1997), this learning process implies a continuous criticism of the concepts and understandings on which people act. In other words, reflexivity changes reality, one of the core axioms of critical realism (see Chapter 2). According to Davis, socially embedded persons develop a need for *ontological security*, because of the continuous changes in our reality. This existential need should preserve their status as an individual—as a person with their own identity.

To illustrate the meaning of the agent-structure analysis we can take the way the current economic crisis is dealt with by bankers, politicians, and academic financial economists. They operate in the financial world, in which they are socially embedded. The leading figures are in regular interaction with each other. They evaluate actual developments on a daily or at least weekly basis. They maintain a *common understanding* of the situation in the financial world. As we all know, this understanding is the typical orthodox and neoclassical view of the world. Bankers, politicians, and academic economists who disagreed with the neoclassical paradigm and analysis had a hard time, and most of them were fired or left the financial world 'voluntarily'. Many people in the financial world are simply followers, and unaware that their views are just one among many other interpretations. Journalists write one article after the other about financial matters in a neoclassical way. Then suddenly, for neoclassically orientated people at least, a crisis hits the financial world, and quite soon the global economy turns into a depression. The 'agents' are shocked and feel the need to talk with people from their neoclassical networks—not with people who always warned of a breakdown, of course. They have formed neoclassical identities, and their common understanding has been shocked by the anomaly of a severe crisis.

Some big men, such as Greenspan, the former chairperson of the FED, and De Grauwe, a famous Belgian macro-economist, openly blamed themselves for their cognitive closure: we were blind and not open to people who warned us. But most spokesmen of the groups mentioned defended and still defend themselves: 'crises are natural'—'nobody could foresee this'—'financial matters have become very complex'—'governments are to be blamed for their high debts; that's the big problem of today'—'as always expansionary monetary policies will help us out'. In this example the learning process has not been impressive until now (December 2013).

In the second place, we will discuss the contribution by George (2008). He assumes that persons have preferences and are able to form a judgement about these preferences, and he calls them first-order and second-order preferences respectively. If a person discovers that the two types of preferences are different, he has an *internal conflict*. George gives the example of a consumer who prefers a high-calorie meal (first order), but judges that a low-calorie meal is better for his health (second order). According to George, a rational person opts for the first-order preference. But the second-order preference is a typical human trait: reflect upon rational behaviour and bring in other considerations, which might lead to different choices.

When clarifying the difference between first-order and second-order preferences, it makes sense to introduce the aspect of time. Then, first-order preferences pop up immediately and second-order preferences are the result of reflection. But George's reflection is not about the person's rationality, but about so-called 'other considerations'. In this construction, the essential meaning of the concept rationality is ignored. Rationality is the capacity of humans to logically arrange information about the costs and benefits of a particular action on the basis of the emotion, which says: 'wait a minute, let me think about this'. If a person is not able to reconcile first-order impulses and second-order considerations, he has an internal or psychic conflict. The framework of interpretation on the basis of which reflection takes place, is based on the person's intuition, and affects the outcome of his self-scrutiny significantly. George seems to mix up rationality and morality when distinguishing between rational impulse and 'other considerations'. This confusion is typical for social economics: everything is socially embedded and psychic problems are completely endogenous and determined by social problems. This clarifies why George refuses to assume the existence of multiple selves. Consequently, the psychic problem could be interpreted as a conflict between different selves within one mind.

But without a careful constitution of the substance of a psychic problem, social economics is unable to show that the social world dominates the psychic world or mind. Our book aims at a careful constitution of what is meant by a typical economic, a typical social, and a typical psychic problem. Only then can the relationships between the three problem areas be researched.

Since we live in a capitalist context we are constantly influenced by advertisements that seduce us to buy goods from commercial firms. George assumes that these types of firms are stimulating first-order preferences, and trying to prevent people from a reflection upon the necessity of particular goods. In mixed societies, George's statement must be modified, since the flow of marketing information has a mixed character. Moreover, it is possible for capitalist firms to stimulate people to reflect and decide to buy fair-trade-like products, for instance.

Some reflections affect behaviour, and, over time, persons might have automatized these reactions and incorporated their first impulse. The second-order preference is the result of new considerations, which are about the new elements of the situation under scrutiny. Let us give the example of a gang of youths to illustrate this process. One of the members is quite new. When he is asked to arm himself to participate in a robbery, his first-order preference might be: no killings, please; I don't want to arm myself. But the pressure of his companions to defend the honour of the gang might lead to his second-order preference: yes, I do what the leadership of the gang requires from me. So with workers, whose first-order preference implies no strike, and with financial specialists, whose first-order preference is not to participate in the construction of intransparent products, meant to seduce people to buy something they don't want.

It seems that George assumes a society that consists of virtuous and socially well-integrated persons. Their first thoughts are intrinsic, which means serving their self-interest in a rational way. Virtuous people, however, always react prudently, and therefore follow their second-order preferences. Daily life is different, however. Social structure is fragmented and many people live in subcultures, all with their own 'morality'. In our sociology chapters we will go into more detail and see that it makes sense to distinguish between different types of morality. George interprets the internal conflicts of people as the conflict between a person and the claims of his social environment. Therefore, he does not make a distinction between different or multiple selves, which might be in conflict with each other. In our treatment of social psychology we will discuss this in more detail. For the moment we can say that this conflict is not a typical psychic problem. It concerns inner considerations about a social problem. Typical psychic problems are about conflicts within a particular person, isolated from his social and economic context. If such an internal conflict is deep, the person will need psychiatric treatment. He might not be able to develop a clear personal identity, and cannot develop a minimum of self-respect. Even if a person is economically rich and beloved and praised by many people around him, he might not be able to solve his psychic problem and become a stable and easily identifiable personality. It means that a social-psychological view on internal problems hinders an appreciation of the construction of 'multiple selves'. Therefore, we should develop an analysis of the mind first. Then we can see whether the use of multiple selves is necessary for successful explanations.

In the third place, we will discuss the contribution by Hirschman (1992). He makes a link between economic history and the history of economics. In earlier times there was no such thing as a common interest on a large scale. Clear national boundaries did not exist, and in so far there were boundaries, they were always subject to dispute. So, every group had an interest in preservation and aggrandizement, always relative to other groups. When economics liberated itself from its social embeddedness, it based its analysis on the idea of the self-interest of a person. In earlier times some rulers considered themselves to be rational, which meant that they were interest-governed. Other rulers were not rational, which meant that they were driven by wild and destructive passions, and were foolishly seeking glory and other excesses. As Hirschman (1977) formulates it: rational rulers are crude, if necessary, and prudent, if necessary. Machiavelli considered appeals to religion, morals, or abstract reason as the opposite of rational rule. The famous German ruler Bismarck characterized his own approach as 'legitimate interest policy' rather than an 'arrogant power policy'. It is important to find out who decides which interests are genuine interests, rather than the personal interest of a wild and passionate ruler. When Bismarck called his policy 'legitimate', the question of which (democratic) rules were applied to legitimize his policy remained.

For Hirschman, the homo oeconomicus developed by orthodox and neoclassical economics is a rational fool, who is not committed socially and never reflects upon his choices. For a good understanding of daily reality we need to fill the utility function with more and different elements. If asked, Hirschman would definitely agree with Smith in his focus on the role of virtues, and oppose the ideas of De Mandeville, who saw vices rather than virtues as important elements that bring us, as an unintended consequence, well-being. In conclusion, we can say that Davis offers the broadest and best ontological construction. It remains unclear how he distinguishes 'economic' from 'social', and whether he would agree that there is essentially no difference between socially embedded economic actors and economically embedded social actors. When we consider the two concepts as referring to aspects of human behaviour, everything might become clearer. George does not recognize the existence of psychic problems, and therefore he calls first-order preferences rational. In second-order preferences positive—not negative—social elements are considered. This means that George's work has a clear ceteris paribus character.

Hirschman (1977) discusses the historical origin of the concept 'interest' and 'self-interest'. Both are constructed as the opposite of the influence of wild passions. This duality can be interpreted as the difference between rational and irrational. Hirschman adds to this 'duality' the difference between vices and virtues. In the self-interest approach the choice between vice and virtue is clearly of an instrumental character. For Hirschman, however, it is clear that economy and society as a whole is benefited by the presence of as many virtuous people as possible.

In Section 9.3 we will discuss the social-economic interpretation of the concept of the institution.

9.3 **Institutions**

9.3.1 INTRODUCTION

In Chapter 6 we explained the evolutionary approach and discussed the contributions by Hodgson (1988, 2001, 2006). He considers institutions to be social phenomena rather than economic ones. Institutions are rules of behaviour, ranging from habits and routines to customs, norms, and values. We must be aware that, in this series, rules have an increasing social and moral aspect. They do not only hold for individuals but also for families, firms, and governments. Rules are part of a framework of rules, which constitutes particular work and lifestyles. A very important framework of rules is the theoretical framework of interpretation, which is in people's minds. In the case of frequent social interaction people tend to develop a common understanding of their situation. This is called culture, which is our source of values and norms. Now we will discuss the work of a few authors who underline the statement that institutions matter.

9.3.2 GREIF ON CULTURE AND INSTITUTIONS

Greif (2006) agrees with the original institutional-economic (OIE) idea that markets and governance systems (or polities, as he calls these systems) are always institutionally embedded—without institutions there are no markets and no governance systems. But, in contrast with the OIE view, he argues that institutions have micro-foundations. It means that institutions on the macro level are based on ideas and rules of individual persons—and institutions emerge out of individual initiative. To illustrate this methodological individualism we can give the example of the institution of micro-finance in Bangladesh. Imagine a small village near a town. A well-known person with some authority in the village suggests that villagers might be able to form a cooperative and finance those people from the village who are willing to erect a small firm. For instance, a few women start a business; they want to transport food from the village to the nearby town. Other people from the village will rent a place on the market in that town to sell the products on a daily basis. Again, other villagers contribute part of their savings. In this way poor people get access to the capital market. Even if the businesses are very small, people can at least make a start. This institution— the cooperative—is based on the fact that the villagers know each other quite well. Some people are well known for their trustworthiness. Trust makes banking an easy job, incomparable with modern (investment) banks. If the new institutions are successful, the idea behind them will spread throughout the country, and after a while micro-finance will have become an important part of the institutions of the financial system of the economy.

According to Greif's analysis, a firm, a sector, or an economy is able to develop institutions that create a stable equilibrium in the system. In the case of a change in one or a few exogenous variables—a natural disaster, a change in political regime, or a large increase in the population of a particular village, for instance—people change their institutions in search of a new stable equilibrium. OIE approaches institutions differently. Institutional change is a process, which means that *change is endogenous.* Particular material circumstances and institutions appear favourable for the generation of new ideas and innovations. This, in turn, improves the quality of production processes and products. The growth of material wealth makes it possible to create even more favourable material circumstances and institutions, and so forth.

The difference between the exogenous and the endogenous explanation is related to the question of whether we see ideas as the result of individual creativity or as the result of rational planning by firms, or by society as a whole. Greif does not only think of technical innovation, which is, to a certain extent at least, subject to planning. But changes in human belief systems, and a change in type of motivation, which results from these changes, cannot be planned at all. We cannot observe these changes empirically but can only hope for them. But when change comes we can try to participate in the further spread of the new ideas and beliefs. For Greif, Western civilization is the result of a process of individualization, triggered by new ideas of persons. This is a paradigm change of the highest order. It broke feudal systems, which created one war after the other. Individualism led to a strong increase in (international) trade.

9.3.3 AALBERS (ET AL.) ON THE SECURITIZATION REVOLUTION

Schrijvers et al. (2010) have edited a series of articles under the title 'The Making of Markets'. They state that there is a paradox between two different approaches: the neoclassical economic approach and the typical political science view. The first focuses on the free market, and only in case of market failure is there room for government interference. The second focuses on the government and only in case of government failure is there room for markets. Both approaches are highly abstract and unrealistic, and the proponents suffer from *rationalist hubris*. Schrijvers et al. pretend to offer an alternative approach: rather than starting with an ideal-type of approach we should start with the actual situation, and give a detailed empirical description. They focus on the question of how market processes influence the formation and change of public interests. Aalbers et al. (2010) have taken the securitization revolution in the Netherlands during the 1990s as their subject matter. Securitization is defined as the transformation of (pieces of) mortgage loans and other types of loans such as consumer credit, into bonds, which are tradable on the secondary capital market. The argumentation for this financial innovation is the idea of the spread of risks. Banks were increasingly inclined to attract new capital, and to evade rules about capital requirements set by supervisory boards. Therefore, they created many new financial products, which were sold to newly erected 'firms': the so-called SPVs (special purpose vehicles). By this judicial trick, the banks, which fell under the jurisdiction of supervisory boards, kept a large amount of risky assets and liabilities off-balance. Since the new products were very complex and intransparent, the supervisors had to deal with growing information asymmetry. Now the important question is how the supervisors reacted to this development. In general, they began to delegate the supervision to the banks themselves: self-control. Unfortunately, the banks were more interested in lower capital reserve requirements rather than a sufficiently high level of solvability. Justification of the behaviour of banks as well as the central banks was and still is the argument that there is competition in the banking market, and banks which lose the confidence of the public will go bankrupt. The Dutch central bank formulated a number of conditions, so as to limit the market for securitized products to professional buyers and sellers only; rather than the public at large. The central bank was highly influenced by the interests formulated by the lobby club of private banks. Public interests, such as the stability of the financial system as a whole, were not served. Aalbers et al. come to the conclusion that the Dutch central bank did not have a coherent vision of how to react to the globalization of the financial world; it suffered from cognitive closure, a concept they borrowed from MacKenzie (2006).

Looking at the ambition of Aalbers and colleagues (2010) we have the following comment. The authors pretend to offer an alternative to unrealistic abstractions, such as the neoclassical economic and the political scientific view. Their alternative is characterized as empirical research of an actual situation. It suggests that this empirical work is not based on an abstract theoretical model. But this is impossible; every researcher needs a paradigm and an analysis of the situation, so as to define the concepts to be observed in a particular situation. Aalbers et al. keep their a priori notions implicit. But in the end they come to the conclusion that the central bank suffers from cognitive closure and a lack of cognitive distance from the lobbies of private banks. However, this conclusion can only be drawn if a framework of interpretation is offered where the concepts cognitive closure and cognitive distance play an important role. Otherwise, we will never be able to empirically observe this 'fact'. For economists who also studied psychology and sociology, understanding of the two concepts is no problem. So, after having presented an overview of the psychological approaches, including our construction of the psychic world, and after an overview of the various sociological approaches, including our construction of the social world, the contribution of Aalbers et al. can be appreciated. Then we observe that almost all financial experts, in the private as well as in the public sector, are educated in neoclassical economics only. For the supervisors the pleas of the private bankers in favour of self-control and the role of competition is convincing; they are not educated and able to oppose the justification, saying that 'if everybody is free to serve his own interests, the unintended outcome of a free market implies a maximization of general welfare'.

9.3.4 ELINOR OSTROM ON THE DIVERSITY OF INSTITUTIONS

Ostrom (2005) discusses the problem of the design of institutions. She stresses the diversity of institutions, which means that neither the market nor the government alone can efficiently institutionalize situations. Every situation requires a mix of institutions, which, in combination, might function well. No market functions well if there is no government to protect property rights, and be co-responsible for the quality of the goods, for instance. No economy can function well if the government takes most of the decisions about investment and production. Even in the most extreme days in the Soviet Union consumers were at least free to buy or not to buy particular shoes, TVs, or furniture.

In orthodox economics the problem of common goods is solved by the idea that every good must have a private owner. This owner will be the actor most motivated and well informed to use the good in the most profitable way. In case of public property rights, the civil servants responsible for a particular service are less motivated, and therefore less informed, about the way the service can be delivered in an optimal way.

Ostrom, however, is more optimistic about the idea of institutional frameworks, which consist of mixtures of principles. Imagine a natural reservation, which is owned by the government. A very rich person wants to buy it, so as to be able to organize a yacht party for his friends once or twice a year. Imagine that the government sells to the rich person the right to, now and then, organize such a party. Moreover, the government asks volunteer organizations to take part in the maintenance of the reservation, and plans places, along the cycle roads, where commercial organizations can have their small restaurants. The area is open to the public, who are required to stick to a series of rules, formulated by the volunteers, and accepted by the government as legal rules. In this way the government takes the lead in the design of institutions, and takes care that the area serves a mix of interests. In her empirical research Ostrom shows that there are more choices than just the straightforward one between public and private-commercial institutions. Design principles can help us to develop *polycentric institutions*.

An illustrative example is described by Huizing and Van Sas (2013). They analyse the problem of doping in the world of sports, and in the cycling world in particular. Imagine a situation, which can be characterized as follows:

(1) Professional cyclists are economic, rational, and social actors.
(2) Doping is not forbidden, or at least there is no monitoring.
(3) There are no rules of fair play.
(4) There are no significant negative health effects.
(5) Doping is costless.
(6) The cyclists are equally talented.

The result is that all cyclists use doping, but this is not a problem. But if doping is costly, and there are definitely negative health effects, there is a prisoner's dilemma. There are different approaches to solving this dilemma. The free market solution says that every individual cyclist is responsible for his well-being, and should choose his optimal mix of performance and health. The government solution is the construction of a list of negatives—drugs that are forbidden (completely or just to a certain extent) and the development of an effective monitoring system. A third solution implies that the association of sportsmen is responsible for the solution to the prisoner's dilemma.[2]

At the moment, a mix of government and cycling authorities are responsible for the monitoring and the penalizing of cyclists who have cheated. A list of negatives and the obligation for the cyclists to constantly let the cycling authorities know where they can be found for a drugs test (the so-called whereabouts) are the two most important instruments for maintaining the rules.

The third solution can be reached by applying the common property resource (CPR) approach, as advocated by Ostrom. The starting point of the analysis is the observation that many professional cyclists know each other, and have a common understanding. Most of them are very much against doping. But almost all of them feel forced to use it, because the others are using it too. Actually, a cyclist has the choice to use doping or to stop his professional career as a cyclist. Now we interpret doping as a *common bad*, as long as it is not forbidden by the government and organizers of competitions. Given the culture of the cyclists they should organize themselves, discuss the problem of doping extensively, and develop a set of rules that fits their common understanding. An example could be the rule that all cyclists who participate in this organization will keep a diary, in which he registers all the drugs he is using. This diary will be accessible to all participants. So, in a particular competition everybody knows from everybody else what sort of dope the others are using. This will stimulate a process of *social control*, where, in this way, notorious doping users are labelled. Every cyclist who is member of the association of cyclists must have the right to request a dope test of other members of the association. This might lead to different competitions, where cyclists are grouped on the basis of their doping level.

In this design we see that various principles are combined: a free market for competitions, where (teams of) cyclists can compete with each other. The (sociological) group of cyclists try to solve a common bad, as does the government, which is an absolute maximum of drugs use.

Kiser and Ostrom (1982) plea for a *universal framework of nested components*. This is a system of parts and wholes, which means a large whole system, consisting of subsystems and subsystems of subsystems. An illustrative example is the global economy. Now we can imagine a large number of nested subsystems, such as the European economy, the Dutch economy, the Dutch health-care system, the Dutch system of hospitals, a particular hospital, and its cardiology department. In all these subsystems we can imagine a design consisting of different control systems, such as government regulation, bodies of consultation, free markets, and groups of volunteers.

Kiser and Ostrom are political scientists. For them institutions are rules meant to control human actions and interactions. Ostrom (2005) states that individuals and groups craft

---

[2] Be aware that there is an important difference between the sport's association and the association of sportsmen.

their own rules on the basis of their cognitive systems, which are also meant to order their behaviour on a relatively subconscious level. Ostrom—like Greif—is a deductivist, who derives theories and empirical hypotheses from a set of axioms and conceptual relationships. According to her we need a universal framework of cognitive systems, on the basis of which we can analyse situations and design our institutions. Unfortunately, universities suffer from the problem of the Babel Tower: many separate perspectives, each with their own language.

There is an important difference between a nested system of subsystems on the one hand, and a system of scientific perspectives on the other. While an economy can be pictured in terms of systems and subsystems, orthodox economics is based on a set of axioms which are about one particular aspect, namely the economic aspect of natural scarcity. To make this analysis more realistic we need to develop other aspect-systems, and present the economy and its subsystems in terms of a system of integrated aspect-systems. This is exactly what this book is trying to do. The problem of the realism of a theory must be tackled on the axiomatic level. Neoclassical economics is built on the idea of an economic and rational actor. Typical sociological analysis is based on the idea of a social actor, and typical psychological analysis is based on the idea that we are all only rational to a certain degree. A political scientist is not asking these questions of human behaviour; he is focused on the problem of controlling behaviour by means of governance systems, which are systems of rules. Our book, however, focuses on the development of a system of integrated aspect-systems. This system tells the controller what to control; in other words, what human drives or motivations must be controlled.

The system in this book makes a distinction between the economic, the social, and the psychic aspect, and tries to integrate the three aspect-systems. If an integrated analysis is made, then a political scientist can try to find out how to control this integrated system; in other words, how to influence the three primary drives of people and how to create a solid foundation for these drives so as to channel human behaviour. When we take the example of the part-whole system just mentioned (from global economy to the cardiology department in a particular Dutch hospital), and we have to design an institutional framework for this group of cardiologists, it is, for instance, very important to find out whether there is (social) rivalry between different groups of cardiologists, or between cardiologists and the group of heart surgeons, or between cardiologists and the group of nurse practitioners. Of course, we must find out which institutions are economically efficient in this particular situation. And, last but not least, the question of whether leading figures of the groups just mentioned are quite irrational or not is relevant. Only then we can find out how to coordinate and control activities.

9.3.5 ACEMOGLU ON ECONOMIC POWER AND INSTITUTIONS

Acemoglu, Robertson (2012) starts his analysis on the emergence of economic institutions with the existence of economically powerful firms who are constantly searching for new opportunities. When pioneers enter an 'empty area', and discover fertile soil, raw materials, and cheap labour, they try to communicate with local people to see whether peaceful relations and voluntary trade is possible. If not, they ask for (military) protection, and start their explorations and exploitations. The next stage is the establishment of local rule that is positive towards foreign investment. In other words, political institutions are established which justify the company's profit-seeking activities. On the basis of established law, economic institutions can be built, such as contract law. The most important matters for the colonists are the protection of property rights and the prevention of the institutionalization of countervailing powers, such as labour unions and welfare-state-like claims. The local economy should become an integrated part of a global free market economy. The justification of this behaviour says that, in this way, economic growth will spread over the world, and the masses can profit from it.

Of course, economic development creates countervailing powers. In the case of industrialization, large groups of workers work very near to others, doing more or less the same jobs. This makes the formation of unions a relatively easy job. In other stages of development, other institutions emerge, serving the interests of the then powerful groups.

So far, this is a concise interpretation of Acemoglu's view on the way the global economy functions—not the way the economy should function. Economic powers rule the world. Some groups, especially the capitalists, use the free market ideology as a justification of their actions. When European colonists travelled to other regions in the world—North America, South America, Africa, South and East Asia—these regions did not, of course, appear to be empty areas. But on the basis of superior military and other types of technology the colonists saw opportunities which were not available to the local people.

We can add to this claim an explanation of how the process of justification took place. Besides capitalists, many Europeans went to primitive cultures and tried to liberate these people from fear of their gods. Christian missionaries and ministers did a good job, but had to face strong resistance from local rulers. Great Britain and France established their governance systems, and tried to reframe the minds of the local people. Even today we can observe the permanent cultural influence of the former colonists.

Acemoglu and Robinson (2012) discuss extensively the issue of why many nations fail to become rich. The authors make a distinction between extractive and inclusive institutions. Extractive institutions are installed and maintained by an economic and political elite, which considers the economy to be a tool that can be used to rule the nation. The mass of the people are just meant to serve the objectives of the elite. If the rulers feel safe enough they might move from strong suppression and force to a more sophisticated approach. Then, the masses can extract more resources from the economy. Inclusive institutions evolve as soon as the mass of the people are involved in the development of political institutions. Most democracies tend to create and maintain an economy with a relatively large free market sector, where individuals can take the initiative to set up a business and the government will protect their property rights. If the institutions of a particular nation are extractive, it might take centuries before they shift into a more inclusive direction. In some cases the extractive institutions are 'imported', as is the case in North Korea. Then a revolution, supported by foreign powers, might help. If the institutions are the result of internal power games between different clans, revolution and foreign support will just promote these internal struggles. The main thesis of the book is the proposition that *institutions are critical* to the question of why some nations succeed, while others fail, in becoming rich. They discuss many historical cases, and show why different economic performances correlate with different institutions.

Acemoglu and Robinson also discuss a number of alternative approaches, which fail to explain the wealth and poverty of nations.

(1) The geography factor. They show that geographically rich areas, such as the Congo remain poor, while there are geographically poor areas that have become rich. They also discuss areas with the same geography, but different economic performances.

(2) The cultural factor. They interpret culture as a series of habits of the people, which characterize the way in which they live their lives—their food and drink, their religious rituals, and the dances they perform in celebration. They reject the Protestant ethics thesis of Weber, which stresses the work ethic of the people. They suggest that everyone who does not work 24/7 is considered as lazy in the Protestant world-view. I consider their portrait of the Protestant views as flawed, and will discuss this matter in the chapters on sociology in more detail.

(3) The ignorance hypothesis. This thesis suggests that poverty is the result of a lack of advice by experts from rich countries. The implicit idea is that there are experts who know why rich countries are rich, and that they know how to make a poor economy into a rich one. Imagine an African dictator, who is surrounded by his clan and rules the nation in a bloody way. Would a neoclassical economist, who advises the dictator to open the economy for foreign investors, really be successful? Economic history gives a clear answer: no. Since political institutions are decisive, every piece of advice must be focused on a reduction in the degree of extraction of the political institutions. Therefore, it is necessary to have a multidisciplinary map of society.

The book is impressive in its exposition of so many cases from world economic history. It is, however, poor in its explanatory power; it does not offer a sophisticated understanding of processes of economic development, and of its critical factors.

In the first place, there is no clearly formulated ontology. It means that the principal concepts, such as economic, social, technology, geography, culture, and institution are not defined and their interrelations are not analysed.

In the second place, although the book stresses the importance of history, it is forced to decide whether geography or culture or institutions is the critical factor. In a more sophisticated analysis, combinations of factors are key in the explanation of growth. Of course, geography matters. Some geographical areas in the world are poor, given the culture of the people. But if people of a different culture visit this area, they might be able to explore and exploit natural resources which appear to be there. As long as nobody is able to find valuable resources an area is poor. But it remains true that some geographical areas are richer than other areas. Norway has found oil, and Sweden has not, although it has the same culture, the same institutions, and the same technology.

In the third place, culture is badly defined. The authors do not refer to basic sociological and psychological literature. There is an overwhelming amount of literature about the definitions of concepts, such as culture and institutions; none of them are used by Acemoglu and Robinson. In Chapters 10 to 13 we will discuss this literature extensively. The theoretical and empirical work on culture by Hofstede, especially, offers us the knowledge necessary for a fruitful approach to the problem of economic development. Acemoglu and Robinson argue that culture is not a critical factor, since Spanish rule in Latin America has the same culture as British rule in North America, although there is a remarkable difference in institutions and economic performance between the two regions. Hofstede's work makes it clear that we cannot speak of a European culture, since the culture of North Europe is significantly different from that of South Europe.[3]

In the fourth place, if there is no explicitly formulated paradigm and analysis, it is impossible to find appropriate empirical indicators. The danger that the hypotheses to be tested are true by definition is real. High income per capita becomes an indicator of the inclusiveness of the institutions. As we have discussed already, there is a significant difference between the economic theoretical idea of well-being of a nation and the GDP per capita. Moreover, a study on extraction cannot ignore inequality within the nation. In this case, the actual figures of the USA over the last decades are striking; apparently the USA institutions seem more extractive than the book by Acemoglu and Robinson suggests.

The analysis by Acemoglu and Robertson is quite radical. It cannot be interpreted as a typical NIE analysis, since it is not based on a neoclassical framework of interpretation. It assumes that markets are characterized by oligopolies, which have much economic and market power. It assumes that capitalists are powerful enough to have a significant effect on government policy. There is room in their analyses for countervailing powers, which means that economic institutions are the result of power battles. The institutions change as soon as power relations change.

There is hardly any room, however, for an independent role for culture and for strong personalities. In sociological terms we can say that Acemoglu and Robertson are supporters of the conflict-sociology, not of the functionalist consensus sociology. Society is not based on consensus; only on temporary compromises (see Chapter 11 for an extensive treatment of the two macro-sociologies). Culture, in the sense of common cognitive understanding, is a reflection of the power battle between different interest groups in society. The most powerful capitalists and firms justify global capitalism as a system that serves the general interest. Smaller firms with a strong interest in their home market

---

[3] If the popular American TV programme on family issues, *Dr. Phil*, became popular in Latin America, that would show a true cultural shift.

might justify some trade protection. It appears it is not difficult to find evidence of foreign firms dumping large amounts of goods on their home market.

Now we will briefly comment on Acemoglu's and Robertson's position. It is clear that they assume that man is economic and rational. The concept 'social' does not refer to a drive or motivation; it just refers to power battles between different groups of people. But the battle itself is of an economic nature. Culture does not play an independent role—there might be cultural battles, but their outcome is determined by the economic power of the various participants. In our sociology chapters we will pay much attention to the interrelationship between culture and power.

In this book I offer an explicitly formulated multi-motivational paradigm (Chapter 14). It leads to a series of definitions of principal concepts, such as the concepts used in the work of Acemoglu and Robertson. His work shows the importance of *institutional inertia*. With a better analysis this inertia can be clearly understood, which makes it also possible to understand why, in some cases, a shift from extractive to inclusive institutions is possible. Because of a lack of micro-foundations, it is difficult to understand how institutional changes from extractive towards inclusive, and from inclusive towards extractive, might occur. Besides the idea of institutional inertia we can introduce the idea of *institutional entropy*. Without regular maintenance inclusive institutions disappear. In Chapter 15 we will discuss four control-mechanisms which can be used to build a theory about institutional maintenance or the lack of it.

For now we will just stress that culture plays an independent role as soon as we assume the existence of creativity and some free will, and we recognize the human capacity to develop moral sentiments. Then, we have brought together the ontological elements necessary for an independent role for culture. For a plausible explanation of the emergence of the welfare state institutions in north-western Europe we cannot do without this.

9.3.6 DOLFSMA AND SPITHOVEN ON SILENT TRADE

Last, we will discuss the difference between the orthodox new institutional economic view (NIE) and the original institutional view (OIE) on institutions. Dolfsma and Spithoven (2008) provide an answer to this question by means of a story, told by Herodotus (440 BC). The story is about a group of traders who approach a village that they had not visited before. Without being able to talk with each other, the different market parties are able to come to an exchange of goods; the case is called 'the silent trade'. NIE economists see the story as proof that markets develop out of an *institution-free situation*. Over time, trade becomes more complex and requires rules of exchange. Practical experience determines which rules make trade more efficient. OIE economists, however, see this story as proof that silent trade starts with a ritual, which is characteristic of the culture of the traders who take the initiative. The first steps must be interpreted as a type of gift exchange, which is a characteristic ritual in the case of intra-village trade. In other words, there is already culture present before an inter-village market emerges. We quote the story now to give the reader the opportunity to interpret the situation herself (Herodotus, 440 BC: book IV, section 196, cited in Dolfsma and Spithoven (2008: 517)):

The Carthaginians say also this that there is a place in Libya, and People living in it, beyond the Pillars of Heracles. When they, the Carthaginians come there and disembark their cargo, they arrange it along the seashore and go back again to their boats and light a smoke signal. The natives, as soon as they see the smoke, come down to the shore and then deposit gold to pay for the merchandise, and retreat again, away from the goods. The Carthaginians disembark and look; if they think that the price deposited is fair for the merchandise, they take it up and go home again. If not they go back to their boats and sit there. The natives approach and bring gold in addition to what they have put there already, until such time the Carthaginians are persuaded to accept what is offered. They say that thus neither party is ill-used; for the Carthaginians do not take the gold until they have the worth of their merchandise, nor do the natives touch the merchandise until the Carthaginians have taken the gold.

Denzau and North (1994) analyse trade beyond the village, as they call it, in a typical NIE way. For them, traders are economic and rational actors, always searching for beneficial exchanges. When trade is beyond the village the traders must find out how to trade and voluntarily exchange goods; in other words, what the exchange conditions in a new situation will be. In this way Denzau and North see traders developing their economic institutions. In practice, however, individuals and groups who are not necessarily traders approach each other. Maybe the persons from the other side are pretending to be traders, but are in fact soldiers of a large army, whose trading is the first step in a process that must end in complete domination. The story of Herodotus is exceptionally peaceful. History shows many examples of different ways of establishing markets. Dutch companies went to the East Indies in the 17th century. After a few visits they asked their bosses for military support. Warships made it clear to the local population that they should trade and that the exchange conditions were to be determined primarily by the Dutch. Neither the local rulers nor the imperialists were simple traders—both tried to dominate the local population, and exploit the resources and the 'labour available'. Dolfsma and Spithoven doubt whether the silent trade story really happened. Important in the NIE–OIE debate, however, is the question of whether inter-village trade starts in an institution-free environment or not. The silent trade case makes it clear that even in very peaceful circumstances culture exists, and might be responsible for the fact that the trade is voluntary, rather than the beginning of large-scale robbery. The rituals that make the market are a perfect form of social communication, although not one word has been exchanged.

Denzau and North interpret the emergence of institutions as a learning process. Three elements play a role. In the first place, the learning process is of an inductive nature. In the second place, the process is irreversible. If dramatic events take place, the emotional and cognitive reactions are stored in the memory of the people. In the third place, there might be sudden shifts in the viewpoints held by actors.

To illustrate their view on learning we can give the following example. The authors assume that the learners are economic and rational actors, and their viewpoint is that all other actors are economic and rational too. In other words, everyone uses the economic world-view as their frame of interpretation. Imagine the Dutch economy is characterized by an excess demand for labour. A specified and estimated neoclassical model tells us that the growth rate of wages is a function of the excess demand for labour and that the coefficient is 0.5. Moreover, the quantity supplied of labour is a function of the quantity demanded for labour, and the coefficient is 1.5. So, the growth rate of the wage rate can be predicted as soon as we know the excess demand. But then firms discover that immigration from Eastern Europe is increasing, leading to a higher coefficient in the second equation. On the basis of this experience they adjust the coefficient in the second equation, which has implications for the prediction of the growth rate of wages in the next period. So far, this case shows that, given a particular viewpoint (the neoclassical one), experience leads the actors to learn and to adjust their behaviour. The increasing immigration does not necessarily lead to a shift in viewpoint.

But after some time social conflicts arise between Dutch locals and East European immigrants, leading to lower productivity of firms and the Dutch economy as a whole. If, as a result of the increasing hostility, the number of immigrants decreases significantly, the neoclassical model should be adjusted again. NIE economists might discover that a realistic explanation cannot be given without the introduction of a social analysis into the economic models, which means a shift in viewpoint.

Given a particular paradigm and analysis, empirical testing might show that important parameters change over time. This is the inductive element in the learning process. But as soon as actors discover that the paradigm is not suitable for their situation, they are open to new ideas. A paradigm shift means a different analysis and model, which is the deductive element in the learning process. In other words, the ongoing discussion about deduction and induction is an artificial and unnecessary methodological divide. Every unit of 'learning', which is a unit of new knowledge, consists of deductive and inductive elements.

With respect to the problem of causation we see that NIE is based on the typical economic and rational actor. These substantial characteristics are the ultimate cause of his actions, while changes in circumstances or constraints are considered as the immediate cause. If NIE economists want to become more realistic, they should extend their paradigm with a social and a psychic element. OIE is of a historical and more evolutionary character. Everything changes all the time, and evolves in unintended directions. Unfortunately, OIE economists are not explicit in their analysis of ever-changing human nature. Even if a particular element constantly changes, it is necessary to carefully define which properties of which element are changing, and in which direction. An important example is the change of the unemployment rate of the Dutch economy over the years, while the definition of unemployment, which is the basis for statisticians to measure or estimate the number of unemployed as well as the size of the labour force, has also been changed over time. To understand the time series of unemployment rates it is necessary to be aware of changes in definitions. Official statistical offices try to solve the problem by making completely new series, based on the latest definition. When we compare Dutch figures of the collective burden in the 1970s, calculated in that period, they appear significantly higher than the figures for that period which are presented now. Applied to our problem of human nature: even if we assume that human nature is moulded by its circumstances, we should carefully formulate the definitions of different types of motivations, and try to discover changes in their properties.

In Section 9.4 we will give a number of examples of socio-economic research.

9.4 Socio-Economics

9.4.1 INTRODUCTION

Socio-economists take the typical economic approach as their starting point, and change and extend the model so as to take social and/or psychological factors into account. We discuss three examples of socio-economic research. In the first place, we look at an article by Van der Lippe and Siegers about the division of labour between husband and wife. They use the typical orthodox economic frame of a preference function and a few constraints as their starting point. They show that not only is the typical economic factor—relative wage rates—important, but also the social norm, which characterizes the culture at a particular moment. The second example is an article by Schenk about the merger and acquisition waves. He does not use the usual assumption of competitive markets, in which many utility or profit maximizers, under the constraint of their budgets, operate. He uses the picture of an oligopolistic market, in which the few suppliers act strategically. Some set the strategy, and others follow and imitate them. A last example is a book by Keizer, in which he analyses wage formation on a macro-labour market which is characterized by bilateral monopoly. In an economy in which the government has committed itself to guarantee full employment, unions can—under particular conditions—develop too much power. This could lead to a structural profit squeeze. Keizer shows that, in the period 1946–1978, important Dutch groups became too optimistic about the making of an extensive welfare state, combined with a low-profit business sector. *Shifts in ideology and militancy* show the overoptimism with respect to the malleability of economy and society. This led to wage and price inflation, and an increasing collective burden. In the 1970s the global economy was hit by two oil crises. Then it became clear that the Dutch economy did not have sufficient buffers to tackle this problem. The lack of solvency appeared to be the cause of a long recession. The similarity with Minsky's explanation of the financial crisis 2006–2008 is striking.

9.4.2 VAN DER LIPPE AND SIEGERS ON THE LABOUR DIVISION BETWEEN MAN AND WOMAN

The research of Van der Lippe and Siegers (1994) is on the labour division between husband and wife with respect to doing housework (home production) or having a paid job (production of market goods). They take as their analytical device the following elements:

(1) They assume that the wife as well as the husband try to maximize their own utilities under a number of restrictions. They formulate a preference function and a number of constraints.
(2) They bring in a social element by assuming that individuals are socialized beings, who derive social utilities from rule following action; so, the economic and rational actor is also a social being.
(3) They use the economic and sociological exchange theory and resource theory.

The economic part of the analysis says that we all strive for as much physical well-being as possible. This well-being is the result of the input of market goods by the husband and the processing of these goods into consumable goods by the wife.

The social part of the analysis says that during our childhood we are subject to a process of socialization, in which we come to understand the different roles we are playing in society. We learn that society expects particular behaviours from an individual, who becomes inclined to adjust to the rules, so as to receive recognition from others (social approval). Social approval depends on income and education-dependent social status (a), behavioural confirmation by adjusting to the normative context (b), and affection from eventual children (c). The basic restriction is the amount of resources available to a particular individual. Now the division of time over the production of market goods and home goods is determined by the principle of comparative advantage, and by the weight of the social approval element in the preference function. In the case of a change in the relative wage rate of the external job, the division will change.

The social norm regarding the division has changed in the Netherlands over the last few decades. Van der Lippe and Siegers construct a continuum from perfect traditional to perfect modern culture. Traditional culture is characterized by the husband producing the market goods, while the woman is responsible for the production of the home goods. Modern culture is characterized by a fifty-fifty distribution of the production of market goods and home goods. Dutch society shows a shift from quite traditional in the direction of a more modern norm. The normative background, which determines the position on the continuum, is affected by the parental background, the year of birth, and the religious background.

The empirical part is about the Netherlands in 1990. The data set that is used contains data from 800 households. Van der Lippe and Siegers estimate the following equation:

$$S = b(0) + b(1).\left[w(w)/w(h)\right] + b(2).N + b(3).\left[w(w)/w(h)\right].N + \ldots$$

S = share of the wife in the amount of paid work
w(w) = wage rate wife
w(h) = wage rate husband
N = position between perfect traditional and perfect modern social norm.

The component with coefficient b(1) shows the effect of the relative wage rate, and the component with coefficient b(2) reflects the effect of the social norm on S. The third component, with coefficient b(3), is an interaction term, which is about the interaction taking place between the relative wage rate and the level of the social norm.

The authors formulate two hypotheses to be tested:

Hypothesis 1: responses of wife and husband to changes in the relative wage rate are larger the more modern the norm of the relevant network.
Hypothesis 2: very traditional and very modern norms leave little room to react to changes in relative wage rates.

The second hypothesis means that the responses are largest at some point in-between, following, for example, a curvilinear path.

This research starts with the familiar preference-restriction framework developed by orthodox economics. When filled with typical economic elements, it offers a great theoretical apparatus, which clarifies the way the economic motivation is operating in the isolated economic world. But the authors recognize the significance of social factors, and specify the social element in the preference function in terms of social approval. Since the subject matter is the division of time of both partners on the labour market and at home, the social norm, which dictates a particular division, functions as one of the restrictions. If we compare this study with regular neoclassical studies, including the home economics of Becker, this is a big step forwards. It offers a clear integrative element: the influence of relative prices, in this case the wages of wife and husband, is affected by the ruling social norm.

The study elicits a few comments, which are meant to show in what ways further progress can be made in this field. The research is about the situation in 1990, but what if the study would explain the division over a particular range of years. Then the evolution in the social norm would have to be explained. In other words, the study under scrutiny takes the social norm in any particular year as the exogenous variable. An explanation of the change in this norm is beyond its scope. A further issue is the fact that Dutch society has been liberalized over the decades. There are two interpretations of female independence. The first says that the wife is free to follow her own preferences. She negotiates with her husband about who is doing what, without any force. The second interpretation says that women should favour financial independence. In case of a divorce, she is financially enforced to search for a paid job. This is a problem, since a woman who has chosen to be a housewife might not have the skills to participate in the market goods production. So, both home production as well as market production should be divided on a fifty-fifty basis. Actually, there are three cultures. The traditional one can be called the conservative culture. The second one is a classical liberal culture: every individual acts upon their own preferences. A third one, which can be called a continental liberal culture, says that every adult should be responsible for him or herself, whether they are married or not.[4] This responsibility also has a financial aspect. Society cannot be responsible for the financial consequences of broken marriages.

A third problem is the absence of any conflict-sociology in the analysis: marriage as a battle—a struggle for domination, mostly by men. The increasing number of divorces gives an indication of the battle and shows that many men and women feel forced to do housework or to search for a paid job. Maybe this view is implicit in the just distinguished socialist view: women must be financially independent of men so as to prevent their domination.

A fourth problem concerns the psychic aspect—the internal struggles within persons when it comes to a decision about having a job outside the home, or doing the housework. Men with low self-respect are sensitive to the expectations of their social environment. Women with low self-respect hesitate to accept an external job, even if their talents and qualifications are positive. The study of Van der Lippe and Siegers can be typified as a typical rational choice theory. A more realistic view might be the behavioural position, in which persons and groups might not be perfectly rational. In Chapter 10 we will discuss the idea of imperfect rationality in more detail. In Chapter 11 we will come back to the idea of rational choice, and see that in sociological rational choice also interesting attempts to discipline integration are taking place.

A last point is related to the microeconomic perspective of the authors. It makes sense to also view the problem of the division from a macroeconomic perspective. If an economy has been in a depression for a long time already, and wages are very low, there is hardly any choice left: both partners have to take every opportunity to work for money, even taking less satisfying jobs. Also, the children must search for a job, and if people are able to sell one or a few organs, or work as a surrogate mother, they might feel forced to do so. So, in many circumstances there is barely room for rational choice, as there is just one option.

An important reason for the authors to leave important elements, such as social conflict and irrationality, out of their analysis might be their focus on quantitative analysis

---

[4] The distinction between classical and continental liberalism is made by Hayek (1978).

and prediction of future developments. In the positivist tradition axioms and so-called auxiliary assumptions are less important. Even if scientists use unrealistic axioms and assumptions, the derived empirical relationships might appear stable across countries and over time. The problem with this methodological view is that stable empirical relationships exist in stable periods only, and disappear as soon as an economy and a society are out of balance—which is the case most of the time. Moreover, even if we have finally found a stable relationship, the problem is how to interpret and understand it. So long as we do not understand the relationship—the theoretical frame behind it does not trigger our emotions—we simply don't know what to do with it. The authors in this research formulate axioms and present them as the relevant elements in the preference function and as relevant restrictions. These axioms determine the way in which we are supposed to interpret the results: women are the most flexible element, at home as well as on the labour market. The interpretation can neither be linked to the self-respect of the partners, nor to domination by the man. These limitations make the empirical part of the study less valuable.

9.4.3 SCHENK ON THE MERGERS AND ACQUISITIONS WAVE

Schenk (2008) focuses on mergers and acquisitions (M&A), which appear in waves and are not successful most of the time. M&A neither improve productivity and profitability nor growth in market share. They appear to have negative consequences also for shareholder returns. This makes the question of why firms continue their M&A strategies relevant, particularly after a period in which many of them appear unsuccessful and the new organizations have to be deconstructed.

A typical neoclassical explanation for the failures runs as follows. There is a market for corporate control. The mechanism that coordinates the activities on this market can be described in the following way. Private equity (PE) firms take over firms which they consider to be underpinning organizations. They appoint new Board members, who restructure the firm. Bad parts go bankrupt, and good parts are—after a few important changes in organization and strategy—sold. In this way prestigious PE firms are guaranteed a big profit. The neoclassical explanation of the recurrent failures of M&A uses the principal-agent approach and indicates that the principals (shareholders)—including the new ones—have imperfect control over the behaviour of the agents (top management).

Schenk disagrees with the neoclassical view on M&A. It is implausible that particular mistakes are made time and again, and in a cyclical way: during the upswing of the M&A wave many principals are optimistic about their chances, and during the downswing many principals discover that control of agents is more difficult than they thought. It seems as if Schenk assumes that principals are forced to react as they do. He discusses a series of behavioural economic explanations and rejects them all. We cannot explain waves by blaming PE boards, and the boards of the firms involved in the M&A process, of suffering from *hubris*. The same holds for explanations in terms of *imitation* of prestigious firms or *rational herding*, which is based on informational externalities.

Schenk prefers an explanation which focuses on the market structure. Many markets are dominated by a few corporations. This structure forces firms to act strategically, which means imitating others. This imitative behaviour intends to reduce the 'risk of falling behind'. In the end he advocates the reintroduction of a public purpose standard in merger control.

Schenk explicitly rejects the neoclassical methodology of utility maximization under the constraints of resources available. But he also rejects explanations of a behavioural type. As already said, his explanation is focused on the oligopolistic character of many important markets. This structure forces participants to behave strategically, while operating under uncertainty. Schenk is unclear about the final goal of decision-makers. Is it maximization of profits (economic drive), or is it maximization of market share (social drive)? In Chapter 13 we will discuss Fligstein's view on the functioning of oligopolistic markets. He suggests that established firms are inclined to operate as a group, and divide the market among themselves. In this approach, the M&A phenomenon seems to take place before a market has been stabilized by the insiders.

Schenk also rejects the neoclassical idea of imperfect control of top managers by principals. We believe, however, that this control is highly imperfect. Principals and agents are member of one and the same network, which makes all members cognitively closed against seeing the main problems, which hinders them making a successful merger or acquisition. (See Kets de Vries, as discussed in Chapter 10, and Fligstein, as discussed in Chapter 13).

Empirical research shows that the most difficult problems are of a cultural kind. If an American firm takes over a Dutch firm, located in the Netherlands, American leadership has to deal with Dutch institutions. This makes American management techniques less effective than American managers expect. So with a German firm, which has taken over an American company located in the USA: cultural problems are almost insurmountable. Germans are used to institutions and leadership styles that are unknown in the USA. The permanent underestimation of the cultural factor leads to permanent overoptimism with respect to the profitability of mergers and acquisitions. After a series of failures firms are forced to break up recent combinations. But most dealmakers remain unaware of the relevance of the cultural factor and they begin to make new plans. Hubris might play a significant role. It is a potential inside all of us, and in times of upswing our hubris become manifest again. In this way we get a Minsky-like explanation of the M&A wave. This overoptimism is based on a strong social drive to grow bigger and bigger. The size gives the top managers the status they want. A more thorough psychological analysis might show that unrealistic calculations are especially accepted as realistic by managers with low self-esteem: they are unable to give themselves the respect they deserve—so others have to give them the desired recognition.

9.4.4 KEIZER ON OVEROPTIMISTIC IDEOLOGIES AND ATTITUDES

In our presentation of post-Keynesian economics we have paid attention to the deregulation of the financial markets during the 1980s and 1990s. Minsky (1982, 1993) warned of an increasing fragility of the financial system. A long period of economic growth makes financial investors overoptimistic, and they shift from risk-averse to risk-loving modes of finance. Minsky is a post-Keynesian and considers our reality to be an open system. This means that we are regularly confronted with unexpected shocks. If our systems, including the financial system, don't have the necessary buffers to dampen the effects of a shock, they might crash. Consequently, even a small shock could have disastrous effects.

More or less the same problem could be detected during the 1960s and 1970s on the West European labour markets. After the Second World War Western Europe recovered in a period of about five to ten years. Then a long period of stable growth began. The experiences from the period 1929–1945 had triggered emotions, such as 'never again such a series of disasters'. Under the influence of Keynes many politicians assumed that a free market economy is not a stable system and that a welfare system is necessary to prevent another process of radicalization, as took place during the 1930s. Justice is not a luxury good, but an important building stone for the achievement of a stable society. When building up a welfare state the assumption was that a stable society would not use the various welfare systems on a large scale. They were just meant as buffers in case of relatively small downswings. During the 1960s optimism, especially in circles of left political parties and unions, grew. 'WWII is a watershed—now we know how to make the business cycle obsolete—now we have found the social technology to combine efficient production with fair distribution.' Strong increases in wages and in the collective burden did not lead to a lower level of growth and employment, as was predicted by neoclassical theory. So, during the second half of the 1960s up to 1973 the left side of society became very optimistic about the social and economic future. With hindsight we might say that these parts of the population were too optimistic and acted irrationally.

When speaking of Europe it is important to make a distinction between the northern and the southern part of Western Europe. In the northern part there was more consensus between employers' organizations and unions about labour conditions and welfare services than in the southern part. Northern unions were more moderate and employers more progressive. Southern unions and left political parties were more militant, and so with right-orientated employers. The ongoing class struggle in the South had negative effects on economic and social performance. The northern economies seemed fine.

Then (the economy is an open system) the Arabs increased the price of oil significantly in 1973 as well as in 1979. The economic-political reaction of Dutch politicians—Keynesian stimulation and wage restraint—was correct. Nevertheless, the reaction in terms of increased production and employment was lower than expected. Why? The economic system appeared too fragile. The continuing increases in labour costs per unit of output had structurally squeezed the profits of the firms. Because the firms had continued their investments and production, their financial bases had become weak. In other words, the buffers in the economic system had become too weak. The oil crises appeared to be the so-called Minsky moments of the economic system. Pessimism made it impossible to continue. Fortunately not all West European economies had become severely fragile—there were important differences. Moreover, the Arabs invested much of their increased income in other parts of the global economy. So, during the 1980s Western Europe was able to recover.

Keizer (1982) contains a theoretical and empirical study about the changes in political ideology or framework of interpretation of the relevant Dutch political parties and in the attitudes of the unions and employers' organizations over the period 1946–1978. He measured these changes and related them to changes in the collective burden and to the rate of change in Dutch wages. These wages affected price inflation, which in turn affected wage inflation. All these relationships appeared significant for the period 1954–1978 (earlier figures were not available at that time). Three elements are important here.

(1) How are changes in ideology measured?
(2) How are changes in militancy measured?
(3) Why do changes in these two variables lead to wage and price inflation?

[Ad 1] Keizer makes a distinction between four categories of political philosophy or ideology. The first, indicated by RR, expresses a *libertarian view*: a free market economy with a government that is responsible for the protection of property rights, and a few pure public goods (dummy: 0).

The second, indicated by R, expresses a *moderate liberal view*: to the libertarian view is added a social minimum for all, including access to basic education and health care (dummy: 1).

The third, indicated by L, expresses a *social democratic and progressive confessional view*: every citizen should equally participate in important services of society. This striving for equality implies a moderate redistribution of income and wealth (dummy: 2).

The fourth category, indicated by LL, expresses a *socialist view*: a democratic society can only function well if the material means of living are thoroughly redistributed from the rich to the poor. Government planning should keep the total investments to a necessary level and the process of redistribution efficient and fair (dummy: 3).

Ideological shifts were measured by means of close reading of the yearly speeches of the parliamentary leaders under the heading 'Algemene Beschouwingen' (General Considerations).

[Ad 2] Also, for the measurement of the shifts in militancy four categories are distinguished.

The first category, indicated by ZZ, reflects an attitude towards the other party, which is based on the *consensus view*. All parties involved have the same long-term interests, and small differences in short-term interests are bridged by means of compromises (dummy: 0).

The second category, indicated by Z, reflects an attitude which is from the *moderate negotiations view*. The parties involved have important interests in common, but about more detailed matters relative power decides whose interests are best served (dummy: 1).

The third category, indicated by H, represents an attitude which is from the *radical variant of the negotiations view*. Important interests conflict with important interests of other parties. It is necessary to develop effective bargaining institutions to keep the battles under control (dummy: 2).

The fourth category, indicated by HH, represents an attitude which fits the *conflict approach*. The most important interests of the different parties are in conflict with each other. It means that the various parties are prepared to use quite radical means to achieve their goals (dummy: 3).

The militancy scores were acquired by close reading of the reactions of the unions and employers' organizations to the political debates. Statements about the degree of disagreement, and the language used to express the relevance of the conflict, were especially taken as indicators of the degree of militancy.

[Ad 3] In an economy with stable growth, we see relatively small fluctuations in the rate of unemployment around an average; unemployment is primarily of a frictional type. If we ignore cyclical movements, and the unions and employers' organizations agree with the existing distribution between capital and labour, the growth in the real wage rate will be more or less equal to the growth in labour productivity. Imagine that the capital market is global and competitive. Then, the interest and profit rate is beyond control of the politicians of our economy. When the government—supported by the unions and employers' organizations—decides to extend the welfare state services, labour should pay for the increasing costs. This means that the growth in the collective burden should not be an explanatory variable in the wage inflation equation. In the Netherlands, however, optimism about the feasibility of a full-fledged welfare state grew. Moreover, the unions and progressive political parties were not convinced of the necessity of not-too-low levels of profit; they called the actual levels 'super-profits'. Keizer's empirical research shows that progressive confessional parties shifted from R to L in 1963, and the Labour Party shifted from L to LL in 1967. With respect to militancy, we see that the progressive-confessional union shifted from ZZ to Z in 1966, and the general union shifted from Z to H in 1969. The general employers' organization moved from ZZ to Z in 1965. If we take all these changes together we can conclude a general shift from R to L and from ZZ to Z.

As already suggested, these shifts were a sign of growing optimism about the malleability of our social and economic reality. But, on a more specific level, there remained disputes about minimum profit levels and the degree of generosity of welfare services, including access to important institutions, such as health care and education. In the Netherlands, famous because of its polder institutions, we saw increasing dispute about the just mentioned economic and social restrictions. Right-wingers had always warned about the negative effects of the implementation of welfare state ideas. Left-wingers had always advocated a transformation of a capitalist economy into something in-between capitalism and centrally planned economy: 'as long as progressive steps forwards do not lead to a downturn, why not try to go further on the road to a mature welfare state?' The answer should have been: every economic unit, including an economy as a whole, needs a *buffer* to dampen eventual shocks. The world is an open system, and firms also need a buffer to ensure a minimum of solvency and liquidity. Nobody can calculate an optimum solvability; the future is principally unknown. But progressive political parties and unions did not believe the right-wing warnings about a structural profit squeeze. When the oil crises came it was as a shock, and the Dutch policy of Keynesian stimulus and wage policy—in itself correct—came too late. Also, the progressive idea of a sharing of wealth growth between workers and capitalists came too late. Business circles did not trust politics and unions anymore. This led to a lack of investments and a growth in unemployment. It took eight years before the left-wingers accepted a significant change in strategy. In 1982 employers' organizations, unions, and the government signed the so-called Wassenaar Akoord, in which they agreed to aim at more sober social services and higher profits, thereby hoping for increasing employment. This Agreement was the beginning of a period of about two decades of recovery for the economy and reform of the welfare state.

To illustrate the battle between the capital, labour, and government share of national income, we have presented a few important statistics about the Dutch economy over the period 1960–2000 in Figure 9.2.[5] We see that the labour share increased

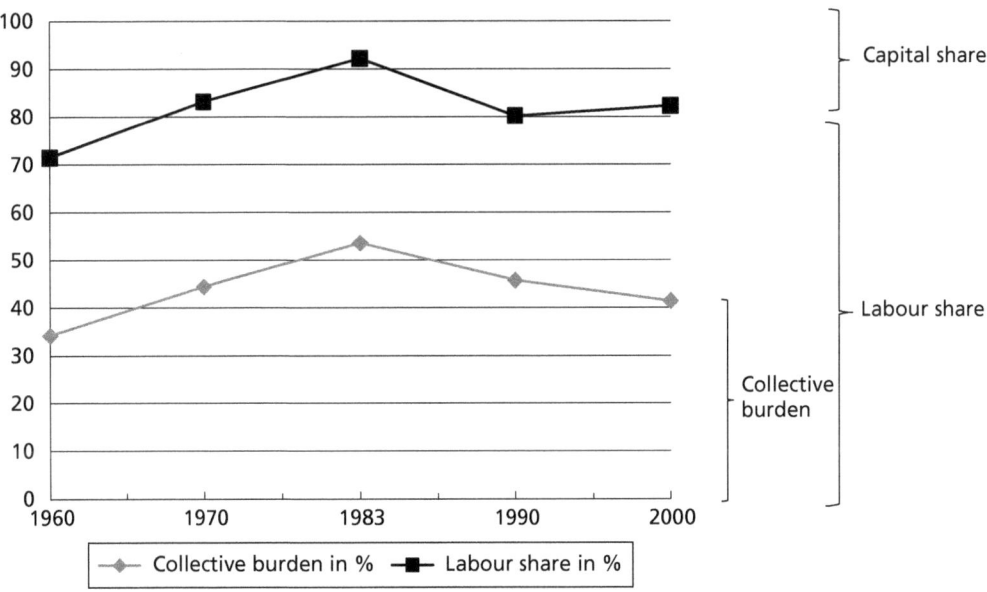

Figure 9.2. Income Distribution of Dutch Economy, 1960–2000

Note: Constructed on the Basis of Numbers Published by the Central Planning Bureau, The Hague, the Netherlands

---

[5] An important and difficult-to-solve problem is the lack of reliable empirical figures. Official agencies, such as the Dutch Central Bureau of Statistics (CBS) and the Dutch Central Planning Bureau (CPB), publish figures about wages, taxes, social premiums, employment, and unemployment on a regular basis.

structurally, primarily because of the structural increase in the collective burden, at the cost of the capital share during the 1960s and 1970s. The opposite development has taken place during the 1980s and 1990s. This structural change in relative factor prices must be considered as the *intermediate cause* of the failure to return quickly to full employment. The *immediate cause* of the crisis during the 1970s was the sharp increases in the oil price. Now we will reveal what was the *ultimate cause* of the crisis during the 1980s.

Keizer (1982, 1986) offers theoretical and empirical evidence for the idea that changes in political preferences—reflecting overoptimism with respect to the controllability of a full-fledged welfare state—led to a structural profit squeeze and a consequent decline in the solvability of the Dutch business sector.

Is it really impossible to reach high levels of justice and efficiency? The answer must be that economic and social processes need to be channelled by effective institutions. Progress can only be made step by step, and every economy must find its optimal mix of justice and efficiency. For the Netherlands we can say that its *labour market institutions were inconsistent*, and therefore ineffective. After the Second World War the Dutch government declared itself responsible for the level of employment and for the building up of a welfare state. In the first half of the 20th century the situation was characterized by free labour markets and an increasing union influence, partly because of increasing legislative support.[6] The main instrument of the unions was the strike. The institutions of that time appeared unable to prevent a severe depression. The post-war deal was the promise of the government to guarantee full employment and a welfare state, in exchange for the promise of the unions not to use the strike as a weapon in wage negotiations. Without such a promise unions would become too strong and claim wage increases that could ruin the economy in the end. During the 1960s a change in ideology and militancy took place. Unions were increasingly prepared to strike, meanwhile putting the government under pressure to maintain full employment. This *institutional inconsistency* has been responsible for the growing weakness of the Dutch business sector. Keizer (1982, 1986) gives an analysis of the power of unions in relation to the power of the employers' organizations. Dutch legislation had made the wage-bargaining

When politicians and union leaders need relevant numbers, however, the figures are not available. It takes years before the agencies publish so-called definitive numbers. Even then corrections take place, sometimes 10 to 20 years later. Moreover, all relevant empirical indicators can be defined and calculated in many ways. During the 1970s the Dutch societal discussion about the level of the labour share was distorted by the fact that official agencies published numbers which were not trusted by progressive parties. Later, the official figures were significantly downgraded (Salverda, 1978).

  [6] In 1907 labour legislation made it possible for the union members to have their own (collective) labour contract. In 1927 new labour legislation offered the opportunity to unionize a firm. The labour law of 1937 allowed that a collective contract between employers and unions could, under particular conditions, be extended to all firms of a particular sector. Taken together, these laws formed a judicial framework which collectivized a very large percentage of the labour force—at least with respect to the process of wage formation.

situation one of bilateral monopoly—in some cases on firm level, in most cases on sector level, but almost always with a clear advice from the national organizations with respect to the desirable wage increase.

Imagine that, in case of bilateral monopoly (see Chapter 4), the union has the right to strike. Bilateral monopoly means that the optimal wage rate for the employer is lower than the optimal wage rate for the union. The bargaining is about the difference. The power analysis runs as follows. Both parties anticipate how long they and their opponent can endure a strike. For the union holds that the strike benefits are higher if the resulting wage increase is higher. While the employer holds that the concession costs are higher if the resulting wage increase is higher. The more time a strike takes, the higher the strike costs for both parties.

Now we have four categories of costs and benefits, which are decisive.

(1) *Strike costs union*: wage sum paid by the strike fund, which is a positive function of the duration of the strike.
(2) *Strike benefits union*: future increase in the wage sum, including eventual negative effects on the level of employment, and a factor which represents the planning horizon and the discount rate of the benefits.
(3) *Strike costs employer*: losses during the strike (related to scale) and the loss of reputation.
(4) *Concession costs employer*: future wage sum increase, including a factor which represents the planning horizon and the discount rate.

As already said, the unions hold that the higher the strike duration, the higher the wage increase must be, in order to keep strike costs below strike benefits. The employer wants to keep the concession costs lower than the strike costs. In other words, the longer the strike duration the lower the concession costs should be. This analysis leads to the following graph (Figure 9.3):

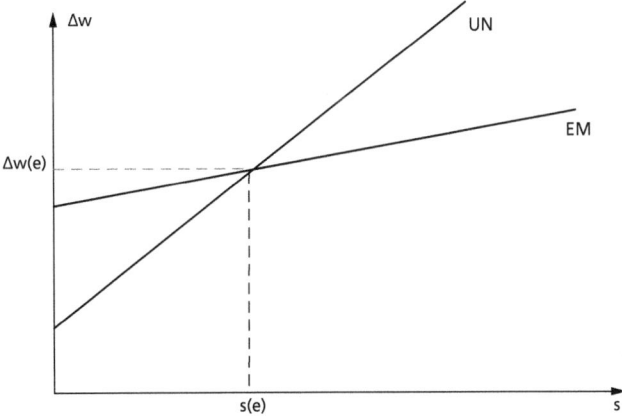

Figure 9.3 Relative Union Power in Case of a Threat of a Strike

On the vertical axis the wage rate increases (Δw) as a result of the strike, and on the horizontal axis the strike duration(s). The line indicated by UN represents the combination of wage increase and strike duration, which holds that the strike benefits for the union are equal to its strike costs. The line indicated by EM represents the combination of wage increase and strike duration, which holds that the strike costs for the employer are equal to his concession costs. The lines represent the model in the minds of the participating union and employer before an eventual strike. It does not picture a process.

Now the situation is as follows. Both parties are assumed to be perfectly informed about their own power as well as about the power of their opponent. So, they know how long each party can maintain a strike. Both come to the conclusion that the wage increase at the level of intersection of both lines is the optimal one. They know this before the union has started the strike. In other words, the strike is not necessary—for both parties it is beneficial not to have a strike at all. The wage increase that is acceptable for both parties is $\Delta w(e)$. This is the only combination of wage increase and strike duration, which implies for both parties an optimal situation. For the union the strike costs are not higher than but equal to the strike benefits. For the employers' organization the strike costs are not higher than but equal to the concession costs. The union would not refuse a wage offer of $\Delta w(e)$. The employers' organization would not refuse to accept the wage claim of $\Delta w(e)$, to prevent the strike costs becoming higher than the concession costs.

Of course, this analysis can be made much more complex. In reality both parties just guess the power of their opponent. The *expected relative power* is decisive—not the actual one. Moreover, if we talk about power, it sounds as if it is something objective and material. But this is not the case. The costs and benefits are based on interpretation and expectation. Two factors need our special attention. The first factor is the wage elasticity of labour demand, which plays an important role in the strike costs of the union. If the government is committed to maintaining full employment, it means that this elasticity is not negative. So, unions can maintain an eventual strike much longer. The increased union power leads to a higher wage increase, which creates some unemployment. The government must step in, and reduces unemployment by means of an increase in effective demand. If the government succeeds in its attempt to increase production and employment, tax revenues will increase as well, bringing the government budget into balance again. But the wage increase might be larger than the increase of the labour productivity, which means that labour costs, including taxes and social premiums, rise. This will definitely be at the cost of the own capital of the firms. An increasing lack of buffers makes the business sector vulnerable to external shocks, even if they are moderate. The second factor might make the problem even worse. Both parties need a *planning horizon* and a *discount rate* to calculate benefits and costs. If unions have a long horizon, it means that the benefits of a particular wage increase are relatively large. In that case unions can maintain a strike for a long time. If the unions do not have a strong time preference and appreciate the increased consumption for their children and grandchildren, again they maintain a strike much longer. Then we can say that the current generation of workers is quite *militant*. The same analysis can be made of the employer or employers' organization. We have seen that Dutch unions became more militant during the 1960s, while this was hardly true of the employers' organizations.

This analysis makes it clear that the combination of strike and employment commitment by the government is a problematic one. The Dutch profit squeeze in the 1970s was based on overoptimistic expectations about the possibility of having economic growth, growth of the welfare state, and a business sector whose financing was increasingly based on external capital.

9.5 The Philosophical Roots of Social Economics

9.5.1 INTRODUCTION

Adam Smith and Amartya Sen can be considered, each in their own way, as the founders of social economics.[7] Smith (1759) constructs an impartial spectator, who is in the minds of the people, and looks critically at the Self. On the basis of *self-critique* a person can develop various types of virtues. Smith *considers self-command* to be the most important virtue. A virtuous person knows what is in his self-interest: being natural, virtuous, and moral. Self-command implies control of the emotions: some emotions, such as sympathy and moral sentiment, are good. Other emotions, such as antipathy and moral resentment, however, are bad, and must be countered by means of *willpower*. In Appendix D we will discuss Smith's contributions in more detail. For the moment we can conclude that his ideas about nature, including human nature and the nature of society, are *naturalistic*. Human beings have the capacity to be economic, to be rational, and to be social. Smith (1744) describes the natural way in which physical nature shows stationary equilibrium. Smith (1759) describes the mechanism of the impartial spectator, by means of which humans interact in such a way that every human being knows how to behave towards each other and towards the Self. Also, Smith (1776) describes the economic nature of a human and the way this leads to well-functioning markets. Smith's work is clearly characterized by methodological individualism. The advantages of his micro-approach are clear: free markets function well in a context in which people are virtuous. The lack of any macro-notion is remarkable, though. Smith's work is not fitted for an explanation of typical macro-phenomena, such business cycles.

Sen (1999, 2002) pays a great deal of attention to a careful analysis of important concepts, such as freedom, order, rationality, market, democracy, and justice. *The liberal idea of freedom* is the absence of government intervention. Some libertarians even reject the government task of protecting private property. The *social justice view* stresses a

---

[7] The choice of these two economists is a little arbitrary. As already mentioned, John Stuart Mill also deserves the title of founder; there are definitely more economists who deserve this title.

positive idea of freedom: having the means to free oneself from want. Sen defines free-dom as *the opportunity to develop capabilities*. They should be developed in such a way that persons function well, as does the whole of society. In line with Scitovsky (1976), Hirschman (1982, 1984) and Davis (2008), Sen makes a distinction between actual behaviour, which results from the confrontation of actual preferences and a limited budget on the one hand, and judgement about the actual preferences, which are called *meta-preferences*, on the other. When people operate on free markets, they experience good and bad practices. By means of a democratic political structure, people can express their meta-preferences. These political preferences are not limited to the consumption of so-called public goods. They are also related to social-moral issues. By means of educa-tion people can learn to profit from experiences and improve the quality of their lives. By means of health care people can reduce their physical and mental limitations. By means of social action people can improve the quality of neighbourhoods, for instance. All these social and political actions make it possible for persons to function well. Sen pays much attention to the conditions under which markets and democracies function well. Both coordination mechanisms appear quite sensitive towards a whole series of restric-tions. In orthodox economics morality and irrationality do not play a role. As soon as we bring in rational actors, who take reasonability seriously, the Paretian optimality conditions do not hold anymore. This phenomenon is called the *Sen paradox*. Because rationality plays a very important role in economics, we pay special attention to the way Sen discusses this concept.

9.5.2 SEN ON RATIONALITY

To Sen (2002), rationality concerns the subjecting of one's choices—actions, objectives, values, priorities—to *reasoned scrutiny*. Sen makes it clear that 'rational' should not be confused with 'logical', or with 'economic' or with 'maximizing behaviour'. He blames neoclassical economics for analysing *rational fools*: individuals who do not have the opportunity to serve interests other than their self-interest.

When the hedonistic interpretation of utility became less dominant, freedom-orientated perspectives should have occupied the empty room. Unfortunately, Samuelson-like interpretations became more popular, among other reasons to make empirical research easier. As discussed already, Samuelson (1938) wanted to get rid of the term utility, as being too subjective. He only accepted the idea of individuals who serve their self-interest as an evolutionary characteristic. So, individuals maximize that which they consider to be their preference, under the restriction of their resources. What they actually do—buying a computer or increasing their financial investments, for instance—reveals their preferences, period. Sen comments on this 'solution' as fol-lows. Samuelson defines that individuals always act out of self-interest—otherwise they would have done something else. Then he concludes that what they are actually doing reveals, apparently, their preferences—in other words, according to Sen: 'to get an empirical rabbit out of a definitional hat' (Sen, 2002: 27).

Sen highlights a difference between three types of rational choice. The first type states that individual subjects are maximizing something. This statement is pure form; there is no content. The second type says that individual subjects are maximizing something economic and social. A third type of rational choice states that subjects are maximizing self-interest. It means that the level of well-being of others is not part of the preference function. It goes without saying that Sen prefers the second type of rational choice. It is remarkable, however, that he does not discuss the type of restrictions. In the first type of rational choice there is no limit to the sort of limitations. This form of rational choice could also be applied to the explanation of natural forces, such as the force of gravitation. The second one suggests that there is not only an economic, but also a social, world. In the economic world the restriction concerns the natural resources available. Since Sen considers man to be a social man, there must be social elements in the preference function as well as social restrictions. He stresses the relevance of *commitments*: persons commit themselves to serve the interests of particular others or other groups. But it is unclear whether commitments are interpreted as a constraint or as part of the preference function; or, as in Sen's words: 'commitment is a reason for action; it can modify the person's goals' (Sen, 2002: 39). Now the problem shifts to the question of what is meant by reason. For Sen, rationality is essentially *reflexivity*. But it remains unclear what he means by reasonability in comparison with rationality. Reflection can only happen if the subject has a point of reference. Sen's anchor point seems to be the genuine rules of morality, which are derived from the Enlightenment philosophy: all persons are equal at the level of substance.

To conclude Sen's philosophy we can say that he adds important psychological and sociological notions to his economic analysis. His work is impressive in its complexity, but, due to the same reason, it is difficult to get a simple overview of what is typical Sen. Two critical remarks can be made.

In the first place, Sen is extensively arguing the necessity of commitments as a solution to problems.[8] But a clear-cut social analysis is missing. In daily life we face many social conflicts and many local solutions, which are called subcultures. If people are committed to their gangs—drugs mafia, union mafia, financial mafia—Sen might not mean this sort of commitment. In Chapter 13 we will discuss the analyses of Fevre, who makes a distinction between 'ersatz' morality and genuine morality. Sen is analysing genuine morality in the sense of Fevre, which is based on the typical Kantian idea of morality: all persons are equal at the level of substance, although they all are different at the level of properties. Then the question is how to bring all these subcultures together under the umbrella of one genuine morality. When we connect genuine morality with the idea of rationality—reasoned scrutiny of one's own choices—we can analyse the idea of reason and reasonability.

---

[8] One of the reasons why Sen's work is difficult to understand is the ease with which he moves from a positive to a normative analysis and back.

In the second place, Sen is not offering a systematic analysis of the mind. Who is responsible for a reasoned scrutiny of the Self? Are there two or more selves? Is there any entity—the 'I', for instance—who takes the decisions after scrutiny? If we were not only analysing the social but also the psychic structure more systematically, the analytical complexity might be reduced. If we bring the social and the psychic analysis together, we might discover that there is a relationship between rationality, reason, and emotion. Now we look at the statement that all people should be reasonable. 'Why should I be reasonable?' could be the reaction of people who feel threatened by increasing modernity—by increasing confrontations with others who are very different on the level of properties. Maybe careful scrutiny of positive and negative emotions might lead to a more acceptable common ground. Cognitive analysis of our condition is not enough. We only understand analyses if they touch us. Otherwise, we don't know how to react to flows of new information. So, genuine progress can only be made by formulating new paradigms, which trigger our positive emotions. An integrated analysis of the three primary aspects of human behaviour—the economic, social, and psychic aspects—might function as such a *progressive paradigm*.

We finish our discussion about social economics with a short discussion of the views of Sen on the current financial and economic crisis. Then we can see whether a different analysis really leads to a different view and helps change the economic situation.

9.5.3 SEN ON THE FINANCIAL AND ECONOMIC CRISIS

According to Sen (2009), the crisis is the result of an unjustified belief in the good functioning of a system of free markets. Especially when market participants behave viciously, there will be a growing lack of confidence with regard to whether parties are willing or able to fulfil contracts. Financial regulation is needed to reduce excessive speculation, for instance. Sen agrees with Keynesian stimulus programmes, but, to him, Smith and Pigou deserve more attention. Smith's work on virtues and Pigou's work on inequality are important for an understanding of the crisis. The underdogs in society deserve more attention from the politicians. In Pigou (1929) we find a psychological approach already applied to business cycle theory. He analyses states of undue optimism and of undue pessimism. In our exposition of post-Keynesian economics, we saw that Minsky (1982) used the terms over-pessimism and under-pessimism, which are identical concepts. For Sen a crisis is a period in which long-term problems can be dealt with. It is a time in which people can reflect upon their conventional wisdoms—their established ideas and conventions.

When we try to reasonably scrutinize Sen's views, we see that his focus is not neoclassical at all. The neoclassical focus on monetary policy—the interest rate is too low—might be the immediate cause, but is definitely not the ultimate cause. For Sen, two other matters besides the reflection upon established ideas are important. First, if virtues turn into vices markets do not function well and crises are the consequence. Second, if there is a crisis, the underdogs are particular victims. Well-developed social services, including education and health care, are of the utmost importance.

With respect to the Netherlands there are hardly signs that economists and politicians really reflect upon their neoclassical prejudices. The Dutch central bank might have taken the issue of virtues seriously by establishing a centre with psychological and sociological expertise. The intention is to give the management of private banks support in their attempts to change the culture. In case of unwillingness the central bank is prepared to refuse particular appointments. With respect to Sen's last point, the ruling Dutch economists and politicians support the ongoing trimming of welfare state elements. In other words, the Dutch are not aiming at solving the crisis, but are trying to use it to reduce government activity significantly under the slogan: 'Never waste a good crisis.'

In Section 9.6 we will draw a few conclusions from our discussion of social economics.

9.6 **Conclusion**

The main message of social economics is the social embeddedness of persons, organizations, and economies. The concept suggests that behaviour is determined by the framework of rules which constitutes the social context. But in some variants of social economics—socio-economics, for instance—we see that the economic context plays an equally important role. Besides economic and social factors, psychological factors play a role as well. Actors are supposed to reflect upon their behaviour. Adam Smith stresses self-command as a very important virtue. Amartya Sen distinguishes between actual preferences and meta-preferences, which are the result of reasoned scrutiny of actual preferences. To Sen, it is important for persons to commit themselves to these judgements.

The concept 'institution' is a central concept, especially in social economics in the narrow sense of the word. Behaviour is institutionalized. It is ruled by habits, routines, customs, and social norms. To understand the evolution of rules, Greif emphasizes that, in contrast to OIE, rules have a micro-foundation. There are always persons, operating in small groups, who begin to change a rule, or adopt a new rule. If a particular situation makes it difficult to stick to a particular rule, interaction between a few persons leads to a step-by-step change. In Chapter 13 we come back to this process.

Victor Ostrom imagines a huge system of nested subsystems, in which every subsystem that is distinguished has its own mix of institutions. Elinor Ostrom pleads for the development of a system which consists of series of interrelated perspectives, so as to prevent Babel Tower-like problems. Our book is an example of a system of perspectives.

It uses the term 'aspect-system', and considers the economic, the psychic, and the social aspect as the three primary aspects of human life.

Three examples are given of the methodological diversity within this 'school'. Van der Lippe and Siegers offer an economic model, which shows that the division of labour between wife and husband is determined by the relative wage rate. They add to this model a sociological part, which says that actors are socialized and strive for social approval. This preference makes actors sensitive to the ruling social norm. After having integrated the two parts, they show that the ruling social norm affects the sensitivity of the actors to changes in the relative wage rate. Schenk discusses several social and psychological approaches to the M&A wave. To him, it is implausible to explain a wave this way. Time and again the same mistakes? He prefers an explanation in terms of market structure. In times of uncertainty managers of an oligopolistic firm prefer to take over a competitor rather than being taken over. Because the results of many takeovers is not positive, Schenk suggests the reintroduction of the so-called public purpose control: M&A are only allowed under particular conditions. Keizer shows that overoptimism with respect to the possibility of combining an extensive welfare state with a low-profit free market sector was responsible for the 1970s crisis in the Netherlands. Lack of own capital was the reason the Dutch economy recovered slowly from the crisis in 1974.

This chapter also makes it clear that a multidisciplinary approach to economic problems is necessary. Remarkable, though, is the fact that, in multidisciplinary schools, such as social economics, the main concepts, such as 'economic', 'psychic', and 'social', are not carefully defined and related to each other on the ontological level. In orthodox economics the term 'economic' is well defined. But as soon as neoclassical economists use the orthodox analysis as a theoretical instrument for their empirical research, they make one serious mistake after another. They misinterpret empirical reality, because they confuse economics as an aspect-system with the economy as a subsystem. Only if we formulate the concepts 'psychic' and 'social' in the same way orthodox economics is doing for the concept 'economic'—namely as a label for an aspect-system—and search for their interrelationship, might we be able to formulate an integrated paradigm, fit for application to some parts of the empirical world. In Chapter 10 we will discuss a series of psychological approaches, and see whether we can design a psychic world.

9.7 **Intermezzo**

Now we have finished the discussion of a series of heterodox economic approaches, it is time to draw a number of conclusions with respect to the divide between orthodoxy and heterodoxy. According to Hodgson, synthesis could be possible if we consider evolutionary economics, in the not-too-narrow sense of the word, as the context in which economic processes of allocation—the subject of orthodox economics—are presented. The results of orthodox economics are thus seen as a special element in the more general evolutionary social-economic science. Our book argues that a synthesis is possible if both camps underline the following statements.

(1) Reality can best be represented as an open system, but human beings cannot live with this idea and will always try to close their system by means of rules of thought and other kinds of rules. So with scientists: they also have to formulate a closed system so as to be able to formulate conditional pieces of knowledge.

(2) Any 'complete' system of knowledge about human behaviour should be explicit about the assumed human drives, the way humans take decisions, and the extent to which they are able to explain empirically observed behaviour. It implies that both internal observation (introspection) and external observation (observation by means of the classical senses) are necessary actions of a human scientist.

(3) This should also be explicit in the dynamic-historical development of its whole: its so-called macro-foundation, on the basis of which macro- as well as micro-analysis can be developed.

(4) We can make a distinction between aspect-systems and subsystems, and we must admit that orthodox economics is an aspect-system, analysing the operation of the economic force or motivation. The orthodox economic system is isolated from two other primary aspect-systems, namely the psychic and the social aspect-system.

(5) Heterodox economics is about a subsystem, which is the economy. However, it is not explicit about human drives. This shortcoming results from the strong influence on heterodox economics of the empiricist or positivist idea that empirical facts are objective and can be established without a specific theoretical apparatus.

(6) When recognizing that reality is an open system, we know that whatever expert system we apply, we have to build in buffers in the system to make them even more stable than experts tell us is necessary.

Orthodoxy should accept the idea of a multi-motivational, dynamic-historical, macro- and open system. Heterodoxy should accept the orthodox structure, in particular during the first stage, when a static closed system of a priori concepts is constituted ontologically.

Parts III and IV are about psychology and sociology. In these we will discover why neoclassical economists have so much difficulty with the formulation of an appropriate macro-foundation. As we saw in Chapter 4, orthodox economics isolates itself from psycho-social phenomena. Consequently, the economy as a whole is just an aggregate of individual actions. It does not stand for a phenomenon with its own ontology and its own properties. In sociology this aggregate is a group in the sociological sense of the word—it exists, it has properties, and it has an independent effect on events on all levels of human action. If we bring psychology into our analysis, the lowest level of analysis and explanation is not the level of the individual anymore. It is the sub-individual level where the psychic conflicts of irrational persons take place. In this way economies as a whole are influenced by combinations of sociological and psychological processes, creating *irrational subcultures*. These cultures especially deliver the necessary interpretation of historical development of economies and societies, upon the basis of which people react. Because of the independent influence of common understandings of the course of history, the macro level also offers a foundation for the micro level – not only for the level of the individual, but also for the sub-individual level. Actually, the micro and the macro level are each other's foundation or embeddedness.

Part III
Psychology for Economists

10 Psychology for Economists

10.1 Introduction

In Chapter 4 we have explained the four axioms of orthodox economics.

First, it assumes that actors are economic in nature. Human beings live in a natural world and their interrelationship is characterized by scarcity of resources. Humans are assumed to be motivated to reduce the tension between needs and resources as much as possible. Second, it assumes that the relationships between humans are of an economic kind only. In other words, social relationships do not exist. By making this assumption, orthodox economists abstract themselves from the problems that are at the core of sociology.

Third, actors are assumed to be perfectly rational. It means that people act according to their true preferences, which are well known and ranked in order of priority. By making this assumption, orthodox economists abstract themselves from the problems that are at the core of psychology. Humans are not perfectly rational, which means that they are not perfectly integrated personalities. Psychologists study the mechanisms that determine the degree to which persons are integrated.

Fourth, orthodox economics is based on the assumption that the laws of logic can be applied. Mathematics is based on logic and can be applied when drawing implications from analysis.

When we take the four axioms together, we see that orthodox analysis represents the ideal-typical economic logic and abstracts from the ideal-typical social logic (sociology) and from the *ideal-typical psychic logic* (psychology).

This text investigates what psychology has to offer orthodox economists.[1] What they need is an analysis of psychic logic, in order to integrate it with the two other logics. In Chapters 11 to 13 we will investigate sociology in order to develop an analysis of the social logic. Our final goal is an integrated analysis of the three primary logics, namely the economic, the social, and the psychic. This gives us a more realistic theoretical instrument, which might function as a theoretical basis for applied research.

In Section 10.2 we will give a short sketch of the origin of psychology. Thereafter we will discuss the main characteristics of a series of approaches or schools of thought in psychology (Section 10.3). The focus will be on their methodology, since this is decisive when it comes to a thorough understanding of their differences. After this discussion

---

[1] Important sources for this chapter were Glassman and Hadad (2004), Wilkinson (2008), Frijda (2007), Rabin (1993, 1998), and Rabin and Thaler (2001).

between the different approaches we continue by looking at the way behavioural economics has tried to link the two sciences (Section 10.4). Experiments and brain research have led to interesting results, and the question of whether this field has already developed a sort of psychic logic will be answered. On the basis of the state of the psychological art, we sketch the contours of a psychic logic, which has a structure comparable with that of the economic logic. In an appendix we present a case about the German monetary trauma, and show how the different psychological interpretations explain this phenomenon.

10.2 **The Origin of Psychology**

Philosophers have discussed the so-called mind–body problem for a very long time. Aristotle advocated the method of *introspection:* become aware of one's own inner world and observe the content of it. Feel the feelings and think about the thoughts, and analyse them. He considered thinking to be a process; a chain of associations where one image follows the other. Idealists tend to consider the mind as a location for ideas which shape the body. Religious idealists even assume the mind is the place where God and the Devil struggle with each other for the soul of the person. Materialists, however, interpreted body and mind as one entity, where the mind is just consciousness of the material world. In the 17th century Descartes came up with a good interpretation of the mind–body relationship. He considered them as two aspects of one and the same phenomenon called the 'human person'.[2]

In the 19th century students in medicine with an interest in philosophy began to study the mind in more detail (Ketcher et al., 1982). We will discuss two scientists who are considered to be the founding fathers of psychology. The first is Wilhelm Wundt, who lived from 1832 until 1920. On the one hand, he criticized Aristotle, saying his method was just introspection. On the other hand, he rejected empiricism, which suggests that empirical reality can be approached objectively and without theory. Wundt advocated a synthesis between introspection and empirical observation. First, he developed an analysis of the structure of the mind, and especially of thought processes. Then he tested theories derived from his structural analysis by means of experiments.

The second is William James, who lived from 1842 until 1910. He made a grand tour through different fields of science, such as chemistry, biology, and medicine. He became increasingly interested in philosophy and began to make a study of the mind, a field

---

[2] Nowadays materialism rules the scientific world. Descartes is accused of dualism, which means the justification of a separation of mind and body. But Descartes was analytically distinguishing the two entities rather than suggesting that mind and body are two separate empirical entities—in the same way that economists are analytically distinguishing between the economic world, the social world, and the psychic world, which is the mind. Damasio (1994) is an important example of a materialist who makes this error. His approach is called monism.

which barely existed at that time. From biology, he knew how Darwin dealt with the mind–body problem. He started his explanation of human behaviour with the body, and explained the existence of emotions in a functional way: they serve the interest of the body to survive. Humans are also inclined to strive for survival group-wise, and develop capacities to communicate with each other—by means of facial expressions, for instance. James considered this approach too materialistic and reductionist. To him, emotions are not linked directly to sensory impressions. He developed the concept of *perception*, and stated that emotions result from perceived or interpreted sense impressions. Some perceptions lead to reflex responses, such as sweating, and others lead to emotional feelings, such as fear. By constituting perception and placing it in-between sensory input and human reaction, James established psychology as an independent science. Or, to formulate it methodologically: he established the ontology of the mind, which implies that there is an interrelationship between body and mind rather than a one-way relationship, where bodily processes influence consciousness (Trigg, 2002). So, we must admit that:

(1) There is no mind without a body.
(2) There is no body without a mind.

In 1890 James published his *Principles of Psychology*, a textbook which is still used.

10.3 **Perspectives in Psychology**

10.3.1 INTRODUCTION

Perception is a core concept of psychology, making psychology a distinguished science rather than a branch of biology. In the same period we see a comparable development in sociology. Weber advocated a research method called 'understanding' (in German: 'Verstehen'). When we want to explain human behaviour we must learn to understand the way people understand their situation. So knowledge of their world-view is necessary for a fruitful explanation of human behaviour. This also holds true for scientists. If we want to understand what scientists mean by particular theories and hypotheses, we must find out the basis on which this theory has been developed. Some psychologists want to explain individual behaviour, while others aim at explaining the functioning of the psyche or mind, and finding out which mechanisms determine psychic logic.

In both cases it is possible to place the human person or the human mind in context. A human person consists of a body and a mind, being two aspects of one and the same phenomenon. The body can be divided into a brain, its control centre, and the rest of the body. The environment of the mind consists of a physical and chemical part, and of a biological and of a social part. Our analysis is presented graphically in Figure 10.1.

For our purpose, the explanation of the functioning of the mind is the central goal rather than explanation of individual behaviour. The mind consists of several entities, which interact with each other. There are flows of emotions, feelings, and thoughts from one entity to another. But we will see that some approaches avoid the mind and link the environment directly with empirically observable behaviour. The following approaches will be discussed.

In Section 10.3.2, we look at *the cognitive approach*, which focuses on human cognition. In the initial period of its existence it focused on thoughts, and studied especially flows of thoughts and their structure, and the way humans store information in their short-term and long-term memories. Later, emotions began to play an important role as well. So the interpretation of the concept of cognition and of the cognitive approach changed: now it refers to *knowing*, whether in terms of thought, or in terms of emotion and intuition. When cognitive economists distinguish between 'cognitive' and 'affective', the term cognitive refers to the early use of cognition, namely deliberate thinking rather than emotionally 'knowing'. By making this distinction it is possible to understand the relationship between the two, and the problems of emotional conflict as well as the role of the ratio in solving it.

In Section 10.3.3, we will discuss *the behaviourist approach*, which focuses on the relationship between the environment of a person and his behaviour. The processes within the human person, especially in the mind, are difficult to observe. The results of introspection are so subjective and unreliable that we must consider the mind to be a black box. Therefore, this approach tries to find stable relationships between stimuli coming from the environment and the responses of individuals. Its findings show that human behaviour is conditioned in several ways.

In Section 10.3.4, we will discuss *the psychodynamic approach*, in which the mind is the place where different entities find their habitat, and interact with each other, positively

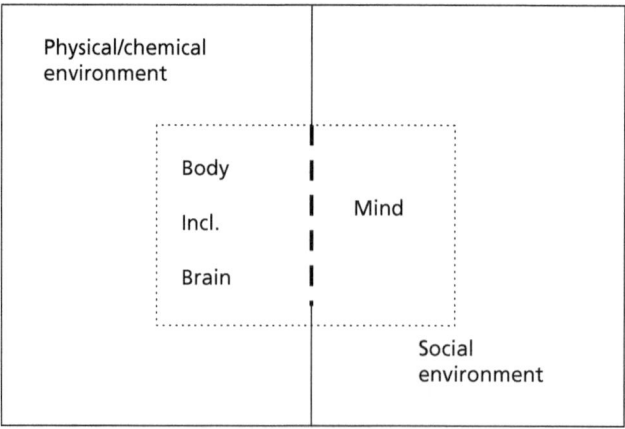

Figure 10.1. A Human Person and His Environment

and negatively. Persons who are able to integrate the different emotional claims, and who are able to choose rationally which needs and desires can be satisfied and which must be blocked, function better and reach a high level of sustainable happiness. The main entities that play a role in the emotional conflicts are the Ego or 'I' of a person, the actual Self that must be controlled, and a true Self or intuition that advises the Ego.[3] So this approach is about the organization of the mind as the control centre of the human person. What are the main emotional conflicts that must be solved? In answering this question two important interrelated features play an important role. First, does history play a role? A person's life has different stages, and each stage is characterized by a particular type of emotional conflict. Second, we can distinguish between two areas or locations in the mind, namely the conscious and the unconscious. In general we can say that, over time, a person becomes increasingly aware of the content of his unconscious. In other words, he becomes increasingly aware of the principal emotional conflicts typical for a human person. Different analyses and theories will stress different elements that are decisive in this respect. As already said, a person who is able to solve those conscious and unconscious emotional conflicts that have become manifest, has a greater chance of living a happy life.

In Section 10.3.5, *the humanist approach* searches for an answer to the question of what makes a person a human person. It has a strong historical element: human life consists of a series of stages of development. Historical development is a process of *self-actualization*. The basic drive of a human being is the manifestation of the true Self. Its step-by-step discovery might be a painful process, but ignoring the true aspects of someone's personality might create more pain and difficult-to-interpret feelings of emptiness.

In Section 10.3.6, *the biological approach* focuses on the body, and especially on the brain. We have seen that it is typical for the mind to interpret sense impressions. But the transport of sense impressions to the control centre, and the activities of the control centre when making a decision, can only take place if physical-chemical processes accommodate these activities. Malfunctioning of the body and especially of the brain affects this accommodation and thereby the human response. Since this process of accommodation is complex and sensitive, the material side of the human person has a significant effect on the personality. The biological approach has an evolutionary bias, which means that the Darwinian idea of survival is accepted as the main human motivation.[4] The body wants to survive and consciousness is a progressive step in its evolution to offer humans an instrument to understand their situation and to communicate with each other, so as to maximize the chance of survival.

Finally, in Section 10.3.7, we will pay attention to *the social psychological approach*. It aims at an understanding of the way culture influences a person's behaviour. Explicit attention is paid to pro-social behaviour such as altruism, as well as to anti-social behaviour such as an expression of aggression.

---

[3] For an extensive treatment of the concept 'Self' see Stevens (1996).

[4] Materialists are not inclined to talk about motivations and innate goals; they consider meta-physics to non-scientific. See Chapter 2 for an exposition of this empiricist attitude.

10.3.2 THE COGNITIVE APPROACH

As we saw in Section 10.2, Aristotle stated that knowledge structures develop by association. When people experience, in the case of increasing demand for labour, that wages tend to increase as well, they are inclined to associate the two variables with each other. If new information is added to the existing structure, the knowledge as a whole becomes more complex and sophisticated. In our example we can think of the experience that increasing demand for labour always follows an increase in the demand for goods. Cognitive scientists try to find out how people store information. They distinguish between a short-term and a long-term memory. When students follow a course in organization theory and learn the content of 20 theories, at the examination they might be able to retrieve most of the theories they have learnt. After a while, however, most of the students are unable to remember all the theories in detail, but some general structure of the course might be stored in the long-term memory, which can be retrieved.

Cognitive psychology aims at a careful description and explanation of processes of encoding and retrieving information, and of processes of learning, unlearning, and forgetting. Every transfer of 'information' implies selection. Limited cognitive capacity drives a person to select information that must be transported and stored, while other information is lost during the transport or not even noticed. In Figure 10.2 we have presented a typical cognitive process.

The structure of knowledge stored in the memory is called a *cognitive map*. We all have maps of many fields of study in mind. Some people principally store facts and correlations between facts. Other people are inclined to store more general knowledge or even meta-knowledge, which is philosophy. For example, when we look at a phenomenon such as liberalism, some people know a lot about various liberal political parties in Europe,

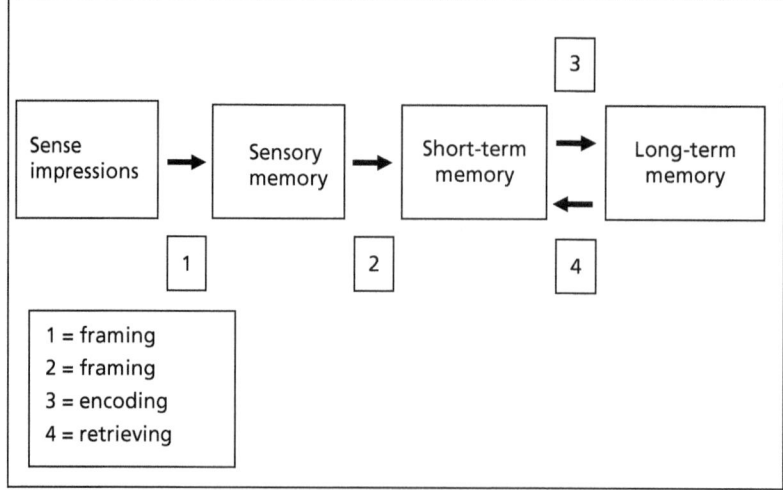

Figure 10.2. A Typical Cognitive Process

and about liberal economic policies in terms of proposed deregulation and privatization. Other people, however, have built hierarchical knowledge structures, and understand liberalism as an idea, on the basis of which an analysis of society can be made. In the literature of cognitive psychology a distinction is made between episodic, semantic, and procedural knowledge. The first is historical, the second theoretical, and the third is of a technical character. Research shows that theoretical knowledge, especially on the paradigmatic and analytical level, is the most difficult part to change. Information that does not fit the existing structure is suppressed. This phenomenon is called *'persistence of set'*. When discussing other approaches we come back to this very important human characteristic.

When thinking of the character of paradigms—ideas that lie at the basis of every analysis—cognitive theorists increasingly admit that emotion plays an important role in accepting or rejecting particular ideas. Heuristics are built on a *belief*, which is a cognitively expressed emotion, connected to strong feelings. Some people have developed negative feelings, while other people have developed positive feelings when hearing the term 'liberalism'. The financial crisis of 2008 and its economic and social consequences has definitely increased the number of people with negative feelings concerning the phenomenon 'liberalism', since many blame the neoliberal idea of deregulated markets for having caused this crisis. So, beliefs are very important and if a person acts in a way that is not in line with his own beliefs, he feels bad. Festinger (1957) called this feeling *cognitive dissonance*.[5]

The cognitive approach is especially interested in the way people show systematic biases in their processing of information. Two errors are worth mentioning here. In the first place, there is the so-called *fundamental attribution error*. Attribution refers to the indication of the causes and consequences of particular behaviour. In other words, it is about the interpretation of a situation. The fundamental error concerns the inclination to underestimate the importance of situational factors, and the overestimation of person-internal factors. A second error is the *self-serving bias*. This bias concerns the inclination to attribute successes to personal factors, and failures to situational factors.

The biases result from distortions in the mental structure, and will be discussed in more detail in the text on the psychodynamic approach. It is remarkable that cognitive psychology has studied learning processes for so long without any reference to emotions and feelings.[6] But now the insight that cognition and emotion are two sides of the same coin is broadly accepted. Although there are many emotions we are not aware of, our thinking is never without emotion and feeling.

---

[5] The economist-sociologist Parsons applied this theory to the level of society as a whole. One of his hypotheses was that the USA could not maintain its discriminatory legislation for long, since it was in dissonance with typical American beliefs concerning the dignity of an individual human being.

[6] Gagné et al. (1993) has been a popular textbook for years, but the terms emotion, feeling, and affect do not play any role in its analysis of learning processes.

10.3.3 THE BEHAVIOURIST APPROACH

Methodologically speaking, behaviourists are materialists who want to reduce their research to empirically observable facts. This means that the mind must be considered as a black box. When ignoring all the information we get from introspection, we are left with information about the environment of a person and his behaviour. By means of experiments, behaviourists try to establish regularities between a change in the environment (*stimulus*) and a consequent change in behaviour (*response*). In this way they discovered that behaviour is strongly conditioned. A famous example is the experiment done by Pavlov. A dog was given food on a regular basis. As soon as the dog saw the food, it began to salivate. Then the experiment introduced a bell: first a bell rang, and after a short period the food was given to the dog. After a couple of times the dog began to salivate when just hearing the bell. In other words, the dog had learned that bell-ringing is followed by the delivery of food. So he starts his preparation for eating food by producing saliva. This learning process is called conditioning, and the test presents an example of what is called *classical conditioning*.

When a bell is ringing there will be no response, except that the dog will look in the direction from which the sound comes. But when the ringing of the bell is followed by the delivery of food, and this connection takes place regularly, the bell-ringing transforms from an unconditioned into a conditioned stimulus.

These tests can be made more complex so as to see whether the subject of experiment is able to learn more complex structures of knowledge.

In the world of advertising the principle of conditioning is applied very often. For instance, Mercedes is offering a very nice car and is able to gain a large market share. Then it broadens its assortment with different kinds of accessories, all with the brand 'Mercedes'. Then it enters the market of clothes and shoes, and offers high-quality products under the brand name 'Mercedes', all marked with the typical Mercedes sign. The company tries to condition the public. In first instance, the brand name and sign are not well known. But the public is excited about the beauty of the car with the brand name 'Mercedes'. Increasingly, the typical Mercedes sign transforms from an unconditioned stimulus into a conditioned stimulus. By linking this sign to other products people look less to the genuine characteristics of the product—the Mercedes logo is enough to make the public 'salivate', thereby stimulating the purchase of shoes and clothes with this sign.[7]

Two phenomena are worth mentioning here. In the first place, we will discuss the incidence of *stimulus generalization*. In the example of the Pavlov experiment we can try another bell, or just a sound or a lamp switching on and off, to see whether the dog interprets the signs in the same way as he learned to interpret the ringing of the bell as

---

[7] A few years ago I saw this example in Torino: a Mercedes showroom with beautiful cars. In the next room all sorts of accessories of Mercedes, and in the third room just clothes and shoes, with the Mercedes logo, of course.

a sign that food is coming. In the second place, and connected to the first phenomenon, we discuss *stimulus discrimination*. Imagine a person who has been head of a department for many years. Regularly, employees terminate their contract; so new employees must be hired. As every job requires particular skills, applicants must send their curriculum vitae to show whether they fulfil the necessary requirements. Sometimes applicants come from Germany, in other cases they come from Bulgaria or from Greece or Turkey. Without having any experience the head is neutral towards the countries the applicants come from. But after a number of bad experiences with Bulgarians the head develops a negative emotion towards Bulgarians. From then on applicants from Bulgaria—whatever their diplomas and experience—become a conditioned stimulus triggering a negative conditioned response: no hiring of Bulgarians. The unconditioned stimulus 'diplomas and experience' is replaced by the negative conditioned stimulus 'Bulgarians'.[8] This stimulus discrimination is also called *stereotyping*.

Now we go back to the Pavlov experiment, and imagine that bell-ringing stops being followed by the delivery of food. How long does it take for the dog to stop salivating when hearing a bell? In general, it takes a long time to uncondition particular stimuli and responses. Fear responses especially are difficult, if not impossible, to be extinguished. For instance, prisoners in a concentration camp who were always beaten at twelve o'clock might feel fear for the rest of their lives when the clock approaches twelve. Another example concerns students who have bad experiences when doing mathematics. As soon as they see a couple of formulas they immediately feel bad, and are inclined to skip them. In this case formulas have become a negative conditioned stimulus. In the case of drug use the body can prepare itself when entering the room where the drug is usually taken. In some cases, the body may already show typical drug symptoms. In other cases, the conditioned response is opposite to the primary effect of the drug itself. Morphine, for instance, normally reduces the sensitivity to painful stimuli. Rats, however—after conditioning—showed increased sensitivity to pain when placed in the conditioned context. An explanation could be that physiological processes, which correspond with the process of conditioning, interact with the body's natural mechanisms for maintaining equilibrium (homeostasis).

Besides classical conditioning we can distinguish *operant conditioning*. This concerns learning with respect to changes in voluntary rather than involuntary responses, as is the case with classical conditioning. Operant conditioning plays a role in the study of how animals or humans solve problems. Thorndike did experiments with a hungry cat, which was confined in a cage. Inside the cage was a lever, and pressing the lever would open the cage. Outside the cage—visible to the cat—was food. Now the research question is how much time and effort does it take for the cat to discover that pressing the lever is the solution. Thorndike formulated a law, the so-called *law of effect*. When the

---

[8] The example of the Bulgarian employees is merely hypothetical. Personally, I have had very positive experiences with students from Bulgaria.

cat discovers—possibly by accident—that pressing the lever leads him to food, he will be inclined to repeat this act.

Skinner (1904–1990) formulated a radical variant of behaviourism. According to him, mental concepts such as free will and (psychic) force cannot be observed empirically and therefore cannot contribute to our explanation. Consequently, scientists should leave them out of their analyses. He did also research in the field of learning with regard to operant conditioning. The focus was on the effect of *reinforcers*, which are stimuli that occur after the response and which alter the probability of the response recurring. Primary reinforcers are based on an innate biological mechanism, while conditioned reinforcers are based on other types of mechanisms, such as money and praise. So if baby Benjamin cries when he feels hungry and his mother reacts immediately by giving him food, Benjamin learns to cry as soon as he feels hungry; crying operates as a primary reinforcer. But if a child of 16 years of age is doing his homework and is 'rewarded' for that by praise of his father, he might be inclined to not do his homework every day. In this case, the praise of his father operates as a negative conditioned reinforcer: the child likes to show his father his independence. The behaviour of the baby is assumed to be a matter of biological survival, while the behaviour of the adolescent is assumed to be a matter of psychic or social survival.

Economists prefer to use the term 'incentive' rather than reinforcer, and, often, they just see money as an effective incentive. The reason is that orthodox economics abstracts itself from the social and from the psychic world. In other words, the only problem is that of scarcity of natural resources, and the only effective incentive is the offering of resources. If we were introducing the two other worlds into our analysis, we would understand why praise affects behaviour, sometimes in a positive, sometimes in a negative, way. In the example of angry and violent young Moroccans in the streets of some Dutch cities it is important to see that a friendly attitude by the police might have a negative effect. An explanation could be that Moroccans are conditioned to have respect for an angry father—being the family authority. They do not respect people who react pleasantly in the face of disobedience. Unfortunately, a behaviourist does not study inner conflicts like the father–son authority conflict, and cannot understand why, in some cases, praise leads to a negative result. As long as we take the mind to be a black box we can only correlate phenomena, and call some events stimulus and other events responses. But the question why a particular event is a stimulus while other events do not lead to any response is beyond the capacity of the behavioural approach. In Section 10.3.4 we will discuss the psychodynamic approach, which deliberately opens the black box to see—introspectively—what is inside.

10.3.4 THE PSYCHODYNAMIC APPROACH

Psychology is literally about the logic of the psychic world, just as sociology is about the logic of the social world and economics is about the logic of the economic world. Since orthodox economics is precisely focused on analysing the mechanism of economic logic, it is important for economists to integrate their analysis with an analysis of the mechanism of the psychic logic. To develop such an analysis we need to open the black box of the mind, and see what's in there. This method is called introspection, and is necessarily subjective. We can have a look in our own mind only; the minds of other people are really black boxes. To establish the ontology of the mind, we must first constitute the entities or elements of the psychic system. Then we must find the essence of the relationships between the various elements that are distinguished. And, last, we can distinguish between different areas or fields within the mind.

Body and mind have needs that must be satisfied. Emotions motivate a person in particular directions and drive him to behave in such a way that needs become satisfied. Economics analyses the behavioural consequences of the assumption of economic motivation, which means that a person is driven to reduce the scarcity of natural resources as much as possible. Sociology analyses behaviour that results from social motivation; in other words, sociological analysis is based on the assumption that we are driven to maximize the status of our group. The psychodynamic approach tries to find out what is meant by psychic motivation. That is, in which direction are we driven in order to solve the typical psychic problem? This section aims at answering this question.

In the sentence 'when I look at my Self', I assume an 'I' and a 'Self'. Freud distinguished between two different aspects of 'I', namely the Ego and the Superego. The Self was called the Id. For him, the Id is a bundle of emotions that are directed to the satisfaction of bodily needs, and has therefore a biological basis. The Superego represents the claims of society upon a person and lets him adjust to the prevailing culture. The Ego has the task of solving the emotional conflicts between the Id and the Superego, and take decisions on how to behave. Jung made a slightly different distinction between the entities in the mind: besides the Ego as the decision-maker he distinguishes between the actual Self and the ideal Self. The actual Self is the bundle of emotions as they manifest themselves at a particular moment. The ideal Self, however, is the essence of the personality, who must increasingly be discovered over time. It is an expression of the notion that at every moment we are driven by emotions and inclined to behave in a particular way. But when we grow older we increasingly develop an intuition about who we truly are. The Ego must solve the conflicts between the ideal or true Self on the one hand, and the actual Self on the other.

The various entities are related to each other, and it is relevant to establish the nature of their interrelationships. Now we distinguish between the actual Self, the true Self, and the 'I'. The actual Self is a bundle of emotions. Body and mind are full of tensions, triggering a force that aims at minimizing the tension. On the one hand, these forces or emotions trigger physical-chemical processes within the body. These processes are beyond the control of the 'I'. But these bodily processes induce feelings, which tell the decision-maker whether the situation is agreeable or not. On the other hand, these forces trigger thoughts, at least in the minds of literate people.[9] The 'I' can be interpreted as a

[9] Babies cannot think, and cannot take decisions. The 'I' is just a potential and has not developed yet. Therefore, all control must come from instinctive actions and from the mother figure.

decision-making centre, who is advised by the true Self as experienced by the 'I', and who is seduced by the thoughts and pressure that come from the emotions that constitute the actual Self. Imagine a student goes to a café, and has a couple of beers. Why? Because the body gives signals saying to the 'I': if you have another beer, it will create very agreeable feelings. But it is also possible that the student feels depressed because his girlfriend dumped him the day before. His mind needs unawareness of this fact and triggers the student to have another beer. But there is a true Self 'under construction'. It functions as an intuition, which constantly advises the 'I', and suggests to the decision-maker that giving in to drinking lots of beer is not in the interest of the person when taking the long-term perspective.

Both Jung and Freud have made a distinction between two areas in the mind: the conscious and the unconscious. Jung has made a distinction between a collective and a personal unconscious (Stevens, 1994). The first area contains the so-called *archetypes*. These are potentials of a neural-psychic character representing the important *themes* in human life. From the very first day a person develops these potentials; so they become increasingly manifest. The personal manifestation of archetypes takes place in the second part of the unconscious: the personal unconscious. Important themes that require much energy are the relationship between mother and child, between parents and children, authority relations in school and on the job, and, above all, the relationship between man and woman. These themes are important sources of emotional conflict and a person who is able to solve these types of conflict is a happy man or woman, and fit to take responsibility in society.

Jung developed an analysis of personalities on the basis of the attitude or focus of a person. Some people feel quite *anxious* unless they have clear indications that they are safe. Others are *curious* about everything new, unless they have clear indications that there is something bad going on. Some people are quite *introverted*, while others are *extravert* in nature. During life people can change mentally, which means that they are able to weaken particular inclinations and strengthen other ones. But the potential capacities of the actual Self determine the starting point and set the limits—it is the scope within which a person develops his attitudes which influences the person's behaviour during the rest of his life.

When people grow up and are sent to school to learn and to practice skills, another difference in character appears. Some people are quite *intuitive* and *emotional* in their learning, while others are quite *intellectual* in attitude and trust the results of deliberate thinking. Later we will come back to this issue; for now it is important to establish that there is a personality with potential attitudes towards the world, including attitudes towards the way of experiencing and learning about the Self and his situation.

Nobody is able to solve his inner conflicts perfectly. One of the possibilities with which to deal with permanent and difficult-to-solve conflicts is to project the problem onto other people and to blame others for misfortunes. This externalization of inner conflicts is called *projection* and is one of the core elements of social logic as discussed in sociology. When trying to understand culture, sociologists interpret it as a set of rules that must limit this externalization (Keizer, 1999). By developing a common view or understanding of the situation, expressed by common myths, and told by common heroes, social conflict based on projection can be limited.

We will finish this section on the psychic-dynamic approach by answering the question: What is the psychic mechanism that determines typical psychic logic? For now, we assume that there are two important sorts of emotional conflict.

The first is the conflict between different emotions within the actual Self. A student wants to study hard, likes to spend time on a number of sports, and enjoys going out with his friends; altogether these activities take up more than 24 hours per day. So far this is a typical economic problem. The psychic problem now is that a person cannot choose. On the one hand, he considers himself to be a hardworking person who has ambitions of having a great career. On the other, he has a very different idea of himself: having a relaxed attitude towards life, for instance. When he follows the first strategy he feels bad about missing so much enjoyment. When he follows the second strategy, he feels bad about this too, and condemns his own decisions. To a certain extent all people experience this ambiguity. Some people, however, experience their life as 'impossible to live', and switch to an imaginary world now and then. This is a very serious disease called psychosis and needs extensive medical and mental treatment (Nietzel, 1998).

The second sort of emotional conflict is that between the actual Self and the true Self as experienced by the 'I'. His actual Self is driving the person in a particular direction, and he lacks willpower to control it. He knows that he is doing the wrong thing, but cannot stop behaving in a way that contrasts with his own long-term interest. The lack of willpower is related to the strength of particular drives. The stronger the drive, the more willpower needed to control it. Such a strong drive is called *neurosis*, and is a very common phenomenon. Leaders of large organizations especially appear relatively neurotic, at the cost of the organization (Kets de Vries, 2006).

Humans are equipped with the capacity to select information that confirms the choices made so far, and forget or even ignore information that shows the strategy chosen to be wrong. In case of the first type of emotional conflict this means that, once a career in the scientific world has been chosen, the person ignores information that makes it clear that a career in the world of business is a very interesting option. In the case of the second type of conflict, a person knows his long-term interest but lacks the willpower to serve that interest. In both cases, once a choice has been made, information is suppressed to protect the true Self as experienced by the 'I'. This means that important information about the true Self is ignored. Since we frame life as a process of discovery of the true Self, the emotional problems might mean the end of this journey.

In Section 10.3.5 we will see that the humanist approach continues from where this story about the psychic-dynamic approach ends.

10.3.5 THE HUMANIST APPROACH

In Section 10.3.4 we saw that, for Freud, the mind is a battlefield where physiologically driven needs and desires, especially of a sexual kind, must be controlled by the constraints set by society. But in this materialist approach there is hardly any room for a typical psychic drive. In other words, there is no person or personality that is driven; just a body. Jung, in contrast, assumes the existence of a true Self that is inspired to manifest itself.[10]

The humanist approach places this true Self in the centre of its analysis. In the course of a lifetime a person discovers his true Self to an increasing extent. Some persons reach a high level, while others appear unable to make much progress. The concept of Self is from James, who had already distinguished between *Self as a subject* (Ego or 'I' in the terminology of the psychodynamic approach) and the *Self as an object* (actual Self and true Self, in the terminology of the psychodynamic approach). Later, Mead developed the idea that the Self is increasingly discovered through interaction with other people. Only in the eyes of others are we able to discover who we are. So we might discover that we are extravert by meeting people who are less extravert or even very introvert. It means that all judgement of personality is relative—there is no absolute yardstick.

The humanist approach has more of an existential nature, and must be seen as a reaction to the materialist variant of psychodynamics and to the behaviourists who completely ignore the inner world. According to materialists, human interpretation is an expression of the material interests of a particular person. According to behaviourists, there is no interpretation at all; there is just a stimulus and a response, and experimental research might show regularities, which reflect processes of conditioning. But humanist psychologists state that there is perception and interpretation, and that this is not completely determined by body and social environment. A human person comes into existence if a particular encounter between a sperm cell and an egg cell leads to the existence of an *embodied spirit* or soul.[11] After his birth he develops his body and Self in permanent interaction with others.[12]

Maslow and Rogers are the big men of the humanist approach. Maslow (1908–1970) has become famous with his so-called *hierarchy of needs*. In this structure needs range from

[10] Jung used the term ideal Self, but I prefer the term true Self to avoid the misunderstanding that the Self is just an idea rather than an embodied 'idea'.

[11] There are philosophies and religions that assume the existence of an eternal soul who is looking for embodiment during a particular period. After the combination has died—the soul has left the body—it searches for new embodiment. For our goal it is not necessary to speculate further about the soul. What we need is the idea that the psychic structure cannot completely be reduced to the physiological structure. In other words, there is a mind where the 'I' lives and decides whether or not to develop the unique personality. Without this idea humans are no different to machines, and there is no room for freedom and responsibility in our analysis. Even the notorious materialist Skinner stated that freedom is a valuable illusion. So we live and do our scientific work on the basis of this *valuable illusion*.

[12] See Nelson (1996) for an application of this approach to economics under the name feminist economics, and see Lutz and Mark (1988) for an exposition of 'humanistic economics'.

physiological needs to the need of self-actualization. The most basic needs are food, drink, and sleep—without these there is no physiological survival. Then there is the level of the safety needs. Safety has a physiological as well as a psychological aspect. Physiologically we are in danger if we walk through a forest, and suddenly a tiger approaches us. Psychologically we are in danger if we lose all our relatives and friends in an earthquake, for instance. We might fall apart, which might make us insane. A third level can be distinguished consisting of needs such as love and belonging. If these needs are satisfied esteem needs become manifest: feelings of being respected by relevant others and self-respect. At the highest level of needs we find the desire to actualize the Self. According to Maslow, the more basic the need, the more powerfully it is experienced, and the more difficult to suppress and ignore.

The hierarchy must not be taken as being too rigid. Different needs may vary in intensity across individuals. Experience shows that many poor people have a strong sense of self-respect. If a rich person throws a piece of bread to a poor person, the latter might be angry rather than grateful. On the other hand, it is possible that rich people never leave the area of so-called deficiency motives: food, safety, love, and esteem. In other words, they never enter the level of meta-needs, which is about the desire to grow as a person.

Rogers (1902–1987) approaches a person in an *organicist* way. A human being is a (living) organism, and develops his Self through interaction with other human beings. The opposite of organicism is the mechanistic approach: the essence of the elements does not change when interacting with other elements. In orthodox economics, economic-rational actors trade with each other. This interaction leads to a change in the economic position of the traders; that's the reason why people trade with each other. But they keep their character of being economic-rational. In a biological-psychological-sociological approach we can assume that interactions really change the manifestation of a personality or of a group. In a romantic relationship this is quite obvious.[13] The lovers help each other constantly in the process of discovering their identity. But members of a department of a particular firm, responsible for marketing, for instance, can also function in such a way that they become a well-functioning 'organ' in the whole of the firm. For all members, organic interrelationships mean that their true selves, as experienced by the 'I', change over time, under the influence of permanent social interaction. Rogers calls this process the *'actualizing tendency'*. He assumes that a human person has the drive to search for his true Self, and to develop its potential. The step-by-step process is painful. Working on a solution to emotional conflicts is energy-consuming. So persons who grow suffer from being tired all the time, and feel depressed regularly: the struggle seems without end. On the other hand, the incongruence between the true Self and the actual Self is the motor towards self-esteem. Acceptance of the true Self gives much release and a deep feeling of satisfaction.[14] Rogers distinguishes between different levels in this respect.

---

[13] But, on the level of countries also, political relationships can affect the identity of a nation significantly. In Europe the relationship between France and Germany affected the whole idea of being French and being German. At the moment, the relationship between Israel and Palestine is an example of a very negative relationship that has harmed the Jewish as well as the Palestinian identity.

[14] In Chinese philosophy this process of self-discovery plays an important role. The Chinese word for 'the road' we have to travel is *tao*, and this is the central concept in Taoism.

A first level is the surface level, where people experience excitement and boredom, both of a short-term character. A second level is the deeper level, where people experience enduring satisfaction. A third level is the deepest level, where people experience being part of the cosmic whole. This deepest sense of harmony is the core of Zen Buddhism, but in Judaism and Christianity also this cosmic whole plays an important role.

Now we will give two examples to illustrate why the humanist approach is relevant for economists.

One of the most striking results in the happiness literature has been found by Easterlin (1974). He discovered that people in countries with a relatively high real income per capita were barely any happier than people in countries with a significantly lower real income per capita. His explanation runs as follows: we all expect to become happier when earning a higher income. If we receive a higher wage we are excited about it. However, this feeling lasts for just a short time. Then we get used to the higher wage level and fall back to the earlier level of happiness. In other words, people who are not poor can barely increase their happiness by means of higher levels of scarce resources. Apparently, the West has not discovered the relevance of self-actualization yet. The finding has become familiar under the term the *Easterlin paradox*.

A second example is the following. If more people learn about the existence of their true Self, and increasingly discover its characteristics and accept them, it might lead to a release that weakens the economic force—less greed—and the social force—less fear of being ejected from the group. It makes people more open-minded and able to really listen to the contributions of other people. It will lead to better-functioning families, firms, and other types of organizations, such as government agencies. More concretely, in autumn 2008 the world faced a severe credit crunch, followed by a financial crisis and economic depression. Then many people involved came out and said that they had known of the increasing fragility of the financial system. Some of them had raised the alarm but had been ignored or even fired. Many others, however, adjusted to the culture of the group, which stated that free markets were a self-regulating system, and that malfunctioning firms would go bankrupt, thereby making room for the more successful firms. Had more people discovered their true Self the debates within the relevant organizations would have been more rational and would have served the long-term interests of the whole of the economic and societal systems. However, they didn't want to give up their economic and social status, and so kept their mouths shut.

The fact that there are hardly people with the courage and determination to stand up against obvious malpractices has a strong negative effect on the quality of the processes of decision-making in all organizations. More attention to the humanist approach has the potential of improving human communication.

10.3.6 THE BIOLOGICAL APPROACH

In Section 10.2 we explained that the body and the mind are two aspects of the same phenomenon. Without a mind there is no body, but without a body there is no mind. Some approaches focus on the aspect-system 'mind', such as the cognitive, the psychodynamic, and the humanist approach. They implicitly assume that the body, including the brain, functions perfectly well, and can accommodate all emotions, feelings, and thoughts. In reality, perfect bodies and perfect brains do not exist. So, all impressions coming from outside the human person trigger materially embedded mental processes. It means that the material properties influence the effect on mental processes significantly.

This section focuses on the role of the brain as the control centre of the body. We can distinguish between different areas, for instance between the *cortex* and the *primitive brain*. The last mentioned area contains two regions, namely the brain stem and the limbic system, an area where the basic drives are located.

The areas that are distinguished all have a specialized function. The cortex is a layer at the surface of the brain, and locates planning and controller functions. Three parts can be distinguished: the frontal lobe, the occipital lobe, and Wernicke's area. In the occipital lobe, transformation of what we sense into a vision takes place. If this lobe is damaged people can see without understanding what they actually see. Wernicke's area makes language meaningful. If this area does not function well, the person has difficulty in understanding text, although every word is clear in itself.

The primitive brain contains a brain stem that is responsible for the transportation of signals from the body to the brain, while the limbic system is responsible for the connection with the cortex. The brain consists of four important areas, namely the thalamus, the hypothalamus, the hippocampus, and the amygdala. The most important area is the hypothalamus, which hosts emotions such as hunger, thirst, and sexual desire. The hippocampus has an important memory function, and the amygdala is related to emotions like fear and rage.

The brain is a piece of bone that hosts an extremely complex system of wires, called the nervous system. This is responsible for the 'communication' between the different areas and functions. It consists of a very large number of wires, which operate like electrical cords. The different wires communicate with each other chemically through so-called neurotransmitters. We can distinguish between two different parts, namely the peripheral system and the control system. The first part is responsible for the transport of the sense impressions to the control centre, and the second part is responsible for the integration of all the 'information' that can be derived from all the messages. So, the organization of the brain shows a separation between a part responsible for the delivery of inputs and the execution of the 'decisions', and a part responsible for the integration of the signals, the development of a strategy, and the taking of decisions. In Figure 10.3 we have presented a picture of the brain with a few important regions and functions. Moreover, we have compared the structure of the brain with the structure of economy and organization.

So, in the brain we find stocks and flows of an electro-chemical nature, which carries emotions and thoughts, both creating feelings.

* * *

Now we can make two types of distinctions (Camerer et al., 2007).

1	2	3	4	5
DESIGN	BRAIN	MIND	ECONOMY	ORGANIZATION AND FUNCTION
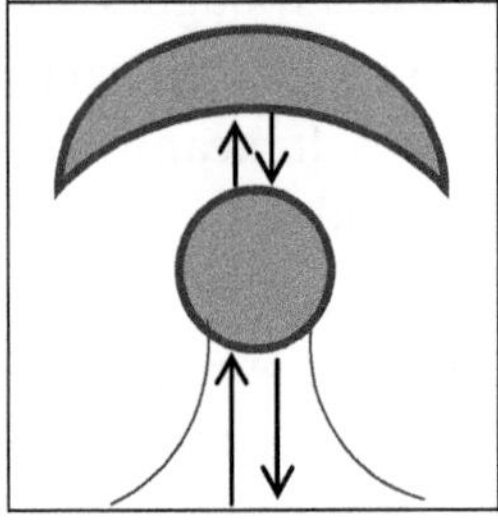	CORTEX	TRUE SELF RATIO	TRUE NEEDS	BOARD: VIEW, MISSION, CONTROL
	LIMBIC SYSTEM	ACTUAL SELF	IMMEDIATE NEEDS	RANK AND FILE: EXECUTION
	BRAIN STEM	SIGNALS	RESOURCES CONSUMPTION	SUPPLIERS: INPUT CUSTOMERS: OUTPUT

Figure 10.3. The Personal System

First, a distinction between *affective* and *cognitive,* and, second, a distinction between *automatic* and *controlled* stocks and flows. Affective stocks and flows reflect emotions, which are forces that result from tensions. These forces drive people in particular directions. If, for instance, there is an emotion called thirst, it drives people to search for drinks. Needs of a physiological as well as of a mental character trigger emotions, which are transported to the control centre (cortex); this centre then decides what to do. In case of a literate person who has learned a language, emotions also trigger thoughts. The more literate a person, the more complex the texts triggered. These texts—so-called cognitive flows—are sent to the control centre, and later to the areas with a memory function, where the texts are stored. So, cognitive flows, although different in category, are triggered by emotions rather than being opposites of each other. Emotions come first and some emotions are followed by cognitions. It means that cognitive processes are always linked to emotions; a fact that is very important to be aware of in education.[15]

A second distinction is between automatic and controlled processes. Automatic processes are unconscious processes in the body and in the mind. When a large dog barks at you, it automatically makes you a little scared. And when your house is on fire, many automatic processes take place in body and mind. They are immediate and uncontrollable. They are to do with physiological processes and with emotions stored in the primitive brain, such as fear and anger. Controlled processes, however, are the opposite: not immediate and uncontrolled. They take some time and the cortex, being the control centre, regulates flows of energy in a particular direction so as to reduce or stimulate particular chemical flows. While the automatic flows are unconscious most of the time, the controlled flows are of a conscious nature.

[15] If students think they are bad at macroeconomics they tend to hate this subdiscipline, and have increasing difficulties in learning and understanding it. When trying to improve their performance, the emotional aspect must be taken into account. The student must build up confidence that macroeconomics is doable for him. Then he must tell himself that more practising will make macroeconomics more agreeable. Finally, the student discovers that mastering a 'difficult' discipline is a lot of fun.

	Affective	Cognitive
Automatic	I	II
Controlled	III	IV

Figure 10.4. Types of Processes in the Brain

In Figure 10.4 we have presented the two distinctions in a matrix. The four combinations express four types of flows.

Technological progress has made it possible to do experiments and find out which parts of the brain are active during particular activities. In this way our knowledge about the organization of the brain has increased significantly. By means of computers we can carefully observe brain activities. Three methods are very popular at the moment:

(1) An EEG, which is an electroencephalograph; it registers electrical activities in the different areas.
(2) Electrical stimulation of particular neurons by means of an implanted electrode.
(3) Computerized imaging techniques such as the PET scan and the MRI scan by means of radio-active tracers injected in the bloodstream and by means of electrical charges in cells in a rapidly changing magnetic field.

Brain research has led to a number of interesting results. We will briefly discuss a couple of them.

In the first place, when *confronted with a new problem* we use, especially, flows from category IV. But the more we learn and practise particular skills, the more we shift from category IV to category I. Since flows from category IV take much physical and mental energy, this shift releases resources, and makes it possible for a person to use more energy for a different activity.

In the second place, *preferences are context-contingent*, which means that the situation influences which brain areas become active, and therefore affects what people prefer. Imagine a man who invests a lot of money but is inclined to reduce risk as much as possible. Then he decides to buy a very fast car, and drives along the motorways in a quite risky way. This example illustrates the fact that a particular person is a risk averter in some circumstances, while being a risk lover in other situations. So with many other preferences: in some contexts a person is an altruist, while in other contexts he is an outright egoist, for instance.

A third finding is about *discrimination*. Tests show that discrimination uses areas in the brain that are cognitively inaccessible. It means that persons are not aware that they are discriminating. Confronted with a person with a very different ethnicity the amygdala signals: be careful. This affective reaction has an effect on the cognitive judgements that follow. Much deliberation is needed to counter these affective and cognitive automatic reactions.

A fourth finding is about the *difference between risk and uncertainty*. While risk can be calculated and expressed in a percentage of probability, uncertainty is a phenomenon that cannot be approached cognitively. When a person is confronted with this uncertainty a brain area that hosts flows from category I particularly is used. But if the person is placed in a situation where he perceives that risks can be calculated, brain areas which specialize in processing flows from category IV are used. This shows that risk and uncertainty are, psychologically speaking, very different phenomena.

A fifth finding is about *myopia*. By assuming perfect rationality economic analysis assumes that economic actors serve the long-term interests of the Self. Brain research shows, however, that the fast-operating affective system focuses on short-term survival, and that we all need a lot of education to develop a cognitive and controlled system, which includes willpower, to operate as a countervailing power.

A last finding shows that *information is grouped* and that there is competition between groups of information. The choice of the group of information that is accepted rather than ignored is based on the winner-takes-all principle: all the information that belongs to the winning group is accepted, while all the information that belongs to the losing group is ignored. Brain research observes this battle in terms of neurons, of course. Groups of neurons conveying particular information are winning battles from other groups of neurons. The winning group of neurons gets access to the control centre, affecting the decisions taken by the control centre. Knowledge transmitted by losing groups of neurons is thrown into the dustbin.

The organization of the brain shows a functional organization. If, by accident, a person's brain is hurt, the damaged areas become dysfunctional. A person cannot move his left leg, or cannot smell, or cannot understand what he observes, for instance. Fortunately, some substitution is possible. This means that some areas can take over some functions, if necessary. It goes without saying—for an economist at least—that substitution is a costly affair. The new function must be practised before the activities become automatized. This finding shows that there is something like an *economics of the brain*. The energy that is needed to execute all the activities is the scarce factor. Energy is a force that makes activities possible; physical as well as mental activities. The more skilled a person is in executing a particular task, the less energy is needed. Automatic processes are not only very fast, but also take less energy than processes which need much deliberation and self-control. When, for example, at a particular meeting the first issue on the agenda takes much energy from the participants, they are inclined to pay less attention to the second issue, which implies that less scarce resources are spent on the discussion about this second issue.

In Section 10.3.7 we discuss the role of the social environment on the psyche of a person.

10.3.7 THE SOCIAL-PSYCHOLOGICAL APPROACH

Psychology is about the psyche, which is embodied, and the brain plays a crucial role in materially accompanying mental processes. However, a human person cannot live alone;

he is the result of an intimate act between a man and a woman, and in his first years he is almost inseparable from the mother figure. In other words, the social aspect plays a very important role in the growth of an individual person. From the very first moment he is part of a group and its culture. Mental processes, emotions as well as thoughts, are shaped by the way the very young are taught. In some cultures more than in others there is a strong influence, and a message saying: 'conform to the group', 'obey the authorities of the group'.

Thinking about reality always takes place in categories, establishing identities versus differences, and substances versus properties. Culture affects which categories must be distinguished: in some cultures the difference between white and black people is crucial while in other cultures children discover this difference after many years.

We can make a distinction between positive and negative social action. Positive social action is called pro-social behaviour, and altruism, which means any behaviour that helps other people, is an example. Negative social action is called aggression, which means any behaviour causing intentional physical or mental harm to another person.

In social psychology there is a permanent debate between scientists who consider pro- and anti-social behaviour to be innate and natural and scientists who consider this behaviour as learned and a matter of nurture. Is it the person or is it the situation that makes a person altruistic or aggressive?

Different approaches give different answers to this question.

The biological approach considers aggressive responses to unpleasant stimuli as an innate drive with an important evolutionary function: physically and mentally strong people survive at the cost of the weaker people. Responses are cognitively mediated, reflecting the person's history with respect to the interpretation of situations in terms of dangerous or safe. Altruistic responses, especially directed to kin, enhance reproductive success. Not only kin altruism, but also reciprocal altruism, can be explained, as is expressed by the Dutch saying: 'wie goed doet, goed ontmoet' ('Good things come to those who do good'). The saying suggests that the golden rule of the United Nations, meant as a normative statement, can also be considered as a positive statement.[16]

The behaviourist approach considers aggression and altruism to be learned behaviour. This means that behaviour is a voluntary response acquired by reinforcement. So, aggression as well as altruism is instrumental: it pays. People can learn that robbing a rich man is a profitable activity, while other people can learn that giving money to the poor feels good: ethical hedonism. Aggression can also result from frustration, which blocks goal-directed responses. There are different types of aggression. If a vending machine is not working properly, aggressive persons may kick the machine, or write an angry letter to the owner, or get depressed (Camerer et al. 2007). Another strategy is called displacement: the release of frustration is postponed and expressed in an 'easier' environment. A good example is the typical sergeant behaviour in an army. If things go

---

[16] The golden rule of the United Nations states: 'Do unto Others as You Would Have Them Do unto You'.

wrong officers blame the sergeants for the mistakes, and as soon as the officers are gone, the sergeants go to the rank and file and shout and punish them, irrespective of who is actually to blame.

The cognitive approach also considers altruism and aggression to be learned behaviour rather than the result of innate drives. The difference between the behaviourists and the cognitive psychologists is that the last mentioned group stresses the role of cognitive learning and the development of cognitive schemata and judgement, while behaviourists stress the (unconscious and affective) processes of conditioning. So, in case of aggression by young people hanging around in the streets, a behaviourist tends to stress the carrot and the stick: punish aggressive behaviour, and reward the non-aggressive youngsters. The cognitive scientists might agree with this policy but consider a change in the codes of the street to be a necessary condition: parents must teach their children well, and society must offer the teenagers a perspective that will change their views and interpretations of their social reality.

The psychodynamic approach assumes the existence of a set of innate drives (the so-called Id), and if the social environment does not accept the expression of some emotions, there is conflict. Tension is created, which must be released. If not, frustrations grow, and look for an outlet. The battle between the Id and the Superego must be solved by the Ego, who is taking the decisions. The Ego disposes of several *defence mechanisms*, so as to reduce aggression. First, the Ego is able to block conscious awareness of the underlying conflicts. Second, the Ego is able to ameliorate the tensions in different ways. Besides displacement, as mentioned earlier, there is the possibility of sublimation: by playing music or making pieces of art, for instance. A last possibility is the release of energy in indirect form, and is called catharsis. It takes place through a process of recalling emotionally charged experiences or through involvement in symbolic activity. But sceptics say that catharsis might release in the short term, but it might be addictive: the more catharsis, the more a person needs it to keep the degree of release at the same level.

The humanist approach considers aggression and altruism as personal characteristics rather than something that is learned and determined by the situation. Everyone is somewhere on their road to discover the ideal or true Self, and feels the pain of incongruence between the true Self and the actual Self. Imagine a teenager who breaks the rules of the family. His parents are wise persons and punish him for that. Then the aggression felt by the teenager is a frustration about his incongruence, as he knows his parents, representing his ideal Self, are right. Imagine a teenager with parents who are unwise persons, and are constantly irritated by his independence. The behaviour of the parents is aggressive and reflects their incongruence. The independence of the teenager creates a priming effect by reminding the parents that they were not that independent in their youth and did not work on the actualization of their Self.

The example of the teenager and the parent stands for many boss–subordinate relationships in our organizations, firms as well as government agencies. In that case unwise bosses fire subordinates who are critical and independent in their attitude.

With respect to altruism it is clear that it adds to the self-actualization of the true altruist, and is genuine rather than instrumental in nature. Altruistic behaviour by people who are not truly altruistic creates inner tensions, which can only be reduced when the person increasingly internalizes the virtuousness of being altruist, or when he increasingly accepts his true Self is not altruistic.

The question whether pro-social and anti-social behaviour is based on innate drives (nature) or is learned (nurture) needs to be studied at a more sophisticated level. It is better to ask how nature and nurture are related to each other. If there is no drive towards a particular behaviour, no situation can trigger it. If the situation never triggers a particular behaviour, why would a person behave that way? It is better to see the drives as latent potential, which can be developed under the influence of particular circumstances. To get to a more sophisticated analysis we make a distinction:

(1) between favourable and unfavourable circumstances;
(2) between a personal character that is curious and trustful and a personal character that is anxious and full of distrust;
(3) between a sensitive versus an insensitive body and mind.

The first is about the situation, the second about the mind, and the third about the body and mind. Now we can construct eight combinations, some of which mean outright altruistic behaviour, and some which mean outright aggressive behaviour. Sensitive, trustful people in favourable circumstances show altruism, and sensitive, fearful people in unfavourable circumstances show aggression. Most people show some altruism, but only in particular circumstances. Their behaviour is quite conditioned, and they have learned to give money if there is an emergency situation and the TV devotes a whole evening to programmes promoting donations. In the case of other 'emergencies' they never give money. With respect to aggression we can imagine that a father who has been beaten by his father beats his son regularly, although on many other occasions he is not that aggressive. In other words, altruistic and aggressive behaviour are very context-contingent in most cases.

* * *

Psychology shows a quite pluralistic picture. There are several approaches, and none dominate the scene. There is competition, and there is cooperation. During the last few decades there has been growing cooperation between cognitive and behaviourist psychologists. With the rise of new techniques of brain research the biological approach has become more popular. There is even a growing cooperation between behavioural, cognitive, and neuroscience: *cognitive neuroscience*. Moreover, there is growing integration of the results of subjective experiences (humanist approach) with the 'objective' results of cognitive neuroscience, which is called *positive psychology*.

When reviewing current trends, less attention is paid to the psychodynamic approach, and the idea of innate negative drives (Glassman and Hadad, 2004). For orthodox economists who have built their core analysis on an innate drive this is bad news. Human motivation is the motor, and without a clear view on the direction of the different drives it becomes impossible to understand the mental processes that are distinguished and described. In Section 10.4 we will see what the import of psychological knowledge into the body of orthodox economic knowledge has brought us so far.

10.4 **Behavioural Economics**

10.4.1 A GENERAL OVERVIEW

Orthodox economics shows under which conditions scarce resources are optimally allocated so as to reach a maximum of efficiency. The ideal economic structure is the perfectly competitive market. Perfect competition is defined in such a way that all goods have just one price, which is a perfect reflection of their natural scarcity. One of the necessary conditions is the existence of perfect information. Economic actors are assumed to be well informed about their own preferences (needs and desires) and about the prices and satisfaction-generating capacities of the goods that are on offer. Even the future is known—we all know what will happen during the rest of our life. This makes it possible to assume that all intertemporal choice problems can be solved.

Every economist ought to know that this is an ideal-typical construction rather than a serious attempt to describe and explain reality. Economic analysis, as we know it from textbooks, relaxes one or a number of constraints as set by the simplest version of the ideal-typical model. The introduction of the assumption of imperfect information has led to important adjustments in economic theory. The typical economics of information considers information as a scarce good, making the analysis more consistent. Economic and rational actors buy an optimal amount of information, on the basis of which they decide to allocate the remaining resources. In case of imperfect information a stochastic world is assumed. Risks can be calculated in terms of probability, and markets develop in which people can buy security.

Simon (1957a,b) considered this solution to the problem of imperfect information as unsatisfactory. His alternative approach runs as follows:

(1) Cognitive capacities are limited; so people can never collect all the information that is available somewhere.
(2) People who spend resources in searching for relevant information continue their search until they are satisfied, rather than keep searching until their calculations of costs and benefits of the additional information tell them that they have reached their optimum.
(3) Since it is impossible to calculate the costs and benefits of information not yet found, it is better not to speak of the maximization of utilities and of optimization

anymore. It is better to characterize the human drive as *satisficing behaviour*, and use the term *bounded rationality* rather than perfect rationality.[17]

The divide between the orthodox approach, expressed in terms of utility maximization and optimal amounts of information on the one hand, and the cognitive approach, expressed in terms of satisficing behaviour and bounded rationality on the other, still exists. The orthodox people stick to the idea of perfect rationality and optimality. They apply the so-called *expected utility theory*, which says that the future can be predicted in terms of probabilities. This means that we can extrapolate regularities of the past into the future and calculate the risks that are always involved. Perfect rationality means that actors maximize the expected utility that can be derived from particular outcomes. A perfectly rational actor sees the following two options as equal:

(1) the reward for a particular effort is 100;
(2) the reward for a particular effort is 50 per cent probability of receiving nothing and 50 per cent probability of receiving 200.[18]

Cognitive scientists stick to their idea that choices are not based on explicit calculation when searching for information. Given the information available people can make calculations of a few options. But the decision to choose between option A and option B, and not between an unknown number of other and different options, is not an economic-rational one. People are uncertain about the realism of their interpretations of the situations and the options available. Therefore, they develop rules on the basis of tradition and experience, which frame their situation. Within a particular framework it is easier to make a calculation that functions as a satisfactory basis for decisions. Experiments of behavioural economists and cognitive psychologists show, however, that people are risk-seeking or risk-averting, dependent on how the situation is framed. Imagine an organization's advisor has her own one-man business and operates in the health-care sector. She regularly participates in a public tender, which takes a week of preparation. Her situation can be framed in two different ways.

Frame 1: she is used to calculating her own labour costs at 4,000 euros per month, and transfers this money to her private account. Now, for next week there are two tenders, and our advisor must choose which one is to be preferred. One tender gives a reward of 500 euros, and the other gives a reward of a 25 per cent probability of 800 euros and a 75 per cent probability of 400 euros.

Frame 2: she has not developed the habit of separating her labour costs, and includes in each tender calculation her labour costs—1,000 euros per week. Then the options are: the first tender definitely gives 500–1,000, and the second tender gives 0.25*800 + 0.75*400–1,000. Experiments show that people always try to avoid losses as much

---

[17] The reader must be aware that bounded rationality is not identical to imperfect rationality, which means that humans are irrational to a certain extent.

[18] In other words, a rational actor is risk-neutral. If we were considering risk aversion as a preference, it would be perfectly in line with orthodox economics.

as possible, and are risk-averse when different levels of gains are compared. In other words, people show *loss aversion*. In our example it means that the advisor is inclined to go for tender 1 in frame 1, and for tender 2 in frame 2. The approach just set out is called *prospect theory* and is meant to offer an alternative to the neoclassical expected utility theory.

The work by Simon was the start of what is called behavioural economics.[19] In the beginning the cognitive approach stressed the limited cognitive capacities of the human mind.

Even today many scientists in this field have a strong 'empirical' inclination, and design experiments to see whether persons are irrational or not. Ariely (2009, 2012) offers us many experiments, which aim to show that we are predictably irrational. In the first mentioned book (2009) he discusses his methodology: science is an empirical endeavour. The reason why he chooses this idea can be found in his first confrontation with the phenomenon of science. His professor in the field of the physiology of the brain asked him to be a research assistant. His job was to prepare experiments, to search for the effect of a stimulus of a particular area in the brain on the behaviour of a guinea pig. As we saw in our discussion of the different psychological approaches in Section 10.3, this setup is actually a combination of the biological approach with behaviourism. We have clarified that both approaches have a strong empirical inclination. They ignore the existence of a mind, of emotions and thoughts, and focus on the correlation between the various brain areas on the one hand and behavioural reactions on the other.

Ariely (2009) admits that introspection and reason do play a role, but he considers empirical inquiry to be the most important part (p. xviii). This is very strange. As we explained in Chapter 2, no empirical research can function without an adequate theoretical foundation. Without theory we don't know what particular empirical phenomena mean, and we cannot understand changes in empirical variables. We also know from Chapter 2 that a priori knowledge alone is insufficient when explaining something about the empirical world. So, a priori and a posteriori cannot do without each other; one is no more important than the other. Therefore, introspection and reason are necessary tools to build a theory that makes it possible to execute the empirical testing of a hypothesis. When analysing the way in which Ariely interprets his experiments, we discover why he stresses the empirical part. He does not define and analyse core concepts, such as economic, rational, and social. He (implicitly) takes the economic world as his point of reference. All behaviour that cannot be explained is called irrational. Economic orthodoxy explains every action on the basis of an economic and rational actor. The concept 'economic' refers to the human drive to maximize utilities by consuming goods. By means of experiments Ariely shows that humans make systematic mistakes in their calculations of benefits and costs; these errors can be predicted, and therefore he considers irrationality

[19] Maital (2007) and Wilkinson (2008) offer many analyses and empirical research in this field of modern behavioural economics. Kahneman and Tversky (1979) and Kahneman (2003) must be considered as classics.

as something empirically visible and predictable. If his introspections had discovered more primary motives, and if he was explicit in his definition of the phenomenon of rationality and the function of reason, he might have discovered that these mistakes are not mistakes at all. We will illustrate this critique by means of a series of experiments, discussed by Ariely (2009: 1–23) under the heading: the truth of relativity.

The first experiment is an advertisement by *The Economist*. It offers an internet subscription for $59, a print-only subscription for $125, and a print plus internet subscription for $125. The persons participating in the experiment opted for the respective options: 16, 0, and 84 per cent. Another group is asked to give their choices, but the second option is left out. Then 68 per cent choose the internet subscription, while 34 per cent prefer the internet plus print edition. The result shows the significant effect of the irrelevant alternative, which is called the decoy. Ariely interprets this effect as a sign of irrationality, and explains it in terms of relativity. In *The Economist* case the attention of the reader of the advertisement is focused on a salient feature, namely the internet subscription is free if it is linked to the print subscription. The idea of getting something for free or a significant discount is always attractive. And in this case it attracts the attention away from a clean weigh up of the pros and cons of the third option: internet only. The problem with this type of research is the following. Ariely uses the orthodox definition of economic, thereby ignoring the social aspect, and shows that the assumption of perfect rationality is not realistic. In this book we explicitly distinguish between the economic, the social, and the psychic motive, and we define rationality as 'control over inner drives'. When we use this framework of interpretation the outcome of the experiment is different. Relativity and comparison are not irrationalities anymore, since the picture of the isolated person who has to solve his economic problem is not the 'absolute' yardstick. When establishing our preferences we use comparison; so when we consider the three options offered by *The Economist* we are still not sure about our preferences. When, having established our true preferences, and try to satisfy them, we cannot perfectly control the drives that are constantly popping up. When designing an experiment, such as that about *The Economist* subscription, we must be aware that we are creating an artificial situation. To reduce the artificiality it is wise to also undertake an experiment in which the guinea pigs are offered more time for their choice. Another experiment could offer the opportunity to discuss the choice with a group of familiar people, and see in which way the discussion affects the process of preference formation. In the experiment, as described by Ariely, the problem of multi-motivated persons cannot be solved. It means that irrationality cannot be made empirically observable.

The second experiment shows a situation in which a person is at the point of buying a pencil with a price of $14. Then a fellow customer whispers in his ear that in another shop the price of exactly the same pencil is $7. The shop is a 15-minute walk away. Most people go for the cheaper pencil. In another situation a customer is at the point of buying a suit for $488, when he discovers that the same suit can be bought for $481 at a shop 15 minutes away. Most people buy the more expensive good. Ariely considers this result to be an indication of human irrationality. But again, our problem with this interpretation is that we don't know the human motivations for this choice. When I asked some people for their choices and also asked them to give their motivations, several answers came up. One reaction was that the person considers the price difference between the suits as acceptable, since various suits are never perfectly identical. Another reaction was that the person conjectured that a 50 per cent difference in case of the pencil suggests an abnormal profit margin for the seller of the $14 pencil. In other words, people have more criteria when buying a good than just the price. In my examples, heterogeneity of goods and possible exploitation of consumers by producers play a role as well.

The third experiment is about an employer and an employee. The salary of the employee is $100,000 per year and he is satisfied with it. Then he discovers that his colleague, who is identical in terms in terms of education, experience, and performance, earns a salary of $120,000. The outcome of the experiment shows that many employees go to their boss and express their dissatisfaction. Ariely interprets this behaviour as irrational. But if we are aware that the actors are not living in the typical economic world, but in an economic-psychic-social world (see Chapter 14), the reaction of most employees perfectly makes sense—there is no irrationality at all. It is plausible to assume that there is a marked difference between the reaction of North American and European employees. In Europe the rule of equal pay for equal output is generally desired and accepted. Discrimination is illegal rather than irrational.

To become less irrational, Ariely discusses the advice by Hong to make the circles of comparisons smaller. If someone buys a Porsche, he knows that it is likely that he will, later on, want a Ferrari. If he just buys a Toyota Prius, he will remain happy with his car. But in this example there is no reference to the motivation behind the purchase of an expensive car. In Chapters 11 to 13 we will discuss sociology and see that social status is considered a strong natural motivator. Social comparison is natural, and the evolution of a culture, including a set of values and norms, is natural too. Of course, some social processes will turn out to be very expensive, or might even be considered immoral—but not irrational. In Section 10.7 we will discuss a different conceptualization of irrationality. There we will carefully distinguish between the meaning of economic, rational, and social. In Chapter 13 we will conceptualize the term 'social'. In Chapter 14 we will integrate our isolated aspect-analyses. Then, it is possible that some social-comparative behaviour is based on envy and anxiety, while other social-comparative behaviour is based on empathy and the willingness to offer every individual the opportunity to participate in society in a respectful way (see also the discussion of the capabilities approach by Sen in Chapter 9).

After the 1980s attention moved increasingly to the role of emotions, however (Elster, 1998; Frijda, 2007). In Greek philosophy the imperfect control of emotions by reason was the essence of the moral problem. Where Plato saw the task of reason to suppress the emotions, Aristotle saw reason as the capacity for distinguishing emotions that contribute to human well-being from emotions that do not serve one's own best interests. The art of life was to find a balance (Norman, 1998).

This Aristotelian idea began to play an important role in behavioural economics. Under the influence of modern psychological research, *self-control*, expressing the relationship between emotions and the capacity to control them, became a central concept (Schelling, 1984; Tiemeijer et al., 2009). The analysis describing the important psychic relationships runs as follows: a human person is permanently exposed to a flow of impressions, which are framed in such a way that they become understandable. Understanding triggers emotions, which set a person in motion; in other words, framed impressions trigger emotions that drive people to act. Many emotions are linked to the needs and desires of an immediate character: feelings of hunger and thirst, of anger or sorrow, of lack of safety, and of cold. Some desires might, if immediately satisfied, evolve into addiction: alcohol, gambling, or sex. There is, fortunately, one emotion that says: 'wait a minute; let's find out whether the satisfaction of this need or desire is really serving my own interest'. Some persons have a strong will and can control themselves relatively easily; others, however, have difficulty in controlling their immediate desires and needs. Now we can call a person with a lack of self-control imperfectly rational or even outright irrational: by satisfying all immediate needs that pop up, he is not serving his own long-term interests.

After this exposition of the shift in meaning of the concept of rationality, we will give a short overview of the main results of empirical and experimental research that has been executed on the basis of behavioural economic theory.

10.4.2 NEUROECONOMICS

Neuroscientists distinguish between two processes, which have very different functions (McClure et al., 2004). The first takes place in the limbic system, associated with the midbrain dopamine system. It processes information about the immediate costs and benefits of a particular phenomenon. The transported information is of an affective and automatic character, runs very fast and does not take much energy. The second is located in the lateral prefrontal and in the posterior parietal cortex. It processes information about delayed benefits and costs of a particular phenomenon, which is of a cognitive and controlled character, runs more slowly and takes much energy (see Section 10.3.6 on the biological approach). Romer (2000) discusses the example of eating peanuts. Many people like the taste of peanuts and often eat them. But some people are allergic to them. Their problem is that the assessment of the taste is a matter of affection; it takes place automatically and fast. But the assessment of peanuts in terms of health effects is a cognitive affair and takes time and energy. So, if a person does not establish a rule of the type 'I never eat peanuts', he is always seduced to eat peanuts, while regretting it later.

A second neuroeconomic finding is the fact that groups of neurons compete with each other (Camerer et al., 2007). Groups of neurons transport bundles of information—units of information that belong to the same category. Information of an affective character, which is unfamiliar to the person, is transported to the cortex for a deliberate and cognitive treatment. But familiar information is processed automatically and is not sent to the cortex—it is already integrated in the existing vision of the person. So familiar groups win the battle against unfamiliar groups, and behaviour is primarily determined by information that fits the existing framework. This process can be illustrated by the following example. A person is an economist, and received training in neoclassical economics. He reads in articles and in newspapers that the financial crisis of 2008 is caused by expansionary monetary policies by the American Federal Reserve System. Since this analysis fits the neoclassical framework, he uncritically consumes this information. In other newspapers he reads about the irrationality of banks and clients being the cause of the crisis. However, in neoclassical economics every actor is assumed to be perfectly rational, and he has never been trained in the meaning of the concept of (ir)rationality. So this information needs elaborate cognitive processing, which takes time and energy. Therefore, our person has a strong interest in ignoring this information.

The two systems, and the fact that affective processes run faster through the system, is often explained in an evolutionary way: survival-required instinctive reaction—no time for deliberation. It explains why many people are still quite myopic.[20]

A last discovery is the fact that the experience of pain is more intense and triggers more reaction than the experience of pleasure. This might also have an evolutionary function: danger requires alertness, while pleasure suggests a safe environment, which makes relaxation possible. Phenomena like loss aversion can be explained in this way.

10.4.3 COGNITIVE SCIENCE

In the text on neuroeconomics we talked about groups of neurons, not of separate individual neurons. They operate group-wise because the mind always approaches reality by means of categorical sense impressions. In a lifelong process we learn to categorize reality and create some order; otherwise we wouldn't understand it. So we have our perceptions of the world rather than a one and only objective picture. This idea of perception or interpretation can also be called *framing* (Kahneman and Tversky, 1979). It shapes our intuition, and is primarily of an immediate and affective character. The framework gives us scope for understanding what's going on, but it also limits us. If we have learned that there are two groups in society, one with career chances and another without, it is impossible to 'see' that many people of the second group did not even try to have a career. If a member of the second group—60 years old—discovers that he had good opportunities in the past, but simply was not open to them, this person has a strong interest in denying this discovery. It would be too painful to realize that he had missed so many opportunities, and that his actual opportunity costs, taken over his whole lifetime, were very high.

---

[20] See Shiller (2002) for an example from investor theory, and see Frey (1978) for an example from voter theory.

The drive to ignore this sort of information is called self-serving bias. This doesn't hold simply for persons, but for organizations too. Imperfectly rational chief executive officers looking to their own interests, develop strategies for their companies that turn out to be bad. Then it is extremely difficult for these leaders to acknowledge that they were the cause of the problem, rather than 'the situation' (Kets de Vries, 2006).

Which factors do determine which frames are constructed? The first factor is called stimulus salience. Parent figures are very important in this respect. They constantly bombard their very young child with sentences such as: Benjamin, look, this is a table, and this is a chair. Benjamin: you being a good boy. So upbringing is a major determinant of the way we look at the world. A second source is education. Professionals are trained to interpret particular phenomena in a particular way. They see things a non-expert cannot see. They know how to tackle particular problems, and have routinized the way in which they do so. A heart surgeon, for instance, knows what to do without having to think deeply about it. This is precisely the characteristic of an expert: sense impressions about 'their' problem are processed by the immediate, affective, and effortless system, which creates room for deliberate attention to the particulars in each individual case. A person perceives sense impressions in such a way that he understands them, and 'knows' how to react. This leads to fast, automated affective reactions, mostly in the unconscious. But if the situation is not completely familiar, controlled and cognitive reactions are triggered and thoughts about the situation arise: 'what shall I do?' Maybe the affective reaction has already led to some behaviour. Then the cognitive part must consider whether the first and immediate reaction was correct or not. The quality of this so-called *corrective thought* can be improved by education; lifelong learning can make a person more rational, although he needs enough willpower to block particular affective reactions, if necessary.

Corrective thought takes place in an analysis of the situation within the framework intuitively adopted most of the time. Professional training especially teaches the student how to solve particular problems. Genuine academic education, however, teaches the student which frameworks of interpretation can be used to understand particular types of problems, and therefore is an important factor in determining frames. So, an academic student will increasingly discover his own intuition, and is offered the chance to change it. But we all have a strong interest in not changing a paradigm, since the psychic and social costs are perceived as prohibitively high. There is (emotional) aversion to move from a liberal to a conservative paradigm, for instance. When the financial crisis of 2008 started, and everyone began to blame the American central bank for having caused it, the previous chairman of this bank, the famous Alan Greenspan, publicly blamed himself for being so foolishly liberal. He had the guts to do so but he was in a relatively easy position as retiree. The current chairman, Ben Bernanke, was in a more difficult position. He was an acknowledged expert in the field of financial crashes and depressions, especially of the economic history of the 1990s. If he had admitted to be blind, it would have been at the cost of his position, economically as well as socially. So, he simply denied having made big policy mistakes. As we saw in Chapter 5 he even decided to cancel the one and only page about Keynes in his famous textbook.

A third and last factor that influences the perception of a particular situation is *selective attention*: some elements are stressed on purpose to attract attention. A person is dressed in a red gown, in an environment where everybody else is dressed in either white or black, for instance. The colour red attracts the attention of all the people in the neighbourhood. Later people remember the situation and think of the person with the red gown.

When framing a particular situation we need *anchors* as points of reference. Neoclassical economists frame the world in terms of economic and perfectly rational actors, who meet each other in markets. If a particular economy shows increasing unemployment, the idea of a free market economy which is always close to equilibrium can function as a point of reference or anchor. It is a benchmark, which shows in which direction we must go in order to decrease unemployment. Imagine the country has institutionalized a system of collective wage bargaining. Models are developed that introduce a system of collective wage bargaining into a model of general equilibrium. Given the anchor, the model shows, unavoidably, that union influence on the level of wages is the cause of unemployment (Keizer, 1993).

Frames and anchors are very important elements in the knowledge that is used when taking important decisions. They are of an intuitive kind and are automatized, affective, and effortless. *Frames are like shelters*: they create emotions associated with safety and being at home. They must be developed into more sophisticated analyses and specified models, although this almost never happens. Most of the time people use intuition and some statistical information at their disposal, which shows some development: a positive or negative trend, for instance. If their intuition suggests a negative trend, while the statistical information suggests a positive trend, most people trust their intuition (Shiller, 2002). The problem of safety in the streets of large cities is a good example. In Dutch cities such as Rotterdam and Almere many people have the idea that criminality is growing, especially the number of violent incidents. For politicians it is difficult to convince the public of the opposite by showing statistics with a positive trend. Why? People trust their intuition: it functions as their personal advisor and is always there. They live in these unsafe areas, and see violent action regularly: 'how dare politicians say that their statistics know better'. Many experts in social science have specialized in empirical research, which is based on a particular paradigm. Most of the time, these researchers do not question their paradigms and do not worry about the limitative character of their work. There are also experts who are statisticians, like econometricians, who are hardly aware of their framework of interpretation. They correlate and calculate probabilities. Their problem is that most people are not open to their information and ignore results of calculations that cannot be understood intuitively.

The evolutionary approach explains the primacy of the affective system by referring to the necessity of a quick reaction in case of danger. This has made living creatures, including humans, myopic. In the literature on voter behaviour, voters are supposed to be myopic. It means that they look at the current situation when judging whether the ruling parties have done a good job or not. Actually, they assume that politicians have always had perfect control of the situation. Politicians use this fact by stimulating the economy about a year before the elections, thereby creating a so-called *political cycle* (Frey, 1978). Financial investors can be very myopic in assuming that particular rises in the price of stocks will continue. Many investors think that they can foresee when the price rise will stop and turn into a decline. In practice, almost all people sell their assets too late (Akerlof and Shiller, 2009).

The assessment of developments in the near future takes place in a different part of the brain compared with the assessment of developments in the far future, which makes it difficult for a person to be perfectly time-consistent. In an experiment people were asked for their preference: 100 euros now or 110 euros a day later. Then, they were asked for their preference: 100 euros in a year or 110 euros in a year and a day. It appeared that people assessed the costs of waiting a day differently: one day of waiting now is more costly than waiting one day in a year's time. In other words, the difference between zero and one is larger than the difference between 365 and 366.

A last consequence of the different processing of affection and cognition is related to the already mentioned difference between risk and uncertainty. Risks can be expressed in terms of probabilities, which can be calculated by means of statistical methods. Suppose that a time series of the rates of return on investments in the AEX assets can be presented as a cycle, and we just left the lowest point: 2 per cent, for instance. Extrapolation leads to an estimated 3 per cent for the next year with a particular probability, which can be calculated. The affective system in our mind approaches the same problem differently. We experience not risk but uncertainty. It triggers negative emotions of fear and anxiety as well as strong positive emotions. In a climate of optimism, for instance, many people become overoptimistic and invest a lot in risky assets: 'no problem, we live in a new era, an era of ever-growing wealth'. The fact that the affective system and the cognitive system are not perfectly coordinated makes it necessary to develop rules of behaviour to control the uncontrolled emotions of the affective system. Within a framework of rules people feel safer and quieter. Within such frames, the cognitive part can more easily make calculations to support the decision-making process. The post-Keynesian plea for financial regulation to avoid financial crises is derived from this type of analysis of the financial world (Minsky, 1982).

10.5 **The Social Factor**

Social psychology is an important part of psychology. Its paradigm says that processes in the mind are significantly affected by or even completely determined by the characteristics of the social world in which an individual person lives. It starts with the parent figures who shape their child's emotional and cognitive structure. Later, the school and the neighbourhood, and even later the organization where our person has a job, are shaping the way he approaches his world. The social world is characterized by group structures: we belong to the rich or to the poor, to the skilled or to the unskilled, to the Christian believers or to the atheists. All these groups are characterized by a subculture, which defines the way group members interpret the world. The group's world-view determines common values and norms, and group members are supposed to stick to the rules. All together, these groups form society, which is integrated to a certain extent. Groups can only function as such if the members attach authority to leading figures, who specify daily practices. A well-functioning group puts pressure upon its members to conform to the rules of the club.

Now we will give a few examples, which illustrate the relevance of the social factor for our understanding of the functioning of economies.

In the first place, we will discuss the problem of blood donation. In the past, in the USA, volunteers regularly gave blood. The reward was something very small, such as a book token or an extra day off. Later the organizations that were demanding blood began to pay the suppliers. They assumed a positive effect on the quantity supplied, but empirical research shows that, quite often, the opposite appeared to be the case. How can we explain this effect? One explanation says that the pricing saw the good transfer from the social to the economic world. Before the pricing the volunteers saw giving blood as pro-social behaviour, creating and maintaining a particular level of self-respect. But the introduction of pricing made the good an economic good, which can be offered as long as the economic benefits are higher than the economic costs. The lower level suggests that the price was simply too low to create a market equilibrium. Moreover, in case of voluntarism, people with poor-quality blood do not participate in the delivery. But when it became an economic market, the blood supplied must be checked to see whether the quality meets minimum standards.

A second example is about tipping. Experience shows that people give tips to waiters in restaurants, even if it is very clear that the tip giver will never return. So, there cannot be any economic motivation. But a social motivation is also problematic as an explanation. In our example, the tip giver has never met the waiter, and has no companions he wishes to impress. The only reason we can think of is self-respect. Particular behaviours have become part of the tip giver's identity. He would despise himself if he did not give a tip. By sticking to this good habit, he maintains his self-respect. If many people derive respect from pro-social behaviour, positive social relationships are stable.

In general we can say that culture has a significant effect on the performance of the economy. If it promotes pro-social behaviour and creates trust among producers and consumers especially, the economy will grow. Culture gives an answer to the question of what is just and what is fair, a core item in sociology. The effects of culture can be illustrated by experiments (Henrich et al., 2007). In an *ultimatum game* there is a proposer, who divides a sum of money between himself and a responder; he latter can accept the offer or reject it. In case of rejection neither the proposer nor the responder receives anything. An economically motivated proposer, who assumes that the responder is also an economically motivated actor, offers the responder just one euro, since he assumes that the other prefers one euro to zero euros. The experiment was held in 15 non-Western countries with much cultural variety. The modal offer appeared to be about 50 per cent, while the mean was 40–45 per cent. About 20 per cent of the responders rejected the offer. In the *dictator's game*, which is the ultimatum game without the opportunity to reject, the modal offers were zero and the mean was 20–30 per cent. In a *public goods game* people were asked to give a voluntary contribution to a fund that would be used to finance a particular public good. Every player received a particular amount of money, and was asked to put some money in the common fund. The result was that most people gave 40–50 per cent of their money, but in case of repetition of the game the offers declined to almost zero. Apparently, people were disappointed with the payments of the others, and decided to stop being 'altruist'.

10.6 **The Psychic World**

Our exposition of the different approaches in psychology has led to the following picture.

The biological approach distinguishes between two neurological processes. The first is responsible for the transmission of automated, uncontrolled, and affective processes, and is located in the limbic system. The second is responsible for the transmission of deliberate, controlled, and cognitive processes, which are located in the cortex. The first process takes hardly any energy, while the second is energy-consuming. When processing sense impressions, groups of neurons compete with each other; those impressions that are familiar to the person win, and the information carried by the losers is ignored (winner-takes-all principle).

The behavioural approach is essentially about the process of conditioning. It says that we learn by association and store the information in the affective memory. The information stored in the intuition is used without much energy.

The cognitive approach distinguishes two systems. One is responsible for the perception of the situation, which means the categorization or framing of information. It functions as an affect and can be called intuition. The other system processes incoming sense impressions deliberately and cognitively. It leads to an analysis of the situation on the basis of the framework, which is constituted by intuition, and is called the cognitive map.

The psychodynamic approach makes an analysis of the mind. According to Freud, the mind is the battlefield between the Id, representing the genetically determined needs of the person, and the Superego, representing the societal needs. The Ego must solve the emotional conflict by reconciling the different needs. Jung, however, makes a distinction between the Self and the ideal Self. The Self represents the way the person actually manifests himself, while the ideal Self is the way the person should manifest himself, according to his own ideas.

Lastly, the humanist approach offers a type of growth theory. What is the goal of a person when all so-called deficiency needs are satisfied? The answer is: discover the true Self and make him manifest to one's own Ego or 'I' and to the world. Humanist psychologists call this self-actualization.

Biological psychologists analyse stocks and flows in the brain, whereas cognitive psychologists analyse the same processes in the mind. Brain and mind are two sides of the same coin, or two aspect-systems of one and the same phenomenon, which is the human person. But if we want to understand these processes, we need to know the prime movers or drives that keep the neurons and emotions moving. This is where the psychodynamic and the humanist approach come in: there is a continuing emotional conflict and we need all our energy to solve these conflicts in such a way that 'we grow'. This means that we increasingly discover our true Self, and learn how to live our life accordingly.

Now, we can distinguish a first brain and mind process the material and the mental aspect of *the actual Self* respectively. A second brain and mind process are the material and the mental aspect of the Ego or 'I' and its *true Self* as experienced by the 'I' or Ego. The true Self as experienced by the 'I' can only manifest itself if important emotional conflicts are solved. Conflict resolution requires energy, which means that very poor persons have difficulty resolving their problems because of a lack of resources to satisfy basic needs such as food, drink, and shelter. Conflict resolution also requires a minimum of recognition by relevant others. If the economic and the social problems are not very severe, there is room for a person to become aware of the Self, and to see whether this discovery leads to *self-respect*. If this respect is below a particular minimum it might lead to an aggressive attitude towards the Self. As a matter of survival a human person is equipped with the capacity to protect the true Self from being discovered. This self-serving bias is reflected materially in the winner-takes-all principle in the neuron competition, and is reflected mentally by so-called cognitive pathology. So, our drive to discover and to develop the true Self is constrained by the self-serving bias.

Now we can fully answer the question of what we mean by the psychic logic, reflecting the behaviour of a typical psychic actor who is imperfectly rational.[21]

The psychic imperfectly rational actor is maximizing his self-respect under the constraint of:

(1) A belt that protects the true Self from discovery of its shadowy sides.[22]
(2) Limited energy available for the execution of decisions taken by the Ego or 'I' to minimize the difference between the actual Self and the true Self as perceived by the 'I' (limited willpower).

---

[21] The term psychic actor does not exist as far as I know. It is meant to play a role in the discussion about the human being as an economic actor versus a social actor. We add a third category to the two categories just mentioned: a human being is a psychic actor, whose behaviour is determined by psychic logic. In Ross (2005), different parts of the mind are seen as bearers of a particular interest. 'Each interest is as clever as a person' (p. 345). Psychic dynamics expresses the fact that humans show ubiquitous preference reversal and time inconsistencies. Nevertheless, we can define a person as a set of basically compatible long-range interests that have co-opted a sufficient army of short-range interests into their coalition to maintain stable psychic equilibrium (Ross, 2005: 351).

Davis (2003) is working along the same lines. According to him, neoclassical economics is based on the idea of a community of selves. In my psychic logic the difference between the short-term desires and long-term interests of the psychic actor is reflected in the distinction between the actual Self (AS) and the true Self (TS). In the long run a person reaches his psychic equilibrium (by definition). See Lagueux (2008) for an extensive discussion of Ross's work.

[22] There is a striking parallel with the scientific-philosophical approach of Lakatos here. He developed the theory of the protective belt, which protects the paradigm of a research programme against easy refutation (Lakatos, 1970).

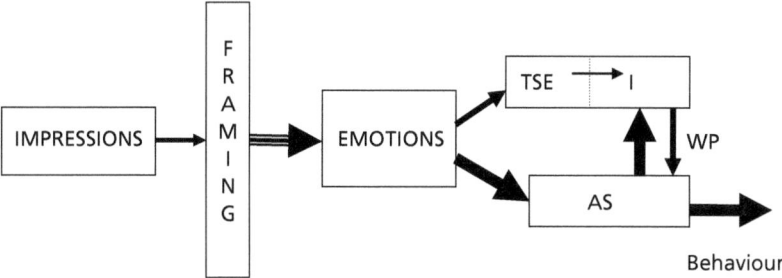

Figure 10.5. The Principle of Psychic Logic

The mechanism operates as follows: sense impressions are framed in a particular way, which leads to emotions. These emotions, called the actual Self (AS), are automatically and effortlessly transported to the brain and to the mind, and lead to action. The emotions also trigger more elaborate and controlled processes, which are transported to the true Self as experienced by the 'I' (TSE) as well as to the 'I'. This centre takes decisions and gives orders to the executive management (willpower), which influences action. The arrow from AS to I suggests that immediate desires are constantly trying to convince the decision making centre of their importance. In Figure 10.5 we have portrayed this process.

If sense impressions give a negative message about the true Self, the TSE adjusts this a little, and the executive management receives new orders to change behaviour in a direction that leads to more self-respect. The more impermeable the protective belt around the TSE and the more willpower, the higher the respect for the TSE. But the impermeability of the belt makes it impossible for the person to grow, thereby maintaining a permanent emotion of emptiness.

The analysis of the mind is of a partial nature, as is typical for economic analysis. The typical economic force is also analysed in isolation. Therefore, we have also analysed the typical psychic force in isolation. When developing a typical social analysis, reflecting social logic, this analysis should also be integrated with the psychic and the economic analysis. If we succeed in this project, we would have developed a unified paradigm and framework of interpretation and analysis that can function as a theoretical basis for human science. To illustrate the relevance of the different psychological approaches to a proper understanding of economic phenomena we end our text with a case study (Appendix 10.1), in which we sketch ideal-typical psychological solutions to an economic problem. These solutions are, as is the case with typical economic solutions, of a partial character, of course.

Appendix 10.1 **Have Germans Experienced a Monetary Trauma?**

A10.1.1 INTRODUCTION

At the moment (December 2013) the EU faces a financial-economic problem: many EU countries, including those who have the euro as their currency, have a budget deficit in per cent of GDP that is higher than is allowed according to the Stability and Growth Pact. Some countries state that this is due to the severe economic crisis. All EU countries had negative growth rates in 2009, and the cause of this depression was a lack of effective demand. So, governments should stimulate their economies by increasing their investments, and the resulting growth of production will lead to increasing tax and social premium payments, and to lower unemployment benefits. This development means lower deficits within a couple of years. Some countries such as Germany, however, advocate significant cuts in government expenditure. Lower deficits lead to lower governmental debts, which create trust among the financial investors. Lower interest rates are the result, which stimulate private investments. At the moment, countries who advocate this policy show surpluses on the current account of their balance of payments: they hope to recover through increasing exports.

In this debate, the Germans play a remarkable role. In an interview in the Dutch newspaper NRC on 20 March 2010, a German former central banker, Otmar Issing, explained the German attitude by referring to the country's history. When Germans talk about monetary management they immediately react very emotionally. They are so traumatized by their economic history that an intellectual debate about the advantages and disadvantages of various monetary policy options is barely possible. Otmar Issing: 'The roots of our fear for monetary instability lie in our history.' To explain this fear in more detail we discuss this history in brief.

A10.1.2 GERMAN FINANCIAL-ECONOMIC HISTORY

When the Germans lost the First World War they had to pay the winners for their destructive activities. These payments were a severe burden for the Germans. The government tried to reconcile the necessity of improving the living of the Germans with the necessity of paying off the external debts. In 1923 the government could not coordinate the two claims any longer and printed so much money that it became worthless. Hyperinflation led to a lower real value of German debts, but also to the impoverishment of the middle class. When, a few years later, a crash on the New York Stock Exchange led to global depression and to impoverishment of the German labour class, the seeds of the next world war were sown.

Mainstream German economists have learned to interpret these events in a monetarist way: governments must strive for budget balance, and central banks must manage money creation by private banks in such a way that inflation is prevented. The German Constitution guarantees monetary stability, which was a hot issue in the period that the Germans introduced the euro at the cost of the strong Deutsch Mark. The almost impossibility for German economists to discuss different policy options is a psychological phenomenon with far-reaching economic consequences. Therefore, it is interesting to see how the different psychological approaches interpret this 'cognitive pathology'.

A10.1.3 SIX PSYCHOLOGICAL INTERPRETATIONS OF THE GERMAN TRAUMA

The text is meant to illustrate ideal-typical interpretations rather than offering solutions based on specific analysis, theory, and empirical testing. Although psychology is meant to explain individual behaviour, it can also be applied to groups and to whole nations as well.

The behaviourist approach interprets German behaviour in terms of conditioning. The Pavlov experiment with a dog shows that bell-ringing—in itself a neutral thing—becomes a conditioned stimulus when it is connected with the delivery of food. Germans have connected the monetary crises of 1923, and the period just before October 1929, with the disasters that followed. So, in the unconscious, uncontrolled, and automatic part of the German mind there is an association between money creation, government, and crisis, which means that they immediately—without elaborately thinking about the relationships—react negatively to large budget deficits. They 'know' how to reduce this deficit, namely through expenditure cuts. Everyone who opposes this policy recipe triggers German irritation. Otmar Issing: 'I'm embarrassed about the fact that so many economists simply don't understand that our democracy is at stake.' A behaviourist solution to this problem is focused on a process of unconditioning, like the Pavlovian dog, who hears the bell but is not offered any food. The Germans must try to detect typical Keynesian situations and learn to accept reasonable budget deficits, and thus discover that this does not lead to monetary chaos at all.

The cognitive approach interprets German behaviour in terms of cognitive mapping. The German mind is framed in a monetarist way. History has taught the Germans that macroeconomic disequilibrium is caused by inflation, which is always and everywhere a monetary phenomenon. Since private bank activities are tightly monitored and controlled by central banks, only monetary financing of government expenditures can cause inflation. Governments should aim at a balanced budget; fortunately the EU has adopted the Stability and Growth Pact, which allows budget deficits of a maximum of 3 per cent in times of recession. The cognitive solution to this problem aims at offering different cognitive maps. If German economics students are going to participate increasingly in foreign exchange programmes outside the Anglo-Saxon world, and discover that different approaches within economics and human science offer serious alternatives to the monetarist view, a new and more sophisticated generation can take over the leading positions within 20 years.

The biological approach analyses brain processes, thereby making a distinction between brain processes that are automatic and uncontrolled on the one hand, and those that are deliberate and controlled on the other. If German economists talk with French economists, for instance, the bundles of neurons that are triggered by French information are ignored since they are anomalies for the German brain. So the French are approached negatively, and are confronted with the information that is transported by winning neurons in the automatic and uncontrolled part of the German brain. The biological solution to the problem searches for a change in the physiological circumstances under which important monetary experts take their decisions. Germans are used to long days of working in a hierarchical atmosphere. Individual Germans should try to shape their environment differently: less hours of work in a more open and relaxed context. The younger generation might even change their food habits: less meat and beer. It could release them, making them more sensitive to the contributions of people who are perceived as different.

The psychodynamic approach focuses on the psychic mechanisms, which might solve the emotional conflicts in the human mind. In the first place, lack of willpower leads to behaviour that is not in the long-term interest of the actor. This is definitely not the case with the monetary emotions of the Germans, who excel in matters of willpower. In the second place, lack of rationality is based on cognitive pathology. Traumatic events have triggered a strong sense of fear when it comes to monetary matters, and Germans' automatic reaction—discipline, government retreat—cannot be corrected by meaningful analysis offered by people with a different view on monetary management. The psychodynamic solution focuses on therapeutic sessions with leading figures, to let Germans discover their true motives, which concern the suppression of fear. Rather than constantly recapitulating typical texts about the necessity of discipline and monetary restraint, leaders could show the results of their reflection to their fellow economists and to the people in general. The typical German map is based on fear and is not effective in all situations. So, the Germans must break through the cognitive and emotional barriers and apply willpower to reach intellectually more satisfying analyses.

The humanist approach stresses that history shows that the German identity, as experienced by Germans, has developed over a long period of antagonistic relationships in Europe. In order to break through the protective belt surrounding the true Self, German economists need positive confrontations with economists who are different, in a power-free environment. Then we can expect them to become more open-minded when it comes to discussions about monetary management. Step by step, German monetary economists will discover their true Self, and advocate more effective public finance policies without fear.

The social-psychological approach stresses that it is social environment that shapes the people's Self. For our problem, it means that the German attitude can be explained by an analysis of the history of social interaction between Germany and its neighbours. Being a large and powerful nation in the middle of Europe, its neighbours have been its enemies for a very long time. Time and again German reaction has been negative and violent. Now they are very reluctant to really get involved in a positive interaction and conversation with other important nations in Europe. Lack of trust in each other, and in each other's world-view, is a barrier that cannot be lowered—also because of ongoing German economic success. German culture is primarily about organization, order, and discipline. Germans have made serious mistakes in the past, which have created severe traumas, and have strengthened their sense of responsibility, but also of reluctance in taking leading positions. This is a new source of frustration. The problem of the Greek budget deficits led Germans to react in panic: 'please, Greeks, discipline your Self', which created Greek irritation. In reaction to the German attitude they reminded the Germans of their Nazi past.

How can we stop these aggressive interactions? Can we organize psychotherapy for a whole nation—or even better, for a whole group of neighbouring nations, in our case the European Union? The best idea is to organize meetings on a regular basis, where important figures from the different nations meet each other in a power-free context, talk about the important problems, and increasingly discover their own cognitive pathologies.

A10.1.4 EPILOGUE

This case is about a German trauma—recognized as such by the Germans themselves. However, we must recognize that all people have traumas of different kinds and to different degrees. When advising Germans to open up, and accept the confrontation with people who are different, we must be honest and admit that it is not only Germans who must learn. Others might learn much from the Germans. We can even speculate that other Europeans might adopt some German views and attitudes, since they have discovered these to be superior. Therefore, the title of this text is a question rather than a statement, expressing the idea that it is not only Germans who experience traumas.

Part IV
Sociology for Economists

IV.1 **Introduction**

In Chapter 3 we discussed the emergence of classical sociology. Industrialization of Western European economies was the immediate cause of the interest in understanding the essence of an industrial society, and the mechanisms that influence its course. Classical sociology assumes, in contrast to classical political economy, the existence of a society of which the economy is just a part. So, the functioning of an economy can only be understood if the interrelationships between economy and society are analysed. Moreover, classical sociology assumes that economic and social processes take place in a historical context. Empirical relationships differ significantly when different stages of development are compared. The most important axiom states that human behaviour is social behaviour. Every individual or organization operates in a social context—always and everywhere. After this general characterization, Chapter 3 discusses the main characteristics of four sociologists, namely Marx, Durkheim, Weber, and Parsons.

Marx interpreted industrial society as an arena where capital and labour struggle for power and resources. The capitalists are the dominant group, and use part of their power to press the government to help them to discipline the labour class, thereby creating and maintaining severe inequalities.

Durkheim, however, interpreted industrial society as a typical modern society. It means that economic growth, resulting from increasing knowledge and specialization, creates a huge problem with regard to order. The fast-growing number of professions creates many different ways of understanding the world. Progressive societies are—by definition—able to organize ongoing communication between these professional groups.

Weber saw many different sorts of conflict—economic, social, political, religious, ethnic, for instance. This makes modern society a very complex phenomenon. If we want to understand human behaviour, we should try to comprehend how different people understand their reality differently. The role of science and technology is very important; they have the potential to make society increasingly rational.

At last we discussed Parsons, who became famous because of his systematic analysis of the different subsystems and aspect-systems within society.

When looking at the three different ideal-types of moral and political philosophy we see that the conservative and socialist views play a large role, relative to the liberal view. As we saw in Chapter 3, the liberal view says that if society leaves individuals free, order will be the spontaneous result. The socialist view, however, says that order will be restored as soon as the inequality between the different groups of people has been levelled out somewhat. Marx is an example in this respect. Conservatives do not interpret order as something that spontaneously arises in some circumstances; it must be deliberately organized. So, a system of rules must be established and strictly maintained. They consider inequality to be a natural phenomenon, which should not be artificially reduced by means of extensive government interventions. Durkheim is an example in this respect.

In order to reach a more thorough understanding of the different views and analyses of economy and society, Chapter 11 will discuss a range of sociological interpretations;

not only those of a macro-character, such as classical sociology, but also analyses of a micro- or network character.

In Section 11.1 we discuss the classical divide between the functionalist and the conflict approach in more detail.

In Section 11.2 we present two different branches within the micro-sociology, namely symbolic interactionism on the one hand, and exchange, network, and rational choice analysis on the other. The first stresses the emergence of culture when people meet each other regularly. The second approach assumes that people act on the basis of a cost/benefit calculation, in the economic as well as in the social context. Within the macro- as well the micro-divides, the interrelationship between power and culture appears to be pivotal.

In Section 11.3 we deal with the interrelationship between the macro- and the micro-approach. In economics there is a serious gap between the two different levels, where the micro methodology dominates the macro one. In macroeconomic textbooks a typical micro-approach, neoclassical analysis, is used rather than a typical macro-approach, such as the post-Keynesian analysis. In sociology, however, the gap between micro- and macro-analysis is bridged by network analysis. We can always argue, however, whether or not the solutions available are satisfying. Of course, the interrelationship between culture and power is at the centre of analysis. Networks transmit pressure by using power from higher to lower levels, and culture is transmitted horizontally by means of persuasion.

We have added two appendices to Chapter 11. The first offers three practical problems, which are analysed by means of the four major sociological interpretations, namely the functionalist, the conflict, the symbolic-interactionist, and the exchange/rational choice approach. The second appendix presents an imaginary discourse between scientists, who all adhere to a different approach. Four experts represent the four major sociological interpretations, and a fifth expert is an orthodox economist. Both appendices try to show how different frames work out in the analysis of practical problems.

In Chapter 12 we deal with the historical approach in sociology. The most important question of social science is at stake: How do we control the ongoing application of technical and cultural inventions without destroying the main source of invention, which is the free individual? Is the idea of modernity realistic enough to achieve continuing progress? The historical approach shows that not only successes but also failures have long-term effects. Postmodernists are sceptical about the reliability of scientific knowledge; it is just a human construction, and therefore highly subjective, social, and uncertain. Straightforward application of the latest inventions is a very risky affair, as problems with nuclear plants and the collapse of the financial system in 2008 clearly show. In this respect, the emergence of post-social theory is an interesting one. It describes a development in which the role of technical systems in the communication between people becomes increasingly important. Foreign currency markets, for instance, are using global computer systems to facilitate 24-hour trade. Do computers that run programmed decision-making processes make the financial system less risky? Or is it just the opposite: if knowledge that lies at the basis of the decision-making software is inadequate in a particular situation, bad decisions can create a lot of trouble. The LTCM-affair in 1997 is a good illustration of this problem. The very large American investment fund LTCM used an inadequately programmed computer for its advice to investors, thereby aggravating the Asian crisis in 1997 significantly. Moreover, we can ask whether the substitution of digital systems for direct human communication is a solution to the classic problem of conflict and aggression. Experience with tax agencies, bank offices, assurance companies, and the like, show that people might develop a strong and negative idea of 'the system', run by an elite, which cannot be called to account.

In Chapter 13 we discuss multidisciplinary sociology, which means the psychological, sociological, and the economic-sociological approach. In the end we will develop a so-called social world, which is the perfect complement of the economic and the psychic world.

In Section 13.2 we discuss the problem of conflict and aggression. Here sociological analysis is based on some psychic-dynamic notions. Sidanius and Pratto (1999) stress the durability of group-based hierarchies. Except in the early hunter-gatherer societies, economic inequality has been paramount and has always been a source of aggression. Feminist theory, when searching for the deeper causes of violence, stresses the way boys and girls are raised. From the very first days we are inclined to stress the differences, so boys are raised on the basis of the idea that they ought to fight against 'the other', and girls are raised on the basis of the idea that they ought to protect their own people, in particular children. Boys are developing a strong ego in ongoing battles with other boys, to impress the girls, for instance. So they learn that rivalling attitudes are rewarded in terms of status. On the level of society as a whole, they stimulate group battles, in terms of wealth, religion, or ethnicity. On the level of organizations, group formation is more differentiated: different groups of medical specialists in hospitals, marketing versus production versus purchasing departments in labour organizations, and alpha versus beta versus gamma researchers in the scientific world. A relevant question in this respect is whether there is any progress in solving the problem of rivalry between groups. Is history an ever ongoing 'panta rei'—a fight that never stops? Or is there a final synthesis between the thesis–anti-thesis clashes?

Section 13.3 discusses developments in economic sociology, which is sociology applied to the economy. Classical sociology is primarily about the economy, and functions as the foundation of economic sociology. Marx, Durkheim, Weber, and Parsons are the great suppliers of paradigms and analyses, on the basis of which much empirical work is executed. The sociology of labour markets is familiar to some labour economists. However, the sociology of financial markets is unknown to financial economists, which is to their detriment. The message of economic sociology is that markets are always and everywhere socially, culturally, and politically embedded. Fligstein (2001) shows how the business sector is socially and culturally connected to the government sector, which is the sector that should control the business sector. Also, on the national and international level there are many arenas where groups fight their status battles, in which their relative power is the decisive factor. But in some areas in the world, notably north-western Europe in the post-war period, consensus emerged with respect to the desirability of a (sober) welfare state. However, in the 1980s and 1990s the political right struck back and it is still trying to dismantle welfare states and ensure an almost complete deregulation of the financial and monetary world. The Anglo-Saxon world reintroduced the classical liberal belief in the intrinsic stability of free market systems. A serious consequence is that the power battles in terms of wealth and ethnicity are back and the more radical parties gain popularity.

The ongoing debate between the role of power and of culture in determining the course of history takes place in every corner of sociology. Communication about justice in a power-free world seems impossible. Culture is always influenced by existing power relations and favours the position of the dominant parties. On the other hand, powerful people can develop ideas that run counter to their own short-run interests. Moreover, an existing culture can influence the social opinions of all people, irrespective of their power position. A very important example is the orientation of employers and the right-wing government in the Netherlands in the beginning of the 20th century. They all agreed to a series of concessions to the unions, although in terms of power there was no reason for doing so.

A very remarkable observation is the fact that virtually nowhere in sociology do the concepts 'scarcity of natural resources', 'economic', or 'rational' play a role comparable to the way in which these concepts are used in economics. It means that the concepts such as social, rivalry, social rationality, and cost/benefit analysis are essentially unclear for an economist. In other words, how can we connect an analysis in terms of power and culture with an analysis in terms of scarcity and economic rationality?

In Section 13.5 we will carefully formulate what we mean by basic concepts such as economic, social, and psychic, leading to a distinction between scarcity, culture, and rationality. We will develop the idea of a social world, analogous to what we did in Chapters 4 and 10, where we developed the idea of the economic and the psychic world respectively. We will pay attention to the debate between Parsons and Robbins, the latter of whom is the most pre-eminent orthodox-economic philosopher. We will also discuss the ideas of Luhman about systems theory and compare his analyses with our distinction between aspect-systems and subsystems. We will come to the conclusion that, in line with work of Weber, Parsons, and Habermas, the idea of sociology—which is the logic of the social—is in line with our idea of the social world as an aspect-system. In this world, processes of grouping and ranking are the major elements responsible for the distribution of power and status. The relationship between the differently ranked groups is characterized by a permanent battle—a battle that is limited in the choice of weapons by the prevailing culture. The mechanism that keeps the various groups 'clean' is the scapegoat mechanism, as described by Girard (1978). In this way, all groups keep themselves culturally sufficiently homogeneous so as not to become weaker as a result of internal divides.

11 Macro- and Micro-Approaches in Sociology

11.1 Macro-Sociology: Functionalism versus the Conflict Approach

As we know, orthodox economics has a classical liberal foundation. Classical sociology, however, is rooted in conservative and socialist views on society. When mentioning names of sociologists without a reference to their book or article, the text is considered as general sociological knowledge. Two important textbooks are Ritzer (2008) and Turner (1998). In particular, Ritzer (2008) has a strong methodological character.

11.1.1 FUNCTIONALISM

A few French sociologists developed conservative analyses, and based their theories upon them. The *conservative paradigm* can be formulated as follows:

(1) Individuals are shaped by society through a process of socialization, which is in contrast to the liberal idea of society as an aggregate of independent individuals.
(2) Society consists of structures and institutions, and of positions and roles, which are hierarchically organized.
(3) Small units, such as families, provide the intimate, face-to-face environments that people need to survive in modern societies.
(4) Since typical modern change has disorganizing effects we need non-rational phenomena, such as ritual, ceremony, and worship, to maintain unity.

In Chapter 3 we have seen that Durkheim and Parsons are considered to be proponents of the functionalist approach, a paradigm that fits the conservative ideology quite well.

Durkheim saw the division of labour as an important source of economic growth, but at the same time as a source of social strife and disintegration. The process of specialization creates an ever-growing separation between (small) groups of professionals, all with their own subculture. The use of typical jargon makes it difficult to communicate with other professionals about the differences in interpretation of their roles and that of the neighbouring professionals. Political scientists have developed corporatist structures to make it possible for the different interest groups to communicate with each other. The famous Dutch Polder model is an example of a corporatist institution that aims at consensus between the various social groups about the ultimate goals of Dutch society.

Parsons worked on a huge system of systems, representing his idea of a functionalist organization of society. As we saw in Chapter 3, Parsons made a distinction between personality system, social system, and cultural system. The personality system aims at keeping personalities integrated, and must be interpreted as an aspect-system of the social system, which aims at keeping society integrated. Both are aspects of the cultural system, which shapes the maps, values, and norms of society, which are all internalized by the participating personalities. There is no explicitly formulated economic aspect, since Parsons wanted to construct a relationship between the micro level of a personality and the macro level of a social and cultural system.

Parsons also developed a completely different system, which can easily be interpreted in terms of the aspect-system or subsystem distinction. He formulated four prerequisites or imperatives of subsystems. It means that subsystems that do not fulfil these necessary conditions will fall apart in the end. We can call the necessary partial systems the aspect-systems of the subsystem. Parsons distinguished between the following four aspect-systems:[1]

(1) The *economic aspect-system*, responsible for a smooth adaptation to the natural environment by taking care of the input–output relationships within this environment. Parsons called this 'adaption' (A).

(2) The *psychic aspect-system*, responsible for the integration of a human person, by supplying him a clear and unambiguous goal. Parsons called this goal attainment (G).

(3) The *social aspect-system*, responsible for the establishment of a generally accepted stratification or hierarchy of groups, so as to keep society integrated. Parsons called this integration (I).

(4) The *political aspect-system*, responsible for the control of the various aspect-systems, subsystems, and the system as a whole. Parsons calls this 'latency' (L).

From Chapters 4 and 5 we know that orthodox economics is an analysis of the economic aspect-system, and from Chapter 10 we know that we can construct an orthodox psychology that offers an analysis of the psychic aspect-system. Later in this chapter we will see that we can construct an orthodox sociology that is an analysis of the social aspect-system. When we give each of these orthodox analyses its own system of control, it is not necessary to distinguish a separate political aspect-system.

Why is the functionalist systems approach considered to be a conservative analysis of society? Systems analysis constructs many levels between the very micro and the very macro level, in order to show that all these levels are part of a whole, the so-called whole system. So, the meaning of a part is determined by the characteristics of the whole. The

---

[1] Although Parsons used a different terminology, there is so much content in his work that suggests aspect-analysis that my interpretation of Parsons' systems approach is a relevant one.

dominant current in science, however, is the reductionist view, stating that all phenomena on a level higher than the lowest micro level can only be understood by studying processes on that lowest level. The systems approach offers (w)holism as an alternative to this reductionism. Liberals tend to reductionism: to reduce societal analysis to the level of the individual and explain his behaviour. Then society can be understood as the aggregate of individual behaviour. Conservatives explain individual behaviour by referring to the characteristics of society as a whole.

Parsons used systems analysis to formulate a series of essences of his structural functionalism:

(1) There is order in the system and the different parts are interdependent.
(2) The system has a tendency to self-maintaining equilibrium.
(3) The system is in stationary equilibrium or is in an orderly process of change.
(4) The system maintains boundaries with its environments.
(5) An optimal allocation, leading to an integrated system, is a process which is necessary for a given state of equilibrium.
(6) Systems tend towards self-maintenance involving the maintenance of boundaries and of the relationships of parts to the whole, control of environmental variations, and control of tendencies to change the system from within.

Parsons was an idealist. That's why he saw the cultural system of maps, values, and norms as the exogenous 'variable', affecting the functioning of other partial systems, while remaining unaffected by them. Applied to the USA, Parsons was optimistic about the effects of the anti-racism campaigns in the 1960s and 1970s. The goals of this campaign fitted the US cultural system as formulated in the Constitution so well, that Parsons could not believe that daily practice would continue to deviate from the culture as officially established and adhered to by a large majority of the American people (Turner, 1998).

Parsons was not only admired, but also criticized. His ahistorical, logical analyses, and his idea that order is something valuable, even if individual freedom and social justice are not realized, were especially not generally accepted.

Whether the critique is right or not, it led at least to changes in the functionalist approach, thereby creating *neo-functionalism*.

Merton was the first who tried to improve functionalism by developing a *disequilibrium theory*. The parallel with the economic market theory is striking. The Walrasian general equilibrium analysis was criticized by macroeconomists, such as Malinvaud (1975), who modelled the Keynesian idea of sustainable disequilibrium in the economy as a whole. On the other hand, microeconomically orientated neo-Austrians stressed the important function of disequilibria in the market processes. They saw it as an important trigger for innovative processes. When analysing not only the subsystem economy, but society as a whole, these issues play an important role as well.

Suppose that our society consists of five institutions, namely economy, family, government, education, and health care. Society is assumed to be in equilibrium. Then there are rumours of a world war, and autonomous consumption and autonomous private investments decrease. This leads to lower production and wages and to higher unemployment. In liberal economics, society is not responsible for the well-being of unemployed people without income. Only if homeless people steal from supermarkets and other organizations or people, will the government step in and put these people in prison. But in our functionally organized society other institutions are responsible for the well-being of the dropouts. If they are ill, they can go into the health-care system. If they have the wrong skills they can go to the education system. The government is responsible for ensuring there is enough demand for labour, and the other institutions are responsible for the necessary inputs that make unemployed people fit for the jobs. Of course, less productive people must accept incomes which might never become higher than a base level.

A functionally organized society needs a refined system of communication between the different institutions and sub-institutions. Coordination of input–output flows takes place on the basis of ongoing *consultation*, in which the different parties inform each other and try to persuade each other of the prices, quantities, and qualities of the inputs and the outputs. *Consensus* about the essential conditions is necessary, as is the willingness to make compromises with respect to the endless flow of practical matters.

Merton considered long-term disequilibrium to be a real option. Empirical research is needed to find out whether functionalist structures perform as they should do.

Alexander, another neo-functionalist, criticized Parsons for his idealism, and for his argument that the cultural system has a primary role in creating consensus in inter-institutional communication. According to him, relative power can prevent culturally necessary adjustments. Referring to the problem of racism in the USA again, we must conclude that the campaigns have reduced discrimination, but there is still much to improve in American daily practice.

11.1.2 CONFLICT APPROACH

German sociologists especially have developed analyses of economy and society on the basis of the socialist view. In Chapter 3 we briefly discussed Rousseau as an ideal-typical socialist philosopher. Later, Fichte, by criticizing Hegel for his idealist dialectics, developed the idea of materialist dialectics, or historical materialism. This means that not ideas but the position of a group in the production structure is decisive with regard to its wealth and power. So an individual worker cannot become rich and powerful by adopting Protestant ideas and lifestyle. In a capitalist society a worker is doomed to become poorer over time, until the stage of the classless society has been reached. Marx built his analysis of the capitalist society upon the basis of this historical materialism. We can summarize *socialist philosophy* as follows:

(1) There is such a thing as society, but as long as productive resources are privately owned, society will be characterized by class conflict.

(2) The capitalist society is the last stage of history before we enter the classless or communist society.

(3) The production structure of a capitalist economy evolves in such a way that an ever-smaller number of haves take an ever-larger amount of income, while an ever-increasing number of have-nots are offered a bare minimum or even nothing.

(4) Increasing inequality is a source of strife and tension between the classes and triggers the development of radical movements; one of them is the socialist movement.

(5) While in a capitalist context, human 'nature' degenerates and becomes competitive and rivalling, offers a classless society individuals the context in which to slowly transform their nature into one of cooperation and solidarity.

In Chapters 3 and 7 we presented an analysis that reflects the ideas of the most influential social scientist, Karl Marx. His materialism made him an economic determinist. The position in the economy is decisive for the position people take in other institutions, among them the cultural institutions.

Later, so-called neo-Marxians criticized Marx's materialism. According to Lukacs and Gramsci, *ideas matter*. In other words, if many people, living in a capitalist society, discover the true nature of the system, and begin to understand that capitalism is basically dehumanizing humans, they will be ready to change the system into something more humane, albeit not necessarily a socialist planning society. Marx claimed, like logical positivists, to develop certain knowledge—so-called hard and objective science. In the eyes of Marx a capitalist has an objective interest in picturing capitalism as a system of free markets, which is a self-maintaining order as long as the government does not intervene. Capitalists have the power to influence the ideas of workers, and make them believe that capitalism is a sort of natural order. The situation of workers is aggravated over time, especially in terms of increasing unemployment, while wages stay at a bare minimum. This is the reason why an increasing number of workers stop believing that capitalism is natural rather than cultural, which means 'man-made'. Workers who discover what their true interests are, are inclined to group together and to form a countervailing power.

Why is capitalism a dehumanizing system? Lukacs refers to the *commodification* of work. Work transforms into a labour service that is for sale; it has become a commodity, like many goods, such as computers or buildings. The human aspect of work is abstracted from the analysis. In our terminology: the psychic and social aspects of a particular action are ignored. Human behaviour is reduced to economic behaviour.

Gramsci emphasizes the relevance of collective ideas, which make it possible to organize enough political will to change the culture of society. This can break the hegemony of capital.[2] Capitalists will lose their cultural leadership, and positive collective ideas about welfare state, for instance, will be taken seriously in the political realm. Marxians who take the role of ideas as triggers for change seriously are called Hegelian Marxians.

---

[2] Remember that the top universities in the USA have many rich donors, and are therefore very wealthy.

During the 1960s, a group of German social scientists formed the so-called Frankfurter Schule. Their approach is called the Critical School, or *critical theory*. They built upon the work by Lukacs and Gramsci about the dehumanization of work. They showed that the combination of materialism and logical positivism has led to the construction of a 'machine' or *System* with its own (formal) rationality. It is as if the System is delinked from ultimate goals of humankind; it aims at its own survival. In other words, all people who have satisficing positions and roles in the System aim at the continuation of it, irrespective of the effects on reasonable goals such as justice and prosperity for all. Who belongs to this System? The workers with tenures in large and medium-sized enterprises and government organizations, the top managers and administrators, and those who own wealth, invested in the organizations just mentioned. In welfare states people with decent social benefits and people who profit from government regulation are also inclined to defend their material interests. In the Netherlands many households profit from considerable tax deduction linked to a mortgage loan. Although the effects appear to increase inequality, political parties don't have the political courage to abolish this tax deduction. The System is actually a huge conglomerate of *vested interests*. The Critical School focuses its critique especially on the capitalist system. Capitalists, including owners of human capital, are the persons who rule the world. In the late capitalist system—the stage we are in now—the System controls society along two lines. On the one hand, it has set up a large subsystem of marketing (Sheehan, 2010). On the other, it has a strong influence on the production of knowledge in our schools and universities. So, the institution of marketing is responsible for the selling of goods that are produced, and the institution of education is responsible for the main input of the System. The formal-rational system is primarily directed towards the satisfaction of needs and desires of those who have the capacity to play an important role in the System. They earn the money needed to buy the output. Those who are considered by the System as inferior do not play a decent role in society. So, in our conflict society the dominant groups use the System to dominate the subordinate groups.

The classical sociological conflict approach is of a historical nature. It means that a particular analysis is always linked to a particular historical stage of development. To illustrate what is meant by economic-historical stages we give two examples: (1) the period of 'early capitalism', characterized by many competitive markets; (2) 'late capitalism', characterized by a series of large globally operating firms, which can barely be controlled by democratic governments. The exploitative nature of capitalism grows over time, but—to an increasing degree—countervailing powers that might become part of the System later on also grow.

Marx was a materialist and an economic determinist. Therefore, he pretended to forecast the future of the System. The ontology of the Critical School is different, however. It assumes that an individual subject, who has a psychic structure which is not completely determined by material forces, exists. In other words, every person has a particular degree of freedom to act differently from what his situation 'dictates'. Marcuse called a society which is largely dictated by the System a *one-dimensional society*. He was professor of social science in Berkeley, and regularly made an appeal to his students to liberate themselves from the dictates of the System. This led to series of student protests against a number of societal problems, such as discrimination. These were the beginning of what is now called the cultural revolution of the 1960s. Marcuse can be summarized by the following statement: 'Be aware that you are part of a continuously distorted system of communication—liberate your Self from that!'

Habermas focuses his attention on the character of knowledge, and the role it plays in the communication between dominant and subordinate groups. He makes a distinction between positivist, humanist, and emancipatory knowledge. The first is directed towards prediction and control, the second aims at understanding, and the third, is directed to the emancipation of the subordinate groups. Knowledge can never be neutral and is always a tool in the hands of a particular group with a particular interest. It is in the long-term interest of all people that the tension between groups is released. Therefore, this release should be adopted by scientists as their most important goal. Only if all people have equal access to the forum of communication can human experience be transformed into reliable knowledge. He calls discourses in a power-free world *rational-communicative action*. Societal discourses are a kind of psychotherapeutic sessions for society as a whole. In a conflict-driven society *we* are irrational, and *we* need a therapist. During the 1970s, Dutch society was sharply divided into two groups: one was in favour of the use of nuclear energy, and the other was furiously against it. Powerful firms led the first group, and activists who claimed to defend the long-term interests of the masses led the second. The government decided to organize an official societal discourse. After a couple of years, the organizers, led by De Brauw, published a report. It defended the use of the two already functioning nuclear plants, but advocated a stop on the building of new ones for a long period. All the (violent) actions stopped immediately, and, even now (December 2013), Dutch society has profited enormously from this consensus.

Wallerstein is a neo-Marxian who has paid much attention to the spread of capitalism all over the world, and to the emergence of a global capitalist society. This *World System* is characterized by a few forces that are in inherent tension with each other. Big business always searches for new markets since every market is threatened by saturation. National governments, however, resist the loss of power. Local people resist since globalization continuously threatens their culture.

The System consists of a *core* and a *periphery*, where the core exploits the periphery by using its cheap raw materials and labour. The stability of the world system is based on the *asymmetrical distribution of gains and losses*. The gains go to the private capitalists, and the losses must be taken over by the local governments, and are paid by the subordinate poor. The financial crisis that started in 2008 might be a good example of this theory. The financial system consists of a few globally operating banks and investment funds. Each of these firms is too big to fail. So the crisis forced the various governments to step in and take over the losses. Banks don't want to participate in the solution to the crisis. They say that they need all their resources to fulfil their primary societal function, which is the financing of the production system by means of bank credit.

Of course, the administrative and managerial top of these institutions is paid extremely well because their networks reserve a limited number of positions for their members. The north-western part of the world particularly exploits the South. The function of the north-western world is the delivery of skilled management and of systems of control. The South offers cheap raw material and labour.

In order to get a more realistic picture, a distinction between the two groups and areas might not suffice. Countries such as China, India, and Brazil show the highest growth rates nowadays. Moreover, we see a distinction between core and periphery in almost every country. The USA is a good example in this respect: many people are marginalized and do not profit from increasing incomes and wealth. In the last few decades only the top 1 per cent have profited from an ongoing increase in labour productivity.

Bauman (2002) makes a distinction between 'globals' and 'locals'. Globals are people who regularly travel over the world, for their work as well as in their function as tourists. They meet many foreign people, who become decreasingly foreign to them. They are used to multi-religious and multi-ethnic situations. When in their homeland they see their own country becoming more and more multicultural and they don't see any problem with this. On the other hand, there are the locals, who never operate globally. They are used to their own culture and see their own culture as natural. Immigrants, especially from countries with a very different culture, are approached negatively, since they do not follow cultural standards. In our modern and globalizing world every economically successful country faces this problem of multiculturalism and the resulting social problem of prejudice and discrimination.

Two important criticisms can be formulated against classical conflict theory.

Dahrendorf recognizes that the world is full of conflict, but the same is true for consensus. It means that our world is not only conflict-driven, but that most people agree with each other with respect to many important matters. In other words, modern societies have some cohesion, maybe enough to permanently improve in quality. For instance, many people accept some degree of inequality, and accept a subordinate position in which a boss has the power to give commands to a subordinate. Accepted differences in power means that power is legitimized and that the officials with power are given the *authority* to take the lead.

Collins stresses the importance of looking for the micro-foundations of macro-sociology as discussed so far. Sociology must be about the ordinary lives of concrete people. He wonders whether the world conceptualized in terms of domination and subordination, of conflict and culture, of power and collective irrationality, is the world in which concrete people live.

In general, we can say that people living in the margin experience the existence of the System and the divide between the haves and have-nots daily. People who are members of the elite and belong to the core of society might not experience 'society' or the System; they experience only their Selves in the context of their family, their sports club, and friends of their student association. The last membership helps them become a member of an interesting network, necessary for a good career. But is there any society? No, there are just a couple of opportunities to live life in an easy or meaningful way.

Collins considers the everyday life of concrete people as the starting point of sociological analysis. He considers macro-systems to be self-constructed and subjective worlds. In this world some people have the power to control the lives of other people, and they execute their power regularly, sometimes in a violent way. In societies characterized by severe inequality, people in dominant positions exploit those who are ranked lower. But, even in such cases, such exploitation is based on behaviour of concrete people, where one official exploits another official. However, people are not completely victims of their situation. Their behaviour is based on the individual drive to maximize their status, and therefore we can say that they construct their situation anew every day. So, each day they can decide to behave differently to the next. An authoritarian boss has the individual freedom to decide to approach his subordinate in a more democratic way, and let him participate in daily consultations about policies to be implemented.

In Section 11.2 we will discuss a couple of typical micro-sociological analyses, and see whether they give us more insight into the question of what is, essentially, a social relationship.

11.2 **Micro-Sociological Approaches**

11.2.1 INTRODUCTION

In this section about micro-sociology, we will first discuss symbolic interactionism, in Section 11.2.2, which is an attempt to conceptualize and analyse processes that take place on the lowest social level in a macro-social context. In Section 11.2.3, we will deal with the exchange, the network, and the rational choice approach. These are attempts to find a common foundation for sociology on the individual level. They assume that individuals are—consciously or unconsciously—calculators. Their behaviour is based on cost/benefit analyses of situations. People adopt social rules as soon as they see that the advantages of adopting and keeping particular rules are larger than the disadvantages.

11.2.2 SYMBOLIC INTERACTIONISM

This sociological approach has its philosophical foundation in *pragmatism*. It assumes that there is no true reality 'out there'; we live in a reality that is created as we act in and towards the world. So, knowledge is not based on universal and absolute truth, but developed out of definitions that seem useful. Dewey is a big man in the world of philosophical pragmatism. According to him, this current is characterized by its focus on interaction between people, which is a dynamic phenomenon. Actors are assumed to have the ability to interpret the world in particular ways.

One of the greatest symbolic interactionists is Mead. Our exposition of this approach will be based mainly on his analysis. He compares and contrasts his approach with macro-sociological structural-functionalism (as explained in Section 11.1) and with psychological behaviourism (as explained in Section 10.3 of Chapter 10). The first states that human behaviour is determined by societal structure as presented in Section 11.1 and the second states that an individual reacts automatically, in a learned way, to stimuli. In other words, there is nothing in-between the stimulus and the response; just a black box, apparently filled with experiences.

According to Mead, societal structure constrains human behaviour, but does not dictate it. Moreover, stimuli affect individual behaviour, but do not completely determine responses. In the black box there is a *mind*, which is the location of thought processes (see Chapter 10 for an exposition of cognitive psychology). Mead also distinguishes a *Self* and a difference between '*I*' and '*Me*'. He is not clear about the psychological concepts; he calls mind, Self, 'I', and 'Me' '*processes*'. It is a negative side effect of the reluctance that pragmatists have when it comes to defining things. Fixing the substance of things in order to observe their properties creates fear of medieval essentialism, in which the essence of things is considered as something objective. However, even if we recognize that knowledge is always a human construction, we need to define things in order to discover function, and see whether their properties change over time. When Mead says that the mind is emerging in a social context, he means that the content of the mind, and especially the flow of thoughts, become increasingly manifest for persons who are in interaction with others. The same is true of the concepts 'Self', 'I', and 'Me': the content can be considered as a process or flow of something. In some analyses the existence of a 'Self', an 'I', and a 'Me' is assumed. In other analyses, such as structural functionalism, these concepts do not exist (see Chapter 10 for a discussion of these concepts; see Chapter 2 for an exposition of the difference between substance and property).

Symbolic interactionism can be summarized in a number of statements:

(1) Human behaviour is interactive and reflective: people reflect upon the results of social interaction.
(2) In the process of socialization the actor shapes and adjusts the information to his own needs.
(3) Interaction takes place by means of symbols, which make it possible for the interacting people to see whether or not there is true communication.
(4) There is choice; humans have the creative capacity to 'define their situation' in ways that might deviate from what is 'dictated' by the social context; the autonomy of actors makes it possible to create new meanings, thereby changing the rules of behaviour.
(5) Large-scale structures are more likely to emerge from micro-processes than the other way around.

(6) When our mother gives birth to us, we enter a socially classified world; we learn the symbols and learn to play roles that belong to our position in the social structure; on a higher level people name each other and themselves according to their position. But, increasingly, we discover some room to search for a position of our choice, and to fulfil the role in a way that fits our definition of the situation: role-making rather than role-taking.

Maybe the most important element in social interaction is the act of *framing*. In the symbolic interactionist approach also, individuals and small groups operate in a social-cultural context. In other words, all members of society are framed by its culture. The formation of *maps* is especially important here—the way one looks at the world and interprets what is important or what is just a minor detail.

Although this societal framing constrains individual behaviour, it does not determine it. There is some room for individual framing, independent of society's culture. Creative individuals use this discretion, and become cultural entrepreneurs. In the Netherlands during the 1960s some women came into contact with each other and discovered that they were highly critical towards the Dutch culture, more specifically with respect to the subordinate role of women. They called themselves 'Dolle Mina' and tried to spread their ideas about cultural change throughout the country. The group appeared to be very successful.

In general, frames of interpretation change in times of extraordinary events. The global economic crisis of 2008 might affect the frames of interpretation of some economists. It is obvious that such a change is very costly for people with vested interests. Imagine a professor of economics, who always taught new classical macroeconomics and monetarism. Suddenly it is clear to him that he has used an unrealistic frame. He must tell his PhD students to stop their work, and he must stop his teaching, and go to the library and study alternative frames of thought. His instinct tells him not to use his ratio and not to recognize his serious mistakes (see Chapter 10 for an explanation of this form of irrationality).

The dynamics of social interaction are a daily happening and not just a matter of dramatic changes in extraordinary times. Imagine a situation in a park along a road. It consists of grass, water, and a footpath and cycle track. The track has been constructed to facilitate the inhabitants of an existing neighbourhood. Then the local government decides to build another neighbourhood, but also decides not to change the situation in the park. Over time we see that an increasing number of the new citizens decide to walk over the grass so as to take a shortcut. It is not forbidden to walk over the grass; so this behaviour, although uncommon, is not illegal. After some time grass disappears from the informal track, and it becomes muddy as a result of heavy rainfalls now and then. Then the local government decides to throw on some sand so as to make it possible to walk there. Now an increasing number of bicyclists decide to take this informal footpath and use it as if it were a cycle track. Some citizens complain and want the government to intervene. The government decides to monitor the situation regularly; however, without much success. Other citizens ask the government to make the sandy footpath a cycle track too, and the government gives in.

In this case we see how a process of action and interaction leads to a particular solution—a solution which is not the result of careful planning but of unintended consequences.

Now we move to the other micro-sociological approaches and see how they fill the space between psychology and macro-sociology.

11.2.3 EXCHANGE, NETWORK, AND RATIONAL CHOICE ANALYSIS

According to Ritzer (2008) these approaches belong to the positivist tradition. Their goal is the prediction and control of future developments. Positivists don't like principles, philosophies, and paradigms.[3] They start with a few concepts—out of the blue—and try to formulate theories, which must be tested empirically. Exchange theorists, such as Homans, take the behaviourist psychology as their starting point. The mind is considered to be a black box, and we can only observe a stimulus (S) experienced by the animal or human person and his reaction (R). The exchange theorist Blau begins his analysis slightly differently. According to him, people are attracted to each other, and, once tied, rewards strengthen and the absence of rewards weakens the bonds. He also pays attention to the development of larger-scale groups, which must stay integrated by means of the development of common norms and values. Emerson wants to analyse the exchange between people in the context of the networks in which they are operating. Then, exchange relations reflect the power and the interdependence of the various parties. This section ends with a discussion about the contribution of rational choice to a better prediction of human behaviour. We will also see that even sociological rational-choice theorists, Coleman in the first place, have a badly developed ontology. Important concepts such as rational and social do not have clear content and meaning in his work.

11.2.3.1 Homans

According to Homans, emergent properties from social interaction can be explained by a series of psychological principles. He admitted that we need Parsonsian macro-sociology, but argues that it offers us a conceptualization and categorization, but not an explanation of human behaviour. He linked behavioural psychology with orthodox economics, and developed his exchange theory upon this combination. According to Skinner, pigeons have an inborn repertoire of behaviour. And so with human beings: over time they learn to automatize their behaviour. When humans are rewarded for particular actions they

---

[3] Even if prediction and control are the goals when searching for knowledge, paradigm and analysis are two necessary elements. In other words, we cannot avoid a careful formulation of the axioms upon which the approaches are built.

tend to repeat these actions. For instance, if someone helps another person, and receives approval for that, the helper is inclined to repeat this behaviour. Homans formulated a couple of propositions.

(1) Successful behaviour leads to repetition.
(2) If stimuli are not very different from earlier successful stimuli, they are also followed by a reaction that will be repeated.
(3) The more a particular good is consumed, the lower the marginal utility (familiar in orthodox economics as the first law of Gossen).
(4) If the result is better than expected, approval follows. If the result is worse than expected, anger is the reaction.
(5) The rationality proposition states that a rational person chooses the strategy with the highest value as perceived by him, which is calculated by taking the result times the chance of getting this result.[4]

Propositions are mostly tested by means of laboratory experiments. Then the situation can be controlled, and it is possible to make ceteris paribus statements. Empirical research is extremely difficult if not impossible, and therefore not very popular.

Homans' most familiar discovery refers to the emergence of culture in the case of regular social interaction. This is called *Homans' law*: if a small set of people have regular face-to-face contact, and they perceive each other as equals, repeated action leads to social interaction patterns that are increasingly loaded morally: we behave according to a rule, and we continue doing so.

Homans' approach is neither psychological, in the sense of an analysis of the psyche, nor explicitly sociological, in the sense of human behaviour, which always takes place in a social context. Lack of social context also means that power differences between groups of people do not exist: 'humans perceive each other as equals'. Humans always remain individuals to the end. His positivist fear of metaphysics has a very high price: no paradigm, no clear analysis, and a series of propositions that might be empirically false. The most severe consequence of an implicit and bad ontology is that the meanings of the term 'cost' and the term 'benefit' are completely unclear.[5] Let us see whether Blau does a better job.

11.2.3.2 Blau

In contrast to Homans, Blau pays attention to the macro level of analysis. Personal exchanges lead to important differences in terms of power and status. Inequality requires

---

[4] By not carefully defining the concept 'economic' there is no difference between the terms economic and rational.

[5] Bad ontology leads to ad hoc explanations. Suddenly, Homans starts to talk about approval and anger, although the mind is a black box. Every theory about human behaviour must be explicit about the mind and the elementary entities of which it consists. Only then we can analyse the flows of thoughts and emotions that accompany behaviour.

justification. If it results from the fact that the dominant party has more valuable input in the exchange, they get rewarded in terms of economic and social utilities as compensation for their readiness to take part. In this way powerful people develop *authority* and the use of their power is legitimized. In small groups, social exchange takes place organically. In large-scale groups, however, 'official' social structures are necessary. Here members of the same group are united by means of consensus, and the values and norms that belong to this consensus. According to Blau, we need other paradigms to explain intergroup processes on the macro level. Organic and informal interaction is not enough to reach consensus and a common understanding; formal structures should be developed to organize necessary interaction.

11.2.3.3 Emerson

Emerson tries to develop a theory of social structure by starting with the operant psychology of the behaviourists. An exchange framework spans different levels of analysis, from micro to macro level. In this way exchange network structures are developed. Networks reflect exchange opportunities rather than just actual exchanges. So, actual exchanges always take place in a network context, which is the social structure. Both parties in an exchange have alternative opportunities. If party A has more and higher valued opportunities than party B, we can say that A has more (structural) power than B, and B is more dependent on A than vice versa. In orthodox economics this analysis is presented in terms of a fallback position and opportunity costs.

Some sociologists criticize this scheme of explanation, in which actual transactions shape and change structure, thereby affecting actual transactions in the next period. Mizruchi states that similarity in behaviour might be the result of structural equivalence or a sign of cohesion. Suppose that a firm has two suppliers with respect to a particular good. The actions of the suppliers are quite similar. Is it competition that drives them to act similarly, or is it a common culture that 'dictates' them to do similar things?[6] Burt warns about another form of structural determinism. In orthodox economics it is always market structure that dictates conduct and performance. Sociology brings in the idea that every actor, purposive or not, operates in a social context. This affects the actor's definition of the situation or map, his consequent values and norms, and also his perception of the costs and the benefits of the various alternative strategies.

Applied to networks, this means that we can expect a large variety of different strategies dependent on the culture of the network. Some networks are quite open and without strict goals; just offering members a floor to exchange information about jobs, education, and the like, such as LinkedIn. Others become more personal, such as Facebook.

---

[6] A familiar example in economics refers to the phenomenon of stable relative wages in a sector comparison. Suppose that secretaries in the agricultural sector earn the same wages as secretaries in the booming high-tech industry. Is it because of competition on the market for secretaries, or is it that national unions and employers' organizations have reached consensus about one national wage rate for secretaries?

But there are also professional networks; some of them are highly ideological, and very precise in who is allowed to be member of the 'club'. In the Dutch world of academic economists there are networks aimed at maintaining power with respect to full professor's positions, and trying to dominate the discussions about the global and European crisis in the Dutch media. This is truly the sociology of network analysis: groups which try to dominate other groups, and threaten members who do not adjust to the dominant views of the exclusive network.

11.2.3.4 Rational Choice Theory

For economists it is interesting to see whether the sociological rational choice approach is similar or different from what they are used to in economics. Let's see how sociologists formulate it.

Friedman and Hechter (1988) have summarized the axioms as follows:

(1) Actors are purposive and have intentionality.
(2) Actors have a preference hierarchy.
(3) Resources are scarce, and actors have different access to resources.
(4) Besides scarce resources there is a second constraint, namely social institutions, which imply positive as well as negative incentives or sanctions.
(5) There is an aggregation mechanism, which aggregates separate individual actions into a social outcome.
(6) Actors are imperfectly informed about their situation.

When we compare and contrast this approach with the typical orthodox economic approach, the similarities are striking. Both are characterized by a strict individualist methodology. Both assume actors who maximize their utilities under particular constraints. In contrast to orthodox economics, however, sociological choice theory assumes that in some circumstances individuals discover the advantage of having norms that must be obeyed. When giving up some control some people gain control over others, who also ought to obey the norm. The *emergence of norms* can be analysed by means of game theory, especially in case of repetitive games. In this way it is possible to find out under which conditions particular norms endure (Ullmann-Margalit, 1977, 1978; Hechter, Opp, and Wippler, 1990).

More generally, game theory is an effective method of analysing dilemmas. We will shortly discuss four dilemmas and see how they can be solved (Heckathorn, 2001). The first is called *the invisible hand game*. As we all know, the invisible hand is owned by an auctioneer, who is constantly asking buyers and sellers about quantities and prices, and decides to bargain when the quantity demanded is equal to the quantity supplied. He does it for all goods that are on offer, and he does it every day. In this way, the economy is in equilibrium. In economics this is called the Walrasian general equilibrium or Pareto equilibrium. It means that all players have reached the best of all possible outcomes. The construction of an auctioneer creates this solution if every player accepts his authority.

The second game is called *the assurance game*. The problem is one of coordinating activities to get a joint endeavour. In other words, for both parties cooperation is the best strategy. For instance, the players must decide whether to sign a contract that appears to be acceptable to all. Imagine the Germans and the French have reached an agreement with respect to Eurozone budget policies. Now they have to decide whether Berlin or Paris will host the celebration of this. If the decision is quite neutral, throwing a dice will help. If the location is an important matter for all players, then it becomes part of negotiations (see the third game). The third game is called *the chicken game*. An important characteristic of this game is the so-called P(unishment) value: if all players defect rather than cooperate, this is disastrous for all parties. But if the other cooperates, defection is the best strategy. In Western Europe labour contracts of many workers are negotiated by unions and employers' organizations. In labour economics literature bilateral monopoly is the market structure, which is used to analyse the process of wage formation. Both parties need an outcome rather than long-enduring strikes. But, in general, employers' organizations plead for wages not to be too high, since labour costs significantly affect the competitiveness of a firm, a sector, or an economy as a whole. Unions, however, tend to plead for relatively high wages, since an economy needs a level of consumption that is high enough for full employment. Relative power is decisive for the bargaining result. In the sociological rational choice literature norms might emerge, but these norms are based on the relative power of the two parties.

Since the norms do not emerge in a particular social context, and are assumed to simply emerge, the sociological rational choice does not offer an ontology that is essentially different from orthodox new institutional economics (see Chapter 4).

The fourth game is called *the prisoner's dilemma*, and, in economics, is very famous. All players are tempted to defect rather than cooperate. The result is equilibrium with a lower gain than the so-called Pareto equilibrium. This means that the free-rider problem is the barrier to an optimal outcome. The players do not trust each other when making an agreement. A familiar example is the production of public goods in the economic world. All members of society must be forced to pay for the production and consumption of these goods; otherwise nobody pays for them.

In Figure 11.1 we have presented the pay-off matrices of the four games. As we know, the *pay-off structure* is decisive for the question of what type of dilemma we are dealing with, and what the possibilities are to solve the dilemma. In all cases we need *norms* that are accepted by all parties. If people deviate from the accepted norm, collective disapproval can penalize the deviant. If we assume a perfectly functioning government, this organization can monitor society completely, and penalize the criminals. But such government does not exist in a world with rational-economic actors. All civil servants are tempted to be corrupt and accept bribes from the deviants.[7]

The number on the left in each cell is the row's pay-off, the number on the right is the column's pay-off. Each player has a choice between cooperation (C) and defection (D).

---

[7] Strictly speaking, the concepts corruption and bribes do not exist in the non-social economic world.

Invisible Hand (Privileged) Game   Chicken Game

	5,5	1,3		3,3	1,5
	3,1	0,0		5,1	0,0

Assurance Game   Prisoner's Dilemma

	5,5	0,3		3,3	0,5
	3,0	1,1		5,0	1,1

Figure 11.1. Social Dilemma Games

Four outcomes are possible in each. These are generally designated Reward (universal cooperation), Sucker (unilateral cooperation), Temptation (unilateral defection), and Punishment (universal defection) (Heckathorn, 2001).

After having discussed a series of micro-sociological analyses and theories, we can draw a few conclusions. Where classical sociology has a strong focus on macro-analysis, in which macro-phenomena are framed as historical phenomena, we see that micro-sociology has a strong focus on analysis of the micro level, whereby macro-phenomena function as a sort of aggregation of micro-behaviour. The relationship between the two different analyses is not clear. This will be the topic in Section 11.3. Moreover, when comparing the symbolic interactionist analysis with the exchange, network, and rational choice theory, a remarkable difference can be noticed. The smallest unit of analysis in the symbolic interactionist approach is the small group, homogeneous in its use of particular symbols, and understandable only to members of its own group. In the other micro-approaches, especially the rational choice theory, the individual is the smallest unit of analysis. In orthodox economics this individual is only constrained by the scarcity of his resources. In the sociological rational choice theory the same individual, even maximizing his utilities, is also constrained by social institutions. It means that the members of a group or society are constrained by the norms that are generally accepted those organizations (see the research by Van der Lippe and Siegers, as described in Chapter 9). Remarkable in this respect is the fact that norms are not necessarily adopted by all individuals, and that it might be possible for all individuals to try to deviate from the 'accepted' norm. Socialization is impossible in the sociological rational choice, because there is no psyche or mind which is equipped with the capacity to develop a conscience. There are no moral sentiments or moral resentments, no aggression or rivalry—the psyche is considered to be a black box—a calculator, which registers costs and benefits. It remains, however, unclear what is counted as a cost and what as a benefit. In other words, if there are no anchors in the psyche, an individual never gets tied to others, either positively or negatively.

Of course, there is no government other than a group of economic-rational actors who try to serve their own interest when developing and executing policies.

The shocking conclusion must be that this approach, analytically strong, misses the essence of sociology and psychology. Its paradigm makes it impossible to improve the economic-rational models of the orthodox economists significantly. In Chapter 13 we will see that the logical-positivist interpretation of rational choice is the cause of this problem, making it impossible to clearly define important concepts such as economic, social, rational, and logical.

11.3 The Relationship between Micro- and Macro-Analysis

11.3.1 INTRODUCTION

In Chapters 3, 4, and 5 we discussed the way in which orthodox economics deals with the relationship between micro- and macro-analysis, and, related to that, with the relationship between agency and structure. The methodology of orthodox economics is individualistic. So every explanation of human behaviour is based on a theory about the nature of a person. Therefore, the basis of microeconomics is also the basis of macroeconomics, which is just an aggregation of the analysis of an individual agent, given his economic constraint. Most heterodox economics approaches, however, start their analysis from the macro level, which is the level of the whole of a thing, mostly a national economy, or the global economy.

In sociology the micro-macro problem was an important topic in the 1930s. In the 1980s it returned and became a widely discussed issue. While mainstream economics is micro-orientated, sociology has a strong macro-orientation. A human being is social in nature rather than just economic. In other words, a personality is basically determined by his social environment, which is a typical macro-idea. As we saw in Section 11.2, some sociologists were dissatisfied with the macro-foundations of their discipline. According to them, groups and societies cannot behave or act without concrete individuals who behave or act. So the search for a theory about human personalities is a very relevant one.

The sociological literature on this topic is extensive but also confusing. While the debates in economics are quite straightforward and relatively easy to follow because of their restrictive character, the sociological debate is much broader, and therefore more complicated. As long as there is barely any consensus among sociologists about concepts to be used, the discussions will not be very productive. A few examples of confusing dual concepts illustrate this problem. In the first place, the term *'normative analysis'* is sometimes meant as a positive analysis of norms, and sometimes used as an analysis of what people ought to do. A second example is the *dual material versus non-material ends.* Since materiality is an aspect of our reality, it is impossible to separate it from ideality. In economics all ends are expressed in utilities, which refer to the level of intensity of our experiences. But is 'utility' material or non-material? The same problem holds for the distinction between *means and ends*. When I go to Amsterdam for a meeting by bike, the meeting is the end and the travel by bike is the means. But what if I like biking, and I hate meetings, but I want to signal to my colleagues that I belong to the group? Then the end has a strong means-aspect and vice versa. It's all about motivation and satisfaction in the end. Where economics focuses on economic motivation only, most sociologists have problems in analysing motives. That's psychology, isn't it? A last problematic duality is the distinction between *subjective and objective*. When I watch a film, it is clear that the 'I' is the subject and the film is the object. But if the watcher tells other people about what he has seen, is that story objective? Not at all, since humans are never able to have knowledge of the object 'an sich'. In other words, everything is subjective to a certain degree, and perfect objectivity does not exist.

Now we will deal with the contributions of Elias, Giddens, Bourdieu, and Habermas.

11.3.2 ELIAS

Elias (1939) places his analyses in a historical perspective. In the early hunting and gathering societies humankind consisted of small groups of nomads. Persons need each other to satisfy their basic needs. Therefore, they are open and interdependent. History can be interpreted as a process of chains of interdependence becoming longer and more differentiated. The patterns of interdependence become more complex, making adjustment to group norms important. In other words, there is a strong interdependence between the personality structure of individuals and the social structure of society. Elias interprets history also in terms of the growing complexity of social constraints, making self-constraint or self-control increasingly important. According to Elias, increasing one's self-control is the essence of a growing *civilization*. People learn to speak correct language, learn table manners, and are introduced into do's and don'ts in social interactions. An example is the way the Chinese government tried to civilize the Chinese people with respect to table manners in the period before the 2008 Olympic Games. Many Chinese were used to belching regularly when dining, something that is seen as uncivilized by Western people.

Power is central in the formation of figurations or social structures. It means that powerful groups have more influence on the process of civilization than the poor. The increasing interdependence also implies that there is growing contact between higher and lower ranks. In these vertical relationships the powerful people force the weaker groups to adjust to the requirements set by the elite. If groups are rivalling on the higher levels in society—warlords who control different parts in Afghanistan, for instance—and they are more or less equally strong, and become increasingly interdependent, there is room for a king who monopolizes the means of physical violence, so as to introduce a system of taxation and rules.

11.3.3 GIDDENS

Giddens (1986) tries to overcome the dichotomy between agency and structure, and, therefore, he developed his *structuration theory*. He distinguishes between *agents, consciousness, and power*. This problem exists at all levels of analysis between the very micro and the very macro level. A child lives his life in a family structure; a worker works in the organization structure of a firm; a minister of a governmental department operates in the structures of his department and of cabinet, parliament, and his own political party.

When analysing a problem by means of an agency-structure distinction, orthodox economists define the agent as an economic and rational individual subject and the structure as a market structure characterized by perfect competition, for example. If demand increases, firms that operate on that particular market react by means of a rise in the price and/or in the quantity supplied. At the end of this analysis the market is back in equilibrium, and the actor has not changed at all; he is still an economic and rational actor, who understands his environment to be that of a market characterized by perfect competition. Giddens would first find out in what way firms which are operating on that market understand their situation. Maybe they have never heard of the typical orthodox market analysis, and just see a few opportunities to make profits. Then agents' consciousness and their understanding of the situation might change under the influence of the strategies actually chosen. For instance, a few firms meet each other regularly and develop a common understanding of the market. They also seek contact with relevant government agencies. All these actors talk with each other about their market regularly, and increasingly act according to the rules of the culture that is emerging. In this way practice affects agents as well as structure.

Giddens stresses the fact that structure does not only constrain agents in their operations. It also enables them to implement strategies that would have been impossible without a structure. Two examples might illustrate this statement. If a person forces himself to save a rather high percentage of his income, this act limits his current consumption. But if the money is invested in a profitable way, his consumption opportunities will increase over time, thanks to the limitations. A second example is about a pond that is frozen because of low temperatures. Then some skilled people do research with respect to the quality of the ice, and make a beautiful ice rink in an area where the ice is thick enough to carry a lot of skaters. Now the ice rink offers the opportunity to skaters to do what they like, but it also limits the skaters in that they cannot go beyond the rink; without the rink most people would have been too uncertain about the quality of the ice to skate at all.

11.3.4 BOURDIEU

Bourdieu (1977)—like Giddens—applies *methodological relationism* to clarify the relation between agency and structure. We saw that Giddens is stressing the interaction between the content of the mind or consciousness and the social structure. Bourdieu, however, stresses the importance of social structure and its effect on the mental structures of the agents. So the mentality and the focus of the agent—Bourdieu calls it *habitus*—is strongly influenced by the *long-term position* he takes in the social structure. Positions are determined by the capital of an agent. Bourdieu distinguishes four types of capital, namely *economic, social, cultural, and symbolic capital*. Economic capital refers to an agent's amount of scarce resources. Social capital expresses the value of the relations of an agent with other persons. Cultural capital reflects the familiarity with and the easy use of cultural forms that are institutionalized. And, lastly, symbolic capital is about the honour and prestige of an agent; in other words, his status.[8]

Bourdieu calls networks of positions *'fields'*. Examples of fields on a macro level are government, economy, religion, art, and education. Micro-level fields are family, a department of a firm, a professional association, and a local environmental action group, for instance. These fields generate a *belief in what is at stake* in a particular field. They guide the strategies of the actors. Actually, fields are arenas of battle, and hierarchically structured. Academic education, for instance, has a strict hierarchy, where a few prestigious professors determine what is at stake in the academic discipline. They have the power to indicate which methodologies are superior and prestigious, and which ones are inferior and must be ignored. In this way, the dominant groups of scientists almost dictate how society approaches its problems. Less powerful scientists are ignored and their language and analysis is constantly ridiculed.

In economics, mainstream economists and econometricians dominate the field. Now that we face a very serious crisis—which was not foreseen by mainstream economists, who constantly ignored the warnings of marginalized economists—the language and analysis of the dominant group dominates the discussions in the political field and in the media. Bourdieu calls this permanent language battle *'distinction'*. It serves to unify and to differentiate, thereby clarifying the difference between the dominant and the subordinate group.

11.3.5 HABERMAS

Habermas is trying to solve the agency-structure dichotomy by realizing that social structure is a network of agents who all permanently communicate with each other in different ways. Not only in the form of conversations, but also in terms of body language or by inviting some people for an important meeting, and excluding others from it. *Communication* is more than an exchange of information about opportunities to sell and to buy. It is essentially about one other's *status* in the group or in society at large.

---

[8] Although Bourdieu accepts the existence of consciousness, there is no room for an 'I' and a Self in his analysis. The consequence is that he does not distinguish psychic capital: amount of respect for the true Self as experienced by the 'I'—maybe the most valuable asset of a person. Moreover, Bourdieu cannot explain why particular personalities function as a motor of change in structures.

Sometimes the communication is explicit about the understanding of the situation, and the roles that belong to particular positions. Most of the time, the communication is quite implicit. Most conversations are about unimportant matters, but the way the persons speak to each other makes it clear, at least to a trained sociologist, who is superior and who is inferior. It also makes it clear that humans differ from machines. Nobody has the desire to show one's superiority to a machine, but they may do to the designer of the machine. Social relationships are not only loaded negatively. Within a group, especially, there is *solidarity*, which is the opposite of *rivalry*, and serves to keep the group united. But even then power relations exist, and the way the group searches for a common understanding and consensus is heavily influenced by the relative power of the various parties and persons. Eventual consensus means that a particular economic, social, and political inequality is accepted and legitimized, including by the powerless people.

Habermas makes a distinction between life world and System. In the *life world* people act and interact. They have conflicts and they cooperate. They are rivalling with each other and they enjoy solidarity with each other. This all takes place in a large number of institutions, such as family, economy, government, health care, and education. Does it lead to a sustainable society?

In all institutions, and on all levels within institutions, there are the more powerful groups and the less powerful groups of people. The more powerful people have a particular interest in stabilizing situations and enlarging their power relative to powerful groups in other institutions. In the institution 'economy', large firms are relatively powerful and spend large budgets on marketing to stabilize and expand their cash flows. Powerful groups of medical specialists, such as cardiologists, constantly try to enlarge their budgets and their salary or profit. The same holds for government agencies: a permanent fight to increase their power by more regulation and higher budgets. Powerful groups not only search for more power by rivalling other groups. They also search for clusters, in which common interests are served. The world of lobbying consists of representatives of powers who constantly try to influence other powers, especially government agencies. The international bank lobby in Brussels is known as the best-organized lobby; it is permanently fighting against the reregulation of financial markets. They try to convince politicians that free financial markets are a stable (!) system, although everyone has discovered that this is not true. The actions and interactions aimed at controlling the mass of the people is, as a whole, called the *System*. Habermas states that this system is growing in power over time, and will increasingly colonize people's life world.

In Figure 11.2 we present the relationships between dominant groups, subordinate groups, and the System graphically.

According to Habermas, a global System is emerging—this system functions far from perfectly and will regularly suffer from *systemic crises*. The current banking crisis, which started in the period 2006–2008, is an example of a global systemic crisis. In this process of the birth of a global System, large parts of the system in progress are also quite unstable for a long time to come. The Euro crisis is an example of a systemic crisis in the subsystem Europe. Because of the growing interdependencies

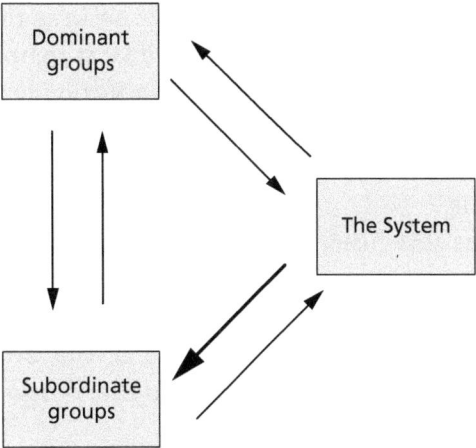

Figure 11.2. Relationship between Dominant Groups, Subordinate Groups, and the System

between European economies, the System Europe 'needs' a transfer from authorities from national governments to the European Union. This transfer has been going on for some time. However, many life worlds in the various countries strongly resist this growing juggernaut. In the Netherlands, the PVV and the SP are the two political parties who most explicitly oppose the growing power of the European System, and try to protect Dutch attainments.

During the next few decades the communication between the different life worlds and the System will be extraordinarily important. The growing use of information and communications technology (ICT) can be of great help, if all parties are really prepared to communicate with each other. Of course, the System will try to control the communication between the different groups in the life world. In authoritarian countries, such as Russia and Iran, the distinction between the life worlds and the System is quite clear. In the Western world the distinction is less clear. Many people who have a good job in organizations which (partly) belong to the System will never become aware of the distinction. But for people who are regularly expelled or constantly ignored, Habermas' distinction is a daily experience. It holds for groups of unemployed persons, who are unable to find a job, despite having searched for a long time (youth unemployment is extremely high in many countries, including in Europe). Women who want to have a part-time job as medical specialist discover that there is a System that says no. Interest-free social scientists, who are genuinely interested in the problems of their discipline and develop critical analyses, have a hard time at universities. These are examples of the fight between the life world and the System, where the System has penetrated the minds of many people who are strongly inclined to adjust to what the System has defined as normal.

* * *

Reflecting upon this section, we come to the following conclusions.

In the first place, there is a methodological divide between the collectivist approach of macro-sociology on the one hand, and the individualist approach of micro-sociology on the other (see Sections 11.1 and 11.2 respectively). Section 11.3 discusses attempts to bridge the gap between macro and micro methodology. All try to bridge the dichotomy between agency and structure, and analyse people who operate in many networks on different levels of analysis.

Elias' paradigm states that history is a process of *increasing interdependencies*. It leads to ever-changing social structures, which press the mental structures of persons to permanently adjust. Increasingly complicated social structures imply ever-stronger social constraints for persons, who are supposed to develop ever-*increasing systems of self-control*. This leads to growing civilization. The elite develop manners that trickle down to lower levels of society.

Elias doesn't like abstract concepts such as individual and society. But the effect of his methodological taste is the lack of a clear ontology. He does not answer the question of what drives people to act. He gives no clear answer to the question of what is 'social', especially in contrast to the concept 'economic'. There is no person with a personality strong enough to have some influence on what is considered as *'civilized'*.

Giddens states that practice shapes social structure and the consciousness of the persons who take the positions and play the roles in this social structure. Moreover, he states that every action (practice) is based on a particular understanding of the situation by the actor. It is obvious that the consciousness of particular effects resulting from particular actions might change the way the person understands the world. In hierarchical social structures the powerful dominate the interpretation of what happens every day.

Bourdieu uses different concepts, and his analysis differs from that of Giddens. In Bourdieu's concept 'distinction', he stresses that social processes are meant to include some persons and exclude particular persons. In other words, the ongoing process of grouping and ranking is typical for social processes. In contrast to Giddens, Bourdieu is more macro-orientated. In Giddens' analysis there is more space for small groups, which influence the course of macro-processes.

Habermas makes a different distinction, namely between System and life world. Using Elias' idea of growing interdependencies, Habermas fears systems of control are going to dominate the daily life of ordinary people. It is true by definition that the powerful groups profit most from 'the System', while the less powerful people suffer from it most. The current economic crisis, again, is a good example. In 2008 the banking crisis led to a global depression. The governments of mostly Western countries paid billions of dollars and euros in order to save the financial subsystem of the global System. The bankers, the most powerful people in the world, kept their positions and their extremely high salaries and bonuses, while many people suffered from the crisis in terms of unemployment and poverty. In Africa about one and a half million babies died in the years immediately following the depression.

Habermas' ideas about communication between the persons with powerful positions and those who occupy lower-ranked positions or do not occupy any position, are unclear.

He developed an idea of *power-free communication*, which has similarities with the ideas of Rawls, who constructed a situation in which people are not aware of the position they occupy in society.[9] But the practical possibility of organizing power-free conversations is impossible, even at universities.

A last example of social processes in a framework of micro and macro levels is presented in Box 11.1.

The explanation of developments on the macro level in the analyses discussed so far is not very clear—it is only historical, not logical. This problem is related to the lack of a clear micro-foundation—a clear ontology about human nature, whether this nature is fixed or variable. The important role of power, on all levels of analysis, is remarkable. It affects the way people understand their situation, and is decisive with regard to actions and interaction. So we can formulate—in line with the orthodox economic strategy— that individuals are driven to maximize their power under a couple of constraints. Two problems must be solved here. In the first place, power seems to be an instrument rather than a goal; an instrument that can be used to reach a series of ultimate goals. In the second place, the question of what the constraints in the maximization process are must be answered. In Chapter 13 we will discuss these issues in more detail.

BOX 11.1 THE EMERGENCE OF THE SYSTEM OF DUTCH LABOUR RELATIONS

In the Netherlands of the 19th century, especially the second half, there were a growing number of workers who regularly met each other in cafes to talk about their social-economic-political situation. A common understanding emerged, and inter-cafe contacts were laid, which led to the foundation of established organizations on a higher level. These organizations organized demonstrations and strikes in firms, and later in sectors of industry. Employers who met each other in clubs were worried about the situation, and began to organize a countervailing power.

  The societal situation became a topic of increasing importance not only in cafes and clubs, but also in churches. Here, persons of different rank met each other regularly. They discovered that the Bible, especially the New Testament, contains texts about social justice. They developed their own organizations, in some cases organizations that united workers and capitalists. During the course of the 20th century these processes of communication reached the national level, and led to changes in labour market institutions. Each interest group had developed its own 'pillar', and on the national level the top of the important pillars constantly communicated with each other on the basis of a common understanding of the social-economic-political situation. These consultations on the Dutch macro level resulted regularly in tracts, formulating common understandings and goals. The leadership of the different interest groups were assumed to communicate the results with their rank and file—thereby relating macro-results with micro-behaviour. This situation still holds, and is one of the most valuable institutional innovations ever.

---

  [9] Rawls (1978) describes a thought experiment in which he tells every participant that his economic and social position in society is completely unknown for the time being. Then he asks them what they see as a fair distribution of power. Rawls assumes that people will be risk-averse and choose a distribution which holds that the growth of the lowest incomes is maximized.

Appendix 11.1 **Practical Problems and the Framing of their Situation**

In this appendix we will show the effect of the choice of a particular approach on the analysis of a particular problem. We first present a problem, followed by four major sociological interpretations of it. By following this procedure three times we want to show that our frames are useful when trying to understand quite different sorts of problems. It goes without saying that a particular frame does not lead to one particular analysis and therapy. The texts are just meant as an illustration of the different types of reasoning.

A11.1.1 PROBLEM I: WAGE STRUCTURE

The salary of the top managers of the University of Los Palatos will rise from an annual $300,000 to $330,000 the following year. A spokesperson justifies the salary increase by arguing that top managers with the same qualifications at other universities are earning more than the top managers at Los Palatos. The deans of the different schools and faculties will be among the beneficiaries of this salary increase. Considering that all departments of the University of Los Palatos face severe budget cuts next year, many employees who do not belong to the top management are shocked by this announcement. They cannot understand how a salary increase for the top management can be justified in a time of general budget cuts faced by the different departments.

A11.1.1.1 A Typical Functionalist Framing of the Situation

The top management has discovered that the salary norm for their position in the university sector is higher than their current level. If employees who fulfil different functions disagree, they must send their complaints to their organizations. If there is no such professional organization, they should first create one; otherwise they have no voice. Thereafter, these organizations can start a discussion with the organizations representing top managers about fair and efficient wage differences. The government, representing the general interest, is supposed to organize these discussions. On the basis of existing functional classifications and general knowledge about the norms that have determined the relationship between function and reward, this tripartite consultation will lead to a solution that must eliminate the discontent among employees who are not top management.

This typical functionalist framing and solving of the problem is based on an analysis of social problems in terms of different functions and the communication between organizations that represent these functions. If all functions in society are well defined and well coordinated through thorough communication between the different functional groups, there will be harmony. In general, all severe social conflicts can be solved through consultation with representative organizations. If problems arise, consultation offers people the opportunity to discuss them on the basis of the values and norms they share. If such a structure does not exist, such problems may lead to severe social conflicts that can only be solved temporarily by a power struggle between the different rivals. Such a fight ends when there are winners and losers. However, as soon as the losers think that relative power has changed to their advantage, they start a new power struggle.

A11.1.1.2 A Typical Conflict-Theory Framing o1f the Situation

The discontent among the rank-and-file workers about the salary increase of the top management is an illustration of the omnipresent conflict between different groups in society. Every organization consists of a number of groups with different interests. They can always argue why their group should get a greater share of the resources. But mostly their argumentation results from an opportunistic choice of those arguments that lead to outcomes favourable to them. In our case, the Los Palatos top management compares itself with the top management of other universities, which may be larger and have different and more complicated tasks. These conflicts are power games; mediation must show the relative power of the parties involved. Conflicts become manifest only if some parties overestimate their relative power. Therefore, reliable information about the positions of the parties involved and experienced mediators are the necessary ingredients for reaching a compromise. A mediator who is trusted by top management as well as by the rank and file must be assigned to make a report giving advice as to the most feasible way to continue. If the conflict is already quite bitter and such a mediator cannot be found, an open battle via strikes and other types of actions must shed light on the real power relations.

This typical conflict-theoretic framing of the problem is implicitly based on the analysis of social problems, in terms of conflict of group interests. A conflict of interest can never be solved; an armistice on the basis of a mutually accepted compromise is the maximally feasible result. It is, like the functionalist one, a macro-approach. All individuals are assumed to reflect perfectly the values and views of their own group. Deviation from group norms is penalized and cannot form the basis of any conflict resolution. But a realistic picture of actual relative power of the different groups involved can be sketched by producing reliable and relevant information. Such a mutually accepted picture can prevent costly power struggles and might lead to temporarily accepted solutions to the problem of the distribution of scarce resources.

A11.1.1.3 A Typical Micro-Interactionist Framing of the Situation

The top managers of the different universities meet each other on a regular basis. Thus, these persons have learned to speak the same language and to speak with one voice. During these meetings they have developed common strategies vis-à-vis the Ministry of Education. According to the top managers, the annual budget cuts that are imposed by the Ministry without prior consultation are not justified. They believe that the budget cuts ignore the fact that, thanks to this budget and to university entrepreneurship, these universities have reached such a high status in the world. The acceptance of a relatively low salary by the top managers in the past apparently sent the wrong signal to the Ministry with respect to the performance of the universities. When facing growing discontent among the rank and file, however, top managers must not only convince each other and the Ministry of their outstanding performance. Their subordinates must also understand that it is in their interest to have a top management whose prestige is represented in its prestigious salaries. Actually, it is an investment in the prestige of the university as a whole. If the top management creates more opportunities to communicate with their employees, they may be able to create a kind of 'corporate identity'. That would stimulate people to interpret the university as a united group, instead of an arena where rank and file and top management are rivals.

The typical micro-interactionist framing of the problem is based on an analysis of group processes within top management. These have consequences for the relationship between different groups within the organization as a whole. In our hypothetical situation, several groups are playing a role. The top management of the Los Palatos University is the principal actor. Other groups, such as the top management of other universities, the Ministry, and the rank and file of Los Palatos University, are also important players, from whom we can expect a reaction. Well-organized communication between the relevant groups can lead to a more effective structure.

A11.1.1.4 A Typical Exchange/Rational Choice Framing of the Situation

If the university really wants to prevent their top managers from quitting for a comparable position at other universities or in the private sector, it must welcome the decision of a salary increase. Other employees would also leave the university to accept another job, if that job is better paid. A quick look at the market for top managers shows that the demand for top managers has increased. An exodus of these people would be disastrous for the university as a whole, but especially for those people with low salaries for whom the markets are characterized by excess of supply rather than excess of demand. They may lose their job without finding a new one. If the university is not able to justify or explain large differences in income, it may consider different and less transparent ways of rewarding its top managers. Attractive means to confer indirect salary increases to top management include parking spaces, car and fuel paid for by the university, payment in shares or options if possible, and prestigious office design. These parts of the reward must tie the productive people to the company. If our top managers become popular among the rank and file and build up a firm-specific prestige, then an exit barrier is created, making further salary increases superfluous.

The typical exchange/rational choice framing of the problem is based on an analysis of what is actually traded. Everything of value can be demanded or supplied. The market situation—excess demand or excess supply—determines price development.

To show that all four approaches are able to frame very different situations we present two further examples.

A11.1.2 PROBLEM II LOGISTICS

The manufacturing company Mac Power faces a series of problems of communication between the Purchasing, the Production, and the Sales Departments. The Board has already taken a number of ad hoc measures, but everyone recognizes the problems to be persistent. The directors of the three departments are not on speaking terms with each other, although each of the directors is quite popular among his/her own staff. The previous director of the Sales Department is the board member who is responsible for the logistics of the firm.

A11.1.2.1 A Typical Functionalist Framing of the Situation

The board member who is in charge of the primary process must organize meetings with the three directors on a regular basis. He is responsible for the coordination between purchasing, production, and sales activities. Therefore, it is necessary to have a platform where corporate strategy is translated in terms of a coordinated sales-production-purchase policy. The Board as a whole must give the board member in charge feedback of his coordinating activities. If the group is able to take decisions that are backed by the Board, the board member in charge must regularly monitor whether there is any deviant behaviour. If so, this kind of behaviour must be openly discussed.

Functionalist framing seeks to determine the functions of the main players in the arena. Those in charge of coordination and control are responsible for the organization of the necessary social interaction. In this approach, transparent communication in a well-designed organization will ultimately lead to consensus about the way the organization must function.

A11.1.2.2 A Typical Conflict-Theory Framing of the Situation

Communication problems are a reflection of the conflicts of interest that always exist between different departments of a firm. The Purchasing Department has developed the idea, or ideology, that a firm can only produce and sell a product once the Purchasing Department has succeeded in buying the necessary inputs on the input markets. While the firm can control the quality of its own production, the quality of its inputs is dependent on the quality of the firm's suppliers. This implies that the Purchasing Department must have an ample budget for an intensive screening of world markets that supply inputs of different quality levels. With their unique knowledge of the input market, the managers of the Purchasing Department must have a big say in the final decision about the characteristics of the good that must be produced. The Sales Department, however, has exactly the opposite idea (ideology) of the situation. It is crucial for the firm to produce a product that can be sold. Reliable knowledge about the output markets is, therefore, essential. Tough restrictions on the budget of the Sales Department would be an illustration of a narrow-minded bookkeeping view. It would basically mean revenue-cutting, which is a threat to the firm as a whole. As a consequence, an appropriate budget for the Sales Department is a necessary condition for the firm to survive.

The Production Department, however, holds the view that the functions of the other departments only support the decisive actions performed by the Production Department. Because production in this context really means 'adding value to', it is natural to give the Production Department the ultimate authority to decide what to produce and how.

In our case, the board member who is in charge of the coordination of the primary process appears to have a marketing background. Full support of the Sales Department brought him to that position. He listens carefully to the pleas of the different directors, but the idea of 'without sales no production' reflects his basic attitude. His proposal to solve the communication problem is definitely a 'victory' for the Sales Department. The other departments, although officially accepting the proposal, immediately start internal discussions on how to get the board member in charge of logistics replaced by a person who has 'ideas' that are more favourable to their own positions.

A11.1.2.3 A Typical Micro-Interactionist Framing of the Situation

The communication problem is basically a cultural clash between the three different departments. Purchasers have developed their own frames, goals, and instruments during their education and in their regular conferences on 'The Problem of Purchasing'. In their experience of their profession, they have always viewed sales managers as their natural opponents, and as speaking a different language. This makes it difficult for purchasers to enjoy closer contact with salesmen. The groups play their different roles when doing business. If a company really wants to improve coordination between the different departments, it must hire a logistician for this task. Such a professional has learned to think as a purchaser as well as a producer and seller. His profession is to develop a language that has the potential to bridge the gap between the different cultures. Logistics frames the relationship between the different departments as a chain, whose strength is determined by the strength of its weakest link. It is the task of a logistician to convince the purchasers, the producers, and the salesmen that they all are important links in this chain, and that their performance is highly dependent on each other's contribution. Regular meetings, not only between the bosses but also among the rank and file, could create an atmosphere that promotes an increasing understanding of their mutual dependence.

Generally speaking, a micro-interactionist analysis clarifies principal bottlenecks in the communication between different professionals and functions. Every specialization has developed its own culture. This gives the experts a sense of identity and meaning, but at the same time makes it difficult for them to adjust smoothly when cooperation with other professions is necessary. A coordinator must be aware of cultural differences and be able to create a new culture that offers different professions meaning in terms of mutual cooperation.

A11.1.2.4 A Typical Exchange/Rational Choice Framing of the Situation

Communication problems between groups will only exist if particular individuals are not fulfilling their tasks well. The board member in charge of the primary process must find out which persons are in constant rivalry. In cooperation with the Personnel

Department, a series of meetings must be organized with these people on an individual basis. Their way of functioning must be judged by comparing it with the standards and the requirements that are formulated in their employment contracts. If their input is, qualitatively as well as quantitatively, less than can be expected, clear commitments must be made about how they function in the future. The monitoring and sanctioning system must be checked to see whether it has functioned well. If the directors of the different departments or some of their staff appear to be insensitive to the renewed attempts to get things done, then replacement or even outplacement must be considered.

Again we see that the exchange approach focuses its analysis on the content of the contracts that have been concluded. If problems arise, they are caused by a lack of clarity with respect to the contract conditions. When all parties are well informed and there are still problems, the sources of trouble must be eliminated. In other words, some people must be fired.

A11.1.3 PROBLEM III AUTONOMY OF THE EUROPEAN CENTRAL BANK

In 1992 the European Union decided to introduce a common currency, the euro, and planned the actual introduction for 2002. This decision implied that a European Central Bank (ECB) had to be created, to be responsible for EU monetary policy. Countries like Germany and the Netherlands insisted upon complete autonomy of the central bank when formulating their monetary strategies and policies. Countries like France, however, supported a platform for regular meetings between the ECB and the governments of the EU member countries. These consultations should guarantee that monetary goals are coordinated with the socio-economic objectives of the various governments. Although the Maastricht Treaty of 1992 is quite clear about the autonomy of the ECB, the conflict between Germany and France especially has not been resolved, and continues to be an issue within the EU.

A11.1.3.1 A Typical Functionalist Framing of the Situation

The European Union is in the midst of a development process. Many sorts of relationships have already been institutionalized. We can also see an evolution with respect to the financial markets. Until 1992 there were only national central banks. They were important institutions, integrated in the culture of the national economies. With the growth of the EU, new financial institutions on a European level had to be created. The next step is the integration of these institutions into a more encompassing European culture and the dissolution of nation-specific institutions like national central banks. Given the processes of Europeanization and globalization, the European Commission will slowly transform into an EU government. Then, it is evident that the function of monetary management, as executed by the European Central Bank, will be coordinated with the socio-economic policies of the European government. Hence, the current conflict between Germany and France is a relatively small issue that will be solved as the evolution of European institutions continues.

Again, the functionalist approach assumes that problems are solved by a well-designed functional organization. Processes such as Europeanization and globalization make a coordinating body on an international level necessary. Since this body is needed, it will eventually emerge. In our case this body is the European government.

A11.1.3.2 A Typical Conflict-Theory Framing of the Situation

The German government represents German interests. German monetary institutions maintain that the interests of the German economy are best served by means of monetary policies that aim at price stability. In this climate German firms are able to compete on the global markets. This will make the Deutsche Mark a very reliable currency that will play an increasingly important role in the global economy. Since the Germans are used to these policies and have profited from them, they promote the same monetary strategies for the European Union. Complete autonomy for the ECB is the best political strategy to reach that goal. The banking world has always been in favour of these sorts of policies; as monetary experts they regard themselves as having the know-how required to reach and maintain monetary and price stability. However, this strategy means that capital interests, more than labour interests, are served.

The French government represents French interests. Because the French economy suffers from cost-push wage inflation quite regularly, the French are not interested in price stability. It would make the situation even worse. The French economy needs some inflation to keep the real wage level on a more competitive level.

So the German–French conflict is a conflict between different economic interests. No consultation can ignore this objective fact. Ongoing talks lead to one compromise after another, to minimize the damage that would result from a more straightforward battle.

Again we see that this analysis presents every problem as the result of an objective conflict of interests. These conflicts can never be solved by consensus. The best outcome that can be reached is a compromise that reflects the relative power of the different parties.

A11.1.3.3 A Typical Micro-Interactionist Framing of the Situation

The economists who advise the German government are mostly German. They were trained in German universities, in a school of economic thought that is highly influenced by German history. Because of a long period of hyperinflation during the 1920s, ultimately leading to the Nazi regime and the Second World War, most German economists define a sound economy as an inflation-free economy. German institutions like the central bank and the Ministry of Finance are especially attracting young graduates who are trained in this way of thinking. The common interest is at stake and Germany cannot afford to have economists in important positions applying non-German views.

The economists who advise the French government are mostly French. They are educated in the kind of economics that is highly influenced by French tradition. An important role for the government is one of the key characteristics of French politics. While representing France in the world, it is constantly aware of French culture and the necessity of being proud of it. Therefore, anonymous markets do not offer France enough opportunities to let the world know that France is a great country with a great culture. So, French monetary policies must be part of the whole of French (foreign) policy. Now the EU is establishing an ECB, exclusion of the French government from this important area must be avoided at all costs. Complete autonomy makes it impossible to be in regular contact with the monetary policy-makers of the ECB and to develop common views that reflect the French viewpoint sufficiently.

To solve this conflict the EU must organize a platform for regular meetings between the various interest groups from the different countries in the EU. Consequently, people are offered a chance to develop a European way of thinking. Europe must not be a big Germany or a copy of France. The EU must develop its own identity, it cannot take someone's nationality as an indicator of all the interests to be represented.

Again we see that the micro-interactionist approach interprets problems in terms of a cultural clash. German history has strongly affected German ideology with respect to monetary policies; so with France, where the government plays a major role in the presentation of French culture on the European and global level. To overcome these problems a European identity and culture must be developed. Then Europeans will learn to speak the same language and to use the same symbols. A European monetary policy is one of the implications of that culture.

A11.1.3.4 A Typical Exchange/Rational Choice Framing of the Situation

The economy is the aggregate of a large number of transactions. To a certain extent rational individual agents give up some control and transfer authority to a body that is supposed to represent the common interest. Such a body, the government, can take decisions on behalf of all those individuals, avoiding inefficiencies, like the prisoner's dilemma. If the government decides to cooperate with a number of other countries—in a monetary system, for instance—this must be interpreted as an important collective transaction. Some groups within the system can have an interest in changing some specifications of the collective transaction. For instance, France disagreed with the budgetary constraints that are part of the Stability Pact, which is linked to the European Economic and Monetary Union (EMU) regulations. These constraints make it difficult for governments to invest, while French culture requires the government to take an active role in this respect. Thus, the French will permanently try to influence decision-making processes via mass media and by voting for political parties that do not share the views of the ruling parties. If these strategies do not have the desired effects, members of these pressure groups must weigh the costs and the benefits of staying under the authority of a government that does not serve their interests sufficiently or leave (exit) that geographical area in search of a more beneficial area.

Appendix 11.2 **A Social Scientific Discourse**

To gain a more profound insight into questions concerning societal order and economic development, we imagine five experts in social science who meet each other to talk about the differences and similarities in their views. All experts espouse a clear ideal-type of approach. Thus, their reactions are not personal, but ideal-typical of a particular school of thought. During the interview a confrontation between the experts takes place. A full transcript of this interesting meeting is given. The five imaginary participants are:

First, Professor Alfredo Pessoa from the University of Rio de Janeiro, Brazil. He has conducted much research on the Latin American industrial relations systems; he typifies himself as a functionalist.

Second, Professor Margaret Barkley from the University of Austin, USA. She is famous for her research in the field of trade protection. She typifies herself as a conflict theorist.

Third, Professor Kurt Muller from the University of Vienna, Austria. He is a famous social psychologist and sociologist and has undertaken research on group dynamics. He typifies himself as a micro-interactionist.

Fourth, Professor Simon MacIntyre from the University of Edinburgh, Scotland. He is a micro-sociologist and proponent of the rational choice approach.

Fifth, Professor Jan Vacek of the University of Chicago, USA. He is a neoclassical economist and has done research in the field of rational expectations.

Interviewer: Welcome all of you. To start with you, Professor Pessoa: When economists state that economic theory is necessary and sufficient to explain the functioning of a free market economy, what is your reaction?

Alfredo Pessoa (functionalist): I would say to these economists that a real-life economy is a set of activities executed by people who are very different from the people who are modelled in economic theory. This implies that the explanations given by economists are not sufficient to understand the phenomena we observe. Let me give an example. When a famous broker on Wall Street appears pessimistic about developments on the stock exchange, many investors react to this news and sell financial assets in an attempt to avoid wealth losses. A model with many independent individuals who supply and demand capital is a poor picture of the reality of today's capital markets. In economic models, markets are stable because of the flexibility of prices that readjust markets if they are temporarily in disequilibrium. But real financial markets are embedded in an institutional structure. Suppliers and demanders do not operate as independent individuals, but are led by the views of prestigious investment funds and globally operating banks. A functional analysis of society, and especially of the economy, must give us more insight into the question of whether the institutional structure of the financial markets is optimal in the sense that those markets can fulfil their societal function optimally.

Jan Vacek (neoclassical economist): May I intervene for a moment? Alfredo, you suggest that economics ignores the institutional structure of markets. But there is a difference between ignoring something and leaving something implicit. Economists only predict the speed of adjustment of prices in case of disequilibrium. Then you need only quantities demanded, quantities supplied, and price levels to find out whether the markets under scrutiny are functioning well.

Interviewer: I'd like to ask Margaret Barkley for her reaction to the position of our typical economist.

Margaret Barkley (conflict theorist): Neoclassical economists basically deny the existence of lasting powerful positions. In economic analysis, monopoly power means profits and profits attract newcomers. Moreover, more competitors mean lower profits. But the reality of our economies is different. A particular market situation gives rise to market power if the number of competitors decline and the surviving competitors become rivals. In these circumstances trade turns into zero- or even negative-sum games. Newcomers have barely any chance to enter the market because of market barriers. Moreover, conflicts over the distribution of scarce resources tend to expand to the political sector. Then, the struggle is not only about the distribution of the produced value added, but also about the decision-making structure, in firms as well as in politics.

Jan Vacek (neoclassical economist): Our discussion was on the effectiveness of the price mechanism in allocating scarce resources in a free market system. Now Margaret is talking about a political power struggle, which is not our subject. So let's turn back to the economy and see what sociology could add to the economic analysis of the free market system. Up to now I've not heard any serious comments. In economics we work with the concept of rational expectations. This means that whatever people outside the economy are planning to do, rational individuals in the economy take these actions into account, so as to escape from the negative effects of political interference as much as possible. Outsiders, like the government, can make the economy less efficient but the tendency of individuals to move in the direction of their optimum is a universal force that will never disappear.

Interviewer: I'd like to ask Kurt Muller for his reaction to the typical economist's position.

Kurt Muller (micro-interactionist): Economists suggest that all kinds of relationships between people have an exchange character. If this were true, the distinction between economic and social relationships would not be relevant—the relationship between a seller and a buyer of pineapples would be of the same character as the relationship between an employer and a worker. Since our daily practice is very different, it is better to make the distinction between economic and social relationships explicitly. It is realistic to assume that, under particular conditions, economic relationships turn into social or social-economic relationships. This has far-reaching consequences for the functioning of free markets. When people offer their labour services on the labour market, they not offer only a service, but are basically identifying themselves with the way they execute their tasks. When the properties of a job have become part of the identity of the worker, not only economic forces but also social and psychic forces are at work. This means that considerations of fairness enter the account of a particular position. If an economist characterizes particular labour conditions to be efficient, they may still be considered unfair by the worker or employer. These considerations are real and have real consequences for the functioning of economy and society.

Jan Vacek (neoclassical economist): If workers consider their market value to be unfair, they must try to find another market where the value is more in line with their ambitions. Further education or skills training is one strategy to increase income.

Margaret Barkley (conflict theorist): Jan, do you really think that every worker has the capacity to improve his skills, and that he is in a situation to find another and better-paying job? Look at the situation of unskilled workers. Their wage is barely enough to maintain a family. Look at their housing, their health care, their working situation; and you simply expect that the labour market offers these people profitable opportunities and that they are well informed about their own capacities and about the opportunities the labour market offers to develop a successful career? As soon as economists broaden their view and take the societal context of people into account, they will discover that free markets need an optimal institutional structure to offer *all* people the chance to have a career.

Kurt Muller (micro-interactionist): I agree with Margaret. Individuals cannot easily break out of their social context. People make friends from the same group. So, an unskilled worker's friends are among the group of unskilled workers. His being unskilled influences his choice of entertainment activities, of the neighbourhood in which he lives, and his views on society and politics. If he is going to change his position in the labour market, he must basically change everything important in his life. Therefore, he needs a particular perspective that shows him a different lifestyle. This is exactly what is missing. If we want unskilled people to change their lives, then social policies focused on the *group* of unskilled people will be much more successful than only preaching that unskilled *individuals* must change their strategies.

Interviewer: I'd like to ask Simon MacIntyre for his reaction to the position of the economist.

Simon MacIntyre (exchange/rational choice theorist): I first want to react to the position taken by Kurt. He said that economic relationships are exchange relationships, while social relationships are of a different kind. I disagree with that. Of course, the relationship between an individual and an apple is different from the relationship between a man and a woman. But what these relationships have in common is that both can be understood as an exchange relationship. The example of the apple is clear. But if a woman marries a man, this contract can be understood by finding out what these people are actually trading. Of course, there are differences. But that also holds for apples versus houses and bridges versus airplanes. They all have value and they all have price. That is what matters. With respect to the position of the economist I must say that his paradigm of the rational individual is a great structuring device. The economist accepts the technological constraints as an expression of physical and chemical structures. However, he must learn to accept the properties of social structures as a given in the cost/benefit accounts of the individuals whose behaviour he is modelling.

Let me give two examples to clarify the relevance of my point. If we plan to make a journey from Amsterdam to Tokyo tomorrow and we want to be there within an hour, then we are beyond our limits. Which kind of limits are we talking about? Technically, we cannot construct planes that have a speed which makes it possible to be in Tokyo within an hour. But there is also a social limit if the flight is already fully booked. Then, we cannot simply kick some people off the plane. Of course, there is a difference in the character of the limit. Even if one tried time and again, technical limits cannot be ignored. Social limits, however, seem easier to disregard. The effects are merely delayed and may not harm the breaker of the social rules, but other people. Economists must become aware that something like social structure is also the outcome of the behaviour of rational individuals and it consequently affects the behaviour of rational individuals. A second example is the following. Suppose a country discovers a significant correlation between criminality and the presence of immigrants from a neighbouring country. The politicians of that country decide to send all these immigrants back to their country of origin. The implementation of such a decision may have far-reaching social effects.

Alfredo Pessoa (functionalist): Simon, of course you're right when saying that social structure affects individual behaviour. But do we need an understanding of individual behaviour in order to understand developments in social structure? No individual is able to create a social process. But every individual is significantly affected by it. Let's take the example of the process of secularization of our Western civilization. There were always people who did not believe in heaven and hell and lived their lives as if there was no God. Why were these people not followed by other people for so many years? And why did so many people in Western Europe during the 1960s leave the Church and claim not to believe in God, heaven, and hell anymore?

Within a period of about two decades we have lost a monitoring device that was quite effective for a very long time. That process cannot be understood as a process whereby an individual rationally decides to reject religious ideas. Now societies must create solidarity without a religious foundation.

Margaret Barkley (conflict theorist): Alfredo, your example illustrates the process of demystification that has taken place in Western societies. Many people began to believe that religion was basically an invention of authorities to defend the status quo. Now most people in the West are secularized, we understand that society is based on naked power rather than on common values. I agree with your remarks about the role of the individual, but you must admit that there is no such thing as 'objective common values'.

Kurt Muller (micro-interactionist): Alfredo, you suggest that religion is a necessary and sufficient condition for having a society with common values. This is not true. I also disagree with your observation that so many people in the West are not believers anymore. I think that the organizational structure has changed; and so with the language used. Nevertheless, our modern society is still a religious society. Look at the economists. They really think that people have become rational, in contrast to earlier times, when they were traditional and primitive. Under the influence of the Enlightenment they have declared all people to be rational. They really believe in a social structure in which no common values are present, except the principle of individual liberty. They believe in the creative powers of free individual persons. The only restriction that an individual must accept in this respect is to grant the same individual freedom to other individuals. But, as I said already, this is no more than a belief.

Jan Vacek (neoclassical economist): A quick comparison between the Western part of the world with the Southern and the Eastern part tells us already that the West is a very attractive area for many people. Most migrants go to Europe, Australia, and North America. I think this has to do with the idea of individual liberty.

Alfredo Pessoa (functionalist): The West is heavily influenced by functionalist ideas. Think of the welfare state, including its systems of industrial relations in Western Europe. These structures are responsible for lasting peace and prosperity.

Interviewer: I think this discussion could last a whole day. However, I do not want to end it before we have dealt with the most important topic of this meeting. As has already been pointed out, this is the question of whether the four sociological approaches are mutually exclusive and whether economics really needs sociology when trying to explain the functioning of real-life economies.

Alfredo Pessoa (functionalist): I admit that the creation and maintenance of consensus was easier in earlier societies than it is today. Now it is more difficult to draw clear-cut lines between the different cultures and economies. Consensus creation takes time and circumstances change so quickly that we don't have the time to institutionalize new relationships. In other words, our conflicts are lasting. But it pays for representative organizations to consult each other constantly, and look for mutually acceptable compromises.

Margaret Barkley (conflict theorist): Although I am still not convinced by your plea for consensus-creating mechanisms, I recognize at least the desirability of conflict-reducing mechanisms. Can we agree that these mechanisms are more or less the same?

Kurt Muller (micro-interactionist): A strong point of the two macro-approaches is their historical character. There has always been a social structure. Thus, searching for the logic of a social relationship is less important than rational choice theorists suggest. A good understanding of changes in the social structure is already be required if one imagines how people have to (re)shape their social relationships under the new circumstances. Suppose bosses and subordinates are used to a top-down command structure. When new technologies are introduced some of the subordinates are fired, and others are retrained to fulfil newly formulated tasks. Parts of these tasks are not familiar to the boss. While his subordinates completed courses in the new techniques, he completed a course in management techniques. To remain effective, the old boss–subordinate culture must be transformed into a different one. The boss must try to base his authority on something other than superiority in technical knowledge or experience.

Alfredo Pessoa (functionalist): Kurt, in your example you sketch a situation of a typical micro-interaction; and you say that it is on this level that social change takes place. But you must admit that this micro-interaction takes place in a macro-context. In your case we can imagine that a transformation from top-down to something of a mix of top-down and bottom-up is more difficult in a society that is characterized by a great power distance and a high rate of masculinity. Imagine we introduce new management techniques in countries where the father is the boss of the family, as the priest is the boss of the church, and the king of the country. In such a macro-context it is more difficult for the boss of a department in a firm to accept more horizontal relationships. When he leaves the firm after five o'clock he will feel inadequate, and dare not to tell his friends about his so-called new leadership style.

Simon MacIntyre (exchange/rational choice theorist): Kurt, I agree with you. But up to now you have not explained to me why your processes of micro-interaction cannot be described in terms of rational behaviour. If social structures are not rational and efficient, individual behaviour will ultimately lead to a change of these structures into more efficient ones. Societies with less efficient structures will lose their competitive battles against other societies, who introduce their superior structures into societies that they have culturally conquered.

Alfredo Pessoa (functionalist): Simon, your position is a fruitful one if applied to more or less voluntary social relationships. Then individuals can choose. But there are also very important social positions that cannot be chosen. If you live in the USA and are black, some discrimination is almost unavoidable. If you are a woman, some sectors of the economy are still a no-go area. Top management of large multinational enterprises is an illustrative example in this respect. In Afghanistan there is hardly any public life for women. These women are free to choose, but only between very stringent constraints.

Jan Vacek (neoclassical economist): I think that this discussion is narrowing the gap between the different approaches in sociology. But Simon, do you really think that phenomena like power and authority fit into a rational choice framework? A rational individual might decide to trust a particular government at a particular moment to a certain extent. But he keeps on monitoring his government and defects from it as soon as he thinks it beneficial. However, as soon as he discovers that the government is cheating him, the trust decreases sharply, I suppose.

Simon MacIntyre (exchange/rational choice theorist): Jan, you are right. But the problem is that a citizen who has transferred his control to a public authority doesn't have the means to really control the government. That power is exactly what he has transferred to the government. Of course, we still lock our doors and bicycles. In the USA, people are allowed to have weapons to defend themselves, but private armies and private police are not part of a regular citizen's portfolio. Kurt, you live in Austria. Suppose the Austrian government decides to accept a number of refugees from Sri Lanka, on the grounds that that these people are of Tamil ethnicity and are really threatened by the Sri Lankan government. How can a citizen check whether the government is right or wrong in its assumptions? A citizen can only trust or distrust the government upon the basis of scant evidence.

Kurt Muller (micro-interactionist): You are right, Simon. But do you also consider the process of framing that takes place mostly during people's youth to be a rational process? Psychologists would not be happy with such an interpretation.

Jan Vacek (neoclassical economist): I have learned a lot from this discussion. However, the outcomes are not a denial of the results of basic economic analysis. They add something to it, making it more realistic. In other words, sociology is not an alternative for, but a necessary complement to, economic theory.

Kurt Muller (micro-interactionist): When we add relevant social factors to the typical economic picture we must take into account the fact that individual preferences are not a given anymore but are the result of human interaction. But it's not only the preferences but also the resources are influenced by someone's social position. Access to rich family members, friends, and banks are important resources and determinants of the perspective of individuals. Institutions frame the perspectives, preferences, and resources of people, and therefore we cannot simply aggregate individual decisions to macro-behaviour. These individual decisions are heavily affected by institutions.

Interviewer: I'd like to wrap up this discussion with the following conclusions. Economic theory offers a strong structuring device to social science. It has stimulated sociologists to think about their micro-foundations. The results of a better macro-micro mix in sociology means that economists are offered important perspectives with respect to the developments in social structure. Now, it is up to the economists to analyse the consequences of these findings for their analysis of the functioning of governments, markets, and economies as a whole.

12 The Historical Approach in Sociology

12.1 Introduction

In Chapter 2 we have discussed the duality of logic and history. Orthodox economics is an attempt to analyse and model the operation of the economic force. The result is called economic *logic;* in other words, the logical implications of an analysis of a world where only the economic force is operating. As we have seen in Chapter 4, the assumption that actors are economic, rational, and non-social offers us such a framework of interpretation. Other schools of thought prefer a historical approach, such as original institutional economics and evolutionary economics. They deny the existence of a fixed human nature, and assume that life is essentially subject to a process of ongoing change. When explaining human behaviour it is essential to know the stage of development of the subject matter. In other words, the *history* of an object of research is decisive for its action. Human behaviour can only be explained when taking the institutional context into account; abstraction from it—as the orthodoxy in economics are doing—creates an unrealistic and useless picture.

In Chapter 11 we saw that Parsons' analytical or systems approach is typical for a logical approach, while symbolic interactionism describes processes, without using any explicitly formulated economic or social or psychic logic. It is interesting to see that Marx uses a clear logic: humans are social beings who group together on the basis of a common economic interest. But he uses this logic to describe the development of systems over time, thereby making a distinction between different stages of development.

Besides the distinction between logic and history, we can make a distinction between *ideality* and *materiality*. They are two aspects of one and the same economic, personal, and social system. Some explanations stress the material aspect, while others also take the ideal aspect explicitly into account when explaining the history of mankind. When discussing the different stages we will see that the two distinctions play an important role. In Section 12.2 we discuss a materialist and an idealist approach and compare them with each other. In Section 12.3 we deal with a number of contributions, which explain the ins and outs of *the modernity project*. The process of globalization is a very important example of modernity and deserves a separate section. Then, in Section 12.4 we explain how people such as Foucault moved from structuralism to post-structuralism. He appeared as the herald of the postmodern era, a period in which the grand narrative of the modern prophets came under severe attack. In Section 12.4 we present the latest offshoot of the modern versus postmodern discourse, which is post-social theory.

12.2 **Two Interpretations of the History of Mankind**

An interpretation, which focuses especially on the material aspect of human life, divides history into periods that differ, especially in terms of production methods and property rights with respect to productive means. In Chapter 3 we discussed the most familiar material interpretation, in which five periods are distinguished.

(1) The hunting and gathering society; nomadic societies organized according to principles of primitive communism.
(2) The simple and increasingly advanced horticultural society; evolution from a nomadic to a settler society.
(3) The simple and increasingly advanced agricultural society; feudal societies; private relationships in production emerge out of communal ownership.
(4) The industrial society, organized according to capitalist principles.
(5) The post-industrial society; order based on a mix of market and government.

Some authors explain the transition from the first to the second stage by referring to increasing population pressure. Apparently, the hunters and gatherers were successful, leading to a healthier population. The increasing pressure led to more scarcity of fertile land, which made people more selfish. They increasingly introduced private landownership. The result was the emergence of differential access to resources. This inequality made it possible for some groups to dominate and compel others to produce economic surpluses. Until now, this stratification of society—meaning the differential control over surplus wealth—has remained.

Another explanation states that population pressure led to the search for more productive methods of production, which led to more surplus and stratification. For an economist there is not much difference between the first explanation (scarcity of fertile land) and the second (surplus of production). Scarcity of land is an incentive for people to develop more productive methods. For a sociologist there is an important difference: in the first explanation there is explicit attention to the changes in the motivational structure and in the institutional context, especially the system of property rights and the social structure. In the second explanation the final change in social variables (stratification) is simply the outcome of an economic process—a completely endogenous variable, and therefore not important for a thorough understanding of the historical process.

Lenski (1970) developed *technological evolutionism*, which attempts to describe and explain the history of modern society. The core of his model consists of a positive relationship between technological progress and inequality, and between inequality and what he called the 'strife' in society. Technological progress has a self-reinforcing character, while inequality has a negative effect on technological progress, because the powerful have a weaker incentive to invent, if there is barely any competition from the mass of poor people.

As said, inequality causes strife in society: unrest, frustration, and resistance. Lenski highlights the difference between *passivist* religions and ideologies on the one hand, and *activist* religions and ideologies on the other. When a particular society is ruled by conservative powers, which control the population with passivist religion and ideology, there is not much technological progress, and strife is caused by natural equality that is suppressed. When a particular society is ruled by progressive powers, which 'control' the population by means of their activist religion or ideology, there is much technological progress. The inequality that results from the application of the latest techniques will be actively tackled by means of redistribution policies. Democratic constitutions, as we see in Europe, induce more activism, and become wealthier, because of the widespread idea of individual freedom and responsibility, and the state seriously tries to limit the strife that comes with increasing inequality. The Nordic countries especially have been extremely successful with their Protestant and social-democratic culture and ideology. In Figure 12.1 we present Lenski's technological evolutionism schematically.

A second interpretation of history focuses on the ideal aspect of human life. In Chapter 2 we briefly discussed the view by Girard, and we will now elaborate on this. Later, many other scientists took the idealist approach to highlight decisive moments in history. For economists Keynes is a good example. He saw that modern capitalism in its later stages of development needed a completely different approach, compared with the dominant neoclassical view. Marx furiously denied being an idealist, but his ideas were severely attacked by the establishment. This created an ongoing ideological debate, which is a waste of time for true materialists.

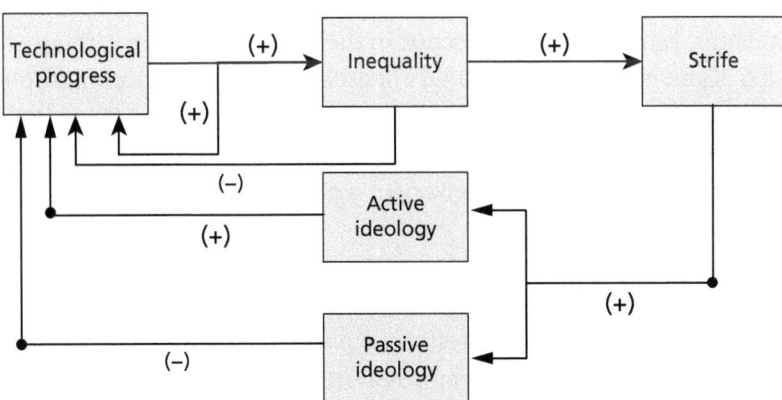

Figure 12.1. Lenski's Technological Evolutionism

As we saw in Chapter 2, Girard makes a distinction between primitivity and modernity. The primitive view states that human behaviour is a reflection of the will of gods who 'possess' parts of the earth, and who are rivals. Every god also possesses groups of people. These people can show their belief by attacking those who belong to another god, whom they regard as a devil. This primitive belief implies strict economic and social constraints. Some trees are sacred, and some animals cannot be used for human consumption; on the contrary they must be fed, even if many people suffer starvation. This belief makes the ongoing rivalry between different groups the central activity. So, the economic problem is subordinate to the social and religious problem. The transition from the primitive stage to the modern stage took a very long period, and actually, even in the most progressive and modern states like north-western Europe, Canada, and New Zealand, the primitive battle of groups goes on, although the weapons which are used are more civilized.

According to Girard, the Jew *Abram*, living in exile together with many other Jews, could not believe in aggressive gods who terrorized their creatures. He created for himself and his family the idea of a god who loves his creatures, and has given them the capacities to develop a good life on earth. He left the land of his exile, and went to a land that was called Palestine. Later, the Jew Jesus came and his pupils exported the idea of a loving god to other parts of the world. Unfortunately, the great idea of people being free and responsible individuals was institutionalized in a strict hierarchically organized institution: the Roman Catholic Church. During the Renaissance an increasing number of individuals tried to escape from clerical doctrines and started to practise Christian ideas. During the Enlightenment, individuals began to develop many ideas about personal and social life, mostly based on Christian and humanist ideas (many humanists, such as Kant and Smith, were devout Christians).

In science we see a permanent debate about the role of subjectivity and metaphysics. Modern science pretends to abstract from both elements as much as possible, so as to minimize the influence of ideas. In the 1920s the Vienna Circle played an important role. Most members were beta-scientists, who tried to abstract from all meta-physical elements in the theory. They adhered to the empiricist ideas of Hume, thereby neglecting the fact that Hume himself became a sceptic in the end of his career: without ideas, there is nothing left. Kant, however, had created a synthesis between the rationalist metaphysics and the empiricist position: we need a framework of 'a priori' concepts in order to be able to empirically observe things 'out there' (see Chapter 2 and Appendix B). Orthodox economics is a good example of a framework of 'a priori' concepts, framing the economic aspect of life.

We have seen that Girard (1978) stresses the variable culture as the main cause of human development. *Ideas rule the world*. Lenski's technological evolutionism sounds materialistic; nevertheless, cultural variables do play an important role in his description of development. His distinction between passivist and activist ideologies, being bottlenecks and triggers respectively, makes it clear that conservative ideologies can hamper improvement in human well-being for centuries.

A recent contribution to this discussion is Diamond (2012). His methodology is quite empiricist—which is the dominating methodology in circles of biologists, psychologists, and anthropologists. Empiricists are very reluctant when it comes to concepts such mind, needs or preferences, emotions, and feelings. Although he recognizes the role of motivation, in his examples of immediate and ultimate motivation, he refers to something empirical: the theft of a pig or of a woman can cause a war between different bands. The ultimate motivation for the theft might be a long period of drought. In other words, motivation is not the inner drive of a person. If a scientist is inclined to stick to empirical realities, he will never understand why someone does something. As long as he does not understand how his subject of research understands the world, he cannot know why his subject interprets something as a cost and what he experiences as a benefit.

Nevertheless, Diamond (2012) considers culture to be an important variable which is not completely determined by the material conditions. He describes an example of an independent cultural phenomenon. In a particular tribe in New Guinea it is still the custom to kill widows by strangling them. So far, no scholar has been able to explain the reason or function of this strangling; there seems to be no benefits for anyone. Since the tribe is quite isolated no external influences have had the chance to stop this practice.

Had Diamond asked himself for the ultimate human motives, he might have found a good reason for this practice, whether the members of the tribe were aware of this reason or not. Also, in modern societies, widows, especially the younger and more attractive ones, are seen as a threat to the stability of the marriages in the tribe. We know from a Bible story that even King David ordered a soldier, who was married to a beautiful woman, to be killed. After the woman had become a widow, David married her. More introspection helps scientists learn more about the basic motives that set humans in motion. More reflection might lead to more rational and reasonable behaviour.

The whole development, from the Jew Abram to the Christian and humanist ideas about the way humans can construct a society that leads to justice and prosperity for all, is a typical modern development. At the end of this chapter we will see the reaction of post-structuralists and postmodernists to the ideas behind this project.

Now we will discuss a number of sociological contributions to the modernity project.

12.3 **Modernity in Sociology**

12.3.1 INTRODUCTION

Primitive societies are ruled by religion and tradition, while modern societies are based on the idea that man has the capacity to increasingly discover the way in which our reality works. This idea implies an increasing control of natural processes, including processes concerning human nature. Modern science is viewed as progressive and leads to a growing body of knowledge. Top scientists work at the frontier and academic education transfers scientifically established knowledge to the next generation.

In the classical sociological literature, various authors have interpreted this process of modernization differently. Marx saw exploitation and alienation, and the transformation from work to labour, as the key element. Weber saw the increasing application of formal rather than value rationality as the core of what is modern. Durkheim emphasized the ongoing process of specialization without sufficient integration as the most typical modern problem. Now we will discuss a number of interpretations of the last few decades.

12.3.2 THE JUGGERNAUT

Giddens analyses the growth of a very large global system, with many parts, which may or may not be in congruence with each other. The system is like a machine with enormous power, which is at the point of running out of control. We give three examples, which illustrate this danger clearly. First, the global food markets are regularly confronted with speculators who have the capacity to determine price fluctuations at the cost of many people, especially in developing countries. Second, emerging global labour markets create mass emigration and immigration. If people from different cultures are supposed to live and work peacefully together, communication should be explicitly organized to avoid cultural clashes in many immigration countries. Third, global financial markets have proven to be unstable, while the financial control system has been deliberately weakened by private financial powers.

To get the machine, often called the juggernaut, under control, it is very important to distinguish between different core subsystems. Giddens indicates the production system, the system of property rights, the marketing system, and education as decisive subsystems. If what is produced has no clear owner, or cannot be sold, the system will get out of control. It is necessary to educate the next generation on how to keep the system running.

Some people have developed the skills necessary to profit from the growing machine: good jobs, high wages. Others face a deterioration of opportunities. For them, the more irregular jobs are left: building, cleaning, and protecting buildings, for instance.

The increasing dependence on the 'machine' makes it necessary to pay a lot of attention to the quality of the expert systems on which it is built, and on the trustworthiness of the people who occupy important positions in the system.

While, in earlier times, people felt more dependent on completely uncontrollable natural events—floods, earthquakes, long periods of drought—nowadays people feel very insecure because of the unreliability of people and the systems they have created. In the past people died because of a heart attack; nowadays people die because of a mistake made by a heart surgeon, or of a refusal by the health insurance company to pay for a sophisticated treatment. In other words, existential or ontological insecurity does not find an outlet in religion; it creates frustration and resentment of a social kind. Beck states that the modern risks are unevenly distributed among the people. The system creates enormous wealth for the very top, while the risks are located particularly at the bottom of society. According to Beck (1992), scientists are not inclined to reflect on what the risks of the systems they have created mean for the victims. Systems of nuclear energy, weapon industry, security systems, deregulated market systems—they all are part of the system as a whole that must be controlled. An important common characteristic is its formal rationality and its irrationality. Formal rationality means that every part is based on specialized expert systems. Irrationality means that the system as a whole has no self-control. Every part of the system keeps itself under control, partly by externalizing a series of problems. A free market system dismisses people who are handicapped but if a government system takes care of these people firms threaten the government with emigration if they are supposed to pay the bill by means of taxation. Value-rational considerations in the sense of Weber are not part of the system; in other words, there are no ultimate goals other than the continuation of the system itself. Scientists have become perfect links in a chain that must not be broken.

12.3.3 THE HOLOCAUST

According to Ahrendt the Holocaust is a perfect example of modernity (Vila, 2000). Later Bauman wrote a classic on this theme (Bauman, 1989). Hitler and a few of his closest comrades had developed the idea that Europe suffered from the presence of too many Jews. It would be a great feat if the German race took the lead in getting rid of them, and would they then rule Europe from then on. They built a military system that was intended to be able to conquer, occupy, and convince Europe of the natural leadership of the German people. They also built a system for the destruction of the Jewish people, and some other groups of people, who were also seen to be a danger to a civilized Europe, such as the Roma and homosexuals. The project was well organized and a very large number of people participated in it, voluntarily or under pressure. Many scientists designed systems of selection, suppression, and destruction, and even many victims participated in it, so as to delay their destruction. In many countries there was at least a large minority that enjoyed the German leadership and actively helped them to reach their ultimate goals.

How was it possible to build such a great and efficiently organized apparatus? The answer must be found in the fact that there are only small minorities of individuals who resist actively when important human values are at stake in their environment. Social and economic motives are very strong and moral resentment appears much stronger than moral sentiment. When jobs and incomes are threatened, as was the case in the 1930s, most people follow a strong leader who promises a way out of the malaise, and are prepared to believe in simple explanations ('look at the financial sector and see how corrupt Jews manage their affairs at the cost of the whole population', 'the Jews are the cause of all evil', for instance). In this way people cannot hear the voice of their conscience anymore.

12.3.4 HABERMAS' WAY OUT

In Chapter 11 we saw that Habermas had made a distinction between System and life world. His concept System can easily be translated into the juggernaut of Giddens. His concept life world is the whole of parts of our daily life, which are not yet dominated by the System.[1] Both terms need more specification in order to understand how the system affects the life world in concrete cases. Only then we can make a distinction between positive and negative effects of the system upon the daily lives of so many people. Only then we can help ordinary people to escape from it or to influence the system into a more desirable direction. According to Habermas, the values of the life world in terms of truth, beauty, and goodness, and attitudes, such as reflection and criticism, can penetrate the formal rational system. In this way people can unmask the would-be world of the PR officials of large organizations.

12.3.5 GLOBALIZATION: PROBLEM OR SOLUTION

The never-ending motivation of multinational organizations to grow is the driver of the process of globalization. Since manufactured risk cannot be controlled completely, there are always problems with local communities who suffer from the constant flow of accidents. This provokes fundamentalism, which is directed against the immoral effects of the formal-rational and amoral cosmopolitan system. As we saw already, according to Bauman (2002) there is a growing divide between globals and locals. The first group consists of the winners in the process of globalization. They constantly move around and land in isolated territories—guarded areas with houses, hotels, luxury shops, and expensive entertainment. The locals are the losers, who are confined to territories denuded of meaning—imprisoned, humiliated, and with a lack of social-cultural life.

There are three groups of theories that attempt to interpret and analyse the process of globalization in a meaningful way.

In the first place, we have cultural theories, which consider the relationship between different cultures to be the most important issue. Some theories say that the various civilizations remain unaffected in their core. In earlier times they were quite separated. Later, we see Western domination. During the last few decades we have faced an increasing clash of civilizations, to use the words of Huntington. Other theories stress that cultures converge, especially because of the dominance of Western lifestyles. The global institutions of marketing are constantly transporting lifestyles from the West to the other parts of the world. McDonald's is a good example in this respect. Everywhere in the world its

---

[1] At the moment (Automn, 2013) there is much discussion in Europe about the way American security agencies are permanently monitoring the lives of ordinary people by means of large digital systems, which were built during the last decades. This is a very good example of the way in which the System tries to increasingly monitor and control the life world of the people.

restaurants have been opened. The firm is always trying to adjust to the local culture. But what it exports to the rest of the world is the idea of efficiency, accountability, predictability, and control by means of technology. Ritzer calls this the *'globalization of nothing'*. McDonald's is exporting form, not content; it tries to export something that must grow—in terms of profits and wealth, and in terms of influence and power. We must realize, however, that form and content are two aspects of the same phenomenon. So exporting form implies exporting content. For instance, workers are supposed to work fast and for long hours, and are responsible for errors they make. This is not just form: the example contains an important cultural element.

Another group of cultural theories observes a process of mixing cultures. New and unique hybrids are emerging out of the increasing communication between different cultures. Media and goods, in particular, offer people the opportunity to create and to innovate. Some critics say that the mixing is primarily related to unproblematic things such as music, sports, and food; never to more problematic issues such as human rights. However, matters of food, sports, and music, and, in particular, the way they are expressed, are not value-neutral. A good example is the way in which the famous Dutch trainer Guus Hiddink coached the South Korean football team: his management style was quite different from what the Koreans were used to. In terms of Hofstede (1980), Hiddink reduced the power distance between him and the players, and approached players more individually rather than just as a collectivity—a true culture shock.

Moreover, there are many examples illustrating the fact that modern media are playing a significant role in several revolutionary situations; for example, the Orange Revolution in Ukraine, and the Arab Spring. Both examples might be interpreted as the beginning of a long process of democratization. But the digital 'revolution' has also created many new opportunities to practise the dark side of life: pornography, racism, paedophilia, and campaigns of hatred.

In the second place, there are economic theories. In sociology this term always means 'theories about the functioning of the economy or parts of it'. These economic theories stress the dominance of the economic system, being a subsystem of the system 'society'. So, the capitalist economic system controls the realm of ideas, the social system, and even the way we look at our body and our mind. The capitalist system develops, mostly through the institutions of marketing, a common morality and institutionalizes a judicial system that determines what is forbidden (Sheehan, 2010). The system incorporates, differentiates, and manages the hierarchy and the differences embedded in it. Medical students have to work very long hours, and gamma-scientists must learn to master quantitative techniques, so as to be able to function well as a link in the system rather than as critical persons, who try to increase the true quality of work and product.

In other words, capitalism can only function well if its rule is generally accepted: those who are productive in the economic system as it is institutionalized participate in society. An important implication says: those who are not productive in the capitalist institutions have bad luck. They are the losers, who—mostly group-wise—desert, migrate, and become nomads. Universities in the Western capitalist system are controlled by the system. Now and then some intellectual communities, who derive their cohesion from being anti-capitalistic, might flourish.

In the third place, there are political theories, which interpret the process of globalization in political terms. The idea is that (national) politicians can make a difference, in contrast to the more radical-economic approach, which assumes that capitalist economic processes cannot be controlled, by either culture or politics. The first is the *neoliberal approach* or Washington consensus. Free markets are stable systems, and small disequilibria disappear through the operation of the price mechanism. In case of excess demand the price goes up until the quantity demanded and quantity supplied have become equal to each other again. In case of excess supply a decrease in the price leads to market equilibrium again. Free market economies are subject to small fluctuations in a number of important macroeconomic variables, such as the volumes of production and employment, and a number of prices, such as the level of the goods prices, the wage level, and the interest rate. If the government does not intervene in the process of price formation, the fluctuations remain small. One of the important stabilizers runs via the government budget. In a stage of expansion tax receipts tend to increase and government expenditures tend to decrease. The resulting budget surplus contributes to a dampening of the increase in the volumes of production and employment; in other words, a turn back to equilibrium. In case of a recession the opposite takes place: a budget deficit stimulates the economy, leading to equilibrium again.

A second political theory is called the *realist approach*. It says that states aggressively pursue their own interests on the global stage. If necessary, they become part of a coalition of countries, or accept a less powerful position and adjust to the political strategies of a strong country. In this approach, states pursue their own interests—or, rather, the interest of the political elite of the country under analysis. An illustrative example is the following. During the economic crisis that began in 2008 we see clusters of countries are operating in cooperation or under the leadership of a powerful country. The Dutch adapt to the Germans, whatever their own views and interests, Mediterranean countries cluster under the leadership of France, and the Anglo-Saxon countries group together under the leadership of the United States. The cultural view is inclined to explain these clusters by referring to their common culture. The economic view is inclined to interpret them by looking at the common economic interests.

12.4 From Structuralism to Post-Structuralism and Postmodernity

12.4.1 STRUCTURALISM AND POST-STRUCTURALISM

Structuralism in classical sociology essentially states that social structure determines social action. Later structuralists began to analyse the structure of human thinking (the *linguistic turn*). They reformulated their position as follows: the position of a person in the social structure determines the way his mind is framed. His understanding of the situation, which is derived from that framework, determines his social actions. Social interaction is a permanent exchange of signs, all loaded with social meaning. *Semiotics* is the discipline that is focused on the meaning of signs. Most of the time people are not conscious of their social actions. We all appear to have a *social structure in our unconscious*— a remnant from the primitive stage—in which we divide humankind in a few groups: our group and other groups. In sociological language it is expressed by: *Us versus Them*, or by: *We versus They*.[2]

Derrida attacked the whole idea of what he called *logo-centrism*, being a search for universal principles that reveals what is true, right, and beautiful. The attempts to find a universal system of thought leads to domination of one group, which is suppressing the other groups. For economics this observation is easy to understand. Many mainstream economists do not consider their approach to be one of several possible perspectives. They dominate the scene, suppressing and marginalizing a whole series of other schools of thought. Orthodox economics claims to have developed a series of universal principles, and equilibrium values are indicated as 'natural' unemployment, 'natural' interest wage, and 'natural' wage rate. In other words, it is in the nature of particular phenomena to act according to the laws of orthodox economic analysis. Derrida advises us to dismantle and deconstruct such thought systems. They are human constructions and it makes sense to uncover hidden assumptions.

Foucault was a typical structuralist in his early years. But over time he developed in the direction of what is now called *post-structuralism*. He rejected the ideas of Weber about the iron cage, and stated that we are not necessarily caught in systems based on formal rationality. He also rejected the ideas of Marx about the one-sided relationship between events on the macro level affecting micro-level events, and not the other way around. He disagreed with the hermeneutic approach, since there are no deep ultimate truths. He did not agree with the phenomenological approach by stating that humans are not autonomous meaning-giving subjects. There is simply no ultimate meaning. And, lastly, he rejected Nietzsche's views on the relationship between power and knowledge. He considered Nietzsche to be an existentialist—giving too much weight to the role of an individual. Foucault had the idea that the relationship should be studied in a sociological framework. Unfortunately, there is no progress in social relationships in terms of increasing justice. Now and then a particular group is able to beat the dominant group, and takes over the leading role. New narcissistic leaders change the rules that decide what is normal and what is deviant. Deviants are socialized, and in case of failure they are pressed to drop out. Criminals—those who ignore the newly established legislative rules—are caught and put into prison. To prevent criminal behaviour

---

[2] Comparison of the idea of the structure of the unconscious with the themes of Jung in Chapter 10 is illuminating.

systems of *total surveillance* are developed, making society a very large prison. As we know, many developing countries have very large and crowded prisons. Besides that, many modern shopping malls and rich neighbourhoods have extended systems of monitoring. So, structuralism states that the behaviour of individual members of a group is determined by the social structure of the group. Post-structuralists are structuralists who discovered that structuralism is too simple, dogmatic, and static. There is simply a continuing battle between bosses and subordinates, where bosses decide the rules of the power game. Now and then there is a regime change, offering the subordinates the opportunity to set the rules, and decide who is criminal and who is not.

12.4.2 POSTMODERNITY

So far we have analysed what we mean by the concept of 'modernity'. In the Western world the capitalist economy has turned into a juggernaut—a dangerous and risky machine, which cannot be controlled anymore. Jameson (1984) sees the logic of capitalism as responsible for the building of a system that, in his later work, has intervened deeply into private spheres, and has offered 'scientific solutions' to 'discovered' problems. The system offers many people—through good jobs and buying fashionable goods—the opportunity to search for a 'satisfying image of the Self'; an image that constantly changes through the marketing activities of the firms.

Postmodernity denies the existence of universal principles, leading to a body of knowledge which is to be trusted. The modern project does not produce objective knowledge; there is—in the words of Lyotard—*no grand narrative*. We must activate the differences between the various bodies of knowledge, and celebrate a range of different perspectives. We must learn to tolerate incommensurability between the different cultures within one part of science. For economics this means that neo-classical economists, who straightforwardly apply the orthodox analysis to practical affairs, must learn that their methodology is not the only one with validity. What they see as explanation and scientific foundation is highly questioned by other economists. Always referring to the individual economic-rational actor is just one way of 'explaining' human behaviour. If they studied several different approaches, they would learn to frame the world in different ways, and learn to appreciate economists who are different.

There are several ways to criticize the postmodern 'project'. The postmodern message is that reality is all about pictures, images, and copies of copies. The institutions of marketing make it clear that the so-called true Self is a selection of images that can be created by means of commodities produced by the modern system. Emotions and affections are not real, since they can be 'produced' by the system. The system can also teach people not to have emotions in particular cases. There is no history, since we cannot know the past. In economics there are books on economic history that tell the student what has happened and why. But the explanations of the past are all based on the outcomes of so-called 'modern science'.

This all is meaningful criticism, but what is left? No story at all? The statement that there are no universal principles might lead to unprincipled practices. Every approach needs a clear ontological foundation. Ontology is a human construction, and therefore subjective and fallible. But we need it since the establishment of essences leads to clear definitions of objects of research. The philosophical current 'essentialism' is very different: every object has an objective and eternal essence—typical for the modern project. The alternative for essentialism is not the cancelling of ontology, as seems to be the case with postmodernity. The subjective alternative is that every person builds his own ontology, on the basis of his intuition as it is shaped by personal experience. If many persons follow this strategy, a power-free and open discourse could help us in the creation of intersubjective truths—truths which can change over time, of course (see Habermas in Chapter 11, Section 11.3).

12.4.3 POST-SOCIAL THEORY

The latest development in postmodern sociology is called post-social theory. It is about the process of desocialization of the social being as we know it from classical sociology. The typical sociological imagination or paradigm—human behaviour is determined by social context—has increasingly been replaced by biological accounts. In contrast with socialization we observe an increasing influence of *objects* in the social world. These objects are indefinite and can be interpreted in different ways. When some people observe a beautiful tree, others see a valuable source of wood. When some people observe a beautiful landscape, others consider this area to be empty, and plan roads and railways through this area.

Comparing the historical development of Europe with that of the USA, we see an important difference with respect to the social aspect of life. In Europe, a state, including a large government apparatus, emerged before capitalism became the dominant economic order. In the USA we see just the opposite: first capitalism emerged, and later—step by step—a government apparatus was built up. So, a different historical development makes the social-political frame of Europeans quite different from the frame of the Americans. Maybe we can say that Americans operated in a post-social world from the beginning. Europeans, on the other hand, lived in a less individualistic culture, and face enormous changes in their cultural pattern as a result of the postmodern desocialization. The European welfare state—a wonderful result of modern thought—has come under attack. The idea of solidarity with other people who are increasingly strangers to each other is very problematic now.

Desocialization is the result of the discovery that our knowledge is not objective. It is a human construct, which is uncertain. It is founded on modern ideas and modern rules of thought. So the large systems in society are fallible too. Social relations appear cultural rather than natural. It becomes increasingly difficult to find out to which groups someone belongs. Important relationships, such as between a married couple and between colleagues, are increasingly liberalized. As a substitute for real and face-to-face contact there are many opportunities via the internet. Relations between people via the internet can become quite intimate without the commitments which belong to intimacy or collegiality. Unfortunately, it is not only family relationships that have become weaker. Labour organizations show the same process of detachment. In labour environments with high-skilled workers especially there is a strong tendency towards 'privatization'. The office offers just a bare minimum and workers are assumed to do much of the work at home, and, in case of a movement to another building, individual workers are responsible for a successful transfer of their books and other personal stuff.

This transformation from complex organizations towards network-like organizations, where workers actually operate as independent one-man businesses, has a significant effect on the mind of individuals. The outside world becomes simply a source of gratification and frustration; not a source of lasting commitment. The Self becomes increasingly fragmented, while living in a fragmented world. The person might be highly skilled but has discovered that his expertise is just a human construction and therefore fallible. As we saw already in a former section, this creates strong feelings of existential insecurity, and undermines the functioning of willpower necessary to satisfy lasting and essential needs. No authorities in the outside world—just human constructions, employed by postmodern Selves—and no inner censors anymore: the destruction of modern control mechanisms is complete now.

One of the researchers in this field is *Knorr-Cetina*. She visited the world of foreign-currency dealing rooms, and tried—in an anthropological way—to understand the way the dealers take their decisions (Knorr-Cetina, 2005). They are constantly looking at their screens, full of numbers and graphs, and have regular contact with dealers at other places around the world. Imagine the price of the dollar decreases by 1 per cent. Will this be part of a series of small fluctuations around a value that holds for months? Or is it the beginning of a severe decline that might hold for weeks? The behaviour of the dealer depends on the way he interprets the general financial-economic developments in the world. But his interpretation has a strong effect on the course of the dollar price. Imagine the dealers in Singapore and Shanghai foresee a long-term decline; then they are inclined to sell dollars in very large proportions. Later, the dealing rooms of Frankfurt, Paris, and London start their business and discover a significant decline in the dollar price. The reaction of Singapore and Shanghai affects the interpretation of the European dealers. In this way small changes in the interpretation somewhere can lead to a huge decline—without any deliberate consultation of a group of top experts. It all just happens in our technically sophisticated expert systems.

12.5 **Conclusions**

In this chapter we described the essentials and properties of three stages in the history of mankind, in particular the primitive, the modern, and the postmodern stage. According to the primitive doctrines, there is a natural order in which rivalling gods rule those empires where their own believers live. This leads to ongoing rivalry between tribes; in the language of today's sociology the battle between *us* versus *them*. Modernity means that people do not believe in gods and devils, but that they are free and responsible for their own well-being. Newton believed in a god who had made reality and, after he had finished his work, disappeared. His creation is wonderful and harmonious and Newton saw it as his responsibility to study the physical aspects of this order. Orthodox economists, such as Menger and Jevons, were excited about Newton's metaphysics, and tried to develop a natural economic order. They took Mill's concept of isolated abstraction and formulated the principles of economics. Menger became the father of the so-called marginal revolution, which is based on the idea of optimality in case of marginal costs being equal to marginal benefits. Neoclassical economics—the empirical application of orthodox economics—is an example of modernity par excellence, and this form of economic structuralism still dominates economic thought. Unfortunately, the sociological debates about post-structuralism and postmodernity are unknown to the mass of economics students. The events in the financial world make it unrealistic to assume perfect rationality. The permanent pressure from neoclassical economists on the government to deregulate labour markets makes clear that they have not learned from experiences with respect to deregulated financial markets. In the 1930s—during the Great Depression—European governments regulated financial and labour markets in such a way that irrationality and social conflict were reduced. A careful study of the modernity and postmodernity literature could help economists in the design of more efficient and fair economic institutions.

13 Multidisciplinary Sociology and the Social World

13.1 Introduction

The term multidisciplinary sociology is not an accepted term: it suggests that sociology is just part of a bigger whole. But most sociologists contend that their discipline is about the whole of society. In the approach put forward in this book, however, most sociology abstracts from the mind and from the problem of scarcity. Therefore, we must consider the term multidisciplinary sociology to be useful. It suggests that there must be a social aspect-system or social world, and there must be a sociology which is enriched by the economic and the psychic aspect of human behaviour. In this chapter we will discuss psychological sociology and economic sociology, and see whether the literature, which can be presented under these headings, meets the conditions of an integration of two aspect-systems. In the end we formulate our social world, and reveal the content of a social aspect-system.

13.2 Psychological Sociology

13.2.1 INTRODUCTION

In this section we will discuss the relationship between the hard core of psychology, which is the logic of the psyche or mind, on the one hand, and the hard core of sociology, which is the logic of the social structure of society, on the other.

The mind is the location of emotions, thoughts, and feelings. The psychic system represents this mind and consists of a number of entities, such as the 'I', the true Self, and the actual Self (see Chapter 10).

We have seen that the biological approach in psychology profits from technical progress, which makes it possible to register accurately which parts of the brain become active when a person is acting or facing a particular situation. The big problem, however, is the relationship between brain and mind.

The social-psychological approach focuses on the relationship between individual behaviour and the social context of the individual. Again, an important problem arises: What is the role of the mind? Mead made a distinction between 'I' and 'Me'. But actually the 'I' theory says that I = Me, thereby avoiding the design of a theory of the mind.

Sociology is about social structure, which means the analysis of grouping and ranking processes. It is about the ongoing rivalry between capitalists and workers, between Islam and the West, and between man and woman, and young and old. Now there is a problem in the interrelationship between social psychology and sociology. One is about the determination of an individual person by the social structure in which he lives. The other is about the social structure: it assumes that an individual is completely determined by the roles which are derived from the social structure. So, the social structure is completely uninfluenced by the person or his mind. This section is an attempt to clarify the interrelationship between the two disciplines.

13.2.2 GROUP-BASED HIERARCHIES

Sidanius and Pratto (1999) make a distinction between psychological (1), social-psychological (2), and social structural explanations (3) of the permanent rivalry between groups.

13.2.2.1 Psychological Explanations

According to Freud, humans are motivated by subconscious non-rational drives, and are inclined to rationalize and justify their behaviour by means of logic and reason. There are a number of explanations for the aggression people feel towards others. In the first place, if economic and psychic constraints make people frustrated, they are inclined to express aggression to those who are to blame for their failure. This phenomenon is called projection. In the second place, children who are raised in an environment characterized by strict obedience and humiliation, tend to develop an authoritarian personality. They are motivated to dominate others as a kind of compensation: now it's my turn. In the third place, uncertainty and anxiety make people conservative. They live in groups with a strong (cultural) world-view, and other groups with different world-views are thus seen as a threat to the safety of the group. The prevailing world-view offers members of the group self-esteem and functions as a buffer against anxiety. In the fourth place, related to the third explanation, people are inclined to derive values from their world-view, which creates a value conflict between groups. In other words, people also consider people from other groups to be morally inferior. In the fifth place, the social-cognitive approach states that stereotyping is an information-saving device. It is impossible to find out whether or not every person can be trusted. So, people are inclined to find easy indicators, which can fulfil the important function of prejudice.

Stereotypical judgement depends on the social context: dominants pay less attention to subordinates, while the latter pay more attention to dominants than to their fellow subordinates. Prejudice fulfils an important function and it is difficult to do away with it. It functions in the same way as paradigms in science. Once a scientist has developed a career on the basis of a series of axioms, and has become famous, not only the axioms are protected by a belt of specific assumptions, but also the vulnerable self-esteem of the scientist (protective belt in the sense of Lakatos).

13.2.2.2 Social-Psychological Explanations

While the psychological explanation stresses psychic problems, which are externalized by blaming others, the social-psychological approach is focused on real social confrontations, such as zero-sum game conflicts with respect to material and symbolic resources. This type of conflict drives people to perceive each other as a threat: the other group are the bad guys, and we have solidarity with each other, since we are the good guys. In ongoing conflicts people need to be convinced of their own goodness. The *social identity theory* assumes a general desire for positive social identity. Football supporters, for instance, prefer a bad match if their club wins the battle in the end, to an exciting match in which their favourite club loses. Tajfel did a series of experiments with small groups. His famous minimal group experiment shows strong prejudice and discriminative behaviour as an attempt to promote *positive self-esteem*. An example will illustrate the most important result of Tajfel's tests. In the Primera Division, Real Madrid and Barcelona consider each other to be the club to be beaten. So fans of Real Madrid prefer a third position in the competition, if Barcelona takes the fourth position, to a second position, if Barcelona occupies the first position.

If the boundaries between different groups in the ranking are not stable, members of the high-status as well as members of the low-status group tend to discriminate in favour of the high-status group. This is especially true of members of a lower-status group, who think that they have a chance to become members of a higher-status group if they behave as if they are already members.

Sidanius and Pratto have criticized the social identity theory for its bias in the explanation of aggression. It focuses on positive self-regard, more than on negative aggression towards 'the other'. It is about *group favouritism* within the context of essentially equal and arbitrary defined social groups. But the social world is full of aggression of one group to a particular other group. This is more than competition; there is much rivalry, and groups are prepared to pay a high price to humiliate the other group. If Barcelona wins 5–0 over Real Madrid in Madrid, this is not just about three points in the competition— it is humiliation. If Iraq attacks Kuwait, a friend of the USA, it is not just because of the oil; it is a challenge to American supremacy. When Muslim terrorists attacked the Twin Towers (9/11), this was not 'just' about all the casualties, but essentially an attack on the American personality.

Sidanius and Pratto have developed a *social dominance theory*, in which they analyse drives and trends towards *hierarchy-enhancing* and *hierarchy-attenuating* forces.

In socialization processes people develop stereotyping as a way to order the social environment, on the basis of which they behave discriminatorily. Even very young children show rivalling behaviour, and in primary schools there is already much bullying. Some children dominate others, and use the others as their slave. This behaviour becomes increasingly sophisticated over time, and the scene of action becomes the office, the factory, and the prison for example; it occurs on every level in the hierarchy. All these behavioural asymmetries lead to institutions which reflect discriminative attitudes.

Hierarchy-attenuating forces are also developed in the first years of a child's life. In the Western culture especially ideas about human rights have been developed. Kant stressed the equality of all men on the level of substance. In other words, we all have something very important in common, which is the fact that we are human. This statement makes sense only if it has consequences for our attitude towards each other. Respect for every individual because of him being human means that some positions and some kinds of treatment are inhumane and therefore not to be tolerated. Familiar examples are slavery, trade in women, torture, humiliation in the office, and imprisonment without any serious trial.

In essence we are all equal. In terms of properties, however, there is much inequality. Some people have very valuable properties, while others have hardly any valuable property, except the fact they are a human person. Inequality-producing processes appear reinforcing—the rich get richer and the poor get poorer. Democracy is an institution that has the potential to function as a countervailing power. A welfare state has emerged on the basis of the idea that inequality must be reduced. North-western Europe has been successful in achieving this goal. Unfortunately, from the 1980s, the inequality-enhancing forces have become stronger again. In the Netherlands health-cost insurance companies advertise separate packages for young and healthy people, thereby ignoring the essence of a social security arrangement. Liberal politicians are in power (2013), and do not resist this trend set by privatized health-cost insurance firms.

Now we will discuss the role of mimesis, legitimizing myths, and rituals in the reduction of violent rivalry.

According to Girard (1978), all cultures have something in common, a view in contrast to that of anthropologists such as Lévi-Strauss, who state that cultures are incommensurable. Girard studied many primitive cultures, the Jewish and Christian cultures, and analysed many classic novels, written in a modern cultural context (see also Lascaris, 1987). He discovered that *mimetic rivalry* is the common and dominant element in all these cultures. Imagine two persons, Peter and John. Now Peter has bought a prestigious computer. Although John was not very interested in computers, now he wants this computer too. Why? In this case the computer plays an important role in the rivalry between two persons. The possession of it is a sign to other people of the status of the owner. So, if your neighbour has a beautiful Ferrari, you might want to have two Ferraris. Then, everyone in your social environment will know who is higher and who is lower in the pecking order. Another example concerns Charles and Richard. Charles is popular among the group of students who study economics. Now he keeps company with Alice, a very beautiful and popular girl. When Richard discovers this relationship he constantly tries to impress Alice, although in the past he did not see her as someone to be desired. This is a pure form of mimesis and typical of negative social relationships.

Achterhuis (1988) analyses Hobbes, Locke, and Rousseau, and concludes that Hobbes and Rousseau especially pay much attention to the phenomenon of mimetic rivalry, and that, while Locke takes the phenomenon seriously, he sees Christianity and the possibility of migrating to other areas of the world as possible solutions to the problem (Achterhuis, 1988). The title of the book by Achterhuis, *The Empire of Scarcity*, suggests that mimetic rivalry makes it impossible to ever solve the problem of scarcity.

Girard concludes from his studies that conflicts become increasingly violent if there are no constraints. All cultures in the world, however different they might seem, try to answer the question of how to limit mimetic rivalry. So the function of the oppression or limitation of violence is the prevention of mimetic rivalry. To put it very straightforwardly and simply: if A takes a higher position compared to B, and A stops the battle and does not buy many prestigious goods anymore, B stops as well, since objects are not subject to battles anymore.

Social practices leading to a particular distribution of status must be legitimized; otherwise the social conflict goes on. This means that, on the level of belief and ideology, and on the level of values and attitudes, practices must be justified. There must be broad consensus about the whole of social practice. The outcomes must be in line with other parts of the ideological, religious, and aesthetic components of a particular culture. The whole of moral, religious, and scientific knowledge must have some degree of pervasiveness: people must see it as 'obviously true'. And, lastly, there must be a link between the desire to establish and maintain a particular group-based hierarchy on the one hand, and the endorsement of hierarchy-enhancing or hierarchy-attenuating policies on the other.

As a matter of illustration we have presented an example in Box 13.1.

Rites quite often fulfil the role of virtual mimetic violence; we make a play in which people sacrifice valuable things, or kill an animal or even a person. The play must end in a solution—the prohibition of a next appropriation mimesis. In practice, appropriation mimeses are followed by conflict mimeses, which means that a few persons band together and decide on who is the cause of their internal rivalry. Then this person is thrown out. By sacrificing this enemy or *scapegoat* internal peace is restored again. When reading the history of economic thought, including the history of the institutions of the communities of economists, the functioning of the scapegoat mechanism is obvious. In the first seventy years of the previous century, American Institutionalists were typical scapegoats. For most economics students, their work was not allowed to be part of the official curricula. During the 1980s and 1990s radical economics and post-Keynesian economics were slowly pushed off the educational and research agendas. Nowadays, neoclassical

---

BOX 13.1 EUROPEAN UNION AND RIVALRY

After the Second World War six West European countries decided to cooperate more closely, economically as well as politically. Two related reasons played an important role. First, a social reason: let the Germans and the French stop their mutual rivalry, which has created a whole series of wars. Second, in line with Keynes' ideas, let's make our enemy our trading partner. In other words, create a common market rather than a common social and military battlefield. The two ideas are strongly related to each other. As long as there is rivalry, there will not be a common market. If we solve the social problem, a common economy might become possible. During the second part of the previous century there was consensus about the building of a common economy, although complete harmonization was not necessary.

Now we are in a severe economic crisis, while the members of the EU have become quite interdependent. Economically speaking, a common macro-policy is desirable and increase in the effective government investment demand is needed. Unfortunately, European politicians from Germany and the Netherlands constantly stress the necessity of cuts in government expenditures. They say that this will lead to lower debts, although all economic history says the opposite: in a depression cuts have a negative effect on the growth of the volume of production, implying lower tax revenues. This economically disastrous policy might be based on a hidden political agenda. The Germans might be trying to become less dependent on Southern Europe by making themselves even more competitive on the world market. In this way they try to remain the strongest economy in Europe. The Dutch might think: we just follow the Germans, which is economically and politically the best strategy for us. Recently, the classical liberal Dutch prime minister stated that the European Union must not be seen as a solution to German–French rivalry, or to an eventual rivalry between North and South. It's just an attempt to create a common market, so as to profit from economies of scale for all the members of the Union.

Now we have two different stories about the EU, expressing two different legitimation myths, and resulting in two very different strategies. For the Dutch classical liberal prime minister the ideal economic order is a capitalist system with a relatively small government. So, expenditure cuts, although economically disastrous, lead us to a small government in the end. Basically, social rivalry does not exist in the framework of interpretation of classical liberals. This makes the existence of a welfare state 'unnecessary'.

economics rules the economics faculties, not only in the Anglo-Saxon world, but increasingly also in Continental Europe. Even after the financial crisis of 2008, also caused by the neoclassical dogmas, there is no strong drive to write better textbooks, which offer an overview of different approaches. The legitimizing myth is still the neoclassical and new institutional economic story about the economic and rational actor and the stability of systems of free markets.

We will finish this section on social psychological explanations with a presentation of *psycho-analytical feminism*, which is an approach to society that starts with the way children are brought up. In primitive societies, characterized by hunting and gathering, men were hunters and fighters and the women were the gatherers of edible plants and the protectors of children. Men were physically stronger, and therefore dominant towards women. This meant that the respective systems of governance were also characterized by *patriarchy*. So, during the first period of their life children were particularly in the company of women. Later, they became more integrated in society—a patriarchal society. In the process of socialization children are inclined to become an independent individual, who is recognized by relevant others as such. Male children are inclined to distance themselves from the mother and choose the side of the father when becoming more integrated in society. Female children develop mixed feelings about the mother role, and therefore about themselves. This means that male domination is maintained.

In modern society this has led to a *controlling attitude* towards people and nature. Modern science has become a principal weapon in this respect. Physical strength has become less important, and modern warfare needs mentally strong men, who are able to use sophisticated technologies. The typical male strategy is that of 'divide and rule' rather than create opportunities to talk and search for common interests. By suggesting differences, males try to set a norm. In USA culture the norm is still a white, young, Protestant Christian, and financially secure male. When institutionalizing a capitalist profit economy, the production process needs outsiders—older, coloured, female—as *surplus people*. In periods of expansion they can be hired in part-time and temporary jobs. In periods of recession and depression they can easily be fired.

In our section on modernity and postmodernity we saw that the modern society has increasingly become a risk society. The modern scientific body of knowledge appears less solid and objective than modern scholars always assumed. It is as if they looked at the universe from a god's-eye view: independent from the object of research. Increasingly, social scientists admit that knowledge is a human construction. Psychological and sociological factors play a role, even in case of learning mathematics and physics. This also means that the whole idea of women playing the role of the mother figure and men playing the role of father figure, and the idea of patriarchy, are human constructions, rather than it being natural to have patriarchal institutions. In a sophisticated and postmodern society different ideas must be analysed and considered. The one and only modern building must be deconstructed, and more and different bodies of knowledge must be constructed; especially constructions on the basis of the essential equality of man and woman.

13.2.2.3 Social-Structural Explanations

In this subsection we will discuss a few *elite theories* and the evolutionary approach to see what they have to say about the nature of group hierarchies.

The *social position approach* says that social structure is always hierarchical and oligarchic, and that the position of a group in the ranking determines its power and influence. All groups strive for dominance, and the highest-ranked group—the elite—tries to control the hierarchy of groups as a whole. Marx developed an economic theory upon the basis of the idea of elites, but assumed that a world without private property of productive resources would mean the end of human rivalry. As long as there is private property of productive means, markets imply an exchange of goods between unequals, which necessarily leads to exploitation. Pareto, however, disagreed with Marx and stated that even in societies without productive private property the leaders of the so-called proletariat would be the elite in the communist society.

Michels developed an elite theory, which is called a neoclassical elite theory. Effective organizations are characterized by a sophisticated system of labour division. It implies much power for the leadership of those organizations. Persons who are part of the leadership become full-time officials, and are constantly looking for partner-leaders who belong to the same network. They stimulate each other to create ever-bigger organizations, which is called *megalomania*. A mission drift takes place, where the original mission is replaced by the survival of the organization in an environment of organizations which all tend to grow as fast as possible. The selection of particular types of leaders is called '*the iron law of Michels*'.

Another neoclassical elite theory comes from Pareto. Like Michels he states that all social systems are inherently undemocratic and ruled by elites, which rationalize their power by using a system of *justifying ideologies*. Persons with particular personalities fit elite positions better than persons with other personalities. Like all people elites are driven by non-logical (= non-economic-rational) forces, especially the *drive to dominate others*.

There is not much difference between Michels and Pareto. For economists it is remarkable that the father of orthodox welfare economics has developed an elite theory which is based on completely different assumptions. His economics was of an axiomatic character, and his idea of an economic and rational (in Pareto's terminology: logical) actor leads to an economic world which might be characterized by perfect efficiency (Pareto-equilibrium). For him it was just an isolated abstraction, modelling the so-called economic force; not a representation of the real world. In his sociological theory he states that the real world is ruled by non-logical (= non-economic-rational) forces, always creating elites which rule the world.

At last, the evolutionary theory discusses the role of rivalry as part of the *human drive to survive*. As we saw in Chapter 6, evolutionary economics uses a Darwinian selection process, in which people constantly adapt to their environment. Only the fittest—best-adapted—people survive. The question is, however, whether individuals or groups do adapt to their environment. Survival can be threatened in many ways. Moreover, the question what must survive is also relevant. So, if there is hunger and thirst, people are physically in danger, and individuals can compete or cooperate with each other to solve their economic problem. But people can also compete with each other, or show solidarity with each other, so as to survive in terms of social status. So, one of the strategies might be the formation of a strong group, which can defeat others and take the harvests and the available wells.

The official strategy of the European Union means that European solidarity is the best guarantee to survival in the long term; a strategy that is focused on *group-inclusive fitness*. This choice is, to a certain extent at least, typical for European civilization, in contrast to the primitive reaction: attack the other, dominate them, and let 'them' do the hard and dirty work for 'us'.

13.3 **Economic Sociology**

13.3.1 INTRODUCTION

Economic sociology is the sociology of the economy, one of the important societal sectors. Classical sociology has laid the theoretical foundations for this type of research. In contrast to orthodox economics, the foundations in economic sociology are of a macro-orientation. In Chapter 11 we briefly discussed the contributions by the neo-Marxians Lukacs and Gramsci as well as by the neo-Weberian Fligstein.

Piore (1996) considers Polanyi (1944) to be the most important economic sociologist of the post-classical period. In his *The Great Transformation of Industrial Society* he makes a distinction between two principles of socio-economic order, or two opposite sides of human endeavour. The first is the market and the human desire for *material well-being*. The second is the human drive for *purpose and meaning*. Human achievement is dependent upon stable and cohesive social relations. According to Piore, unstable markets, such as the markets for labour, land, and financial resources, undermine the *social fabric* that gives meaning to people's lives.

When looking at Europe Piore makes a distinction between three stages of historical development of industrial society.

The first stage is the period 1800–1850, characterized by social stability, decreasing institutional constraints, and the emergence of free markets.

The second stage is the period 1850–1914, in which social forces gradually reinforce themselves through political struggles. The establishment of the first unions and the socialist claims for democracy are examples in this respect.

The third stage is the period 1914–1945, in which social forces strongly react against the instabilities of the free markets. The communist revolution in Russia (1917) and the fascist revolution in Germany (1933) are the most remarkable events in this case.

When we extend his analysis and typify the post-war period, we see that 1945–1980 is characterized by a reinstitutionalization of the market economy. The most important legislation necessary for this process had already begun, in the 1930s. After the Second World War, the welfare state was built.

From 1980–2008 we see again a period of deregulation—of financial as well as of labour markets. As we all know, the system of free financial markets created a large bubble, with many people, including many large banks, bearing an unbearable debt burden. Now the important question is whether social forces are strong enough to get the financial and labour markets reregulated. In the political debates there is some attention to the legislative rules necessary for stable financial markets. With respect to the labour markets many economists plea for more deregulation, making labour markets more flexible. But this advice will not contribute to the stability of our economic system; on the contrary.

In contrast to orthodox economics Piore approaches behaviour as a process. There is no outcome or equilibrium, no beginning and no end. It is a process of creation and learning, and it generates interpretation and meaning, which directs the process. Stories capture the identity of actors and institutions, which evolve over time. According to Piore we can frame the problem of economic sociology now as follows: search for an economic system that fulfils the necessary requirements for markets as well as for social stability and cohesion.

Before we discuss the work of a few economic sociologists, we want to make a critical remark about the idea of process. Adherents to this idea always interpret economic or social logic as the opposite; as something which is wrong. But this is not true. Analyses based on economic logic, for instance, assume the existence of an economic force (Chapter 4). Over time the strength of this force can change: from weak to strong, for instance. If so, we can only understand change if we first have established what is subject to a process of change. This is the case with every concept: the definition of it stresses its essence, while its properties can change all the time. The essence exists until the phenomenon, caught by the concept, does not exist anymore, and is assumed to never return again. Another example might clarify this even better. A particular phenomenon can be conceptualized as 'grey'. We can define it by saying that it is a combination of black and white. Now there can be a process that increasingly makes the colour of a particular good, let's take a sweater, lighter grey. Now we can interpret this process in terms of black and white: the colour of the sweater contains ever more white. But without the idea of grey being a combination of white and black we cannot describe the process that is going on. So with the principles of Polanyi: if social forces become stronger in particular periods, while the strength of the economic force is decreasing, we cannot describe processes without exactly knowing what we mean by economic force and social force. Economic logic and social logic exactly offer us a definition and analysis of the operation of a force in isolation. Definition as well as property are human constructions. Of course, it is possible to change definition during processes of change, if the constructor thinks that a different definition is a better one. But it is very important to be aware of such a shift when interpreting descriptions of processes of change.

13.3.2 NEW ECONOMIC SOCIOLOGY

Swedberg (1994: 255) makes a *sociological analysis of markets*: 'markets as social structures'. Most laymen interpret the concept of market in a strict economic way. The quest for economic gain will definitely be an important motive for people to work, and to save and invest. But the typical sociological approach also makes sense. Households, firms, governments, and markets can be considered as social structures, having their own mechanisms of coordination and distribution. People group together and form organizations, which operate on markets. Everywhere people group together they are inclined to form social structures: horizontal and vertical relationships between positions, each having a particular role. Economists explain vertical relationships—hierarchies—in terms of transaction costs. Sociologists are referring to the drive of people to *dominate* the other, and to have control over the other. Large companies have more power, and therefore people want to see their organization grow, whether it is profit maximizing or not. The leadership of an organization especially gains in prestige, and therefore their salaries grow faster compared with salaries in smaller organizations.

Granovetter (1985) discusses the phenomenon of *embeddedness* in case of economic actions within social structures. We can understand this idea as follows. The psychic and the social force affect human behaviour like the economic force is doing. All these forces lead to the formation of institutions, which are the context or framework within which all actions take place—including the actions in the real-life economy.

It means that markets as a subject matter are not the playing field of economists only. Psychologists and sociologists also deal with important aspects of human behaviour on markets. We will discuss Fligstein's theory of fields in more detail, to illustrate the way in which the sociology of markets makes sense.

Fligstein (2001) calls his approach a political/cultural approach. The analysis starts with a few actors who make plans to produce a particular product, because their research has shown that there are many potential customers for it. Maybe there is just one actor who simply starts the production of that good, and tries to sell it. Later other firms imitate him, and so we can speak of a market. But as soon as there is a producer the question arises whether or not it is allowed to start a particular production process. It might cause negative effects for others. And so the government steps in and formulates a number of conditions under which that particular production process is allowed. The producer(s) are inclined to go to the government agency that is responsible for this market to consult and negotiate and try to convince the civil servants of the general interest of their product and its production. Over time, regular face-to-face contact between producers and the civil servants who are responsible for the necessary legal framework, leads to a *common understanding of the situation*. This common interpretation implies consensus about the rules of the game. For instance, if there are new entrants—foreign competitors, who are not familiar with the informal customs, for instance—the established producers might develop a policy that hampers the actions of the challengers.

Fligstein makes a distinction between *incumbents* and *challengers*. The incumbents are the insiders, who cooperate with each other in their policy towards the challengers. Only if the challengers show their commitment to the culture of the market, and accept a more subordinate position, might they be allowed to produce and sell on that particular market. Otherwise they are constantly attacked by the incumbents, until they leave the market. These sorts of attacks are executed in many ways: creating bad news about the newcomers by suggesting that they ignore local culture (1), physical barriers across the entrance of offices and factories of the challengers (2), espionage with respect to important firm secrets (3), robbery (4), threats towards the top managers, for instance by accusing them of illegal activities (5).

The whole of the market and the government agencies that are involved in the institutionalization of it is called 'the field'. The main goal of the incumbent players is the creation of *stability*, since a stable market is the best guarantee of survival and growth.

The culture of the market consists of a common understanding and the rules that are derived from it.

So far the story is about one particular market. But, during history, market economies have gone through a series of stages. They always begin with a few markets, where people from different communities meet each other in their search for profitable trades. In this way local cultures affect each other, thereby forming, to a certain degree at least, a regional or even national culture. In some countries, unions, representing the labour force, begin to play an important role in the process of culture formation. In other countries it takes more time for workers to establish their unions. The same holds for the development of a government apparatus: in some countries we see a sophisticated government growing faster than in other countries. This cultural difference in the early stages of development of markets appears very persistent over time. In the USA economic policy is highly affected by firm lobbies. In Europe unions and politicians play a significant role in the formulation and reformulation of economic policy. Fligstein distinguishes four types of rules.

(1) Property rights; every good or service must have an owner or a group of owners; there must be an institution, which is responsible for the enforcement of this rule.
(2) Governance structure; expressing which positions are authorized to fulfil which role. If persons fulfil their role badly they undermine the authority that belongs to that particular position. This reduces the legitimacy of the actions of that person, and of the authority of that particular position.
(3) Rules of exchange; making clear who is responsible for the correct execution of the transaction; if IKEA has outsourced the transport of a good, and the organizer has outsourced the actual execution of the ride, including the transport of the good from the car into the house of the customer, for the customer especially it is important to know at what moment he becomes responsible for the good that must be delivered.
(4) Conceptions of control; representing the ways in which particular situations are understood. In Europe we saw that the *stakeholders' view* dominated the strategies of the firms for a long time: 1945–1980. During this period, profits were squeezed and the labour movement had a powerful representation, leading to the building up of costly welfare systems. During the period 1980–2008, the *shareholder view* gained ground, which can be interpreted as a coup by the capitalists, who wanted to become the dominant party again. So with the conceptions of control of governments in their role of the management of a country. In the period 1945–1980 European policies were a mix of Keynesian and Beveridgean policies. After 1980, however, the neoclassical and monetarist views began to dominate the political scene. Although we all face the negative effects of the free market system nowadays, European politicians, under heavy pressure of the Germans, stick to neoclassical and monetarist thinking.

When we compare the way *financial sociology* is analysing the market for corporate control with the typical financial economics approach we see the following difference. The economic analysis states that capitalists, such as investment funds, hedge funds, and private equity, force firms to deploy their assets 'properly'. If the profitability of capital is not maximized, the funds buy shares in order to force boards to change their strategies. In this approach labour and society as a whole are given particular functions—they must serve the ambitions of capital: maximization of its profitability. Otherwise capital flows to more profitable areas. According to the sociological analysis, however, control by financial institutions makes a firm vulnerable to *financial manipulation*. For instance, hedge funds spread bad news about a particular firm, with the effect that share prices drop. Then a fund buys a package of shares and exercises pressure upon the administration of the firm to change its strategy in the direction of short-term shareholder value. Therefore, it has to be restructured and many workers are fired. The new leadership makes deals with the government agencies responsible for this segment of society about the rules of the game. If they succeed they sell the shares after a couple of years with a large capital gain.

The new economic sociology is characterized by its emphasis on the organization's drive to survive and its attempts to reduce its resource dependence (Swedberg, 2003). In this approach there is an important role for the use of power compared with the typical economic focus on competition. Capital, labour, and government struggle for control over the organization of a firm or market, so as to determine how the organization will survive, and on which terms. The neoclassical picture of competitive markets, in which governments are protecting property rights, and are maintaining competition and other rules of the game, is replaced by a picture where powerful organizations, quite often in cooperation with governments, are able to change the rules of the competitive game to their advantage.

In Section 13.3.3 we will discuss an economic-sociological approach, which stresses the role of culture.

13.3.3 CULTURE MATTERS

Culture is at its strongest when people are not aware of it, and see the cultural representations as natural (Bauman, 1990). People from a classical liberal background have learned to see individuals rather than groups. They consider individual freedom as something natural, and lack of individual freedom as oppression. A homeless person is considered as a person who chose to leave his home, and apparently prefers to live without any responsibility. People with an orthodox religious background are able to see God's intervention in so many things, while atheists simply don't see it. Orthodox economists are able to establish a natural unemployment rate, a natural interest rate, and a natural wage rate. It implies that they know when the actual rates deviate from the natural ones, and governments apparently have intervened too much. In other words, a global free market is the natural state of the world, including small governments, which protect natural property rights. If there is a severe economic crisis, maybe governments should intervene temporarily. But a structural solution can only mean a smaller government without debts.

In sociology there is no support for this view. Sociology is about rival groups, where group membership is not voluntary most of the time. On the basis of unconscious images of Self and society people develop—group-wise—their preferences, attitudes, and opinions. So *culture helps to frame choice-situations*, in which people can make their cost/benefit analyses. In other words, culture determines what people consider as costs and what they experience as benefits. In case of problems they become aware of their routines, and they try to solve their problems by changing a couple of routines or norms. If this doesn't help and the problems grow, more fundamental questions are posed—in other words, people become aware of their more basic frameworks of interpretation. The history of labour relations offers many examples of very serious accidents, leading to more fundamental changes. In the Netherlands it was a railroad strike (1903), and in Sweden it was a series of bloody fights between workers and the police in 1938, which triggered fundamental changes in the relationship between workers and capitalists. Sociologically speaking, the Dutch and the Swedish systems moved from a conflict society towards a consensus society, with far-reaching positive economic consequences (Magnusson, 2006; Windmuller, 1969).

Neoclassical economics contains the implicit idea that competitive markets, as described in their textbooks, shape the culture of a market society. Free markets function better than regulated markets, and that is the reason why people become increasingly classical liberal. Through experiments it has become clear that economics students are more selfish and short-term orientated than students from other social sciences (Frey and Meier, 2003). Apparently, the field attracts particular personalities and it shapes and justifies particular behaviour.

Di Maggio (1994), however, describes a series of deviations from the typical economic approach, which stresses (short-term) maximization of utilities and profits.

(1) In case of dense social interaction *informal reciprocity* emerges (Homans, 1961).
(2) Every contract between individuals or private organizations has a *non-contractual basis* (Durkheim, 1899): when we sign a contract, we commit ourselves to stick to the conditions as agreed in the contract. In other words, we promise each other not to shirk.
(3) In case of unforeseen emergencies *personal relationships* between the parties involved help solve the problem of the interpretation of the contract.
(4) When a long-term relationship exists between the contract parties, the parties do not only increasingly trust each other, they also develop a *sense of obligation*—a *loyalty* that makes it difficult to constantly look for other parties that might be a little better and cheaper.

Societies are characterized by cultural dimensions, which have existed for many years. This means that current powers cannot change these cultural characteristics overnight, and must respect the consequences. Hofstede (1980) defines culture as *mental programming*, a process that takes place in early childhood. He distinguishes between culture, human nature, and personality. Culture is learned—not inherited. Human nature refers to the universal level in someone's mental software, inherited from his genes, which is the operating system that determines the potential physiological and psychological functioning. It is about the human ability to feel fear, anger, love, and sadness, about the need to associate with others, to play and exercise, and about the facility to observe the environment and talk about it with other humans. The personality of an individual can be conceptualized as a unique set of mental programmes, with traits that are partly inherited and partly learned. While culture is very important for every organization, personality is especially relevant when selecting managers for positions at the top. Here leaders can make a difference and influence corporate culture significantly. Kets de Vries (2006) shows that narcissistic personalities especially reach the top, to the detriment of the organization as a whole.

Culture expresses itself by means of symbols (symbolic interactionism). For instance, words, gestures, pictures, or objects carry a particular meaning, which is only recognized by those who share that particular culture. Every culture has its heroes: persons who possess characteristics that are highly praised and who serve as role models. Culture maintenance takes place by means of rituals: collective activities, which are technically and economically superfluous, but socially essential. Examples of rituals are the way people greet each other and pay respect to each other, and social and religious ceremonies. Again, they are visible to everyone, but only understood by the insiders. Cultures frame the world in which people live. The choice of values and strategies are derived from this frame, even if a person is not aware of his frame. In the economic culture of the USA, wealth inequality, unemployment, and poverty do not have so much priority as in Continental Europe. In the Anglo-Saxon world it is all about government debt, when analysing the current crisis. Social problems are ignored most of the time. In Continental Europe, however, the social conflict plays an important role in analyses of non-economic experts.

Hofstede (1980) did research on cultural differences between countries by taking data sets, which were constructed by interviewing employees of the computer firm IBM all over the world. He constructed four dimensions, which he saw as characteristic for culture.

(1) *Power distance*: the distance between the different hierarchical layers is large or small according to the perception of the dominant as well as the subordinate level. Eastern cultures appear to have more power distance than Western cultures. But if we go from the Netherlands to Belgium we sense a cultural shock: the typical Belgian organization has significantly more power distance than the typical Dutch organization.

(2) *Individualism versus collectivism*: in some cultures people think in terms of *we* rather than in terms of 'I'. For instance, a Japanese person sees himself as more Japanese than a Danish person sees himself as Danish. People from individualist countries have fewer problems with working in a multicultural environment, and prefer a more personal approach rather than a 'one size fits all' approach.

(3) *Femininity versus masculinity*: femininity refers to a holistic view on nature, including human nature. Persons operate on the basis of the idea that their personality can only grow in an atmosphere of cooperation and solidarity rather than competition and rivalry. Masculinity refers to a world-view where persons think in terms of control; especially the control of the group over its physical and social environment. Social conflicts are difficult to solve in masculine societies. Mediterranean countries are more masculine than Northern European countries, which have been able to solve their social conflict to a certain extent.

(4) *Uncertainty avoidance*: in some areas of the world history shows many violent conflicts, and so institutions of those countries are strongly focused on the prevention of conflicts, so as to make people feel more secure. In other areas culture is more relaxed with respect to the uncertainties of life. If migration is not an option, strict rules might be an answer to the problem.

Later research showed that East Asia could not be characterized easily by means of the four dimensions discussed. Bond and Hofstede (1996) developed another dimension that expresses people's inclination to set long-term or short-term goals. So, a fifth dimension had to be added.

(5) *Long-term orientation*: cultures in the West appear short-term orientated, in contrast to Asian cultures.

There is empirical evidence for the proposition that culture matters when explaining economic performance. Keizer (1982) explains, theoretically as well as empirically, that ideology and militancy of important social groups, such as political parties, unions, and employers' organizations significantly contribute to the explanation of wage and price inflation in the Netherlands over the period 1946–1978. Keizer and Spithoven (2009) show empirical evidence for the cultural factor when explaining income distribution in the Netherlands. Keizer and Spithoven (2010) show significant coefficients when relating the difference in economic performance between North and South Europe with different scores on the Hofstede dimensions.

13.3.4 SOCIOLOGY OF LABOUR MARKETS

We can conceptualize a global labour market, and develop statistics, showing its characteristics. As long as there is history, this market shows large unemployment rates and very low wages for many people. The distribution of jobs, wages, and other kinds of rewards, such as working conditions and holidays, has always been very unequal—with strong variation with regard to space and time. Some people are more talented than others, and some people are offered more opportunities to develop their talents than others. Markets coordinate supply of and demand for jobs, which are clusters of tasks. Moreover, market processes lead to the clustering of jobs into *segments* of the labour market. But how do these processes of clustering tasks and jobs actually take place? To answer this question it is important to see these processes not only as economically, but also as socially, driven. Imagine an organization where the personnel as a whole is responsible for the cleaning of offices, including their kitchens and toilets. There are no separate jobs, clustering the cleaning activities. A typical economic approach claims that this is inefficient practice. But many workers might be socially motivated to refuse this idea. A person who is qualified as an executive officer may not be willing to clean the kitchen, if lower-qualified people are eating at that particular moment. But from an economic-sociological point of view this might work out very efficiently. The bosses discover what it means to do low-skilled and low-status work. They also might discover that regular breaks in their management work increase their productivity significantly. It is possible for the vertical relationships to become healthier, and for a true team spirit to emerge.

To reach this stage, important barriers must be overcome. The *difference in status* is especially important. Members of dominant groups don't like to be confronted with members of groups that take a much lower position in the ranking. Everyone wants to interact with people of the same or higher ranking.

The army is an illustrative example in this respect. Many 'workers' enter the army without any specific skills—just some general knowledge at the primary-school level. Others enter the army and get some specific training on a higher level, based on general knowledge at high-school level. Then the highest level: some people get professional education in warfare, and then they enter the army at the highest level of entry. So, there are different segments in the army, and it is extremely difficult to move from one level to a higher level. So with the labour market: only if someone is from Oxford or Cambridge, or from Harvard or Princeton, are particular clusters open for him. These academic institutions are much more than suppliers of knowledge alone. They also teach particular world-views as superior and they do it almost always implicitly. People who study financial economics are taught and mentally programmed to smoothly fit into the financial capitalist system, and have learned to see free markets as the superior economic order, or even the natural order. In the Netherlands there is a social battle going on for decades between universities offering academic education and schools offering higher professional education. Economically, the first is of a higher level. But the second group does not accept the difference in status, and is constantly trying to imitate university practices. Now they also have full professors and PhD students. Their disciplines are called applied sciences, and they suggest that they are doing practically relevant work, while the university staff do some theoretical stuff in a sphere of 'l'art pour l'art'. Reading Kant and Popper leads us to conclude that this view cannot withstand criticism: empirical research without any theoretical tools is impossible. Therefore, we must interpret the battle as of a social nature.

So, mobility within a particular segment is much greater than between segments. The economist Mill has already analysed the phenomenon of non-competing groups. Sociologically, non-competing groups should be called non-rivalling groups. Employers or top managers have an interest in the categorization of the labour market into separate groups according to the principle 'divide and rule'.

Doeringer and Piore (1990) have developed a *segmented labour market theory*. They distinguish between a primary and a secondary market, two segments with different characteristics. The *primary market* offers good working conditions, relatively high wages, and tenures. The *secondary market* offers the opposite: dirty and dangerous working conditions, temporary work, and relatively low wages. The regular business cycles have an impact, especially on the workers in the secondary market. In case of expansion more workers are hired, and in case of recession some of the workers are fired. They form a *buffer*, which makes it profitable for the upper class to limit the losses in bad times. In case of a true depression the same message holds: many people are thrown back into poverty without any educational or health-care service.

In the Third World there is a large gap between the formal and the informal sector, which is the sector of *not-registered activities*. This work is actually black work without any social protection, and abuse of women and children takes place on a regular basis, in line with the rules of the capitalist game: humans are reduced to commodities, and will be bought and sold if the (black) market price leads to profitable business for the mafia.

In Western Europe 'labour' has organized itself in order to develop countervailing power against dehumanization. The union movement has fought for political democracy, economic democracy, and for full employment, fair wages, and a system of social protection. In Northern Europe they have been successful, in contrast to Southern Europe, where employers and workers could not reach a common view on the future. Lack of social peace is still a bottleneck preventing these countries from growing.

Orthodox-neoclassical economists would immediately ask why economic and rational actors leave so much cash on the table. Flexible prices and substitution processes would lead to a complete restructuring of clusters of tasks and jobs. It would mean a closing of the gaps between segments and a significant increase in economic efficiency and profits. Orthodox sociologists would react, however, by arguing that there are social constraints preventing this solution. People are inclined to group together, and to ensure as much distance from lower-ranked groups as possible, preferably also physical distance. They interpret such a result as social efficiency.

13.3.5 SOCIOLOGY OF FINANCIAL MARKETS

Before the introduction of money we had so-called barter economies: goods were traded in exchange for other goods. Some goods appeared to be efficient in functioning as money: silver and gold, for example. Later these metals were increasingly hoarded in the cellars of banks, in exchange for notes and coins or even for checking-deposits.

With the ongoing extension of the realm of markets, more goods were expressed in market value, which could easily be counted in terms of money. Even the value of a human life could be expressed in money and be compared with the value of an ice cream. Money facilitated this process of rationalization, which is so characteristic for a modern society.

It made wealth accumulation easier, and large amounts of debt became a possibility, creating opportunities for people without wealth to take initiatives, to become wealthier.

The growth of money and capital markets have attracted many people who are not interested in borrowing money or capital to finance profitable activities. Their aim is just to become rich by means of speculation. On every market one can speculate on price fluctuations, whether it is the market for shares or bonds, or the market for gold or food. It goes without saying that on some markets speculation is socially more problematic than on other markets. Food price fluctuations create the strongest social unrest, especially in the Third World. But oil price speculation also creates hatred against capitalists and capitalism as a social-economic order.

Analyses of fluctuations in stock and bond prices make it clear that people regularly show *herding behaviour*. If the price of a particular asset begins to rise, many financial investors are inclined to invest in this good: 'apparently well-informed people expect a price increase in the near future; so step in!'

This behaviour can be explained by the typical economic approach: some people think that other people are better informed than they are—so they follow like a herd of sheep. There is also a psychological aspect in herd behaviour. In times of uncertainty especially people are inclined to imitate the behaviour of others. They prefer to make a bad choice like many others, rather than make a bad choice while most others make a good choice. The last result affects self-respect significantly. Finally, there is a sociological aspect with respect to herd behaviour. The prestige of a particular fund is at stake when the fund goes down at a time when most other funds are doing well.

Another point with respect to the social aspect in the financial world is indicated by Warner and Molotch (1993). Every day the world is confronted with an enormous amount of information. Media are constantly spreading news, but have to select relevant from less relevant information. *Selection needs interpretation.* That's the reason why the media can never be objective or neutral towards views and interests.

The Anglo-Saxon press, for instance, is highly affected in its selection by capitalist interests and the views that justify the capitalist system. They dominate the global financial world, and have a huge influence on the texts in the European and Asian press as well. The current crisis is interpreted as a crisis of government debts, while it started as a banking crisis. The governments had to solve the problems created by the deregulated financial markets, and had to operate as a lender of last resort. To defend their belief in the free market system many financial experts took their chance and began to direct their focus to the governments as being the cause of all evil. German and Dutch experts and politicians particularly are the victims of this brainwashing. In Chapter 10 we have seen what a psychological interpretation of 'irrationality' means. Most people are not even aware of their own paradigms and other prejudices which narrow their scope. Instinctively, people protect their axioms of life against criticism by means of a Lakatosian belt.

A last point to be mentioned is related to the phenomenon of *prior knowledge.* Some positions give the persons who occupy such position a lead with respect to relevant information. That makes it tempting for them to use this information to their own advantage. Although it is legally forbidden, many of them use prior knowledge in their decisions to sell or to buy financial assets.

* * *

Now we have discussed the sociology of markets, it is interesting to compare the analysis with a typical economic analysis of markets. According to this view markets are competitive as long as governments do not intervene in the process of price formation. Wages are highly influenced by the marginal labour productivity of the worker. They reflect the scarcity of the labour service and can be seen as something natural. If a worker is paid less than his natural wage, he might go to a competitor, who is willing to pay him a higher wage. In the typical sociological approach, however, wages do not tend to keep to a natural level, and do not express the scarcity of labour services. Instead, they reflect a scarcity that results from a socially created situation. If the institutions that are highly influenced by power relations change, relative prices will change too.

Suppose that irrational socially biased recruiters of a particular firm attract many workers, so as to build up a new organization. Over time these people develop a culture, including a series of norms and routines. Within this institutional framework people are supposed to operate as efficiently as possible. In a later stage new workers must be attracted. For the recruiters the institutional framework is a given, and they search for workers who fit this inefficient framework. In this case it is difficult to attract people who have the highest marginal productivity, as meant by economic analysis.

We can also imagine a researcher who is searching for solutions in a different direction compared with other researchers, who show herding behaviour and constantly adapt to the prevailing institutions of the research community. Very talented people are simply fired or never hired, since they do not fit into particular social groups, which are used to operate within inefficient institutions. Neoclassical economists believe that inefficient institutions will not survive in the competitive struggle. But the sociological reaction is that competitors are subject to the same psychic-social biases, making markets and market economies less efficient.

Actually we also need the development of a *sociological macroeconomics*. Classical sociology offers us a few paradigms, on the basis of which macroeconomic analysis could be developed. The current crisis is much in need of such types of analyses. Only Marx developed an extensive analysis of the capitalist system, and neo-Marxians have improved his analysis with a more important role for culture. Durkheim, Weber, and Parsons have laid important foundations for an economic analysis, but no more than that.

13.3.6 NETWORKS IN ECONOMIC LIFE

In our discussion of networks we have seen that one's position in a network both *empowers and constrains* the person. Connections are based on mutual trust, obligation, and dependence. The *identity* of people is shaped by multiple role settings, which predict attitudes and behaviours.

Granovetter (1985) stresses the strength of weak ties. As we see with LinkedIn, for instance, it is easy to participate, and the network functions more as a website full of economically relevant information. The social aspect—trust, obligation—is relatively weak. That makes the network an effective start for many people who do not belong to networks with strong ties, such as a membership of the Dutch student association 'The Corps', which is full of obligations, but has more meaning for the members.

Also, ethnic economies are characterized by strong ties, mostly running via family lines. So if a person appears to be able to set up a flourishing business in a different country, many family members hope to come over and profit from his initiative (Light and Karageorgis, 1994).

When compared with firms, a network offers less uncertainty reduction and stability. It makes the economy more flexible, but for the persons who are actually all running one-man businesses, it is just a modern way of competing, rivalling and cooperating—a life full of uncertainties.[1] For the economy as a whole, more flexibility always means less stability; a concern for governments.

We can distinguish between several kinds of networks. First, we can distinguish *industrial districts*. They are a form of spatial clustering, making it possible to have frequent face-to-face contact between different types of professionals. To illustrate this issue, we can take the Dutch multinational Philips, which was located in Eindhoven for over a hundred years. It decided to move their headquarters to Amsterdam, to the famous Zuidas. The reason was the desire to be close to prestigious firms which deliver banking, legal, and accounting services. Maybe the proximity of Airport Schiphol played a role as well.

Second, we can distinguish *R&D networks*. Some combinations of scientific disciplines appear successful when they are regularly meeting each other; especially when they are—like industrial districts—located near each other. Face-to-face contact has an important advantage over other ways of contact, such as through digital media. Economic relationships transform more easily into social relationships. It appears that disciplines that cooperate most easily are not necessarily the disciplines that should cooperate with each other from a scientific point of view. This holds especially true for gamma-sciences.

Third, there are *business groups*, aiming at a reduction of competition and of resource dependence (Granovetter, 1994). The cooperation leads to long-term contracts, but also to social elements such as obligation and reciprocity. Most of the time the group has a strict financial control system, to serve its long-term interests.

Lastly, we can distinguish *strategic alliances*, such as the merger between KLM and Air France—aimed to curb potential opportunism. Most of the time the cooperation starts at some point and, in case of success, the contract is repeated and extended.

---

[1] Today's universities have been transformed into networks. A number of scientists who share a room might not have any meaningful communication, while being in each other's space quite often. But every scientist is almost permanently in contact with other members of their network, who have their area somewhere in the world. A negative externality is the lack of coherence of the educational programmes.

We will end this subsection with a critique by Fevre (2003) on the new economic sociology. He criticizes the new economic sociology for its focus on the idea of norms serving the promotion of economic ends. Historically, we observe periods of markets becoming increasingly free, followed by periods in which markets are becoming increasingly institutionalized. In terms of morality we see that free markets lead to an increase in vice, perversion, crime, and starvation. According to Sennett (1998), they even lead to the corrosion of character. Firms with demoralized top managers and workers show a bad economic performance. To improve the results of the firm, different approaches can be applied to improve the discipline of the top and of the workers that must execute the orders of the managers. Taylor developed the so-called *scientific management approach*, in which all necessary actions of the workers are spelled out and closely monitored. Humans are considered to be extensions of their machines, and should perfectly adjust to the conditions necessary for excellent economic results. Later we look at the so-called *human relations school*, which tries to manipulate workers in a more sophisticated way. Humans are considered as defective and malleable. In this approach programmes are developed to increase morale in a demoralized world, thereby making the firm more productive. Fevre wants to make a clear difference between forms of manufactured morality or culture, which have an instrumental character, on the one hand (he calls it *ersatz morality*), and *genuine morality* on the other.

Genuine principles of morality are of an ontological character, which are not dependent on the situation. They refer to universal human rights, as already formulated by Kant. Applied to the economy, they set norms for a minimum of decency with respect to wage levels and working conditions. Many labour conditions do not meet the standards as formulated by the ILO (the UN International Labour Organization). When applying genuine moral principles, labour productivity does not necessarily rise; on the contrary, often this negatively impacts the productivity of the firm. Only if all or most firms apply these principles, will the productivity of the economy as a whole increase.

Fevre calls his approach 'the new sociology of economic behaviour'. In Figure 13.1 we have presented his critique.

Now we will briefly summarize Chapters 11, 12, and 13 in a methodological assessment of sociology for economists, and explain why we end this chapter with a last section on the so-called social world.

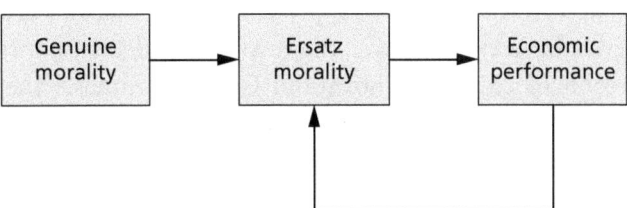

Figure 13.1 Fevre's Different Types of Morality

13.4 **Methodological Assessment**

In the first place, we have seen that during the second half of the 19th century and the first half of the 20th century economics diverged increasingly from (economic) sociology. While sociology continued its search for satisfying explanations of the functioning of the real-life economy, isolated economics itself, to an increasing extent, from sociological and psychological influences. This isolation did not only take place on the level of analysis, but also in terms of persons. Economists such as Weber and Parsons were excluded from the economics community, while sociologists and political philosophers, such as Walras and Pareto, were included, because some of their analyses were typical of economic orthodoxy.

This divergence is responsible for the lack of debate between the two disciplines. Chapters 11, 12, and 13 give a review of the results of sociological development, while Chapters 4 and 5 gave us an overview of the developments within orthodox economics. In sociology these debates were fruitful and led to increasing consensus between the different approaches. Functionalism adapted to critique from conflict theorists, and increasingly took the possibility of disequilibria, the role of power, and the necessity of empirical application into account. The conflict theoreticians increasingly took into account the role of ideology and culture. Moreover, sociological development shows a convergence between micro- and macro-approaches. Network analysis especially delivers a structure that makes it possible to show the interrelationship between the two extreme levels of analysis.

An important element in the micro-macro problem is the so-called agency-structure problem. In economics this problem is solved by assuming that the agent is the economic and rational actor, and the structure is that of the (competitive) market. Both elements are considered to be constant, which are not realistic assumptions. In sociology the problem is solved by assuming that agent as well as structure is the result of action on the basis of a particular understanding of the situation. Compared with orthodox economics we come to the conclusion that human nature might change because of a change in the understanding of the situation. In other words, if the framework of interpretation changes, it might lead to a change in human nature, which triggers a change in human behaviour. Since every structure is a configuration of positions, occupied by humans, it changes in case of a change in the framework of interpretation.

In the second place, in the historical approach different stories are told about the way human societies have evolved over the years. The idealist approach interprets progress as the result of cultural innovation. Girard's mimesis theory is the best example in this respect. Solution to the problem of human rivalry opens the door for peaceful solidarity, cooperation, and competition between persons, organizations, and countries, with ever-growing prosperity as a result. The materialist approach interprets progress as the result of technical innovation. Lenski's technological evolutionism is the best example in this respect. Both types of innovation lead to more knowledge, and to a Malthusian growth of the population. Growing population, together with growing prosperity, increases the demand for space. Migration of some people to other areas is one solution. But most people prefer to group together for reasons of existential anxiety, and accept the disadvantages of growing interdependence. According to Elias this will lead to more and tighter social constraints, which require more self-control; in other words, civilization. So, people must pay a price, but ever-growing prosperity by applying cultural and technical knowledge is the goal. On the basis of modern scientific tools, Western cultures especially appeared to be able to build a huge System, based on formal rationality. Without explicit recognition of the psychological and sociological context within which economic processes are embedded, this System can only be interpreted as a great tool that makes us rich. However, when we take psycho-social processes into account, the effects of the building of the modern System might turn out to be a nightmare. There is not only a problem of imperfect information, but also of different goals when constructing systems. According to Functionalists, the main problem is the large number of specializations that must cooperate well in order to build a huge system. But according to (social) conflict theorists the various groups want to dominate other groups, also by means of control of the System.

Now we live in a postmodern period, in which the fallibility of modern systems is recognized. One reason for the increasing risks is the fallibility of technical knowledge; the problems in the production of nuclear energy are illustrative. A second reason has to do with the unreliability of human behaviour; again the production of nuclear energy is a very good example.

In the third place, psychological sociology shows us that social relationships have a psychological foundation. In Chapter 4 we have seen that one category of emotions or drives was the economic motivation. In Chapter 10 we have seen that another category of emotions was the psychic motivation or drive to have as much self-respect as possible. So far, in this chapter, we have discussed what sociology has to offer economists. They seriously try to be realistic in their analyses and theories, in contrast to orthodox economists, who focus on just one aspect of human behaviour. On the basis of this overview we can conclude that sociologists, like economists, cannot resist the temptation to explain real life by means of a partial analysis most of the time. In some cases there is true multidisciplinarity. For instance, Bourdieu's four types of capital, are economic, social, cultural, and symbolic capital, and it would be great to develop four partial analyses based on these concepts. For economic capital we can simply copy an economics textbook. Social and cultural capital must be considered as investments, necessary to produce economic and symbolic capital. We have seen that Bourdieu has forgotten to mention psychic capital, which is the value a person attaches to himself. So if economists and psychologists are offering these partial analyses of economic and psychic capital respectively, there is a place for sociologists who develop a partial analysis of symbolic capital. This idea is in line with contributions of classical sociologists, such as Weber and Parsons. Weber made a distinction between different types of action, among them actions focused on status or prestige. Parsons made a distinction between different aspects, among them the social aspect, which is related to the ranking of different groups. Habermas and Girard are contemporary sociologists, who construct a particular meaning for the term 'social', which does not just refer to society at large, or to all sorts of relationships between humans. Habermas has developed a theory of communication, in which this concept is defined as exchange of information between humans, essentially meant as an exchange of symbols. Communication is about recognition and respect, or about the absence of it. Girard interprets every human action as a matter of mimesis. In other words, life is about the rivalry between humans, as members of hierarchically ranked groups. At last we see that, in the new economic sociology of markets, the idea of superior versus inferior, or incumbents versus challengers, is the central element in its analyses.

Therefore, we will end up our treatment of sociology with Section 13.5, focusing on what we call 'the social world'. Here we will present an analysis in which the social motivation of individuals is the foundation of typical micro- and typical macro-sociology. The sociology of the social world is an aspect-science; not an attempt to explain the daily reality of human relationships. It goes without saying that the analysis of the social world must be integrated with the analyses of the economic and the psychic world. Only then have we developed a theoretical instrument, which might function as a foundation for empirical research.

13.5 **The Social World**

13.5.1 INTRODUCTION

In Chapter 10 we have seen that human persons are motivated to survive and to manifest themselves. In this manifestation approach economics is about the scarce resources needed to reach this goal. Sociology should focus on the manifestation of the Self to other humans. Social behaviour must be defined as the constant flow of signals to other persons and groups about one's position in the hierarchical ranking, reflecting the status of the actor. It makes sociology into an aspect-science, in the same way we made psychology into an aspect-science.

To explain the concept 'social' more extensively we first sketch an *original state* of mankind, so as to find a starting point for human social relationships. This sketch is meant to give us a general ontology, from which we can derive a typical social ontology. The original state is a *core family*, consisting of a father, a mother, and a number of children. This core family lives within the context of its extended family. The task of the father figure is to protect the family against external threat and to hunt for food. The task of the mother figure is to take care of the children and to protect them against other sorts of threat. Children must learn how to live their life from their surrounding adults, primarily the father and the mother. It is love and fear that keeps family members together; love to prevent loneliness, fear of not finding food, drink, and shelter, fear of the threats of nature (wild animals, poisonous plants, dangerous landscapes and rivers), and fear of other groups of humans. In this world humans try to survive and are inclined to manifest themselves in particular ways. In the social world they are inclined to manifest their selves especially to members of relevant groups of humans who might be enemies. This social manifestation aims at the acquisition of recognition or status. As economics explains human behaviour by focusing on the economic aspect, and models the human drive in terms of maximization of utilities through the consumption of goods, so sociology focuses on the social aspect, and must model the human drive in terms of maximization of status.

In the chapter on orthodox economics we have explained the meaning of the research strategy of isolated abstraction. We distinguish between three worlds, namely the economic, the psychic, and the social world. The economic world is based on the idea of an economic, rational, and non-social actor. The psychic world is based on the idea of a non-economic, non-social, and imperfectly rational actor. In this chapter we discuss the characteristics of the social world, which is based on the idea of the non-economic, non-rational, and social actor.

13.5.2 THE BASIC AXIOMS OF THE SOCIAL WORLD

Our construction of the so-called social world is meant to model the operation of the social force.[2] So we must exclude the other two primary forces, namely the economic force and the psychic force. Therefore, we assume that all actors have solved their economic problem and live in affluence. Increase in the amount of resources does not lead to an increase in economic utilities anymore. In other words, it is not economically efficient to put more effort into productive activities. We also assume that all actors have solved their psychic problem, and act perfectly rationally.

A different construction, which might be a better one, is the assumption of the absence of the ratio, which is the capacity to be rational. Then we are just driven by forces, and behave accordingly, without any intervention of an entity or authority inside the human mind that says: 'wait a minute, is this action in my long-term interest?' We choose to sketch a primitive model of the social world, in which actors have not developed their rational capacity. Then we introduce the idea of growing rationality as the outcome of a social learning process.[3] By abstracting from the economic problem, our analysis will be focused completely on the operation of the social force, and the increasing control of it.

---

[2] Evidence of the social force being strong is given by Sidanius and Pratto (1999).
[3] Max Weber interpreted history as a process of rationalization. In his interpretation rationality is not only linked to persons, but also to social systems, including society as a whole.

13.5.3 THE TECHNIQUE OF PRODUCING STATUS IN THE SOCIAL WORLD

In our sketch of the original state we see that humans are just social beings. They live group-wise, and identify themselves as a member of a group. The basic group is the core family, living within the context of an extended family. It is here that a child tries to get his recognition; first from the mother figure, and later from the father figure. When the child becomes an adolescent, she tries to get recognition from friends, and from teachers and other adults who play an important role in her life. In this way social patterns emerge: horizontal and vertical relationships. In this pattern of groups we distinguish between people of the same group with the same level of status, and people of a higher and of a lower group, having a higher and lower level of status, respectively.

As long as the groups are small the status cannot be very high, and people who are highly esteemed in a large group are ranked higher relative to people who are highly esteemed in a relatively small group.[4] This is the social reason why there is an inherent tendency towards the *formation of ever-larger groups*. If a couple of families live in one and the same area, there are two social tendencies. On the one hand there is *rivalry* between the groups in terms of status. Regularly, there is a clash between the two groups, to see which group is the better one and thus requires more recognition and status. On the other hand, there is a tendency of the stronger one to *take over authority* of the other group, and to unite both groups under its own leadership.[5] History shows a development from family to tribe to nation to supranational bodies. This is the outcome of a continuing process of the grouping and ranking of people.

The process of grouping is meant to make persons uniform and homogeneous in a particular respect. This homogeneity is necessary for relevant others to identify the group, and for the group to acquire respect and status from other group(s). This acquisition refers to the process of ranking: social status cannot be given to a group by the group itself; only by the opponent. We will illustrate this by means of an example from the world of science. A few private universities in the USA have become very rich and famous. The various faculties profit from this, irrespective the scientific quality of their output. These universities are famous because scientists from other universities, including from Europe, attach prestige to these universities. So, if, for instance, the Economics Faculty of Harvard University changes its research policy, other economics faculties throughout the world are inclined to imitate this change, irrespective of whether it increases the quality of the output or not.

---

[4] In the real world the size of the group is just one of the determinants of the level of status. Economic importance of the activities of the group is another one.

[5] If groups are firms our analysis is basically the sociology of external organization, and explains the processes of mergers and acquisitions as well as processes of rivalling opponents out of the arena (where economic analysis is about out-competing competitors and expelling them from the market). A topical example is the strategy of Russia to build a new 'Soviet Union'.

13.5.4 US VERSUS THEM

Behaviour is social behaviour, which means that all actions are meant to communicate to relevant others that the communicator is prestigious. Politically relevant distinctions are the rivalry between males and females, between seniors and youngsters, and between ethnically or religiously different groups. In the rivalry between countries differences in wealth, size of the population, and military strength are important indicators of difference in status. On the micro level of the small groups, clothes and other products are effective means of identification. Experts in advertising know exactly the sensitivities of the different generations and different classes: the yuppies, the aristocrats, the punks, and the rappers, for example.

Some memberships are natural, like the membership of groups based *on race, age, and sex*. Other memberships, like that of a political party or golf club, are more voluntary, although social pressure can be strong. But every member of every group has an interest in a certain degree of homogeneity within the group. A group can only be socially powerful if it can be identified quite easily. Cohesion of the group is maintained by a strong sense of internal solidarity and loyalty. It means that it is costly for the group to have many deviants. To avoid *deviation* a well-functioning group is characterized by strong *social control*. Those who do not exactly underscore the axioms of the group culture are forced to adjust. If the deviant behaviour appears persistent, the sinner is exorcised in the end. He is blamed for all the problems the group is facing. By *excommunicating* the deviant, the group tries to restore control and become powerful again. This method of purification is called the *scapegoat mechanism*, where the person who is thrown out is considered as the scapegoat. Quite often the only sin of the scapegoat is him being different. This social mechanism is a selection mechanism, such as the price mechanism in the economic world. If goods become more expensive they become a threat to the survival of a person, and through substitution by another and cheaper good, the optimal situation is restored. In the social world persons who are a threat to the identity of the group and its social power must make room for others.

History shows many important examples of this social mechanism. Jesus was the scapegoat in the eyes of the Jewish people, and was sentenced to crucifixion. In Europe, quite often the Jewish were the scapegoats, and during the Second World War 6 million of them were killed. In the 1990s the Hutus slaughtered many Tutsis in Rwanda. But the scapegoat mechanism does not only take place in big social divides on a national level. On every level, there is *social divide*. In every family, in every organization, and in every neighbourhood scapegoats are exorcised in particular ways. A child who grows up in a strictly religious family, but increasingly expresses his doubts about the dogmas that rule the family's culture, will be pressed to adjust. If not, he will be exorcised. Other examples are: (1) a member of a marketing department of a particular firm, who protests against particular practices, in which customers are fooled—the DSB case is illustrative in this respect;[6] (2) a post-Keynesian economist in an economics department, who is

---

[6] DSB was a fast-growing Dutch bank, which went bankrupt because of scandals.

surrounded by econometricians, and is constantly ignored—the financial crisis 2008 is illustrative in this case.

While groups maintain internal solidarity, they also maintain external rivalry. The rivalry is necessary, because *status reflects a relationship*: the status battle needs two or more groups who are enemies of each other. For instance, Barcelona and Madrid need each other in their process of identification, and so with Amsterdam and Rotterdam, and Thessaloniki and Athens. The ongoing rivalry keeps them going: panta rei.[7] If a particular rivalry ends for whatever reason, this is a threat to the unity of the groups. All the energy necessary in the status battle must be directed in another direction. Internal divides are fuelled. When the Soviet Union broke apart, the USA needed a new rival, and the Pentagon, the CIA, and the FBI were strongly interested in finding a new one. About ten years later the Muslim world, at least the more radical parts, became the next enemy. China also became a new rival, particularly because of its impressive economic growth and population growth. At the moment (2013) there is rivalry—more than competition—with respect to the relative price of their currencies. Although the global economy needs currency price stability, and China has linked her renminbi to the dollar, the Western world, under the leadership of the USA, is constantly blaming China for its destabilizing policies.

13.5.5 THE MORAL CONSTRAINT

In the beginning were primitive tribes. They were ruled by big men, who had the authority to distribute resources among the members, so as to guarantee some equality (see Chapter 2; for a detailed description of primitive culture see Sanderson, 1999). With respect to culture, priests and medicine men maintained the tribes' traditions, reflecting the wisdom of the ancestors. Through the telling of myths and the application of rituals they took care of the transmission of their tradition to the next generation. The main message of a primitive tradition was the idea of gods who need to be beseeched by regular sacrifices. Other tribes were ruled by rival gods, who were devils. One's own god could be best pleased by attacking other tribes. This idea is the beginning of human rivalry, and in many religions, even today, this message is an essential part. The ongoing rivalry is a major source of anxiety and existential fear. Many myths can only be understood by assuming that, in earlier times, massacres took place on a regular basis (Girard, 1978).

We will shortly repeat the history of the social world, as constructed by Girard. In Mesopotamia lived a man named Abram. He did not believe that there were many gods, who were constantly rivalling each other. According to him there must be one god, who

---

[7] Panta rei is an expression from the Greek philosopher Herakleitos; he referred to this human rivalry, which keeps human societies going.

has created our reality on the basis of the principle of *love, not rivalry*. He moved to another area, namely Palestine, in order to make a new start. He appeared as the beginning of Jewish religion and philosophy. A few thousands of years later the Jew Jesus told his people that the Jewish message of love was not only meant for Jews, but for all people. He claimed to be the Christ, who liberates people from the idea of rivalry, and introduced the idea of love, interpreted as mutual sympathy, and promised social peace and prosperity for all who apply this principle. Later humanists adopted the same idea, but stripped its religious element from it.

So, Western civilization became humanization according to the Christian and humanist belief. It meant the introduction of a different view of human life, implying a new morality. In the primitive world the moral imperative was to serve the best interest of the own group at the cost of the interests of the rival group. Western civilization implies a morality that aims at ending the rivalry.

Of course, the introduction of a new philosophy of life, including a new morality, does not take place in a few days or a few years. It took a few centuries to enlighten people throughout the world. This philosophy is still a thin layer, which disappears as soon as important interests are at stake. In that sense history can be interpreted as a slow process—a few steps forward followed by a few steps backward—of *increasing reasonability*.

Actually, there are many ethnic groups and nations, each with their own culture. All these cultures must be considered as mixes of primitive and humane elements. Globalization means that there is growing interaction between these groups. As long as the various cultures differ significantly, conflicts might increase in number and strength. But, increasing interaction might also lead to more mutual understanding.

Immanuel Kant deliberately thought about the idea of a *universal morality*. He developed an ethical theory on the basis of human reason. His approach consists of two ideas. The first is the idea that human beings have the *capacity to be rational*. It refers to the capacity to deliberately analyse a situation, set goals, and choose instruments to reach these goals. The second idea is the assumption that human beings have the *capacity to be moral*. It concerns the capacity to acknowledge that, on the level of substance or essence, all individuals are equal.

This notion has a number of important implications. In the first place, one must accept that other people may have the same preferences—the *universality condition*. In the second place, one must accept that each person is an end in himself. In other words, respect each other as a human being. This is not the same as accepting all the goals held by each other—the *impartiality condition*. If Peter wants to kill John, a third person must support John in his attempt to prevent Peter from killing him. But the morally necessary support of John is not because it is John, but because John is the person who is threatened. So, individual persons are limited in their choice of ends. But within these moral limitations persons are autonomous in choosing their goals.

Now a basic assumption is that persons with a capacity to be rational and to be moral—that is, having the capacity to be reasonable—ought to act reasonably. *Kant's moral law is: act morally*—do your duty. The UN golden rule is a nice expression of Kantian reasonability: 'Do unto Others, as You Would Have Them Do unto You.'[8]

Although humans are equal in terms of essence or substance, in terms of properties there are many differences between them. So it makes sense to see how we can specify the inalienable human rights and duties.

Rawls and others have analysed moral problems on a Kantian basis in a (hypothetical) contract framework. Rawls assumes a society with many persons who are all completely ignorant with respect to their economic and social position (Rawls, 1971). These persons are asked for their opinion with respect to the fairness of distribution of scarce resources. He assumes that people are risk averters and opt for the 'maximum' distribution, which is the distribution where the lowest income or wealth is maximized. In other words, inequality is accepted only in so far as it leads to a higher minimum level of income or wealth.

13.5.6 SOCIAL DESIRE VERSUS ECONOMIC NEED

Orthodox economics assumes that social relationships do not exist. In neoclassical economics the orthodox analysis is straightforwardly applied to the real world. All activities are interpreted as economic utility-maximizing behaviour. Preferences are given, and expressed by means of a utility function. Economics is considered to be neutral between ends. So it's up to the individual or organization to decide about the content of this preference function—not economic science. In this way the discussion about the character of the motives behind human behaviour is avoided; every action is considered as an economic action. So the question of whether a person buys a car to impress his neighbour, or simply because he likes it is an irrelevant one. If a chief executive of a large firm receives a salary of 5 million euros, the explanation is: 'it's the market'. If a landless peasant in Latin America receives a wage of 1 dollar per hour worked, the explanation is the same. In reality, however, some market transactions are generally accepted, but others arouse strong moral resentment.

In the case of a Latin American landowner all people involved in the matter know that the land is unequally distributed, and concentrated in the hands of a few families. Poor peasants cannot buy a piece of land, and are dependent on landlords. Renting a piece of land is quite expensive for the average peasant, making it almost impossible for them to make a decent living. This fact creates moral resentments among the peasants, who group together and express their anger. Landlords feel challenged by aggressive peasant movements. They approach an individual peasant not as an individual human, for whom he is responsible to a certain degree, but as a member of the enemy. This status

---

[8] Kant was a Protestant Christian and founded his ideas of morality on biblical notions. Kant (1788) is about the essence or substance of morality, not about its properties.

battle makes it difficult to solve the problem of poverty. A more equal land distribution might lead to more prosperity for all. Unfortunately, both groups are caught in the social conflict, which is a negative-sum game in the end.

This example shows that an analytical distinction between the economic and the social aspect of human behaviour makes sense when trying to understand the real world. To clarify the qualitative difference between the economic and the social aspect of a transaction, we come back to what has been said about the approach by Girard. As we know already, he has analysed the social aspect thoroughly and illustrated it with many examples from classical and modern literature (Girard, 1961). The economic analysis presents a transaction as a direct relationship between subject and object. Girard analyses transactions as a triangle: two subjects or groups of subjects and the object. Suppose that subject 1 needs object A. Subject 2 notices this need, and from then on he desires object A. He desires it, because for him object A has become an interesting instrument to use to rival with subject 1. He can show the rival his superiority by buying a higher-quality copy of object A, for instance. This copying behaviour is called *mimesis*. In this way other people are not just sources of information about needs and the way they can be satisfied. Others are the opponents in an endless rivalry game. In traditional societies the problem of rivalry and of mimesis is reduced by the development of castes and classes. At the top was the aristocracy, which was supposed to run society in a virtuous way. Rights and duties were more or less clear. And so with the lower classes, which had to obey the rules as implemented by the elite. In the public space it was immediately clear who was a member of which class. Since it was nearly impossible to move from one class to another, there was no rivalry. Social peace was guaranteed as long as all classes accepted the rules of the game. Only severe economic inequality or disrespectful behaviour were reasons for the lower classes to protest; not the unequal distribution in power and status per se. The rivalry between different societies, however, was extreme. History shows an almost permanent series of conflicts; one war after the other.

With the emergence of modern society this idea of natural inequality of classes was increasingly questioned. In Western Europe the Renaissance brought a more secular view of our reality, and the Enlightenment stressed the idea of the autonomous individual, whose intrinsic value is independent of his behaviour. In this emerging modern cultural environment, individuals were increasingly allowed to strive for self-enhancement. Over the last few centuries this has led to an ongoing improvement in techniques of production, resulting in ever-growing economic prosperity.

Modern production methods are based on new insights in technical and economic-organizational processes. Adam Smith (1776) saw specialization as a very important source of productivity increase. Émile Durkheim (1893), however, saw also disadvantages: specialization creates new opportunities for rivals to rival with each other. According to him, modernization leads to differentiation, which is a threat to organizations and societies and can lead to them falling apart. To maintain or restore communication between the different functions in society explicit organization of the important functions is necessary. Only then can communication between groups be organized.

This *corporatist way* of organizing society not only keeps the different parties informed about important societal matters, but especially dampens rivalry and reaches solutions which are socially acceptable. Today *communitarians* advocate more democratic platforms of consultation, again, especially meant to maintain or restore an integrated society. Only then can society be efficient and fair.

13.5.7 IRRATIONAL PERSONS AND IRRATIONAL SOCIETIES

In Chapter 10 the concept of irrationality is discussed in a psychological context. An irrational person is defined as a person who is protecting himself against information that can be experienced as a threat to his self-respect. As far as it is impossible to ignore this information, an irrational person lacks the willpower to behave according to the requirements of the true Self as experienced by the person (see Section 10.6 for an elaborate account of these two components of irrationality).

This concept can also be applied to groups and to societies as a whole. The social world is characterized by an ongoing status battle, where the more prestigious group permanently shows the other group(s) their inferiority. Groups which are able to ignore all information that shows that members of the other group are not inferior, are perfectly irrational. Note that the superiority and inferiority has to do with a valuation of persons and of groups on the level of substance, not on the level of properties. Suppose that a person earns a salary of 1 million euros per year, and another person earns a salary of 10,000 euros per year. In terms of property, it is obvious that the first person earns more money than the second, but does it mean that the first person is a better human and deserves more prestige in terms of human dignity? In the social world the valuation has to do with basic respect, irrespective of the various properties that play a role in life.[9]

Besides the principal difference between substance and property, people with high grades and high salaries, functioning in the top of society, regularly forget why they are successful. They tend to explain it by referring to their personal efforts rather than by referring to the rules of the societal game, which are determined by the elite itself. If Ajax wins from Feijenoord while the referee is systematically benefiting Ajax, there is no reason for Ajax fans to feel superior to Feijenoord fans. So with the leading figures in the financial world: they became very rich at the cost of the mass of the people, simply because they have the power to decide upon the necessary job requirements, for instance.[10]

[9] In practice, large differences in properties trigger emotions leading to differences in terms of substance, as experienced by people. The leader of the Dutch political party PVV, Geert Wilders, expresses his views about the properties of the Islam in a way that many people experience as very disrespectful, and actually suggests that there is a social difference too ('c'est le ton qui fait la musique').

[10] As soon as we integrate the social world with the economic world individual economic performance induces more or less prestige, of course. But in this integrated approach social prestige also has an effect on economic performance: discrimination in segmented labour markets, for example.

How can groups become more rational? Two reasons play a role in this respect, an endogenous and an exogenous one. In the first place, the status battle can turn into a complete massacre, which is so frightening that the people involved might think of methods to avoid another clash. Theoretically, it is possible that there is no interaction between the two groups at all, except the signals expressing superiority and inferiority. In practice, however, there are always members of each of the two groups who are not perfectly adjusted to their own group; they are imperfectly socialized and have developed feelings of sympathy for members of the other group. Smith's concept of sympathy refers to a moral emotion, which functions as an incentive for the deviants to morally persuade others: 'guys, we should stop rivalling '. In the second place, in real life the social world is psychic-economically embedded. Suppose two rivals live close to each other, and have a common economic problem. The rivalry prevents an efficient economic solution. The costs of the rivalry can become so high that some peace talks are organized. These talks contain a social aspect, which is that regular communication might lead to growing mutual understanding. In such a context it is easier for the parties involved to bargain in an economic way, and to make deals which are beneficial for both groups.

Some areas are more successful than others in their attempt to get the status battle under control. Western Europe has shown some success in dampening the rivalry between France and Germany, and between England and France, and so with the battle between Protestants and Roman Catholics and between Christians and humanists. In north-western Europe even the relationships between young and old, and between men and women, has changed over time in the direction of less rivalry and more solidarity.

Can we detect a structural decline in rivalry over time? *Progressive philosophy* answers this question positively; at least, holders of such a view expect harmony between the different classes in the end. They defend the idea of substantial equality between people (Kant, Hegel, Habermas, Rawls, for instance), and expect increasing awareness among people of this fundamental fact. Dialectical philosophers describe a dialectic process. Applied to the social world, this means that adherents to the idea of equality will be able to convince more people of this idea than the conservative adherents to the idea of fundamental inequality can. Fukuyama (1992) is an example: he considers the liberal-democratic structure of society to be the winner.[11] Democratically elected politicians, chosen by liberally orientated people, run countries which favour a free market economy, including a safety net for those who are really unable to sufficiently serve their own interests. Habermas (1987) developed ideas about how to organize communication between rival groups in such a way that they increasingly learn to understand each other: communicative-rational action, as it is called. There is a striking parallel with discussions in the philosophy of science about the necessary discourse between different research programmes, which aim at the explanation of the same phenomena.

---

[11] Be aware that Fukuyama lives in the eastern part of the United States, and uses the word liberal in the Continental European sense of the word—not in the Anglo-Saxon way (see Hayek (1978) for an exposition of the term 'liberal'.).

Differences in views are caused by the choice of a different paradigm, which makes programmes incommensurable. Ongoing conversation, including moral persuasion, must lead to intersubjective agreement in the end. If harmony appears to be impossible, at least more mutual understanding and tolerance with respect to remaining differences might be the result. This tolerance is exactly what is needed for ending social rivalry. What is left is a healthy economic competition between a few strategies in search of a rational society.

Now we have defined a rational person and a rational society. A rational person has overcome his cognitive dissonance, and a rational society has overcome its *social dissonance,* which is the primitive status battle. Only in a rational society can people learn to trust each other; we are all members of one and the same club: the human race. The trust that connects 'us', while there is no 'them', is founded on the trust in one's own Self.. This is the perfectly reasonable person, who has discovered and learned to respect his true Self, and lives in a *perfectly reasonable society,* where everybody can trust each other perfectly.

Part V
Towards an Integration of the Three Worlds

V.1 **Introduction**

We have seen that the most important methodological difference between orthodox and heterodox economics concerns the idea of isolated abstraction. Orthodox economics is an ideal-typical approach. It means that it reflects a particular idea, which is the idea of 'economic'. The founding fathers consider economics to be the expression of the fundamental problem of scarcity, which means that there is a tension between economic needs and their satisfaction. Since resources are limited, there is not enough to satisfy all the economic needs, making it necessary for subjects to choose: only some needs will be satisfied. The analysis that is built upon this idea offers us a description and explanation of human behaviour in a world where the economic aspect is the only one that counts. This means that the other two primary aspects, namely the psychic and the social aspect, are abstracted. So, subjects have no psychic problems, which means that they have no internal conflicts, and their preference-orderings are undisputable for the subject. Moreover, the subjects have no problems of a social nature, which means that there are no social conflicts between groups of people. Everyone approaches every subject as an economic subject only.

Heterodox economists rejected this research strategy from the beginning. It is not difficult to understand why: from the very first moment neoclassical economists have used the orthodox analysis as a theoretical basis for their empirical research. The functioning of free markets was especially considered as a great area where orthodox economics could offer us important empirical knowledge. The use of an isolated abstraction as a theoretical foundation for empirical research without any further justification might be the most serious error made in the history of economics. In our chapters about heterodox economics we have seen that psychic and social factors play an important role in these approaches. Unfortunately, heterodoxy does not offer a satisfying alternative framework of interpretation and analysis. Although very rich in theory and hypothesis, it is weak in the formulation of human motivation. It criticizes the orthodoxy in this respect—human motivation being a constant and restrictive motivational force—but it does not offer a variable and less restrictive alternative. The meaning of the idea of 'psychic' and of 'social' remains unclear. The two concepts cannot play a role in a realistic analysis of human behaviour as long as the ideal-typical constitution of the mind and of the social arena is not established and analysed. Therefore, we have developed the construction of the psychic and the social world—analogous to the construction of the economic world. In this part we will bring the three worlds together, and we will sketch their interrelationships. Then we will make the picture more realistic by adding a few important aspects to it, namely the evolution of technology and institutions, the historicity of human life, the ecological aspect, the intrinsic openness of nature in general, and the macro view on the three-motivational world.

In this introduction we will clarify the issues which are necessary complements to the closed and mechanistic multi-motivational world. In Chapter 14 we will integrate the economic, the psychic, and the social world. In Chapter 15 we will discuss a series of important concepts, whose meanings are determined by our integrated world.

V.2 **Technology and Institution**

The focus of the simplest picture is an individual subject—be it a person, a family, a firm, a non-commercial organization, or an government agency—placed within a particular structure. In the economic world this structure is about the characteristics of nature, as far as it offers resources. In the psychic world this structure is about the structure of the mind, and in the social world the basic structure is determined by the group structure in which people live. Over time, subjects develop technologies and institutions so as to transform combinations of input into output in an increasingly effective way.

V.3 **Historicity**

If we were considering the construction of an integrated model of three worlds as the end of our methodological work, it might seem as if we would accept that our reality is determined by a few universal and eternal mechanisms. Then stationary models would suffice in the same way as we accept the idea that planets circle around the sun as they did in the past. Even in astronomy historicity plays a role, however. Some events have a significant influence on the course of history. Very positive or very negative experiences are stored in the minds of the subjects, and their memory will play a role in their actions for the rest of their lives. The existence of history means that our model is subject to change on all levels. In the first place, our integrated model is still partial in the sense that the physical/chemical aspect only plays a role as a restriction. Second, the dynamics of human motivations might show difficult-to-predict changes in motivation and behaviour.

V.4 **Ecology**

Economics is about the relationship between human subjects and their natural environment. But this relationship is viewed from a human perspective only: How can we, humans, profit from natural resources? Not only is the idea of a human person quite unrealistic—just economic and rational—but the idea of nature is also biased: whatever we use or destroy, without any recognition of their value in their own right, we will always find perfect substitutes. Nature as a whole will always remain an unlimited resource. Ecology takes a different view about this relationship. Animals, plants, and other things have their own right to exist. To a certain extent, humans and animals, for instance, are competitors. So, we have the right to defend ourselves and the right to eat meat. But as soon as humans become materially comfortable there is room for more cooperation and respect.

V.5 **Openness of Systems**

Our analysis is a multi-level analysis. On all levels—from human motivation to the system as a whole—there is uncertainty about the relationships we have constructed. In the physical/chemical world, many, although not all, relationships appear quite stable. The situation in the human world is quite different, however. Humans have the capacity to reflect upon their situation, and develop rules of behaviour, which make the situation more predictable. People who acknowledge openness and the existence of uncertainty, which is different from calculable risk, are inclined to build buffers of everything that might become scarce quite unexpectedly (the precautionary motive). In heterodox macroeconomics we saw that, in a free market economy, those subjects who are rational build up stocks, which can be used in times of decline.

V.6 **Macro-Analysis**

In the orthodox approach the micro level—the level of a person in his situation—is not only the level of analysis, but also the level of explanation. It means that behaviour on other levels is explained by reference to what happens on the micro level. We know from Chapter 5 that orthodox macroeconomics is just the aggregate of microeconomics: all markets are cleared by their own flexible prices. Heterodox macroeconomics, however, assumes that the macro level is not only a level of analysis, but also the level of explanation. A person is always and everywhere part of a group, and influenced by common flows of information and experiences. So, we can expect common reactions. This axiom makes macro-analysis a solid macro-foundation for micro-analysis. This foundation also explains the dynamics of the primary human motivations.

Since the three isolated worlds are closed systems, their integration will also be a closed system, whose functioning is determined by a series of mechanisms. In Chapter 14 we will present the interrelationships between the three isolated and closed systems. In more advanced models it is possible to build in some of the complicating but significant matters that we have just discussed.

14 The Integration of the Three Worlds

14.1 The Economic World

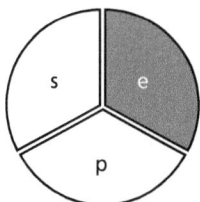

In our chapter about orthodox economics we have sketched the construction of the economic world.[1] Now we briefly repeat the axioms that constitute this world.

(1) Human beings are considered to be economic actors. It means that these actors have economic needs, which cannot be satisfied completely. So, the actor must choose on the basis of his preference-ordering and the scarce resources available to him. Thus, the term 'economic' refers to the omnipresent natural scarcity of resources and the human drive to minimize this scarcity as much as possible.

(2) Human beings are also considered to be rational actors, which means that every subject has perfect control over his actual drives or emotions. He is able to select which needs must be satisfied so as to serve his long-term interests.

(3) Human beings are assumed to be atomistic or non-social, which means that all relationships between humans are of an economic nature only. Humans use each other as long as the relationship offers both parties net economic benefits.

(4) The economic world is subject to a mechanism that determines the outcomes—in this case the price mechanism, which creates equilibrium on all markets. This closed and mechanistic world shows relationships between elements, which can be described by means of classical logic, and the mathematical analysis, which is derived from it (economic logic).

Analytically, we can present this world in the simplest way by formulating a preference-ordering (1) and two restrictions, namely the amount of resources (2) and the level of

[1] The letters in the circle mean social world (s), psychic world (p), and economic world (e) respectively.

production technology (3). The confrontation between preferences and constraints determines the action of the actor. As long as we assume perfect competition (including perfect information), there is no experience within the system that leads to change. As soon as we assume imperfect information, all the elements just mentioned can be changed. People can change their preferences if they discover that particular goods do not have the effects expected, for instance. People can save part of their income and invest it in human or physical capital. The effect might be a relaxation of the resource restriction. People can also profit from improvements in their production and consumption technology. In Figure 14.1 we have presented this picture schematically.

Now we will answer the question of how the allocation and distribution of scarce resources takes place. In Chapter 4 about orthodox microeconomics we have seen that the idea of scarcity leads to an analysis of the world in terms of supply, demand, price, and equilibrium. In the simplest model, which implies perfect competition, all actors are in their Pareto-optimum: given their resources they have maximized their (economic) utility. In Figure 14.2 we have presented this model graphically.

In Figure 14.2a we have pictured a micro-goods market. It shows that part of the quantity demanded is selected out. For them there is no trade. For many goods markets this

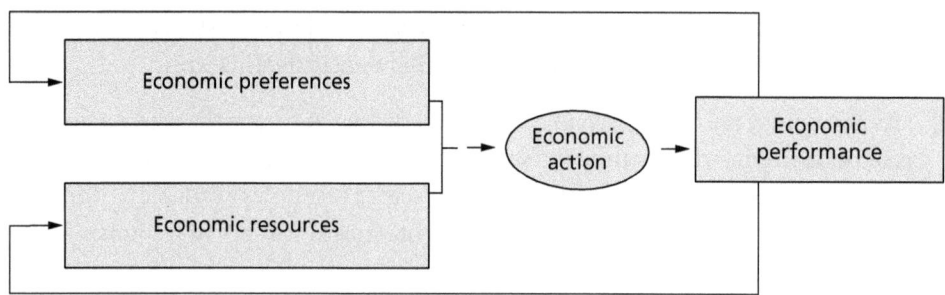

Figure 14.1. Economic World with Imperfect Information

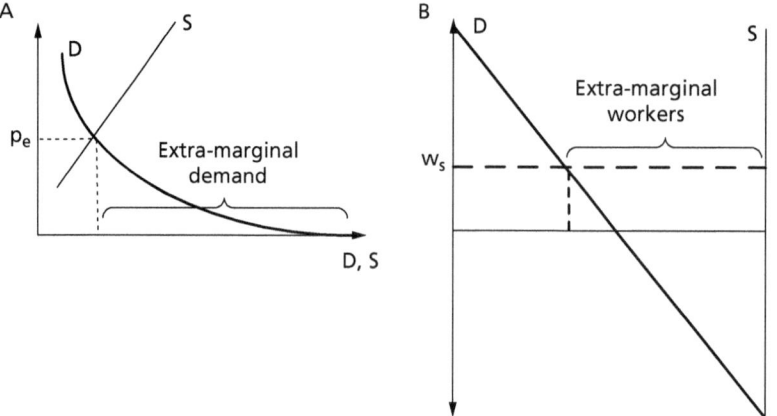

Figure 14.2. A: Selection Mechanism Micro-Goods Market; B: Selection Mechanism Macro-Labour Market

is not a serious problem. In a poor country the impossibility for some people to buy their daily bread is a serious problem, of course.

In Figure 14.2b we have pictured a macro-labour market. We know that most people hold that they are not wealthy and dependent on having a job. On the horizontal axis we have pictured groups of dependent people according to their marginal productivity (curve D). Curve S expresses the quantity supplied of labour, which is the labour force. The horizontal line w_s expresses the subsistence level of the wage rate. Figure 14.2b shows that many people have a marginal productivity, which is not high enough to have a job. Since there are no social institutions in the economic world, there will always be people who cannot earn a living for themselves. Some people will die, while others wander around and take goods from others (criminality does not exist in the economic world).[2] The mafia will flourish, and groups of guerrillas regularly attack wealthy resorts. According to new institutional economics (NIE) economic and rational actors are inclined to negotiate and adopt rules of exchange and governance. Locally, traders can be successful in the conclusion of contracts of a temporary nature. When traders become acquainted with others especially, they learn to operate on the basis of calculated risk. Over time, areas of 'trust' can evolve, but in a world of economic, rational, and non-social subjects, breaching of contracts and robbery by third parties will always be a threat. A system of private property rights is generally considered to be the most important institution. Without such an institution the economic world becomes a cowboy economy, which makes every initiative a precarious business. But why should economic and rational outcasts agree with this institution? The economic world does not offer any possibility of significantly and structurally reducing violence. Therefore, we need to abandon the axiom of non-sociality.

14.2 **The Social World**

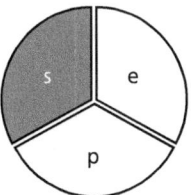

---

[2] Introductory textbooks always assume perfect monitoring and protection of private property rights—mostly implicitly.

In Chapter 13 we sketched our construction of the social world. The axioms that constitute this world are the following.

(1) Human individual actors are assumed to be social. The way they perceive their preferences and resources are determined by the common understanding of the group in which they live. The ultimate goal of the group is the maximization of its status, relative to the status of rival groups. Individuals also strive for as much status or social approval as possible within the group. But in interactions between groups, members of a group show solidarity to each other.

(2) Human individual actors, as well as the group in which they operate, are assumed to be perfectly rational. This means that they have perfect control over their actual needs or emotions. They are able to select those needs that must be satisfied to serve the long-term group interest.

(3) Human actors are non-economic, which means that there is no scarcity of natural resources.

(4) The social world is closed and determined by the arena mechanism. The relationships can be described by means of the rules of classical logic, including the mathematics which is based on it (social logic).

As long as we assume perfect rivalry and perfect solidarity, including perfect information, the social system is in equilibrium. It means that the status differences are determined, and that there are neither external nor internal factors which can change the status structure. As soon as we assume imperfect information, equilibrium will be incidental. Every interaction gives new experiences, and can lead to different reactions of the various groups. We can imagine that weaker groups train harder in existing battle techniques, or that some members of the group are planning to work on new battle technologies. We can also imagine that some members of the various groups begin to deviate from the social norms, and communicate with members of other groups in a positive way. In Figure 14.3 we have presented the simplest analysis of the social world schematically.

The arena mechanism creates social equilibrium, and determines group membership and the status ranking. In the simplest model all members of a group are perfectly adjusted to the culture of the group. So, there is perfect solidarity and perfect rivalry. Consequently, the group has maximized its status.

Now we formulate a few conditions, which constitute the arena. In the first place, we assume that there is a *difference in the level of status-battle technology*. Given these different levels there is social equilibrium, in which the ranking is determined. Everybody who is prepared to accept the group norms is welcome, and together the group members work hard on a permanent improvement of their social technology. If the difference between the group's status and the status of the group one level higher becomes greater, more resources will be necessary for the status battle and its technology. The same happens if the status difference between the a group and the group one level lower

GROUP A

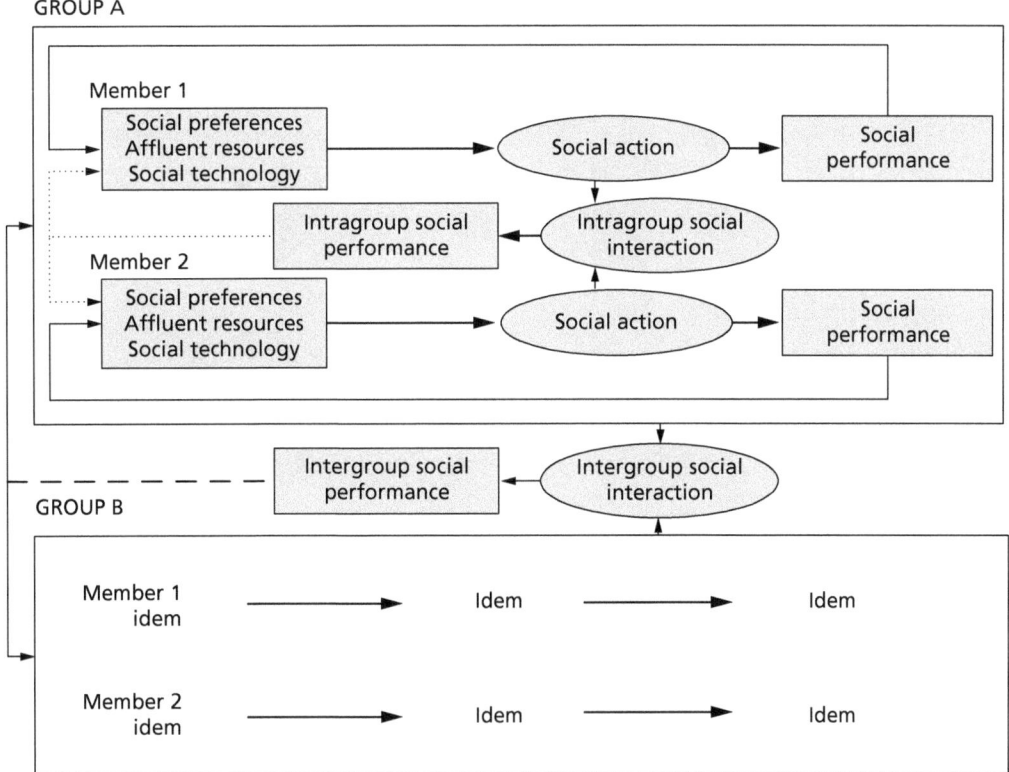

Figure 14.3. The Social World

decreases. A second restriction says that *not all group members are perfectly adjusted to the group norms.* Some persons show deviant behaviour on a regular scale. Others might interpret this as group weakness, and a threat to its relative status. If this is the case, the group might become more hierarchically organized. The leadership may design more specified rules and pay for more resources to monitor and to penalize deviants. If the threat of status loss is large and the members' deviation quite serious, the group might exorcise particular members. They are considered as scapegoats, who are to be blamed for the group's loss of status. We have pictured this mechanism in Figure 14.4. Circle A presents group A with its core position a. The group members take a position within the circle; some are positioned close to the core position (the most loyal members), while others take a more deviant position. Circle B presents group B with its core position b. In this group also some members are more loyal than others. This social mechanism leads to the following theory: *the smaller the status difference, the smaller the room for deviation from the group norms.* In the left part we have presented the situation with a relatively large status difference, while in the right part the situation of a relatively small status difference is presented. The exorcised members become strangers—people who are ignored by the groups (Bauman, 1998).

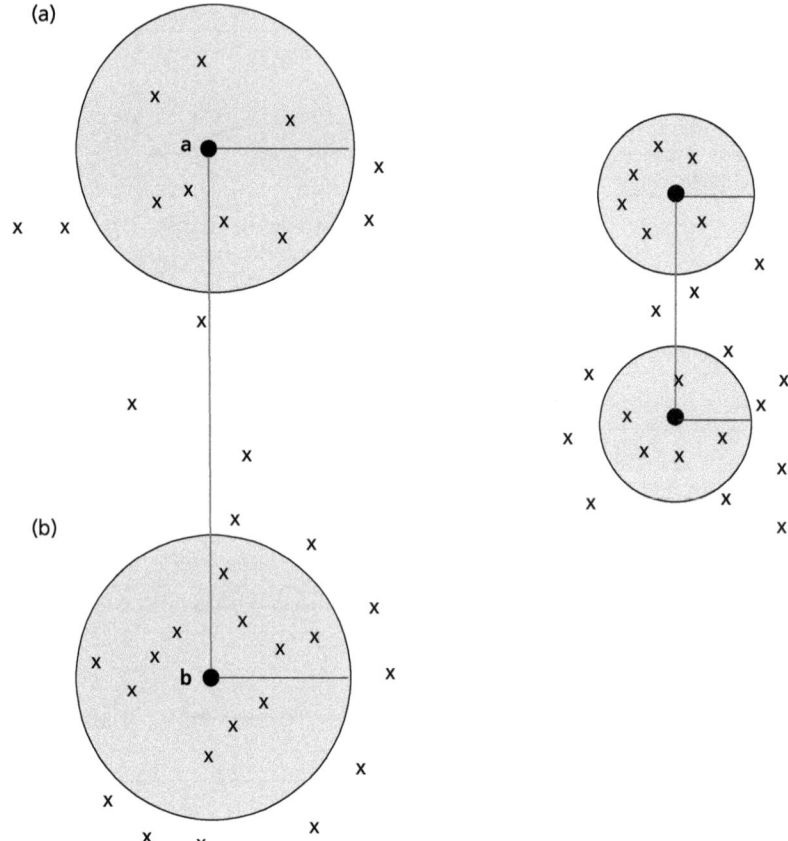

Figure 14.4. The Arena Mechanism in the Social World

In a more complex model we can assume that social actors might develop feelings of sympathy, not only for members of their own group, but also for members of other groups.

Suppose that a war between two (groups of) countries leads to very large number of deaths. Members who are very close to the core position develop strong feelings of resentment towards the enemy. But members who deviate to a certain extent from that position, and know members of the rival group on a personal basis, might also develop positive feelings for victims from the opponent group. Deviants from the participating groups might group together and agree to put pressure upon their own leadership to reach an armistice.[3] Then peace talks can be arranged, and the participants might be successful in the formulation of a series of rules which should guarantee less cruel ways of social conflict. These rules can function as a *moral constraint* in the next rounds of contests. So, in a more sophisticated picture we should add 'institutions' to the series of restrictions.

---

[3] Follett (2012) is a great novel situated in the context of the First World War, and exactly describes this case.

14.3 **The Psychic World**

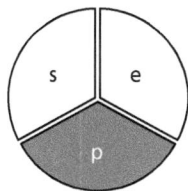

In Chapter 10 we developed a psychic world, and offered a map of the human mind. A set of four axioms constitute this world.

(1) Human actors are assumed to be imperfectly rational. It means that every actor has imperfect control over his actual emotions.

(2) Humans are assumed to be non-economic, which means that there is no scarcity of natural resources.

(3) Humans are assumed to be non-social, which means that there is neither human rivalry nor human solidarity.

(4) The psychic world is an isolated and closed world, which is determined by the psychic mechanism. The relationships between the various entities in the mind can be described by means of classical logic and the mathematics that is based on it (psychic logic).

Before we explain more elaborately what we mean by irrationality, we must discuss the elements that form the mind system. In the first place, we distinguish between an *actual Self* and a *true Self*. The actual Self (AS) encompasses all of a person's needs and emotions, which manifest themselves at a particular moment. If there is no emotion that says to these drives 'wait a minute', the AS determines the behaviour of our person. The true Self (TS) is the entity that represents the true preferences of a person. They emerge if a person thoroughly reflects upon his personality. These second-order preferences are not immediate in their manifestation. They let the person know what he should do, according to his own intuition. A third entity is the 'I', representing the personality as a whole. This element possesses a stock of energy, willpower, which can be used to control the AS. Imperfect rationality means that willpower is a scarce good, and insufficient to perfectly control the AS. All the three elements can be interpreted as *stocks of energy*. The AS of a baby is very clear: warmth and milk from the mother. The way in which she communicates with her mother already expresses her personality traits, which have a strong influence on the development of the TS. Over time, the TS develops under the influence of the parent figures and the characteristics of its circumstances.[4] We can imagine the mind as if it is a firm. The 'I' is the boss, the TS functions as its personal advisor, especially about strategic issues. The AS represents the rank and file of the firm. As long as there is no monitoring at all, they do what they like: they will shirk work all the time. It does not necessarily mean that they are lazy people; it means that they serve their own interests, and work according to their own views on the firm interest or on self-interest. So, the boss takes the decisions and tries to affect the behaviour of the rank and file in the direction which he thinks is desirable.

In Figure 14.5 we have schematically presented the mind in a situation of imperfect information. The 'I' possesses the ratio of a person, which is embedded in the person's intuition. Over the years, this intuition will develop under the influence of education and experience. In philosophical terms the *intuition represents a person's paradigm,* which consists of a series of basic statements, which are the person's framework of interpretation. These determine the way a person reacts to particular changes in his situation. TSE stands for the true Self as experienced by the 'I', and ASE stands for the actual Self as experienced by the 'I'. This 'I' tries to control the ASE as much as is needed by means of his willpower. So the actions are determined by the ASE as far as it is controlled by the 'I' (ASEC).

The psychic mechanism can be illustrated by looking again at the metaphor of a firm. Suppose the results of the firm are satisficing. The boss decides to save on monitoring costs. New initiatives are developed, but the preparation of the plans and their execution occurs less carefully than before. Optimism turns into overoptimism and makes decision-makers less alert. This goes on until the results are significantly worse than before. The difference between the TSE and the controlled ASE (ASEC) has grown, which triggers the use of more willpower to narrow the gap. Monitoring becomes tougher and the analysis more careful again. Why these reactions? Because the self-respect of the boss is at stake in the case of worse results. It's not because of the economic results—there is affluence in the economic environment of the mind. It's not because of the prestige of the boss—social recognition is not at stake, since there is no social environment. Self-respect

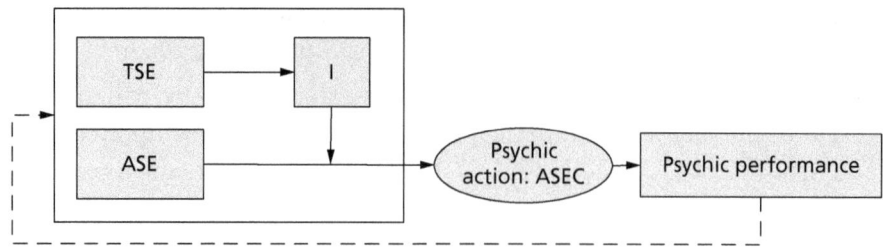

Figure 14.5. The Psychic World

---

[4] Strictly speaking, there are no other people living in the psychic world of a particular person. When discussing the psychic world of a baby a mother figure is a conditio sine qua non. In reality, hardly anybody can live without other humans in his environment, of course.

can be seen as the only source of psychic utilities, which are maximized under the constraint of limited willpower. In the case of perfect information the person is able to find psychic equilibrium, given the level of willpower. As soon as the level of willpower is enough to achieve perfect self-control, we have reached an ideal world: there are no economic, social, and psychic problems anymore.

If we assume imperfect information, we don't know for sure which emotions and feelings belong to the TSE, and which to the ASE. The personality 'I' experiences inner voices, but which are the voices of the TSE, and which of the ASE? The mechanism in the simple model just says that the TSE is the advisor, who deliberately thinks about the situation on the basis of the paradigm of the person. The ASE just drives the person to particular kinds of behaviour. For the person, it is clear what he should do if he wants to serve his long-term interest and to what degree he has to constrain the ASE, and in what way. Imperfect information, however, means that the person has difficulty interpreting the drives. Different inner voices compete to get the attention of the 'I', so as to control the other voices and emotions behind the voices. This is the more sophisticated inner conflict. In Figure 14.6 we have pictured an additional flow, which must be added to the simple model. The immediate drives (AS) try to convince the 'I' of their necessity, by influencing the messages from the TSE to the 'I'. Now there is a conflict

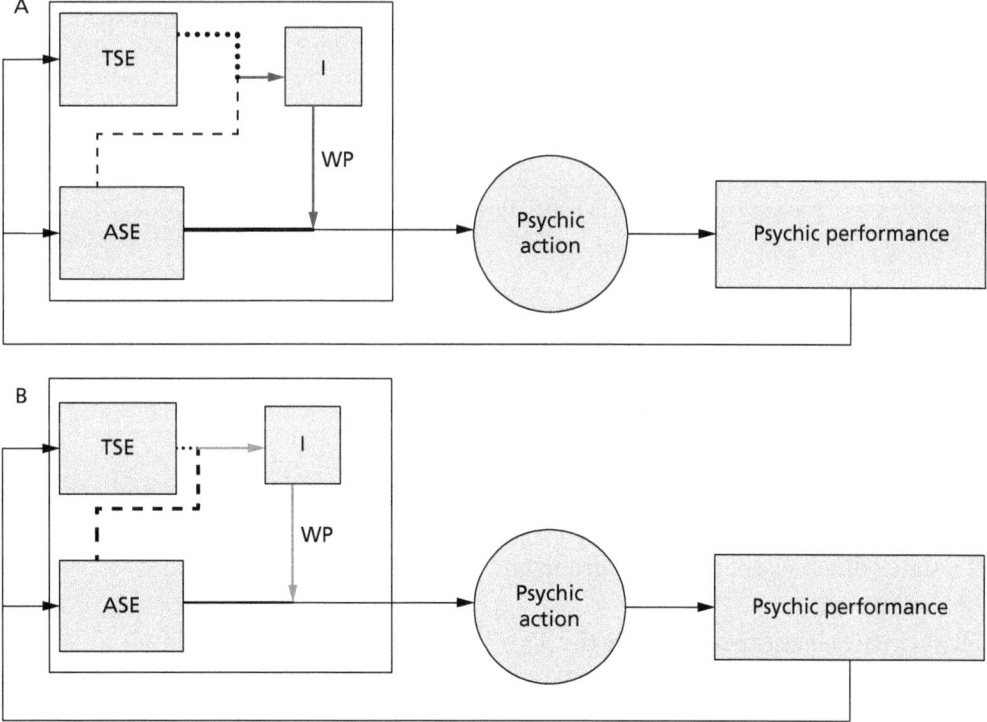

Figure 14.6. A: Psychic World with Imperfect Information—Strong Personality; B: Psychic World with Imperfect Information—Weak Personality

between the TS and the TSE, and between the AS and the ASE. Actually, short-term interests suggest to the person that they are representing the TS. In this way they protect the TSE against a change as a result of observed anomalies. In our discussion about the securitization revolution this phenomenon was called *cognitive closure*. Change of the TSE would be disastrous for the survival of vested interests of a particular person or organization. In science this phenomenon happens time and again. In the current crisis neoclassical economists face one anomaly after the other. But hardly any of them are prepared to switch from their neoclassical paradigm. In Figure 14.6 we have presented this second element of irrationality: the attempts of the actual Self to prevent the 'I' from changing his idea of the true Self.

In our text on the biological approach we saw that brain researchers talk about competition between groups of neurons, and that neurons that represent automatized and uncontrolled reactions are faster and win their battles against those that represent the deliberate and controlled reactions most of the time. If a person wants to become more rational, she can develop personal institutions, which means that she adopts rules of behaviour for different types of situations. So, if rules that result from deliberation become automatized, they might be victorious over other automatized emotions. In this way psychic institutions are of great help in improving self-control.

We can summarize the three allocation mechanisms by means of the following three equations, expressing the economic, the social, and the psychic mechanism respectively.

$$P = f(D - S) \tag{1}$$

$$ID = f(SD) \tag{2}$$

$$WP = f(ASE - TSE) \tag{3}$$

P = price of a particular good;
D = quantity demanded for the good;
S = quantity supplied of the good;
ID = ideological distance between the position of the marginal member and the core position;
SD = status difference between the group and its rival;
WP = willpower;
ASE = actual Self as experienced by the 'I';
TSE = true Self as experienced by the 'I'.

Now we will discuss the various combinations of two worlds, namely the economic-psychic, the economic-social, and the psychic-social world.

14.4 **The Psychic-Economic World**

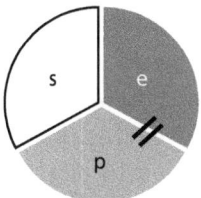

We take the picture of the economic world as our starting point and replace the perfectly integrated decision-maker by our mind system with its elements TSE, ASE, and 'I', which are equipped with variable willpower. In Figure 14.7 we present psychic-economic processes schematically.

Economic preferences are economically motivated. Psychic preferences are focused on self-respect: investment and consumption, which serve to maintain self-respect on as high a level as possible. Psychic consumption is a signal to the person that he is successful. Some psychic consumption patterns are the result of ASE drives; others are affected by the TSE, which means that actual behaviour is determined by the controlled ASE drives (ASEC). With respect to the resources, we also make a distinction between economic and psychic resources. The first type concerns machines, hammers, guns, raw materials, and so on. The second type consists of the energy with which a person is striving for self-respect. Willpower can be interpreted as a stock of energy available for controlling the actual Self. Some persons use all their psychic resources in an attempt to derive self-respect from it. Others invest in the growth of willpower, and are able to postpone current psychic consumption. In the end this willpower investment appears profitable in terms of self-respect. It creates room for

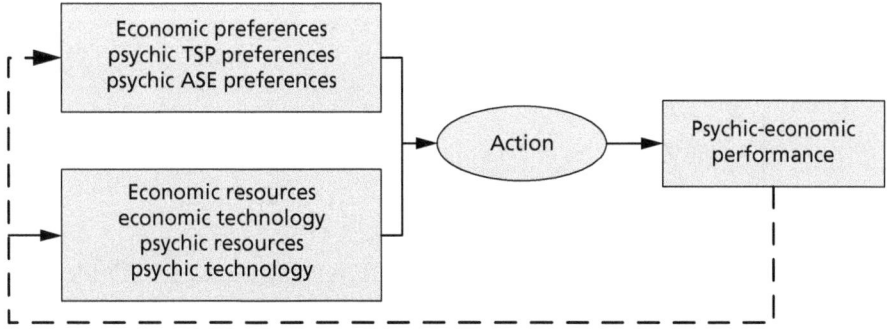

Figure 14.7. Representation of a Psychic-Economic Process

the development of personal talents, the use of it creating much self-respect in the end. Even during the period of investment and sacrifice, persons have much self-respect already: status in their own eyes. The meaning of the concept technology is clear: economic technology is related to the technology that improves the relationship between inputs and outputs in the economic world, where actors are perfectly rational. Psychic technology improves the relationship between the inputs and outputs in the production of willpower. Since we are also applying the language of the economic analysis to the description of mind processes, we can picture the production and consumption of willpower in a typical economic way. In Figure 14.8 we have drawn a supply and demand curve on the market for rationality. The demand curve shows that a person who wants to be more rational must pay a price in terms of willpower. The lower the price the higher the quantity demanded. The supply curve shows that it is costly to increase someone's rationality. There is an optimal level of willpower, leading to an *optimal level of rationality*. We saw in the model of the economic world that the assumption of perfect competition, and especially the element of perfect information, contradicts the idea of the model, which says that everything is scarce. Now we see that the axiom of perfect rationality is also a foreign element in the economic world. As soon as the psychic world becomes part of the model, economic actors will economize on the investments and use of willpower in the same way that they think that they can economize on information.

Last, we will discuss the consequences of the assumption of imperfect information in the psychic-economic world. Economic-rational actors who discover that their experiences are not as expected apply the model of the economic world to decide what to do. Are their tastes different from what they thought? Are the characteristics of the good different from what they read on the packaging? If so, they substitute another good for the bad good, and try again. But economic-irrational actors react

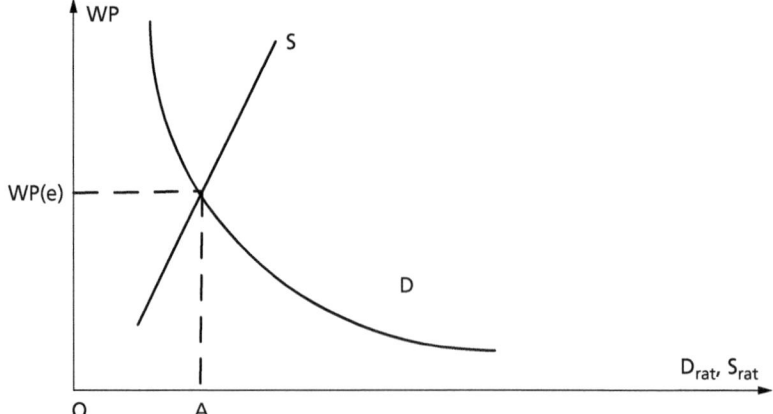

Figure 14.8. Supply (S_{rat}) and Demand (D_{rat}) for Rationality

differently. Irrational people might continue their consumption, because they don't want to sacrifice resources to improve the quality of their choices. They also might have stringent opinions about their current life strategies. So deliberate self-research is not necessary. They even might simply ignore the bad experiences and start to believe they were not bad experiences at all. The first form of imperfect rationality is the result of imperfect willpower. This might be the result of a lack of perspective, which implies that training and using willpower are perceived as costs without future benefits. The last example suggests that irrational actors are able to use an unrealistic framework of analysis, thereby systematically ignoring the anomalies it gives. It seems that many people are able to fool themselves all of the time. It also shows that man is not a truth-searcher; not an ideal-type of a scientist. Man is able to protect views which have so far offered him much self-respect against any form of critique. While lack of willpower might be the result of a lack of perspective, cognitive closure is the result of automatizing the one and only framework for all problems all of the time. The more automatized the framework of interpretation, the less consciously open to reasonable scrutiny it will be. It is difficult to explain the problem of the protection of the vulnerable Self in terms of typical economic analysis. In the case of dramatic events it might come to the surface. But then the ASE is inclined to block the process of cognitive disclosure. It tries, mostly with success, to convince the 'I' not to react.

The psychic-economic world offers a psychic-economic person more possibilities to improve the quality of his life by changing behavioural patterns. In other words, there are more resource and substitution effects, since his portfolio has extended significantly. Rationality has become a scarce good, and the production of it needs resources and a technology, which can transform a series of inputs into the output, called willpower. This good can be used not only for the control of the ASE, but also to break through the protective belt of the TSE. It is about the will to be courageous and honest to her Self rather than be completely ruled by the lust to survive at the cost of transparency.

14.5 **The Social-Economic World**

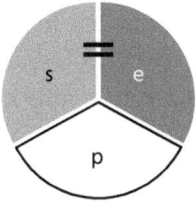

In this world the actors are assumed to be economic, rational, and social. Humans are social beings in the positive sense of solidarity between members of a group and in the negative sense of rivalry between groups. It means that we analyse economic and rational actors in their social context. Therefore, we place the schedule of the economic world into the schedule of the social world. Figure 14.9 shows the result. We see that all members of all groups are economic and rational subjects, aiming at the maximization of economic utilities under the constraint of scarce natural resources. They compete and they cooperate with each other. In one extreme case they all compete with each other, whatever their group membership, and in another extreme case they just compete and cooperate with members of the same group.

We also see that all individuals rival or have solidarity with each other—in the extreme cases there is just one battle between two groups or there are many battles, in which many groups participate. In a first very simple case, each individual is member of only one group, while in a second case each individual is a member of many groups, battling in many areas. To illustrate what is meant by persons who participate in many status battles, we will give a couple of examples now.

Peter Johnson is married to Joanne Peterson and they have two children, Gary and Anne. Peter is head of the Financial Department of Mendelsohn & Sons, a producer of pianos. Joanne is a housewife. They live in London, and Peter is fan of Arsenal. Now Peter might participate in a whole series of status battles. In the first place, he battles with his wife: he does not want Joanne to have also a paid job; he is the breadwinner, period. As the head of a department Peter is battling with heads of other departments in the company for which he works. He is also fighting against his subordinates, who are constantly challenging him. On Saturday Peter wears typical Arsenal clothes and attends the weekly match, but when Arsenal has to play against Chelsea, also a club from London, the confrontations between the supporters of the clubs show true rivalry. In election time Peter used to vote for the Liberal Democrats, although he lives in a typical Conservative neighbourhood. This example can be extended by a large number of other battles, to be fought by one person who is a member of many groups.

Another example is the attack of the USA on Iraq in 2003. They wanted to kill Saddam Hussein, and to install a democratic regime which would accept the rules of the free market economy, including the oil market. But Hussein did not threaten the oil production and export of the Middle East region. The American president, Bush Junior, just wanted to finish the job of his father, when he threw Hussein out of Kuwait. Hussein constantly challenged the Americans politically, and the invasion in Iraq was simply meant to teach the challenger a lesson. Many economists, the liberals as well as radicals, explain the invasion as an attempt to secure oil delivery. When looking at the level of the costs and the loss of prestige of the Americans it seems highly unlikely that oil was the only reason for the invasion.

In this social-economic world, the social and the economic aspects of human behaviour affect each other in every action. Social battles are costly operations, and therefore economically limited. If a union calls for a strike, it is not only meant as a means to get

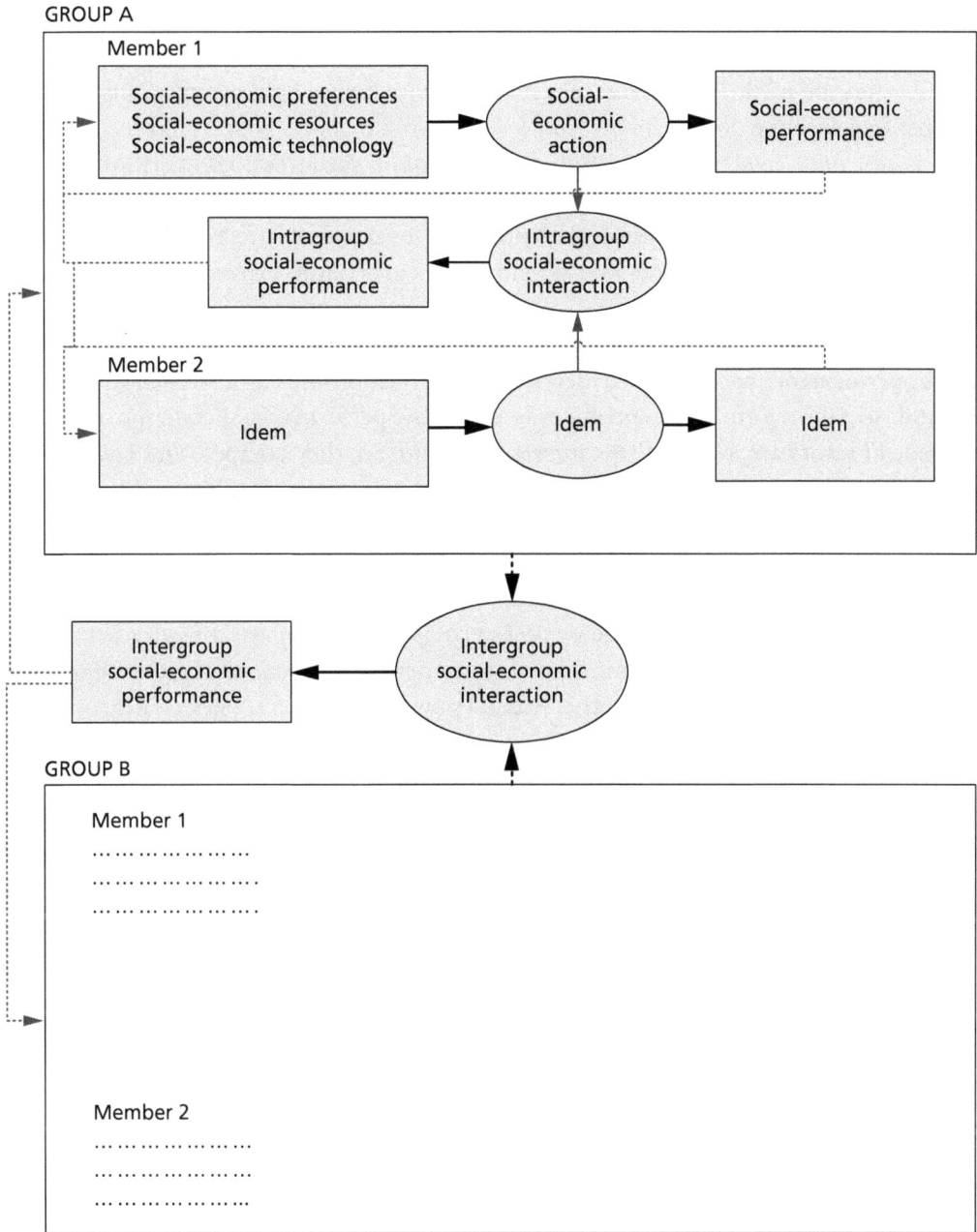

Figure 14.9. Competition and Rivalry in the Social-Economic World

an increase in the wage rate. It is also an attempt to test the power of the employers, and to show the world that the union is an organization which must be taken seriously. Nevertheless, if the strike fund is almost exhausted, the union must consider stopping the strike. Suppose the workers are very committed to their cause, and accept a large decline in the 'wage' they receive from their union during the strike; this makes union success more likely. The last few years we saw many actions from Greek workers against the austerity policy of the government, which was under heavy pressure from the IMF, the EU, and the ECB. The workers' general reaction was: we fight against injustice, not against wage decline.

It is not only rivalry that is limited by economic resources; competition is also limited by social resources. If the price of rice rises because of speculation by some traders, many people might (violently) protest. Governments are put under pressure to intervene in the free market and set particular maximum prices or organize large buffer stocks.

We can imagine that actors compete and cooperate on markets and that their economic performance contributes to their status. The relationship can also be the other way around: social performance contributes to economic performance. Economic, rational, and social actors are aware of this interrelationship. So, they compete and rival at the same time. The analysis by Fligstein about markets, discussed in Chapter 13, is a nice illustration of a permanent status battle on markets, in which private and public players collude and try to dominate market processes. Here, real-life markets are economic markets and social arenas at the same time.

In a simple model, characterized by *perfect competition* and *perfect rivalry*, actors are in a social-economic equilibrium. All actors are perfectly informed about each other's competitiveness, and about each other's social power. In case of imperfect information, the combination of the market and the arena mechanism is responsible for a smooth adjustment process in case of new information. In equilibrium, every actor is using his social-economic resources and technologies to improve his situation. In a more advanced model we can add an institutional part. On the basis of experience, a subject or a group of subjects can decide to adopt rules of behaviour: habits, routines, customs. In this way, economic and social institutions arise and form the context of the economic and social processes.

This social-economic analysis gives us the opportunity to show resource and substitution effects, which are neither part of the social nor of the economic world. We will give a few examples to illustrate the existence of these effects.

(1) In the course of the 19th century Continental Europe recovered from the Napoleonic Wars. The Industrial Revolution created economic growth and growing inequality. It triggered feelings of rivalry among the rank and file. It meant that unskilled workers were motivated to organize social resources: more meetings, socialist education, and increasing fighting spirit. Later, when employers increasingly gave in to, or even cooperated with, the unions in the development of positive social institutions, attitudes of the workers changed from negative to positive. Negative social resources turned into positive social and economic resources.

(2) The same social-economic process can be observed within families. Feminists started a battle of the sexes in the 1960s. They called men the oppressors of women,

and discussed problems such as rape within marriage, and other forms of oppression. In the Western world feminists were quite successful, because the idea of substantial equality between all people was already a cornerstone of Western civilization. Slowly the battle turned into more economic cooperation: a lot of feminist energy was used to get a paid job on a level as high as possible. Growth of resources, progress in social and economic technology, and institutional change took place in a process full of interactions.

In both cases we see that a typical social process of emancipation transforms latent potential into manifest action, creating resources which can be used in the economic processes.

14.6 **The Psychic-Social World**

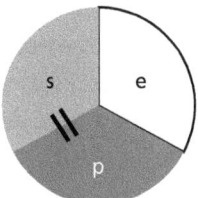

This world is based on the idea that actors are imperfectly rational, social, and non-economic. Non-economic means that natural resources are affluent, while the psychic aspect means that mental resources, combined with mental technologies, are too limited to produce sufficient willpower. The world is closed, and determined by the typical psychic and the typical social mechanism. It implies that relationships, derived from the analysis, can be described by means of logic and the mathematics that is derived from this.

An integration of the two worlds means that conflicts in the mind of persons are socially embedded, and that social structure results from the interaction between imperfectly rational persons. This picture is less unrealistic than one might think in the first instance. The deregulation of the Western financial system during the 1980s and 1990s offered the banks the opportunity to multiply the credit they offered to clients. The leverage mechanism was used on an unprecedented scale. Many (quasi)-banks let their solvency decline towards 2–3 per cent. When we look at a particular bank we can consider this subject to be an imperfectly rational subject. Every client could see that insolvent banks are fragile, and vulnerable to setbacks. Many top bankers meet up with top bankers of other banks on a regular basis. They all read the same newspapers, are all using the same sources of analysis, and were all educated in the same type of institutions. In this way, they have developed a common framework of interpretation, and by regularly meeting each other, they execute social control so as to prevent important persons from deviating too greatly from the rules. So, a *subculture* develops, in which it is possible that critical voices are strangled. Independent thinkers are 'losing their effectiveness', as is the expression in the world of finance and business. They are fired, which makes the social group homogeneous again.

In Figure 14.10 we have presented a schedule which shows the interrelationship between the two mechanisms. Every person and every group has an internal psychic mechanism, and an external social mechanism. So, actor 1 and actor 2 stand for a subject—be it a person or a group of persons. The TSE of the group expresses the identity of the group (culture). When the group is dissatisfied with its 'psychic' performance—for instance, Ajax plays quite defensively, which is very much against its identity—in the evaluations the people in charge will consider important changes. It might lead to a change in identity (TSE) or in a change of actual behaviour (ASE). Suppose actors 1 and 2 are groups—both imperfectly rational. They socially interact and try to show the world that they are ranked higher than their opponent. Imagine two departments of a television broadcasting company, namely the production department and the marketing department. The production department has attracted a number of professional journalists. They form a team who has meetings on a daily basis. Over time, they have developed a common understanding about the *quality* of TV productions. The marketing department has also attracted a number of specialists, who are responsible for the *popularity* of TV programmes. The production department considers the marketing department to be their rival, and vice versa. This example is borrowed from the famous Danish drama *Borgen* (series 1, episode 3), where

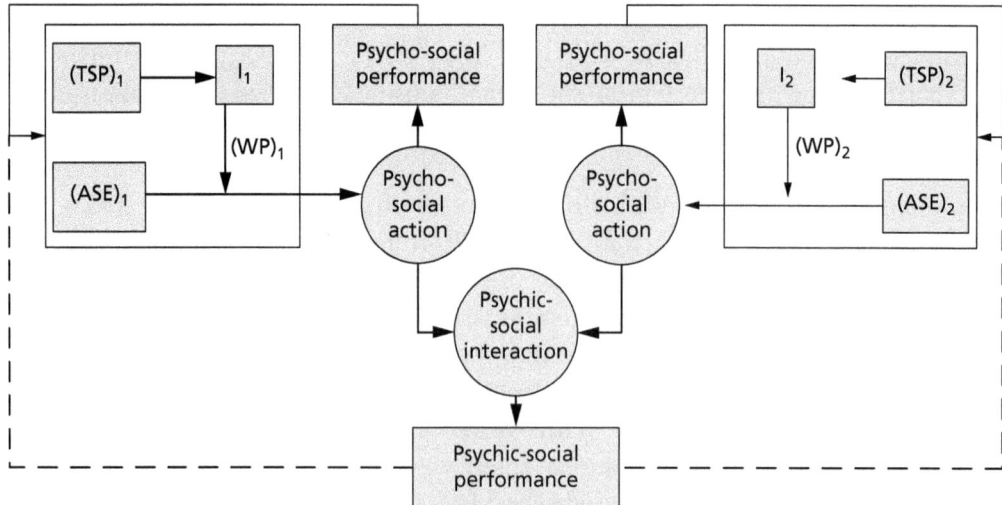

Figure 14.10. The Mechanisms in the Psychic-Social World

we see the company appointing a production director who has a typical marketing frame. Finally, the conflict becomes manifest, and the production director with the marketing mindset is fired by the Board, because all the production experts supported their boss unanimously. The conflict is typically social, but psychic elements aggravate the problem. The director's style of leadership is a permanent humiliation for the man who is head of the team of journalists—his ASE is too strong to be perfectly controlled. The way the head of the team handles the problem is shocking. He appears to be a man with a very low level of self-respect, who is unable to withstand the regular humiliations, which triggers the arrogant director to continue his ineffective approach.

For a good understanding of the situation in the TV series, it is necessary to start with the fact that the broadcasting company (TV1) is competing with another company (TV2). The competition is fierce, which means that both companies have an economic problem. That is the reason why the Board of TV1 appointed a production director with a marketing background. But our analysis of the psychic-social world shows that even if there are no economic problems at all—we live in a world of affluence—the psychic and social drives fuel a mechanism, which might create long-term imbalances.

Imagine two groups meet each other regularly, and experience each other as a serious rival. Members of the groups are imperfectly rational, and the group as a whole, led by imperfectly rational leaders, operates irrationally in their social interactions. Western Europe can be considered as a region characterized by affluence for many people. In so far as there is scarcity of resources, it is mostly socially created scarcity. People imitate the behaviour of those who are higher in the social ranking. This imitative behaviour is a costly affair, and can be justified by the social benefits in case of a higher position in the status ranking. Suppose the unions are representing wealthy insiders, while employers are representing wealthy firms. Nevertheless, the fights can be tough, because prestige is at stake. Meanwhile, the leaderships of the organizations involved are very busy with their own 'problems': meeting each other in pleasant places and exchanging valuable opportunities for friends and for the children of current leaders. Corrupt practices create moral resentments among the rank and file of the union. Workers might become sick of their union, and erect a new one. So with employers' organizations. In the psychic-social world the two mechanisms strengthen each other's effects: *increasing rivalry is fed by increasing irrationality, and vice versa.* But can we say that decreasing rivalry leads to increasing rationality, and vice versa? Under some conditions this seems the case. If the higher-ranked persons and groups decide not to show their superiority so often, this might weaken the moral resentments of the lower ranked. But if the lower-ranked people decide not to show their resentment so often, that might trigger the higher ranked negatively, who humiliate the lower-ranked even more.

Now we assume that not all members of a group are perfectly adjusted to the cultural views and norms of the group. Suppose that prestigious people become a little deviant, and invite members of the rival group for talks. There are two reasons why prestigious persons might take such an initiative. In the first place, they might perceive the losses of the battle for their own people as too high. In the second place, they might have discovered that members of the enemy are not that bad. The second discovery is extremely important: people who are different are not necessarily bad. If rational persons of both rival groups regularly meet with each other, they develop a common understanding of their situation. Then they can try to convince their groups to stop the rivalry and to begin more positive relationships. In 1989 Gorbachev decided to stop the Cold War against the USA. At that moment he was convinced that a planned economy such as the Soviet one, could never win the status battle against a capitalist economy such as the American one. He announced an important strategic change: a restructuring of the economy (perestroika) and more openness of society (glasnost). Of course, the malfunctioning of the centrally planned economy played an important role, but without the status battle the Soviet Union would have had ample resources to feed and to clothe its population. The population could not profit from the continuous progress in production technology because of the extremely high military budget. In a perfectly social world the huge losses resulting from the status battle is a reason for social actors to imagine that the rivalry must have a terrible effect on people of the other group as well. This development of positive emotions—moral sentiments—is the beginning of a moral restriction 'do unto others as you would have them do unto you'. In the case of irrational people this reaction is less probable. Their closed minds prevent them interpreting the situation of the other in an unbiased way. Then, rational and moral leaders have a hard time convincing the members of their group that being more reasonable is in their own long-term interest. If leaders try too hard, irrational members might exorcise them. History, including contemporary history, shows that irrationality and immorality are like two liquids, which, put together, form an extremely explosive and toxic one.

14.7 The Psychic-Economic-Social World

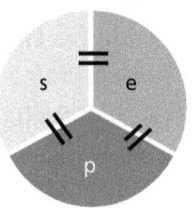

Now we bring the three analytically distinguished aspect-systems together. As long as the physical-chemical-biological world is not explicitly distinguished, our world is still a partial system, which is based on the ceteris paribus clause—in this case the assumption of a given natural world. When studying ecological problems, our multidisciplinary economic approach, as developed so far, is not useful. But our model shows exactly where the points of contact are if we want to transform the economic world into the ecological world. In Chapter 4 on orthodox economics we have paid some attention to this problem. Our three-motivational model shows that environmental problems are not only the consequence of scarcity of natural resources. If our mentality and morality show progress, they will contribute significantly to a more balanced relationship between man and nature.

In Figure 14.11 we have brought the three worlds together in one scheme. We have numbered the relevant relationships and characterized them one by one.

1. The TSE is a kind of strategic department for the Board ('I'), and put pressure on the Board to take the long-term interest of the person seriously.
2. The ASE can be interpreted as the rank and file of a firm. The assumption is that they act according to their own interest, which is immediate satisfaction. But they are sensitive towards the pressure of the Board to fulfil firm tasks properly; otherwise they know they will be 'fired'.
3. The Board takes decisions about the preference-ordering and puts pressure on the ASE—by means of its willpower—not to react too impulsively.
4. Under circumstances of imperfect information, it is difficult for the Board to find out what best serves the long-term interest of the firm. Should they take the experiences of the rank and file seriously, or is the advice of the strategic department (see 1) the most reliable voice.
5. In so far as the Board attaches value to the experiences of the rank and file, they justify this in discussions with the strategic department and with the social-political environment of the firm.
6. The psychic part is about the establishment of the preference-ordering, and the mental energy invested in the psychic conflict about this ordering. Concrete action, however, requires resources of a mental, economic, and social nature.
7. Under the influence of experiences, actors can also decide to spend resources on the improvement of the quality of the technology used so far.
8. Given the psychic, economic, and social technology, these resources are transformed into output. This means action which produces a particular performance.
9. The experiences lead to regular reflection by the actor. His mind frequently evaluates its internal and external policy. Should I spend more resources on the improvement of my TSE? There are many instruments that might be effective in this respect. And so with the other elements which constitute the mind system. From an economic point of view the actor can decide to strive for an increase in the economic resources and for technological progress.
10. From a social point of view the performance gives rise to regular evaluation, which might lead to a substitution of social resources for economic and psychic resources, and to an improvement of social technology. The figure shows a situation with two

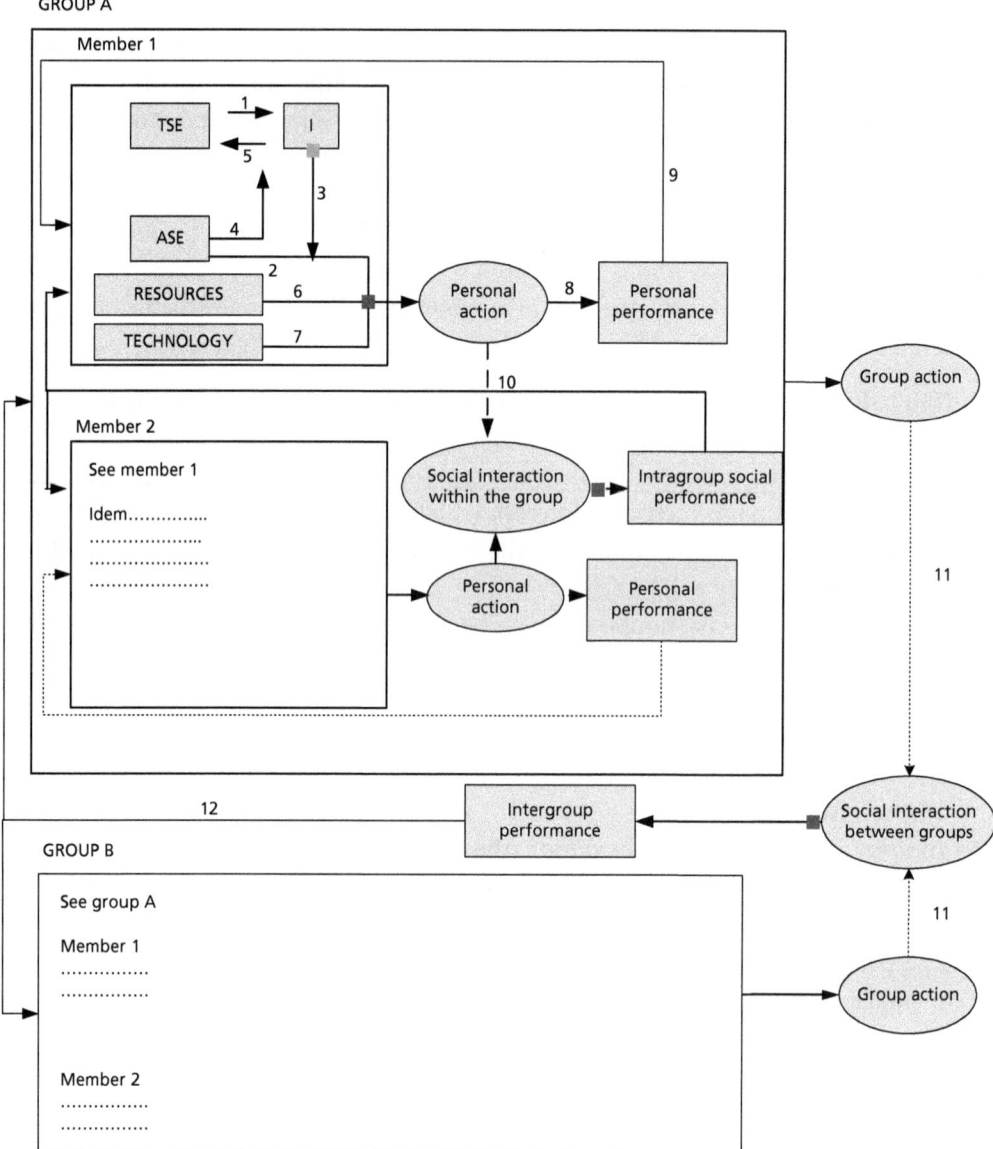

Figure 14.11 The Psychic-Economic-Social World

groups (A and B), and two members in each group (1 and 2). Within the group the actions of the members are part of social interaction. The effects of social interaction on the common understanding within the group trigger members to reflect upon their preferences, resources, and technology.

11. The group action, which is the result of all the actions of members of the group taken together, is part of the interaction between groups. This interaction has consequences for the way both groups perceive their common reality, as a harmonious or a more conflicting one.

12. If the intergroup structure changes, it might affect the psychic, economic, and social actions of subjects.

In this scheme the psychic conflict takes place within the 'I', being under pressure by the TSE as well as by the ASE (1 and 4). The 'solution' is indicated by the use of willpower by the 'I' (3 and 5). The economic conflict also takes place within the 'I'. When the 'I' puts pressure upon the ASE, it takes the amount of resources and the level of technology into account. Every system has its own evaluation procedures. The psychic, social, and economic conflicts create psychic, social, and economic disutilities respectively, thereby inducing pressure upon the decision-maker to change his decisions. All these reflections and evaluations do not only lead to changes in behaviour. They also affect the institutional framework adopted by persons and groups. The solution to the psychic conflict might mean that a person commits himself to applying a new set of rules. For instance, a person can decide to stop drinking alcohol, or force himself to automatically transfer part of his income to a savings account. To train his willpower he can develop a lifestyle which improves his mental and physical health. Besides a stronger will, he could try to improve his open-mindedness. The problem, however, is that people with closed minds do not perceive their minds to be closed. Later we come back to this issue. The solution to the actor's economic problem becomes easier if he has no inner conflicts. He can decide to educate himself and search for a better job. He can also try to achieve a lower level of consumption.

To clarify a way of solving an intragroup conflict, we can give the following example. Imagine a group of economists, some of them are econometricians, and others are institutionally orientated. Then one of the econometricians talks with an institutional economist about a part of the educational programme. Another econometrician hears his colleague saying that he will skip a particular mathematical part. This leads to a vicious discussion between the two econometricians: "how dare you say that—you know what we agreed upon!" Later the two econometricians discuss this issue in a more harmonious way, and the person who promised the institutional economist he would skip a mathematical text does not keep his promise. It goes without saying that this action triggers animosity between the two different groups of economists. The example shows that important processes of change involve an extremely large number of tiny fights—each not very important, but, taken together, representing a revolution.

The model as a whole makes it clear that the resource and substitution effects, so familiar in orthodox economics, can be interpreted in a much wider sense. Now we move from a very material idea of natural resources towards a concept which includes human energy, generated by mental and social processes. Depressed people have less energy than other people, and people who are socially appreciated have more energy than people who must fight against social prejudice. Persons cannot only be inspired and energetic by means of mental processes. Social processes, for instance on the national level, can also inspire persons and groups to actions which are completely impossible without socially orientated inspiration. Sportsmen who represent a country or politicians and CEOs of large companies might be inspired by all the positive energy in society. The current economic crisis in Europe results from a lack of confidence of consumers and investors in the short- and medium-term future of the economy. Dutch neoclassically orientated economists advised their government to cut their expenditures, and to further deregulate markets. This leads to lower resources in the hands of government as well as private subjects. Now, neoclassical politicians try to create a positive and energetic climate, and call upon private consumers and investors to stop being depressed, and spend. With an integrated model we see immediately how contradictory this policy advice is. The governments create lower growth rates, but ask the people to spend. A genuinely economic and rational actor would become depressed. But we live in a world with imperfectly rational persons. So, we never know what will be the effect of this government policy. The approach defended by Keynes is based on the idea that depressed people will only become more optimistic and spend if the government sets the example. The government is the only economic subject that is large enough to really create the inspiration necessary for a recovery. Moreover, many government investments are complementary to private investments. In the neoclassical analysis, these two types of investments are assumed to crowd each other out. At the moment (December 2013) Dutch employers try to convince the Liberal Party to stop expenditure cuts in important fields such as infrastructure and education. This illustrates all the more the cognitive closure of classical-liberal politicians at the moment.

15 Applications of the MDE World Approach

In this chapter we will give a number of examples, which illustrate the complex inter-relationship between the three primary aspects of human behaviour.

15.1 Discrimination as an Economic and Social Cost

Imagine a country whose society seems quite stable and the economy flourishing. Nevertheless, there are some people, mostly women, who feel dissatisfied with their position in society. It makes them feel bad, and their self-respect is low. However, every-thing happens according to generally accepted norms, which makes it difficult to complain. The only way of protesting seems to be wearing deviating clothes. Some of these women get together and talk about their feelings and their ideas about equality between men and women. Such small groups might be like butterflies in China, who cause a desert storm in America in the end. Women come into action, and psychic conflicts turn into social conflicts—in this case the battle of the sexes. Female emanci-pation increased significantly in north-western Europe during the last few decades of the 20th century, while in other parts of Europe women were expected to have a job, besides their job in the household. In the Muslim world, the pressure from women organizations to treat men and women equally is increasing. The resistance against these 'Western' ideas, however, is increasing too. In Afghanistan the Taliban is killing many 'disloyal' people, while the national women's football team practise their skills in Kabul at the same time.

The economic effects of female emancipation are clear: it allows people to apply the Ricardian rule of comparative advantage to the division of labour between men and women. This economic law assumes a society which is completely sex-neutral, but our description and explanation of the social world made it clear that this is far from true. In every firm women must fight, not just compete, to be hired and to be treated equally. Many men hate to be commanded by a woman. Men do not like to fight against other men under the chairpersonship of a woman. In such situations women function as strangers, who show that, from an economic point of view, cooperation is more effective than fight-ing: they should therefore leave the room. So, even economically productive women are not hired. But women who imitate men in their fighting behaviour, and also humiliate lower-ranked people, might even fuel the status battle. If we look at the psychic conflicts in the minds of men and women, it would be a revolution to appoint increasingly cooperative women and men. It might dampen social rivalry in the labour organizations, and lead to a release of energy which could be used to find a solution to economic problems.

15.2 A Cost-Benefit Analysis of (In)Equality

In Western Europe there is an ongoing debate between economists and social scientists about the price or value of equality. Economists who tell the liberal story mostly use the neoclassical paradigm as their theoretical foundation. Economic actors are supposed to be able to serve their own interest. Free markets coordinate their demand and supply decisions in such a way that the allocation process is optimal for the economy as a whole. The outcome, in terms of distribution of resources among people, depends on the distribution of the earning capacities among people. Some are talented or are lucky, while others are less talented or have bad luck. If governments try to make the distribution more equal, it is at the cost of the efficiency of the economy as whole. In other words, equality has a price. A transfer from rich to poor means an incentive for the rich as well as the poor to reduce their efforts. The discussion among liberal economists is reduced to finding out the lowest supply price of equality. The politicians must answer the question: How willing are they to pay for equality? Equilibrium equality is reached where the supply and demand curves cross each other.

In the MDE world, however, where not only the economic aspect is considered, but also the psychic and social aspect of human behaviour, the analysis is different. In this world there is no natural degree of equality, and government incidence is not considered as something alien. Now we take the economic world as our starting point, and assume that the labour market is in equilibrium, as was sketched by Figure 14.2b in Chapter 14. There are many people without capital, who are dependent on their labour service. In an economic world, where workers are assumed to be perfectly heterogeneous, the market value of the marginal product of extra-marginal workers is lower than the subsistence wage. So, there is no place for these people in a market society. Economic and rational actors have no problem considering these people to be a waste. They can be put into a bin and destroyed.[1] In the MDE world, however, bad economic performance is not accepted

---

[1] Since the economic world is just a thought experiment, we will never observe these destructive economic actions; it is only the logical implication of the assumptions which are made. If we add the two other aspects to it, we can explain how the combination of the three aspects might lead to such destruction. This is observed in reality so often. The destruction of 6 million Jews in the Second World War and the organizations responsible for the disappearance of so many opponents of the Argentinean regime at the end of the 1970s are just two examples from a terribly long list of the dark side of human history.

by the mass of the people. They do not interpret the outcome as something natural, like the weather. The economy is interpreted—as in our model—as also an arena, where powerful people play their status games and refuse to take responsibility for their irrationality. The extra-marginal workers react psychically as well as socially. Some people feel very bad about themselves, and become apathetic and reduce the pain by taking alcohol or drugs. Others group together and share their anger. When the anger grows, the group looks to channel it effectively. Demonstrations, occupations, and political actions might turn out to be effective means.

Now we sketch four situations, which might be stable for a particular period of time.

15.3 **Four More or Less Persistent Systems**

In the first place, we discuss a *capitalist society*, which is characterized by a large free market sector and a small government. The system is primarily focused on the protection of private property and a proper system of money issuance. If the government is too weak to protect the properties of the rich elite, the members erect their own private armies. Many people become apathetic and protesters are imprisoned or even killed. It might appear a successful policy, as we have seen in Chile in the 1970s. It can also lead to a private army of the poor, including people who pretend to operate on behalf of the poor. Colombia is a good example in this respect. For many decades the progressive opposition, who advocated social-democratic ideas, were oppressed so heavily that the most militant among them continued their social-democratic opposition as a group of guerrillas in the forests of the Amazon (FARC). At the moment (December 2013), the government and FARC are prepared to talk about a peace settlement. The government has implemented some social reforms already, and FARC still faces important losses. So, both parties might win in case of peace. It goes without saying that peace is a good thing, from the psychic as well as from the social and economic perspective. We see that in the case of Chile, as well as in the case of Colombia, a capitalist system can be stable for a long time, while we cannot say that there is equilibrium. In Chile many people felt oppressed, and even today groups take action to express their anger about what happened over the last decades. In Colombia many people supported FARC at the moment they went underground. But its popularity did not grow, forcing the organization to search for an armistice at the very least.

In the second place we discuss a *socialist society*, which is characterized by a large government sector and a small private sector. Different power centres compete with each other, mostly at the cost of the masses. Each of the power centres has adopted a mission, and many members of such a centre believe in the importance and rightness of their work. If it is necessary to shoot or even kill those who lost their effectiveness, this act is not seen as a moral problem. Actually, many people have a job in the socialist system, and do not bother about the social and moral aspects of the functioning of their system. They are all small links in a chain, and nobody can induce important changes. If some people are still fighting for change—improvement in the transparency of the system, for instance—they know of the negative effects this has for them and for their family. Large systems always make individual people feel powerless, leading to low self-esteem—whether the system is a capitalist or a socialist one. Nevertheless, history shows that socialist systems can be very stable. The Soviet Union, China, North Korea, and Cuba are illustrative in this respect.

In the third place, there are also *conservative societies*, which are held together by a strong culture represented by a cultural elite. These societies are not focused on economic success for the mass of the people. The elite in power find their legitimation in religious, ethnic, and nationalist ideas. They organize many manifestations to celebrate their identity: being Islamic, or Tutsi (Rwanda at the end of 20th century), or being Russian—not from the Caucasus (Putin in current Russia). Many opponents are just killed or put in prison; in Russia many of them end up in a labour camp somewhere in Siberia.

When applying the idea of the economic world to the real world and calculating the price of equality, redistribution of resources is always a costly affair. But if we apply the idea of our MDE world to the real world, increasing equality not only has costs, but also benefits. It might lead to less social conflict, which means that more resources can be used in economically profitable businesses. It might also lead to less psychic tensions in the minds of the members of the rank and file. People who face injustice and feel the lack of power to do something about it, feel low self-esteem; they suffer from the emotion of being a loser. Where there is more social justice, more people have self-respect, which is a major determinant of lasting satisfaction.

All these examples are about societies characterized by serious social conflicts, which have very negative effects on the economic and psychic performance of the country. Some regions appear more successful in the reduction of social rivalry than others. In our fourth type of society we discuss countries which were relatively successful in their attempt to overcome social conflict. This type of country is called the *welfare state society*.[2] It is based on the idea that economic prosperity and social justice can be realized at the same time. If the idea of social justice especially is realized, many psychic and social resources can be used for the fostering of economic prosperity. We have seen that north-western Europe, especially the Nordic countries, have been the most successful countries in this respect. They show the highest scores on the Human Development Index, and happiness research shows that people living in this part of the world score highest in terms of lasting satisfaction. With this last example we will show that even in a very harmonious societal structure the same psychic, social, and economic problems play an important role. The difference to other regions is one of degree, especially the degree in which people have learned to limit social rivalry. It means that more resources are available

---

[2] For an extensive treatment of the various types of welfare states, see Esping-Andersen (1990).

to be used for long-term social and economic development. As soon as we have introduced the dynamics of human motivation and the aspect of historicity, we will see that well-functioning societies have mechanisms which maintain this good functionality, but also mechanisms which makes it probable that 'empires' always decline after a period of peace and prosperity.

By means of an example we will show also that, in societies which are not characterized by social conflict on the macro level, life in the economy consists of an endless flow of social and psychic problems, which have a significant effect on the economic performance of families, firms, and economies as a whole.

The context of our case is Sweden during the 1950s. There were hardly social conflicts at that time, and the economy began to grow steadily. Two brothers, living in the Uppsala region, decide to erect a construction firm. The eldest brother, Ulf, works hard and excels in calculation and logistics, while the younger brother, Martin, likes the social aspect of life: meeting clients and colleagues from the construction sector. The firm appears to be an economic success and grows. Clients come from all parts of the country and this leads to long working hours for the two directors. The eldest brother feels good if the calculations appear correct, while the younger brother feels good as long he is not forced to work particularly hard. Fortunately for him, it is difficult for Ulf to monitor him closely. Over time it becomes increasingly clear that it is not only the two brothers who have very different attitudes, but also their respective families. Ulf marries an orthodox Protestant wife, while Martin falls in love with a Catholic girl. Pretty soon the girl falls pregnant, and Martin decides to marry her.

Twenty years later the two brothers are succeeded by their eldest sons, Richard and Eric respectively. They differ from each other in almost every respect. Now the firm has grown and has built up financial buffers as a matter of precaution, the two directors quarrel about almost everything. Eric wants to make their office more luxurious: 'this is good for the prestige of the company'. He also wants to have a few business seats in the stadium of the local football club. What is more, potential clients must be invited to enjoy to 'Stockholm by night'. Richard prefers a very different style of doing business. The bonuses should be given to all the personnel—not just to the administrative elite. Moreover, the firm should also employ a number of people who are less productive due to physical handicaps.

Then, quite suddenly, the sales drop significantly. There is an oil crisis going on, and government agencies and housing corporations decide to cut their expenditures, thereby reducing the number of orders. Our company is one of the first companies to have a problem in paying the bills in time. Richard, our director with the Protestant background, blames Eric for his luxurious attitude and policy. But Eric, our director with the Catholic background, refers to the ongoing macro crisis, and to the change in arena structure: a few big firms have built up positive relations with relevant government agencies. Moreover, they are colluding and have divided the market among themselves.

Just before the brothers have to declare the firm bankrupt one of the big firms appears to be prepared to take over their firm, thereby offering the two brothers a very nice sum of money in exchange for leaving the company. Our Catholic director is very happy—over the years his self-respect has grown and he interprets this bonus as a sign of his value. Now he can buy a beautiful sailing boat, a wish he has for a long time. Our Protestant director, however, feels bad about the takeover. He blames himself for his lack of control of the behaviour of his co-director. He considers using his bonus as capital for a new firm—definitely without any member of the family.

In the case of the family firm we see that psychic and social factors play a significant role in how people act and react. Protestants, more than Catholics, are inclined to do what they think is right. Catholics, more than Protestants, attach more value to status. Without any social prestige it is impossible to participate in a market. The story ends with a takeover: some takeovers are unavoidable, even if strong personalities appear able to create social peace by acting justly. But in our case the firm was one of the first to be threatened by bankruptcy when the crisis broke out. In explanation of that fact, psychic and social factors play a significant role. In Section 15.4 we will discuss a number of concepts and their meaning in a MDE world.

15.4 Meaning of Concepts in the MDE World

As we have seen, the meaning of concepts depends crucially on the context in which they are used. The meaning of the concept of institution has a meaning in new institutional economics which differs substantially from the meaning of the same concept in original institutional economics. The same holds for all concepts; it makes sense to recognize whether a particular concept is used in the context of the economic world, or in the social or psychic world. Now we have developed an integrated paradigm the concepts have a meaning, which is determined by their MDE context. We will discuss a number of them, and show their multi-motivational basis.

15.4.1 UTILITIES (PREFERENCES), RESOURCES, AND TECHNOLOGY

In the first place, we discuss the concepts utilities (preferences), resources, and technology. We distinguish between the psychic, the social, and the economic aspect of human behaviour. This means that humans face three primary problems. Reduction of a problem induces utilities. So, we can distinguish three types of utilities, namely psychic, social, and economic utilities. They are, to a certain extent at least, interrelated, and can be substituted. They cannot, however, be reduced to each other.

With respect to the concept resources, we make the same distinction: psychic, social, and economic resources. Again, they are interrelated, they are imperfect substitutes, but cannot be reduced to each other.

Imagine a worker in a pharmaceutical company discovers malpractices by the Board. The problem for the worker is how to prove it in court in a way that is acceptable to the judge. The economic costs will be quite high if he tries. The social costs will be high too: his colleagues will definitely exorcise him. The psychic costs will be high, if he decides to accept the role of whistle-blower. But if he decides not to take action, while he is able to pay the (economic) costs, the psychic costs are very high. Psychic resources refer to the willpower, which a person can use in a fight. A person with a high level of self-respect and willpower is able to organize energy for this sort of activity—energy which is not available for other activities, such as doing the cooking.

Social resources refer to human energy, which become available in situations where social conflict and social harmony play a vital role. In the following example we make it clear what we mean by social resources.

Home care is a growing business in the Dutch health-care system. But the government cuts its health expenditures year after year. The number of volunteers in this sector is growing as well. Now they increasingly organize themselves into volunteer associations, so as to professionalize their work. The enthusiasm created by regular consultations among volunteers is a good example of a social resource. A culture emerges, which creates a common understanding, leading to a sense of belonging. It gives the work of volunteers meaning, which would not have happened in a different institutional setting.

The meaning of the concept technology is also different from the meaning it has in the economic world. This technology is about the application of physical and chemical knowledge to make production processes more efficient. Psychic and social technology is not part of the modern discussions about innovation and the desirability of government subsidies in this field. In our integrated world they are. Here the mind is an integrated part of the world under scrutiny. *Psychic technology* is about the knowledge and skills a person has to improve the functioning of the mind. There is a market for persons who want to become closer to their true Self, and increase the strength and effectiveness of their willpower. This market offers rationality as a good. We have seen that rationality is not the opposite of emotionality. Later we will come back to the meaning of the concept 'rationality' in our integrated world. *Social technology* is about the knowledge and skills of members of groups—employees of a firm, professionals of a particular school of thought, members of a particular church, the indigenous population of a particular country—to keep peace within their group, and to search for possibilities to create peace between rival groups. Imagine a person who hates one of her colleagues because he belongs to a different school of thought. She has no energy to go to that person in a constructive way to find out whether this person is really disgusting or not. Other persons in her group might have the social energy to learn themselves that persons in the rival group might be different, but are, nevertheless, also sources of wisdom. Some parts of the Bible can be interpreted as an introduction into the technique of peace-making. Other parts, however, seem to fuel human rivalry: the technique of how to keep rivalry alive. In the Netherlands some student associations teach their members how to form a close network—implicitly suggesting that non-members should not be treated with solidarity. It is generally known that one of the largest Dutch banks is 'occupied' by alumni of one particular student association. In this way rivalry is kept alive. It is also generally known that the social conflicts in the largest Dutch union, the FNV, is essentially a fight of members of the Labour Party against members of the Socialist Party. It is a continuing status battle, in which compromises are just temporarily concluded. In these fights we see that the fighters—especially the more militant socialists—have large amounts of energy available for this battle. In these examples the social aspect is very important, but—as is always true—not the only influential one. The psychic and economic aspects play a role as well. For the students who become members of that particular association, especially in the beginning, the economic aspect—getting a well-paid job, for instance—plays an important role as well. For the union holds that the fighters are also psychically motivated: they follow their heart (in our terminology they listen to their TSE), and fight for a good cause.

While psychic technology can be improved in such a way that a person becomes more rational, groups can also improve their technology to increase social harmony and solidarity: within as well as between groups. The *Dutch Polder model* is a good example of social technology. Unfortunately, the actual Dutch consultation economy needs some maintenance. The renewal of groups which are represented—consumers and environmental associations also have a say now—can be seen as an example of social-technological progress. If we combined psychic and social technological developments, the results might surprise us.

15.4.2 RATIONALITY

In the second place, we will discuss the concept rationality in more detail. In moral philosophy the concept is linked to self-control. Later, especially in sociology, the term also came to be applied to larger groups, such as firms and societies. Also, here the concept is about control by means of the ratio, which is the human capacity to make a logically consistent analysis of a situation, and to use it for concrete action. Logic is the language of the ratio, and the analysis is based on an intuition, which is characteristic of the personality of the subject and significantly affected by his experience.

Orthodox economists only use the term economic rationality, which refers to rational persons who live in the economic world. Orthodox sociologists only use the term social rationality, which refers to rational persons and groups operating in the social world. And so with orthodox psychologists: rationality refers to rational persons living in the psychic world. When we apply the term to subjects living in the integrated world, it refers to control of this world. Then, a rational firm means that it is able to execute its mission in a way which is efficient and fair. It is not necessary that employees of the firm be perfectly rational persons; it is enough that all employees function as perfectly rational functionaries. Apparently the firm has developed a perfect system of socialization, tying imperfectly rational persons together in a perfectly functioning team.

If a group is imperfectly rational and dysfunctional, individual members can take the initiative to improve cohesion. By regularly communicating about the mission they have in common, they build a strong culture. The common view on their situation leads to a series of moral constraints, channelling the behaviour of the members of the group. These constraints can be adopted to restore internal cohesion. An important question is whether a socially stronger group is inclined to use its increase in power to put more energy into the rivalry with its opponents or do just the opposite? We can imagine that a small and not-too-powerful group will use its excess supply of social energy to rival with the group just above it in the ranking. But if a group is large and powerful already, increasing cohesiveness might give the group the trust that attempts to seek out more cooperation and solidarity will not turn out to be destructive. We can even imagine that two powerful firms decide on a merger, so as to be able to dominate a particular market and its governance agencies, which are responsible for its functioning. Imagine that the merger is a success, and the new firm dominates the market, thus increasing profits. This success gives the Board the opportunity to change its strategy. More profits lead to more financial buffers, which makes a longer planning horizon possible. If the Board consists of people with rather open minds, who feel responsible because of their power, the firm's strategy might become more sustainable. If the Board consists of people with rather closed minds, the firm might go on playing power games, which could presumably enable it to dominate its field.

15.4.3 MORALITY

In the third place, we discuss the term morality in more detail. We have seen that the social world is defined as the world in which social beings fight their status battles. From Girard we adopted the idea that morality was developed as a reaction to experiences of extreme violence: 'we should not want it—it might destroy us in the end'. Morality is presented as an instrument in the survival kit—in the religious variant morality should please god(s), and in the secular variant morality should protect us against the almost limitless anger and fear inside each of us. Secularization meant the disappearance of god(s) and the crowning of man as the king of reality. Half a century ago, however, we saw the beginning of what we now call *ecological awareness*. Our universe evolves, and the positive influence of humans on it might be very tiny. The modern idea of humans being the kings of the universe has led us to a whole System of risky systems, which might run out of control (Beck, 1992). So, we also need morality in our relationship with nature. Of course, human responsibility for the environment can only be limited. Nevertheless, it makes sense to take ecological considerations into account.

The history of Western moral philosophy can be characterized by three distinct approaches, namely Greek philosophy (1), the approach of the Enlightenment, and especially of Kant (2), and the utilitarian approach, especially of Bentham (3).

Greek moral philosophy tries to answer the question of how to live a *virtuous life*. According to Plato, the most important virtue is self-control, which is focused on a total suppression of passions. Aristotle, however, interpreted self-control as the capacity to select which passions are virtuous and which are not. He advocated a modest and moderate lifestyle. So, drinking alcohol is no problem as long as it is not too much. And so with many passions: keep to the middle of the road. Currently, McCloskey and Nussbaum are advocating research on virtues and their effect on economic and societal life. The overall question remains how to control emotions.

In the period of the Enlightenment moral philosophy took a different turn. A good example is Kant, who developed the idea of the *categorical imperative*. Kant distinguishes three categories, which cannot be reduced to each other. Morality is one of them and has the nature of an imperative: 'Thou shall do this . . . and thou shall never do that.' So, Kant's moral theory is not about concrete behaviour, which should be called morally good or morally bad. His theory is about the question of what makes a statement a moral statement. In other words, what is the substance or definition of morality rather than what are its evolving properties. Kant's argument about moral substance runs as follows. What humans have in common is the fact that they are humans; in that sense they are all equal. Humans are not animals, plants, or pieces of rock, and should not be treated as such. This means that humans should treat each other as humans, which implies a way which maintains at least a bare minimum of respect. In our social world terminology: we should minimize human rivalry as much as we can. We can do this by developing a framework of moral rules, which limit human exploitation and humiliation. The events in the Abu Ghraib prison in Baghdad in 2003, where American soldiers treated naked Iraqis as leashed dogs, is a perfect example of human rivalry and immorality in the sense of Kant. If we put rationality (psychic control) and morality (social control) together, we have constructed the concepts reason and reasonability. A reasonable person is a person who is rational and moral in the sense of Kant; and so with the concept of reasonable society, which is rational and moral in the sense of Kant. So his approach gives us a strictly impartial morality: the moral rules hold for all individuals. The golden rule of the United Nations is not only based on biblical notions, but is also in line with Kant's approach. While this approach sounds so intellectual—so without emotion—actually it is based on a very strong emotion. We come back to this issue later.

A third approach in moral philosophy is called *utilitarianism*. It criticizes the previous ideas about morality, by stressing that it is not the intention, but the consequences, which makes particular behaviour moral or not. Good effects can be expressed in terms of utilities, and bad effects in terms of disutilities. Bentham has become the most familiar utilitarian. He said that we must aim at a maximum of happiness (expressed in utilities) for a maximum number of people. Of course, the production of happiness is not an easy business. People can take too much of particular goods, making them addicted. Particular lifestyles produce series of excitements, but not lasting satisfaction. When we imagine that only intentions play a role in our decision about what is moral behaviour, we see that our analysis does not lead to satisficing results. If a person gives money to the poor, making them happier than they were before, it is a moral act without knowing what the motivation of the money-giver is. Maybe the giver hopes that everybody will praise him as a responsible person. But this motivation does not make the act non-moral.

If we compare the three approaches, we can make the following comments. The virtue approach is essentially about the preferences of the people. Some preferences are morally good (virtuous) and other preferences are morally bad (vicious). But moral preferences might be a necessary but not a sufficient condition for labelling behaviour as moral. The Kant approach leads to the interpretation of morality as a constraint—a person is doing good because he thinks that he should, whether he likes it or not. The utilitarian approach is essentially about the utility people derive from particular behaviour. The difference between the Greeks and the utilitarians is not essential, especially not when we take the distinction of Mill into account: besides pleasure utilities (hedonism) we can also distinguish moral and aesthetic utilities. In other words, virtues also create utilities. So, what is left is the distinction between preference and restriction. Now it makes sense to recall Nietzsche's view on Christian morality. He considered Christians to be slaves: people who act according to some rules, which limit their possibilities to express and manifest themselves. But what if persons learn the wisdom of some moral rules over the course of their life, and adopt them voluntarily, and learn to enjoy the practising of it? In the language of the utilitarians we can say that the application of moral rules create (moral) utilities. Then these persons have learned to internalize moral rules and *transform this restriction into a preference.*

15.4.4 INSTITUTIONS

In the fourth place, we discuss the concept of institution. Institutions are rules of behaviour, which result from a permanent process of learning. Actors form habits as they act in ways which satisfy. Why change a winning team? The answer to this question is: circumstances may have changed. In the case of a football team we can imagine that a very successful team must be changed, because a few top players are becoming older and slower. Or the opponents have developed successful methods of defence, which require counteraction by different players. Perhaps several other teams have adopted a totally different view on the phenomenon football. Barcelona, advised by the famous Cruyff, redefined the idea of what football is, and began to educate a new generation of players in the new philosophy. Now Barcelona and Spain have reigned in the world of football for a decade or so. A few years ago, opponent Bayern Munich attracted Van Gaal as coach. He was one of the successful coaches of Barcelona, and introduced his ideas in Munich. Recently (2013), the new coach of Bayern was Guardiola, the most successful Barcelona coach ever; altogether a good example of innovation diffusion.

This football story shows that institutions—although meant to stabilize situations, so as to make them more predictable—must permanently evolve in order to remain successful. Otherwise a successful team will not be successful in the end. Good habits become bad habits, and routines become ineffective—just under the pressure of changing circumstances. Nevertheless, there are institutions which should not be changed too quickly. In our football case the outcomes of the matches are not only the result of the quality of the players and of the team. Institutions designed to reduce doping in the sport, or to reduce referee bribing, are progressive institutions, and should not disappear because of changed power relations.

In the world of business these practices are common occurrences. Institutions can channel malpractices as well as good practices. In large parts of the world women are still discriminated against—their preferences are not important. Strong institutions maintain these malpractices—Veblen's institution 'habit of thought' is the most important barrier to progress. Recent experiences in the Muslim world shows that bad institutions can be challenged, but that it will take much time and energy to create stable progressive institutions.

Institutions in our MDE world are multi-motivated. Imagine a person decides to build up more buffers of psychic energy by doing fitness exercises on a very regular and frequent basis. He forces himself to exercise every day. This is especially meant to build up his willpower. This rule might also give the person more energy to manage his department in a more open way, or participate in a long strike. More endurance has many applications, and rules that make the person more persevering are helpful with regard to him reaching his targets. Institutions on a personal level are like virtues—living a virtuous life gives much lasting satisfaction. But on the level of an organization also we can develop virtues—then we speak of culture, and of institutions in which it is specified.

Rules are meant to keep control over important processes. The MDE world brings psychic, social, and economic control together. If a woman wants to take part in boxing lessons, so as to invest in willpower, she also faces the social and the economic aspect. If she lives in a radical Muslim culture, the rulers might forbid her to take these lessons. If the woman is economically dependent on her father or husband, and he is not willing or able to finance the lessons, boxing is an impossibility. Besides the distinction in three aspects or motivations, we can also distinguish between the personal, the organizational, and the public level. Imagine that the European Union governs European society. In this scenario there is a European mind with a particular identity. The European citizens perceive themselves as European and act accordingly. Then, severe economic problems arise—worse in some regions than in others. The EU designs and executes a policy which arouses moral sentiments as well as moral resentments—in some regions moral sentiments dominate, while in other regions it is resentments. Especially in the areas most hurt by the EU policy moral resentment also creates a lack of self-respect—an intense feeling of being a loser. Some people become apathetic, but others have a stronger personality, and transform their negative feelings into aggressive or even outright violent behaviour. While it is 'natural' that superiors use their subordinates as a way to work off their feelings, groups of subordinates can also work off their feelings on the bosses—in firms, as well as in society at large against government agencies or banks. Psychic and social conflicts can make economic solutions to economic problems impossible.

Dramatic positive events can trigger a return to more healthy relationships. Dramatic negative events can aggravate the three typical problems. Too much cultural difference between two areas in one organizational whole might change the experienced true Self (TSE) of the European citizens: we are not European citizens anymore. For instance, because of the enduring European crisis Germans tend to stress the German identity; and so with the Greeks in Greece. The social problems in Europe might aggravate the internal social problems in Spain: Basque Country versus Madrid and Catalonia versus Madrid. If the central government foresees this threat, they might consider a stimulus programme, in which the two areas play an important role. An important condition for such a policy is that leading politicians have a strong personality—people who can control their more primitive emotions, such as: 'now we have the chance to teach the separatists a lesson'.

A last example of an integrated analysis is about the current economic situation in Japan (2013). The story starts with the burst of the bubble on the stock market in 1989. It was the end of a long period of (over)optimism. This period started with the introduction of the Nikkei Index in 1949. The burst of the bubble was the beginning of a deep psychic crisis. Brooke, a high-ranked employee of the GLG Japan Core Alpha Fund, and generally recognized as a Japan expert, describes this crisis in terms derived from the famous psychiatrist Kübler-Ross (Van Lotringen, 2013). The population went through all the stages of grief: denial, anger, negotiation, depression, and acceptation. Now Japan is at the brink of a new revival. The banks took about twenty years to restructure and to recapitalize themselves, but are able to fulfil their regular tasks again. The new prime minister, Abe, appears able to create a positive political climate. The population seems ready for a new start. The monetary policy has become very expansionary, which means that the central bank is trying to increase the amount of money in circulation significantly. Via a lower value of the yen in relation to the dollar the Japanese hope for an increase of their exports, which is expected to stimulate economic growth, employment, and tax receipts.

Brooke offers a macro-psychic-economic explanation of Japanese economic development over the last 60 years. On the basis of our integrated MDE approach we can expect improvement in the quality of his explanation if we add the social factor to his analysis. In the first place, we should pay more attention to internal social rivalry and solidarity. The big Japanese companies were more or less private welfare states for their employees, while the Japanese workers without secured employment were treated as second-rate citizens. Social peace can only be secured if a modest sober welfare state be more democratically organized. In the second place, we should pay more attention to external rivalry and solidarity. The history of East Asia shows that Japan has manifested itself in a negative way, thereby triggering rivalry. When Japan surrendered in 1945 the military expression of rivalry in East Asia stopped. In contrast to Western Europe, East Asia did not decide to build an East Asian Union, so as to reduce the chance of another war. The German attitude towards their former European enemies was quite different. The Nazis most responsible for atrocities were brought to court, and a new Germany restructured its foreign policies completely. Europe was helped financially by the Americans, and the

Germans paid the state of Israel large amounts of compensation. In East Asia, however, there is still animosity among the relations between the Japanese and the people of the countries which were occupied by them during the Second World War (Buruma, 2013). It would be a good idea to ask the Japanese emperor to visit these countries, and show them a totally different attitude, compared with the superior attitude shown by the Japanese during the Second World War. East Asians should take more initiatives to develop their identities in line with an emerging and more positive East Asian identity.

At present, economists discuss Japanese problems primarily from the neoclassical/monetarist perspective. The current approach is based on a monetarist view: an economy in a recession needs an expansionary monetary policy, executed by a central bank which is independent of the government. Abe hopes to create so much money that the yen depreciates in relation to the dollar, so that exports will grow. But according to this approach, the largest economy of East Asia, and third in the global ranking, hopes to climb up the ladder at the cost of other economies—a policy also executed by the EU. In both cases poor countries are supposed to help out rich countries. This is not a progressive policy; neither from a psychic nor from a social and economic point of view. At the end of this chapter we will make a few remarks about the current global economic crisis, and especially about the crisis in the EU from our MDE perspective.

15.4.5 ECOLOGY

In the fifth place, we discuss the ecological context of our approach. In the orthodox economic approach nature has a connotation of constancy. There are strict laws of nature, and the more laws we discover, the better we can control nature, and use it to the advantage of economic and rational actors. But also here history plays a role. Concrete materials change over time, and cultivation of land makes nature different from what it was in the past. Nature appears less predictable than some scientists still assume. There are definitely laws, and we can use nature to our own advantage—but there are limits to this one-sided approach. The other side means that there is an organic interrelationship between humans and non-humans. If we do not just approach nature from an economic point—try to dominate nature—but commit ourselves to an interrelationship with non-humans, it might benefit all parties. Also, the psychic aspect plays a role in our ecological view. If we abandon the typical Western idea of domination, and accept the emotion of being small relative to the whole of nature, we might lose the overstressed idea of controlling everything. It might even lead to more self-respect rather than less—acting on the basis of a more realistic view makes failures less dramatic. It also makes us less sensitive to the seduction of making overoptimistic plans (see the Minsky view on the financial world in Chapter 8; see also the text of Keizer on the welfare state hubris in Chapter 9). It is a generally accepted idea that children should regularly touch animals, plants, and mud. Living in a world of concrete does not make the world a comfort zone.

Modern urban and rural planners know that it is not only humans who need a place where they can develop their talents. Trees need space and soil; and so with rivers. If we place our MDE world in an ecological environment, the analysis gives the opportunity to apply the three aspects of human science to make it clear that humans and non-humans profit from the recognition of the ecological aspect. Achterhuis (1988) makes it clear that human rivalry as analysed by Girard is a major force making the economic scarcity problem unsolvable. One of the consequences is that social-economic actors will always need more natural resources, which makes the ecological problem practically insolvable. We can formulate these relationships more positively. It means that a reduction of the problem of human rivalry, including the psychic imbalances needed for the continuation of this rivalry, would create more room for an ecologically balanced approach to economic problems.

In Section 15.4.6 we will discuss the next step in making the MDE model more realistic: the opening of our closed and deterministic system.

15.4.6 THE OPENNESS OF SYSTEMS

Our systems are constructions, which try to show how parts of our reality work. When we construct a closed system, we mean to say that the world which is constituted, described, and explained, is ruled by a limited number of laws. These laws are derived from an analysis of the forces and mechanisms which determine how the system works. They describe adjustment processes, which always bring systems, once in disequilibrium, back to equilibrium. When we construct an open system, we mean to say that our world is always subject to unexpected changes, from within the system as well as from outside it. In other words, reality, which is modelled by an open system, is difficult to predict—there might be laws we don't know yet. There might also be discontinuity in the (closed) relationships. Let's imagine a simple 'relationship': a few observations of two empirical entities, A and B. It is usual in econometric research to intrapolate and to extrapolate, and to estimate the coefficients of the relationships we find. In our discussion of the Phillips curve we have seen that, if the author had not dismissed so many observations, the relationship would not have been stable at all. Moreover, ten years after its 'discovery', the curve broke adrift. So, if we close the world in order to create a controllable model, we must know that reality is essentially an open system for us. It means that we always face uncertainty, and we should always be aware of it and take precautionary measures, so as to deal with it.

In natural sciences the relationships which are discovered are more reliable and future developments more predictable. But even in this field of science, it makes sense to realize that the natural system is an open system. Sudden and unexpected changes are possible and we should build buffers in our natural technology. In human sciences the openness of reality is more obvious. But the reason why human systems are more difficult to predict and control—human creativity, capacity to reflect emotionally and cognitively—is also the reason why humans might develop sustainable systems. Human subjects have a strong motivation to reduce uncertainty. They are able to develop ingenious systems to protect themselves against the unexpected: dikes, well-founded homes, and the police and army, for example. Humans have developed very complex systems of rules—institutions—to make behaviour more predictable and controllable. Many rules are automatized, which makes behaviour habitual. Some rules were so important that they gained a moral connotation and became customs. Examples of customs are protocols and routines in professional environments.

We can imagine reality as a large hierarchical system of subsystems. Every subsystem has its function in the whole, but if a subsystem fails, other systems might be able to take over its function. Systems which cannot easily be substituted must have buffers to protect them against the unknown future. If we take the economy as an example, it cannot be replaced by a different system which fulfils its function. But there are many firms which might be necessary for persons or small groups, but which need not be backed by the government, who is responsible for the economy as a whole. If the shareholders of a firm consider their firm to be necessary, they should take care of financial buffers. So with persons and families: if people consider some systems as necessary and irreplaceable, they should take measures to make those systems shock-proof. If an economy is relatively open, it is vulnerable to negative shocks coming from outside the economy. This makes it all the more urgent for the government to protect the economy by means of large buffers: stocks of gold, for instance. If the wider economic system is in disarray, the government can decide to stimulate its economy—if necessary by increasing its own investments. It can also decide not to become too dependent on other economies with respect to necessary goods, such as food and energy.

If the community believes that bankrupt persons and families should be supported within a series of conditions, it must develop support systems. Now we move from the economy to the larger system society. If persons living in a particular society have strong moral sentiments, they can develop systems of charity. If persons or families are not self-supporting, charity funds can step in and give systematic support, and train the people in the need to improve their capacities to take responsibility for their life again. If this is impossible—seriously handicapped people, for instance—charity funds can decide to adopt these people financially as well as in terms of emotional care. If the charity system is inadequate, the community can decide to develop a collective support system, which is a system of solidarity. A reason might be the experience that too many people are not reasonable and do not participate in the charity system. People who barely participate in the financing of the charity system might think that a solidarity system is more adequate, since in that case the distribution of the support can be organized in a fair way.

The threat of social disintegration might also come from outside the community. In the case of large flows of immigrants from countries with a significantly different culture, disintegration increases. This leads to an undermining of the solidarity system and makes peaceful cohabitation in the neighbourhoods of towns and cities more problematic. Two reactions to maintain social cohesion are possible. In the first place, a reduction of the flow of immigrants, meanwhile taking the integration of these people more seri-ously. In the second place, more attention to the extent of integration of one's own popu-lation, to make them able to support the newcomers in their integration.

Persons must prepare their mind for unforeseen events—events which cannot be expected and explained by the vested frames of thought and emotion. Without *buffers in the mind* persons might become frightened and aggressive. It makes sense for persons to be emotionally as well as cognitively prepared to tackle the unexpected. A buffer in the mind can be interpreted as a stock of energy, which prevents a person from reacting irrationally if his vested interests are at stake.

Aggression can be directed to the person himself by further closing the mind in an attempt not to be hurt. If hurt by unforeseen events—humiliated by the boss, sudden lay-off, wife or husband has an affair—some might also hurt themselves physically, in some cases even committing suicide. Aggression can also be directed externally—police end a peaceful demonstration violently, children permanently disobey their father. In these cases the person might become aggressive by robbing a shop or by humiliating subor-dinates. As soon as the Self is at stake and the mind closes even further, the interpreta-tion of Self and environment become even more biased. More attention is paid to the strength of the protective belt. When neoclassical economists discovered that a free mar-ket economy can fall into a depression, they were shocked. When Keynes came up with a revolution in economics and explained the possibility of a depression in a free market economy, the defence to protect the paradigm came a year later. Keynes published his *General Theory* in 1936, and the then neoclassical economist Hicks published his inter-pretation of Keynes' theory in 1937. In his article Hicks 'showed' that a depression is just an extreme case—not the normal situation. In other words, Keynes' theory is not general at all. Hicks' analysis—the so-called IS-LM analysis—became one of the cornerstones of neoclassical macroeconomics, and was extensively presented and discussed in almost all textbooks. His analysis was a reaction to the approach of Keynes, which has never been discussed widely in textbooks. The reaction of the community of neoclassical economists is a typical closure of the mind—a clear example of *apology*, which is the art of defence. So, if persons and communities are themselves able to open their minds step by step, and become more pluralistic, this will increase their self-respect. Communication with other sides of the Self as well as communication with other people can only be developed if a person attaches respect to his Self—it makes him less sensitive to economic and social success in terms of money and status. A scientist who is not addicted to his income and scientific status, can afford to discover that he was wrong, and that he supervised his PhD students in an incorrect way.

A higher level of independent self-respect opens the door for open persons, groups, economies, and societies to what is outside. On all levels, the resistance against increas-ing openness will be strong because of *short-term survival instincts*, economically and socially as well psychically. But the long-term advantages are important. A relaxed attitude towards economic gain and social status, especially by people who are not low ranked, offers room to become inspired and develop and use talents to the advantage of the larger whole—that is, to experience *meaning* in particular daily activities. *Inspiration cannot be produced, but people can open their Selves to be inspired.* Such open persons can open groups and can develop more harmonious relationships with nature, thereby leaving room to rivers in times of flood, for instance.

15.4.7 MACRO-ANALYSIS

Our integrated world is based on a three-motivational foundation. In orthodox economics the economic world is based on one motivation, and the strength of the motivation is not explicitly analysed. This makes the model suited for a typical micro-methodology, an extreme variant of methodological individualism. In our MDE world, however, it is possible to also analyse micro-level behaviour in a macro-analysis. Then macro-developments affect not only resources and technology available to individuals, but can also affect the total human energy available and the relative strength of the three motivations. This idea represents methodological collectivism. So, our MDE paradigm makes it possible to analyse the interactions between the different levels. *The micro and the macro level are each other's foundation.*

Subjects operate in a particular institutional context, and given resources and technology available they act. The institutional context includes rules, which should make persons and organizations more rational. These rules are the result of a historical development, in which persons and organizations tried to reduce their uncertainty. The aggregation of all the actions with respect to the rules of conduct affects the institutional context in the following period. The aggregation of all the actions with respect to concrete behaviour (rather than actions of communication and commitment) determines macro-behaviour. Within the institutional boundaries subjects can make choices by means of more or less sophisticated cost-benefit calculations (see the discussion on Davis in Chapter 9).

Now we can imagine a historical process, in which phenomena on the macro level develop from a first family to a global society. At the moment that male–female interaction leads to a new person, a family is created: the first human organization (marriage is interpreted as a market contract). Later we see that a few families can form a clan or tribe. Then a couple of tribes can form a village, and a few villages can transform into a town. In this way the organization of human society becomes increasingly complex—which is not surprising, given the growth of the population and the complexity of its technology of production.

Our three-motivation model says that human actions are determined by the three primary motivations. The economic motivation dominates the literature in new institutional economic history. The social motivation plays a role in sociological historical theories. But most sociological analyses leave motivation implicit, while stressing that historical development results from the application of technical knowledge, and—if needed—in the production of high-tech military equipment. It is true by definition that the most powerful organizations win the battles. So, the relevant question is: What is power and what makes particular persons and organizations so powerful? The typical MDE answer is the following. Subjects can develop resources of an economic, a social, and a psychic nature. Economic resources are human capital, money, machines, and roads, for instance. Social resources are the skills of people to impress others, and the energy people have available to constantly work on their status in the eyes of relevant others. Psychic resources are the skills of people to convince and to motivate themselves to reach particular goals. Powerful people are powerful because they possess the psychic, the social, and the economic capital to reach their goals.

There is, however, a serious problem in this power analysis. The three types of power cannot be reduced to one form of power, because their dimensions are not homogeneous. If a person has the psychic capital to reduce his superficial desires and is able to kick some of his bad habits, social and economic capital cannot function as a substitute for this psychic capital. Actually, every person or organization should search for effective combinations of the various sorts of capital. They all are necessary inputs in the production of lasting happiness. The physical and orthodox economic laws, as discussed in Chapter 4, can be applied here.

This power analysis can also be applied to large entities, such as Great Britain. The country has a TSE, and the 'I' of GB permanently doubts whether membership of the EU network contributes to typical GB goals. Why should GB become a prestigious country in the eyes of other EU members, while EU membership requires so much repudiation of the typical GB identity. Even if a GB exit would mean that the country's economic capital decreases, and the British people become less prestigious in the eyes of the remaining EU members, many British people would still vote for an exit: psychic capital prevails. What British people experience as typical Brits cannot be substituted by economic and social capital.

In macroeconomics and macro-sociology there is no place for psychology. That's a pity, because the course of history is affected by the psychic state of persons and organizations, and vice versa. Imperfect rationality can lead to inadequate reactions to remarkable events. So, if many people in a particular country are traumatized by the experience of terrible events, their reactions to particular developments are difficult to predict. Currently (June 2013), there are mass demonstrations in Brazil. Up to now economic growth was impressive; nevertheless many people are dissatisfied with respect to current government policies. It has to do with discoveries of corruption, fraud, and prestigious projects, which makes a large number of people very angry. Perhaps just because economic development is impressive, people have the social energy necessary to demonstrate. Sick of all the traumatizing experiences, they get angry with the officials who take care of themselves rather than solving the problems in the favelas.

On every level we find psychic conflicts, but it is impossible for a country to have a psychic conflict which is not experienced as such by individuals. If all people are rational, economic and social conflicts do not affect the psyche of the individuals. But if conflicts on a macro level create internal conflicts within persons—which is, generally speaking, the case—a country can suffer from pain in its psyche (see the example of Great Britain, who is constantly swithering about being in or out the EU).

A last point which should be discussed is whether a society exists at all, or is just in the minds of collectivist-orientated people. If we come to the conclusion that a society exists, we can ask the more specific question of whether a European society, or even a global society, exists. If the answer is positive, we should ask whether there is a European or even a global psyche or mind. Even if these questions cannot be answered, they are still relevant. According to the late Margaret Thatcher—prime minister of Great Britain during the 1970s—there is no such thing as society. There are individual persons, and voluntary organizations, and that's it. In Brussels she was always defending the idea that British society is very different from that in other European countries, which makes the idea of a European Political Union an undesirable utopia. Sociology states that if there is a thing such as society in the minds of the members, then *society is at least real in its consequences.* So, when asking the British, the Germans, the Dutch, they all say that there is a British, German, Dutch society respectively. So, these societies exist in their consequences. If we ask people living in Europe whether a European society exists, the answers might shock European federalists. When looking at the number of voters who participate in the election of members of the European Parliament, there is no reason for optimism. People act according to their experienced identity. As long as citizens are not addressed as Europeans by non-Europeans, it remains difficult for them to develop feelings of being a European citizen. The same problem holds for the concept of global society, and the way people act as global citizens. So, is there a global society? Most people might say that this society is emerging, and the United Nations is representing this development. But global elections sound quite utopian at the moment.

We can also ask ourselves whether there is such a thing as economy. Many people in Europe do not perceive themselves to be Europeans. When they travel through Europe they present themselves as Italians, as Serbs, or as Germans. Wherever they are, they feel, think, and act on the basis of national or even more local identities. An important example is the experience that Dutch economists, who express their views in the established media, operate as Dutch economists, commenting on Dutch economic developments, rather than as European economists, commenting on the Dutch economy as an intrinsic part of the EU economy. Although Dutch politicians and civil servants are quite active in Brussels, these activities are barely discussed. Dutch politicians and economists take the policies of the European Commission as given—as the context within Dutch policies should be designed. The policy stands of Dutch politicians and civil servants who are operating in Brussels—strict application of the tight budget rules, reached by huge government expenditure cuts—are based on a perspective which frames the Dutch economy as a small and open economy competing on the global market, rather than as a department of the European economy, which is in trouble. Back in The Hague they implement the policies as defended in Brussels. Meanwhile, the economy shrinks and the budget deficits barely diminish (December, 2013).

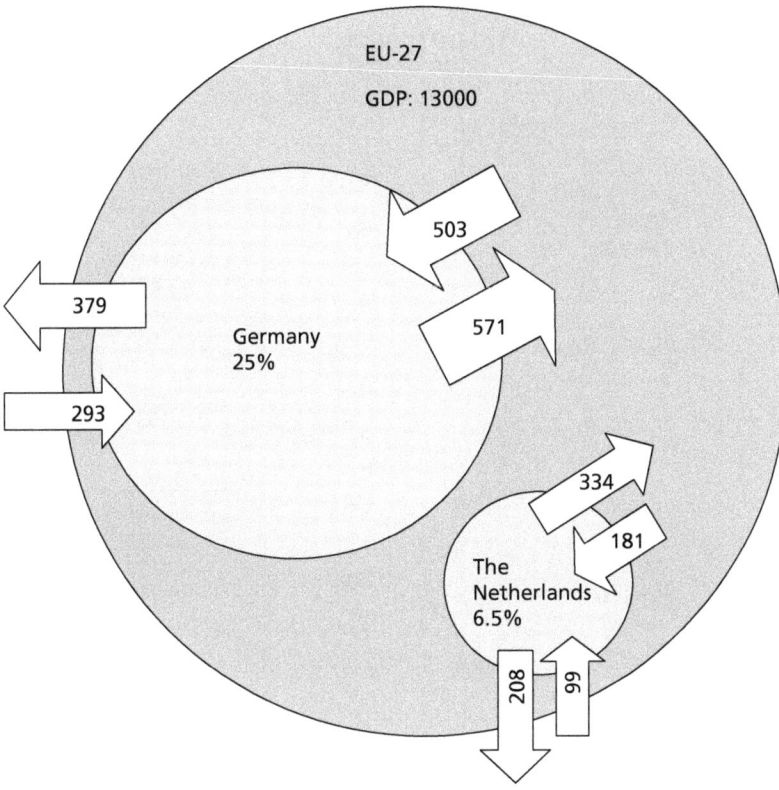

Figure 15.1. European Union, its GDP, and the Import and Export Trade of the Netherlands and Germany, Year 2010

Note: Numbers Expressed in Billions of Euros
Source: IMF: World Economic Outlook

So far, we have talked about society and economy as phenomena in the minds of people. We can, however, also try to catch these concepts in more empirical ways. Imagine that the European economy consists of many small economies, which trade with each other only on a small scale. Their interdependence can be ignored as all these small economies have their own interests, and their independent policies. But this is not the case with the EU economy. The various national economies are highly interrelated, although the dependence on the whole of the EU economy differs between the various members. We have presented diagrams which show the importance of the EU for Germany and the Netherlands (Figure 15.1), and the importance of the EU economy for the whole of the global economy (Figure 15.2). So, if economists keep taking the national level as their level of analysis and policy, while the empirical facts hint at the EU economy as the best level of analysis and policy, serious policy failures might be the result. Figure 15.2 shows that a badly managed EU economy might be disastrous for the global economy. In this respect it is easy to understand why non-EU countries are disappointed about the EU policy stance. Now the EU consists of a series of countries which all try to recover through increasing exports, even countries with a structural surplus on their balance of

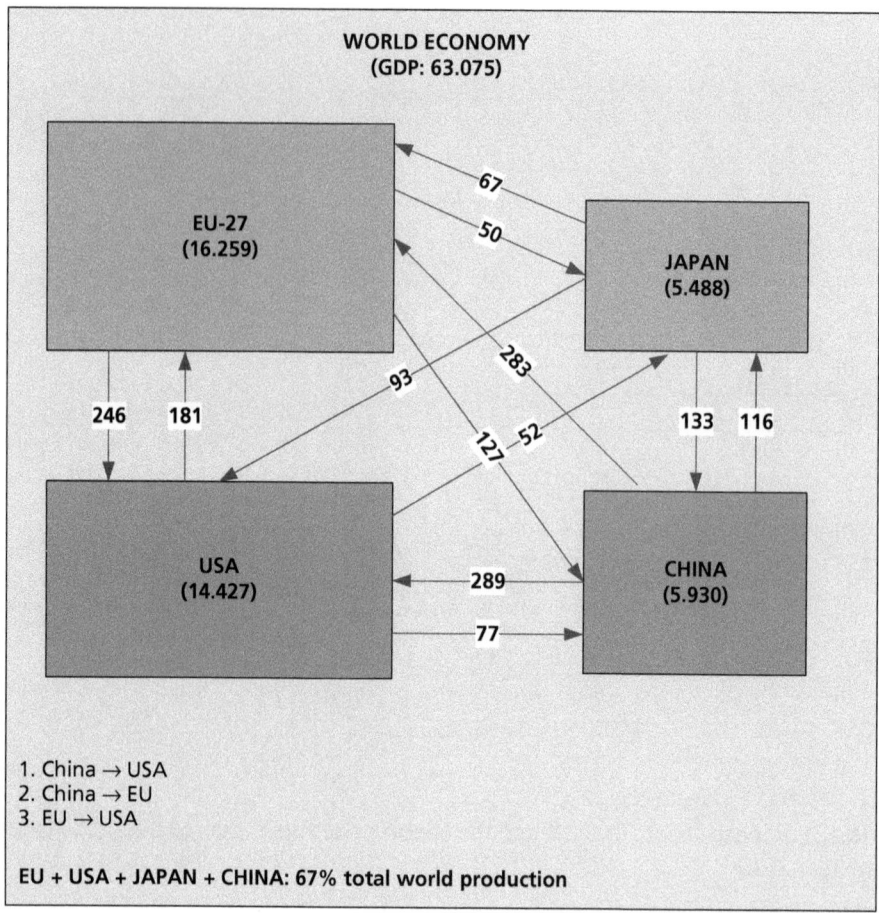

Figure 15.2. Global Economy, Year 2010

Source: IMF, World Economic Outlook

payments (Germany, the Netherlands, Finland). We saw already that Japan implements the same policy. If we imagine that the USA, because of its deficits on the balance of payments and government budget, also opts for such policy, we cannot be optimistic about the global economy in the years to come.

Multidisciplinary macroeconomics should be applied at the right level of analysis. Since the EU economy is a rather closed economy, we should apply our MDE approach to the EU level. With respect to the current economic crisis, delegation of authority to the EU level is unnecessary. The current depression is not the result of bad internal developments. The crisis is coming from the USA, where the credit crunch started and led to a global depression in 2009. The USA and China stimulated their economies—China especially through an increase in their effective demand. The EU did not contribute significantly to the global recovery. The member-states just hoped for an increase in their national exports.

The Eurozone should have decided that the economies with a surplus on the balance of payments stimulate their effective demand, and especially their government investments, and finance these investments via the European Central Bank. This easy economic-rational solution of post-Keynesian origin appears non-debatable, because of the closed minds of the ruling economists and politicians. Their social and economic orientation is their own national economy. That is the reason why collective rationality on the EU level cannot be realized, thereby making rational national solutions illusionary.

As long as there is no EU mind, it stimulates social rivalry within countries if politicians collude and strive for delegation of political authority to a higher level because of its perceived economic advantage. The independence of the personal and national mind is therefore too important for people. It also implies that the decision to accept new member-states must be taken carefully. Politicians should also apply the rules of entry to the insiders. They may have undergone important institutional changes, which might not fit the aimed EU mind and society. Given the absence of an EU mind and the problems in the formation of it, further integration might be undermined by members who try to become less dependent on other member-states. If Germany chose this strategy, the EU would disintegrate. Even in that case it might be important to accept political disintegration without psychological and social disintegration. Social rivalry between groups in a region which is so densely populated might create disasters. It is extremely important that the social discourse on EU level in the sense of Habermas continues more intensively than is the case at this moment. Moral and political philosophers, human scientists, artists, non-governmental organizations fighting for rights of particular groups of people, and environmental action groups should confront each other with their ideas and performances. The result of these social actions might be a more articulated idea of what Europe is or should be. It does not mean that consensus about one style being superior to the others grows. It might also lead to the acceptance of a multicultural picture and the maintenance of a significant degree of autonomy among the various nations.

15.4.8 PARSIMONY

Orthodox economics is based on the paradigm of an economic and rational actor. Psychic and social elements do not exist. Neoclassical economists have adopted this paradigm, and its logical implications, as their theoretical instrument, on the basis of which empirical research can be executed. Neoclassical economists are reluctant to relax their paradigm: they try to explain everything they observe within the limits set by it. Irrationality and sociality do not exist. Empirical research gives them coefficients, which describe the elasticity with which particular variables react to changes in other variables. Private and public actors can take the values of these coefficients into account in their planning. The quantitative methods have become increasingly complex, so as to reach more precision. Unfortunately, precision can only be reached in periods of stability. Hirschman (1977) warns against too much parsimony and pleads for a more realistic, and therefore a more complex, picture of reality. This means that, for the next few decades, we need a different type of economics—*a post-crisis economics*.

The big problem with the neoclassical strategy is the *lack of realism of its paradigm*. When we carefully define what we mean by irrationality and by negative and positive sociality, we know by introspection that a paradigm which takes these phenomena into account is more realistic. We have constructed our MDE world in an attempt to take the phenomena just mentioned into account. When we make this world dynamic and historical, and formulate it as an open rather than as a closed world, our model becomes extremely complex. Fortunately, the aim of our open MDE system can never be the delivery of precision; this is always and everywhere impossible in an open system. Even if we close our MDE system temporarily, so as to understand basic mechanisms, precise predictions will be impossible in human science. Such a goal is an expression of the hubris of modern human scientists, who think that control over human behaviour is possible. In the first place, the MDE model is very suited for the development of scenarios which might trigger important discussions between senior scientists over future developments. In the second place, the model is suited for well-argued simplification. If a firm wants to analyse the market for matches or for dinky toys, it might be possible to deal with rationality and sociality in a not so complex way. In the third place, well-argued simplification leads to analyses and models which might be very useful for private as well as public actors. They can develop methods of calculation, which could be useful for the time being. In the fourth place, in times of social and economic stability the model offers many points of impact, leading to a list of important buffers, which must keep society on track.

If experts, working in so many corners of society, train themselves in the MDE way of thinking, and develop skills to approach problems from different viewpoints they might be very effective in the development of more specific analyses and calculation methods relevant for the problems at hand.

Part VI
Conclusions

16 Conclusions

A thorough discussion of psychological and sociological analysis has offered us the building blocks needed for the creation of a synthesis between orthodox and heterodox economics. For the construction of a new structure of knowledge about human behaviour knowledge about the philosophy of science is essential. Part I is therefore about the basics of the philosophy of science and a methodological account of the history of social sciences, among them economics. Part II is about orthodox and heterodox economics. Parts III and IV are about psychology and sociology respectively. Part V discusses the integration of economics, psychology, and sociology, dealing with a synthesis of the typical economic, the typical psychological, and the typical sociological approach.

In this last chapter we draw a number of conclusions. After having discussed so many approaches it is our experience that most approaches make sense, but only to a certain extent. Moreover, we have dealt with the problem that every approach has its own language. This means that, in an attempt to integrate the three sciences, we had to solve a huge Babel Tower problem. Because the book is primarily meant for economists, we took orthodox economics as our starting point. This perspective developed as an isolated abstraction, which isolates the economic aspect from other relevant aspects. In the most abstract picture of reality in which humans are distinguished we discover three primary relationships: (1) the relationship between man and nature (economics); (2) the relationship between man and man (sociology); (3) the relationship between man and his Self (psychology). In taking the isolated abstraction of the economic aspect as our point of departure, it is obvious that the next steps are the formulation of the isolated abstractions of the psychic and the social aspect respectively.

Our journey through heterodox economics, psychology, and sociology taught us that the construction of an integrated paradigm on the level of the primary motivations of humans is not enough by far. For us, it is an important and necessary step towards an integrated understanding of human behaviour. The lessons we learnt from this journey are numerous. The most important lessons are:

(1) Neoclassical economics uses the orthodox aspect-analysis as their theoretical foundation for their research on the real-life economy, which is a subsystem. This is the most important criticism from heterodox economists.

(2) There is no genuine orthodox and neoclassical macroeconomics. Almost all textbooks on macroeconomics consider an economy to be an aggregation of individual activities, which are explained by the interaction between an individual, with his constant economic and rational nature, and his environment, which only consists of natural resources. Neoclassical 'macro'economists consider national

economies as firms, which operate on a competitive market. In case of disequilibria prices should adjust until equilibrium has been restored again.

(3) Some heterodox economic perspectives take a real-life economy as their starting point. They do not take an individual with a constant nature as their basis; on the contrary, human nature is considered to be a variable (as malleable), and dependent on the historical development of the economy and of the society, of which the economy is part, as a whole. At present we live in a late capitalist stage, and analyses should take this context into account.

(4) The isolated economic world of the orthodox and neoclassical economists is a closed and determined world. Its functioning can be understood by a few mechanisms, in particular the price mechanisms on the various markets. Heterodox economics, except the radical economic approach, considers the real-life world as an open system, which is not determined in its functioning by just a few mechanisms. An open system is characterized by a permanent bombardment of small or sometimes large shocks. Without having a few strong equilibrium-restoring mechanisms, the open world creates strong feelings of uncertainty. Fortunately, humans have an instinct and an intuition, which function as guides. These drive them to apply rules, so as to reduce the anxiety associated with a situation.

(5) Heterodox economics, psychology, and sociology teach neoclassical economists a number of important lessons. The first is the idea that real life is not only dynamic, but also historical. We have seen that German monetary views have been strongly affected by events in the 1920s. The resistance against the production of nuclear energy is significantly affected by dramatic accidents in Russia and Japan, for instance. Every person knows many examples of events in his own life that make it impossible to do particular things, and events that have stimulated him to change his behaviour in a positive way. The second is the idea that behaviour on a more micro level and on a more macro level influence each other significantly. Neoclassical economics is based on a strict micro-foundation. The question for a sound macro-foundation for neoclassical economics has never been asked. Analyses about interactions between different levels have never been formulated satisfactorily. The main reason for this failure is the reluctance to analyse phenomena which cannot be observed empirically. In our chapter on the philosophy of science we have made it clear that this reluctance is not tenable. The third is the idea of the openness of real-life systems. It stresses the unbridgeable gap between calculable risk and incalculable uncertainty. In case of risk, markets develop so as to make it possible for firms to buy risks from people who are risk averters. This is not possible in a case of genuine uncertainty. Insurance companies make always exceptions for unforeseen disasters such as earthquakes, social unrest, and financial crises. This means that, basically, every person should take precautionary measures so as to reduce the cost in case of the unpredictable.

(6) The macro-foundation of the heterodox-economic and sociological theory needs improvement. A historical theory with institutions as the prime movers of societal

and economic development is not enough. Also, the idea of technological progress, as interpreted in orthodox economics, does not deliver a satisfying explanation of history. The process of ongoing change needs a mover in terms of primary human motivations. These are not just a constant anymore, such as in orthodox economics. They form an integrated whole of three forces, each with its own strength and direction. These forces are limited and controlled by three integrated restrictions. This creates three different sorts of technologies and institutions, which are multi-motivated.

(7) The economic world consists of economic, rational, and non-social actors, who maximize their economic utilities under the constraint of their scarce resources. Its principal equilibrium-restoring mechanism is the price adjustment on a free market and in a free market economy in case of disequilibrium. Textbooks explaining this mechanism are almost never clear about the restrictions of this market analysis. It is built upon four axioms, which make the scope of this approach clear. Scope means room and restriction. The user of this analysis must know in what situations the theoretical instrument can be applied to the real world, and when it is unrealistic to do so. The four restrictions are the following: an individual is economic (1), rational (2), and non-social (3), and classical logic can be used when the model is written in mathematical form (4). No book clarifies the meaning of the four concepts, seducing the reader to apply the model always and everywhere.

(8) The psychic world consists of imperfectly rational, non-economic, and non-social actors, who maximize their self-respect under the constraint of scarce willpower. Its principal equilibrium-restoring mechanism is the change in the use of willpower so as to reduce the difference between the actual Self and the true Self, and the degree to which the true Self, as experienced by the 'I' of a person, is protected against falsification by anomalies.

(9) The social world consists of social, non-economic, and rational actors, who maximize their (social) status under the constraint of scarce moral energy. Its principal equilibrium-restoring mechanism is the change in the homogeneity of the group in case of an increase in rivalry between the group and its most important challenger. Every group is characterized by a common understanding of its situation. Some members are closer to the core understanding, while others deviate more from group standards. In case of increasing social tension, members who deviate are put under pressure to adjust or leave the group.

(10) The three isolated worlds cannot be applied to the real world. An integrated analysis shows the interrelationships between the main variables of the three partial worlds. Moreover, it is necessary to use the integrated paradigm to construct a macro-foundation, which goes beyond the statement that technological progress and institutional change are the prime movers of history. As already said in Section 5.5 the model of the three integrated worlds must be opened so as to allow the bombardments of shocks, which keep systems in their adjusting phases, while never reaching equilibrium.

Now we will discuss a series of more specific conclusions by going through the different chapters.

Chapter 2 presents the basics of philosophy of science. Ontology, epistemology, and methodology are discussed. In Chapter 4 we apply these concepts to orthodox analysis. It appears that this is characterized by its strictly economic ontology: there are no social and psychic problems in the economic world. It is a world which is closed and can be described and explained by a few mechanisms. Orthodox economics has introspection as its principal epistemology. Neoclassical economics, however, also uses empirical observation as an important source of knowledge. From a methodological point of view, orthodox and neoclassical economics are applying the typical micro-orientated individualist approach. In Chapters 6, 7, 8, and 9 we discuss different heterodox perspectives. We show that, in most approaches, empirical observation rather than introspection plays a dominant role. Some heterodox perspectives are micro- and others are macro-orientated. Excepting the radical economic approach, heterodoxy is about reality being an open system. We conclude that many philosophical concepts are used as a series of duals, which appear quite unproductive. No meaningful knowledge structure can do without an axiomatic basis. Without an empirical counterpart, however, the knowledge structure is like a semi-manufactured product. Human behaviour can be interpreted as the result of a confrontation between the internal world (mind) and the outer (empirical) world. This makes internal observation (introspection) equally important relative to external or empirical observation. Lastly, the concepts of the closed versus the open system are duals by definition. The idea of an open system is more realistic, but if we do not locally and temporarily close the system, we can never find the mechanisms which significantly affect our real-life world. At the empirical surface we observe the result of the operation of several mechanisms which steer human behaviour. These mechanisms can only be understood by partial analysis of an isolated and closed world.

We have established that the orthodox and neoclassical world is based on a micro-foundation: the constant economic and rational nature of a human individual. Various heterodox approaches are based on a macro-foundation, which depends on the stage of historical development of the economy as a whole. A more realistic approach states that events on the micro and on the macro level are each other's foundation or bedding. The same holds for the epistemological strive between axiomatic realism versus empirical evidence: they are each other's foundation. And so with the ontological divide between the economic, the social, and the psychic nature of a human: they are each other's bedding. Economic behaviour is socially embedded. Social behaviour is economically embedded, and so forth.

Chapter 3 discusses the history of economics and sociology. There is an ongoing clash between the idea of real-life analysis, the idea of isolated aspect-analysis, or a combination of the two. Classical political economy claims to give a real-life analysis, while orthodox economics is focused on an analysis of the economic aspect of human behaviour. Neoclassical economics tries to combine the two ideas. Over time we see that neoclassical economics moves in the direction of more empirical research, thereby increasingly avoiding an explicit account of its axiomatic structure. The origin and development of sociology is discussed as well. Classical sociology is a typical macro-historical perspective. It offers an explanation of the societal context in which real-life economies operate. Weber and Parsons were important economists who were not appreciated by the dominant neoclassical school. Therefore, their work is still not taught in economics programmes. Their methodological contributions are crucial, however. Weber developed an alternative to empirical prediction. According to him, the real-life world is too complex to be understood by just looking at the empirical surface. His alternative was focused on an understanding of behaviour. We can only understand behaviour if we know why people do particular things. By discovering the way people understand their reality, we learn to understand how reality functions. The neoclassical approach assumes that preferences are givens, but that is an unrealistic assumption, made to isolate the economic preference. Parsons has worked on an integration of the different aspects of real life. But even sociologists do not pay much attention to the person who is considered by the American Sociological Association to be the best sociologist of the 20th century.

In Chapter 4 we discuss the simple and the more sophisticated versions of orthodox economics extensively. The analysis is meant to offer pure economics, as Pareto and Walras did. In this economic world prices perfectly reflect natural scarcity. It appears that four axioms and nine other types of conditions must be met in order to make this statement a realistic one. All these conditions together create a situation of perfect competition. In more sophisticated versions even a monopolistic market can be considered as competitive, as long as entry and exit is not costly. The strict condition of perfect information is relaxed. Imperfect information implies that calculations are not certain but probable. There is always a risk that the outcome is different than expected. The economic world has now become a stochastic world. Statistical theory can be applied to find significant correlations and the estimation of probable values of particular coefficients. Risk-loving actors accept high-profitability–high-risk outcomes, whereas risk-averting actors prefer low-profitability–low-risk outcomes. An insurance market can coordinate the needs and desires of these two groups of people.

Neoclassical economists use orthodox economics as the theoretical foundation of their empirical research. Their argument runs as follows. Irrational firms will not survive on the competitive markets. Firms who take social considerations, such as discrimination, into account will also lose against firms which do not discriminate. Ergo, the effects of irrationality and sociality will always remain small, and not relevant for an understanding of the functioning of a market. In our chapters about heterodox economics and about psychology and sociology, we have shown that psychic and social factors—especially in combination—affect the functioning of the free market mechanism significantly.

Also, in prisoner's dilemma-like situations, the orthodox solution is problematic. In the economic world the government operates as a deus ex machina, which is an exogenous and benign authority. It can solve the dilemmas by setting efficiency-enhancing rules. By negating irrationality and sociality as real-life phenomena, orthodox economics ignores efficient solutions along psychic and social lines. It makes the approach blind to very serious problems, such as financial mafia-like organizations. Over the years orthodox economists have tried to model a democratic political sector under the label of public choice. Such an organization structure appears to be a fragile system, which needs further institutionalization. The famous Arrow paradox shows that a democratic economic world cannot function well. There are no Pareto-like solutions, and even the agenda-sequence affects the results. When introducing the idea of social man, a culture might grow which reduces the possible outcomes of democratic decision-making significantly.

In the presentation of heterodox economics we discuss original institutional economics (OIE). In this approach, institutions are social phenomena. Much later, new institutional economics (NIE) was developed by people such as North and Williamson; this is the orthodox and neoclassical approach to the phenomena of institutions. Here institutions are economically motivated phenomena. It is very interesting to see that two headmen of NIE have increasingly taken over the social elements of OIE. Apparently, it does not make sense to study the institutions of the economic world. Rules without any social and moral connotations cannot function properly.

In Chapter 5 we discussed orthodox macroeconomics, including the results of empirical research, which is built upon it. As already concluded, this type of macroeconomics is just the aggregation of individuals and micro-markets. Economic and rational actors are at their optimum and, if circumstances change, they adapt and reach, again, their optimum. Macroeconomic theory is about wealth (or income) and substitution effects. Every actor is small relative to the economy as a whole. When applying the orthodox model to the one and only genuine macro economy, which is the global economy, all countries are assumed to be firms which are operating on a large global market. They all have to take care of their competitiveness. So, in case of disequilibrium a country should decrease labour costs, and especially the collective burden part of these costs. There is no room for complementarities and strong interdependencies between firms and countries. When discussing heterodox macroeconomics we saw that the Netherlands, for instance, should not always consider itself to be a firm operating on a competitive global market. The current European depression might need another metaphor, such as the Netherlands as a department of the firm the European Union, which is large relative to the global economy.

In Chapters 6, 7, 8, and 9 we present heterodox economics. It appears a very rich source of analyses and theories. In Chapter 6 the evolutionary and the Austrian view are discussed. Both use an ontology which says that reality is open, organic, evolving, and historical. Evolutionary economics focuses on the process of selection of those who survive and those who don't. It has a Darwinian as well as a Lamarckian character. Darwin stressed the necessity of adaptation to changing circumstances, while Lamarck added to this process the possibilities of individuals and groups changing the environment. Current evolutionists avoid the use of the concept of survival, since this is based on a drive which cannot be observed empirically. This avoidance is not a satisfactory solution, but just circumvents the important question of what should survive. In very poor countries life is a struggle against death. But in most circumstances status and self-respect also play a large role. In the Austrian approach the entrepreneur plays an important role in the process of competition and selection. He is the creator of novelties, which are the source of economic growth. The Austrians are strictly individualistic and reject almost every idea about government regulation. This is in contrast to the evolutionary perspective, which is pragmatic in its stance towards government incidence. The strict non-social character of the Austrian view makes its analyses and theories less valuable for straight application to the real world. The American Tea Party shows that they regularly operate on the basis of a typical 19th-century America idea of the world. When applied to the crisis which is still going on in Europe, the Austrian advice encourages a long process of cutting government expenditures until entrepreneurs change their expectations and invest again. The evolutionary economists advise the government to stimulate R&D and education. Then entrepreneurs will change their expectations and increase their investments.

Chapter 7 discusses the radical economic view. This approach can be considered as an update of the economics of Marx, and includes influences of other heterodox views. The radical ontology says that reality is a closed and determined world, inhabited by economic, rational, and social actors. Reality is also historical. It means that it can be described by a series of laws of motion rather than by universal and eternal laws, as is the case with orthodox economic laws. Marx adhered to the (historical) materialist philosophy, which means that human interests and views are determined by the position of the person in the production process. History shows that the struggle between the haves and the have-nots is the common denominator. A capitalist system is determined by the struggle between (human) capitalists and workers. Historical development is of a dialectical character, which means that conflicts are only solved by the victory of the strongest. Attempts to reach consensus are a waste of time and the acceptance of compromises is just temporary. Technological progress changes the structure of society and the economy, and those groups which do not adjust to the latest techniques of production do not survive. Two things are important here. In the first place, the axioms basically determine the main outcome of radical analysis, which is the statement that capitalism as a system will not survive. In that sense, radical analysis has the same properties as the orthodox economic analysis: axioms determine the outcomes. There have also been debates about more practical issues, such as the possibility of calculating the value of the capital stock—on a firm level as well as on the global level. In the famous Cambridge Controversy, neoclassical economists recognized radical objections against neoclassical analytical procedures. The experience that the measurement of the capital stock is problematic makes it difficult for radical economists to show—via a structural increase of the capital coefficient—that the capitalist system is intrinsically unstable. In the second place, in the radical approach social man is not a person with some independence. Individual behaviour is determined by the position of the group in the production process. Individuals are not agents who operate in a particular structure; there is just structure, and this structure determines the interests and understandings of the group to which an individual belongs. So, only macro-sociology counts. When discussing sociology (Chapter 11) we saw that micro-sociology is equally important. When we look at the social-economic history of Europe we see that agents have formed new groups, independent of their economic position, and have changed the structure of the economy and society significantly. The European welfare state is a mix of various systems, and has appeared relatively stable over a number of decades already. Radical economists doubt whether the welfare state is a stable system. The process of globalization especially undermines this state in the very long run. The financial crisis of 2008 shows this instability. A radical analysis of the global economy focuses on the large excess supply of savings, which actors are looking to profitably invest. But lack of demand for consumption goods makes it impossible to actually borrow the excess supply of capital. Low interest rates do not lead to a lower volume of capital supplied, and a higher volume of capital demanded. Therefore, the capital market is the main source of structural disequilibrium, which makes it impossible to solve the disequilibrium on the labour and the goods market. Although the radical approach can be criticized in its unrealistic axioms, students must be confronted with the challenges the view offers to the mainstream community.

Chapter 8 is about the post-Keynesian perspective. This school of thought is an attempt to make permanent updates to the economics of Keynes. Keynes' ontology says that reality is an open and organic system. Its history consists of subsequent stages of development. Each stage has its own characteristics. The analysis of Keynes is an attempt to capture the capitalist system in the Western world during the first half of the 20th century. Keynes called this stage 'managed capitalism', which indicates his view that large corporations, unions, and governments have a decisive influence on the course of the economy. When the world faced the Great Crash and the Great Depression neoclassical economists were astounded. This was impossible in their economic world. They advised governments to stick to the gold standard and to cut government expenditures. Countries such as the Netherlands followed this strategy, which aggravated the crisis. In 1936 Keynes published *The General Theory* and offered a theory which explained the phenomenon of persistent unemployment. The typical neoclassical therapy—wage decline—did not work. The reason why Keynes was successful, in contrast to the neoclassical theory, can be found in his expectations theory. According to the neoclassical approach, deviations from the trend in the growth of the production and income level are relatively small. In this context, the concept 'small' means so small that the equilibrium-restoring mechanism stays intact. So a negative deviation—recession—will never turn into a depression. This means that consumers will continue their consumption—including if incomes show a small negative deviation from the expected trend—because their expectations remain optimistic about the medium and long term. According to Keynes, however, a decline in income and employment can be interpreted in a more pessimistic way. Especially in case of great shocks, such as the crash on Wall Street in 1929, consumers might react with a decline in consumption. This reaction aggravates the crisis, and there are no mechanisms in a capitalist free market system that counter this movement. Leijonhufvud constructed two corridors. The first channels the cyclical movement around the trend in the growth of production, which belongs to full employment. Its general characteristic is optimism. The second corridor channels a cyclical movement around a trend which is significantly lower and produces persistent unemployment. Its general characteristic is pessimism. Minsky criticizes the idea of stable corridors. He developed a financial instability hypothesis, which suggests that the instability of the capitalist system is intrinsic, and does not come from outside the system. In a long period of economic growth people become increasingly optimistic. Since humans are imperfectly rational they cross the line between optimism and overoptimism. Minsky describes this development in terms of changes in the mode of finance, namely from hedging via speculation to Ponzi schemes. This process goes on until the system has become so fragile that even small shocks can be the immediate cause of a great crash. The post-Keynesian perspective is a typical macro-approach. Eichner and Kregel have developed some microeconomic analyses of firms and markets on the basis of this macro-foundation. This is a scarce element in the economics literature, and should be extended and become part of a complete dynamic-historical analysis of the interactions between phenomena on the macro and the micro level, including the level of human motivations. In the discussions under the labels of social economics and economic sociology we saw that the issues of the micro- and macro-interaction and of the agency-structure type are important elements. Post-Keynesians should cooperate with these communities so as to improve the social element in their analyses. It would improve the quality significantly.

In Chapter 9 we discussed the social economic approach. The name already shows that the principal axiom of this perspective is the statement that economic processes are socially embedded. The micro-macro problem is approached in terms of agency versus structure. Typical micro-approaches start their analyses with a statement about the nature of an agent or actor. In this case the nature of the agent is economic and social. The concept rationality is not much used, which is a pity. Typical macro-approaches start their analyses with a statement about the structure of the situation under scrutiny. This can be a particular stage in the development of the capitalist system. It can also be a state of the collective mind: the economy is in a depression, for instance. Davis has constructed a model of the social individual: an individual who operates in a social structure, but has a large amount of discretion in his decisions about how to act. This means that, besides a social identity, there is room for a personal identity. In other words, people matter. The dominant idea of social economics is, however, that institutions matter. They form frameworks of rules, which have moral connotations most of the time. Greif stresses the necessity of micro-foundations for a proper institutional theory. Our book pretends to offer such micro-foundation. In Chapter 14 we have explained how we can interpret the phenomenon of institutions in a multi-motivated way.

Dolfsma and Spithoven argue that an institution-free world does not exist, thereby using the story by Herodotus about the so-called silent trade. In other words, the attempts of the neoclassically orientated new institutional economics to explain institutions are not realistic. A multi-motivated paradigm can also be used as a foundation of the work by Ostrom on the diversity of institutions. A separate position in the field of social economics is taken by Acemoglu, who argues that power relations determine institutional patterns rather than these patterns being culturally embedded. The problem with this position is, however, that power is about instruments, while culture is about goals. It is important to notice that the distinction between instruments and goals is an analytical one; it does not mean an empirical separation. In other words, a particular phenomenon can be an instrument and a goal at the same time. If we take our multi-motivational paradigm, we should immediately ask Acemoglu to make a distinction between economic, social, and psychic power. In that case his power approach might not significantly deviate from our MDE approach.

Keizer offers a theoretical and empirical analysis of Dutch inflation over the period 1946–1978. He attributes this phenomenon to the changes in ideology of several political parties and of changes in the militancy of unions and employers' organizations. Behind these changes we find a growing overoptimism with respect to the possibilities of uniting capitalist production with social-democratic government planning. The first blueprints used by the construction of the Dutch welfare state show an almost utopian idea of human solidarity. Today the Dutch welfare state is more sober and realistic.

Sen can be considered as the philosopher of social economics. He discusses in detail important social-economic concepts, such as rationality, morality, and reason, and links reasonability to his main concepts, namely freedom and human capability. His ideas of rationality and morality are identical to the ideas developed in our chapters on psychology and sociology respectively. On the whole we must conclude that social economics is a wide and flourishing field. But from a methodological point of view there are still some serious problems. Much research is empirically orientated, while the theoretical foundation is unclear. An example is the conclusion of Aalbers et al., who have empirically observed that cognitive closure is an important cause of the financial crisis. There is, however, barely any psychological theory in their text (Aalbers et al., 2010). In other words, this observation comes out of the blue. The authors keep their axioms implicit, and in the end they surprise the reader with their 'empirical' finding. The social-economic school needs an explicitly formulated paradigm and analysis, and should clarify what it means by principal concepts, such as economic, social, and rational. If social and personal identities are not specified in terms of human motivations, scientific progress will become difficult.

Chapter 10 discusses a series of schools of thought in psychology. The reason why psychology is important for economists has to do with the axiom of perfect rationality of actors in the orthodox economic world. This axiom is meant to leave psychic problems out of a typical economic analysis. Simon (1957a, b) argued that rationality was bounded by the limits of human cognitive capacity. So actors can only be rational within the limits of the information which is collected. People continue collecting information until they feel that they are sufficiently informed. Unfortunately, this behavioural-cognitive approach does not discuss the concept rationality itself; only the fact that it is bounded. We have seen that this omission is caused by the empiricist nature of the behavioural approach. In philosophy and in other parts of psychology imperfect rationality refers to limited willpower and the drive to protect the true Self from discovery. People have a particular idea of their true Self, and are inclined to ignore information which might ruin a positive picture.

The cognitive approach focuses on processes of perception, and of storing and retrieving knowledge. Over time, the connotation of the term 'cognitive' has changed. Now it means something like 'knowing', which includes emotional and intuitive implicit knowledge. The behaviourist approach does not recognize introspection as an acceptable source of knowledge and therefore it considers the mind to be a black box. The most important finding is the process of conditioning. If we are used to having dinner at 18.00 hours, we are inclined to feel hungry from 17.45 onwards. When we break with the habit of having dinner at 18.00 sharp, it takes a long time for us to stop feeling hungry at 17.45. The approach stresses the relevance of uncontrolled, automatic, and affective reactions. The psycho-dynamic and humanist approach use introspection as an important source of knowledge. Their ontology says that there is a mind, in which one or a few selves operate, and in which the 'I' of the person functions as a decision-maker. They see the essence of a psychic problem as the tension between different selves. By means of willpower the tensions can be reduced. The mind is the area where intuition, feelings, thoughts, and emotions find their home. Like economy and society, the mind is a battlefield, and only perfectly integrated persons are rational, which means that they have solved all their psychic problems. It goes without saying that these perfectly rational actors only exist in the orthodox economic world. The biological approach does not focus on the mind, but on the brain. Mind and brain are two aspects of the same phenomenon. Without a mind there is no brain, and without a brain there is no mind. Neuro-scientific research shows that cognitive thought processes take place in a different part of the brain in comparison with the automatic, uncontrolled, and affective processes. The first type is located in the cortex and the second type in the limbic system. It is obvious that brain damage can distort processes of coordination between the two different types of processes, making behaviour difficult to understand.

While the biological approach focuses on the influence of physiological factors on human behaviour, the social-psychological perspective focuses on the influence of the social environment. If we combined social psychology with micro-sociology, and micro-sociology with macro-sociology, this would be true scientific progress. There is interesting psycho-analytical research about the mind of Adolf Hitler, for instance. Moreover, there is important research about the collective mind of German society during the 1920s and 1930s. A comparison between the two suggests that the two minds interacted positively with each other. Social-psychological and micro-sociological processes link individual minds with the collective mind. If this type of analyses would be applied to various sectors of society, such as the financial world or the world of politics, the results might be astonishing.

The chapter ends with the construction of a psychic world analogous to the way the economic world has been constructed. Typical economic conflicts are solved by market competition and auctioneer-like processes of coordination. Typical psychic conflicts are solved through the willpower of the 'I' of a person. In this way a person can minimize her psychic tensions by pressing the actual Self to behave according to the institutions which are established by the true Self, as experienced by the 'I' of a person. Why should a person press his actual Self, when it takes much energy? This is because of the drive to maximize self-respect. This is the level of respect a person has in his own eyes. Without expending more energy on willpower, tensions grow and find an often negative outlet. Some people with low self-esteem commit suicide. Others focus their aggression on other people. Hitler directed his aggression towards different groups. In the first place, the countries that had humiliated Germany in the peace treaty of Versailles. Second, the Slav people who were definitely inferior to the German race. Third, the Jewish people, who were the principal internal threat and could therefore function as scapegoats. It is clear that one man cannot execute his extremely violent plans without the help of many people, who also feel humiliated because of whatever reason. When it became clear that Hitler had failed, he committed suicide.

This chapter makes clear that imperfect rationality is the rule, and perfect rationality is just an ideal-typical concept, which cannot be found in daily life. When systematically applied to the explanation of the behaviour of functionaries in firms and government agencies, many mainstream theories must be adjusted. Kets de Vries is a forerunner in this respect. Another major point with respect to human (ir)rationality is about the discovery that a learning process has an emotional foundation. The experienced true Self warns the decision-taking centre of an inconvenient tension between the true Self and the actual Self. But, regularly, this centre cannot distinguish the voice of the actual Self from the voice of the true Self. This is not only a cognitive problem, but also an emotional one: the 'I' is unwilling to use its willpower. It all turns back to the issue of the self-serving bias, in which the positive self-respect is protected against anomalies which show that the person has made serious mistakes. A last point to be made in this respect is the following. In Chapter 2 we made a distinction between four different elements in a knowledge structure. Meaningful pieces of knowledge cannot consist of less than these four elements, which are paradigm, analysis, theory, and hypothesis (PATH). In Chapter 10 we discussed the four types of psychic entities, as distinguished by Jung, which are intuition, feeling, thought, and sensation. According to Jung, there are virtually no persons who are good at using all these knowledge-carriers. Some are especially focused on intuition and feeling, while others are characterized by thought and sensation. If we apply these specializations to scientists, it means that most scientists specialize in one or two of the four elements in the PATH structure. Among economists, we see that some people prefer empirical-statistical research, and others are storytellers or ontologists. As long as specialists have a thorough understanding of the common PATH structure of economics, there is no problem. Unfortunately, there is an ongoing methodological rivalry between the different groups. Some people are reluctant to apply quantitative methods; partly because of their emotion, which says that self-respect is not served by admitting the relevance of mathematics and statistics. Most people doing empirical research today exorcise other people. When reading their texts, there is hardly any reference to the paradigm and basic analysis that is used. 'That's philosophy, not science' is the frequent apology. Emotional barriers prevent members of staff at universities becoming adult scientists, who master all stages of construction of knowledge structures. This book pretends to contribute to the goal of solving this Babel Tower problem.

Chapters 11, 12, and 13 are about sociology. Chapter 11 makes a comparison between the various macro- and micro-sociological approaches. Functionalism stresses the necessity of culture, which makes society function well. Conflict theory states that conflict is a necessary element in a progressive society. Relative power is and should be decisive with respect to the direction in which society is going and should go. Those groups that are able to profit most from technological progress are the most powerful, and can decide which institutions rule society. The two main macro-perspectives, functionalism and conflict theory, are less antagonistic than they were in the past. If there is not any common understanding society will fall apart after a series of conflicts. In the debate between the two macro-approaches, the scientific controversy between culture versus power is at the centre. The same controversy plays a role in the debates between the two main micro-approaches, which are symbolic interactionism and the exchange/rational choice perspective. The first is focused on the formation of culture in small groups of people who perceive each other as equals. On the basis of a common understanding the group takes its decisions about strategic issues, such as goals and instruments of policy. In this way culture affects what is experienced as costs and what as benefits. The second is focused on the choice of individual subjects under the constraints of scarce resources and restrictions of a moral kind. The subjects are supposed to be economic and positive social actors. Irrationality and negative social motivations do not play a role in this type of analysis. Subjects are independent in their preference-formation as long as they stick to the moral rules of their society. It means that each subject is able to reach his goals proportional to the amount of scarce resources they possess. Some are more powerful than others. This means that the more powerful have more resources to influence the societal debate about the common understanding, and the consequent morality. Two remarks must be made here. In the first place, we see that in symbolic interactionism the preferences of individual subjects change under the influence of frequent social interaction. This is not the case in exchange/rational choice behaviour. In some cases the moral constraint leads to social approval, an additional element in the preference function. Even then the common understanding has apparently not led to an internalization of this understanding. Suppose a person walks down the street and discovers that she is alone. She is eating a Milky Way, and throws its wrapping onto the street. Of course, she would never have done this if she had not been alone. An analysis of a true internalization of a moral rule requires the construction of a mind, including a potential conscience. The two micro-sociological approaches have never developed a sophisticated analysis of the mind, however. A second remark about the relationship between culture and power is that it manifests itself as a process of ongoing interaction. But, for an improvement of the quality of this analysis, we should, as we just saw, include a psychic analysis. This process of interaction can be placed in a network analysis. Some interactions are horizontal:

several heads of department meet each other and exchange information of an economic and social nature. Growing common understanding leads to a culture that every head tries to implement in his department. Now the result of horizontal interaction affects the content of vertical interaction. In this way culture can move from one sector of society to another, and from one society to another. Micro-level events lead to cultural change—also on the macro level in the end. Economics profits from network analysis this point in time. One problem is not yet solved in this area. This is the lack of careful definitions of concepts such as economic, social, and rational. Without a carefully conceived language, network analysis cannot make much progress.

In Chapter 12, attention is paid to principal historical developments. The thread that runs through it is continuing technological and cultural progress. The main problem is how to control this development without destroying the main source of progress, which is the free individual. Progress is a process of ups and downs. Also, failures have long-term effects. The financial innovations are illustrative. The more failures, the stronger the inclination to make the control systems more complex. Liberally orientated people are inclined to deregulate as much as possible and to accept the consequent failures. Socialist-orientated people are inclined to regulate in such a way that large risks are significantly reduced. In our conclusions with respect to Chapter 15 we come back to the issue of institutional design in a multidisciplinary world. At the moment we live in a culture in which technical control systems are preferred to control by humans. By building ever-larger systems of control, human responsibility is increasingly minimized. In sociology this problem is indicated as the problem of the juggernaut. People are increasingly losing control over a very large control system, which consists of a very large number of subsystems. The technicians who programme the control systems are not perfectly aware of the needs and possibilities of the people who must use them.[1] The work by scientists at universities is highly programmed by systems. The education programme prescribes subjects and textbooks, and research must fit 'the literature' as promoted by prestigious journals. Nobody, except a few, can influence the system, which determines which journal is prestigious and which is not.[2] For, economics holds that policies at 'prestigious' universities in the USA must be followed.

Modern life, including for high-skilled people, is dominated by ongoing adjustment. Everyone has become a link in a machine which produces something that is beyond control—including beyond the control of people who receive extremely high salaries for their work in controlling complex systems. In the future we will increasingly face

---

[1] Many scientific staff at Dutch universities don't have their own space where they can do their work. The 'system' has declared it is not responsible for this omission, and there are no administrators who defend the basic interests of those who are supposed to produce high-quality products. The system also just accepts student assessments as an indicator of quality. These assessments are about their own facilities most of the time.

[2] Maas (2013) discusses the role of Samuelson in the increasing role of quantitative methods. Samuelson favoured less philosophy and analysis and more technicalities, necessary for the empirical application of orthodox economics. My discussion of Samuelson's work shows my negative assessment of this view (see Section 5.6).

one crisis after the other, creating increasing feelings of uncertainty among people. The postmodern reaction is the idea of deconstruction. The modern juggernaut is a human construction more than a system which is based on objective knowledge. So let us try to decentralize systems. Those who dream about a United States of Europe must get a wake-up call. Brussels must develop in the direction of a centre of reliable information and coordination—not a centre which decides about the level of pension premiums and benefits, about tax rates and the level of government expenditures, for instance. Cooperation yes—supranational power no. At the moment the European economy is in a depression, and needs an increase in its effective demand. It is not difficult for open-minded economists to agree with this policy position. Then, independent members of the European community can voluntarily decide to increase their government investments. Those countries with a surplus on the balance of payments can especially do this—all countries will profit from it. If there are a few countries which do not cooperate, they might profit less. All countries remain responsible for their own buffers in case of serious accidents. When Europe was hit by the global financial crisis, members such as Greece did not have the buffers necessary to cope with the situation. When global financial markets 'decided' to punish the Greeks for their statistical lies, Europe decided to stand by Greece's side. However, rather than help the Greeks to improve their production and pay-off capacity, neoclassical economists and politicians decided to break down the Greek economy. Here, we see how dangerous it is for a country to become dependent on a large and badly functioning system. The postmodern advice to the Greeks would be to stop paying off loans, to leave the EU, to vote for politicians of new and small political parties, to become a member of newly erected and small unions, work hard, invest in numerous opportunities, and publicly invite members of the rich Greek elite to finance these investments.

Modern sociology is about increasing interdependencies—about increasing complexity, risk, and uncertainty. What would be the reaction of neoclassical economists to these empirically observable phenomena, such as increasing interdependence? They blame the governments, which helped the private banking sector out of the problems they themselves had created. In the United States groups of libertarians (Austrian economists) advised the government to accept the bankruptcy of banks, and build a new and libertarian society on the rubble. As we saw in Chapter 6, the Austrians ignore psychology and sociology, thereby ignoring the irrationality and negative sociality of humans. When taking these characteristics into account, the mess which would result from series of bankruptcies might be insurmountable. The typical neoclassical and Austrian way out—competition—has become defective precisely because of these psychic and social factors. A better way out is a step-by-step dismantling of extremely large systems, such as banks, firms, and governance systems. Computer technology can support information and coordination systems relatively easily. A European pension system, for instance, should be a network of national systems; a network which just registers rights European citizens have built up in the past. Technological progress—in the area of IT in this case—can be of help in both cases: centralization or decentralization. It is the psychic-social factor that should help us in the dismantling of too large systems without sufficient buffers.

In Chapter 13, multidisciplinary sociology is discussed. This is not a familiar term, but in this book it refers to the link between sociology and psychology and the link between sociology and economics. When linking sociology with psychology it becomes clear why group-based hierarchies are so unstable. Inequality always creates conflicts, which can be controlled only under particular circumstances. It has to do with the strength of human social and psychic motivation. Neoclassical economics has difficulty explaining very costly and sometimes violent expressions of anger. Our multidisciplinary approach brings these empirically observable phenomena within our horizon. The combination of sociology with economics leads to analyses which are not very different from those we discussed in Chapter 9 under the label social economics. Fligstein argues convincingly that social behaviour dismantles the economic market mechanism. The judicial difference between the private sector and public sector is very important in neoclassical economics. In economic sociology, however, strong social networks are built, bringing private and public actors into one group. Economic and social forces drive people to cross these boundaries, as soon as it is to their advantage to do so. Even truly economic actors become increasingly dragged into a social process, thereby undermining competitive forces. Those actors who refuse to take part in the social process of rivalry, make themselves ineffective and are exorcised. The financial world is full of illustrations of this observation.

When a sociologist uses the term economic he refers to the economy as a sector of real-life society. Sociologists have never developed an isolated world which is determined by the social force. Although some sociologists, such as Weber and Parsons, talk about aspects and about social aspect, they never constructed a social world, thereby abstracting from the economic and the psychic aspect. This means that the typical economic and the typical psychic problem are not playing a role in the explanation of human behaviour. Even the social aspect is not explicitly formulated, which means that most sociological theory explains movements without any mover, with social approval as a possible exception. Chapter 13 contains a first and simple construction of a social world inhabited by non-economic, social, and rational actors. They maximize their (social) status under the constraint of moral rules. In the simplest model the status of a person is identical to the status of the group to which the persons belong. The group status is always relative to the status of the other group(s). In this model there is always equilibrium. In more sophisticated versions many members deviate from the core standards, while some people deviate even more than others. The equilibrium-restoring mechanism functions as follows: if the status difference between two groups becomes smaller, the group higher in the ranking intensifies its social strategy. Members are pressed to adjust to the rules of the core culture so as to make their group more homogeneous and therewith socially stronger. If members are unwilling to adjust they are exorcised. In this isolated world economic resources and people's willpower are strong. In real life, resources are scarce, and economic performance and social performance have a positive effect on each other.

In Chapter 13 we also discussed the necessity of making the analysis historical and open. A historical analysis of the social world means that, over time, moral constraints might become stricter and evolve into preferences. Then people internalize the moral duties, and make them their own goals. Of course, the opposite is also possible: the constraints become increasingly relaxed.

Chapter 14 integrates the three isolated worlds. First, an analysis is given of the psychic-economic world. Imperfectly rational and economic actors inhabit this world. Resources are allocated in an optimal way, but the choice of needs which are satisfied takes place in an imperfectly rational way. Apparently, there is an 'optimal' degree of rationality. Actors overestimate the costs of using their willpower. In daily language we call these people lazy. Second, we have constructed a social-economic world. All actors are rational, social, and economic. Competition and rivalry rule this world. Resources are optimally allocated between social and economic actions. It is important to notice that these types of actions cannot be separated in an empirical way. The American decision to attack Iraq in 1990 was because of the oil *and* because of American status, which was at stake. Third, an analysis is constructed of the psychic-social world, which is inhabited by non-economic, imperfectly rational, and social actors. This world is characterized by affluence of economic resources, and psychic and social conflicts rule this world. The two types of conflict are interrelated. Imagine that irrational actors, including organizations and countries, are facing internal rivalry. A very popular solution to this problem is the creation of an external rival. Then all the energy available must be organized for battle against the common enemy. But this common enemy is also irrational and in need of an external opponent. Then the chance of a real battle is high. The battle itself fuels mutual moral resentments, thereby creating a vicious circle. To break through this circle dramatic events are needed, which trigger mutual moral sentiments. The UN golden rule is an appeal to all people in the world to develop sympathy (empathy) for each other. If two rivals are facing one and the same tsunami, they might start cooperating, creating positive sentiments. When the Second World War came to an end, countries in Europe, including Germany and Italy, decided to erect a European Economic Community, the forerunner of the current EU. Now the EU economy is in a crisis old resentments become manifest again. But, on the whole, the EU has given Europe peace for many years. Fourth, we have integrated the three primary aspects into the psychic-social-economic world. The psychic-social conflicts, as sketched in the third construction, become more complex because of the scarcity of the economic resources. The fights do not necessarily become more enduring and more violent. Battles might be very expensive, and poor economic actors have to stop their rivalry when funds dry up. Poor unions are a good example, but, if strikers feel humiliated, unexpected energy resources become available, leading to unexpected results.

This integrated world is a typical multidisciplinary world, in which there is an energy constraint on the human drive to maximize human preference functions. The elements in the preference function as well in the constraints are based on three motivations: an economic, a social, and a psychic motivation. When we make this static picture dynamic and historical, we see that there is an interrelationship between preference and constraint. Moral restrictions can become internalized and part of the preference function. A child learns about moral rules, and listens to her parents and applies these rules because her parents insist upon it. Later, the adult adopts some of the rules as her own rules and applies them when nobody can monitor her behaviour. Psychic preferences can become moral constraints. We can imagine that people are highly involved in particular matters, such as environment protection or fairly paid jobs for handicapped people. Over time, the person loses motivation and changes his preferences towards the direction of economic success. Then the preference, which was based on self-respect, changes into a restriction: 'I should give some money to a foundation, which is protecting the environment.' The analysis will contain many resource and substitution effects, as we know from the analysis of the economic world. But, as we saw in post-Keynesian economics, there must be ample attention for complementarities and strong interdependencies.

In Chapter 15 we discussed the meaning of a series of important concepts, well known from orthodox economics, in the so-called multidisciplinary economic world (MDE world). Moreover, we dealt with a series of steps necessary to get from a static, micro model of a closed world to a dynamic, historical micro-macro model of an open world. With respect to concepts such as preferences, resources, technology, and institutions they all are seen as having a much wider meaning. They include the psychic and social motivation, and the constraints of the model are also of a psychic and social nature. The concept social has not only a positive, but also a negative meaning. Solidarity is a positive phenomenon only in the context of the culture which prevails. So, if groups of Afghan men oppress Afghan women, the mutual relations between men are positive and show solidarity. The relationship between men and women is of a negative nature, as soon as women become aware of the oppressiveness of the relationship.

Our MDE model uses familiar concepts, such as rationality, morality, and reason. As we know, the meaning of a concept is determined by its context. This implies that the concepts, as mentioned, have a wider meaning than we are used to. The meaning of rationality is not limited to persons anymore. Also, groups or even the emerging global society can be judged in terms of rationality. So with the concept of morality, which is not necessarily limited to our fellow humans. It can also be applied to a person's Self ('be loyal to your Self'), or to animals, plants, or impressive areas of nature. When we consider the three worlds as one perfectly integrated whole, and specify their interrelationships, there is no principal difference between rationality and morality anymore. It has become 'reasonability'. Quite often, rationality and reason have a connotation which is the opposite of emotion. In our chapter on psychology we have argued that emotion and cognition are two aspects of the same phenomenon. No thought without emotion, and no emotion without thought, except in young children and some mentally handicapped people. Emotions drive people, including their thoughts. The emotion which warns people of danger says: 'wait a minute, let's think about it'. This emotion can be developed by means of training. It makes people more rational, but not less emotional. Over time, people develop an intuition, which can be considered as an experienced instinct. It is an emotion structured by the basic personality traits, as far as they become manifest under the influence of salient experiences. For students in economics, it is obvious that the pictures in the neoclassical textbooks affect their intuitions significantly.

The fact that emotion and personality are important determinants of learning has far-reaching consequences for educational formats. In Chapter 6 we discussed the problem-based learning method, which appears to be a quite progressive technology, and deserves diffusion.

A last feature of the MDE world to be dealt with is the fact that several social-economic systems persist for a long time. In the orthodox world a capitalist economy is a stable system, and the government is considered as a deus ex machina, taking care of property rights, and possibly also a few facilities for homeless people. Neoclassical economics suggests that a significantly larger government influence makes the system unstable. However, the welfare states in north-western Europe have already existed for more than half a century. In the Arab world conservative societies have also existed for a very long time. All the orthodox/neoclassical ideas and policy conclusions need to be re-verified in the light of the MDE characteristics.

We end this book with five essential conclusions.

First, the most serious mistake of neoclassical economics is the straight application of orthodox economics, which is an aspect-system, to the explanation of the economy, which is a subsystem.

Second, the development of two other relevant aspect-systems, namely the psychic and the social system, and the integration of the three worlds, is an important step towards a realistic human science. But it is, by far, not enough. The model should become a dynamic-historical model, which includes a macro-'foundation', and should also function in an open reality.

Third, there are no objective, absolute ontologies which deliver yardsticks that are fixed for all situations. Every scientist should create his own construction, including sets of goals and instruments, dependent on the specific context in which the problem under scrutiny is situated. Scientific knowledge will always be subjective, and therefore fallible; so with our systems developed upon scientific expertise.

Fourth, I adopt the ontology of the discretionary room within the mind of a person, which makes every person free and responsible to a certain extent.

Fifth, this book offers the generation of economics students to come many opportunities to improve and to specify the three worlds approach. There is much work to do.

Appendices

■ APPENDIX A   THE LOGICAL WORLD

A.1 **Introduction**

When discussing the problem of logic, it becomes increasingly clear that the term *logic* is a vague and fuzzy concept. In our daily language we use it when we mean to say that we understand the mechanism(s) behind a particular phenomenon. When we study logic as a field of science, however, most of the time we refer to classical or orthodox logic. It is based on a series of axioms, which are the foundation upon which this scientific discipline is based.[1]

A.2 **Origin**

Aristotle (384–322 BC) was one of the first philosophers to deal extensively with logic. For him, logic is a tool by means of which we can argue convincingly. He analysed sentences by highlighting the difference between subject and predicate. For instance, in the sentence 'all human beings are mortal', the part 'human beings' is the subject, while the part 'mortal' is the predicate. Syntactically the sentence is correct: there is a subject and there is a predicate that says something about the subject. Whether the sentence is true and has meaning are different questions. Aristotle developed the syllogism, which is a tool to derive conclusions from a series of assumptions. The truth of the conclusion is a logical implication of the truth of the assumptions. Later, Chrysippus (280–206 BC) introduced so-called logical connectives, such as 'and', 'or', 'if', and 'then'. This made him able to analyse complex statements and the logical structure of large texts (propositional calculus).

A.3 **Orthodox or Classical Logic**

For centuries Aristotle's analyses dominated the study of logic. Then Leibniz (1646–1716) came up with the idea to abstract from concrete sentences and to use algebraic equations in our search for the logical structure in our language. He formulated a law, stating: a = b. According to him, this identity is the basis of all logic. He derived four axioms (or laws) from this identity, which were sufficient to analyse an infinitely large number of sentences. These axioms are:

(1) a = a; this is an expression of the *law of identity*;
(2) if a = b and b = c, then a = c; this is the *law of substitution*;
(3) a = not (not a); this is the *law of non-contradiction* [¬ (a & ¬ a)];
(4) a is b = not -b is not -a; this is the *law of the excluded middle* [a v ¬ a].

While the first two laws are about the identity of a particular element, the third and fourth laws are basically saying that something is 'true *or* false'—not 'true *and* false' and not something 'in between true and false'.

---

[1] Cryan, Shatil, and Mablin (2001) give a nice overview of the core of logic.

This set of laws describe *typical* logic. It is the basis for a system of *rules of thought*. Leibniz appeared to be able to isolate these rules from the practical grammar, which is embedded in interpretation and judgement. This is the logical world, describing the rules that are necessary conditions for understandable thought. These rules are not sufficient conditions, since we cannot check whether our logical statements are true in the empirical sense. Many philosophers followed Leibniz, of which Kant is the most important one. Kant (1781) interpreted the axioms of logic as a description of the structure of thinking: the human mind is not able to understand texts that do not meet these logical conditions. Actually, Kant was saying that our mind frames information in such a way that we will never be able to directly observe 'reality'—our observation always runs via the logical framework that is set by the mind.

Mathematicians tried to use the logical axioms to see whether or not they could function as a foundation for mathematics. Frege (1848–1925) introduced so-called quantifiers, such as 'all', 'some', 'most', to link logic and mathematics. But others, especially Hilbert (1862–1943), tried to prove the independence of typical mathematical axioms, such as statements about the existence of numbers (1 + 1 = 2) and lines (two lines are parallel if these intersect each other in infinity), from typical logical axioms. However, Gödel (1906–1978) showed that any system of axioms is incomplete or inconsistent. Take, for instance, the sentence: 'the law of identity cannot be proven'. If this statement is true, then logic is an incomplete system, namely, based on an axiom that cannot be related to other axioms; it can just be assumed. If this statement is false, then the system is inconsistent.

The result found by Gödel can be interpreted as follows: logicians have discovered that human thinking has a logical aspect. This can be presented as an aspect-system. This system is based on the assumption that every 'thing' has an identity. We can never logically prove the truth of this identity axiom. It is saying that the world is knowable—it identifies itself to us. If someone is denying it, we cannot prove that he is wrong. Mathematicians have discovered that, in our imagination, not only logical axioms but also typical mathematical symbols like lines and numbers play a role. We cannot prove their existence (logically); we can only assume their existence on the basis of our experience of understanding what we mean when we talk about one, two, and three. A simple acceptance leads to the adoption of a large number of other statements when applying logic to the typical mathematical axioms.

A.4 **Paradoxes**

Human thinking is subject to restriction, like all other aspects of human life. An important function of logic is the discovery of contradictions or paradoxes.

The *Zeno or movement paradox* shows our difficulty when dealing with the problem of finity versus infinity. If we lag behind someone else in a particular race, we can never pass the other: the time we need to bridge the gap is used by the other to stay ahead. If we are faster, we will approach but never reach the other. This paradox shows our difficulty in imagining finity and infinity. The reasoning sounds logical. In many races, however, we see athletes lagging behind but running faster: at a particular moment they pass the other. This matter of experience can only be explained when avoiding the finity/infinity trap.

Another paradox is the so-called *heap paradox*. This is about a heap of sand. When we take one grain of sand from the heap, it is still a heap. When we continue taking away grains of sand from the heap, we end up with one grain, which is definitely not a heap. But when does the set of grains stop being a heap? We can solve this problem only by making an agreement on the definition of a heap of sand. This paradox makes it clear that an identity is not fixed. Everything is in constant change and, in our real world, in contrast to our logical world, it is not necessarily be true that a = a.

A third paradox is called a *self-referential paradox*. If a proposition states something about itself, it can be wrong or self-evident. For example: 'this sentence is false'. This is paradoxical. But the sentence 'this axiom is true' does not offer something relevant; it just stresses the character of the axiom to which the sentence refers, namely it cannot be proven and is assumed because of its self-evident character. So the axiom 'a = a' is self-evident, while the statement (a) = (not -a) is a contradiction, which cannot be accepted as part of our system of logic.

So far we can draw the conclusion that the logical world is an *isolated world* that describes just one aspect of the real world. If we want to develop a 'logical' system that can be applied to real-world problems, we might adjust this classical or orthodox world, so as to make it more practical.

A.5 **Applied Logic**

This is exactly what happened in the world of logicians and mathematicians. Two important experiences played a role in the development of logical and mathematical systems. In the first place, the acknowledgement that our information and knowledge of reality is very limited. In the second place, the discovery that our brain capacity is not only limited, but also framed in a particular way. In terms of physical and chemical processes (the hardware) we just have limited control over it. In terms of thinking and feeling (the operating system and other software) we all are framed in ways which are affected by our personality and by the cultural context which surrounds us. One important implication is the discovery that, in practice, our thinking does not take place like a logically programmed machine. The search for relevant information takes place within particular frames of interpretation and analysis. These frames (or Weberian world-views) organize information available in an efficient and directive way. Within these frames, humans are rational in the sense of logically arranging the positive and negative effects of particular strategies. But the 'choice' of frame is not a straightforward rational-logical affair.

This is the reason why logicians and mathematicians have tried to develop alternative approaches to the problem of modelling human thinking. We will discuss two alternative logics, namely 'fuzzy logic' and 'intuitionistic logic'.

Fuzzy logic rejects the law of the excluded middle and allows as truth values any real number between 0 and 1, where 0 stands for completely false and 1 stands for completely true. So something is true or false to a certain extent only. Related to this problem is the problem of *fuzzy concepts*. Basically, every concept is just an attempt to approach the indicated reality; it is never reality itself. When we discuss important phenomena such as unemployment or inflation it is not exactly clear what we mean by these terms. If experts try to define and measure them, there appear large differences.

Intuitionistic logic, as developed by Brouwer (1881–1966) and others, not only rejects the law of the excluded middle but also the double negative elimination (p = ¬ ¬ p). This type of logic accepts a position of 'I don't know', besides true or false.

When analysing the mind, classical logic imagines the mind as a logical machine. New approaches picture the mind as a neural net, which can be in any of a variety of states. In a logical machine, thinking is the same as *formal deduction*: deriving logical implications from premises. But how do we develop premises? In a neural net; however, first a process of categorization takes place. The emergence of categories is the result of the coming together of personality traits and cultural circumstances. Over time people become increasingly experienced, making the framework of interpretation more specific. When observing situations, we find relationships between different categories. When we feel pain when touching a very hot thing and we experience this phenomenon a few times, we tend to draw a general conclusion that we will always feel pain when touching a very hot thing. This is called *'inductive inference'* and leads to pattern recognition and arouses positive sentiments connected to the idea that we understand something. Particular relationships are recognized as being part of a bigger whole, giving these particulars meaning. In case of relationships between entities, it is (classical) statistics rather than (classical) mathematics that plays a role.

A.6 **Conclusion**

Applied logic, mathematics, and statistics are facing the problem of uncertainty and severe lack of information and knowledge. This has led to the emergence of fuzzy and intuitionistic mathematics. The common denominator is their attempt to make the classical approach more practical. Philosophers and mathematicians such as Ludwig Wittgenstein and John Maynard Keynes (also a famous non-classical economist) tried to say something systematic about interpretation and judgement, and about probability and belief in a non-classical way.

Now we can understand what is meant by the axiom of orthodox economics, saying that classical logic can be applied. Although there is no authority that can fix the meaning of the word 'classical' here—again a fuzzy concept—it is quite accepted to see the four laws of Leibniz as the hard core of classical or orthodox logic.

■ APPENDIX B KANT FOR ECONOMISTS

B.1 **Introduction**

I see, I touch, I hear, I smell, I taste . . . but who is 'I'? He is the thinker who not only thinks about what he sees, touches, hears, smells, and tastes, but also about the way he is thinking about these sense experiences. The 'I' discovers that he is always applying particular rules of thought. Some of these rules are just habits, making thinking easier. But other rules are necessary in order to make the results of our thinking understandable. Rules of the first sort are culturally bounded, but rules of the second group appear to be universal.

Some philosophers, such as Locke and Hume, saw the *sense experiences* as the primary source of knowledge. By means of observation we can discover empirical relations between particular phenomena. This knowledge will help us in getting more control over different sorts of processes, which constitute reality. Other philosophers, however, saw the *ratio* as the primary source of knowledge (Descartes, Leibniz). The ratio was supposed to be able to discover a logically ordered world of objects, which are causally related to each other.

The empirical world is the world that can be sensed. What is sensed is the behaviour of the causally related objects. Changing circumstances lead to the changing behaviour of objects. Explanation of these relationships require, however, reference to the world of objects where the driving forces behind the observable behaviour determine the interactions.

In his *Critique of Pure Reason* Kant formulates a *synthesis* between the empiricist approach by Locke and Hume on the one hand, and the rationalist approach by Descartes and Leibniz on the other. According to Kant, experiences of the human mind are the result of a flow of sense experiences that are processed and ordered by the ratio. So the 'I' who thinks about his experiences will never be confronted with the sense experiences themselves, only with the logically structured experiences. In this appendix we will first discuss empiricism and rationalism in more detail. Then we will explain and interpret the synthesis by Kant. After that, we will deal with the relevance of Kant for economists. We will show that the typical economic analysis is a straightforward application of rationalism, while the practice of empirical testing of economic theory refers to the empiricist view. Does this mean that Kant would agree with the typical economic research strategy? We will argue that this is unlikely to be the case.[2]

B.2 **Empiricism**

In reaction to Christian belief and to early rationalist approaches in Greek philosophy, some philosophers tried to develop an alternative. Their ideal was to develop a body of knowledge that was genuinely *objective*. Here, objectivity means: knowledge of the behaviour of objects without any interference of other elements, such as gods or prejudiced people. Let the objects speak for themselves and we just register what they say. When a human being is born, his mind is a

---

[2] A sophisticated introduction into Kant's main contributions is given by Scruton (1996).

blank sheet; a priori knowledge does not exist. From the very first day we receive information about reality via our senses. The mind registers this information and stores it in a systematic way. Knowledge about relationships is developed in an inductive way. Suppose the price of apples goes up, followed by a decline in the quantity of apples sold. Then the price of bikes goes up, followed by a decline in the quantity of bikes sold. If this happens for many goods, we would be inclined to generalize our experience: if the price of a particular good goes up, the quantity sold of that good will decline. Such a general formulation is called a *covering law*: if A, then B.

What if A is followed by B only now and then? Then the covering law must be refined. Statistical research might show that there is a third variable playing a role. Then the law might be: if A and C, then B. Carefully executed statistical research will finally lead to a whole series of *empirical laws*, describing stable empirical relationships between observable variables. In economics, empiricist-orientated people claim to have found a number of empirical laws. Examples are:

(1) Phillips claimed to have found an inverse relationship between the nominal wage rate and the unemployment rate.
(2) Okun claimed to have found a proportional relationship between excess demand on the goods market and excess demand on the labour market.
(3) Calmfors and Driffill claimed to have found a hump-shaped relationship between the unemployment rate and the degree of centralization of wage negotiations.

If scientists are able to find many stable relationships, it would make the world more predictable and controllable. This is exactly the purpose of the so-called modern project: we, humankind, do not need the subjectivity of persons and authorities to increasingly understand and control the universe. By carefully registering what everybody can see, hear, touch, smell, and taste, the world will be known by all of us—and can be changed to our own advantage. This makes the world a better place.

B.3 Rationalism

According to Descartes, we can have doubts about almost everything, except about the fact that we think. When we observe different sorts of phenomena there is always uncertainty about what we have actually observed. Everyone has a different opinion about it—senses are important but unreliable sources of knowledge. They must be directed by something that is superior and this is the human ratio. The way it works is equal for everyone and therefore we can trust the results of our thinking about sense impressions. Leibniz contributed significantly to the study of the rules that everybody applies when thinking correctly, that is, logically (see Appendix A on the logical world). These rules or axioms are the foundation of classical logic and offer us a structure that makes the results of our thinking understandable. While logic can be interpreted as the form of our thinking, Leibniz also offered an analysis of the content of our thinking. According to him, the world consists of objects. He distinguished two aspects: every object has substance and has properties. So there is a world of substances. Each substance which can be distinguished has a character, which is a set of necessary elements. It makes the substance what it is—it defines the object. There is another world, the world of properties. This is the world as we observe it. When approaching an object with our senses we observe properties. But before establishing properties we must know the substance, which is the definition of our object; otherwise we don't know which object we are talking about when describing the properties. For instance, a cup can be defined as a thing that is meant to contain liquid. If we accept this definition, every object that does not fit this definition is not a cup. But when discussing properties, we (empirically) observe, for instance, that some cups are blue and others are yellow. Another example: we can define an object as an actor who maximizes utilities in his relationship with his natural environment; this is the meaning of the concept 'economic' or economic substance. We can also observe a series of properties: our economic actor is rich, possesses a house, or is a devout Christian. Whatever happens, the substance remains the same, while properties are subject to change.[3] These changes can be described empirically—a person becomes richer over time, for instance. Different changes might empirically correlate: an increase in the price of computers is followed by a decrease in the quantity demanded. But a causal explanation must refer to the underlying world of substances, including the causal relations between the different substances. This world is ruled by universal laws, which describe these causal relationships between substances. For instance, when the substance 'human being' is surrounded by the substance 'natural resources', this relationship is characterized by the drive of a human being to use the resources to his own advantage. This example is the core of orthodox economic theory. The relationship between different sorts of natural objects are determined by natural laws: the law of gravity or chemical laws, describing the way liquids, gases, and fixed materials react to each other. The relationship between various human beings is ruled by social laws. Homans' law is an example in this respect: wherever humans who perceive each other as equals meet each other regularly, a set of common views, values, and norms emerge. In this way we can think of a world of *substances that are causally related to each other via the operation of a series of forces.*

Scientific research must find out, by thinking about the results of introspection or so-called internal observation, which forces rule what kind of substantial relationships. So we learn increasingly about the way the world of objects, which is the objective world, functions. Leibniz and other rationalists discussed primarily the physical and chemical world. Later rationalist economists and sociologists approached the human world in a comparable way, as we have seen in the examples given above.

B.4 **Kant's Transcendental Synthesis**

In his *Critique of Pure Reason* Kant tries to formulate a synthesis between the two approaches, empiricism and rationalism. Is the ratio or are the senses the primary source of knowledge? Kant was impressed by Hume's contributions. But Hume himself already admitted that he could not solve the so-called *problem of induction*. We can observe large numbers of incidents, but they will always remain just a very small part of the whole of occurrences that had to be observed to

---

[3] According to the evolutionary approach, even the substance of objects changes over time. If we assume that everything—character as well as properties—are subject to change, we need a dynamic analysis of the world of objects too. Nowadays the distinction between substance and properties has increasingly become blurred, which is a rich source of confusion. As a good example of this problem: the definition of unemployment in the Netherlands has changed over the period 1945–2009. It led to a significant change in the statistics as published by the Central Bureau of Statistics, making all empirical research based on the unemployment statistics flawed. The same happened with the concept of the 'collective burden'. A good understanding of Kant makes researchers more aware of this problem.

reliably formulate a general law. Moreover, Kant made it clear to the empiricists that observation can never take place by senses only—the human person necessarily uses his ratio when thinking about the impressions that come from the senses. The ratio transforms chemical processes into structured thoughts, which have meaning. The two elements, sense experience and the process of structuring, are two *aspects* of one and the same process. The first is to be considered as the content, while the second can be interpreted as form. This famous distinction, first introduced by Aristotle, clarifies the one-sidedness of empiricism (only content) and rationalism (only form). According to Kant, content without form is blind, while form without content is empty. We can never separate the two aspects—we can only analytically distinguish the two.

As already said, the mind structures sense impressions. This implies that we can never get into contact with reality 'out there' directly. We only experience reality as it is shaped by our ratio. If we accept this, we must admit that knowledge is not objective (directly coming from objects), but influenced by the subjects who observe. This makes the result *subjective*. Kant tries to save the objectivity of knowledge by adopting an axiom that is called *transcendental idealism*. It means that reality is ruled by the same laws as the human mind. In other words, the mind structures sense data in exact *correspondence* with the way reality itself is structured. The term transcendental idealism must be understood as follows: transcendental means 'beyond empirical enquiry' and idealism means that reality is ruled by ideas. Here, the idea that is reflected in the structure of human thinking is identical to the idea as is reflected in our reality. Reality 'out there' is perfectly reflected in our mind structure.

Kant's discovery of the human laws of understanding is now called the Copernican Revolution in philosophy. These laws tell us something about the architecture of the mind (internal reality). They are not the result of external observation (empirical enquiry); they result from internal observation or introspection. The laws of understanding shape the empirical results. Knowledge that results from internal observation is called 'a priori' knowledge, in contrast to knowledge that is acquired by external observation, which is called 'a posteriori' knowledge. Before Kant only analytical statements were considered to be of an 'a priori' kind. For example, the statement 'a movie consists of a series of moving pictures'. Such a statement cannot be confirmed or falsified by empirical observation, since the statement is true by definition. The definition of a movie logically implies the truth of the analytical statement. From Kant we know that also synthetic statements can be of an a priori kind. Famous examples of statements of an 'a priori' and synthetic type are about the existence of substance as distinguished from property, the categorization of reality or the establishment of identity and the differences between the various identities, the existence of cause and effect, the basic axioms of logic and of mathematics, and our intuition of time and space.

When analysing the world of substances we must make a distinction between different types of substances and we must establish which forces set which substances in motion. A falling stone, a running woman, a consumer who buys a computer, an employee who is fired: all these actors 'move', but what is the mover and in which direction do these actors move? A causal explanation of a change in the behaviour needs a universal law about the unvarying character of the substance, which is subject to our research. But it appears to be very difficult to reach consensus about general formulations of the forces that characterize the relationship between different substances and establish an unvarying order.

In social science several attempts have been made to construct a picture of a world of substances that is ruled by one force. In orthodox economics a distinction is made between two substances, namely human beings and natural resources. The relationship is assumed to be characterized by scarcity. The human being is assumed to be driven by the propensity to reduce scarcity of natural resources as much as possible. In orthodox sociology a distinction is made between different groups of people. The relationship is assumed to be characterized by a drive to maximize one's own status, that is, one's position in the hierarchical ranking. This implies group-internal relationships characterized by solidarity and group-external relationships of a rivalling nature. In Section B.5 we will deal with the theoretical and empirical character of economics in more detail.

B.5 **Kant Applied to Economics**

As explained in the previous sections substances cannot be observed. We need to determine different substances first, in order to be able to observe a set of properties of an object. Then these properties can be interpreted as an empirical manifestation of that particular substance. If we observe a human being we must first have established what a human being is. If we observe a person as unemployed, we must first have established what unemployment is. In other words, we must first develop a framework of interpretation before we can start our observations. Orthodox economics offers us a framework of interpretation. In order to answer the question of whether this framework is not only a necessary but also a sufficient condition for careful observation and explanation of human behaviour, we first explicate how this framework has been constructed.

In the second half of the 19th and the first half of the 20th century a number of philosophers/economists worked on a project that did lead to an economics that could establish a series of universal laws. It resulted in a construction which is now called 'the economic world'. In this world two different sorts of substances are assumed, namely human beings and natural resources. These human beings are actors, who face just one problem, namely scarcity. The definition of scarcity is: actors want more natural resources than they have at their disposal. This difference creates a tension, which sets people in motion. It means that they are motivated to reduce this tension as much as possible. This drive can be typified as 'the economic force'. In order to analyse the operation of this economic force, they have to ignore the effect of other forces that drive people.

To ignore the psychic force, economists assumed human behaviour to be rational. Human beings were supposed to have solved all their 'internal' problems, and become integrated persons (individuals—not to be divided). They know exactly who they are and what they need, and collect an optimal amount of information about the quality and prices of goods available which can satisfy their needs. Emotions play a role when consuming goods and intuition plays a role when taking economic decisions. But phenomena such as uncertainty and addiction are excluded.

To ignore the social force, it is assumed that social relationships do not exist (actors are like atoms, which do not cluster into molecules).

The construction of the economic world is a sophisticated thought experiment. It has led to the formulation of a series of universal laws, like the law of diminishing marginal utility and the law of diminishing marginal returns. However, by isolating the economic force from the operation of two other relevant forces, we cannot use the economic theoretical apparatus when observing and explaining human behaviour. Therefore, we need to introduce an analysis of the two other forces into this economic world.

B.6 **What is Wrong with Economic Naturalism?**

While economic philosophers were discussing the nature of their construction many economists were applying economic world theories to real-life situations. The idea that in economies, especially in free market economies, the economic force is the dominant one is called *economic naturalism*. Almost all economics textbooks reflect this idea: empirical phenomena can be explained by economic theory; we do not need psychology and sociology to clarify developments in real-life economies. Of course, these books make exceptions now and then. But on the level of analysis and theory the economic force is the only force that is recognized. This practice leads to serious flaws. Every action that belongs to the real-life economy—a person is buying a book, a woman is selling labour services, a union is declaring a strike—is interpreted as an economic, rational, and non-social action, which is directed towards the maximization of economic utilities of the actor. In real life, however, the actions that are mentioned might be described differently. If a person buys a book it might be a message towards members of the same group that the buyer is an intelligent person who reads difficult texts. If a woman is supplying her labour service, orthodox economics interprets this action as a sacrifice and a cost, but in reality it is possible that the person likes the job since it enhances her self-respect. Moreover, she benefits from it because of the social contacts on the job. If we make a careful analysis of the operation of the psychic and of the social force, not only does the set of goals become more sophisticated, but different restrictions play an important role in the analysis.

An example of the sort of mistakes that result from an economic-natural approach is the following. When measuring economic growth monetary incomes are taken as an indicator of the value that is produced during a particular period. But a careful analysis of empirical phenomena, like having a job, on the basis of a multi-aspect approach, shows that economic naturalism leads to large miscalculations. The values that are really consumed—also including social and psychic utilities—are very difficult to observe. An endless flow of activities in the household and informal sector are not taken into account. Moreover, many activities create disutilities for the person or for his enemy: these sorts of effects are never taken into account. An inadequate set of instruments makes attempts to observe the true consumer value into a desperate affair.

B.7 **Towards an Empirical Economic Science**

So far the text shows how orthodox economics has applied Kantian epistemology. It is not an easy task to carefully distinguish between elements that are part of the definition and elements that are to be considered as the property of a particular good, however. It appears subject to an ongoing debate among different people. Different specifications of substance-property combinations lead to different observations and different explanations. So every approach has not only its own explanation, but also its own reality. This is an outcome that might have surprised Kant and his followers. But it is exactly the outcome of debates within the philosophy of science in the 19th and 20th century. It shows that Kant was too optimistic about the possibility of developing objective knowledge. Especially in social sciences, concepts appear vague. Their specification depends on the ontology chosen. In economics there is a continuing dispute about the ontology that is used by orthodox economics. The so-called economic world is constructed on the basis of a few axioms. Actors are assumed to be economic, rational, non-social, and to apply classical logic.

In this world they are economic actors in the sense of always being motivated to maximize their (economic) utilities under the constraint of the natural resources available.

When explaining processes in real-life economies, not only this economic force, but also a social and a psychic force, play a role in the determination of human behaviour. In order to explain the existence of three primary forces we must imagine reality or the universe as a thing. Then we distinguish between humans and other things. In this world three primary types of relationships can be distinguished:

(1) The relationship between humans and the other things.
(2) The relationship between different human beings, who recognize each other as such—in the positive as well as in the negative sense.
(3) The relationship between a human being and his Self.

Here, the first relationship is of an economic nature, the second is of a social, and the third of a psychic nature. While the typical economic approach regards the individual level as the only level acceptable from an ontological point of view, we distinguish three levels. The economic aspect is linked to the individual level, the social aspect to the super-individual, and the psychic aspect is linked to the sub-individual level. So in the world of objects we can distinguish different sorts of substances: sub-individual parts, such as the thinking versus the feeling 'I' or the masculine versus the feminine part within a person (1), the individual 'I' that is related towards his natural environment (2), and the super-individual part, such as unions versus employers or men versus women (3). At all levels causal relationships exist, which create forces that set people in motion. Besides the familiar economic force, we can distinguish a social force which drives people to strive for a (social) status as much as possible and a psychic force that drives people to an integrated Self that maximizes the respect towards the Self (self-respect).

B.8 **Conclusion**

To explain empirical reality (the world of properties), we must first specify a proper world of substances. This world defines the different types of substances that constitute the real world, including the forces that characterize the different relationships. Only with a proper ontology can empirical researchers hope for some success.

■ APPENDIX C JUNG FOR ECONOMISTS

C.1 **Introduction**

Neoclassical economics is based on a number of axioms, one of which is the assumption of perfect rationality. A perfectly rational person has enough willpower to act according to the preferences of the true Self. By using the term true Self it is suggested that there are more selves, which strive for different things. A realistic account of human behaviour needs a fundamental analysis of the essential elements of the psyche. As the term 'psychology' suggests, its essential task is to search for the logic of the psyche, which means the search for mechanisms that keep the psyche in balance.

In this appendix we will discuss ways of designing a psyche, so as to be able to develop ideas about this mechanism. Therefore, we present the psyche as part of a biological system, called 'human person'. In particular, we will discuss the way Carl Jung has designed and analysed the psyche as such. Jung is the representative of psychology par excellence (Stevens, 1994). Many schools of thought within psychology do not analyse the psyche or have adopted very restrictive assumptions about its abilities. Jung, however, is one of a few *analytical psychologists* who refused to abstract from the analysis almost everything important. Even more than Freud and Adler, he focused on the *ontological aspects of the psyche*, making his approach a very valuable start for an understanding of the functioning of a psyche or mind.[4] In Section C.2 we will approach the human person as a biological system, consisting of a psyche or mind and a body, both aspect-systems of the whole system called 'human person'. We will discuss the elements constituting the psychic system according to Jung in Section C.3. In Section C.5, C.6, and C.7 we discuss Jung about homeostasis, rationality, and psycho-dynamics respectively. In Section C.4 we will deal with a number of *psychic types* that are distinguished. In Section C.8 we will pay attention to the core of psychological analysis and answer the question of what we mean by the logic of the psyche. In Section C.9 we will apply the ideas of Jung to a series of economic phenomena, illustrating that the analytical psychology of Jung can contribute significantly to a better understanding of economic phenomena.

C.2 **The Human Person as a Biological System**

Biological systems are characterized by their teleological character. Plants, animals, and humans have a *built-in drive to wholeness*; they can be interpreted as a bundle of potentials or drives that become manifest when triggered by particular circumstances. Economists are used to approaching a human person as an economic man, driven by an economic force, aimed at a reduction of

---

[4] In modern psychology monism rather dualism dominates the discussion. Descartes has been blamed for a dualistic approach by separating mind and body (Damasio, 1994). But this accusation is wrong: Descartes explicitly denied being a dualist. He only distinguished analytically between the mind and the body. In other words, he considered them aspect-systems rather than subsystems. When doing this we go beyond the dualism-monism controversy, and recognize that there is no mind without a body, *and* there is no body without a mind.

scarcity of natural resources as much as possible. But there are more forces that co-determine human behaviour.

In social science we are used to distinguishing between three primary forces, namely the economic, the social, and the psychic force. In this text we distinguish a biological force, which is a synthesis of the physiological and the psychic force.

The organic character of biological systems implies that different forces, connected to different emotions and needs, have a dialectical relationship with each other: they are in conflict with each other, but since they need each other to let the system as a whole function well, they are also inclined to search for synthesis. This tendency towards balance is called homeostasis, and is well known in physics. In economics the law of increasing, constant, and decreasing marginal utility and marginal returns are expressions of this law.

In Section C.3 we will discuss the constitution of a psyche as an aspect-system of the whole system 'human person'.

C.3 **Archetypes and Complexes in the Unconscious**

According to Jung, every psyche consists of a *collective unconscious*, a *personal unconscious,* and a *personal conscious*. In order to understand what is meant by a collective unconscious we must imagine our reality as a biological system; in other words, the universe or cosmos has a body and a mind. This collective mind is located in all living creatures. We stick our analysis to human persons: they all carry the human heritage—all the experiences of man from their creation until now. In the modern evolutionary-economic and Austrian literature the concept of tacit knowledge comes close to this idea of a collective unconscious. It is the location where humans have stored their so-called *archetypes*. These are potentials of a psycho-neuro-logical character—altogether they tell the story of human life. When a child grows up, circumstances trigger these potentials or forces, and drive his behaviour and experiences. These experiences trigger and develop more specific archetypes, called *'complexes'*, which are located in the personal unconscious. Life as it is lived every day results from a confrontation between complexes in the unconscious and outer circumstances. If a child is born into a poor family the primary needs that result from manifest complexes cannot easily be satisfied. Lack of food and lack of attention from the parents has a negative effect on the physical and psychic growth of the child. If there is no mother figure during the first years, this affects psychic growth very negatively. Every stage of life is characterized by a particular set of complexes that are manifest, and must be developed and satisfied. If this does not happen, the psyche will remain unbalanced, which is harmful for the growth and integration of the psyche.

Now we will give a few examples of archetypes and complexes, to illustrate in which ways they regulate the human life cycle. In the first years a child is strongly connected to the mother figure, and develops a strong mother complex. But after some years an ego complex emerges, which is responsible for a growing distance between child and mother. During this stage a child begins to explore the world around him, and the father figure becomes increasingly important as a guide in this process. In this way a person develops two complexes or centres of consciousness: the Ego or 'I' of a person and the Self of a person. He is able to look at himself; the sentence 'I look at my Self' expresses nicely the fact that the two entities are distinguished from each other, and increasingly establish an interrelationship. The relationship between the two complexes can be clarified as follows: in the process of development the Ego of the child must increasingly take over the task of the protection of the Self from the mother. So, the Ego becomes increasingly the 'executive' of the Self, and if things happen that are against the interests of the Self, the ego must be able to avoid particular behaviours and situations.[5]

When the ego screens the desires that claim immediate satisfaction, it must select those desires or needs that are urgent and in the long-term interest of the Self, and reject those that are bad for the long-term interest. In this permanent conflict two complexes are formed: the *persona*, representing the desires and needs that are acceptable in a particular cultural context or even forced by this context on someone, and the *shadow*, representing the desires and needs whose satisfaction is a threat to the survival of the person. In other words, the persona is the mask of the person, or the public relations officer, and the shadow is the enemy of the true Self. The shadow complex is formed through continuing familial repression and cultural indoctrination; of course, the formation of this complex is based on the universal shadow archetype, which lives in the collective unconscious.[6]

A fourth example of a specific archetype is the gender complex. In each person lives a complex that has some masculine and some feminine properties. In Buddhism we find the distinction between yin and yang, which represents comparable properties. In a man we do not only find some masculinity, but also some hidden feminine properties. These are called his *anima*. In a woman we do not only find some femininity, but also some hidden masculine properties. These are called *animus*. There is an ongoing conflict between the persona and the anima or animus. Over time, a person must solve this conflict by creating a synthesis between the two powers. As with all inner conflicts, not reconciling the antagonisms threatens the development of an integrated personality. As long as a person is a self-divided person, much energy is used to fight these conflicts, and the *focus* (or attitude or disposition) is directed to these conflicts, rather than to the solution to social and economic conflicts.

In Section C.4 we will discuss a series of psychic types, and we will see that different capacities of the mind lead to different personalities.

C.4 **Psychic Types**

Jung distinguishes four *psychic capacities*, which fulfil different functions. The first function is *sensation*, and it tells the person that something exists—an object or a threat, for instance. The second function is *'thinking'*, which tells the person what it is that exists. A third function is *'feeling'*, telling the person whether that which exists is agreeable or not. And the fourth function is *intuition*, telling the person when 'it' comes and where 'it' is going. Besides these four functions Jung distinguishes between two attitudes or dispositions, namely an extroverted and an

---

[5] Keizer (2015) offers a slightly different picture of the mind. A distinction has been made between two selves, namely a true Self and an actual Self. In this constitution the 'I' or ego is 'advised' by the true Self, and screens the claims of the actual Self to see whether the satisfaction of them is in the long-term interest of the true Self. In some other analyses a superego is introduced to represent a moral complex inside the mind of a person. This complex can be interpreted as an important part of the true Self, and will be highly affected by the prevailing culture in which the child grows up.

[6] Girard has written many books and articles about ancient myths and primitive religions which all show the universality of these archetypes. He explains the so-called scapegoat mechanism that reflects the social logic by referring to the tacit knowledge of primitive man (Girard, 1978).

introverted focus. When taking the four functions and two foci together we can construct eight types of personalities. Because the capacity to develop skills is scarce, Jung assumes that every person can develop only two functions and one type of focus. Since thinking and feeling are two different rationalizing functions, a person always chooses one of these two. The same holds for sensation and intuition, which are non-rational functions; a person chooses one of these two. It means that a person is a thinker who uses his intuition, or a person who uses his feelings and sensations. Now we are left with four types of personalities:

(1) An extraverted personality who trusts his well-developed capacity of feeling and his sensation.
(2) An extraverted personality who trusts his well-developed capacity of thinking and his intuition.
(3) An introverted personality who trusts his well-developed capacity of feeling and his sensation.
(4) An introverted personality who trusts his well-developed capacity of thinking and his intuition.

It looks as if Jung is saying that sensitive persons have a comparative disadvantage in doing philosophical work. Jung's distinction between non-rational and rational capacities is based on the idea that rationality and intuition are separate capacities. In practice, however, the four psychic capacities might better be considered as different *aspects* of one and the same phenomenon, which is the human epistemological or knowledge-acquisition capacity.

In Section C.5 we will discuss the problems which result from homeostatic imbalance, and see how we can interpret the concept of rationality, which is so important in economic analysis.

C.5 **Homeostatic Imbalance**

The satisfaction of certain archetypal needs is essential to the development of the programme of a person's life. If these essential needs cannot be satisfied, a psychic imbalance develops. For instance, the mother figure malfunctioned in the early years of childhood. Or the father figure wasn't there when the child needed introduction into the external world. Then the ego might remain relatively weak, with far-reaching consequences for the person's social skills, for instance. Persons with a weak ego are inclined to compensate for it by satisfying a strong need for social recognition: if the person is unable to respect their own Self, others must fill this gap. Two psychic imbalances have become well known in the analytical psychological literature, namely psychosis and neurosis. Jung interprets these two mental illnesses in terms of the functions and foci discussed in Section C.4. In case of extreme introversion, where the person is using his thinking and his intuition especially, there is a chance of developing a psychosis. The person lives primarily in his inner world, which is quite separated from the external world. This separation creates a continuous flow of misunderstandings when interpreting the behaviour of others—a very painful experience. In a case of extreme extroversion, where the person is particularly using his feeling and sensations, there is a chance of developing a neurosis. A neurosis is an emotion connected to a particular need or desire, which is not under control of the person. He is unaware of this problem because of a lack of inner reflection. Therefore, he is not using any willpower to correct his behaviour.

Strong introversion can lead to a withdrawal from the outer world; a move which can be interpreted as a form of *autism*.[7] Strong extroversion can lead to a lack of connection with the unconscious, rootlessness, and a loss of intuition. With respect to the gender complex it is obvious that a man who is unable to see his 'anima', or a woman who is unable to see her 'animus', has a serious problem in understanding people who have more self-knowledge and self-acceptance.

In Section C.6 we will discuss the concept of perfect rationality, as used by the typical economic analysis, in Jungian terms.

C.6 A Jungian Conception of Perfect Rationality

Our ontology of the mind leads to the following elements in the psychic system:

(1) An 'I' who is the decision-maker; when thinking, the 'I' uses its ratio, which is the capacity to structure information in a logically consistent way.

(2) A True Self, as experienced by the 'I' (TSE), advises the 'I'. This is the person's source of intuitive knowledge of himself and his situation, and can therefore also be called 'intuition'. The Jungian psychic capacities play an important role here.

(3) An Actual Self (AS), who is a bundle of emotions, connected to needs and desires of a psychic or physical nature, and claiming immediate satisfaction. This actual Self receives sense impressions from the outer world. The sensation of these impressions leads to feelings in a way that is influenced by the personality of the person. These feelings are an important incentive to behave in particular ways. Emotions trigger feelings and thoughts, and both are sent to the decision-maker.

(4) A system of framing, which structures the 'information' before it reaches the 'I'. This act of framing has two functions. First, it makes information understandable, thereby making it possible for the person to react. Second, the framing should protect the person against discoveries, which are unwanted by the AS—in other words, a typical irrational element.

(5) The decision-maker 'I' has some willpower, which helps him to execute his decisions by influencing the emotions of the actual Self.

This system must be read as follows: a person is permanently bombarded with impressions. He receives signals from the body about physiological needs that want to be satisfied. From the mind he receives signals about psychic needs, such as safety. These impressions are framed in such a way that they become understandable and acceptable to the person. Understanding means: knowing the meaning of a particular phenomenon; being able to see something functioning as an important part of a bigger whole. Only if a person understands impressions are emotions triggered which set him in motion. In other words, without understanding, a particular phenomenon does not trigger emotions, and without emotions there will not be any behavioural reaction to that phenomenon.

Emotions are connected to all sorts of needs, and some of them claim immediate satisfaction. But there are also emotions reminding the person of the importance of his long-term interest.

---

[7] In France there is a group of economists who call neoclassical economists autistic. Although I personally don't like to use words with a strong negative connotation, this is exactly what is at stake. Neoclassical economists live in their own economic world, and are isolated from the real world, ignoring social and psychic problems. The French group calls its own approach 'post-autistic economics'.

These emotions produce feelings and thoughts and send these to the decision-making 'I'. We can imagine that the emotions which serve long-term interests say to the 'I': 'wait a second', 'let's first think about the long-term consequences for the satisfaction of this particular need'. So it triggers the 'I' to use its ratio and make a more careful analysis of the costs and benefits of a particular action.

The analysis made by the ratio is based on a paradigm, which is delivered by the intuition of the true Self, as experienced by the 'I'. So this true Self offers a map of the world or a world-view, including a picture of the personality of the person. On the basis of a specified 'model' of the situation the 'I' decides whether or not to use willpower in an attempt to influence actual behaviour.

In a previous section we have seen that Jung makes a distinction between the personal conscious (1), the personal unconscious (2), and the collective unconscious (3). The wall between the three worlds is porous, which means that the three worlds are, at least to a certain extent, open to each other. This means that the archetypes in the collective unconscious and the resulting complexes in the personal unconscious are constantly affecting the processes in the conscious. These influences can be interpreted as a permanent bombardment of exogenous shocks, affecting the development of the intuition of the experienced true Self and of the needs and desires of the actual Self. In this way the archetypes and complexes give the life of a person its structure.

C.7 **The Psychic System in Motion**

In the living world systems and subsystems are teleological in nature and therefore not only characterized by their structure, but also by their goal. We have just sketched the structure of the mind: its elements and their interrelationships. The goal of the personal system as a whole can be formulated as follows: *survival and manifestation of the Self.*

We have made a distinction between three aspects of human behaviour. In the relationship between the human person and non-human elements in reality—the typical economic aspect of life—the person wants to reduce his scarcity of natural resources as much as possible; in other words, the person wants to be as wealthy as possible. In the relationship between the person and other human persons—the typical social relationship—the person wants to reach a position in the ranking as high as possible; in other words, the person strives for a maximum of social recognition or status. In the relationship between the person and his Self—the typical psychic relationship—the person strives for a maximum of self-respect; in other words, he wants to maximize his status in his own eyes. This division into three aspects of human life fits nicely with the idea of survival and manifestation. The economic, the social, and the psychic goal are all inputs necessary for the output or ultimate goal: *manifestation of the Self.*[8] In the evolutionary approach, as we find in many parts of social science including economics, the main drive is assumed to be 'survival'. But the question 'what must survive' has never been answered. In biology survival means 'life, not death'; but when it comes to human behaviour it makes sense to distinguish

---

[8] In the ecological view we should formulate the goal in terms of manifestation of the Self and the enjoyment of the manifestation of other beings. Later in this appendix we will see that the essential true Self strives for wholeness, which is similar to the ecological view.

between economic survival (no poverty), social survival (no humiliation or exclusion), and psychic survival (no self-hatred). Existential philosophy is about the Self in his manifestation to the world so as to leave an eternal footprint. Now we can define perfect rationality as the perfect and eternal footprint of the true Self.

C.8 **What Do We Mean by Psychic Logic?**

As economics is about the economic logic, and sociology is about the social logic, so is psychology about the psychic logic. In economics the economic motivation explains why a change in the economic situation –a lower price for bikes, for instance—leads to a change in economic behaviour, which means a higher quantity of bikes demanded. So we can construct a psychic logic, where the psychic motivation to maximize self-respect explains why a change in the psychic situation—a decline in willpower, for instance—leads to a change in psychic behaviour, which means less control of the emotion that says 'take another glass of beer', for example. If the person gives in and drinks another glass of beer, it is because of the short-term satisfaction that beer consumption gives to the drinker, or because of the status it gives the drinker in the group to which he belongs (social status). On the other hand, this behaviour leads to a lower level of self-respect: the true Self says: don't drink too much beer; nevertheless the 'I' cannot prevent the person drinking another beer. After a series of bad experiences the 'I' can decide to invest in willpower, so as to prevent these bad experiences in the future. Such investments promote long-term psychic growth. In other words, the person becomes more rational over time.

In our model of the mind, we have isolated the psyche from its economic and its social environment. It does not give us a realistic picture, and we can improve the quality of our knowledge significantly by connecting this analysis with a typical economic and a typical social analysis. But the focus of this text is directed to the typical psychic factor. It means that we assume that our person grows up in a very rich environment, with family and colleagues and friends, who all think highly of him. What then can still go wrong?

Rich persons have solved their economic problem. People in prestigious positions have solved their social problem. The typical psychic problem is a lack of self-respect, and the solution to the economic and to the social problem contributes definitely to the solution of the psychic problem. But on the essential level *genuine self-respect can only be given by a person himself.* Even if all efforts to get out of the misery of being poor fails, and even if nobody appreciates you as a person very much, a person can be convinced of the value of his true Self, and keep on acting according to his guidelines. This autonomous component of self-respect is the basis for a true life—not economic success and the applause of other people.

Besides a lack of autonomous self-respect persons have insufficient willpower to perform so well as to compensate for that lack of autonomous self-respect. Lack of willpower leaves emotional conflicts unresolved. The result is a kind of *border liner attitude* of trying to satisfy all desires that pop up as soon as possible. The long term is just the aggregate of short-term solutions and the personality is far from integrated.

Another problem is the *imperfection of the intuition* of the true Self as experienced by the decision-making 'I'. As said, the intuition is based on a particular paradigm, which is settled in the (un)conscious. Paradigms are composed of a set of axioms characterizing the essence of life. What if impressions are framed in such a way that an increasing number of anomalies become manifest? Then the person has a strong interest in searching for explanations for these anomalies within the existing framework. So small adjustments are applied or the anomalies are considered as incidents or the result of errors in the observation. It is very human to prevent paradigmatic changes, and to surround the established paradigm with a protective belt, since the costs of changing the structure of someone's intuition are extremely high.[9]

* * *

The three primary problems in life, the economic, the social, and the psychic problem are *substitutable* to a certain extent. Less focus on the economic and the social problem makes more energy available for a stronger focus on the development of the true Self, and for more investments in willpower necessary to reach this goal. This search means an increasing *open-mindedness*. This means that a person accepts a more porous protective belt around his intuition or established paradigm. Closed-mindedness is the result of protecting the actual intuition that led to so much economic and social success. But it prevents the search for the true intuition of the person and an increase in autonomous self-respect.

As already said, perfect rationality means the perfect manifestation of the true Self. Since life is a discovery process we will never be able to fully understand our true Self. We must accept that we just meet the true Self as actually experienced.

The two causes of imperfect rationality—lack of willpower and biased framing—are related to each other. If willpower (WP) is weak the bias in the framing (BIAS) compensates for the loss of self-respect.

We express this negative relationship graphically in Figure C1.
The curve expresses a type of protective belt around the intuitively experienced Self and prevents a decline in self-respect that is below a minimum necessary for psychic survival. The higher the position of the curve the more the person has closed their mind to a more realistic picture of the world, including the true Self; in other words, the less rational the person.

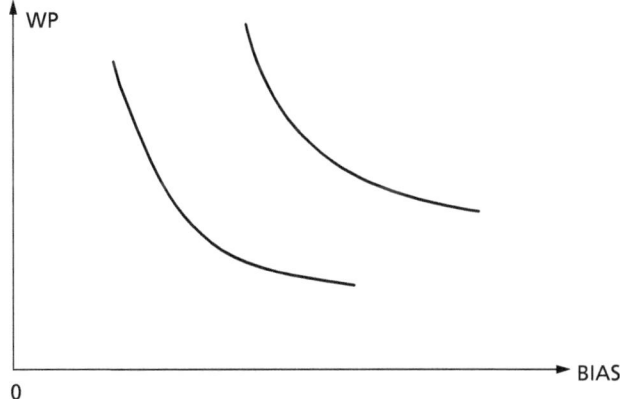

Figure C.1. The Trade-Off between Willpower and the Frame Bias

___

[9] The concept of protective belt is borrowed from the scientific-philosophical analysis of Lakatos. He defends the position that it is not irrational not to immediately change the paradigm in case of one or a few anomalies (Lakatos, 1970).

C.9 **Jungian Analysis Applied to Economic Phenomena**

As we all know, there is an essential difference between economics and the economy. When talking about economic phenomena we mean everything that happens in the economy: the behaviour of consumers, investors, workers, and management, for instance. Economics studies economic phenomena from a typical economic point of view, leaving out the typical social and the typical psychic elements. Because Jung's analysis comes quite close to what can be called the typical psychic analysis (leaving out the other types of factors), it makes sense to show how this analysis can contribute to a better understanding of economic phenomena.

A first example is the explanation of consumer behaviour. In neoclassical economics the preferences of the people are given, and so with the information about prices and qualities of the various goods which are offered. Given the budget, every consumer can calculate the number of different goods that must be bought in order to reach optimal allocation of scarce resources. In reality, preferences as well as information about what is on offer, are not givens at all. In our modern economies a very large institution of marketing has emerged. According to the typical economic explanation, the function of this institution is the delivery of information about preferences and the quality and price of goods. According to the typical sociological explanation, the organizations in the marketing industry are creating a culture that stimulates consumption. According to a Jungian approach, the institution of marketing is trying to influence the battle between the different complexes in the personal unconscious in such a way that consumption is stimulated. Clothing firms organize fashion shows which express independence or masculinity, or show one belongs to a prestigious group. In some cases, consumption of particular goods can help people to find homeostatic balance in their psyche. It is in the interest of the marketing industry, however, that the solutions they offer are short-term solutions only. Otherwise, consumption would decline. So advertising must continuously suggest that the solutions found are inadequate, and that the latest fashion is a better solution to the problem of psychic imbalance.

A second example is about the explanation of worker behaviour in their bargaining about labour conditions. The Dutch union of medical specialists is a good example. Its power is based on the skills of the specialists to solve health problems. At present most specialists are males, who behave in quite a masculine way, thereby denying their anima. In a less powerful situation males are less seduced to misbehave and exploit situations. Were their psyches more in balance they would change their behaviour and become more caring creatures, who do not exploit their power so much.

A third example is about financial investor behaviour. In the last two decades the Western financial world has been confronted with aggressively operating hedge funds and private equity. These organizations develop strategies focused on the maximization of short-term capital gains and profits, by buying shares, restructuring firms, and selling the newly formed organizations. These strategies are also profitable by ignoring the interests of people who cannot defend themselves sufficiently. It is not that difficult to seek short-term gain while ignoring the long-term gains of other stakeholders. Daily life is full of situations where people have short-term power. If we all constantly exploited our short-term powers, life would be hell. But some people do not have a balanced psyche, so if they discover a way to become filthy rich, they cannot control themselves.

A last example is about the explanation of the behaviour of leaders of large companies. Over the last few decades many mergers and acquisitions have taken place. Economic logic tells us that scale matters, and so a merger can be profitable. But empirical research shows that, in many cases, the merger appears unprofitable in the end. The drive to be the captain of a huge empire is so strong that some analyses, about differences in cultures between the candidates, for instance, are ignored. Again, people placed in a very powerful position often cannot withstand the triggering of unconscious complexes. In many cases captains of industry are confronted with a number of serious objections against particular strategies. But the typical psychic process of repression makes it possible for the captain to decide against economic logic.

In Section C.10 we will draw some conclusions.

C.10 **Conclusion**

Carl Jung must be considered to be a typical psychologist. He is searching for the logic of the mind in a way which is comparable with the way in which orthodox economics searches for the logic of the economic world. This makes him a valuable source of knowledge for economists. In his constitution of the mind he does not completely abstract the mind from the body; it is important to see that physiology plays an important role in his design.

In Jung's construction the archetypes in the collective unconscious play a decisive role in the whole of factors which determine human behaviour. They manifest themselves in the minds of individual persons through a series of complexes. During childhood, the role of the mother and the father figure are the most important ones. During adulthood, the relationship between man and woman and between senior and junior, or between boss and subordinate, are the decisive positions. It goes without saying that the experiences in the first structure affect experiences in the second configuration significantly.

The psyche of a person is in balance if he has dealt with the various complexes in a harmonious way. Otherwise, the person becomes neurotic in some respects. In our Western world many people have developed one or more neuroses, which affect the quality of their decisions negatively.

With respect to autism we must take into account the fact that many people are autistic to a certain extent only. Among scientists, autism is widespread. Many scientists are very good in one aspect of science, while bad in other important aspects. In gamma-science especially this is a serious problem. Some gamma-people are alpha types, and try to avoid beta-elements in their scientific research. Other gamma-people are beta types, and try to avoid the alpha-aspects in their field. In economics it is obvious that econometricians try to avoid a discussion about the paradigm and the analysis upon which their hypotheses are based. On the other hand, economic philosophers don't like to explain differential and difference equations, which describe mathematically the course of a business cycle. The way in which economics has developed itself makes it clear that the econometricians are the dominant group at the moment.

In orthodox economics individuals are assumed to be perfectly rational. This assumption is made in order to isolate the economic problem from the typical psychic problem. The architecture of the mind, as constituted by Jung, helps us better understand what rationality of an individual person means. Perfect rationality means that human willpower is not scarce, and that a person has discovered his true Self and is able to manifest his true Self to the world, including himself. Of course, nobody will ever become perfectly rational. Human life is like a journey. We experience and we grow—and suddenly it is over.

APPENDIX D ADAM SMITH AS A FOUNDING FATHER OF MULTIDISCIPLINARY ECONOMICS

D.1 Introduction

Many economists see Adam Smith as the founding father of economics. In dogmen-historical textbooks Smith is portrayed as the first classical political economist; the first scientist who made a study of the mechanism that explains the functioning of a market and of the role of the government in this respect. In the second half of the 19th and the first half of the 20th century orthodox/neoclassical economists pretended to have improved his analysis by abstracting it from its capitalist framework, and focusing on the universal laws behind an economic mechanism. In the second half of the 20th century behavioural economists criticized neoclassical economics, but considered Adam Smith to be a typical behavioural economist. They criticized the neoclassical approach, particularly with regard to its use of the axiom of perfect rationality, and claimed that Adam Smith had developed an idea of rationality that differed significantly from the neoclassical picture.[10]

Methodology is always decisive in understanding why various schools of thought differ so much in their analyses and theories. Smith admired Newton's attempts to find universal laws that could describe the behaviour of planets; the search for natural constants, which determine the relationship between geographical distance and the mass of an object, for instance. In Smith's work on human behaviour we see that he is searching for universal laws about human nature and their consequences for the mechanisms that determine human behaviour.

In this appendix we will first briefly discuss the content of the work by Adam Smith, in Section D.2. Then we will present the reactions of the Institutionalists and the neoclassical economists in Section D.3. In Section D.4 we will show why behavioural economists claim Adam Smith to be their founding father. After a methodological intermezzo in section D.5, we continue in Section D.6 with an interpretation of Smith as a multidisciplinary economist since he adheres to the neoclassical methodology of searching for universal laws, but supports the behavioural idea of psychic and social factors as relevant when trying to understand the functioning of real-life economies.

D.2 The Legacy of Adam Smith

This section draws in part on Hanson (2010), which has compared and contrasted the three main books by Adam Smith, namely his *History of Astronomy*, his *Moral Sentiments* and his *Wealth of Nations*.

---

[10] Smith did not use the term rationality. But he discussed the problem of self-command thoroughly. For him, command was a moral concept based on moral feelings or sentiment. In those days rationality was the opposite of emotion and feeling. In the most recent behavioural literature the two terms are not considered as opposites anymore (Keizer, 2015).

In his first major work—*The History of Astronomy*—Smith commits himself to the scientific philosophy of Newton: the search for universal laws and the predominant role of *human imagination* in it (Smith, 1756). When doing research we need ideas and analyses to see whether they produce theories that can be empirically falsified. Many centuries later, famous philosophers such as Popper and Lakatos advocated philosophies that Adam Smith had already formulated. The recognition of the importance of imagination means that Smith is not an empiricist, as he is regularly interpreted to be. Every research starts with an idea about the substance of a particular phenomenon. On the basis of this ontology an analysis can be developed, leading to series of theories, which can be tested empirically.

In his second book—*The Theory of Moral Sentiments*—Smith tried to become the Newton of social science (Smith, 1759). He developed the idea of an *impartial spectator*, an imaginary man who represents the norms and values of society. This man looks at every person and tells him how to behave towards his fellow humans. The ideas of how to behave evolve, since every man is assumed to have the capacity to imagine how other humans feel in their particular situation—*sympathy*. This capacity constantly produces moral sentiments and moral resentments. Through social interaction a group develops a particular culture, and the impartial spectator represents it. Smith borrowed many ideas from Hume and Hutcheson, but he added a psychological analysis to this micro-sociological analysis (Hanson, 2010). He imagined that every person has such an impartial spectator in his mind. So, independent of what people in his environment actually are saying, every person must try to look at the Self to see whether he can become more virtuous. According to Smith, the most important virtue is *self-command*. It can be reached by controlling emotions by means of willpower so as to serve the long-term interest of the Self. Nobody has perfect knowledge of the essence of their own personality. Over time we increasingly discover personal characteristics that might reflect the true Self. Smith considers prudence, beneficence, and justice as principal virtues, which can be developed by means of self-command.

In his third book—*The Wealth of Nations*—Smith searches for the mechanism that rules market behaviour (Smith, 1776). The idea of *virtuous man*, as developed in his second book, is used to find out how the idea of self-interest can be used for this goal. To understand Smith well, we must know that he was a devout Christian, but—as always with great thinkers—he was not impressed by the institutions of the Church. They were inclined to interpret self-interest as egoism, that is, as the opposite of altruism. The Church preached altruism, of course. Smith, however, considered the inclination to serve the Self not only as natural, but also as virtuous and morally good. When discussing the market mechanism Smith states that it is natural for the butcher, the brewer, and the baker to serve their own interests. It is as if there is an invisible hand that steers society, such that not only the self-interest of the individuals are served, but also the general interest of society as a whole! To understand this implication it is necessary to realize how Smith had interpreted this self-interested person in his second book. There, he made a distinction between virtuous men of inferior prudence and virtuous men of superior prudence. Ordinary people are supposed to be 'inferior-prudent', which means: taking care of their own health, fortune, reputation, and being trustworthy, not greedy, not corrupt, and not striving for self-advancement at any cost. Besides ordinary people in every society there are great leaders, who are able and willing to use their talents for the service of the general interest.

So, Smith' optimism with respect to the functioning of free markets is based on the idea that it is natural for humans to be at least 'inferior-prudent'. The financial crisis of 2008 has shown that this assumption is not always and everywhere a realistic one.

In Section D.3 we will discuss how economics as a science has reacted to the ideas of Smith and his followers.

D.3 **Institutionalism and Neoclassicism**

Classical political economy became increasingly analytical over time. Ricardo, for instance, developed an abstract theory of international trade and factor income distribution. Some economists criticized the increasing lack of empirical relevance, especially the Institutionalists. Others criticized classical political economy for being an analysis of 19th-century Western capitalism rather than a universal theory. Scientifically, the second reaction became the dominant one: orthodox economics. It led to the development of an economic analysis that aims at the modelling of an economic force, thereby abstracting from the operation of other forces, such as the psychic and the social force (Keizer, 2015). By assuming that relationships between people are only of an economic nature, orthodox economics distinguished itself from sociology. By assuming that persons are perfectly rational, neoclassical economics also distinguishes itself from psychology. This research strategy is called 'isolated abstraction'. In this division of labour between different branches of social science, economics had the task of analysing problems of scarcity, isolated from problems of social status and irrationality. The result was a sophisticated analysis of the essence of scarcity. However, empirical reality is different. In real life the three primary problems of human beings, namely the economic, the social, and the psychic problem, are highly interconnected. So, empirical research requires a theoretical instrument integrating the analysis of all three primary problems.

After the Second World War neoclassical economics increasingly used the orthodox analysis as the theoretical foundation for their empirical analysis. It is not surprising that most of this research turned out to be a failure.

D.4 **Behavioural Economics**

Herbert Simon was one of the first who criticized the neoclassical idea of perfect rationality and perfect information (Simon, 1957a,b). According to him, human cognitive capacity is limited and cannot process all the information about a relevant situation. People stop searching for information, which is relevant when taking a particular decision, when they are satisfied, rather than continuing until they have gathered all relevant information. Also, the neoclassical notion of 'optimal amount of information' is flawed, since nobody can calculate the benefit of the extra-marginal unit of information that is not yet been gathered. Simon speaks of satisficing behaviour rather than maximizing behaviour, and of bounded rationality rather than perfect rationality.

Over the years, behavioural economics has evolved and increasingly includes emotions in its analysis. An important implication of this evolution is the shift in meaning of the concept of rationality. The original meaning—limited cognitive capacities—was increasingly replaced by the idea of lack of control of emotions. We have seen that Smith argued that self-command was the principal virtue, and therefore we can call Smith a behavioural economist avant la lettre.

This book discusses behavioural economics and the meaning of rationality. When looking at the different schools of thought in psychology, behavioural economics is quite biased in its choice of psychological theory. It is about cognition and emotion, but there is no *prime driver*. As long as behavioural economists do not formulate the driving force of a person with respect to his Self, something very important is missing. Now, behavioural economics provides a variety of descriptions of processes and experiments, but is unable to deliver satisfactory explanations. Therefore, this book summarizes other important schools of thought in psychology, such as the humanist approach and the psycho-dynamic approach. When integrating their ontology into our psychological framework, the concept of rationality takes on a different meaning. Then it's not only about self-command, but also the drive to protect the Self from information that could reduce self-respect too greatly.

D.5 Economic Methodology

There is a strong current in economics that considers empirical research as the foundation for theoretical research. Those who subscribe to this argue one must: look at the facts, search for stable relationships between empirical variables, and as soon as these have been found them, try to find a theory that can explain these stable relationships. Lack of methodological knowledge is the cause of the popularity of this procedure. A long time ago there was an epistemological debate between philosophers of science about the relationship between theory and reality; in other words, between the ratio or the senses being the primary source of knowledge. Immanuel Kant has solved this problem by stating that the two sources need each other. The senses give us the raw material and the ratio gives us the necessary framing of this material so as to make it understandable. Nevertheless, time and again rationalists and empiricists suggest that rational analysis *or* sense impression is the sole basis for fruitful research. In economics, the empiricist approach is very strong at the moment: here only empirically measurable variables are allowed to play a role in the analysis. This is a threat to its quality, and behavioural economics does not counter this development.

Adam Smith, although quite often interpreted as an inductivist and empiricist, has a different methodology. In his *History of Astronomy* he states that every scientific research starts with imagination. Newton imagined a world of moving objects, and assumed that these objects were attracted to each other (gravitational force). So far there is no empirics in his theory; just an image that functions as a framework of interpretation and analysis. In his *The Theory of Moral Sentiments* Smith imagined society as a set of interrelated individuals, who all are driven by the desire to be socially recognized. He also assumed that every individual has the capacity to sympathize with other people; that is, to imagine how other people feel in their situation. Then he imagined an impartial spectator who is constantly judging persons on the basis of norms and values. These moral anchorpoints emerge out of continuing interaction between people, who all have moral sentiments and resentments on the basis of their sympathies and antipathies, respectively. As mentioned in Section D.2 Smith borrows heavily from Hutcheson and Hume. But Smith adds to this analysis of the social world a psychological theory (Hanson, 2010). He imagines a psyche or mind in which two entities live: an impartial spectator and a Self. The spectator is not a concrete person with interest-biased expectations. Every person is assumed to construct an imaginary person who is impartial in his judgement of the Self. Smith cannot be considered as an existential philosopher, since his individuals are motivated to adjust to what society expects from them. But they are not asking other persons what to do; they form their own opinions about what society at large needs. This is the way adult persons constantly try to be virtuous persons.

When writing his *Wealth of Nations* Smith had these virtuous persons in mind—rather than those who are greedy, opportunistic, and corrupt.

D.6 Adam Smith as the Founding Father of Multidisciplinary Economics

Smith is generally considered to be the founding father of economics. However, most approaches within economics differ quite significantly from his work. Orthodox/neoclassical economics has searched for and found a universal principle, which is the human drive to reduce scarcity as much as possible. A whole series of principles are logical implications from this, such as the law of decreasing marginal utility and the law of decreasing marginal returns. Unfortunately, they do not take into account the social and the psychic world. Post-Keynesian economics tried to develop a different economics by the introduction of uncertainty and irrationality. The social world is almost absent, however. Behavioural economics is a reaction to the lack of empirical validity of neoclassical economics. Unfortunately, more empirical analysis does not necessarily lead to more realistic theory. From methodology we know that empirical research makes sense only if it is based on a realistic analysis. Adam Smith has shown that understanding of economies needs a theoretical apparatus in which social, psychic, and economic motivation are integrated. Of course, his work is just a beginning and contains many flaws. But considering him as the founding father implies a commitment: economists, focus on a multidisciplinary approach.

REFERENCES

Aalbers, M.B., E. Engelen, A. Glasmacher (2010), De staat en de securisatierevolutie: de institutionele verankering van de nieuwe obligatiemarkt, in: E. Schrijvers et al. (eds.), Markten maken (The Making of Markets), Special Issue of *Beleid en Maatschappij*, jaargang 37, 3.

Acemoglu, D., J.A. Robinson (2012), *Why Nations Fail; The Origins of Power, Prosperity and Poverty*, London: Profile Books Ltd.

Achterhuis, H. (1988), *Het rijk van de schaarste*, Baarn: Ambo.

Akerlof, G.A., R.J. Shiller (2009), *Animal Spirits. How Human Psychology Drives the Economy, and Why it Matters for Global Capitalism*, Princeton: Princeton University Press.

Akerlof, G.A., J.Yellen (1990), The Fair Wage-Effort Hypothesis and Unemployment, *Quarterly Journal of Economics*, vol. 105 (2), 255–283.

Alchian, A.A., H. Demsetz (1972), Production, Information Costs and Economic Organization, *American Economic Review*, 62 (5), 777–795.

Alchian, A.A., A.S. Phelps (eds.) (1970), *Microeconomic Foundations of Employment and Inflation Theory*, New York: Norton.

Anielsky, M., J. Rowe (1999), The Genuine Progress Indicator—1998 Update, Redefining Progress (see website of 'Redefining Progress').

Ariely, D. (2009), *Predictably Irrational*, Second Edition, New York: Harper Collins Publishers.

Ariely, D. (2012), *The (Honest) Truth about Dishonesty*, New York: Harper Collins Publishers.

Arrow, K. (1951), *Social Choice and Individual Values*, New York: Wiley.

Backhouse, R.E. (2002), *The Penguin History of Economics*, London: Penguin Books.

Bauman, Z. (1989), *Modernity and the Holocaust*, Ithaca, NY: Cornell University Press.

Bauman, Z. (1990), *Thinking Sociologically*, Oxford: Blackwell Publishers.

Bauman, Z. (1998), *Globalization: The Human Consequences*, Cambridge: Polity Press.

Beck, U. (1992), *Risk Society: Towards a New Modernity*, London: Sage.

Bhaskar, R. (1975), *A Realist Theory of Science*, London: Verso.

Blanchard, O. (1997), *Macroeconomics*, London: Prentice-Hall.

Blanchard, O., A. Amighini, F. Giavazzi (2011), *Macroeconomics: A European Perspective*, London: Prentice-Hall.

Bond, M.H., G. Hofstede (1996), *The Confucian Connection. From Cultural Roots to Economic Growth*; website Geert Hofstede (10-12-2013).

Bourdieu, P. (1977), *Outline of a Theory of Practice*, London: Cambridge University Press.

Bowles, S., H. Gintis (2011), *A Cooperative Species, Human Reciprocity and its Evolution*, Princeton: Princeton University Press.

Buchanan, J.M., G. Tullock (1962), *The Calculus of Consent, Logical Foundations of Constitutional Democracy*, Ann Arbor, MI: University of Michigan Press.

Buruma, I. (2013), Dynastieke zonden bepalen het lot van Oost-Azie, *NRC*, 13-12-2013.

Camerer, C., G. Loewenstein, D. Prelec (2007), Neuroeconomics: How Neuroscience Can Inform Economics, in: S. Maital et al. (eds.), *Recent Developments in Behavioral Economics*, The International Library of Critical Writings in Economics Series, Cheltenham: Edward Elgar.

Clark, M. (1936), *Preface to Social Economics: Essays on Economic Theory and Social Economics*, London: Farrar & Rinehart.

Coase, R.H. (1937), The Nature of the Firm, *Economica*, (4) 16, 386–405.

Coase, R.H. (1960), The Problem of Social Cost, *Journal of Law and Economics*, 3, 1–44.

Cohen, A.J., G.C. Harcourt (2003), Whatever Happened to the Cambridge Capital Theory Controversies?, *Journal of Economic Perspectives*, 17 (1), 199–214.

Cohen, G.A. (1995), *Self-Ownership, Freedom and Equality*, Studies in Marxism and Social Theory, Cambridge: Cambridge University Press.

Coleman, J.S. (1994), A Rational Choice Perspective on Economic Sociology, in: N.J. Smelser and R. Swedberg (eds.), *The Handbook of Economic Sociology*, Princeton: Princeton University Press.

Commons, J.R. (1924), *The Legal Foundations of Capitalism*, New York: Macmillan.

Crotty, J. (2009), Structural Causes of the Global Financial Crisis: A Critical Assessment of the 'New Financial Architecture', *Cambridge Journal of Economics*, Special Issue: The Global Financial Crisis, 33 (4), 539–562.

Cryan, D., S. Shatil, B. Mablin (2001), *Logic*, London: Icon Books.

Daly, H., J. Cobb (1989), *For the Common Good*, Boston: Beacon Press.

Damasio, A. (1994), *Descartes' Error*, London: Penguin Books.

Davis, J. (2003), *The Theory of the Individual in Economics*, London: Routledge.

Davis, J. (2008), The Conception of the Socially Embedded Individual, in: J. Davis, W. Dolfsma (eds.), *The Elgar Companion to Social Economics*, Cheltenham: Edward Elgar.

Davis, J., W. Dolfsma (eds.) (2008), *The Elgar Companion to Social Economics*, Cheltenham: Edward Elgar.

Denzau, A.T., D.C. North (1994), Shared Mental Models: Ideology and Institutions, *Kyklos*, 47 (1), 3–31.

Diamond, J. (2012), *The World until Yesterday*, London: Penguin Books.

DiMaggio, P. (1994), Culture and Economy, in: N.J. Smelser, R. Swedberg (eds.), *The Handbook of Economic Sociology*, Princeton: Princeton University Press.

Doel, J. van den (1978), *Demokratie en welvaartstheorie*, Second Edition, Alphen aan de Rijn: Samson.

Doeringer, P.D., M. Piore (1985), *Internal Labor Markets and Manpower Analysis*, Massachusetts: D.C. Heath and Company.

Dolfsma, W., A. Spithoven (2008), 'Silent Trade' and the Supposed Continuum between OIE and NIE, *Journal of Economic Issues*, 42 (2), 517–525.

Dow, S.C. (2002), *Economic Methodology, an Inquiry*, Oxford: Oxford University Press.

Dow, S.C. (2012), *Foundations for a New Economic Thinking: A Collection of Essays*, London: Palgrave Macmillan.

Downs, A. (1957), *An Economic Theory of Democracy*, New York: Harper & Row.

Downs, A. (1967), *Inside Bureaucracy*, Boston: Little, Brown.

Dunleavy, P. (1991), *Democracy, Bureaucracy and Public Choice: Economic Explanations in Political Science*, Hemel Hempstead: Harvester Wheatsheaf.

Easterlin, R.A. (1974), Does Economic Growth Improve the Human Lot? Some Empirical Evidence, in: P.A. David, M.W. Reder (eds.), *Nations and Households in Economic Growth: Essays in Honor of Moses Abramovitz*, New York: Academic Press, Inc.

Eichner, A.S., J. Kregel (1975), An Essay on Post-Keynesian Theory: A New Paradigm in Economics, *Journal of Economic Literature*, 13 (4), 1293–1314.

Ekelund, R.B., R.F. Hebert (1990), *A History of Economic Theory and Method*, Fourth Edition, New York: McGraw-Hill.

Elster, J. (1998), Emotions in Economic Theory, *Journal of Economic Literature*, 36 (1), 47–74.

Endeburg, G. (1998), *Kennis, macht en overmacht*, Zutphen: Eburon.

Esping-Andersen, G. (1990), *The Three Worlds of Welfare Capitalism*, Cambridge: Polity Press.

Festinger, A. (1957), *A Theory of Cognitive Dissonance*, Stanford: Stanford University Press.

Fevre, R. (2003), *The New Sociology of Economic Behaviour*, London: Sage Publications.

Fisher, I. (1911), *The Purchasing Power of Money*, New York: Macmillan.

Fligstein, N. (1998), Is Globalisation the Cause of the Crisis of Welfare States? Unpublished paper, University of California, Berkeley, October.

Fligstein, N. (2001), *The Architecture of Markets*, Princeton: Princeton University Press.

Follett, K. (1989), *The Pillars of the Earth*, London: Macmillan Ltd.

Follett, K. (2012), *Fall of Giants*, London: Macmillan Ltd.

Frank, R.H. (1994), *Microeconomics and Behavior*, Second Edition, New York: McGraw-Hill, Inc.

Frankfurt, H.G. (1971), Freedom of the Will and the Concept of a Person, *Journal of Philosophy*, 68, 5–20.

Frey, B.S. (1978), *Modern Political Economy*, Oxford: Martin Robertson.

Frey, B.S. (1983), *Democratic Economic Policy*, Oxford: Martin Robertson.

Frey, B.S., S. Meier (2003), Are Political Economists Selfish and Indoctrinated? Evidence from a Natural Experiment, *Economic Inquiry*, 41, 448–462.

Friedman, D., M. Hechter (1988), The Contribution of Rational Choice Theory to Macrosociological Research, *Sociological Theory*, 6, 201–218.

Friedman, M. (1953), The Methodology of Positive Economics, in: *Essays in Positive Economics*, Chicago: Chicago University Press.

Friedman, M. (1956), The Quantity Theory of Money: A Restatement, in: *Studies in the Quantity Theory of Money*, Chicago: Chicago University Press.

Friedman, M. (1968), The Role of Monetary Policy, *The American Economic Review*, 68 (1), 1–17.

Friedman, M., A. Schwartz (1963), *A Monetary History of the United States, 1867–1960*, Princeton: Princeton University Press, for NBER.

Frijda, N. (2007), *The Laws of Emotion*, London: Lawrence Erlbaum Associates.

Fukuyama, F. (1992), *The End of History and the Last Man*, New York: Free Press.

Gagne, R. et al. (1993), *The Cognitive Psychology of School Learning*, Second Edition, New York: Harper Collins College Publishers.

George, D. (2008), The Social Dimension of Internal Conflict, in: J. Davis, W. Dolfsma (eds.), *The Elgar Companion to Social Economics*, Cheltenham: Edward Elgar.

Giddens, A. (1986), *The Constitution of Society: An Outline of the Theory of Structuration*, Oxford: Oxford University Press.

Girard, R. (1961), *Messonge romantiques et verité romanesque*, Paris: Grasset. [English version: *Deceit, Desire and the Novel*, Baltimore: Johns Hopkins University].

Girard, R. (1978), *Des Choses caches depuis la fondation du monde*, Paris: Grasset. [English version: *Things Hidden since the Formation of the World*, Stanford: Stanford University Press].

Glassman, W., M. Hadad (2004), *Approaches to Psychology*, Fourth Edition, Open University Press, London: McGraw-Hill.

Granovetter, M. (1985), Economic Action and Social Structure: The Problem of Embeddedness, *American Journal of Sociology*, 91 (3), 481–510.

Greif, A. (2006), *Institutions and the Path to the Modern Economy: Lessons from Medieval Trade*, Cambridge: Cambridge University Press.

Habermas, J. (1987), *Theory of Communicative Action*, vol. 2, Cambridge: Cambridge Polity Press.

Hall, R.E., C.E. Jones (1999), Why Some Countries Produce So Much More Output Per Worker than Others? *The Quarterly Journal of Economics*, 114 (1), 83–116.

Hanson, J. (2010), *Adam Smith and the Ideal of the Free Market*, unpublished honours thesis, UCU-Utrecht.

Harrod, R.F. (1939), An Essay in Dynamic Theory, *The Economic Journal*, 49, 14–33.

Harrod, R.F. (1948), *Towards a Dynamic Economics*, London: Macmillan.

Hayek, F. A. von (1931), *Prices and Production*, London: Routledge and Kegan Paul.

Hayek, F. (1978), *New Studies in Philosophy, Politics, Economics and the History of Ideas*, London: Kegan Paul.

Hayek, F. (1984), *1980s Unemployment and the Unions*, London: The Institute of Economic Affairs.

Hechter, M., K-D. Opp, R. Wippler (eds.) (1990), *Social Institutions: Their Emergence, Maintenance and Effects*, New York: Aldine.

Heckathorn, D.D. (2001), Sociological Rational Choice, in: G. Ritzer, B. Smart (eds.), *Handbook of Social Theory*, London: Sage Publications.

Henrich, J. et al. (2007), 'Economic Man' in Cross-Cultural Perspective: Behavioral Experiments in 15 Small-Scale Societies, in: S. Maital et al. (eds.), *Recent Developments in Behavioral Economics*, The International Library of Critical Writings in Economics Series, Cheltenham: Edward Elgar.

Hicks, J.R. (1937), Mr. Keynes and the Classics: A Suggested Interpretation, *Econometrica*, 5 (2), 147–159.

Hicks, J.R. (1963), *The Theory of Wages*, Second Edition, London: Macmillan.

Hines, A.G. (1964), Unemployment and the Rate of Change in the Money Wage Rates in the United Kingdom 1893–1962, *Review of Economic Studies*, 29 (1), no. 85, 253–266.

Hirschman, A.O. (1977), *The Passions and the Interests*, Princeton: Princeton University Press.

Hirschman, A.O. (1984), Against Parsimony: Three Easy Ways of Complicating Some Categories of Economic Discourse, *American Economic Review*, AEA Papers and Proceedings, May, 21–26.

Hirschman, A.O. (1992), *Rival Views of Market Society*, Cambridge, MA: Harvard University Press.

Hobbes, Th. ([1651] 1983), *Leviathan*, London: Everyman's Library.

Hodgson, G.M. (1988), *Economics and Institutions, A Manifesto for a Modern Institutional Economics*, Cambridge: Polity Press.

Hodgson, G.M. (2001), *How Economics Forgot History*, Abingdon: Routledge.

Hodgson, G.M. (2006), 'What are Institutions?', *Journal of Economic Issues*, 40 (1), 1–25.

Hofstede, G. (1980), *Culture's Consequences*, London: Sage.

Homans, G.C. (1961), *Social Behavior: Its Elementary Forms*, New York: Harcourt, Brace & World.

Hotelling, H. (1929), Stability in Competition, *The Economic Journal*, 39, 41–57.

Howitt, P. (2002), On Keynesian Economics and the Economics of Keynes: A Study in Monetary Theory, in: X. Greffe, J. Lallement, M. de Vroey (eds.), *Dictionnaire des grandes oeuvres economique*, Editions Dalloz.

Huffschmid, J. (2007), *Hedge Funds and Private Equity*, paper presented at the conference on the Political Economy of the Financial World, Utrecht University School of Economics, Utrecht, the Netherlands, 7 November.

Huizing, D., E. van Sas (2013), *Een rechtseconomische analyse van de dopingproblematiek in de sportwereld*, Bachelor's thesis, Utrecht: Utrecht University School of Economics.

Jespersen, J. (2009), *Macroeconomic Methodology, A Post-Keynesian Perspective*, Cheltenham: Edward Elgar.

Kahneman, D., A. Tversky (1979), Prospect Theory: An Analysis of Decision under Risk, *Econometrica*, 47, 263–291.

Kant, I. (1781), *Critique of Pure Reason*, New York: Prometheus Books.

Kant, I. (2004), *Kritiek van de zuivere rede*, Meppel: Boom.

Kant, I. ([1788] 2008), *Critique of Practical Reason*. Cheshire: A&D Publishing.

Keizer, P. (1982), *Inflatie als politiek-economisch verschijnsel. Een theoretisch en empirisch onderzoek naar de invloed van ideologie en militantie op inflatie*, Leiden: Stenfert Kroese.

Keizer, P. (1984), *Inflatietheorie and anti-inflatiepolitiek*, Groningen: Wolters-Noordhoff.

Keizer, P. (1986), Wage Formation in the Context of Collective Bargaining, *De Economist*, 134 (2), 191–213.

Keizer, P. (1990), Comment on D. Bellante Labor Markets and the Welfare State, in: K. Groenveld, J.A. Maks, J. Muysken (eds.), *Economic Policy and the Market Process: Austrian and Mainstream Economics*, Amsterdam: North-Holland.

Keizer, P. (1993), Union Economics: A Methodological Critique, in: *Die Okonomische Wissenschaft und ihr Betrieb*, Okonomie und Gesellschaft, Jahrbuch 10, Frankfurt, New York: Campus Verlag.

Keizer, P. (2007), Hayek, Buchanan en Sen over vrijheid, bespreking van het boek 'Markt, democratie en vrijheid', *Maandschrift Economie*, 54, 492–498.

Keizer, P. (1999), vrijheid, van de hand van J. de Beus: Capitalism, Rivalry and Solidarity, *International Journal of Social Economics*, 26 (6), 752–762.

Keizer, P. (2005), A Socio-Economic Framework of Interpretation and Analysis, *International Journal of Social Economics*, 32 (1/2), 155–173.

Keizer, P. (2015), *Multidisciplinary Economics, a Methodological Account*, Oxford: Oxford University Press.

Keizer, P., A. Spithoven (2009), Cultural Foundation of Distribution of Income: The Dutch Case, *Journal of Economic Issues*, 43 (2), 517–526.

Keizer, P., A. Spithoven (2010), *Income Equality, Productivity and Corporatism: A Comparison between Continental West-European Countries*, Working Paper, Tjalling Koopmans Institute.

Kets de Vries, M. (2006), *The Leader on the Couch: A Clinical Approach to Changing People and Organizations*, Chicester: John Wiley & Sons.

Keynes, J.N. (1980), *The Scope and Method of Political Economy*, London: Macmillan.

Keynes, J.M. (1936), *The General Theory of Employment, Interest and Money*, London: Macmillan, St Martin's Press.

Keynes, J.M. (1943), The Objective of International Price Stability, *The Economic Journal*, 53, 185–187.

Kirzner, I.M. (1973), *Competition and Entrepreneurship*, Chicago: Chicago University Press.

Kiser, L.L., E. Ostrom (1982), The Three Worlds of Action: A Meta-Theoretical Synthesis of Institutional Approaches, in: E. Ostrom (ed.), *Strategies of Political Inquiry*, New York, Sage.

Knight, F.H. (1921), *Risk, Uncertainty and Profit*, Boston: Houghton Mifflin.

Knorr-Cetina, K. (2005), How are Global Markets Global? The Architecture of a Flow World, in: K. Knorr Cetina, A. Prada (eds.), *The Sociology of Financial Markets*, Oxford: Oxford University Press.

Ketcher, D. et al. (1982), *Elements of Psychology*, New York: Alfred Knopf, Inc.

Kregel, J. (2009), Why Don't the Bailouts Work? Design of a New Financial System versus Return to Normalcy, *Cambridge Journal of Economics*, 33, 653–663.

Kuhn, T.S. (1970), *The Structure of Scientific Revolutions*. Chicago: University of Chicago Press.

Kuipers, S.K. (1985), *Het Moderne Geldwezen, III, De Geldtheorie*, Vijftiende druk, bewerking, Amsterdam: Noord-Hollandsche Uitgeverij.

Kuipers, S.K., B.S. Wilpstra (1983), *Conjunctuur- en groeitheorie, visies op de werking van een markteconomie*, Leiden: Stenfert Kroese.

Lagueux, M. (2008), Are We Witnessing a Revolution in Methodology of Economics? About Don Ross's Recent Book on Microexplanation, *Erasmus Journal for Philosophy and Economics*, 1 (1), 24–55.

Lakatos, I. (1970), Falsification and the Methodology of Scientific Research Programmes. In I. Lakatos, R.A. Musgrave (eds.), *Criticism and the Growth of Knowledge*, Cambridge: Cambridge University Press.

Lange, O., F.M. Taylor (1938), *On the Economic Theory of Socialism*, Minneapolis: University of Minnesota Press.

Langlois, R.N. (1984), Internal Organization in a Dynamic Context: Some Theoretical Considerations, in: M. Jussawalla, H. Ebenfield (eds.), *Communication and Information*, Amsterdam: North-Holland.

Lascaris, A. (1987), *Uitzicht voor een oude wereld: West-Europa op een keerpunt*, Kampen: Kok Agora.

Layard, R. (2005), *Happiness, Lessons from a New Science*, London: Penguin Books Ltd.

Leijonhufvud, A. (1968), *Keynesian Economics and the Economics of Keynes*, New York: Oxford University Press.

Leijonhufvud, A. (2009), Out of the Corridor: Keynes and the Crisis, *Cambridge Journal of Economics*, 33, 741–759.

Lenski, G.E. (1970), *Human Societies: A Macro Level Introduction to Sociology*, New York: McGraw-Hill.

Light, I., S. Karageorgis (1994), The Ethnic Economy, in: N.J. Smelser, R. Swedberg (eds.), *Handbook of Economic Sociology*, Princeton: Princeton University Press.

Lippe, T. van der, J.Siegers (1994), Division of Household and Paid Labour between Partners: Effects of Relative Wage Rates and Social Norms, *Kyklos*, 47, 109–135.

Lipsey, R.G. (1960), The Relation between Unemployment and the Rate of Change in the Money Wage Rate in the United Kingdom 1862–1957: A Further Analysis, *Economica*, New Series, 27, 105–108.

Locke, J. (1689), *Essay Concerning Human Understanding*, London.

Lotringen, C. van (2013), Herrijzenis van Japan is structureel, *Het Financieele Dagblad*, 18-06-2013.

Lutz, M.A., K. Lux (1988), *Humanistic Economics, The New Challenge*, New York: The Bootstrap Press.

McClure, S.M., D.I. Laibson, G. Loewenstein, J.D. Cohen (2004), Separate Neural Systems, Value Immediate and Delayed Monetary Rewards, *Science*, 306 (15), 503–507.

MacKenzie, D. (2006), The Credit Crisis as a Problem in the Sociology of Knowledge, *American Journal of Sociology*, 116 (6), 1778–1841.

Magnusson, L. (2006), The Swedish Model in Historical Context, *Kobe University Economic Review*, 52, 1–8.

Maital, S. (2007), Introduction, in: *Recent Developments in Behavioral Economics*, Cheltenham: The International Library of Critical Writings in Economics, Elgar Reference Collection.

Malthus, R. ([1798] 1970), *An Essay on the Principle of Population*, Baltimore: Penguin.

Mandel, E. (1974), *Inleiding in de marxistiese economie*, Nijmegen: Sunschrift 20, Socialistiese Uitgeverij.

Marx, K. (1872), *Capital*, 3 vols, trans. E. Untermann, ed. F. Engels, Chicago: Chicago University Press.

Menger, C. (1883), *Untersuchungen uber die Methode der Socialwissenschaften und der politischen Okonomie insbesondere*, Leipzig: Dunker und Humblot.

Mill, J.S. (1874), *Essays on Some Unsettled Questions of Political Economy*, London: Longmans, Reader & Dyer.

Mill, J.S. ([1848] 1985), Principles of Political Economy with Some of their Applications to Social Philosophy, vols 2 and 3, in: *Collected Works of John Stuart Mill*, Seventh Edition, London: Routledge & Kegan Paul.

Minsky, H.P. (1982), *Inflation, Recession and Economic Policy*, Brighton: Harvester; Armonk, NY: M.E.Sharpe.

Minsky, H.P. (1993), The Financial Instability Hypothesis, in: P. Arestis, M. Sawyer (eds.), *Handbook of Radical Political Economy*, Aldershot: Edward Elgar.

Mises, L. von (1949), *Human Action: A Treatise on Economics*, New Haven: Yale University Press.

Mizruchi, M.S., L. Brewster Stearns (1994), Money, Banking and Financial Markets, in: N. J. Smelser, R. Swedberg (eds.), *The Handbook of Economic Sociology*, Princeton: Princeton University Press.

Mueller, D.C. (1989), *Public Choice II*, Cambridge: Cambridge University Press.

Nentjes, A. (1983), *De ontwikkeling van de economische theorie*, Groningen: Wolters-Noordhoff.

Negishi, T. (1979), *Microeconomic Foundations of Keynesian Macroeconomics*, Amsterdam: North Holland.

Nickell, S.J., M. Andrews, (1983), Unions, Real Wages and Employment in Britain 1951–1979, *Oxford Economic Papers*, Supplement, 35, 183–206.

Nietzel, M.T. et al. (1998), *Abnormal Psychology*, London: Allyn & Bacon.

Niskanen, W.A. (1971), *Bureaucracy and Representative Government*, Chicago: Aldine Atherton.

Niskanen, W.A. (1973), *Bureaucracy, Servant or Master*, London: Institute of Economic Affairs.

Nooteboom, B. (2004), Inter-firm Collaboration, Learning and Networks, London: Taylor & Francis.

Norman, R. (1998), *The Moral Philosophers*, Second Edition, Oxford: Oxford University Press.

North, D.C. (1981), *Structure and Change in Economic History*, New York: W.W. Norton & Company.

North, D.C. (2005), *Understanding the Process of Economic Change*, Princeton: Princeton University Press.

O'Boyle, E.J. (1996), *Social Economics, Premises, Findings and Policies*, London: Routledge.

Olson, M. (1965), *The Logic of Collective Action, Public Goods and the Theory of Groups*, Cambridge, MA: Harvard University Press.

Ostrom, E. (1990), *Governing the Commons: The Evolution of Institutions of Collective Action*, Cambridge: Cambridge University Press.

Ostrom, E. (2005), *Understanding Institutional Diversity*, Princeton: Princeton University Press.

Parijs, Van Ph. (1996), *Solidariteit voor de 21ste eeuw*, Leuven and Apeldoorn: Garent.

Parsons, T. (1937), *The Structure of Social Action*, New York: McGraw-Hill.

Parsons, T. (1951), *The Social System*, New York: Free Press.

Parsons, T. (1978), *Action Theory and the Human Condition*, New York: Free Press.

Perlof, J.M. (2012), *Microeconomics*, Sixth Edition, Boston: Pearson (Global Edition).

Peterson, W.C. (1994), *Silent Depression, Twenty-Five Years of Wage Squeeze and Middle Class Decline*, New York: W. W. Norton & Company.

Phelps, E.S. (1972), *Inflation Policy and Unemployment Theory*, London: Wiley.

Phillips, A.W. (1958), The Relationship between Unemployment and the Rate of Change in the Money Wage Rate in the United Kingdom, 1861–1957, *Economica*, 25, 283–293.

Pigou, A.C. (1929), *Industrial Fluctuations*, London: Macmillan.

Piketty, T. (2014), *Capital in the Twenty-First Century*, trans. A. Goldhammer, Cambridge, MA: The Belknap Press of Harvard University Press.

Piore, M. (1996), Review of the Handbook of Economic Sociology, *Journal of Economic Literature*, 34, 741–754.

Polanyi, K. (1944), *The Great Transformation*, Boston: Beacon Press.

Popper, K. (1968), *The Logic of Scientific Discovery*. London: Hutchinson.

Rabin, M. (1993), Fairness in Game Theory and Economics, *American Economic Review*, 1281–1302.

Rabin, M. (1998), Economic Psychology, a Review of the Literature, *Journal of Economic Literature*, 11–46.

Rabin, M., R.H. Thaler (2001), Anomalies, Risk Aversion, *Journal of Economic Perspectives*, 15 (1), 219–232.

Rawls, J. (1971), *A Theory of Justice*, Oxford: Oxford University Press.

Ritzer, G. (2008), *Modern Sociological Theory*, Seventh Edition, New York: McGraw-Hill.

Robbins, L. (1932), *An Essay on the Nature and Significance of Economic Science*, London: Macmillan & Co.

Romer, P.M. (1990), Endogenous Technological Change, *Journal of Political Economy*, October, 71–103.

Romer, P.M. (2000), Thinking and Feeling, *The American Economic Review*, Papers and Proceedings, 90 (2), 439–443.

Romme, S. (1999), Redistributing Power in the Classroom, in: J. Troy, M. Pettigrew, P.K. Keizer, J. Hommes (eds.), *Learning in a Changing Environment*, Dordrecht: Kluwer.

Rousseau, J.J. (1755), *Discourse sur l'origine et les fondements de l'inegalite parmi des hommes*, Amsterdam: Marc Michel Rey.

Ross, D. (2005), *Economic Theory and Cognitive Science: Microexplanation*, Cambridge, MA: The MIT Press.

Salverda, W. (1978), Haalt de arbeidsinkomensquote de 100%?, unpublished paper.

Samuelson, P.A. (1938), A Note on the Pure Theory of Consumer's Behaviour, *Economica*, 5, 61–71.

Samuelson, P.A. (1950), Consumption Theory in Terms of Revealed Preference, *Economica* 15, 243–253.

Samuelson, P.A., W. Nordhaus (1995), *Economics*, Fifteenth Edition, New York: McGraw-Hill, Inc.

Sanderson, S. K. (1999), *Macrosociology, An Introduction to Human Societies*, Fourth Edition, New York: Addison, Wesley, Longman.

Saros, D.E. (2008), The Turnover Continuum: A Marxist Analysis of Capitalist Fluctuations, *Review of Radical Political Economics*, 40, 189–210.

Schelling, T. (1984), Self-Command in Practice, in Policy, and in a Theory of Rational Choice, *American Economic Review*, 74 (2), 1–11.

Schenk, H. (2008), Firms, Managers, and Restructuring: Implications of a Social Economics View, in: J. Davis, W. Dolfsma (eds.), *The Elgar Companion to Social Economics*, Cheltenham, Edward Elgar.

Schrijvers, E. et al. (2010), Markten maken (The Making of Markets), Special Issue of *Beleid en Maatschappij*, 37 (3), 195–287.

Schumpeter, J. A. (1943), *Capitalism, Socialism and Democracy*, London: Unwin University Books.

Scruton, R. (1996), *Kant*, Oxford: Oxford University Press.

Sen, A. (1977), Rational Fools: A Critique of the Behavioural Foundations of Economic Theory, *Philosophy and Public Affairs*, 6, 317–344.

Sen, A. (1999), *Development as Freedom*, Oxford: Oxford University Press.

Sen, A. (2002), *Rationality and Freedom*, Cambridge, MA: The Belknap Press of the Harvard University Press.

Sen, A. (2009), Capitalism after the Crisis, *The New York Review of Books*, 56 (5).

Sennett, R. (1998), *The Corrosion of Character: The Personal Consequences of Work in the New Capitalism*, New York: W.W. Norton.

Shackle, G.L.S. (1955), *Uncertainty in Economics*, Cambridge: Cambridge University Press.

Shand, A.H. (1990), *Free Market Morality, The Political Economy of the Austrian School*, London: Routledge.

Shapiro, C., J. Stiglitz (1984), Equilibrium Unemployment as a Worker Discipline Device, *American Economic Review*, 74 (3), 433–444.

Sheehan, B. (2010), *The Economics of Abundance, Affluent Consumption and Global Economy*, Cheltenham: Edward Elgar.

Shiller, R.J. (2007), Bubbles, Human Judgment and Expert Opinion, in: S. Maital et al., *Recent Developments in Behavioral Economics*, The International Library of Critical Writings in Economics Series, Cheltenham: Edward Elgar.

Sidanius, J., F. Pratto (1999), *Social Dominance*, Cambridge: Cambridge University Press.

Simon, H. (1957a), *Models of Man: Social and Rational*, New York: Wiley.

Simon, H. (1957b), Theories of Decision-Making in Economics and Behavioural Science, *American Economic Review*, 49, 252–283.

Skidelsky, R. (2009), *Keynes, the Return of the Master*, London: Allen Lane Penguin Books.

Smelser, N., R. Swedberg (1994), The Sociological Perspective on the Economy, in *The Handbook of Economic Sociology*, Princeton: Princeton University Press.

Smith, A. ([1756] 1795), The History of Astronomy, in: W.P.D. Eightman, J.C. Bryce (eds.), *Essays on Philosophical Subjects*, London.

Smith, A. ([1759] 1982), *The Theory of Moral Sentiments*, Indianapolis: Liberty Fund.

Smith, A. ([1776] 1994), *An Inquiry into the Nature and Causes of the Wealth of Nations*, New York: The Modern Library.

Solow, R.M. (1985), Insiders and Outsiders in Wage Determination, *The Scandinavian Journal of Economics*, 87 (2), 411–428.

Stevens, A. (1994), *Jung*, Past Masters Series, Oxford: Oxford University Press.

Stevens, R. (1996), *Understanding the Self*, New York: Sage Publications.

Stiglitz, J., M. Weiss (1981), Credit Rationing with Markets with Imperfect Competition, *American Economic Review*, 71, 393–410.

Swaan, A. de (1973), *Coalition Theories and Cabinet Formation*, San Francisco: Jossey-Bass.

Swaan, A. de (1988), *In Care of the State*, Oxford: Oxford University Press.

Swedberg, R. (1994), Markets as Social Structures, in: N.J. Smelser, R. Swedberg (eds.), *The Handbook of Economic Sociology*, Princeton: Princeton University Press.

Swedberg, R. (2003), *Principles of Economic Sociology*, Princeton: Princeton University Press.

Taylor, J. (1993), Discretion versus Policy Rules in Practice, Carnegie-Rochester Conference Series on Public Policy, 195–227.

Tiemeijer, W.L. et al. (2009), *De menselijke beslisser*, Amsterdam: Amsterdam University Press.

Tilly, C., C. Tilly (1994), Capitalist Work and Labor Markets, in: N.J. Smelser, R. Swedberg (eds.), *The Handbook of Economic Sociology*, Princeton: Princeton University Press.

Tinbergen, J. (1935), Annual Survey: Suggestions on Quantitative Business Cycle Theory, *Econometrica*, 3 (3), 241–308.

Trigg, R. (2002), *Philosophy Matters*, Oxford: Blackwell Publishers.

Turner, J.H. (1998), *The Structure of Sociological Theory*, Sixth Edition, Belmont, CA: Wadsworth Publishing Company.

Tversky, A., D. Kahneman (1986), Rational Choice and the Framing of Decisions, *Journal of Business*, 59 (4), S251–S278.

Ullmann-Margalit, E. (1977), *The Emergence of Norms*, Oxford: Clarendon Press.

Ullmann-Margalit, E. (1978), Invisible Hand Explanations, *Synthese*, 39, 282–286.

United Nations Development Programme, *Human Development Reports*, Website: http://hdr.undp.org/en/countries.

Usher, D. (1982), *The Economic Prerequisite of Democracy*, Oxford: Basil Blackwell.

Veblen, Th. (1899), The Preconceptions of Economic Science, *Quarterly Journal of Economics*, 13/14, 1–16.

Veenhoven, R. (1984), *Conditions of Happiness*, Dordrecht: D. Reidel.

Vila, D. (ed.) (2000), *The Cambridge Companion to Hannah Ahrendt*, Cambridge: Cambridge University Press.

Visser, P. (1989), *Overlegeconomie*, Assen/Maastricht: Van Gorcum.

Warner, K., H.L. Molotch (1993), Information in the Marketplace: Media Explanations of the '87 Crash, *Social Problems*, 40, 167–188.

Weber, M. (1904), *The Methodology of the Social Sciences*. New York: Free Press.

Weber, M. ([1922] 1965), *Economy and Society*, Totowa, NJ: Bedminster.

Welsh, P. (1987), Keynes' Employment Function and the Marginal Productivity of Labour, *Journal of Post-Keynesian Economics*, 9 (4), 507–515.

Wicksell, K. (1898), *Interest and Prices* [*Geldzins und Guterpreise*], New York: Sentry Press.

Wilkinson, N. (2008), *An Introduction to Behavioral Economics*, London: Palgrave Macmillan.

Williamson, O.E. (1967), Hierarchical Control and Optimum Firm Size, *Journal of Political Economy*, 75 (2), 123–138.

Williamson, O.E. (1975), *Markets and Hierarchies*, New York: Free Press.

Williamson, O.E. (1998), Transaction Cost Economics: How It Works; Where It Is Headed, *The Economist* 146 (1), 23–58.

Windmuller, J. (1969), *Labor Relations in The Netherlands*, Ithaca, NY: Cornell University Press.

■ INDEX